Praise for *Winston and Clementine*

"In a wonderfully candid exchange of letters over nearly sixty years, two strong, fascinating and endearing personalities discuss their lives and fortunes as molded by the great events of the twentieth century. Superbly edited by their daughter, the correspondence between Winston and Clementine Churchill is on one level an intimate revelation of the mysteries and fulfillments of marriage and on another a permanent contribution to the history of our times."

—**Arthur M. Schlesinger, Jr.**

"The Churchills' youngest and last surviving child, Mary Soames, has done a singular service in editing the couple's personal correspondence . . . The result is an invaluable historical record that is also fascinating reading—a delightful tour through the lives of two remarkable people who shaped the way we live now . . . Reading their letters is a reminder not just of headier days but of the human moments that had everything to do with how history turned out." —*Newsweek*

"These private letters, expertly edited by their youngest daughter, evoke times and places and people, the characters of both correspondents, and above all a warm and lasting love." —*Atlantic Monthly*

"Beautifully edited and set in context by the Churchills' youngest daughter, Mary Soames, *Winston and Clementine: The Personal Letters of the Churchills* not only illuminates the couple's ardent and playful lifelong love but also offers a sweeping yet accessible view of British politics in the 20th century."

—*Washington Post Book World*

"These letters are a bonanza for Churchillians and a fascinating read for any student of our century. They're spontaneous, candid and frequently charming . . . the letters contain all the drama of wartime, world travel and the making of a great political career despite some serious reverses." —*Seattle Times*

"Beyond showing a picture of love and an assessment of character, the letters afford a splendid perspective on world history in the making." —*Boston Globe*

"We shall never in the future see anything like [*Winston and Clementine*] again."

—*Sunday Times*

"Mary Soames has done very well . . . a worthy tribute to 'the golden thread of love.'"

—*Times Literary Supplement*

Winston and Clementine

THE PERSONAL LETTERS
OF THE
CHURCHILLS

EDITED BY
THEIR DAUGHTER

Mary Soames

A MARINER BOOK
Houghton Mifflin Company
BOSTON · NEW YORK

First Mariner Books edition 2001

First Published in Great Britain in 1998 by Doubleday,
a division of Transworld Publishers Ltd.

For information about permission to reproduce selections
from this book, write Permissions, Houghton Mifflin Company,
215 Park Avenue South, New York, New York 10003.

Visit our Web site: www.houghtonmifflinbooks.com.

Library of Congress Cataloging-in-Publication Data
Churchill, Winston, Sir, 1874–1965.
[Speaking for themselves]
Winston and Clementine : the personal letters of the Churchills
/ edited by their daughter Mary Soames.
p.   cm.
Originally published: Speaking for themselves. London ;
New York : Doubleday, 1998.
Includes bibliographical references and index.
ISBN 0-395-96319-2
ISBN 0-618-08251-4 (pbk.)
1. Churchill, Winston, Sir, 1874–1965 — Correspondence. 2. Churchill,
Clementine, Lady, 1885–1977 — Correspondence. 3. Prime ministers'
spouses — Great Britain — Correspondence. 4. Prime ministers — Great
Britain — Correspondence. 5. Married people — Great Britain — Correspondence.
I. Churchill, Clementine, Lady, 1885–1977. II. Soames, Mary. III. Title.
DA566.9.C5A4   1999
941.084'092'2—dc21
[b]   99-18699   CIP

Printed in the United States of America

QUM 10 9 8 7 6 5 4 3 2 1

Contents

CONTENTS

List of Illustrations

The following illustrations are reproduced by permission of the Master and Fellows of Churchill College, Cambridge: 2, 23, 24, 49, 58, 60, 61, 62, 63, 64, 65, 83, 109, 111.

The publishers have made every effort to trace the owners of illustrations reproduced in this book. In cases where they have been unsuccessful they invite copyright holders to contact them direct.

List of Maps

Preface

I first had sight of this remarkable correspondence when my mother sent her personal archives to me in 1963, so that I could use them for writing her life. My brother Randolph was at that time already working on the official life of our father, and in the vast collection of papers which comprises the Churchill archive was also a large number of letters between our parents: together, these form a written dialogue between Winston and Clementine Churchill from 1908 to 1964 – the year before my father's death – totalling some 1,700 letters, notes, telegrams and memoranda.

This material formed the basis of the biography I wrote of my mother[1]: it was also available to Randolph, and after his death in 1968 – having completed only two volumes of the biography – to Martin (now Sir Martin) Gilbert, who took on the task of completing Winston Churchill's authorized life. To the eight volumes of biography, Sir Martin added the Companion Volumes, which contain a vast selection of the papers and correspondence from all sources upon which he built his magisterial work (further volumes from 1940 are in preparation). He also wrote a single-volume biography published in 1991. A considerable number of my parents' letters to each other appear in these volumes.

Much of the correspondence which forms the stuff of this present book has appeared either in part or in whole in the above-mentioned works, and in limited quotation elsewhere. However numerous letters, not previously seen by me, have come to light in the Chartwell and Churchill Papers: chiefly telegrams between my parents during my mother's two long cruises (1934–5 and 1938–9); telegrams and messages between them in the Second World War, mostly during the wartime conferences; and also a considerable number of post-1945 letters. Searches at the Public Record Office at Kew also resulted in some valuable finds, and unexpected nuggets came from folders held at No. 10 Downing Street (but now at Kew).

When, over thirty years ago, I first read this archive as a whole, it made a powerful impression on me, and as the years went by, I became convinced that the letters should one day be presented in the form of the lifelong dialogue which they essentially are. This dormant idea was fanned into life when the late Dr Frederick Woods FRSA, bibliographer of the works of Sir Winston Churchill (who already had access to, and was working on, the papers at Churchill College, Cambridge), suggested that he should edit

[1] *Clementine Churchill by Her Daughter Mary Soames*, 1979.

the letters, and that I should write an introduction and commentaries to accompany them. We had signed a joint contract with Doubleday for this work, when the whole project was halted by Dr Woods' tragic death from cancer in February 1995.

At this sad and difficult moment, Ann Hoffmann, who had worked with me on my mother's biography as researcher and literary assistant, and with whom I had kept in touch, to my great good fortune, was willing to take on this new work. In addition to the high professional skills which she brought to my rescue, Ann was already, from our collaboration of so many years before, familiar with the papers, and our family scenario.

And so, to the letters – and the two people who wrote them to each other over a period of fifty-six years.

The most striking characteristic of this correspondence is its spontaneity and naturalness: these letters were written for each other's eyes alone, with no thought of a curious posterity looking over their shoulders. Now and then Clementine begs Winston to lock letters away and not leave them lying about – her concern was that the servants might read them; and in a letter of 18 December 1915, written from the Western Front at a moment of great personal torment and bitterness, Winston asks Clementine to burn two letters: 'I was depressed and my thought was not organised.... Everyone has hours of reaction; & there is no reason why written record shd remain...'. The letters do not survive. But the value of this correspondence lies in the fact that in the thoughts, judgements and sentiments expressed, they are truly 'speaking for themselves' – in the context and mood of the moment.

There are also the letters, nearly all from Clementine, where she gives her considered view about a person, a situation or a problem (domestic or political); and some in which she urges Winston to or from a particular course of action. These letters, notes or memoranda were sometimes written even when they were under the same roof, and would meet during the course of the day or evening. This may seem odd – but Clementine was not a good arguer: she quickly became vehement and over-emphatic, often spoiling her case by exaggeration. Winston under such fire presented a defensive obstinacy – which further exasperated her. Such discussions sometimes ended in an explosion and a 'sweep-out': once she actually shied a dish of spinach at him: it missed, but left a tell-tale mark on the wall. He also could wax furious – but rarely did the sun go down on their anger. Throughout their long exchange there are some touching Winston notes – probably slipped under her bedroom door – expressing contrition and love, and signed with penitent pigs or pugs; in her letters too, Clementine recognized ruefully the painful effects her own flare-ups of temper and passion could produce.

The 'house post' (✉) advocacy worked rather well: she wrote a reasoned case; he paid attention. Nor were these in-house communications always about controversial issues – Clementine really hated disturbing Winston while he was working, particularly during the war; nor did she want to lumber their precious times *à deux* with mundane domestic arrangements.

The letters reveal the dissimilarities of Winston and Clementine's natures: in their taste for people; in the hours they kept; in their pleasures and choice of holidays – indeed, an outsider may be forgiven for wondering what held them together. The answer to that is also in the letters: it was the love between them, which quickly kindled, and took deep root, that was the key to their enduring and heroic partnership. I use the adjective 'heroic' deliberately, for their relationship was not always an easy one, but love, loyalty and – from both of them – a deep commitment to their marriage brought them through the tumultuous years. The fact that both could express their love was like dew on the grass, and not confined to the written page: the warm embrace; the 'paw' held out; the rallying cry of 'WOW' (capable of so many inflections) – such were the expressions of their open affection for each other – to which those closest to them, and even casual acquaintances, bore witness.

Another crucial bond between them was politics: from the first, political life appealed to Clementine, and she accepted its excitements, hazards and frustrations. She rarely resented the demands of Winston's public life, although from the earliest days of their marriage, parliamentary and public engagements were often the cause of separations; but an absence of even two days was marked by an exchange of sometimes several letters – a reflection also on the postal services at that time. The telephone was certainly installed in most of the houses in which they stayed, but it was still a fairly unwieldy instrument, and often situated in a passage, hall or other somewhat public place; it was the means of conveying essential information (arrivals, departures, births, deaths), not a channel for chat or confidences – and indeed, it never became such for them.

Clementine espoused radical Liberalism with enthusiasm and partisanship. The reforming zeal of the Liberal Government swept to power in 1906 appealed to the noble and puritan elements in her nature: asked many years later what had been the happiest time of her life, she answered without hesitation: those early ardent days of her marriage, when she felt part of the crusade for social reform, and relished Winston's involvement in it.

There can hardly have been a time when politics and social life in Britain were more fascinating or more closely intertwined than in the opening decade of the twentieth century, and Clementine, although at times inhibited by her natural shyness and reserve, for the most part thrived in the world of Winston's friends and colleagues, which ran the gamut from the old Liberal establishment; through the brilliant Asquithian circle; the rising star – Lloyd George; the dedicated intellectual civil servants who masterminded the Government's policies; writers; and political journalists. There was the patrician world of the Marlboroughs (Spencer-Churchills, Winston's cousins), the Cecils and the Cavendishes. And across the increasingly bitter divide between the Liberal and Tory parties, Winston never broke his link of friendship with such as F. E. Smith and A. J. Balfour. It was a galaxy indeed.

Clementine's interest and involvement in the big issues of those days is patently clear. It was not that she always agreed with him; indeed, part of the invaluable contribution she made to Winston's career was her ability to differ from his views. She was not necessarily always right – nor did he always take her advice – but her capacity and will to voice a contrary or moderating opinion was of immeasurable importance, and never more so than in the years of his greatest power.

Clementine possessed that most important ingredient in a politician's make-up – a good political instinct. She was also, on the whole, a better judge of people than Winston. She did not approve of, or like, several of his friends; this made for arguments, and it truly pained Winston that she was not more appreciative of some of his close cronies. Yet although her dissent or criticism at times annoyed Winston, he always wanted her opinion – whether of policies, people or proofs.

I have often reflected how different might have been the course of my father's life and career had he married a socially eager or trivial-minded woman. He would always, through his talents and thrusting nature, have made his mark in politics: but his energies might have been distracted or – who knows? – the rapier of his destiny blunted or tarnished, had he married a woman of lesser character and principle.

Winston was a loving husband, and he always wanted Clementine to 'be there'; but his self-centredness, combined with his total commitment to politics, did not make him a very companionable one. Moreover, by the standards of his time and class he was not a rich man, and he kept his family by his pen. The urgent necessity for this, and his amazing capacity for work, emerge constantly in his letters. And then, there was painting: discovered as a God-sent therapeutic ploy in the summer of the Dardanelles crisis (1915), it became a lifetime occupation, pleasure and distraction. To this absorbing pastime must be added the endlessly happy hours at Chartwell: bricklaying; masterminding the landscape and (until after the Second World War) his small-scale, but usually disastrous, farming activities. His 'Chartwell Bulletins', dictated and typewritten, are appended to many letters describing in detail his projects; and the lives of the domestic farm animals and the predations of wildlife form a continuing and dramatic saga. Winston – ever candid – wrote to Clementine (4 April 1928): 'I am always "there"; but I am afraid that vy often my business & my toys have made me a poor companion.'

The effect of presenting the exchange of letters between a husband and wife is of course to highlight their absences from each other. In the early years of their marriage, times apart were mostly caused by the births of their children: in those days, for the upper classes, three weeks in bed was *de rigueur*, followed by a period of convalescence. Clementine always took some time to recover, and she nursed all five of her children. Family holidays for the nursery were a great feature, with rented houses often shared happily with Jack and Goonie Churchill (Winston's brother and his wife) and their parallel nursery: both the Papas – Winston and Jack – coming down at weekends from Parliament and City respectively. The intervening weekdays invariably saw letters between Winston and Clementine.

During Winston's first tenure as First Lord of the Admiralty (1911–15), the yacht *Enchantress* became a virtual annexe to his office, where, despite his being prone to seasickness, he spent days at a time. He relished being 'at sea', and in touch with the ships and the men who were the linchpins of his thoughts and schemes for the Navy. Their almost daily letters then often travelled faster than by post, by hand of messenger or Private Secretary carrying the official pouches.

When they married the world was largely at peace – the threat of the cataclysm to come crystallized late: but in Britain these were years of social convulsion and industrial strife, and as the Liberal Government sought to thrust forward its radical programme, and to raise the necessary finance, formidable opposition reared up from established interests. The passions aroused by the People's Budget (1909) were followed by bitterness as the Parliament Bill took form and was finally passed (1911); Home Rule for Ireland always engendered bitter controversy – now it was sliding into violence. Meanwhile the suffragettes shrieked at meetings and physically attacked ministers – all these are part and parcel of the stuff of Winston and Clementine's letters, along with family, domestic and social news.

In 1915 came the débâcle of the Dardanelles campaign, for whose concept and implementation Winston bore a large (but not sole) responsibility, as a result of which he resigned from the Government in November 1915 and, taking up his Oxfordshire Yeomanry commission, proceeded as a major to the Western Front, serving with the Grenadiers and later commanding the 6th Battalion, Royal Scots Fusiliers. The letters between Winston and Clementine from mid-November to early May 1916, when he was almost continuously in the front line, are among the most moving and gripping of their long correspondence, and are deeply significant in what they reveal of their relationship, and of the tensions and rivalries on the political front.

Winston then was at the lowest ebb ever of his fortunes; he felt deserted by political colleagues, and the weight of the Dardanelles catastrophe with its heavy loss of life, and the foundering of a brilliant strategy which might have significantly shortened the war, bowed him down. Clementine was to prove his lifeline: he poured his heart out to her, and she – although bitter, griefstruck by the events which had laid his fortunes so low, and gripped by fears for his safety – rose to heights of nobility and strength in the measured advice she gave him (often against her own deepest wishes); and she sustained him by her love and her belief in his destiny.

Winston and Clementine's holiday life evolved to encompass plans apart. In the early Twenties, Clementine, who was a keen and excellent tennis player, for several years made spring visits to Nice or Cannes to take part in high-class amateur tennis tournaments. Winston sought sunshine painting scenes, and he used to stay with long-time friends in the South of France: Clementine was always invited but, although she sometimes joined him on these visits, increasingly she came to dislike Riviera life and all it stood for. In fact the socially glittering (but mainly inconsequential) *monde* there was not Winston's natural habitat either – but, more easy-going than Clementine, he tolerated the assorted company better. Moreover, he largely led his own life – working on his current book, and painting away the daylight hours. At night, there was also for him the lure of the casino: he loved gambling. Clementine herself sometimes played – and she wrote some amusing accounts of her (mis)fortunes; but she came to have a revulsion from what to her was a pernicious pursuit, and she always feared its potential hold on Winston. And so, as the years went by, when Winston headed for the South of France, Clementine made her own plans: either staying at Chartwell, or going on a round of visits with Diana and Sarah, who were increasingly companionable: the former in her early twenties, and the latter emerging from the cocoon of schooldays and soon 'coming out'.

But of course there were places and friends they took pleasure in visiting together. Clementine loved travelling, and over the years she and Winston made several Mediterranean cruises and journeys to the Middle East. Visits to Florence and Venice were always a success, with painting for him and sightseeing for her.

Clementine possessed great vitality and enthusiasm, but these attractive characteristics were not matched by physical and nervous staying power – and she was a perennial worrier. She was aware of this, writing to Winston (29 January 1927): 'It is a great fault in me that small things should have the power to harass & agonise me.' Although throughout her long life she suffered from relatively few clinical ailments, she often succumbed to what a one-time family friend (Alastair Forbes) perceptively described as 'high metal fatigue'. Consequently, at sometimes fairly frequent intervals she would retreat to a health cure establishment to revive her flagging energy and regain her poise. Winston was always sympathetic and solicitous, and kept in constant touch. Naturally at these times, their letters spoke a good deal about her health and the regime she was undergoing: but, cast down in body and spirit although she may have been, she rarely ceased to follow the news, commenting upon it with her usual pithiness.

Of this whole correspondence (the present volume being but a selection), all the letters are handwritten up to August 1918, when Winston's first dictated and typewritten letter to Clementine appears. Her (far fewer) type-written ones come much later on, and are usually memoranda dealing with domestic matters, visitors or other arrangements. Winston invariably wrote loving openings and endings to his dictated letters in 'his own paw', and often interventions or quite long postscripts; his Chartwell Bulletins nearly always had a handwritten covering letter. To Winston dictation was a natural function; his thought and feelings flowed unhampered by the essential channel of a secretary. He experimented with various audio systems over the years, but they were always a dismal failure. 'There's nothing to beat "Miss",' he would say. However, Clementine became restive if too many letters were typewritten.

Both of them were frequent 'telegraphers' and must have tested the tele-graph services to the hilt, in the days when telegrams were mostly written out by hand at the local Post Office – especially if strange Churchillian words such as 'WOW' appeared in the text. If Winston was much beset by speeches and bookwork and had fallen behind in letter-writing, he would try to fill the gap with a series of telegrams to his absent 'cat' – who, on one occasion, responded scratchily: 'Please don't telegraph – I hate telegrams just saying "all well rainy weather Love Winston." '

During the Second World War absences from each other were fewer, and chiefly occurred when Winston was on his journeyings to, from, and at conferences. Despite the enormous pressure of his work, Winston was an amazingly good correspondent, his letters and telegrams bringing her news about the current talks. Home front news from Clementine was, of necessity, less enthralling, though sometimes punctuated by the crump of bombs.

Telegrams then kept them in touch, and often formed the only speedy link between them: sent always in code, and of course seen by other eyes (unlike their letters) – and there were no reproaches now! Through these staccato messages one senses the pressures, the secrecy and the controlled, but acute, anxiety of those at home. It is easy to forget the dangers and discomforts of wartime travel. Journeys with the Navy, or aboard the *Queen Mary* (the great passenger liner converted into a troop carrier) were the most tolerable – though the risk of enemy detection and attack was ever present; but air travel could be spartan: to the risks of enemy action were added the technical limitations of aircraft then in use. Early in the war, flight range was severely limited by refuelling necessity; the main body of the aircraft was not heated; there was no cabin pressurization (oxygen could be supplied only exceptionally, by a mask attached to a mobile cylinder); routeing was governed by many factors, and sometimes changed during a journey (at sea, for instance, to avoid reported submarines); until European countries were liberated, long detours had to be made on flights to North Africa and the Middle East. Many of these factors emerge quite casually in the letters, as do also the severe discomforts for even VIP passengers, travelling in aircraft designed essentially for war purposes. Recorded gratefully, too, are the improvements which appeared on successive journeys: the much better facilities of the York aircraft being superseded by those of Skymaster.

The insistence of my publishers that this correspondence must be contained in a single volume has meant that many letters have had to be omitted and others drastically cut. This has been for me a painful process, but, ably assisted by Ann Hoffmann, I established a yardstick: some letters are repetitious or simply not as interesting as others; discussion of travel or domestic plans; letters concerning family and financial arrangements; too many references to minor health problems and their remedies; lists of luncheon or dinner guests – all these were candidates for cutting. Clementine's lively but extremely long travelogues of her journeys to the Far East and the West Indies in the 1930s merit a book of their own, but here have had to suffer severe curtailment, as have passages in Winston's Chartwell Bulletins.

This book is *my selection* of the letters between my parents. The definitive edition remains to be done – a mammoth task indeed. Meanwhile the entire archive (the Chartwell Papers, the Churchill Papers and the Baroness Spencer-Churchill Papers) is available for inspection at the Churchill Archives Centre, Churchill College, Cambridge, and the Second World War telegrams at the Public Record Office, Kew.

I am satisfied that the letters presented here show my parents as the human beings they were. In speaking for themselves they have revealed their characters and their relationship: we see them in their ardent and debonair exchanges in the early years of their marriage; we see them maturing in the years of endeavour, and the flowering of Winston's political career; we feel them bearing the anguish of the trauma of the Dardanelles, and Winston's crashing fall from power. After the First World War the letters tell of the interim years of peace: of Clementine's long and deep-seated disenchantment with Winston's 'Chartwell Dream'; of the money troubles which were a nagging cause of worry, particularly to her. We come to wonder at Winston's amazing zest for work and play; the children grow up, causing their parents the usual hopes, fears and disappointments; we share in family griefs.

Their letters in their last decade together form the coda to their lives. Winston felt deeply the fading of his great powers, his giant's constitution ineluctably undermined by a series of strokes (a major one in 1953): he reluctantly and finally relinquished the reins of office in 1955. But he still had books to complete; Chartwell; his racehorses; and – of course – painting. He fought his last election (albeit in muted form) in 1959, and continued to set great store by his attendance in the House of Commons. Sadly, he said to

Diana in 1960: 'My life is over, but it is not yet ended.'[2] And the dusk deepened for him when he retired from his parliamentary seat in 1964.

Clementine, although ten years younger than Winston, was exhausted emotionally and physically by the time they reached this last lap of the road together: she had hoped he would retire after 1945, not battle on as Leader of the Opposition – let alone undertake another spell as Prime Minister. She trudged on valiantly – but at a cost: her own nature, as well as ailments deriving principally from nervous tension and over-anxiety, made this last stint of Winston's public life increasingly hard for her. Her beautiful and *soignée* appearance at all times, and the effect she usually gave of serenity, were artefacts of a long lifetime of self-control. Of course there were sunshine times: Chartwell had become less of a financial burden and more of a pleasure to her; the prospect of its continuing future (since 1946) as a National Trust property encouraged her to undertake long-term projects. Grandchildren of a wide span of ages were a delight and a stimulation; she travelled with friends, and enjoyed four sea voyages with Winston on Ari Onassis' yacht, the *Christina*. In September 1958 they celebrated, amid joy shared by many, their Golden Wedding. In the New Year of 1959 they both made a last visit to Marrakech with a group of old friends; Winston would soon give up painting, but he painted a scene from the terrace of his hotel bedroom.

And still in absences there were letters – although not so full of news and views as of old: now it was weather reports; visits from friends; news of grandchildren – and health. In these last years Clementine's pen ran dry, and she became a somewhat meagre correspondent. Winston, however, struggled on, drawing her attention to his 'own paw' efforts: the letters are short, and the writing wavery, but his notes constantly assure her of his love and tender concern.

Our grandparents tied their precious letters in neat bundles with pink tape; Winston and Clementine's letters of a lifetime lie in folders, and are part of our national archive: but were they to have been traditionally packeted, surely one may feel after reading them, that the thread which binds the bundles is the golden thread of love.

MARY SOAMES
London
March 1998

[2] Martin Gilbert, *Churchill: A Life*, 1991, p. 956.

Acknowledgements

I am most grateful to my nephew, Winston S. Churchill, and to C & T Publications Ltd, for permission to use my father's letters and other material of which they hold the copyright. I wish also to express my thanks to the Master Fellows and Scholars of Churchill College in the University of Cambridge, for allowing me and my researcher access to the Chartwell Papers, the Churchill Papers and the Baroness Spencer-Churchill Papers, and for their permission to use material from these papers which lies within their copyright.

The principal sources for the historical commentaries, footnotes and bio-graphical notes which accompany these letters are the eight volumes of my father's official biography, *Winston S. Churchill*, begun by my brother Randolph S. Churchill (Volumes I and II) and continued after his death in 1968 by Martin Gilbert (later Sir Martin Gilbert CBE); the accompanying *Companion Volumes* I–V; *The Churchill War Papers*, Volumes I and II; and, also by Martin Gilbert, the one-volume biography, *Churchill: A Life*.

I would like to express my appreciation in particular for the wealth of detailed information contained in the *Companion Volumes*, which has been of immense assistance to me in commenting upon and annotating my parents' letters. I wish to thank Sir Martin also for allowing me to use a number of his excellent maps, and to make short quotations from his works. And most especially am I grateful to him for reading the finished typescript with particular regard to my commentaries.

I am immensely grateful to Dr Piers Brendon, Keeper of the Archives at Churchill College, Cambridge, since February 1995, for his great help, support and advice to myself and my literary assistant, Ann Hoffmann, on so many matters throughout the preparation of this book. We both wish also to express our warmest thanks to the Archives Centre team at Churchill College, led by Alan Kucia, for their unfailing helpfulness in our researches. In partic-ular I would like to thank Tamsin Pert for her dedicated diligence in searching out letters lurking in unexpected files.

I am most appreciative of the hospitality shown to myself and Ann Hoffmann by Sir Alec Broers, Master of Churchill College, 1990–6, and now Vice-Chancellor of the University of Cambridge, and Lady Broers at the Master's Lodge. My warm thanks also to the Bursar and his staff for accom-modating Ann Hoffmann in college on her several subsequent visits.

My heartfelt gratitude goes to my 'home team'. First to Ann Hoffmann, who again has been my right hand, and has borne the main burden: transcribing over 1,700 letters from manuscript; researching and constructing the greater number of the footnotes; and compiling the index. She has assisted me in the difficult task of deciding which letters to cut or omit. I have greatly valued her professional knowledge and advice, her unremitting hard work, and her resolute cheerfulness. When time pressed towards the end, Idina Le Geyt helped us enormously by researching some elusive matters in the British Library, the London Library, the Public Record Office and elsewhere; she has unearthed some nuggets, and we are extremely grateful and appreciative of her skill and efforts.

Then to my Private Secretary, Nonie Chapman, who in addition to all she does for me normally has typed and retyped my draft commentaries, biographical notes, etc., and has maintained a close liaison with Ann Hoffmann; she has also done some valuable 'field' research in Kent and Surrey, and in so many other ways has helped this work on its way: I am truly grateful.

My thanks to Mike Shaw of Curtis Brown, my literary agent, who has so wisely advised me in many aspects of the production of this book. And to Anthea Morton-Saner, also of Curtis Brown, for her advice, especially in matters concerning copyright.

I wish to express my gratitude to the Doubleday team: especially to Sally Gaminara for her support, enthusiasm and understanding; to Claire Ward, who designed the jacket; and to Julia Lloyd, who designed the photographic section and the text pages. My thanks also to Gillian Bromley, the copy editor, for her eagle eye and meticulous care; and to Sheila Corr, the picture researcher, for her enthusiasm, and for finding some little-used photographs and matching them so often with the contents of the letters; and for her judicious choice of cats, pigs and pugs.

Grace Hamblin OBE, my parents' secretary for over forty years and the first National Trust Administrator at Chartwell, 1966–73, has helped me so much in remembering details of our family and domestic (particularly Chartwell) life, and by contacting former secretaries and staff for further information. Carole Kenwright, the Property Manager for the National Trust at Chartwell, has been most helpful, and I thank her. John Taylor-Smith of Taylor-Smith Books in Westerham most kindly gave me the rare and invaluable booklet, *Churchill, Townsman of Westerham* by Percy G. Reid.

I wish to thank most warmly John Holroyd CB, the Secretary for Appointments at No. 10 Downing Street, who informed me that there were folders of telegrams between Winston and Clementine Churchill sent during Second World War overseas conferences through official channels. Mr Holroyd allowed me to inspect these folders at No. 10 (they are now at the Public Record Office), and I found some most valuable additions to those already in my possession.

The following people have so kindly taken time and trouble to supply me with information on various subjects: Lady Ashburton; the Countess of Avon; Pam Botley; Sir Edward Cazalet; Mrs Peter Cazalet; Lord Cobbold; Clare Fleck, archivist at Knebworth House; His Excellency The French Ambassador, Monsieur Jean Guéginou; Sir Nicholas Henderson; the Duke of Marlborough; Sonia Melchett; Diana Neill; Jasper Ridley; Kenneth Rose; Graham Snelling, of the National Horse Racing Museum, Newmarket; Hugo Vickers.

I am grateful for assistance given to my researchers by the staff of the British Library; the British Library Newspaper Library, Colindale; the House of Lords Record Office; the London Library; Tunbridge Wells Public Library; and the Public Record Office; and by Dr Peter Simkins of the Imperial War Museum Research and Information Office.

The provenance of each illustration and the copyright holder (where known) are given on pp. vii–xii. But I wish to thank especially, for supplying, and for permission to use, various pictures, my first cousin Peregrine Spencer Churchill and my nephew Winston S. Churchill (The Broadwater Collection).

We have in all cases diligently tried to verify sources and copyright holders of all the pictures used, but this has in some cases proved extremely difficult or even impossible, particularly where photographs have come from private collections (often pasted down in albums); or where no clue to their original provenance exists. We apologize therefore for any omissions or errors which may have been inadvertently committed.

A book such as this owes much to the help, advice and encouragement of many people – and I am grateful to them all.

M.S.

Editor's Note

The greater number of the letters between Winston Churchill (WSC) and Clementine Hozier, later Churchill (CSC), has been drawn from the following sources, housed at the Churchill Archives Centre, Churchill College, Cambridge:

◇ the Chartwell Papers: WSC papers up to his resignation July 1945 (CHAR);
☐ the Churchill Papers: WSC papers post-resignation July 1945 (CHUR);
○ the Baroness Spencer-Churchill Papers (CSCT).

The corresponding symbol appears at the head of each letter.

A few Second World War telegrams are at the Public Record Office, Kew, in the Cabinet Papers and Premier Papers series; source references will be found below each telegram.

In some cases the original of a letter may be housed in one archive and a carbon copy in another, in which case the source of the original is given. Likewise, typed copies of some wartime telegrams (originals at the Public Record Office) are in the collections at Churchill College.

Most of the letters have been transcribed from photocopies of handwritten originals. Those from typed transcripts have been checked against the originals.

All letters are handwritten unless otherwise stated. The ✍ symbol indicates a handwritten insertion or addition to a typewritten letter.

Some WSC letters bear no salutation or end message/signature. In most cases this is because the only surviving archive copy is a carbon copy of a typewritten letter, not the original as sent.

Where WSC uses official headed writing paper, and we are aware that he is writing from elsewhere, the actual location, where known, is given in square brackets.

The symbol ✉ indicates that a letter or memorandum was sent by 'house post', i. e. when WSC and CSC were under the same roof.

Dates have been standardized throughout. A date within square brackets denotes either one supplied by the Editor for an undated letter, or a correction by the Editor.

In order to save space, some liberties have been taken with the use of ellipses (omission dots). In general, the conventional . . . indicates the omission of one or more words; at the end of a paragraph, however, . . . signifies the omission of the following paragraph or, in some cases, of more than one paragraph.

Both Winston and Clementine Churchill were erratic spellers: place names, names of people they knew quite well and ordinary words all suffered at the pens of these two highly educated people. Although I have hated tidying up these idiosyncrasies, I have followed the example of Sir Martin Gilbert and restored the majority of such words and names to their conventionally correct form; I have retained, however, WSC's abbreviations 'vy', 'cld' or 'cd', 'gt', '&', etc., and Clementine's much-favoured use of dashes rather than full stops. Punctuation also has been sometimes amended for easier comprehension.

Nicknames were much used within the family and close friends, and a glossary will be found on pages 663–5, together with the code names under which WSC/CSC travelled during the Second World War.

The symbol * in the text denotes that the person concerned has an entry in the Biographical Notes section (pp. 648–62). All other persons of relevance have a footnote on their first mention, with subsequent footnotes only when it is necessary to supply additional information relevant to the text. Readers should consult the index for these references.

The courtesy titles of Rt Hon./Hon./Honourable have been omitted throughout.

Most political 'labels' and terms are explained in the text or footnotes as they arise. However, the word 'Unionist' appears so often, either as an adjective or referring to the political theme or body of opinion, that I offer an explanation here, culled from *The Companion to British History*: 'In Britain, those who advocated the continuance of the parliamentary union of Britain and Ireland. They were formed from a coalition of Tories and Liberal Unionists in 1886, and the Tory Party later called itself both conservative and unionist . . . After the creation of Eire, unionism remained significant in relation to the six counties of Ulster.'

It is inevitable that much of the individual character of handwritten letters must be lost when they are reproduced in print. Sample pages of Winston and Clementine's letters are illustrated here, both in the plate section and as endpapers. Unfortunately lack of space has permitted the inclusion of only a small percentage of the hundreds of delightful pigs, pugs, cats and other animals with which they adorned their letters (often with witty comments) throughout their married life.

There was no time in their life together when outside events and politics were not present in Winston and Clementine's private life. Because of this, I have provided summaries of public events and political issues which are mentioned in their letters, or by which their lives or attitudes were influenced. In the footnotes and fuller Biographical Notes, I have tried to sketch the people who played their part in the crowded scene in which my parents moved. I am keenly aware that, for reasons of space, my treatment of sometimes complex issues, and my evaluation of the various personalities, verges on the simplistic: I hope, nevertheless, that they may provide a guide for my readers to the background of my parents' lives, and the circumstances in which these letters were written.

M.S.

SELECT FAMILY TREE

Showing Family Members & Connections *appearing in the* Letters
as at January 1998

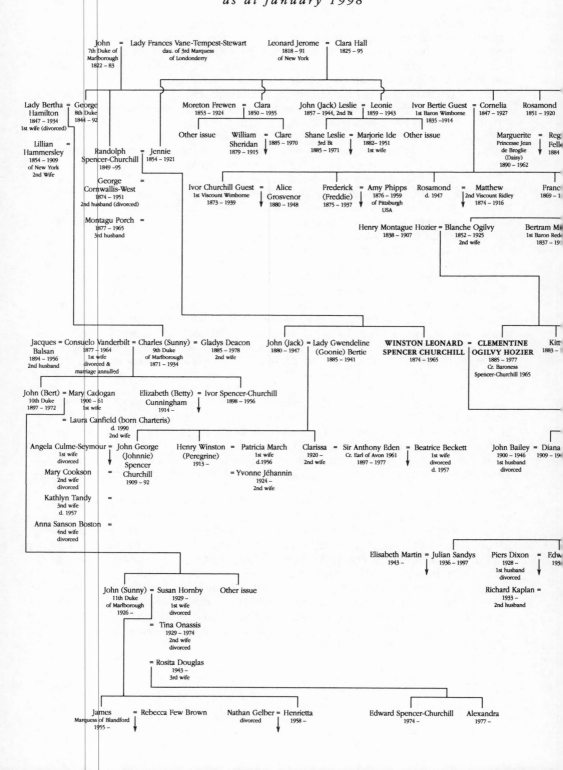

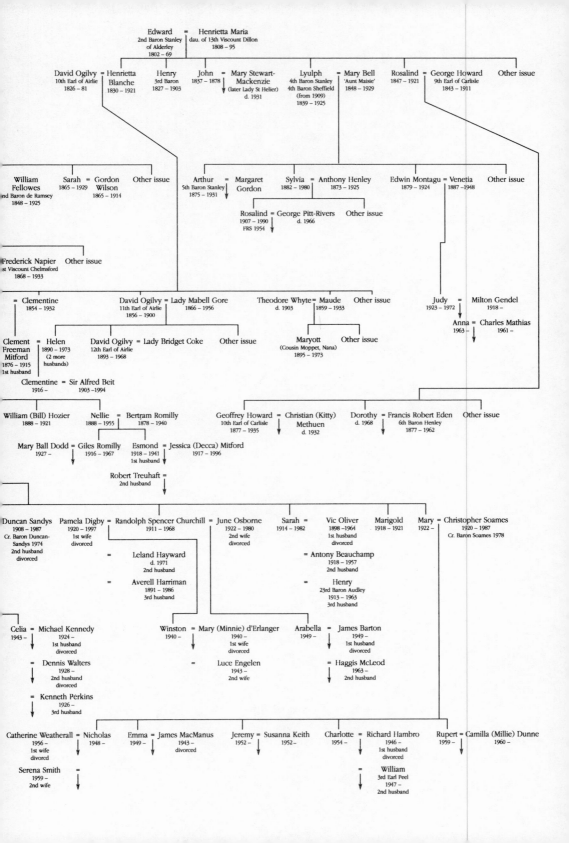

Edward = Henrietta Maria
2nd Baron Stanley | dau. of 13th Viscount Dillon
of Alderley | 1808 – 95
1802 – 69

David Ogilvy = Henrietta Blanche | Henry | John = Mary Stewart-Mackenzie | Lyulph = Mary Bell | Rosalind = George Howard | Other issue
10th Earl of Airlie | 1830 – 1921 | 3rd Baron | 1837 – 1878 | (later Lady St Helier) | 4th Baron Stanley | 'Aunt Maisie' | 1847 – 1921 | 9th Earl of Carlisle
1826 – 81 | | 1827 – 1903 | | d. 1931 | 4th Baron Sheffield (from 1909) 1839 – 1925 | 1848 – 1929 | | 1843 – 1911

William Fellowes | Sarah = Gordon Wilson | Other issue | Arthur = Margaret Gordon | Sylvia = Anthony Henley | Edwin Montagu = Venetia | Other issue
2nd Baron de Ramsey | 1865 – 1929 | 1865 – 1914 | | 5th Baron Stanley | 1875 – 1931 | 1882 – 1980 | 1873 – 1925 | 1879 – 1924 | 1887 –1948
1848 – 1925

Rosalind = George Pitt-Rivers | Other issue
1907 – 1990 | d. 1966
FRS 1954

Frederick Napier | Other issue
1st Viscount Chelmsford
1868 – 1933

Judy = Milton Gendel
1923 – 1972 | 1918 –

Anna = Charles Mathias
1963 – | 1961 –

= Clementine | David Ogilvy = Lady Mabell Gore | Theodore Whyte = Maude | Other issue
1854 – 1932 | 11th Earl of Airlie | 1866 – 1956 | d. 1903 | 1859 – 1933
| 1856 – 1900

Clement Freeman Mitford | = Helen | David Ogilvy = Lady Bridget Coke | Other issue
1876 – 1915 | 1890 – 1973 | 12th Earl of Airlie | 1893 – 1968
1st husband | (2 more husbands) |

Maryott | Other issue
(Cousin Moppet, Nana)
1895 – 1973

Clementine = Sir Alfred Beit
1916 – | 1903 –1994

William (Bill) Hozier | Nellie = Bertram Romilly | Geoffrey Howard = Christian (Kitty) Methuen | Dorothy = Francis Robert Eden | Other issue
1888 – 1921 | 1888 – 1955 | 1878 – 1940 | 10th Earl of Carlisle | d. 1932 | d. 1968 | 6th Baron Henley
| | | 1877 – 1935 | | | 1877 – 1962

Mary Ball Dodd = Giles Romilly | Esmond = Jessica (Decca) Mitford
1927 – | 1916 – 1967 | 1918 – 1941 | 1917 – 1996
| | 1st husband

Robert Treuhaft =
2nd husband

Duncan Sandys | Pamela Digby = Randolph Spencer Churchill | June Osborne | Sarah = Vic Oliver | Marigold | Mary = Christopher Soames
1908 – 1987 | 1920 – 1997 | 1911 – 1968 | 1922 – 1980 | 1914 – 1982 | 1898 –1964 | 1918 – 1921 | 1922 – | 1920 – 1987
Cr. Baron Duncan-Sandys 1974 | 1st wife divorced | | 2nd wife | | 1st husband divorced | | | Cr. Baron Soames 1978
2nd husband divorced

= Leland Hayward | = Antony Beauchamp
d. 1971 | 1918 – 1957
2nd husband | 2nd husband

= Averell Harriman | = Henry
1891 – 1986 | 23rd Baron Audley
3rd husband | 1913 – 1963
| 3rd husband

Celia = Michael Kennedy | Winston = Mary (Minnie) d'Erlanger | Arabella = James Barton
1943 – | 1924 – | 1940 – | 1940 – | 1949 – | 1949 –
| 1st husband divorced | | 1st wife divorced | | 1st husband divorced

= Dennis Walters | = Luce Engelen | = Haggis McLeod
1928 – | 1943 – | 1963 –
2nd husband divorced | 2nd wife | 2nd husband

= Kenneth Perkins
1926 –
3rd husband

Catherine Weatherall = Nicholas | Emma = James MacManus | Jeremy = Susanna Keith | Charlotte = Richard Hambro | Rupert = Camilla (Millie) Dunne
1956 – | 1948 – | 1949 – | 1943 – | 1952 – | 1952 – | 1954 – | 1946 – | 1959 – | 1960 –
1st wife divorced | | | divorced | | | | 1st husband

Serena Smith =
1959 –
2nd wife

= William
3rd Earl Peel
1947 –
2nd husband

Introduction

Winston Churchill and Clementine Hozier met for the first time at a ball at Crewe House[1] in London, in the summer of 1904. He was in his twenty-ninth year and she was nineteen years old.

Winston Churchill was born in 1874 at Blenheim Palace, the home of his grandparents, the 7th Duke and Duchess of Marlborough. He was the elder of the two sons of Lord Randolph Churchill* and Jennie Jerome (Lady Randolph Churchill*), one of three beautiful daughters of the American financier and newspaper owner Leonard Jerome of New York and his wife Clara.

After schooldays at Harrow, where scholastically young Winston showed little promise of brilliance to come – though often coming top of the class in history and geography – he opted for the Army and passed (at his second attempt) into the Royal Military College at Sandhurst. Commissioned as an officer in the 4th Hussars, a cavalry regiment, Winston at once sought excitement and action. During a prolonged period of leave he and a brother officer found both in Cuba, where the Spaniards were fighting a guerrilla uprising. Winston came under enemy fire for the first time on his twenty-first birthday, 30 November 1895.

In the autumn of the following year the 4th Hussars were posted to India. Winston soon became a first-class polo player; he also discovered the beauty of the butterflies. More importantly, during his nearly two years in India, he was seized with a great desire to learn: his mother found it difficult to satisfy his voracious appetite for books, with which she tried to keep him supplied. Constantly on the look-out for action, Winston hastened to take part, both as a war correspondent and as an officer, in the North-West Frontier campaign of 1897. His first book, *The Story of the Malakand Field Force*, published in 1898, is his account of that campaign. The book attracted considerable attention and was in general favourably commented upon.

Then a new field of action caught his restless attention: the Sudan and Egypt, where Lord Kitchener[2] was fighting the Mahdi[3]. Through a

---

[1] Home of the Earl (later Marquess) of Crewe (1858–1945), a prominent Liberal politician, and his second wife, Lady Margaret (Peggy) Primrose, younger daughter of the 5th Earl of Rosebery, whom he married in 1889.
[2] Kitchener, Horatio Herbert (1850–1916) KG, OM, PC, GCMG. Field Marshal, 1909; cr. Earl Kitchener of Khartoum, 1914. At this date Sirdar of the Egyptian army. Later Chief of Staff to Lord Roberts in South Africa, 1899–1900; C.-in-C. India, 1902–9; British Agent and Consul-General, Egypt, 1911–14; Secretary of State for War, 1914–15. Drowned at sea.
[3] Mohammed Ahmed (1848–85), Moslem Messiah.

combination of his mother's manipulations and the exertions of her friend Lady Jeune (later Lady St Helier)[4], and not least his own in enlisting the recommendation of the Prime Minister, Lord Salisbury[5], his wish was achieved. He joined the Army of the Nile, attached as a 'supernumerary' lieutenant to the 21st Lancers, in time to take part in one of the last cavalry charges of history, at Omdurman on 2 September 1898. His letters describing the battle were published in the *Morning Post*, and on his return to India he began a two-volume account of the Egyptian campaign, *The River War*, published in November 1899.

Politics now beckoned. Resigning his commission, in early July 1899 Winston fought a by-election as a Conservative Unionist at Oldham, Lancashire, where he was narrowly defeated. In October that year, the Boer War broke out, and he went out to South Africa as a correspondent for the *Morning Post*. On arrival in Cape Town he obtained a commission in the Lancashire Hussars and then proceeded to Natal. There followed a series of dramatic events.

On 15 November 1899 Churchill was aboard an armoured train making a reconnaissance into Boer-held territory, under the command of Captain Aylmer Haldane[6], when it was ambushed and derailed by Boers. During the skirmish, in which Churchill played a prominent and gallant part, Haldane, Churchill and fifty other officers were taken prisoner. But imprisonment irked Winston, and on 12 December he escaped[7] and headed eastwards towards the frontier with Portuguese Mozambique, a journey of some 300 miles through hostile country. After a series of adventures he arrived in Durban on 23 December to find himself a popular hero – his capture, imprisonment and escape, coupled with speculation as to his whereabouts and fate in the interval, having been reported around the world.

While he was in South Africa, Winston's one and only novel – *Savrola* – was published, followed by *London to Ladysmith via Pretoria* and, a little later, *Ian Hamilton's March*. Returning to England in July 1900, he stood once again at Oldham in the General Election of that autumn and was this time victorious, making his maiden speech in the House of Commons in the New Year of 1901.

In 1903 when Joseph Chamberlain[8] proclaimed his belief in Protection and Tariff Reform, and a drift towards Protection became evident in the Conservative Party, Winston, as a Free Trader, found himself increasingly out of sympathy with Conservative policies and mood. In May 1904 he crossed

---

[4] Mary Stewart-Mackenzie, whose first husband was Col. John Stanley, son of 2nd Baron Stanley of Alderley. Her second husband, Sir F. H. Jeune, was created Lord St Helier in 1905. A brilliant society hostess and Clementine's great-aunt by marriage, she died in 1931.
[5] Robert Gascoyne-Cecil, 3rd Marquess of Salisbury (1830–1903). Prime Minister 1885–6, 1886–92 and 1895–1902.
[6] Capt. (later Gen. Sir) James Aylmer Haldane (1862–1950) GCMG, KCB, DSO. Soldier and writer. C.-in-C. Mesopotamia, 1920–2.
[7] Two fellow prisoners, Capt. Haldane and RSM A. Brockie, with whom he had planned to escape, were prevented from doing so, and WSC, after waiting outside the prison wall as long as he dared, set off alone. Haldane and Brockie escaped three months later. Haldane later became embittered and accused WSC of abandoning his co-planners, although in his original account he made no such accusations. For full details of the escape and controversy, see Randolph S. Churchill, *Winston S. Churchill, Companion Vol. I*, 1967, pp. 1087–1116.
[8] Joseph Chamberlain (1836–1914), Secretary of State for the Colonies 1895–1903.

the floor of the House to sit with the Liberals. This defection caused him to be regarded as a renegade in the eyes of his own party, and by many others as a traitor to his class.

Politics was more passionate in those days and permeated social life. Winston found the doors of many of the great Tory houses closed to him; the Liberals, however, were enchanted by their new acquisition, and at Crewe House he was a welcome guest at the ball in the early summer of 1904.

Winston arrived at the ball with his mother, Jennie (now Mrs Cornwallis-West). Across the room, standing alone in a doorway, he saw a girl of great beauty.

Clementine was the second of the four children of Sir Henry Hozier* and Lady Blanche Ogilvy, daughter of the 10th Earl of Airlie. At the time of their marriage in 1878 she was twenty-six and he forty. Unlike his bride, the groom was not of noble stock, and despite a brilliant military career and the prospect of a secure future (he had been appointed Secretary to the Corporation of Lloyd's in 1874), Hozier was not a rich man. This, together with the difference in age and the fact that he had recently been divorced, did not make the marriage a particularly satisfactory one from a worldly point of view. But her parents may have acquiesced in the engagement with feelings of relief, for Blanche was already in her mid-twenties and combined with her great beauty and charm a wayward and tempestuous disposition.

With hindsight one realizes that Blanche and Henry's natures were too dissimilar for mutual happiness. An early and serious reason for discontentment on her side was her husband's declared determination not to have children; Blanche was deeply maternal by instinct. It was five years before the birth of her first child, Kitty, in 1883; Clementine followed in 1885, and the twins, Bill and Nellie, in 1888. We now know that it is extremely unlikely that Henry Hozier was the father of all – or indeed any – of these children. However, the marriage staggered on in an atmosphere of mounting bitterness until 1891, when, after threatening divorce, Hozier (against whom also there was firm proof of adultery) agreed to a separation.

In her later life Clementine became convinced that she was not the child of Henry Hozier, and she would occasionally privately speculate as to whether Kitty and the twins also were not his. But she had no inkling of all this in her youth, and although instinctively frightened of him – for his influence lowered over their family life – yet as she grew up she became increasingly interested in her presumed father, realizing what a brilliant and unusual man he was. It was a lifelong regret to her that Henry Hozier's death in 1907 precluded his knowing Winston.

What was her origin? It may be that Hozier believed his two elder children, Kitty and Clementine, to be his progeny; certainly he behaved in a possessive way towards them, while totally ignoring the existence of the twins. There is no doubt that Blanche Hozier was promiscuous; and at the time when her husband was threatening to divorce her, gossip had it that she had at least nine lovers[9].

One of Blanche's lovers was said to be her own brother-in-law, 'Bertie'

---

[9] Wilfrid Scawen Blunt, 'Secret Memoirs', vols. XIV, FM 31/75, 29 May 1891 and XV, FM 32/1975, p. 36.

Mitford[10], who had married her younger sister Lady Clementine Ogilvy in 1874. Mitford had entered the Foreign Office at the age of twenty-one and served in St Petersburg, Peking and Japan, writing several fascinating books about these places. A body of latter-day opinion believes him to have been Clementine's father.

There is another candidate, however, who must be considered for reasons which cannot be ignored. Blanche Hozier herself told Wilfrid Scawen Blunt[11], a former lover and long-time friend, that the father of her two elder children was Captain William Middleton[12] of the 12th Lancers, known as 'Bay' because of his bronzed hair and russet-coloured eyes. He was one of Lady Randolph's friends from hunting days in Ireland[13] and, coincidentally, she and Blanche Hozier were close friends during the earlier years of the latter's marriage. In Lady Randolph's London diary Middleton was clearly Blanche's lover[14].

Given Lady Blanche's promiscuity and the conflicting evidence, I find it difficult to take a dogmatic view about Clementine's paternity. Before the advent of DNA tests such questions must often be the subject of conjecture. As so often, the French express it so well: *Je n'y ai pas tenu la chandelle*. For the generation about which I am writing it seems more elegant for the dead to be allowed to keep their secrets.

After the Hoziers separated in 1891, Blanche was badly off, and a considerable degree of social stigma then attached to a woman living apart from her husband. She and her children and their governess lived in a series of rented furnished lodgings; but their peripatetic way of life may well have derived from Blanche's own capricious and restless nature. Summer holidays were spent at Airlie Castle, staying with Blanche's mother, the Dowager Countess of Airlie*. Visits were made also to the seaside, at Seaford in Sussex, and to the children's Stanley cousins in London and Cheshire, where Clementine formed lifelong ties of affection, especially with Sylvia (Henley*) and Venetia Stanley (Montagu*).

In the summer of 1899, with an unpredictable suddenness which marked so many events in the Hozier children's lives, their mother whisked them off to France. Her husband was defaulting on the meagre allowance he paid her, and Blanche was in debt; but the real reason for the decision to leave England was that she had cause to think that Hozier, despite his habitual neglect of his family, might try to regain custody of the two elder children. They settled in Dieppe, on the Normandy coast. But the family's life there was destined to be disrupted and darkened: in February 1900 Kitty fell ill with typhoid, and after a fortnight's harrowing illness died, just over a month short of her seventeenth birthday.

Kitty's death marked the end of a whole period in Clementine's life: she

[10] Algernon Bertram Freeman-Mitford (1837–1916), later 1st Baron Redesdale. Appointed GCVO for public services in 1905.
[11] Wilfrid Scawen Blunt (1840–1922), poet, Arabist and passionate protagonist of Home Rule for Ireland. He was a brilliant man and a great womanizer.
[12] Capt. William Middleton (1846–92). A brilliant horseman and dashing rider to hounds. Killed steeplechasing.
[13] Lord Randolph had been Private Secretary to his father, the 7th Duke of Marlborough, when the latter was Lord Lieutenant of Ireland, 1876–80, and he and Jennie had lived in Dublin for four years.
[14] John Pearson, *Citadel of the Heart*, 1991, p. 118.

had lost her dearest friend and companion; Kitty also had been her mother's favourite, and Clementine now was a lonely figure in the family (the twins were still children); she lacked her elder sister's spirits and self-assurance, and in early adolescence showed little sign of the beauty she was to become.

After Kitty's death, Blanche Hozier took her family back to England, settling in Berkhamsted, in Hertfordshire, so that the children could continue their education there. Whereas most girls of her class were still at this time governess-taught, Clementine benefited greatly from the higher and more purposeful level of education she received at the Berkhamsted School for Girls, where she mixed with a wider world of companions.

As Clementine approached her later teens, her mother became concerned as to how to launch her into the society to which by birth she belonged. Warm-hearted Lady St Helier (her great-aunt), who lived in considerable grandeur in London, came to the rescue, taking Clementine to balls and including her in dinner parties.

The next few years were however neither easy nor happy for Clementine: although now increasingly beautiful and much admired, she was by nature rather shy and reserved; and at home there was continual tension between herself and her mother. To augment her meagre allowance she gave French lessons, and also worked for some time for a cousin who had a small dress-making business.

At the ball at Crewe House in 1904 Winston had asked his mother to introduce him to the girl whose beauty had so impressed him across the crowded ballroom: the introduction effected, however, Winston simply stood rooted to the spot staring at her, not uttering a word. Clementine, greatly embarrassed, signalled to a beau, who promptly came up and asked her to dance, remarking as he swept her away that he was surprised to see her talking to 'that frightful fellow Winston Churchill'. After this unpropitious meeting it would be four years before their paths crossed again.

Clementine did not lack for admirers. She had a *fidèle serviteur* in Sidney Peel[15], a man of brilliance and distinction who loved her devotedly; twice they were secretly engaged: but instinctively she knew the difference between friendship and love. In 1906 she became officially engaged to Lionel Earle[16], a distinguished civil servant nearly twice her age, but after a few weeks she began to have grave doubts, and (to her eternal credit) Lady Blanche supported her in her decision to break off the engagement, although it would have been a good solid match for an impecunious girl.

Winston was never a 'ladies' man', yet he greatly admired beautiful, spirited women and had over these last years formed several attachments. His first great love was Pamela Plowden, daughter of the Resident at Hyderabad, whom he had met as a young subaltern in India; in 1902 she married the Earl of Lytton[17], but their friendship would be lifelong. Presently Winston

[15] Col. Sir Sidney Cornwallis Peel (1870–1938), third son of 1st Viscount Peel. In 1914 he married Lady Adelia (Delia) Spencer. Created 1st Bt Peel, 1936.
[16] Lionel Earle (1866–1948), knighted, 1916.
[17] Victor Lytton (1876–1947), 2nd Earl of Lytton, 1891. Held various government appointments including Under-Secretary of State for India, 1920–2; Acting Viceroy of India, April–August 1925. Married, 1902, Pamela Plowden (1874–1971). Their heir, Anthony, Viscount Knebworth, was killed in a flying accident in 1933, aged thirty; their younger son killed in action at Alamein, 1942. The title was inherited by Lord Lytton's younger brother, Neville (3rd Earl of Lytton, 1879–1951).

courted another beautiful woman, Muriel Wilson[18], daughter of a Hull shipowner; she rejected him (it is said she did not think he had much of a future); they too always remained friends. He also proposed to Ethel Barrymore, the famous actress, but she said she felt unable to cope with the world of politics – and politics would always be his world, and his first passion.

In December 1905, after twenty years of Conservative rule, Balfour[19], whose Government was being seriously weakened by the split over Protection, resigned and was succeeded by the Liberal leader, Sir Henry Campbell-Bannerman, who offered Winston his first governmental post, as Under-Secretary of State at the Colonial Office. In the General Election of the following year (1906) the Liberal Party swept back to power with a large majority over all other parties. Sir Henry resigned on account of ill-health in early April 1908 and was succeeded by Herbert H. Asquith*, in whose new Government Churchill, aged thirty-three, entered the Cabinet as President of the Board of Trade.

A few weeks earlier, at a dinner party given by Lady St Helier, Winston had met Clementine again. In retrospect the romance of the coincidence is compelling: Clementine had been invited by her great-aunt at the very last moment, to prevent the company being an unlucky thirteen. Clementine was tired, had no clean white gloves (an imperative in those days), and felt disinclined to accept the invitation. But her mother scolded her, reminded her of Great-Aunt Mary's many kindnesses, and hounded her off. Likewise, the Under-Secretary of State for the Colonies felt averse to the prospect of a society dinner that evening, but was nagged by his firm and faithful Private Secretary Eddie Marsh* into proper behaviour. Winston arrived late at the dinner party, and, after profuse apologies, found his place – next to Clementine Hozier; and this time he did not spoil his chances.

At her son's behest Lady Randolph invited her old friend Lady Blanche and Clementine to her home, Salisbury Hall (near St Albans), for the weekend of 11–12 April. Much was now afoot in Winston's life: he was seriously in love, and his appointment as President of the Board of Trade was made that weekend. But fate decreed that almost immediately the lovers should be parted. On being appointed a minister, a Member of Parliament then had to seek re-election; Winston had therefore to fight a by-election in his seat at North West Manchester, which he had won as a Liberal in the General Election. Clementine, for her part, was pledged to leave on 13 April to go with her mother to Nordrach in Germany, to collect her sister Nellie, then in the last weeks of a rigorous cure for tuberculosis. On their way home the three of them planned to visit old Lady Airlie at her summer home in Florence. It must have been hard indeed for Clementine to leave England just then. As for Lady St Helier, she thought Blanche Hozier had taken leave of her senses in removing her daughter at this juncture.

Now began the long dialogue in letters between Winston and Clementine which was to extend over half a century.

[18] Muriel Wilson (1871–1964). Married (1917) Maj. Richard Warde.
[19] Arthur James Balfour (1848–1930), created 1st Earl of Balfour, 1922. Conservative statesman and philosopher. Entered Parliament 1874. Prime Minister, 1902–5. Succeeded WSC as First Lord of the Admiralty, 1915. Foreign Secretary, 1916–19; Lord President of the Council, 1919–22 and 1925–9. Died unmarried.

Chapter I

COURTSHIP AND MARRIAGE

O From WSC   12 Bolton Street, W.
16 April 1908

I am back here for a night and a day in order to 'kiss hands' on appointment, & I seize this fleeting hour of leisure to write & tell you how much I liked our long talk on Sunday, and what a comfort & pleasure it was to me to meet a girl with so much intellectual quality & such strong reserves of noble sentiment. I hope we shall meet again and come to know each other better and like each other more: and I see no reason why this should not be so. Time passes quickly and the six weeks you are to be abroad will soon be over. Write therefore and tell me what your plans are, how your days are occupied, & above all when you are coming home. Meanwhile I will let you know from time to time how I am getting on here in the storm; and we may lay the foundations of a frank & clear-eyed friendship which I certainly should value and cherish with many serious feelings of respect.

So far the Manchester contest has been quite Napoleonic in its openings & development. The three days I have been in the city have produced a most happy change in the spirits of my friends, & not less satisfactory adjustments of the various political forces. Jews, Irish, Unionist Free Traders – the three doubtful elements – wh were all alleged to be estranged, have come or are coming back into line, & I have little fear of their not voting solidly for me on Friday.

The Socialist candidate is not making much progress as he is deserted by the Labour party. He will however deprive me of a good many votes, and this is the most disquieting feature in a situation otherwise good and rapidly improving. Even with the risk that a contrary result may be proclaimed before this letter overtakes you, I must say I feel confident of a substantial success. Lady Dorothy[1] arrived of her own accord – alone & independent. I teased her by refusing to give a decided answer about women's votes, she left at once for the North in a most obstinate temper. However on reading my answers given in public, back she came and is fighting away like Diana for the Greeks – a vy remarkable lady in every respect. But my eye what a tyrant! Mind of marble – calm, unerring, precise, ruthless in its logic devoid of flexibility – a thing to admire, but not to bruise yourself against. Yet – a dear!

I never put too much trust in formulas & classifications. The human mind & still more human speech are vy inadequate to do justice to the infinite variety & complexity of phenomena. Women so rarely realise this. When they begin to think they are so frightfully cock-sure. Now nature never deals in black or white. It is always some shade of grey. She never draws a line without smudging it. And there must be a certain element of give & play even about the most profound & assured convictions. But perhaps you will say this is only the sophistry of a political opportunist. Will you? Well I shall not mind, so that you say it in a nice letter to

Yours vy sincerely
Winston S. Churchill

[1] Lady Dorothy Howard, daughter of the 9th Earl of Carlisle and his wife Rosalind (Stanley). CSC's cousin. In 1913 she married Francis Robert Eden, 6th Baron Henley (1877–1962). She died 1968.

O From CSC   Nordrach-Colonie
Thursday 23 [April 1908]   Badischer Schwarzwald

Your letter found me here only yesterday – Seemingly, our maid at home thought there was no hurry in forwarding letters – if it were not for the excitement of reading about Manchester every day in the belated newspapers I should feel as if I were living in another world than the delightful one we inhabited together for a day at Salisbury Hall –

All day long here, people are struggling to get well – Many with absolute success as in the case of Nellie whom Mother & I carry off to Milan on the 30th. Most of the time there will have to be devoted to getting clothes for Nellie who after 9 months here looks like a suffragette after a hot scrimmage ...

I feel so envious of Dorothy Howard – It must be very exciting to feel one has the power of influencing people, ever so little. One more day & we shall know the result of the Election – I feel as much excited as if I were a candidate.

Lately I have felt as if I wanted something to keep the mind about which you say kind things to me, steady & balanced, so I studied every word of Lord Cromer[1] to the very end – But now I have begun your book[2] – so instinct with life & vitality – This letter will reach you after the storm & stress of Manchester is over, otherwise I would not take up a minute of your time –

I don't know if wishing & hoping can influence human affairs – if so – poor Joynson-Hicks![3]

Yours very sincerely
Clementine Hozier

[1] Evelyn Baring, 1st Earl of Cromer (1841–1917). Agent and Consul-General in Egypt, 1883–1907. His *Modern Egypt*, 2 vols, was published in 1908.

[2] Probably WSC's *Lord Randolph Churchill* (1906), which he had promised to send her.
[3] William Joynson-Hicks, Conservative, won by 429 votes. Polling day was 23 April.

○ From WSC   Taplow[1]
27 April [1908]

I was under the dull clouds of reaction on Saturday after all the effort &
excitement of that tiresome election, and my pen did not run smoothly or
easily. This morning however I am again buoyant, and refreshed by a
quiet & cheery Sunday here, I set myself to write you a few lines.

It was a real pleasure to me to get your letter & telegram. I am glad to
think you watched the battle from afar with eye sympathetic to my
fortunes. It was a vy hard contest & but for those sulky Irish Catholics
changing sides at the last moment under priestly pressure, the result would
have been different. Now I have to begin all over again – probably
another long & exhausting election. Is it not provoking!

The Liberal party is I must say a good party to fight with. Such loyalty &
kindness in misfortune I never saw. I might have won them a great victory
from the way they treat me. Eight or nine safe seats have been placed at
my disposal already. From my own point of view indeed the election may
well prove a blessing in disguise. It is an awful hindrance to anyone in my
position to be always forced to fight for his life & always having to make
his opinions on national politics conform to local exigencies. If I had won
Manchester now, I should probably have lost it at the general election.
Losing it now I shall I hope get a seat wh will make me secure for many
years. Still I don't pretend not to be vexed. Defeat however consoled
explained or discounted is odious. Such howls of triumph from the Tory
Press; such grief of my poor friends & helpers; such injury to many
important affairs. There is only one salve – everything in human power
was done.

We are having hateful weather here – blizzards, frost, raw wind –
perfectly vile to everyone:... How I wish I could get away to Florence &
the sun. But here I am bound upon the wheel of things.

Lady Dorothy fought like Joan of Arc before Orleans. The dirtiest slum,
the roughest crowd, the ugliest street corner. She is a wonderful woman –
tireless, fearless, convinced, inflexible – yet preserving all her
womanliness.

How I should have liked you to have been there. You would have
enjoyed it I think. We had a jolly party and it was a whirling week. Life for
all its incompleteness is rather fun sometimes.

Write to me again – I am a solitary creature in the midst of crowds.
Be kind to me.

Yours vy sincerely
W

[1] Taplow, Bucks, home of William Henry Grenfell, 1st Baron Desborough (1855–1945), and his
wife Ethel (Ettie) Fane.

O From CSC   Hotel Como
Sunday 3 May [1908]   Milan

Your letter reached me just before we left Nordrach. Manchester was a
horrible disappointment. But I am not surprised that the Liberal Party
treated you as if you had won them a victory, for I am sure they felt that
no one but you would have lost so few votes under the circumstances.

I hate to think of you having the fatigue and worry of another election.

We have not had any newspapers for 2 days so I don't know what is
happening in Dundee – or anywhere else. I have lost the thread. I do
hope all is going as you wish –

We have been here three days and after the bitter cold of Nordrach, it
feels like Heaven. As a matter of fact the town is modern and not very
interesting but the sun makes everything beautiful and happy –
Everywhere are the most gorgeous azaleas in full bloom. . . .

Mother has a mania for buying animals wherever she goes – It is most
inconvenient when travelling – In Paris she bought 2 Java sparrows from a
boy in the street – It was only by saying that she must choose between me
& the sparrows that she consented to leave them behind – Yesterday she
wanted a little Italian mongrel, called a 'lupetto' – Fortunately the
quarantine prevented that – Today love-birds are the danger – I have not
yet thought of a good objection to them –

Thursday we go to Florence[1]. I do hope you will have a record
majority –

Yours very sincerely
Clementine Hozier

[1] To stay with CSC's grandmother, Blanche, Countess of Airlie.

After his rejection by the voters of North West Manchester, Winston soon
found himself another seat – Dundee, in Scotland – where in early May he
fought his third by-election, and this time won by a sizeable majority. He
was to represent Dundee for fourteen years.

During June and July Winston and Clementine saw one another several
times, but since in those days unmarried girls did not dine or lunch alone
with men their meetings were confined to social occasions. They both had
pre-arranged plans for the early part of the summer recess, but arranged to
meet at Salisbury Hall in the middle of August. Meanwhile Clementine went
to stay near Cowes, on the Isle of Wight, where she was a somewhat *distrait*
guest at various balls and entertainments. Before the marriage of his younger
brother Jack Churchill* to Lady Gwendeline Bertie (always called 'Goonie')[1],
Winston went to stay at Burley-on-the-Hill at Oakham in Rutland, which had
been rented by his cousins Freddie Guest* and Henry Guest. In the early
hours of 6 August a fire broke out after everyone had retired to bed, and a
whole wing of the house was burned to the ground. Clementine, at Cowes,
heard garbled reports about the fire and was frantic with worry until she read
a full account of the event in *The Times*. Greatly relieved at the knowledge
that Winston was unharmed (although he had played a leading part in

rescuing pictures and other valuables from the conflagration), she cast discretion to the winds and telegraphed him her relief and joy.

[1] Lady Gwendeline Bertie (1885-1941), daughter of the 7th Earl of Abingdon.

○ From WSC   Nuneham Park[1]
7 August 1908   Oxford

This is only to be a line to tell you how much I am looking forward to seeing you on Monday. But I have a change of plan to propose wh I hope you will like. Let us all go to Blenheim for Monday & Tuesday & then go on, on Wednesday to Salisbury Hall. Sunny [9th Duke of Marlborough*, WSC's cousin] wants us all to come & my mother will look after you – & so will I. I want so much to show you that beautiful place & in its gardens we shall find lots of places to talk in, & lots of things to talk about. My mother will have already wired you & Sunny will do so tomorrow. There will be no one else there except perhaps F. E. Smith* and his wife.

Jack has been married to-day – <u>civilly</u>.[2] The service is tomorrow at Oxford: but we all swooped down in motor-cars upon the little town of Abingdon and did the deed before the Registrar – for all the world as if it was an elopement – with irate parents panting on the path. Afterwards we were shown over the Town hall & its relics & treasures – quite considerable for so small a place – & then back go bride & bridegroom <u>to their respective houses</u> until tomorrow. Both were 'entirely composed' & the business was despatched with a celerity and ease that was almost appalling.

I was delighted to get your telegram this morning & to find that you had not forgotten me. The fire was great fun & we all enjoyed it thoroughly. It is a pity such jolly entertainments are so costly. Alas for the archives. They soared to glory in about ten minutes. The pictures were of small value, & many, with all the tapestries & about ½ the good furniture were saved. I must tell you all about it when we meet. My eyes smart still & writing is tiring.

It is a strange thing to be locked in deadly grapple with that cruel element. I had no conception – except from reading – of the power & majesty of a great conflagration. Whole rooms sprang into flame as by enchantment. Chairs & tables burnt up like matches. Floors collapsed & ceilings crashed down. The roof descended in a molten shower. Every window spouted fire, & from the centre of the house a volcano roared skyward in a whirlwind of sparks.... It is only the archives that must be mourned inconsolably. Poor Eddie Marsh* lost everything (including many of my papers) through not packing up when I told him to. I saved all my things by making Reynolds [his manservant] throw them out of the window. It was lucky that the fire was discovered before we had <u>all</u> gone to sleep – or more life might have been lost – than one canary bird; & even as it was there were moments of danger for some.

Your telegram to my mother has just arrived.

It is my fault that the plan has changed. I thought it would be so nice to go to Blenheim, & I proposed it myself to Sunny. If you have a serious reason for not wishing to go there, I will telegraph to him in the morning & try to stop arrangements; but I fear he will already have asked F. E. Smith & his wife to balance us.

I do hope that your reluctance is only due to not quite understanding the change & fancying there was to be a great function or to very naturally requiring some more formal invitation; & not to any dislike of Sunny or harsh unfavourable judgement wh you have been led – perhaps on imperfect information – to form of him. He is my greatest friend, & it would pain me vy much – if that were so. But I am sure it is not. Write & tell me all about it & about your days at Cowes; & what you have been thinking of; & whether you would have thought of me at all – if the newspapers had not jogged your memory! You know the answer that I want to this.

Always yours
W.

¹ Home of Mr and Mrs Lewis Harcourt, where some of the escapees from Burley had taken refuge. A prominent Liberal politician, 'Lulu' Harcourt (1863-1922) was created 1st Viscount Harcourt in 1916.
² The bride was a Roman Catholic.

○ From WSC   Nuneham
8 August [1908]

My dear – I have just come back from throwing an old slipper into Jack's departing motor-car. It was a vy pretty wedding. No swarms of London fly-catchers. No one came who did not really care, & the only spectators were tenants & countryfolk. Only children for bridesmaids & Yeomanry with crossed swords for pomp. The bride looked lovely & her father & mother were sad indeed to lose her. But the triumphant Jack bore her off amid showers of rice & pursuing cheers – let us pray – to happiness & honour all her life.

I was vy glad to get your telegram this morning that you will come to Blenheim on Monday. There will be no one at all except my mother & the Smiths & Mr Clark my secretary of the Board of Trade, & the duke and his little son – just blossomed, or rather poured into Eton jackets. You need have had no apprehensions, for I am as wise as an owl when I try, & never take steps of which I am not sure.

Here at Nuneham we have the debris of the wedding party & also of Burley on the Hill. The Harcourts are most kind & hospitable and are entertaining all sorts of aunts, cousins & nieces collected for the event. Among the former – Leonie¹ – who brings me news from Cowes – of a young lady who made a great impression at a dance four nights ago on all beholders. I wonder who it could have been!...

I shall go over to Blenheim quite early on Monday, & mind you come by the first possible train. It is quite an easy journey from Southampton to Oxford via Didcot. I will meet you at Oxford in a motor-car if you will telegraph to me here what time you arrive.

You have not distinguished yourself very much as a correspondent; for no line of your handwriting has as yet glinted from among my letter-bag. But I suppose you were waiting for me – & I was hampered & hindered by Cruel Catastrophe. Alack!

Sunny made a charming speech after the breakfast & showed all his courtly address to the greatest advantage. I hope you will like my friend, & fascinate him with those strange mysterious eyes of yours, whose secret I have been trying so hard to learn. His life has been grievously mutilated[2], there are many to blame him – not altogether without cause. But any clever woman whom he loved could have acquired a supreme influence over his nature & he would have been as happy as he now is sad.

He is quite different from me, understanding women thoroughly, getting into touch with them at once, & absolutely dependent upon feminine influence of some kind for the peace & harmony of his soul. Whereas I am stupid & clumsy in that relation, and naturally quite self-reliant & self contained. Yet by such vy different paths we both arrive at loneliness!

I think you will be amused at Blenheim. It has many glories in the fullness of summer. Pools of water, gardens of roses, a noble lake shrouded by giant trees; tapestries, pictures & monuments within. And on Wednesday we will motor on to Salisbury Hall to humbler if homelier surroundings. For the rest I will do what I can to divert the hours, when better company fails. Till Monday then & may the Fates play fair.

Yours always
W

[1] Lady Leslie (1859–1943), younger sister of Lady Randolph, and WSC's aunt, who had married Sir John Leslie Bt of Castle Leslie, Co. Monaghan.
[2] His wife, the beautiful Consuelo Vanderbilt, whom he had married in 1895, had left him in 1906. See Biographical Notes under 'Balsan'.

O From CSC   Nubia House
Saturday night 8 [August 1908]   Cowes

I was so glad to get your delightful letter this morning – I retired with it into the garden, but for a long time before opening it I amused myself by wondering what would be inside –

I have been able to think of nothing but the fire & the terrible danger you have been in – The first news I heard was a rumour that the house was burnt down – That was all – My dear my heart stood still with terror –

All the same I did not need that horrible emotion to 'jog my memory' –

We all went to the ball the next night which I hated – I was extremely odious to several young partners not on purpose, but because they would interrupt my train of thought with irrelevant patter about yachts, racing, the weather, Cowes gossip etc. – So I was obliged to feign deafness –

Please do not think there is any real reason for my not at first wanting to go to Blenheim. It was only a sudden access of shyness –

We all went in a yacht to-day to a lovely place called Bembridge where most of the party played golf. I went on to Portsmouth to see Bill (my brother)[1] who is laid up in hospital with very bad rheumatism – I am rather worried about him – He looked very pale & lonely. . . .

Farewell till Monday –
Yours
Clementine H.

[1] William Hozier (1888–1921), at this date a sub-lieutenant in the Royal Navy.

The house party which assembled at Blenheim on Monday 10 August was composed of Winston and Lady Randolph Churchill*, Clementine, the F. E. Smiths* and Winston's Private Secretary.

Winston made an assignation with Clementine to walk in the rose garden the following morning after breakfast. He was (predictably) late, and Clementine – (predictably) punctual – was considerably ruffled by such cavalier behaviour; she seriously considered returning to London. The Duke, interpreting her mood, sent a sharp note upstairs to the dawdling Winston and, deploying all his charm, whirled Clementine off in his buggy for a tour of the park. On their return to the Palace, Winston was anxiously waiting.

That afternoon Winston and Clementine went for a walk and, overtaken by a shower, took refuge in the little Temple of Diana overlooking the Great Lake; there Winston proposed, and was accepted. Clementine enjoined secrecy upon him until she had told her mother, but as they returned to the house they met the Duke and other guests on the lawn; unable to contain his joy, Winston blurted out their happy news.

During the next few days the Blenheim maids and footmen were kept busy bearing notes up and down the long wide corridors.

○ From WSC ✉   Blenheim Palace
[12 August 1908]

My dearest,

How are you? I send you my best love to salute you: & I am getting up at once in order if you like to walk to the rose garden after breakfast & pick a bunch before you start. You will have to leave here about 10.30 & I will come with you to Oxford.

Shall I not give you a letter for your Mother?

Always
W.

○ From CSC ✉   Blenheim Palace
[12 August 1908]

My dearest
    I am very well – Yes please give me a letter to take to Mother –
    I should love to go to the rose garden.

                                                              Yours always
                                                              Clementine

After both visiting Lady Blanche at her home, 51 Abingdon Villas, in Kensington, and obtaining her consent and blessing, all three travelled back to Blenheim the same afternoon.
    Once more love notes flew along the corridors.

○ From WSC ✉   Blenheim Palace
[undated, probably 13 August 1908]

My dearest – I hope you have slept like a stone. I did not get to bed till 1 o'clock; for Sunny kept me long in discussion about his affairs wh go less prosperously than ours. But from 1 onwards I slept the sleep of the just, & this morning am fresh & fit. Tell me how you feel & whether you mean to get up for breakfast. The purpose of this letter is also to send you heaps of love and four kisses
    X X X X

                                                              from
                                                 Your always devoted
                                                              Winston

○ From CSC ✉   Blenheim Palace
[undated, probably 13 August 1908]

My darling
    I never slept so well & I had the most heavenly dreams
    I am coming down presently – Mother is quite worn out as we have been talking for the last 2 hours –
    Je t'aime passionnément – I feel less shy in French.

                                                              Clementine

The engagement was announced on Saturday 15 August, and Winston and Clementine spent that weekend at Salisbury Hall, with Lady Randolph Churchill*.

○ From WSC ⊠   [Salisbury Hall]
[undated]

My beloved – Get up! I want so much to see you. Let us go for a walk
before lunch. I slept till 10.30! Several interesting letters have arrived wh I
will show you. The sun shines bright, & my heart throbs to see you again
– sweet – precious –

                                                    Your devoted
                                                    W.

○ From CSC ⊠   Salisbury Hall
[undated]

Darling – I am surrounded by millions of letters which I am trying to
answer. I will be down in about an hour or a little more –
    I love you

                                                    Clementine

○ From WSC   12 Bolton Street
[undated]

My dearest & most truly beloved –
    I send you the King's telegram wh I have <u>dutifully</u> answered.
    There are no words to convey to you the feelings of love & joy by wh
my being is possessed. May God who has given to me so much more than
I ever knew how to ask keep you safe & sound.

                                                    Your loving
                                                    Winston

○ From CSC   Batsford Park[1]
[undated, probably August 1908]   Moreton-in-Marsh

My darling,
    I do long for you so much –
    I wonder how I have lived 23 years without you – Everything that
happened before about 5 months ago seems unreal – I had a very tedious
morning writing & writing till my fingers were cramped & inky – After
luncheon Uncle Berty [Mitford] said I needed some fresh air, so he took
me & Uncle Algernon[2] in his motor to Stratford where there were
numberless Americans looking at Shakespeare's birthplace etc – I fidgeted
inwardly as I thought I should miss the post. However I am just in time to
catch it and to tell you that I <u>love</u> you, but how much I shan't tell you –
you must guess.

Uncle Algernon likes you but is vexed to find how easily I have become a Liberal. He put me thro' a searching political catechism –
Goodbye my dearest one.

Yours always
Clementine

¹ Home of the Mitford (later Redesdale) family.
² Rt Revd Monsignor Algernon Stanley (1843–1928), son of 2nd Baron Stanley of Alderley.

O From CSC
[undated]

51 Abingdon Villas
Kensington

My Darling

Thinking about you has been the only pleasant thing today.

I have tried on so many garments (all of which I am told are indispensable)....

My tailor told me he approved of you & had paid 10/6d to hear you make a speech about the war at Birmingham – After that I felt I could not bargain with him any more....

I said nothing pleasant happened to-day but I was wrong – Nellie came home. We were very glad to see each other again.

Dearest I was so happy driving with you last night to the station

I long to see you again – Wednesday Thursday Friday 3 long days –

Goodbye my darling I feel there is no room for anyone but you in my heart – you fill every corner –

Clementine

Winston and Clementine were married at St Margaret's, Westminster, on 12 September 1908. Although it was the time of year when many people were away from London, the church was packed, and there was a large and enthusiastic crowd outside. The Bishop of St Asaph conducted the service, and the address was given by Bishop Welldon, Dean of Manchester – Winston's former Headmaster at Harrow. The old bishop must have been something of a prophet; in his address he said:

There must be in the statesman's life many times when he depends upon the love, the insight, the penetrating sympathy and devotion of his wife. The influence which the wives of our statesmen have exercised for good upon their husbands' lives is an unwritten chapter of English history ...

Chapter II

SETTING OUT

W inston and Clementine began their married life in Winston's bachelor house, 12 Bolton Street, W1, but in March 1909 they acquired a good family house: 33 Eccleston Square, SW1. By this time there was a certain urgency, as Clementine was expecting her first child in July. Between moves they stayed at Winston's cousin Freddie Guest's* house, 22 Carlton House Terrace.

On the political front the Liberal Government was forging ahead with its radical policies, laying in effect the foundation of the modern welfare state. At the Board of Trade Churchill was fully occupied with legislative measures which touched closely the working lives of millions of men and women. On taking over his new office Churchill sought to carry on the initiatives set in motion by Lloyd George*, whom he had succeeded, measures which included the Port of London Bill, setting up the Port of London Authority, and the Coal Mines (Eight Hours) Bill, limiting miners' working hours underground and improving safety.

It was the Board of Trade's role to assist in conciliation and arbitration of industrial disputes. The economic depression having caused several major employers to announce wage reductions, Churchill soon had his hands full with strikes and lock-outs: in January, the shipwrights; in February, the engineers; in May, in the shipyards on the Tyne, Merseyside and the Clyde; and later that summer the cotton spinners and weavers.

An ongoing problem was that of 'sweated labour', principally in the tailoring and dressmaking trades, but also in the docks. In April 1909 Churchill introduced the Trade Boards Act, setting up Trade Boards in scheduled trades with powers to establish minimum rates of pay and impose fines on employers who did not conform.

Unemployment had risen sharply in 1907–8, and to grapple with this problem Churchill, influenced by the work of Beatrice and Sidney Webb[1] and taking note also of German models, pioneered the creation of labour exchanges[2]. He laid the foundations of a scheme for compulsory unemployment insurance, and of old age pensions; these were carried forward by Lloyd George, as Chancellor of the Exchequer, and became a built-in part of Liberal legislation.

But all these measures had to be paid for. When Lloyd George introduced his so-called 'People's Budget' in April 1909, raising death duties and introducing not only super-tax but taxes on tobacco and liquor, motor cars and petrol, and – most controversially – land value duties, passions in Parliament and throughout the country rose to fever pitch. In July Clementine was among those who heard Lloyd George's famous 'Limehouse' speech, in which he whipped up public opinion with a savage attack on landlords. During the late summer and autumn the prospect grew that the Lords would reject the Finance Bill; and indeed, though passed by a large majority in the Commons on 4 November, it was defeated in the House of Lords on 30 November. Asquith* (Prime Minister since April) declared the Lords' action 'a break of the Constitution and a usurpation of the rights of the Commons'[3]. On 3 December the King granted a dissolution of Parliament, and preparations began for a General Election in the New Year. The Liberals' battle-cry was 'The Peers against the People'.

It was against this background of political activity and excitement that Winston and Clementine began their married life. He was used to the hurly-burly of politics; Clementine came new to it, but threw herself into the fray with enthusiasm. The demands of his work, and the birth of their first child, Diana, in 1909, meant that they were apart for fairly frequent, if brief, periods. But the shortest absence (a day or two) saw letters flying to and fro. Even in country districts there were three or four posts per day, and the young Churchills put them, and the telegraph service, to the test.

In these next letters we see the first use of the pet names by which they would address each other, and the lively drawings which would decorate their signatures for the rest of their lives.

Winston started as 'Amber Dog', then 'Pug'; gradually this motif was superseded by 'Pig'. And pigs and pugs happy or sad, rampant or frivolous – even the occasional lion or peacock – decorated many of his letters to his wife.

Clementine was the 'Cat' or 'Kat'. The rudimentary felines (pregnant when appropriate) accompanying her signature conveyed her mood to Winston. Occasionally she appeared as a strange hybrid, 'Clem Pussy Bird'. Their first baby-to-be was known as the 'Puppy Kitten' or 'P.K.'

[1] Sidney Webb, later 1st Baron Passfield (1859–1947), and his wife Beatrice (born Potter) (1858–1943). English social reformers and founders of the London School of Economics and the *New Statesman*.
[2] The forerunners of today's Job Centres.
[3] The Lords' rejection of the Budget shattered the tradition that control over raising and spending revenue was the exclusive prerogative of the House of Commons.

O From WSC   [Board of Trade]
21 April 1909

My darling,
I have missed you a great deal. Your room is vy empty. The poor pug pules disconsolate. Sweet cat – I will come tomorrow by the 6.15. Make them meet me. It will be delightful to be back again in beautiful Blenheim. . . .
The House marches steadily; & I think they will keep their engagements.
The marble basin has arrived. Your window is up – a great improvement. All the bookcases are in position . . . The dining room gleams in creamy white. The living room is prepared. The bath room well advanced. Altogether there will be a fine show for you on Monday.

I hope you read the debate last night on the B of Trade Status Bill. If not – get today's Times. . . .

I am to introduce my P.P.I. Insurance Bill tomorrow under the 10 minutes rule: & I will come down to Blenheim afterwards.

I am going to dine with Mamma who has also asked F.E [Smith*]. Late as usual!

So with fondest love and a bouquet of discriminating & judiciously placed kisses to my sweet & beloved Clemmie-cat

believe me your loving & devoted
Husband

○ From CSC   Blenheim Palace
21 April [1909]

My Darling,

Do try & come down here tomorrow instead of Friday – It is perfectly lovely but I can't enjoy it properly without you, whereas Lloyd George* can quite well manage his Disestablishment Bill alone –

A large gold crown has been fixed over the head of the Lady of the (Consuelo) fountain[1], while the attendant nymphs below are provided with golden tambourines –

The whole group now looks like a Pagan representation of the Assumption of the Virgin Mary attended by fallen members of the Salvation Army –

Sunny [Marlborough*] (much pleased), Goonie & I looked on while the crowns and tambourines were being fixed – Sunny after looking for a long time at the Lady of the fountain remarked that she was not a well modelled woman & that most of _his_ friends were better made! We then disparaged the Venus de Medici –

Goonie & I having spent the first part of the day together have now retired to write to Jack [Churchill*] & you. . . .

Here are several things <u>not</u> to forget. Wallpaper & mantelpiece & grate for your bedroom. . . .

I do hope you are quite comfortable at Carlton [House Terrace] – I telegraphed to Edith to find some curtains for your windows last night – I hope she did –

Goodbye my darling Winston
Your loving
Clemmie

The Wow   The Woo

---

[1] The fountain described is in the Italian Garden at Blenheim.

○ From CSC   Blenheim Palace
27 April [1909]

My Darling One

To my horror I find I have nearly missed the post, so this is only a
scrawl to bring you my love –

I had a long afternoon with Baxter & carpets – The green carpet is
lovely & will do beautifully for library....

In your room Nathan Laski's carpet, in mine blue bedroom carpet from
Bolton Street – (just enough) I tried hard to make the red stair carpet do
for the dining room, but it is really too shabby – The edges of stairs have
made ridges along it – & there are awful stains (not my dog this time![1]) ...
Green sickly looking carpet out of Jack's bedroom in Bolton Street does
Puppy Kitten rooms – Another bit does the Cook's room – A big rug (from
dining room in Bolton Street?) does my little sitting room, the edges done
with blue polished linoleum continued out of hall –

The whole house is now carpeted except one big servants room (which
can be done with cheap linoleum for about £2) <u>and</u> the Dining room! for
which new carpet will have to be got – I have written to the people who
are making the blue stair carpet to ask what it will cost to cover dining
room entirely with the blue – (4/6d a yard)....

I wonder if you will go to Alice Guest's[2] party tomorrow – Also there is
Lord Brooke's wedding but I expect you will be much harassed on
Thursday –

Goodbye my little Puggie Wow

I hope you are comfie – <u>Please</u> do some exercises in the morning to
please your loving little

                                                          Clemmie Kat

   . . .

[1] This is the only mention of CSC possessing a dog. There are no clues to this – I think – unique
animal's breed or name.
[1] Alice Guest (1880–1948), born Grosvenor, daughter of 2nd Baron Ebury. Wife of Ivor Churchill
Guest, 1st Viscount Wimborne.

○ From WSC   [House of Commons]
28 April [1909]

My darling – I write this line from the Bench. The Trade Boards Bill has
been beautifully received & will be passed without division. A Balfour &
Alfred Lyttelton[1] were most friendly to it, & all opposition has faded away.
But the House was tired & jaded and speaking to them was hard work.

You certainly have made a most judicious selection of carpets & I
entirely approve it.... The work is going on vy well. The book<u>shelves</u> are
being put in the cases & the colour is being most attractively polished.

Tomorrow is the day of wrath! I feel this Budget will be kill or cure:
Either we shall secure ample pounds for great reforms next year, or the
Lords will force a Dissolution in September.

I breakfasted yesterday with Cassel[2]. He wants us both to come to his

mountain villa. Post is just going so with best love & kisses, believe me
ever

Your loving & devoted
husband
W.

[1] Alfred Lyttelton, PC, KC (1857–1913), barrister and Liberal Unionist MP. Secretary of State for the Colonies, 1903–5. His first wife, Laura Tennant (d. 1886) was Margot Asquith's sister.
[2] Sir Ernest Cassel (1852–1921). Financier and philanthropist, of German Jewish origin, and a great figure in English society. Friend of Edward VII.

O From CSC   Blenheim Palace
29 April [1909]

My Darling

I am delighted that the Trade Boards Bill went so swimmingly, such amiable speeches from Mr Balfour & A. Lyttelton....

I hope you communicated with the scrubbing people in Victoria Street & ordered them to scrub forthwith; the furniture begins arriving at 9 a.m. tomorrow – A perpetual stream of vans will unload themselves all Friday & Saturday. I have written to Reynolds[1] & also to Edith the housemaid to tell them to be on the spot....

I am longing to see the library – Wouldn't it be rather fun to put the books in on Sunday? Do let me come up & we can do it together all day – We could cover the shelves with sheets afterwards to keep the dust off while the room is being cleaned....

Goodbye my dearest & best beloved little pug – I wish I had been near you during part of this fateful day –

Your loving
Clemmie

I hope you enjoyed Alice's party. It seemed very gay from the papers.

[1] George Reynolds, WSC's manservant.

Both Winston and Jack Churchill* held commissions in the Queen's Own Oxfordshire Yeomanry, and the summer camps were a great feature of the training. The ladies lodged agreeably in neighbouring mansions: often at Blenheim Palace and, as in 1909, with the Harcourts at Nuneham Park.

Goonie and Jack's first baby, John George, was born on 31 May, and Clementine gave birth to her first child, Diana, in London on 11 July. Although the birth was straightforward, Clementine took some time recovering and stayed with friends and relations during much of the later summer and autumn.

O From WSC   Camp Goring
30 [31] May 1909

My darling sweet –

    . . .
    I daresay you read in the papers about the Field day. My poor face was
roasted like a chestnut and burns dreadfully. We had an amusing day.
There were lots of soldiers & pseudo soldiers galloping about, & the 8
regiments of Yeomanry made a brave show. But the field day was not in
my judgment well carried out . . . These military men vy often fail
altogether to see the simple truths underlying the relationships of all armed
forces, & how the levers of power can be used upon them. Do you know
I would greatly like to have some practice in the handling of large forces. I
have much confidence in my judgment on things, when I see clearly, but
on nothing do I seem to <u>feel</u> the truth more than in tactical combinations.
It is a vain and foolish thing to say – but <u>you</u> will not laugh at it. I am sure
I have the root of the matter in me – but never I fear in this state of
existence will it have a chance of flowering – in bright red blossom.
    So Jack [Churchill*] & Goonie have their P.K.! Jack like a little turkey-
cock with satisfaction. 'Alone I did it' sort of air.
    It seems to have been a most smooth & successful affair. Goonie dined
out, walked home slept soundly till 2. Then felt the premonitory sensations
wh precede the act of destiny. And at 4 or 5 all was gloriously over – &
another soul – escaping from its rest or unrest in the oceans of the spirit
world crept timidly up on to a frail raft of consciousness & sense – there to
float – for a while. She hardly had any pain & Phillips [the doctor] was
most skilful.
    My dear Bird – this happy event will be a great help to you & will
encourage you. I rather shrink from it – because I don't like your having to
bear pain & face this ordeal. But we are in the grip of circumstances, &
out of pain joy will spring & from passing weakness new strengths arise.
    Bourke Cockran[1] – a great friend of mine – has just arrived in England
from U.S.A. He is a remarkable fellow – perhaps the finest orator in
America, with a gigantic C. J. [Charles James] Fox head – & a mind that has
influenced my thought in more than one important direction. I have asked
him to lunch on Friday at H. of C. & shall go to London that day to get my
Money Resolution on the Trade Boards Bill.
    But what do you say to coming up too & giving us both (& his pretty
young wife) lunch at Eccleston? We could settle up lots of things & see
each other . . . Do think about this: & let me know whether it is feasible.
    <u>Now</u> it is pouring here – but I am going to take my whole squadron out
on a gallop over the Downs – Tomorrow there is a field day against the
Berkshire. So that Thursday must be the day for Pussy to come to
luncheon, if she thinks it worthwhile. . . .
    Goodbye my beloved Clemmie I would so much like to kiss your dear
lips & to curl up snugly in your arms, but I am glad you have found a nice
refuge from paint & worries for these few days [at Blenheim Palace].

Goodbye my darling. Write – send by the bearer – a line of news & love to your dear loving

Husband
W.

[1] William Bourke Cockran (1854–1923), American Democrat politician, whom WSC had met on his first trip to the USA.

O From CSC
1 June [1909]

Stoke Court[1]
Stoke Poges, Bucks

My own Darling

Your letter came as such a joyful surprise, as I was in the schoolroom here playing games with my small cousins –

My hostess, Dorothy not expecting me till this evening has gone to London for the day – No wire has reached me from you – I would have come in spite of rain as I am longing to see my small pug & to kiss his sunburnt face....

I read about the Field Day. It sounds most interesting – I should like to have seen it with you –

It is wonderful Goonie having her Baby so easily –

I feel it is <u>nothing</u> now & only wish there was not another month to wait –

I will come up to London Friday morning & Dan Leno[2] shall be put on her mettle to provide a good luncheon, so arrange with your friend & his wife. I would like very much to come Thursday to the camp, if it is fine....

There was great excitement at Nuneham over the advent of Goonie's P.K. Mrs Harcourt is rather an expert in these matters & discoursed on them rather to the Embarrassment of the young men to say nothing of the Kat.

Goodbye my precious Darling.

Your loving
Clemmie X X X

[1] Home of Dorothy Allhusen, CSC's cousin and daughter of Lady St Helier by her first husband, Col. John Stanley.
[2] The Churchills' nickname for their cook. The British music hall performer Dan Leno (George Galvin, 1860-1904) was famous for his comic songs and pantomime dame roles.

O From WSC
[undated, probably 30 July 1909] 3.15

Board of Trade

My beloved – We are in close grapple[1]. But I think it is going to come right. The differences are now reduced to mere hagglings.

I hope my sweet woo-Kat is not sprawling in the Miserable Valley.

This will be a great event if it comes off.

Cabinet quivered with excitement about it this morning –

Your loving & devoted
Winston

[1] WSC was at the centre of negotiations with coalminers' leaders. A strike threatened to halt all coal production.

○ From WSC   Board of Trade
[undated, probably 30 July 1909] 6.15 p.m.

We are on the verge of a complete settlement.
Smillie the warlike miners' leader has been over-ruled by his followers & has resigned after a fierce struggle.
The settlement is practically on my terms.
It will take 2 hours yet.

Your ever loving husband
W

As part of her convalescence after Diana's birth Clementine, with her mother and sister Nellie, was staying at Carpenter's at Southwater in Sussex, a small house on Wilfrid Scawen Blunt's estate which he used to lend to the Hozier family. Diana (the P.K.), together with her nanny, had remained in London – 'keeping house' with her father.

○ From CSC   Carpenter's
Sunday morning [29 August 1909]   Southwater

My Darling,
It is quite wild, savage & altogether delightful here. – The house is quite as rough as the shanty on the desert island in The Admirable Crichton[1] ....
The butter is yellower, the cream thicker & the honey sweeter (the neighbour keeps a bee) than anywhere else in the world. Mother, Nellie, Alice and the faithful Minnie all wait hand & foot on the Kat who is purring loudly – Occasionally she gives a plaintive mew for her Pug & P.K. (especially for her Pug), but except for that she is very happy....
Goodbye my Best Beloved I love you and send you countless kisses – I hope my sweet Pug is having a delightful Sunday. Your telegram just arrived this second –

Your loving
Clem-Pussy-Bird

(You haven't called me that for a long time)

. . .

[1] A play by J. M. Barrie, first performed in 1902.

O From WSC   Board of Trade
31 August 1909

Beloved
    ... I have had no letter from you today – but only one from Nellie.
Please thank her for me. I do trust dearest that you are making steady
progress. Do send me a telegram in the morning – in case you have not
written.
    The P.K. is vy well – but the nurse is rather inclined to glower at me as
if I was a tiresome interloper. I missed seeing her (the P.K.) take her bath
this morning. But tomorrow I propose to officiate!
    If you read the Daily Mail of today you will see a vy sad case – Mrs
Whitley – the wife of one of the Whips – stealing potted meat! poor thing
she went off her head. He is broken by it & has fled to Italy with her.
    Mind my sweet pussie cat not to steal potted meat.
    The news about the Lords is flickering – but seems to harden towards
rejection [of the Budget].
    'Those whom the gods wish to destroy, first they make mad.'
    Please telegraph early, & whether I can bring anything down for you.
                                                        & with best love
                                                            I remain
                                                Your loving & devoted
                                                                W.

...

O From WSC
6 September 1909

My sweet Clemmie, I am in the train on my way to Swindon & I shall ride
tomorrow with the Cavalry....
    I have just seen the P.K. She is flourishing & weighs 10 tons! The nurse
says she has written to you about the perambulator. Will you settle what is
to be done.
    I am rather tired tonight my beloved & weary – as I woke so early. But I
think the fresh air tomorrow will do me good. A day on a horse is always
a great pick-me-up. I did enjoy my Sunday with you in the wild wood
house, & Eccleston seems so deserted without you that I am glad to be out
of it.
    Dearest Clemmie do try to gather your strength. Don't spend it as it
comes. Let it accumulate. Remember my two rules – No walk of more than
½ a mile: no risk of catching cold. There will be so much to do in the
autumn & if there is an Election – you will have to play a great part. All
these last 8 months you have been weighed down with your tremendous
effort. But when you are quite recovered I shall find you such a lot of
work to do – that you will call me a beast. My darling I do so want your
life to be a full & sweet one, I want it to be worthy of all the beauties of
your nature. I am so much centred in my politics, that I often feel I must
be a dull companion, to anyone who is not in the trade too. It gives me so
much joy to make you happy – & often wish I were more various in my

topics. Still the best is to be true to oneself – unless you happen to have a vy tiresome self! Good night my sweet Clemmie, give my love to your Mamma & Nellinita – and keep yourself the fondest wishes of my heart – now & always.

Your loving husband
W

. . .

After the Carpenter's interlude Clementine, reunited with the P.K., went north to stay with her Stanley relations at Alderley Park, Cheshire. In her letters she refers affectionately to the Stanley women as 'the Alderney cows' and to her great-uncle Lyulph Stanley* as 'the Alderney Bull'.

Winston, at the personal invitation of Kaiser Wilhelm II, was attending the German army manoeuvres.

○ From CSC   Alderley Park,
11 September [1909]   Chelford

My Darling

I am so glad you had a comfortable journey & that you are having fun – I toiled thro' the Rosebery[1] speech which the Kat thought tedious – His alternative to the Budget proposals i.e. cutting down the Civil Service, spending less on Ireland & encouraging self reliance & thrift in the working classes would seem hardly to provide the necessary cash; but then 'being a Peer . . . I do not regard myself as a financier'! His delicate & refined nature has been kept aloof since early youth (by a thrifty marriage) from the sordid consideration of how to make both ends meet. . . .

There are six babies here, the eldest is 4 years & the youngest 4 days old! None of them are fit to hold a candle to our P.K. or even to unloose the latchet of her shoe – There are also numberless dogs & a most beautiful little gray bear – He stands about 3 foot high & has a most lovely soft coat & makes nice little grunty noises – He tried to get inside the beehives yesterday & was badly stung – He comes out for walks with the dogs & plays with them – When they annoy him he climbs a tree – The Alderney cows are all very friendly – Venetia Stanley [Montagu*] is staying with the Asquiths – A letter came from her yesterday describing how both the P.M. & Herbert Gladstone[2] are black & blue from the repeated pummellings of the 3 suffragettes.[3] Uncle Lyulph [Stanley*] (the Alderney Bull) says <u>he</u> would have no mercy on them, he would feed them with a stomach pump, put them in the punishment cells, give them penal servitude, hard labour etc etc. . . .

Birmingham is not far from here & I am longing to hear the P.M.'s speech on the 17th – Do you think we could get tickets? . . . Aunt Maisie[4] is longing to go –

My Beloved Pug take great care of yourself – your Kat sends you all her love with a great many kisses

The Clem-Pussy-Bird

kat and kitten

[1] Archibald Philip Primrose, 5th Earl of Rosebery (1847–1929). Liberal. Prime Minister, 1894–5. A friend of Lord Randolph Churchill, about whom he wrote a memoir. Married Hannah, daughter and heiress of Baron Meyer de Rothschild.
[2] Herbert Gladstone (1854–1930), 1st Viscount Gladstone, son of William Ewart Gladstone, the Liberal statesman, at this date Secretary of State for Home Affairs. First Governor-General of South Africa, 1910-14.
[3] The Prime Minister had been molested by three suffragettes, one of whom struck him repeatedly, on leaving Lympne church the previous Sunday, 5 September, and later that afternoon by the same women at Littlestone Golf Club. Two large stones were thrown through the window of the Asquiths' dining room, where Mr and Mrs Asquith were sitting with guests, at 10 p.m. that night.
[4] Wife of 4th Baron Sheffield (Stanley of Alderley).

O From CSC   Alderley Park
Sunday 12 September [1909]

My Darling,
How I wish we were together today – It is just 5 o'clock – This time last year we were steaming out of Paddington on our way to Blenheim – The Pug was reading an account of the wedding presents in the Westminster aloud to the Kat!

Then the Pug embraced the Kat, but unfortunately another train was just passing us quite slowly & its occupants caught him in the very act -

My Beloved Winston I hope you are having a very happy holiday I do long to see you again – Tell Eddie [Marsh*] & Freddie [Guest*] that if they don't return you to me in the pink of health I will never forgive them....

Our Nurse is purring with joy because of the compliments which are showered on our P.K., who is universally proclaimed (below stairs) to be the finest specimen ever brought within these walls....

Your most loving
Clemmie Kat
Miaow

No letter from one bad little Pug yet

The Kat's tail is gradually getting its curl back as you see from the picture!

○ From WSC   Strassburg [Strasbourg]
12 September 1909

My darling Clemmie,

A year to-day my lovely white pussy-cat came to me, & I hope & pray she may find on this September morning no cause – however vague or secret – for regrets. The bells of this old city are ringing now & they recall to my mind the chimes which saluted our wedding & the crowds of cheering people. A year has gone – & if it has not brought you all the glowing & perfect joy which fancy paints, still it has brought a clear bright light of happiness & some great things. My precious & beloved Clemmie my earnest desire is to enter still more completely into your dear heart & nature & to curl myself up in your darling arms. I feel so safe with you & I do not keep the slightest disguise. You have been so sweet & good to me that I cannot say how grateful I feel to you for your dear nature, & matchless beauty. Not please disdain the caresses of your devoted pug. Kiss especially the beautiful P.K. for me. I wonder what she will grow into, & whether she will be lucky or unlucky to have been dragged out of chaos. She ought to have some rare qualities both of mind & body. But these do not always mean happiness or peace. Still I think a bright star shines for her....

Rosebery's speech has come in this morning's Times – What poor stuff! & so inaccurate in fact – over over & over again he betrays the almost childish unacquaintance with the common details of the Budget. He does not urge the Lords to reject it. On the other hand he warns them against it – But the execution of the speech, its argument, its phrasing, seem to me feeble beyond words....

We have no servant & in spite of my portmanteau & its excellent arrangements, there is a regular whirlpool of linen & clothes all over my room. Alack....

> Always my own darling
> Clem-puss-bird
> Your loving husband
> W

...

○ From WSC   Kronprinz Hotel
15 September 1909   Wurzburg

My darling, We have been out all day watching these great manoeuvres.... I have a very nice horse from the Emperor's stable, & am able to ride about wherever I choose with a suitable retinue. As I am supposed to be an 'Excellency' I get a vy good place. Freddie on the other hand is ill-used. These people are so amazingly routinière that anything the least out of the ordinary – anything they have not considered officially & for months – upsets them dreadfully.... I saw the Emperor today & had a few minutes' talk with him. He is vy sallow – but otherwise looks quite well....

We have had a banquet tonight at the Bavarian palace. A crowd of princes & princelets & the foreign officers of various countries. It began at 6 p.m. & was extremely dull. . . .

This army is a terrible engine. It marches sometimes 35 miles in a day. It is in number as the sands of the sea – & with all the modern conveniences. There is a complete divorce between the two sides of German life – the Imperialists & the Socialists. Nothing unites them. They are two different nations. With us there are so many shades. Here it is all black & white (the Prussian colours). I think another 50 years will see a wiser & a gentler world. But we shall not be spectators of it. Only the P.K. will glitter in a happier scene. How easily men could make things much better than they are – if they only all tried together! Much as war attracts me & fascinates my mind with its tremendous situations – I feel more deeply every year – & can measure the feeling here in the midst of arms – what vile & wicked folly & barbarism it all is.

Sweet cat – I kiss your vision as it rises before my mind. Your dear heart throbs often in my own. God bless you darling keep you safe & sound. Kiss the P.K. for me all over.

With fondest love
W.

this is the galloping pug – for European travel.

O From CSC   Alderley Park
16 September [1909]

My Darling

Your sweet letter is a great joy to me – The year I have lived with you has been far the happiest in my life, & even if it had not been it would have been well worth living.

I do long to see my little Pug again –

Yesterday was a bad day, for the P.K. was not well – It was nothing serious & to-day she is better, but her little pale pinched face frightened me –

She has had a good night & the nurse says she will be <u>quite</u> well tomorrow. . . .

I see someone in The Times objects to your going to the German Manoeuvres. The Poor Pug cannot disport himself in any corner of Europe without comment –

The Kat is writing in the chill of dawn – She wakes up so early & would so like to be cuddled & kissed by her warm delicious little Pug -

Your very loving
Clemmie-Kat

O From CSC   Alderley Park
18 September 1909

My Darling
    After all Aunt Maisie & I did go to the Bingley Hall Meeting....
    The P.M. made a splendid speech. He looked grim & determined as he
said his last words rather low & very slowly leaning over the platform: We
are not only ready, but anxious – we are not only anxious but <u>eager</u> to
take up the challenge –
    The meeting was in a state of wild excitement – We came out by a side
door – A steward said to the crowd 'There's Mrs Churchill' & they all
cheered the pug – Two boys leant into the carriage & said Give him our
love – Those poor people love & trust you absolutely I felt so proud....
    I shall come up to London Tuesday – The Alderney cows want us to
come here this next Friday (or Saturday) to Monday. Please send me a
telegram if you would like this as if so I will leave the P.K. here in the
interval –
    Goodbye my Darling I send you a great many kisses

                                                           Clemmie Kat

...

O From WSC   Hotel Russischer Hof
[undated, probably 19 September 1909]   Ulm

My darling,
    I am returning & will be with you on Wednesday morning early. How
shall I find you? I do hope you will have made good progress during this
fortnight....
    Yesterday we visited the battlefield of Blenheim[1]. It is not difficult to
follow the positions of the armies. In the village of Blenheim we found an
amiable curate & an intelligent postman, both of whom knew about the
battle & were able to point out the features of the field ... the old bank
of the river – wh was the right of the French position – can be clearly
seen; & the Nebel stream which the Allied army had to cross, & the
ground of the great cavalry charge, & the wooded hills through wh Prince
Eugene fought his way – all are recognisable....
    The manoeuvres finished with a tremendous cannonade in a fog. I had
only two minutes' speech with the Emperor – just to say goodbye & thank
him for letting me come. He was vy friendly – 'My dear Winston' & so on
– but I saw nothing of him. Perhaps it was just as well. I rather dreaded
the responsibility of a talk on politics. It is so easy to say something
misunderstandable – & Foreign affairs are not – after all – my show. I met
however Enver Bey[2] <u>the</u> Young Turk who made the revolution. A
charming fellow – vy good looking & thoroughly capable. We made
friends at once. He is a great power in Turkey – though behind the
Throne. I had a vy useful talk with him about Baghdad railway....
    Now my sweet Clemmie I must finish – For we are to start out. I hope

to find a letter from you at Paris if not at Nancy. It is 4 days since I had 'signe de vie'. The Pug is therefore disconsolate.

Your ever loving
W.

...

[1] The battle of Blenheim, in which WSC's ancestor the 1st Duke of Marlborough and Prince Eugene of Savoy won a famous victory over the French on 13 August 1704.
[2] Enver Pasha (1881–1922), a Young Turk leader in the revolution of 1908. Turkish Minister for War, 1914.

That autumn Winston had to go to Dundee to attend to constituency matters. When in London, he was consumed with ministerial and parliamentary work, and so Clementine took Diana and her nannie to spend some weeks at the Crest Hotel in Crowborough, Sussex; Winston joined her at weekends.

Their letters from now on regularly contain references to the suffragettes, whose campaign had escalated since the defeat in 1907 of a Private Member's Bill purporting to give women the vote. Increasingly the activists were disrupting political meetings, tying themselves to railings outside Buckingham Palace and No. 10 Downing Street, and harassing and attacking ministers physically. Asquith* was resolutely opposed to women's suffrage and constantly attracted their most violent hostility. Winston, not convinced about giving women the vote, never campaigned against it. At Bristol Station in November 1909 a woman attacked him with a dog whip and tried to force him backwards on to the railway line, into the path of an oncoming train; Clementine jumped over a pile of luggage and pulled him back.

Clementine supported women's suffrage, but like many others deplored the violent tactics of the militants.

O From WSC   Queen's Hotel
17 October 1909   Dundee

My darling,

This hotel is a great trial to me. Yesterday morning I had half eaten a kipper when a huge maggot crept out & flashed his teeth at me! To-day I could find nothing nourishing for lunch but pancakes. Such are the trials wh great & good men endure in the service of their country!

The meeting yesterday passed off vy well. I made a dull but solid speech wh was received most respectfully by a large audience who had gathered at this tiny village among the hills from all parts of Perth & Fifeshire. The Suffragettes arrived in a motor-car and were much pelted with mud by angry ploughmen – within the meeting all was still.

I find everyone here in high spirits & full of fight.... There are many inquiries after you, & I have tactfully explained that you are recuperating.

You must read Wells's new book, Ann Veronica[1]. Massingham tells me (this is most secret) that Wells has been behaving very badly with a young Girton girl of the new emancipated school – & that vy serious consequences have followed. The book apparently is suggested by the intrigue – These literary gents!!...

I hope the Burgundy has reached you safely & that you are lapping it with judicious determination....

My sweet cat – devote yourself to the accumulation of health. Dullness is salutary in certain circumstances. I wish you were here, but I am sure you will not afterwards regret this period of repose.

The post goes early, & I want to have a walk before it gets dark, so I will end now with fondest love & many kisses from your devoted loving husband

W

...

[1] H. G. Wells' feminist novel *Ann Veronica*, about a 'new' free woman seeking free love, created something of a public scandal when first published in 1909.

○ From WSC   [Dundee]
18 October [1909]

My darling – I write you this in gt haste between two meetings & in the midst of a scrambled dinner.

I hope you will not be angry with me for having answered the suffragettes sternly. I shall never try to crush your convictions. I must claim an equal liberty for myself. I have told them that I cannot help them while the present tactics are continued. I am sorry for them. The feeling here is vy hot against them. The women's meeting I addressed later – 1,500 – absolutely orderly & enthusiastic – was unanimous against the rowdyism. The Women's Lib. Association has doubled its membership in the last 12 months. They were full of solicitude for you: & I told them you would be at their head on the day of battle.

My sweet cat – my heart goes out to you tonight. I feel a vivid realisation of all you are to me: & of the good & comforting influence you have brought into my life. It is a much better life now. Then too I think of this beautiful pussy cat that purrs & prinks itself before me, & I feel as proud & conceited as those peacocks to possess it....

I am terribly hard up for something to say tonight & tomorrow.

Ever – my darling your
loving husband
W.

Kiss the P.K. for me.

○ From CSC   The Crest Hotel
18 October [1909]   Crowborough

My Darling,

How uncomfortable you must be! After your experience at the Queen's this will seem like the Ritz!

Your gossip about Wells is very exciting – I long to confide it to Hodgy Podgy[1] but restrain myself.

Perhaps she will be called in to succour the poor Girton girl. I thought that Institution turned out only stern & masculine specimens –

The Burgundy has arrived & for it, I have forsaken the bottle of claret I began the first evening which is still ½ finished! ...

I am glad you were not interrupted & that the suffragettes were foiled – Bermondsey[2] looks rather hopeless by the papers; perhaps if we lose it, the Lords' wavering courage will rise again –

Goodbye my sweet Pug
Your own little
solitary Clemmy Kat

The picture ... represents one small cat in one large desert –
I explain this as I can't do it by perspective –

[1] Nurse Hodgson, Diana's nurse.
[2] Where a by-election was to take place on 28 October. See p. 36.

○ From WSC   Board of Trade
26 October 1909

My darling – I am afraid you must be having odious weather. Here it is the vy lowest level of concentrated malice. I have been at work all day – first on my preface[1], then at the Cabinet Committee on Somaliland.... Lady Carlisle[2] marched in upon me this morning on the cause of the Suffragettes & I had a long & formidable discussion – of an amiable nature however – with her. She – it seems – took a lenient view of my speech, as being at any rate free from mockery, but Dorothy & Geoffrey [Howard][3] are completely estranged, & neither would come – so she said – to see me!

Dan Leno has distinguished herself by cooking too well for words. Ivor [Churchill Guest*] & F. E. [Smith*] dined last night & were entranced by her excellence. F.E. is positive the Lords mean to chuck the Bill. My eye!!!

Mamma rang me up on the telephone this morning to ask if you & I would come and spend next Sunday – their last at Salisbury Hall – with them. I feel rather sentimental about that place – & the organ & the galloping horse & all that. How does it strike you? You must telegraph vy early on receipt of this as I have to communicate with her. Whatever you like.

It is such fun riding with you, & when you are able to gallop really fast over beautiful turf it will be a great joy to us both.

My sweet – I felt vy lonely in my bed last night & thought often of you. I do hope you are not too dull – a little is good; & that you are really gathering strength.

I sent you a cheque yesterday for £60 – I was so sorry to have seemed snappish when I was hurrying off. I was not really a bit. But I thought the train looked hopeless. I am trying hard to be punctual....

With fondest love to you & the P.K.
Your devoted husband
W

...

P.S. Mind you do whatever you like about Salisbury [Hall]. I would just as soon come to Crowboro'. I loved last Sunday.

W

[1] The preface to his book *Liberalism and the Social Problem*, published in 1909.
[2] Countess of Carlisle, Rosalind (d. 1921), daughter of 2nd Lord Stanley of Alderley. Married, 1864, 9th Earl of Carlisle. A formidable character of strong radical views and a campaigning teetotaller. CSC's great-aunt.
[3] Daughter and son of Lady Carlisle. Lady Dorothy Howard had helped WSC fight the N.W. Manchester by-election in 1908.

O From WSC   Board of Trade
27 October 1909

My darling – I am glad you like the idea of revisiting Salisbury [Hall] – tho' I enjoyed last Sunday so much that I was in two minds about it....

From the 5th Nov to 23rd no House of Commons. Tell it not in Gath. We will have some fun. The State banquets & Mansion House occur in that period – & I must speak at Bristol on the 13th (you too!) So we shall I think have to stay in England – But we will discuss plans together – the less expensive the better. I have just paid Maple £500 & [Dr] Phillips 75. The Pug is décassé [out of funds] for the moment. The 'Separate account' wh I lately established is separated indeed from its parent.

But the book will be out in 10 days & that will bring an extra £150 in....

I must arrange some riding for you on your return to London. Almost immediately you could ride in the Row with me on a quite meek horse....

Kiss the P.K. & think often of your faithful, loving & devoted husband

W

After reading Balfour's speech

○ From CSC
28 October [1909]

The Crest Hotel
Crowborough

My Darling,

. . .

I am so much excited about Bermondsey[1] – I quite dread the Daily Mail tomorrow there will be such a howl of triumph if Dumphreys gets in –

I am so sorry the poor Pug is ruined for the house. How about staying quietly at Eccleston Square during the holiday? . . .

We went, Hodgy Podgy, P.K. & all to have tea with Lady Conan Doyle[2]. The P.K. had exquisite company manners & looked too lovely making the little Conan Doyle child look such a fat lump.

Your loving
Clemmie Kat

. . .

[1] The Bermondsey by-election held on 28 October 1909 was won by the Conservative candidate John M. T. Dumphreys, with a majority of 987 votes.
[2] Wife of the author Sir Arthur Conan Doyle, who lived in Crowborough.

○ From CSC
3 November [1909]

The Crest Hotel
Crowborough

My Beloved Darling One

Your letter has just come & I am writing you a line to tell you how much I think of my Pug all day & of all the struggles, difficulties & complications he is encountering just now, more than ever –

My dear, I want you quite to forget my perverseness last Sunday. I feel much mortified with myself for having been found wanting in such a little thing – My crowning joy will be when I feel I can really be a help to you in your life & a comfort to you in disappointments & deceptions –

Would you like me to return now, in case you want to have a little dinner or anything like that before the H of C adjourns?

The P.K. sends you a heavenly smile – She is lying in her little cot & her darling little face looks like a creamy rosebud crowned with gold –

Goodbye & Good Cheer my Sweet heart

Your own
Clemmie Kat

. . .

○ From WSC
3 November 1909

Board of Trade

Secret

My darling – I was not seriously downcast yesterday – only I realise that there are forces at work wh are not so friendly or so fair as I had been in the past inclined to hope.

We had an exciting Cabinet this morning on the question of what we should do if the Lords reject – as is now assumed. I took a vy clear line & was almost alone at first, but gradually they all came round to my view. . . .

I am in full wrestle about my Assurance Bill wh hangs in the balance. One difficulty after another crops up. . . .

Goodnight my sweet darling Clemmie, with all my fondest love to you & the P.K.

Your loving husband
W

a tranquil pug

P.S. I have not spoken to a single cat of any sort except my mother!!!!!

○ From CSC   The Crest Hotel
4 November [1909]   Crowborough

My Darling
I gave the P.K. her bath to-night – Hodgy Podgy says I did it quite nicely & I want to do it always now, & she, H.P., is quite jealous –

I have found a lovely new ride for us on Saturday –

I hope you will have a nice dinner party to-night – I do wish I was there. . . .

Good-night my Darling Pug – I must have lessons in Kat-drawing as your pugs are so much better than my Kats

Your loving
Clemmie

. . .

○ From WSC   Board of Trade
10 November 1909

My darling – The P.M. was evidently much pleased by my consulting him on my speech. He has authorised me to make what will be a most memorable pronouncement upon the consequences of rejection. . . .

Dearest it worries me vy much that you should seem to nurse such absolutely wild suspicions wh are so dishonouring to all the love & loyalty I bear you, & will please God bear you while I breathe – They are unworthy of you & me. And they fill my mind with feelings of embarrassment to wh I have been a stranger since I was a schoolboy. I know that they originate in the fond love you have for me, and therefore they make me feel tenderly towards you & anxious always to deserve that most precious possession of my life. But at the same time they depress me & vex me – & without reason.

We do not live in a world of small intrigues, but of serious & important affairs. I could not conceive myself forming any other attachment than that to which I have fastened the happiness of my life here below. And it offends my best nature that you should – against your true instinct – indulge small emotions & wounding doubts. You ought to trust me for I do not love & will never love any woman in the world but you, and my chief desire is to link myself to you week by week by bonds which shall ever become more intimate & profound.

Beloved I kiss your memory – Your sweetness & beauty have cast a glory upon my life. You will find me always Your

loving & devoted husband
W

wistful but unashamed.

It is hardly surprising that since they spent so much time apart in these earliest years of their marriage, misunderstandings and anxieties should from time to time have slipped between them. I have found no clue to the 'rufflement' which appears in the last letter to which Winston reacts so strongly – albeit with urgent tenderness. Whatever it was, it vanished from view, and when my mother read this letter again over fifty years after it was written she could not remember what it had been about.

Chapter III

HOME OFFICE

Winston, Clementine and little Diana spent Christmas 1909 and the New Year at Blenheim, and then Winston and Clementine hurried north to Dundee for the General Election campaign[1]. It was the first of the fifteen electoral battles that they would fight together.

Winston won at Dundee, with a handsome majority; but the Government lost 104 seats and the Liberals their absolute control: the great Liberal majority of 1906 had vanished. In the ensuing Government reconstruction Asquith* appointed Winston as Home Secretary. At thirty-five, he became the youngest holder of that office since Sir Robert Peel.

The Home Secretary's brief embraced a wide spectrum: prisons and prisoners, the police, and the grim duty of signing death sentences. He was also responsible for the working conditions of seven million people in shops, factories and workshops, and a million more in the mines.

As well as his specific concerns as Home Secretary, Churchill was much involved in the preparation and parliamentary business of the National Insurance Bill and the Parliament Bill. Moreover, Asquith often entrusted him with the winding-up of major debates (especially after dinner)[2].

The most important Bill attaching to his own office was the Coal Mines Bill, introduced in March 1911. Concerned largely with safety and welfare arrangements, this Bill also regulated the employment of women and children in the mines. Another piece of Home Office legislation was the Shops Bill, which incorporated a multitude of provisions to ameliorate the working conditions of shop workers.

At the end of April 1910 the Finance Bill (Budget) passed through the House of Commons, and was passed by the House of Lords without a division, but the Government was determined to rid the Lords of their power of veto over Commons legislation, and to that end had already introduced the Parliament Bill. Bitter political strife continued, interrupted only by national mourning occasioned by the sudden death of King Edward VII on 6 May.

That summer one of Winston's cousins, Henry Guest[3] was contesting a by-election in East Dorset. Winston was unable to absent himself from his ministerial duties and sent Clementine to the 'fighting front', armed with a speech that she was to read for him. She stayed with the Wimbornes at Canford Manor.

[1] 14 January–9 February. At this time General Elections were normally held every seven years; the interval changed to five years in 1911 (but the provision was waived during the First World War).

Polling days were staggered over a period of up to four weeks until the election of December 1918, when under the New Reform Act (January 1918) they were to be held on one day.
[2] See WSC's letter of 22 April 1911, p. 43.
[3] Lt-Col. Henry Guest (1874–1957), second son of 1st Baron Wimborne and brother of Ivor and Freddie.

O From CSC   Canford Manor
Tuesday [?28 June 1910]   Wimborne

My Darling
    One line after an exhausting but not unsuccessful day –
    The open air Meeting at Swanage yesterday was great fun – Lots of people –
    Your Kat delivered your speech in great style – Sylvia [Henley*] stood at the back of the crowd & heard every word – The only nuisance is that it has been printed & scattered broadcast over the constituency – So henceforth I shall have to rack my own brain for words & thoughts. We spent to-day canvassing in Swanage, but did not come across a single doubtful. Everybody was rabid one way or the other. Last night I heard Henry [Guest, the candidate] speak at Wimborne – blunt – sincere – short – clear – Freddy [Guest*, his brother] spoke really well & was cheered again & again....
    They are calling me to start for meeting.
    This letter is incoherent

                                                                    Your most loving
                                                                    Clemmy Kat

On his accession, King George V, anxious to try to solve the constitutional impasse between Lords and Commons, had convened an All-Party Constitutional Conference. But by early November, after twenty-one sittings, no workable compromise had been found. Asquith therefore decided to call another General Election specifically to decide the issue of the reform of the House of Lords. He had wrung from the King a secret pledge that, if the Liberal Party won the election and the Lords blocked the passage of the Parliament Bill, the King would create enough new peers to ensure its passage. Thus on 28 November Parliament was dissolved, and the second General Election of that year took place before Christmas. The position of the parties was almost unchanged from the January election.
    Clementine was now in the early months of pregnancy with her second child (known to them both as 'The Chumbolly'[1]).

[1] Possibly derived from the name of a beautiful flower that grows in N.W. India, where WSC had served almost 15 years earlier, or from the Persian language (Farsi) meaning a healthy, chubby new-born baby (Winston S. Churchill, *His Father's Son: The Life of Randolph S. Churchill*, 1996, p. 3).

O From WSC   Warter Priory[1]
19 December [1910]   York

Beloved –
   'Tis late, but as we start early tomorrow I scratch this line.
   A nice party – puissant presentable, radical in preponderance – a rare
combination. I wish you were here. It is quite reminiscent to me of circles
long vanished from my life. Nearly all men.... Tomorrow pheasants in
thousands – the vy best wot ever was seen. Tonight Poker – I lost a little –
but the play was low.
   On the whole survey how much more power and great business are to
me, than this kind of thing, pleasant tho it seems by contrast to our
humble modes of entertainment.
   I expect I will have a headache tomorrow night after firing so many
cartridges. All the glitter of the world appeals to me: but not thank God in
comparison with serious things.
   How naughty of the Kat to be enrhumed. Tell [Dr] Beauchamp to
telegraph fully & take the greatest care. I will be back on Wed[y]....
   I told Johnson to send you some flowers

                                              Goodnight dearest
                                              Your pug in clover. W.

[1] Home of Lord and Lady Nunburnholme, where WSC stayed for shooting.

O From CSC   33 Eccleston Square
19 December [1910]

My Own Darling
   After lunching with your Mamma to-day & doing a little Christmas
shopping I again retired to bed – I dozed off – When I woke up, imagine
my surprise & delight to see my room transformed into a Paradise of
exquisite flowers & a lovely melon sitting near the bed – You are a sweet
Darling Lamb Bird!! I have never seen anything like the flowers – Pink
Chrysanthemums in one huge bowl, golden ones in another, fragrant
mimosa, lilies of the valley, great fat pink carnations, branches of lilac,
blue forget-me-nots, white waxen hyacinths, sweet smelling violets cover
every table & make my room like a Spring Garden – The Puppy Kitten
squeaked with surprise when she came in – As for the melon it is <u>too</u>
delicious –
   What a <u>splendid</u> Majority at Romford[1] – And the dirty dogs bragged that
they would win it – The 'result' was tucked away in a corner of the Tory
evening papers.
   Goodbye my beloved Pig Pug – Come back safe on Wednesday ...

                                              Your loving
                                              Clemmie

[1] The results were: Liberal, 22,119; Unionist, 18,850.

○ From CSC   33 Eccleston Square
20 December [1910]

My Own Darling Pug

Now that I feel better, I do so wish I was at Warter with you enjoying the Flesh Pots of Egypt!

It sounds a delightful party & your frivolous Kat would have purred with pleasure....

Dearest you work so hard & have so little fun in your life – I wish you had more of this sort of thing....

Goodbye my Sweet darling

Your loving
Clemmie

I hope you will shoot the high flyers & not have a head-ache.

To while away the last wearisome weeks before the birth of the Chumbolly, Clementine went to stay with her great-uncle Lyulph [Stanley* of Alderley] and Aunt Maisie at their seaside home, Penrhos, near Holyhead.

○ From WSC   House of Commons
19 April [1911]

My beloved, Your P sat up on his tail till 4.45 this morning & delivered a fiery harangue at 2.30; with many smaller interventions. After a night in the train and a long day's work you may imagine how tired I was when I crawled into bed at 5 a.m. Today Cabinet & lunch with P.M. committee on Parlt. Bill amendts –. I am still rather tired.

George[1] has written to Mamma offering to come back. She has on my advice written to him telling him he is welcome if he comes back freely of his own will. He did not like my letter....

A thousand kisses from your devoted & loving husband

W.

[1] George Cornwallis-West, whom Lady Randolph had married in 1900. She divorced him in 1913.

○ From CSC   Penrhos
20 April [1911]   Holyhead

My Sweet Pug

Thank you for your letter.

I am glad George W. has come to his senses, but unless he is going to be really nice & make your Mamma happy, one wld think there might be little advantage in his coming back.

However if he does return, after such a public desertion he will have to behave properly I suppose?...

A lovely Sunshiny day again, so we are out the whole time. In the evening Venetia [Stanley/Montagu*] & I play Aunt Maisie & Sylvia [Henley*] at Bridge.... Tonight Violet [Asquith*] arrives with one or two Brothers in tow. Tomorrow we all go to hear Redmond[1] speak in Holyhead....
Later
...

I hope you are enjoying the House of C. You seem to be having the Lion's share of whatever is going on – I am getting rather restless & wishing for my 'Basket'. But I will be patient – It will seem quite a short time to wait for Chum Bolly when I get home next Monday. He engages a great deal of my thoughts & so do you my Darling One –

Your loving
Clemmie 'Kat'

[1] John Edward Redmond (1856–1918). Irish politician and barrister; Chairman of Nationalist Party, 1900. Declined to serve in Asquith's Coalition Government (1915) but supported the war. Opposed to Sinn Fein and deplored the Irish rebellion.

O From WSC   [Home Office]
22 April 1911

My Beloved – You will see from the enclosed Hansard what a little pig Winterton[1] made of himself. I ought not to have called out his name in my position – but the House was thoroughly good-tempered & I did not expect him to take such a nasty line....
   On Thursday night the P.M. [Asquith*] was vy bad: & I squirmed with embarrassment. He could hardly speak: & many people noticed his condition. He continues most friendly & benevolent, & entrusts me with everything after dinner. Up till that time he is at his best – but thereafter! It is an awful pity & only the persistent freemasonry of the House of Commons prevents a scandal. I like the old boy and admire both his intellect & his character. But what risks to run. We only got him away the other night just before Balfour began the negotiations wh I conducted, but wh otherwise wd have fallen to him – with disastrous consequences. The next day he was serene efficient undisturbed.
   ... I played golf better this afternoon – & slept 10 hours last night. We shall be up all night Monday – & I am going to put the screw on the Parliament Bill as it has never been put before in the next few days. We must get on. No peace till after the shock....
   Wire me when you return & bring your P.K. & C.B. with you my sweet darling Clem pussie bird –

Your loving & devoted husband
W.

[1] Edward Turnour, 6th Earl Winterton (1883–1962). Unionist MP from 1904; held various government appointments. As an Irish peer he did not sit in the House of Lords. During the debate on an amendment to the Parliament Bill, in the early hours of 20 April 1911, there was a running fire of interruptions. Winterton accused WSC of making disorderly interruptions and of bawling out his name in a way meant to be discourteous, and called for the Speaker; WSC denied the charge.

○ From CSC   Penrhos
22 April [1911]

My own Darling

. . .

Lord Winterton's behaviour is detestable – He contributes nothing to any
debate but his offensive insolence –

The Meeting last night was great fun – The Welsh have a very good
opinion of themselves – Redmond played quite second fiddle to Ellis-
Griffith[1]! The Chairman said how happy they all were to welcome Two
Great Leaders, The Leader of the Welsh Party Mr Ellis-Griffith (in a loud
trombone voice) & the leader of the Irish party Mr Redmond (this quite
casually –) Ellis-Griffith then made a speech persuading the audience to
allow Home Rule to precede Welsh Disestablishment. . . .

Redmond then followed with great common sense – The gist was how
much more powerful & united we should be in spirit after Home Rule
etc. . . . In a moment of excitement however he said 'We Irish & Welsh, we
haven't one drop of British Blood in our veins.' Fervent cheers from the
audience. . . .

Ellis-Griffith spoke again before the end – this time in Welsh for more
than 20 minutes while the audience rocked with laughter & Redmond
looked a little sulky –

We ended up with really beautiful singing –

Goodbye my Darling Winston I hope you will have pleasant golf & a
good rest after your tiring week – Your loving

                                                                          Clemmie Kat

[1] Sir Ellis Jones Ellis-Griffith (1860–1926), knighted 1911. Cr. 1st Bt Ellis-Griffith, 1918. Liberal MP
for Anglesey since 1895.

The Chumbolly – Randolph Spencer Churchill – was born at 33 Eccleston
Square on 28 May. A few days later Winston joined his fellow officers for the
perennial Yeomanry camp – this time at Blenheim.

○ From WSC   Blenheim Camp
2 June [1911]

My sweet and beloved Clemmie,

The weather is gorgeous and the whole Park in gala glories. I have been
out drilling all the morning & my poor face is already a sufferer from the
sun – The air however is deliciously cool. We have 3 regiments here – two
just outside the ornamental gardens, & the 3rd over by Bladon.

. . . Many congratulations are offered me upon the son. With that lack of
jealousy wh ennobles my nature, I lay them all at your feet.

My precious pussy cat, I do trust & hope that you are being good, & not
sitting up or fussing yourself. Just get well & strong & enjoy the richness
wh this new event will I know have brought into your life. The Chumbolly

must do his duty and help you with your milk. You are to tell him so from me. At his age greediness & even swinishness at table are virtues.

We are all going to bathe in the lake this morning. The water is said to be quite warm. No cats allowed. How I wish you were here – it wd be such fun for you. . . .

Always my darling your own loving Winston.

. . . This goes to you by the King's messenger who is taking the box.

○ From CSC   33 Eccleston Square
[undated, probably 3 June 1911]

My own Darling Winston

Blenheim sounds gay & entrancing, & I long to be there sharing all the fun & glitter. But I am very happy here, contemplating the beautiful Chumbolly who grows more darling & handsome every hour, & puts on weight with every meal; so that soon he will be a little round ball of fat.

Just now I was kissing him, when catching sight of my nose he suddenly fastened upon it & began to suck it, no doubt thinking it was another part of my person!

My room is more of a bower than ever & just now arrived quantities of delicious fruit & flowers from you my Darling Pug. . . . Your Mama came to see me yesterday. . . . She is rather fussed about whether you can take her in my place (as I am going in the King's Box[1]) to the Coronation. She wanted to write & ask Lord Beauchamp [His Majesty's Steward] about it; but I asked her to write & ask you about it first, as I am sure it will be better if you arrange it.[2] . . .

Goodbye my Own Darling – I love you so much & send you countless kisses.

Your own
Clemmie

. . .

I feel much better to-day. Yesterday was rather miserable because of the quantities of milk –

[1] CSC had thought she would have to miss the Coronation of King George V and Queen Mary on 22 June, since Randolph would be only a few weeks old; however, the King invited her to his private box in Westminster Abbey and sent a royal brougham to convey her to and from the ceremony.
[2] One notices veiled criticism of Lady Randolph's seat-bargaining tactics.

HOME OFFICE

○ From WSC   [Blenheim]
5 June 1911

<u>Secret</u>
Lock up or destroy

My dearest,
    ...
    I am so glad you are both progressing so well. Ten ounces since last
Tuesday is indeed good. I hope he is helping you as well as himself!....
    We all marched past this morning. Walk, trot & gallop. Jack [Churchill*]
& I took our squadrons at the real pace and exacted the spontaneous
plaudits of the crowd. The Berkshires who followed cd not keep up &
grumbled. After the march past I made the general form the whole Brigade
into Brigade Mass and gallop 1200 strong the whole length of the park in
one solid square of men & horses. It went awfully well. He was
delighted....
    Yes, Balfour has written to A[squith*] protesting agst F.E. [Smith*] being
made a P.C. & to F.E. to tell him so ... the main purpose is pretty plain.
They want to keep him (F.E.) back.
    The result is unimportant either way. If F.E. does not get it, he will not
forgive Balfour. If he does, Balfour will not forgive him[1]. But what an
insight into the fatuous & arrogant mind of the Hotel Cecil[2], wh even at its
last gasp, would rather inflict any amount of injury upon the Tory party
than share power with any able man of provincial origin. So may it long
continue.
    And now my sweet little darling with my fondest love I sign myself your
                                                        devoted friend & husband
                                                                            W.
    ...

[1] F. E. Smith was made a Privy Counsellor in the Coronation Honours announced 20 June 1911.
[2] A sarcastic jibe referring to the predominance and influence in the Tory party of the Cecil
(Salisbury) family. The joke originated in 1900, when no fewer than four close family members
were to be found in Lord Salisbury's Government, apart from himself. A further droll touch was
provided by the opening of the 800-room Hotel Cecil, on the site of the 1st Earl of Salisbury's
town house (Kenneth Rose, *The Later Cecils*, 1975).

○ From CSC   33 Eccleston Square
Tuesday 6 June [1911]

My Darling Winston,
    I am so much interested by all you tell me in your delightful letter....
    I wonder what the P.M. will do about A. J. B. [Balfour]'s letter? I am
afraid that he is rather inclined to please Tory Swells & F. E. [Smith] is not
a natural favourite with him – He grudgingly admires his talents....
    Please be kind to the poor boy of 18 who jumped over the gaol wall at
Bedford & swam twice across the Ouse followed by every policeman in
the town & was finally caught when he fell down from exhaustion – It was
in the Sunday papers –

Nellie has just arrived, looking so pretty & happy & I am gradually hearing all the amusing details of her visit to Blenheim –

She is much interested in Chumbolly & watched him in his bath & having his Supper –

All my Love to you Darling Pug –

Your loving
Clemmie

○ From WSC   Yewhurst[1]
18 June 1911   East Grinstead

My darling,

It has been a vy windy day but we have played 2 rounds of golf notwithstanding. General Botha[2] plays! He is a beginner but getting on. He also plays tennis & Bridge – the latter excellently. I have never seen him in these pursuits before. In the evening he tells us about his military exploits – always with great modesty & deep knowledge of all that counts in war. The great & lion-like man is now thank God a pillar of the British Empire.

Mrs Botha is here too. She is a remarkable woman – of superior intelligence & strong character – & still quite womanly. The war was no subalterns' outing to these two. They fought it through with genuine sorrow & inflexible determination. She carried messages to her husband during the negotiations for peace, & was present in the camps during the siege of Ladysmith & at other important operations. We are all thoroughly friendly now and these fierce memories scorch no longer. 'Battles' as I said in the House of Commons on the night I first met <u>you</u> at Crewe's 'will be remembered only to celebrate the martial virtues of two brave races.' So it has come to pass already....

I shall be up about 11.30 tomorrow.

I hope you have enjoyed your excursion to the sofa this afternoon.

All my fondest love.
W.

[1] Home of Sir Abe Bailey, 1st Bt (1864–1940). South African. One of the principal Transvaal mine owners. He had been a friend of Lord Randolph Churchill and had known WSC for many years.
[2] Louis Botha (1862–1919), South African statesman and soldier. C.-in-C. Boer forces during Boer War. In 1907 he became Prime Minister of Transvaal Colony, and in 1910 the first premier of the Union of South Africa.

After the Coronation Winston went to stay with Maxine Elliott* at Hartsbourne Manor, near Bushey Heath, where she entertained a wide swathe of society in memorable style. Clementine stayed in London, anchored to a ravenous Randolph.

O From WSC   Hartsbourne Manor
25 June 1911   Bushey Heath

My darling Clemmie,

It rained all the morning so I stayed in bed & ruminated amid my boxes. At luncheon Barrie[1] arrived – but I am vy sorry to say that he went off again unexpectedly this afternoon without my ever having a talk with him. I am vexed at this because I am sure I like him – and always something crops up to prevent my getting to know him.

Curzon[2] cd not come – ill – but Mamma is here and Muriel [Wilson] comes to dinner. Maxine is so nice. She has a new bullfinch – arrived only last night & already it sits on her shoulder and eats seeds out of her mouth. See how much these innocent little birds know!...

The general turn out on Friday [State Drive] made a good impression. Everyone admired the cat [CSC], the carriage, the horse and the tiger [liveried boy on box] – separately but in combination.... It really was great fun, & I am sure you will long look back to our drive & will like to tell the P.K. and the Chumbolly all about it – so it will become a tradition in the family & they will hand it on to others whom we shall not see. Dear one, I have thought of you with tender love to-day. May all blessings be yours & all good fortune....

With fondest love,
Your own ever loving
Husband
W.

Do ask Grey[3] to be godfather. I am sure it is a vy good idea, & will give him great pleasure. I am always hearing nice things he has said about me. He likes and wistfully admires our little circle. What do you think?

...

[1] J. M. Barrie (1860–1937), Scottish novelist and dramatist. The most famous of his plays was *Peter Pan* (1904). Cr. baronet, 1913.
[2] George Nathaniel Curzon (1859–1925), cr. Earl Curzon of Kedleston, 1911, and 1st Marquess, 1921. Son of 4th Baron Scarsdale. Entered Parliament, 1886; sat as Irish representative peer (Baron Curzon) from 1908. Viceroy and Governor-General of India, 1898–1905. Lord Privy Seal, 1915; member of War Cabinet and Lord President of the Council, 1916; Secretary of State for Foreign Affairs, 1919–24; Leader of House of Lords, 1916–25. Married (1) 1895, Mary Leiter of Washington, DC (d.1906); (2) 1917, Grace Duggan, daughter of a US diplomat and widow of a wealthy Argentinian rancher (see p. 252 n. 3.)
[3] Sir Edward Grey, later 1st Viscount Grey of Fallodon (1862–1933). Liberal statesman. Secretary of State for Foreign Affairs, 1905–16. His first wife, Dorothy, died in 1906 after a carriage accident; in 1922 he married Pamela, widow of the 1st Baron Glenconner.

Towards the end of June Clementine took Diana, Randolph and their nannie to stay in lodgings in Seaford, Sussex. Lady Blanche was also staying there with an old friend, Mrs Jack.

O From CSC   [Seaford]
Monday 26 June [1911]

My Own Darling

I was so much delighted at so soon, getting a lovely long letter from
you –

I have written to Sir Edward Grey & I hope he will consent. Then we
must find a Fairy Godmother for the Chum-Bolly.

As soon as I come back we will entice Barrie to luncheon or dinner but
he is dreadfully shy & has to be much coaxed. We must have him alone or
with only one other choice person as he is always silent when invited to
perform....

I have ruminated much on Friday's triumphal Drive – It is a very
wonderful thing to have happened – But you are a very wonderful Person,
my Darling, because besides being famous and exciting, you are a sweet
cuddly comfortable Pug, & I love you....

Goodbye my Sweet & Beloved Winston
Your loving Clemmie

. . .

O From WSC   33 Eccleston Square
26 June [1911]

He returns to the maison. No cat! No Puppy Kitten!! No Chumbolly!!! All
gone. Where have you all decamped to? What are you conspiring against
me? What league have you formed. Be gentle – be loyal – return soon –
fat, strong & beautiful & I will forgive this exodus.

The Home Office vote was productive of a snappish attack from Alfred
Lyttelton raking up all the old stale things – Sidney St., Tonypandy & the
Dartmoor shepherd[1] – to wh I made a quite satisfactory impromptu reply.
Thereafter a straggling debate on all the turns & twists of factory law....

No letter has yet arrived from you my dearest one I shall look for it
tomorrow....

I have written a tart speech for the King to deliver to the Eton boys –
putting these fashionable young cubs on their mettle – He is awfully
pleased with it. All his ideas of naval discipline were gratified as I
expected they wd be.

I am just off (vy late – not my fault) to Gala: & then to Grosvenor
House. They say Bendor [Westminster*] will not be there to entertain the
King & Queen. He has gone off without leaving an address to see a friend
whom we all know by sight[2]! This is thought to be cool even for a duke.

Always your loving devoted
Winston

---

[1] All subjects with which to taunt WSC. See Randolph S. Churchill, *Winston S. Churchill*, Vol. II,
1967, pp. 378–80, 391, 407–10.
[2] Gertie Millar, the celebrated musical comedy star and the Duke's current paramour.

O From CSC   [Seaford]
Tuesday 27 June [1911]

Only one line my Darling from an exhausted Kat, returned from Brighton
after being tortured (mostly mentally, I must admit) by a fierce dentist....
    I see the King & Queen ran no risks of meeting Gertie Millar receiving
them at the top of the stairs & stayed away from the Ball last night –
    Chumbolly is <u>so</u> greedy – I do hope the Dairy won't give out....

                                                                          Your loving
                                                                          Clemmie

What fun about the K's speech to the Eton Boys!

O From WSC   [Home Office]
29 June 1911

My beloved, I am just back from a long day's drive with the King to the
City & back through North London. They put me in the State coach
immediately in front of the royal escort – with D[s] of Devonshire & Mary
Minto [Countess of Minto]. Of course all the whole route I was cheered
and in places booed vigorously. It was rather embarrassing for these two
Tory dames. They got awfully depressed when the cheering was vy loud,
but bucked up a little around the Mansion House where there were hostile
demonstrations. They were vy civil but rather fussed – I did not
acknowledge any cheering & paid no attention at all to the crowds.
    The King was most friendly & the Queen asked much after you & urged
the importance of a full rest before beginning gaieties.
    Tonight we have a dinner of the Other Club[1]. – Kitchener in the chair.
<u>Secret</u> We are going to send him to Egypt – How pleased he wd be to
know! But nothing is finally settled[2].
    I have some worrying things on hand – first Haldane[3] has got my
promise to make an appointment wh I fear will be regarded as a job, ...
2nd a vy disagreeable Death Sentence, wh will take me a good many hours
– a woman who murdered her 2 year old illegitimate child under vy bad
circumstances.
    This is what we settled about the Veto Bill. As soon as it leaves the
Lords we shall tell them through their leaders that we have the guarantees
[as to the creation of peers], & that we shall use them <u>at once</u> unless they
undertake to pass the bill. We shall not deal with the Lords Amendts.
in H. of C. until the new Peers are actually made or the others have
surrendered, so that if they fight, the Bill will go back not to the present
H. of L but to a new one in which we shall have a majority!!! Secret
information points to the fact that the Tory leaders do not mean to fight
and are only looking for some means of saving their faces. But it will
make no difference to us whatever they do.
    Last night I gave L.G. [Lloyd George*] dinner at the Café Royal and we
had a vy good talk. He was full of your praises – said you were my
'salvation' & that your beauty was the least thing about you. We renewed
treaties of alliance for another seven years.
    My precious one – I will come down to you on Saturday motoring from

Walton Heath [Golf Club] and arriving for dinner. I will inspect the infantry next day. Let them all be drawn up in line of brigade masses. It will be so nice to see you all again. This house is vy silent without you; & I am reverting to my bachelor type with melancholy rapidity.

My dearest I am rather tired tonight – the long drive in uniform & the ceaseless clamour have been a good day's labour. I am off to a pleasant dinner of our Club – tomorrow golaf [*sic*].

Goodnight my dearest one,
Always your everloving husband,
W

...

[1] The Other Club, founded in May 1911 by WSC and F. E. Smith in opposition to 'The Club' which would not receive Liberals, met fortnightly to dine at the Savoy Hotel while Parliament was in session. Other Club dinners became one of WSC's most congenial and perennial pleasures.
[2] Kitchener was British Agent and Consul-General, Egypt, 1911–14.
[3] Richard Burdon Haldane (1856–1928), cr. 1st Viscount Haldane, 1911. Liberal politician, barrister, philosopher and writer. Secretary of State for War, 1905–12.

During that sweltering summer – of high celebration over the Coronation, of parliamentary feuding, and of industrial unrest – a chill warning of deadly dangers ahead was sounded from abroad, which alerted those who had ears to hear: the Agadir Incident[1]. For a few weeks tension rose, and war seemed a real possibility; but the moment of crisis passed. The implications were not lost on those responsible for the defence of Britain.

[1] In July French troops occupied Fez, the Moroccan capital, in order to quell a rebellion against the Sultan. Germany, suspecting that French annexation of Morocco might be imminent, sent a gunboat, the *Panther,* to the port of Agadir as a challenge. No hostilities took place, but shock waves ran through Europe, and there was much *va-et-vient* between governments behind the scenes.

○ From WSC   House of Commons
3 July 1911

My darling,

All is well here. Hull is peaceful and the strike has been settled. It is impossible to deny that violence has played its part in this – but that was not my fault. The House supported me warmly to-day on the sending of the Police.

The German action in Morocco has caused a flutter. The French want us to send a 'bâtiment' [warship] to Agadir. This would be a serious step on wh we shd not engage without being ready to go all lengths if necessary. There is to be a special Cabinet tomorrow on the question. . . .

My cold is pronounced but simple. What a bore to catch cold in July!

I enjoyed my Sunday so much, it was a wonderful thing to see the whole family rallied & marshalled under a single roof. I was so glad that you were making such good progress. It will be wise of you to stay for another fortnight. There is nothing like making a complete recovery. A set back is so disheartening. I fear it will seem a little dull – but it is worth it....

Write to me regularly – & think often of your own

loving & devoted husband
W.

○ From CSC   [Seaford]
Tuesday 4 July 1911

My Darling

    . . .

Yesterday, after your departure I hired a motor & took Diana with me to Newhaven to see Mother off to Dieppe[1]. It was a lovely day & Diana was so much excited by the steamer & the harbour & the general bustle – Nellie was there, also seeing Mother off, . . . & I took her back with me, & had a happy day with her here; but Alas! this morning she flitted, attracted like a moth by the glitter of London –

Nurse Hodgson took her departure yesterday; I miss her very much.

A small annoyance, but all the same vexatious, is, that the Nursery maid by whose cherub like countenance I was charmed into engaging, is turning out to be a little pig & not a cherub at all – She does not help the Nurse a bit & grumbles the whole time, finds these lodgings not good enough . . . etc. etc. – A worse fault is that she is careless when in charge of Diana whom she now ought to look after & lets her fall down. . . .

I write & tell you of these small incidents which will seem to you trivial, but down here they seem vastly more important than Germany's misconduct in Morocco. . . .

I do hope we are going to be firm with those treacherous Germans – I wonder if this is a little piece of the Kaiser's work, perhaps done without consulting his Ministers?

Your very loving
Clemmie who
sends you many warm kisses –
Do come back next Sunday, my precious
Darling –

[1] In 1910 Lady Blanche had bought a charming house in Dieppe – St Antoine, 16 rue des Fontaines; it would be her home base for the rest of her life.

○ From WSC   [Home Office]
5 July 1911

My darling,

I have got a vile cold in the head wh makes me thoroughly uncomfortable, & so far remedies have proved very inefficacious. . . .

I am sorry the nursemaid is a hussy. 'Don't hesitate to sack,' as Balfour wd have it. I hope to come down to you for the Sunday – but I wd much rather not dine out. Let us dine together quietly. . . .

L.G. [Lloyd George*], Grey, Haldane & I dined together last night and made good progress in the Home Rule problem. But I hope we may yet get some aid from the other side. Meanwhile the Lords go on tearing the Veto Bill to shreds. I shall be vy glad when the crisis actually comes.

We decided to use pretty plain language to Germany and to tell her that if she thinks Morocco can be divided up without John Bull, she is jolly well mistaken. . . .

> With my fondest love (I am in no condition to offer kisses)
> Your ever devoted husband
> W.

○ From WSC   [Home Office]
11 July 1911

My dearest one –

I bought some toys for the P.K. last night – but she is so little that it is difficult to know what will amuse her. Be careful not to let her suck the paint off the Noah's Ark animals. I hovered long on the verge of buying plain white wood animals – but decided at last to risk the coloured ones. They are so much more interesting. The Shopman expressed himself hopefully about the nourishing qualities of the paint & of the numbers sold – and presumably sucked without misadventure. But do not trust to this. . . .

All is going smoothly here. Very nice dinner last night with Ivor & Alice [Guest*]. Pretty pleasant friendly people. . . . Ivor considers himself still an invalid for all purposes except pleasure!

Alice interested me a great deal in her talk about her doctor in Germany, who completely cured her depression. I think this man might be useful to me – if my black dog[1] returns. He seems quite away from me now – It is such a relief. All the colours came back into the picture. Brightest of all your dear face – my Darling. . . .

> With fondest love,
> Always your devoted
> W.

[1] WSC's own name for his bouts of depression.

As Home Secretary, Winston had a traditional and important role to play in the investiture of the Prince of Wales, which took place at Caernarvon Castle on 13 July.

○ From WSC   H.M. Yacht Victoria & Albert
13 July 1911

My darling,
    We motored vy pleasantly from Chester to Penrhos yesterday.... The
yacht arrived about 7 & I went on board at once. The King sent for me & I
had a long talk with him about the most important things. All quite
satisfactory from our point of view, but of course there is a good deal of
tension underneath[1]. We have rehearsed the ceremony today with the little
prince[2]. He is a vy nice boy – quite simple & terribly kept in order. The
King has learned a lot since he acceded to the Throne & seems to be très
dans son assiette. The Queen, whom I sat next to, is rather alarming & not
so easy to converse with as her lord – who does most of the work
himself....
    This is a beautiful ship, & last night in this perfect weather & with the
full moon we might have been lying in the bay of Naples....
    The Holyhead ladies choir came aft and sang extremely well after
dinner.

With fondest love my darling Clemmie
I remain your devoted
W.

---

[1] On account of the continuing Lords v. Commons crisis.
[2] HRH Prince Edward (1894–1972). King Edward VIII from January to December 1936, when he
abdicated, taking the title of HRH the Duke of Windsor.

○ From WSC   [Penrhos]
14 July 1911

My darling Clemmie,
    It was indeed a beautiful and moving ceremony wh I witnessed
yesterday. The little prince looked & spoke as well as it was possible for
anyone to do. The enthusiasm was sincere & unbounded. The great radical
crowds gave the King & his son the best of welcomes. It was a most
happy event & will long live in the memories of all who took part in it.
    My reading of the Patent was much praised & I thought went well. I
returned after the ceremony to the Yacht & dined again on board. The
P.M. was also bidden. He had a good & useful talk with the King. I am vy
glad I suggested this meeting. Things are clearly tending to a pretty sharp
crisis. What are you to do with men whose obstinacy & pride have blinded
them to their interests and to any counsel of reason. It would not be
surprising if we actually have to create the 500 [peers]. We shall not boggle
about it when it comes to the pinch.
    ... It is vy pleasant here. The weather perfect: the garden delicious. We
all bathe each morning and lie & bask on the hot rocks. How I wish you
were here my dearest, & how glorious you wd look in your thinnest
Venetian bathing dress! The P.M. is in great form – apparently without a
care in the world quite happy talking to the young. Sylvia [Henley*] is here

as well as Blanche and Mrs Goodenough[1]. Eddie [Marsh*] leaves tonight. I shall be in London early Monday morning.

. . .

> With fondest love
> Ever your devoted
> W.

P.S. Much chaff by Violet [Asquith*] & the P.M. of Venetia [Stanley/ Montagu*] – who is alleged to have flirted with McKenna[2] to the effect that on his saying to her at Golf 'Come along me little mascot' she replied (she denies this) 'I wish I were – & then I could hang on your watch chain'. Wrath of Venetia. Do not spread this. It is a good joke for a few people only.

[1] Sylvia, Blanche and Margaret (Goodenough), all daughters of the 4th Baron Stanley of Alderley, now 4th Baron Sheffield.
[2] Reginald McKenna (1863–1941), First Lord of the Admiralty, 1908-11; Home Secretary, 1911; Chancellor of the Exchequer, 1915–16.

At the end of July Clementine and Venetia Stanley (Montagu*), later joined by Jack (Churchill*) and Goonie, set out for a holiday in the Bavarian Alps. It was planned that Winston would join them as soon as his ministerial and parliamentary duties allowed; but the parliamentary crisis and proliferating strikes on the industrial front thwarted his intention.

Despite the verdict of two General Elections and the passing of the Parliament Bill by the House of Commons on 15 May, the Conservative peers fought on bitterly – capitulating only when the Government revealed the King's pledge to create enough Liberal peers to ensure the Bill's passage through the House of Lords. The Bill was passed by them on 10 August.

After her Bavarian visit, therefore, Clementine returned home; and later in September she and Winston set out on a Scottish tour in their new car – a 15-20 Napier, purchased by Winston in her absence for £610, and the cause of mutual excitement and delight.

○ From WSC   Balmoral Castle
24 September 1911

Secret.
My dearest,
    Here I am in the traditional 'Ministers room' with all the portraits of departed Premiers & other political worthies on the walls around me. The party in the House is unexciting: principally Connaughts[1], Soveral[2] & Sir Francis Hopwood[3]. Also Dr Laking[4] who informed me that he had brought you into the world some years ago. This morning we attended church where a considerable sermon was preached us, ...
    The King talks much to me about affairs. L.G. [Lloyd George*] when here seems to have made a less good impression than last year. He electrified Their Majesties by observing that he thought it wd be a great

pity if war did not come now. They are of course repeating this statement somewhat freely. I shall practise caution. The King at first even put on a shocked air – but this soon wore off....

Everyone is most civil & friendly & life is vy quiet & easy. I wish you were here. It would be jolly. There is very little formality and much comfort.

Give my respects to your Grandmamma. I am going to bring the motor up here, & shall hope to reach you in it for luncheon on Wednesday.

Your ever loving husband,
W.

---

[1] Duke and Duchess of Connaught and Strathearn: Prince Arthur (1850–1942), third son of Queen Victoria, married, 1879, Princess Louise (1849–1917), daughter of Prince Frederick Charles of Prussia.
[2] Marquis de Soveral (1853–1922), Portuguese Minister to London, 1897–1910.
[3] Sir Francis Hopwood, later 1st Baron Southborough (1860–1947). Permanent Under-Secretary of State for the Colonies, 1907–11.
[4] Francis Henry Laking (1847–1914), 1st Bt. Physician in Ordinary and Surgeon Apothecary to Queen Victoria, King Edward VII and King George V.

O From CSC   Airlie Castle[1]
[undated, September 1911]   Alyth

My Darling,

    . . .

I am very happy here, tho' I am kept in great subjection by Granny who tho' infirm in body is active & even agile in mind.

She has now left off being a Tory & pretends to be non-party & above politics....

My little cousin Helen Mitford (née Ogilvy)[2] has just given birth 3 weeks too soon to a baby, a girl – Granny is 'relieved' to find that it is not an idiot & that it has the usual number of toes & fingers, because Helen married her first cousin, & Granny has therefore poured the vials of her wrath upon her –

I have finished the Crown Princess's [Auto]Biography[3] –

It tells of ill-bred people in an ill-bred manner & makes you wonder what is the use of long descent and high tradition....

Do tell me all about Balmoral.

I am so much excited about the motor & am looking forward to being fetched in it.

Many kisses my Darling from

Your loving
Clemmie.

---

[1] Ministers' wives were not invited to Balmoral, so while WSC was there CSC stayed with her grandmother, the Dowager Countess of Airlie.
[2] Helen Mitford (1890–1973), born Lady Helen Ogilvy, daughter of 11th Earl of Airlie. In 1909 she married Clement Freeman Mitford, son and heir of 1st Lord Redesdale.
[3] Louise of Tuscany, *My Own Story*, 1911.

O From CSC   Airlie Castle
25 September 1911

My Darling Winston
    Your telegram has just arrived –
    I hope you are happy my Sweet Pug & that you are being properly
petted, & that you will secure a huge stag – I am very happy here –
Granny is become much kinder with age tho' she points out all my defects
for my 'good' –
    She likes you, finds my handwriting detestable, & observed while
looking at me severely & stroking her lace lappets, that 'a gentlewoman of
consequence should not write like a housemaid'[1] –
    She is going to give me samples of the handwritings she most admires
so that I may try & copy them – Lord Melbourne & Lord Palmerston are
her favourite guides in this –
    She sends you her love & is looking forward to see you on Wednesday
for luncheon which is at 1.30 <u>to the second</u> by <u>Greenwich time</u>.
    Afterwards we fly away to Archerfield[2] in the new motor....
    I am just going to drive over to Cortachy Castle to luncheon with Aunt
Mabell[3], (the young Lady Airlie, & Granny's daughter in law -) She is a
sister of Lady Salisbury's who is staying there now – Granny instructs me
to 'walk delicately' as Aunt Mabell & my cousin are sunk in the most
stagnant bog of Toryism –
    Goodbye my Darling
    Send me a telegram when to expect you Wednesday & I will walk along
the road a mile & meet you & drive up in the new motor....
                                                          Your own loving
                                                          Clemmie.

[1] Her grandmother evidently employed highly educated housemaids.
[2] Home of Mr and Mrs H. H. Asquith near North Berwick.
[3] Born Lady Mabell Gore, daughter of the 5th Earl of Arran. She married the 11th Earl of Airlie in
1886. Died 1956. Her memoirs, *Thatched with Gold*, were edited and published posthumously.

During their visit to the Asquiths, the Prime Minister invited Winston Churchill
to become First Lord of the Admiralty – an offer which was eagerly accepted.

Chapter IV

ADMIRALTY

Winston Churchill became First Lord of the Admiralty on 23 October 1911. Until the Great War the Lords Commissioners of the Admiralty, and principally the First Lord, enjoyed the use of the Admiralty yacht *Enchantress* to facilitate their visits to the British fleet. Duty and pleasure easily combined on such voyages, and it was quite in order for civilian guests to be on board.

Winston made the fullest use of this amenity: in the three years before the war he spent in all eight months afloat, visiting every important ship, dockyard, shipyard and naval establishment in the British Isles and in the Mediterranean.

Admiralty House, a beautiful eighteenth-century house next to the Admiralty in Whitehall, overlooking Horse Guards Parade and St James's Park, was the official residence of the First Lord. The Churchills delayed moving there, however, because they could not afford the extra servants required (up to twelve as opposed to the five at Eccleston Square).

Nineteen-twelve opened for Clementine with visits to Blenheim and Burley-on-the-Hill for hunting, a sport to which she had become much addicted.

○ From CSC   Blenheim Palace
Wednesday evening [3 January 1912]

My Darling,
    I have just come back from a long day's hunting – The meet was at Stow-on-the-Wold, 25 miles away. It was the greatest fun – Sunny took charge of me & gave me a hand over the stone walls – We found at once, & had a lovely run over the vale. Sunny took me out of the crowd quite on one side & all the morning we were at the top of the hunt ... We went over some quite big places ... I took all the fences after Sunny – No one was in at the death, but Captain Daly gave me the brush – The hounds settled the fox all by themselves & when the huntsmen came up there was nothing left but the brush, which the hounds had very considerately left for me! ...
    Do my Dearest Darling take great care of yourself & arrive tomorrow not an exhausted weary pug, but sleek – & with your tail curled well over your head.

I wonder what the chauffeur[1] has done – your telegram I found, on coming in – I wonder if he was malingering? Mind you make him give back his livery which cost a lot of money –

List
1 suit of clothes
1 overcoat lined with fleece
1 cap
1 pair of boots
1 pair of gauntlets

Your own loving
Clemmie who loves
you my Sweet Darling
more than the Whole World

. . .

[1] Probably the chauffeur/valet Smart, who is mentioned again on p. 67 (letter of 23 June 1912).

○ From WSC   [Admiralty]
23 January 1912 11 p.m.

My Beloved darling,
    . . .
    The Belfast situation[1] has developed. The Orangemen have obtained the hall the night before & will evidently attempt to hold it over the 8th. The W. Office is preparing 3 Brigades (2 from Ireland & 1 from England) to keep order – I don't like this, & am holding up the orders. I am quite ready to leave the Orange folk stewing in their hall, while we have a 4 miles triumphal procession through the Nationalist quarter & speak in security at the St. Mary's [Hall].
    This is the way that things will I think eventually solve themselves. Ld Pirrie[2] arrived to-day much perturbed. He wd advise the abandonment of the meeting. I told him that coûte que coûte I shall begin punctually at 8 o'clock on the 8th of February to speak on Home Rule in Belfast.
    . . .
    I hope you have had a good day – no telegram! bad Cat – but no news is good news. Do not do foolish things –
    Tell Freddie [Guest*] to come to Belfast.
    . . .

Always your devoted husband
Winston.

. . .

[1] WSC had promised to address the Ulster Liberal Association on Home Rule at a meeting in Belfast. When this became known a great hullabaloo was raised by the Unionists and Orangemen.
[2] William James Pirrie, Baron (later 1st Viscount) (1847–1924). Shipbuilder and former Lord Mayor of Belfast; appointed HM Lieutenant for City of Belfast, 1911.

○ From CSC   Burley-on-the-Hill
24 January [1912]   Oakham

My Own Darling

    . . .

    I am so glad about what you say about St Mary's Hall – The vital thing is
that you make your speech (as you say) in Belfast on the day, & at the
hour – The matter of the Hall is of very small importance, & if lives were
lost in sticking to the letter instead of to the spirit of your undertaking, it
would lose in power & dignity –
Lord Pirrie must be rather faint-hearted.
    My Darling – I was so happy to get your letter. Last night before I fell
asleep I thought of you & wanted to kiss you & tell you how I love
you. . . . I shall be back on Friday for luncheon, so unless you want to very
specially, don't ask anyone, for I want to hear all your news . . .
    Lovely hunting yesterday with the Belvoir – Lots of fences & a long run.
Today I was too tired – But I hope tomorrow to hunt with Mr Ferney's
[Foxhounds]. But Alack it looks like freezing –

                                                  Your loving
                                                    Clemmie

    . . .

○ From WSC   [Admiralty]
24 January 1912

My Beloved,
    The plan on wh I have decided after full consultation is to hold the
meeting in the Nationalist quarter & ostentatiously defer to Londonderry's
demand[1]. A whole block of old houses will be pulled down & a beautiful
tent erected [on the Celtic Football Ground] with sounding boards etc. to
hold 10,000. All the Protestant ticket holders, who were coming to the
Ulster Hall will be acccommodated here, guarded not by troops but by
thousands of Nationalists. We shall make a great torchlight procession
down the Falls road 8 miles long surrounded by the Nationalist army; until
we reach the Hall. The police will draw a cordon between the two parts of
the city. The Orange faction will be left to brood morosely over their
illegal & uncontested possession of the Ulster Hall. Dirty dogs. 'Chained
like suffragettes to the railings.' . . .
    I am entirely satisfied with the developments.
    They are doubtful about your coming. But we will see how things
shape. Do not be too venturesome hunting. Keep some of your luck
unused.
    . . .
    Love to the babies,

                              Always your loving & devoted – tho vy weary
                                                    Winston S.C.

Handwriting as slovenly as yours!! & not nearly as pretty.
Many kisses.

[1] WSC had had quite a brisk exchange with his kinsman Lord Londonderry on the subject of the Belfast meeting and its proposed venue. The Ulster Hall was where Lord Randolph Churchill (a passionate Unionist) had made his famous 'Ulster will fight and Ulster will be right' speech on 22 February 1886. Charles Stewart Vane-Tempest-Stewart, 6th Marquess of Londonderry (1852-1915), was a cousin of WSC through the marriage of Lady Frances Vane-Tempest-Stewart, daughter of the 3rd Marquess, to the 7th Duke of Marlborough.

Winston, accompanied by Clementine, carried out his intended engagement in Belfast. A vast hostile crowd surrounded the Grand Central Hotel where they were staying, and people thronged round their car on the way to the Celtic Football Ground and, despite police protection, nearly overturned it; but when they reached the Roman Catholic Falls area of the city the yells and imprecations turned to cheers. Despite deluging rain the football ground and marquee were thronged with 5,000 people, mostly Irish Nationalists. Churchill addressed them for an hour.

Early in 1912 Clementine was again with child, but possibly as a result of her hunting activities and the strain and excitement of the Belfast visit, she suffered a miscarriage towards the end of March. This marked the beginning of many months of ill-health.

○ From WSC   H.M.S. Enchantress
24 March [1912]   Portland

My Beloved Clemmie,
      . . .
   My darling I do hope that you are not fretting & that all is going on well. It is probably for the best. . . . No wonder you have not felt well for the last month. Poor lamb. Anyhow you will be able to have a jolly year & hunt again in the winter. And there is plenty of time.

   The strike[1] seems vy remote from Portland with its well disciplined fleet & mountains of coal. It will be a great relief to learn that it is settled. We have so many difficulties to contend with. Still I think we shall surmount them. Governments are vy tough organisations. They stand wear & tear & are made to stand it.

   I hope Diana is dutiful & that Randolph perseveres in growth & teeth cutting.

   Unless some crisis occurs I shall not return till Wednesday.

   I hope you will be well enough to come down to Portsmouth on Friday – we will lie in the Solent & it will do you a lot of good.

   Goodnight my darling & sweetest Kat

                                        Always your loving husband
                                                        W.

[1] A national coalminers' strike for a minimum wage had begun on 1 March 1912; by 11 March 850,000 miners were out. The Coal Miners (Minimum Wage) Act, introduced in Parliament on 19 March, was passed on 29 March, and the strike ended on 11 April after a ballot failed to produce the necessary two-thirds majority to continue.

○ From CSC   33 Eccleston Square
25 March [1912]

My Own Darling
   Yesterday was such a Soft Spring Day, that I longed to be out in the
sunshine instead of lying flat on my back looking at the tops of the sooty
trees in the Square –
   It is so strange to have all the same sensations that one has after a real
Baby, but with no result. I hope I shall never have such another accident
again –
   I shall not, I fear be able to go to Portsmouth next Friday, as Doctor
Phillips wants me to stay flat till Saturday....
   What will happen if the Owners & Miners don't agree?...
                                         Tender love you my Darling from
                                                   your very loving
                                                       Clemmie

○ From WSC   H.M.S. Enchantress
[undated, 26 March 1912]

My dearest,
   I have just got back after a long day's cannonading, wh was well worth
seeing. The electric turrets of the Invincible have given so much trouble
that it was a question whether they shd not be replaced by hydraulics.
£150,000 it wd cost! I had them tested as they have never been tested
before – making one gun fire 8 rounds in succession. I stayed in the turret
myself to see what happened. All went well. It will be hard to condemn
the system on the results of to-day.
   The squadron of 4 ships all firing at once was most impressive – , a
stern & terrible picture of the wrath of man.
   The strike looks awfully black. Here all proceeds with clockwork
regularity. Elsewhere uncertainty & confusion over cloud the sky. I do not
feel I have missed much by not attending the Cabinet today. Events will
soon begin to govern them.
   We all return tomorrow by the 10.10.: & I will come to see you as soon
as I can on arrival. Your letter came this morning just as I was starting. It is
hard for you to be cooped up like this. My fondest love.
                                         Your ever devoted husband,
                                                       W.

○ From CSC ✉   33 Eccleston Square
27 March [1912]

My own Darling
   Welcome Home! I send this little line to greet you in case you have to
go straight from the station to work – The strike looks so black that I feel
dawn must soon be coming. The Times behaves very well at last:

supporting the Prime Minister in today's Leader – It actually insinuates (did you see) that Balfour is a person of limited intelligence. Come as quick as you can ...

Feeling recovered, Clementine flitted to Paris with some friends.

O From CSC   Hôtel Bristol
17 April [1912]   Paris

My Darling
   I had a very pleasant journey yesterday with Mrs Beatty[1] who is so nice – I found Rosie & Mat[2] here – Poor Mat still looks to me dreadfully ill, but don't say I said so ...
   It is so bright & warm, not a breath of wind & a cloudless sky. The [solar] eclipse was weird & it became very dark for a few moments. Everyone out in the street with bits of smoked glass. The light was strange & metallic like lighting on the stage.
   Rosie has gone off to see a friend & I am resting –
   The horror of the Titanic[3] overshadows everything.
   Goodbye my Darling.
      ...

                                                        Your very loving
                                                               Clem

[1] Wife of Rear-Admiral David Beatty, later 1st Earl Beatty. She was Ethel Marshall Field of Chicago; d. 1932.
[2] Matthew White Ridley, 2nd Viscount Ridley (1874–1916), and his wife Rosamond (born Guest), youngest daughter of the 1st Baron Wimborne. She was WSC's cousin and Randolph's godmother.
[3] The luxury liner SS *Titanic*, on her maiden voyage from Southampton to New York, struck an iceberg south of Newfoundland and sank on the night of 14–15 April 1912, with a loss of 1,513 lives.

O From WSC   [33 Eccleston Square]
18 April 1912

My darling,
   I have just returned here after a flying surprise visit to see the P.K. Just to bed at 6.30 ... Both the chicks are well and truculent. Diana & I went through the Peter Rabbit picture book together & Randolph gurgled.... He looks vy strong & prosperous.
   A vy busy day. Bill [CSC's brother] arrived yesterday, so I slept in your bed & accommodated him in my room. He has been gambling and has won a hundred pounds. You are not to know this.
   Apparently you inspire an awe which no one else can rival in the breast of the young officer. He has gone down to Portsmouth tonight....
   What good letters you write! Your description of the metallic light of the eclipse is perfectly correct. I noticed it myself. It also got much colder.

The Titanic disaster is the prevailing theme here. The story is a good one. The strict observance of the great traditions of the sea towards women & children reflects nothing but honour upon our civilisation. Even I hope it may mollify some of the young unmarried lady teachers who are so bitter in their sex antagonism, and think men so base & vile. They are rather snuffy about Bruce Ismay – Chairman of the line – who, it is thought – on the facts available – shd have gone down with the ship & her crew. I cannot help feeling proud of our race & its traditions as proved by this event. Boatloads of women & children tossing on the sea – safe & sound – & the rest – Silence. Honour to their memory.

Sweet & beloved cat – wire your wishes. The yacht will be at Dover on Saturday and I am inspecting there....

Always your loving & devoted husband
W.

...

O From CSC
18 April [1912]
Hotel Bristol
Paris

My Darling

...

I am coming back because I am not well – Rosie has been too kind for words –

Yesterday, after being out for less than an hour I was quite worn out & felt rather ill, so she found out who is the best woman's doctor in Paris & he came to see me this morning –

He says that from the condition of my inside he would have guessed the miscarriage happened 3 days instead of 3 weeks ago....

... I asked the French Doctor if there was anything seriously wrong. He said Not yet, but that if I did not take care I would be very ill & have to have an operation....

I feel bitter against Dr Phillips – It was his duty to warn us – If I am fortunate enough to have another baby I shall not have him again – But don't write to him or do anything till we meet.

I arrive at Victoria at 7.10 tomorrow evening – If you can spare the time do come & meet me....

... I shall be happy again when I see you my Darling –

Your loving
Clem

I sent £15 to Daily Mail for Titanic out of the £60 you gave me.

O From WSC
20 April 1912
H.M.S. Enchantress
Dover

My darling

Your telegram reached me here in good time. I hope the doctor's report will come tonight. There is nothing for it but a vy careful month. Did you get the flowers I ordered from Solomons? I hope they were fresh & beautiful.

Here we have had a fine day & the view of the harbour from the batteries on the hills was splendid. The sea turquoise – and the moles & piers all mapped in like a plan. I have been walking round the whole place & have found out several things –

One – that the boom defences wh they are supposed to have to close the entrances of the harbour simply do not exist!...

... The whole [*Titanic*] episode fascinates me. It shows that in spite of all the inequalities and artificialities of our modern life, at the bottom – tested to its foundations, our civilisation is humane, Christian, & absolutely democratic. How differently Imperial Rome or Ancient Greece wd have settled the problem.

The swells, and potentates would have gone off with their concubines & pet slaves & soldier guards, & then the sailors wd have had their chance headed by the captain, as for the rest – whoever cd bribe the crew the most wd have had the preference & the rest cd go to hell – But such ethics can neither build Titanics with science nor lose them with honour.

I feel vy selfish playing about here and you tied by the leg in town. My fondest love. Goodnight my dearest Clem

Your devoted loving husband
W.

O From WSC   H.M.S. Enchantress
8 May 1912

My darling –

Fog intermittent but rolling up every hour or so in deep banks has prevented all firing today. The Admiral missed his chance like a noodle and when there was a lucid interval his fires were low & he cd not move. The King came out in the submarine bringing a little puppy kitten prince[1] and I had them taken for a two-mile dive. I am getting quite experienced in submarines & the novelty & sense of danger are wearing off together. The boat dives vy well – I cd not let him go alone.

... We took the yacht all round the Fleet & the ships looked magnificent. The air full of aeroplanes, the water black with Dreadnoughts....

I return with Mr Balfour tomorrow night, but only arrive in time for the Home Rule division, & shall not see you till after 11 – about 11.30. Can you wait up so long – you poor sleepy puss to give me a kiss?...

How are you getting on? No letter has arrived from you. I do hope that your stern adherence to the doctors' most strict rules will be working a good result, and that you are recharging your electric batteries of energy & health.

We are all to dine on the Royal Yacht tonight.

That Beast Briggs[2] was not at all grateful for the fine appointment I have given him; but thank God I shall see his face no more. He has both character & ability, but is a thoroughly disagreeable man, & his mind is pinched & his soul is sore & sour & sulky & surly & generally <u>swinish</u>.

Let me draw a line between him &
my fondest love to my own dear darling Clemmie
Winston

[1] Prince Albert, later Duke of York (1895–1952). Succeeded his brother, King Edward VIII, in December 1936 as King George VI.
[2] Rear-Admiral Charles Briggs (1858–1951), Third Sea Lord and Controller of the Navy. Appointed Vice-Admiral in command of the 4th Squadron Home Fleet, 1912–14. Knighted 1913.

O From WSC   H.M.S. Enchantress
12 May 1912

My dearest darling,

I shall return tomorrow, but whether in time for dinner or not depends on the weather here. 4 torpedo boat destroyers are to go out and fire at the gallop from the saddle and it may be misty early in the day. I will therefore telegraph as soon as I know....

I have done some important things today – sacked Briggs, appointed Moore[1] in his stead, & a new Commodore of Destroyers, & a new Director of Naval Ordnance. Generally I have cleared off a lot of difficult & serious matters wh were hanging & flapping week after week.

The King talked more stupidly about the Navy than I have ever heard him before. Really it is disheartening to hear the cheap & silly drivel with wh he lets himself be filled up....

Goodnight my sweet pussy cat

Always your loving husband
W.

[1] Archibald Wilson Moore (1862–1934), Third Sea Lord, 1912–14; Admiral, 1919. Knighted 1914.

O From CSC   33 Eccleston Square
Saturday Night [22 June 1912?]

My Sweet Darling

Such lovely flowers! Such luscious peaches!

I love you very much. I hope you had fun in the swimming bath & that you will have a delicious balmy Sunday among trees & flowers – Give everyone my love –

Goonie [Jack Churchill's* wife] & Venetia [Stanley/Montagu*] have been here, both nice friendly tame Cats. The naughty old 'Sage' [Asquith*] took Venetia for a long motor drive in the country yesterday after Auction Bridge with Pig & Kat. I must say, if I were still a young damsel at large, I would take my walks abroad with a younger swain! Burn this you bad Pig instead of leaving it lying about, or just stuck inside your writing case.

I feel better! Come back early Monday or you may find me frisking about on the Roofs (or is it rooves).

. . .

○ From WSC   Knebworth House[1]
Sunday [23 June 1912]   Knebworth

My darling one,

Your dear letter gave me the greatest pleasure.

Smart has behaved atrociously. He refused to sleep in the bedroom provided & made an awful row down stairs, so I finally sent him off to London. Pamela was much upset.... The room was used only last week by Prince Arthur of Connaught's servant & the Admiralty messenger who used it after Smart's departure made no sort of complaint....

We have had some dancing lessons to day from the pretty little Miss Park Palings [*sic*] – I got on quite well at the threestep. I have an idea that we might form a dancing club – just for friends – & dance every fortnight in the winter months, with good teachers, so as really to dance well & with well trained people. Does the project attract you?...

We bathed & talked & danced. How I wish you cd have been here. But alas – Everyone asks after you & I think the Lyttons were much disappointed at your not coming.

My sweet one, I will come & see you as soon as I return.

Always your loving
W.

[1] Hertfordshire home of the 2nd Earl of Lytton and his wife Pamela (born Plowden).

○ From WSC   H.M.S. Enchantress
9 July 1912   Spithead

My darling One,

It was good of you to send me your telegram; but I have been feeling your pain & discomfort all day by reflexion....

But my darling I am so sorry for you. How I wish you cd have been here....

The submarine attack was vy dangerous owing to the traffic & the submarine fouled a little yacht. Luckily she swam to the surface all right – but how near a tragedy! The Fleet is just going to weigh & steam off to sea. I have been on the run since 7 o'clock this morning & I am tired out.

Margot[1] has enjoyed herself. She wanted to stay tonight – but I have no room & discouraged her. How she talks – anything & everything that comes into her head slips off her indiscreet tongue. Such views – & such expression of them.

The P.M. is quite indefatigable & has been on his legs all day. He loves this sort of life & is well suited to it. He would have made a much better Admiral than most I have to get along with.

Prince Louis[2] looked vy imposing on his splendid Thunderer.

I am coming up in [Sir Ernest] Cassel's special train tomorrow & arrive at a little after 10 tomorrow. Meanwhile Fondest Love, & may God give you a quiet & restful life.

Ever your devoted
W.

[1] Margaret ('Margot') Asquith, later Countess of Oxford and Asquith (1864–1945), daughter of Sir Charles Tennant, 1st Bt. She married H. H. Asquith as his second wife in 1894.
[2] Prince Louis of Battenberg, later Mountbatten, and 1st Marquess of Milford Haven (1854–1921). At this date First Sea Lord.

○ From CSC   33 Eccleston Square
Sunday [14 July 1912]

My own Darling

I feel so much delighted over Hanley[1]. Coming just now, with all the anxiety & doubt, which all must feel about the unknown but impending Insurance Act it is a real triumph – I suppose it is almost the first time in the world that every single person in the country will have to perform a definite action as the result of a single act of Parliament. Every single person must be affected by it as everybody must be employed or else employ someone.... Did you read the rude speech of the Governor of the Bank of England when Lloyd George* was his guest at a city banquet – ?

My dear Darling Amber Pug – Do not let the glamour of elegance & refinement & the return of old associations blind you. The charming people you are meeting to-day – they do not represent Toryism, they are just the cream on the top – Below, they are ignorant, vulgar, prejudiced – They can't bear the idea of the lower classes being independent & free – They want them to sweat for them when they are well & to accept flannel & skilly as a dole if they fall ill, & to touch their caps & drop curtsies when the great people go by – Goodbye my Darling I love you very much.

. . .

[1] In the by-election held on 13 July the Liberals gained the seat from Labour. Liberal, 6,647; Unionist, 5,993; Labour, 1,694.

Clementine's health at last seemed to be on the mend, and in late July she took the children to stay for a few weeks at Rest Harrow, near Sandwich in Kent, lent to them by Waldorf and Nancy Astor[1]. Winston visited his nursery party whenever possible.

[1] Waldorf Astor, later 2nd Viscount Astor (1879–1952), great-grandson of the US millionaire John Jacob Astor. He and his Virginian wife Nancy, born Langhorne (1879–1964), were prominent in British politics. Owner of the *Observer* newspaper. Conservative MP for Plymouth from 1910; on his succession to the peerage in 1919, Lady Astor became MP for his constituency and the first woman to take her seat in the House of Commons.

O From CSC   Rest Harrow
Tuesday Evening [30 July 1912]   Sandwich

My Darling

Two windy days since you departed, but tonight I think the weather is abating.

Neville Lytton[1] & Nellie turned up yesterday evening late, just before dinner & we had a merry evening – singing songs, dancing one-steps & flute playing by Neville. This morning Neville, Bill & Nellie bathed, but your Kat was good & sat looking on with her tail just dipping enviously in the water. This afternoon we motored to Ramsgate & sat on the sands listening to the Niggers [minstrels].

Come down soon my dear one – I think it is going to be lovely & hot & I am longing to talk with you, walk with you, bathe with you, sing with you

Your own Clemmie

. . .

[1] Neville Lytton, later 3rd Earl of Lytton (1879–1951). Artist and writer. His first wife was Judith Blunt, daughter of Wilfrid Scawen Blunt; they were divorced in 1923.

O From WSC   H.M.S. Enchantress
30 January 1913

Beloved Clemmie,

All has gone off admirably. The P.M. in gt form, the suffragettes foiled, & the Dundonians[1] highly delighted. I made, with vy little trouble, an almost impromptu speech, which was well received & generally commended. . . .

There were many inquiries about the Kat & her motor smash[2]. They are good folk up here & soberly appreciate their friends.

I hope you will take the Admiralty function[3] in hand this week & be in a position to tell me what you propose when I return.

I was stupid last night – but you know what a prey I am to nerves & prepossessions. It is a great comfort to me to feel <u>absolute</u> confidence in your love & cherishment for your poor P.D. [Pug Dog]

With many kisses & devoted love always your loving husband

W

. . .

P.S. I wish you were here; I shd like to kiss your dear face . . . and make you purr softly in my arms.

Don't be disloyal to me in thought. I have no one but you to break the loneliness of a bustling & bustled existence.

Write to me to Queensferry on receipt of this. It will reach me Sat[y] morning & tell me how much you care about your poor

W.

X.X.X. Here are three kisses one for each of you. Don't waste them. They are good ones.

[1] The Prime Minister and WSC had addressed a meeting at Kinnaird Hall, Dundee, on 30 January.
[2] On 18 January CSC had been involved in a collision in fog near Melton Mowbray, Leicestershire. She narrowly escaped serious injury, but received some cuts on her face and was considerably shaken.
[3] The Churchills had now decided to move into Admiralty House, which they did in April.

○ From CSC   33 Eccleston Square
31 January [1913]

My Darling One

I am very glad that the Dundee function went off so well – I read your speech with appreciation and interest. The Daily News (for once in a way) is delighted with you.

A small incident, which did not escape the Kat's watchful eye was that you did not arrive at the Kinnaird Hall till the 'Prime' had got well under way. I wonder if this was due to your train being late or because there was no Mrs Grimalkin [old she-cat] to mew at you!

I liked the P.M.'s speech but I thought the joke about your 'shrinking modesty' rather a stale one.

I have spent yesterday & to-day mornings in grapple with the Admiralty installation & the Office of Works officials. I am afraid altho' we are allowed to 'choose' our bedroom furniture it will be difficult to get anything attractive as the 'choosing' is to be done out of a grim catalogue; so far I have <u>avoided</u>, but not chosen anything.

I really think they ought to have a woman at the head of the Office of Works – someone like your Mama. Perhaps if I had married Lionel[1] the furniture in the catalogues would be prettier, but then that would be no use as I shouldn't be going to live at the Admiralty! However I really think it will be <u>very</u> comfortable. . . .

My sweet Darling Winston I love you so much & what I want & enjoy is that you should feel quite comfortable and at home with me – You know I never have any arrière pensée that does not immediately come to the top and boil over; so that when I get excited & cross, I always say more than I feel & mean instead of less – There are never any dregs left behind.

The only times I feel a little low is when the breaks in the 'bustling & bustled existence' are few & far between. I suppose they are not <u>really</u> few, but I am a very greedy Kat and I like a great deal of cream.

I have kept the three precious kisses all to myself, as I appreciate them more than the P.K. & C.B.

Please give my love to the 'Prime' & to Violet and a very special message to the Prime. . . .

                                           Goodbye my sweet precious
                                                     Your own Kat
                                                              . . .

[1] Lionel Earle, to whom CSC was engaged briefly in 1906. Permanent Secretary to HM Office of Works, 1912–33.

○ From WSC   H.M.S. Enchantress
1 February 1913   Forth Bridge

My precious One – Your dear letter gave me the greatest pleasure & comfort.

The wind has turned completely & is now off the shore, so that we hope to have a fairly prosperous passage to the south ... We start tonight & hope to arrive Monday early. I shall be with you for lunch....

Be vy careful not to open suspicious parcels[1] arriving by post without precautions. On the other hand do not leave them lying unopened in the House. They shd be dealt with carefully & promptly. These harpies are quite capable of trying to burn us out. Telephone to Scotland Yard if you are doubtful about any packet.

Since you have kept the 3 kisses for yourself, I send you 2 more for the P.K. & C.B. XIX and out of a store that will never be exhausted send you an additional six x x x x x x

Always your loving & devoted
W

[1] This warning seems painfully contemporary. Also, because of kidnap threats, the Churchill children had police protection on their walks in the parks. The militant suffragettes were now adopting increasingly violent tactics including arson, resulting from a setback in legislation granting certain categories of women the vote in early 1913.

O From CSC   Burley-on-the Hill[1]
7 February [1913]

The children send you love & 6 kisses
from Diana & 3 from the more stingy
Randolph.

My darling

I hope that you are wise in insisting upon the acceleration. I rather gathered that you did not think these Canadian ships <u>absolutely</u> essential but that you were pledged to Borden[2] ...

Do not, now that you have fought so grimly & won so much risk defeat for a thing which in itself is not vital (always providing that 'l'honneur est sauf'). You have shewn throughout such wonderful calm & even temper.

I feel rather sad & subdued at not being able to hunt[3]. I went to the Meet this morning & felt like a Cat with a mouse just out of reach. The wind whistled round this great gloomy barrack of a House....

Amy is kind, but more Suffragetty, Christian Sciency & Yankee Doodle than ever. Poor Freddie [Guest*] is a Sheep in Lion's clothing –

Your loving
Clemmie

...

[1] Where CSC was again staying with Freddie Guest and his American wife Amy, born Phipps, of Pittsburgh, USA.
[2] Sir Robert (Laird) Borden (1854–1937), at this date Prime Minister of Canada. Throughout 1913 WSC and Borden discussed the idea that Canada should pay for the construction of three Dreadnoughts. In early 1914 it became clear that the Canadian Senate would not pass the plan.
[3] CSC was somewhat fragile after her miscarriage the previous year and still recovering from the car accident.

O From CSC   33 Eccleston Square
4 April [1913]

My Darling Winston

I hope you are having a glorious time with your Ships – Please be a good one, & don't do any work besides the Inspecting as you <u>must</u> be tired after last week's efforts.

Last night I spent a most pleasant evening with Mr Evan Charteris[1], Margot [Asquith] & Count Mensdorff. We dined at the Ritz & went to see a most thrilling & delightful old fashioned play, Diplomacy, full of lovely women spies, purloined State documents, Russian counts etc – Margot said to me on the way home: 'are you going to ask me on the Yacht? I asked Henry if he would like me to come & he said "Yes, but I should like to be invited by Winston" – ' Don't you think the simplest way will be to ask the P.M., Margot & Violet [Asquith*] & let them settle it between themselves? – Margot was very nice & simple, but she looked rather sad. She said pathetically: 'It <u>is</u> my turn this year. I have never been on the Yacht'!

Tomorrow I go to the Wharf[2] – I wish you were going too so that we could play 'golaf' [sic] on those beautiful Huntercombe links. Diana & Randolph ask for you & are displeased at your absence –

Your very loving
Clemmy
. . .

[1] Evan (later Sir Evan) Charteris (1864–1940), sixth son of the 10th Earl of Wemyss. Barrister and art connoisseur.
[2] The Asquiths' home on the river Thames at Sutton Courtenay, Berkshire.

O From WSC   H.M.S. Enchantress
6 April 1913   Portsmouth

My darling,

We have got back here after a good passage from Devonport & remain in harbour till tomorrow evening, when we sail for Chatham. The naval members of the Board having had quite enough of the sea have taken themselves off till Monday ...

I hope you & the P.M. will be well looked after at the Wharf, now that [the] three creatures [suffragettes] are in their pens.

The penal sentence on Mrs P.[1] will enable the Government to deal with her from time to time as they please. It is as good as the Cat & Mouse Bill[2] itself.

There is no news here, but of ships & guns. I always like this port. I stay placidly in my nice cabin working all the morning, walk round the Dockyard in the afternoon & then home to tea & a couple of hours more work before dinner. The papers in files & bags & boxes come rolling in. One never seems to do more than keep abreast of them.

It will be nice coming back to the Admiralty. I like the idea of those spacious rooms. I am sure you will take to it when you get there. I am afraid it all means vy hard work for you – Poor lamb. But remember I am going to turn over my new leaf! That I promise – the only mystery is 'What is written on the other side'. It may be only 'ditto ditto'!

I do hope you will have an enjoyable weekend with the Asquiths. Do not commit yourself & the yacht unnecessarily to Margot, if you can help it. But I know how discreet you are.

Good night my sweet darling – Fondest love & kisses from your
ever loving & devoted
W.

...

¹ Mrs Emmeline Pankhurst (1858–1928), founder of the Women's Social and Political Union, who in 1905 launched the militant suffragette campaign. She was supported by her two daughters, Christabel and Sylvia. At this date she had just received a three-year prison sentence for inciting her supporters to place explosives in the house of the Chancellor of the Exchequer (Lloyd George); she was to serve only one year, part of which she devoted to a hunger strike.
² The forcible feeding of prisoners on hunger strike, permitted for some time, had aroused considerable criticism. The Royal Assent to Prisoners (Temporary Discharge for Ill-health) Act, 1913, known as the 'Cat and Mouse' Bill, authorized the release of women weakened by hunger strike and their re-arrest once their health was restored.

O From CSC
Sunday 6 April [1913]

The Wharf,
Sutton Courtenay

My Darling Winston

A very pleasant Sunday here – The Prime & Violet [Asquith*] picked me up, yesterday morning at Eccleston Square & as I was whisked away, I felt it was the end of a chapter in my life – Leaving a house where one has lived nearly 4 years is as much of an event in a 'Kat's' life, as changing from Home Office to Admiralty for a Statesman!

We stopped on our way to Huntercombe & lunched at 'Skindles' where we had 'all the delicacies of the season' – Plover's eggs, (I hope you will not have had a surfeit of these on the Yacht, as they are to smile at you on your return) – salmon, lamb, asparagus, rhubarb.

Then we proceeded on our way & played <u>very</u> badly. We said it was the wind, but I suspect it was Skindles –

This morning we played again, ... Mr Montagu¹ is here, a very agreeable person. His heart, I think, is divided between the Violet & the Venetia [Stanley/Montagu*], but he will have to be contented with one of his own race or forfeit all his worldly goods! <u>He</u> might be prepared to make the sacrifice – Elizabeth² is here, returned from having her already bright intellect burnished at Munich – She is very attractive & has become almost pretty –

Tomorrow I fly back by the early morning train as I am longing to take possession of our Mansion –

My Darling – I feel that it's such a long time since I've seen you – It may be partly because I haven't written to you any nice letters but only tedious scrawls about whether to lunch or not to lunch....

I went to Mr Steel's³ wedding – He looked radiantly happy – I hope he will come back from his honeymoon at the end of his leave! They both looked as tho' they meant 'to sail away for a year & a day'.

Your loving
Clemmie

...

[1] Edwin Montagu (1879–1924), second son of 1st Baron Swaythling. At this date Parliamentary Under-Secretary of State for India. In 1915 he married Venetia Stanley; she renounced Christianity and adopted her husband's Jewish faith in order that he should not forfeit his inheritance.
[2] Elizabeth Asquith (d. 1945), daughter of H. H. Asquith and his second wife, Margot. In 1919 she married Prince Antoine Bibesco of Romania. She wrote plays, poems and novels.
[3] Gerald Arthur Steel, WSC's Assistant Private Secretary, 1911–15.

○ From WSC   H.M.S. Enchantress
7 April 1913   Chatham

My darling,
    Two beautiful letters arrived on Sat^y night & Sund^y Morning respectively from you. I expect you are now in the vy throes of moving & it is just as well that I am away. The passage round here was quite good & we all made it without misadventure. Brab[1] is staying till tomorrow. He has I think enjoyed himself, & has been treated with the greatest ceremony. He is a wonderful man for 70. I shall be vy glad to look & feel like that when I am 60 – if I ever get so far along the road....
    I return Wed^y morning in time for the Cabinet. Greet me at the Admiralty then.

Your ever loving husband,
W.

My dear sweet – I have thought vy tenderly of you while I have been cruising. XX is for yourself & X & X are for Diana & Randolph. Don't misappropriate them.

[1] Maj.-Gen. Sir John Palmer Brabazon (1843–1922). He was WSC's first commanding officer, 4th Hussars, 1893.

○ From CSC   [Admiralty House]
28 April 1913

My Darling,
    I think of you prowling round the Dockyard & going on board all the men of war in the harbour & then retiring to the Board Room with the firm resolve of reflecting upon Ireland & her needs instead of on Germany & her doom – I hope you will come home refreshed & bearing inside you the most lovely glossy egg [speech] full of meat ready to be laid on Tuesday.
    Violet [Asquith*] is coming, a delighted telegram came from her yesterday. Margot [Asquith] came to see me at tea time & was very pleasant. I had an embarrassing five minutes when I found she did not know that the 'Prime' was coming to the Mediterranean. She said 'How I wish Henry was going away with you at Whitsuntide – it would do him so

much good.' I replied 'But he is coming.' She was enchanted, but she seemed a little hurt when she found Violet was going too & that she had been discounted. There was a pause & then she said 'Oh I see' & changed the subject. From Violet's telegram I could see that the 'Prime' had not said a word to her about it & that it was quite a new idea[1]....

Your loving
Clemmie

...

[1] In May 1913 Mr and Mrs Asquith *and* Violet were all three guests of the Churchills for a Mediterranean cruise which took in a visit to Malta and witnessing naval exercises at sea.

○ From WSC   H.M.S. *Enchantress*
[undated, probably 23 July 1913]   S. Queensferry

Clemmie darling –
We did not sail for Scapa yesterday after all, because the C. in C. is coming South & all we have to do is to meet him off the Forth ... By all means ask K [Kitchener] to lunch next week – Tuesday wd be a good day. Let us be just à trois. I have some things to talk to him about[1].

The party has settled down quite happily & I think they have made up their minds to enjoy themselves. The weather too is bright & clear & there is every prospect of the manoeuvres beginning at least on smooth water.

Tender love to you my sweet one & to both those little kittens – especially that radiant Randolph. Diana is a darling too: & I repent to have expressed a preference. But somehow he seems a more genial generous nature: while she is mysterious & self conscious. They are vy beautiful & will win us honour some day when everyone is admiring her & grumbling about him.

My dearest you are vy precious to me and I rejoice indeed to have won & kept your loving heart. May it never cool towards me is my prayer & that I may deserve your love my resolve.

Write daily –

Always your loving husband
W

[1] Lord Kitchener was at this time Agent and Consul-General in Egypt, and in 1914 would be Secretary of State for War. WSC was keen to establish a good working relationship since there had been a long-standing coolness between them going back to 1898 when 'K' had not wanted WSC to join his army in the Sudan. After Omdurman, WSC had criticized Kitchener sharply over the treatment of the Dervish wounded and the desecration of the Mahdi's tomb.

○ From CSC   In the train. 9 o'clock a.m.
Saturday [26 July 1913]

My Darling Winston
I heard that Diana wasn't quite well, nothing serious – but I felt anxious & longed to see them both, so I telegraphed to Maxine [Elliott*] & Nellie & I are off to Birchington-on-Sea to spend Sunday on the sands with the P.K.s. If you get back in time you must go to Maxine's & make up for my

defection – I am disappointed to miss Sunday there as it is always such fun, but I felt I must go & see the Kittens & especially little Diana who went away with such a pale face....

I lunched with Sir Edward Grey at 'Eccleston' yesterday – He has made the library charming – masses of roses from Fallodon[1]. The Crewes were there & the Asquiths & the Japanese Ambassador & his pretty wife ...

I long to hear from you about the Manoeuvres – It is difficult to follow what is happening from the papers. I am so glad you feel better –

Tender Love
from your
Clemmie
...

Worse writing <u>even</u> than usual owing to a shaky train

[1] Home of Sir Edward Grey at Christon Bank, Northumberland. When the Churchills had moved into Admiralty House, Sir Edward had taken a lease on 33 Eccleston Square.

While Winston went to Balmoral for his annual ministerial visit, Clementine, Goonie, Nellie and little Diana stayed on board *Enchantress* at Greenock and amused themselves with local expeditions.

O From WSC   Balmoral Castle
20 September 1913

My beloved,

I am writing in one of the Keepers' Lodges to wh I have returned after stalking & where I am waiting for the Prince of Wales. Quite the best day's sport I have had in this country – 4 good stags & home early! Three were running & one of these a really difficult shot – downhill, half covered, & running fast. Not a bad performance for I have not fired a shot since last year....

Last night I had a long talk with the young Prince [of Wales, aged nineteen] and we went through all my Admiralty boxes together. He is so nice, & we have made rather friends. They are worried a little about him, as he has become so vy spartan – rising at 6 & eating hardly anything. He requires to fall in love with a pretty cat, who will prevent him from getting too strenuous.

The King has been extremely cordial & intimate in his conversations with me, and I am glad to think that I reassured him a good deal about the general position....

Altogether it has been most pleasant, & not at all dull or embarrassing. I am glad I came – tho' leaving the yacht was as always a wrench to me.

I am delighted that you are happy & placid and that Goonie & Nellinita are with you.

I will meet you in the grey dawn of Monday in London, & we will lunch together at the Ritz ...

I have done quantities of work and have also written at length to the P.M.

Tender love my darling one to you & sweet Diana from your ever devoted husband
W
. . .

○ From WSC   H.M.S. Enchantress
19 October 1913   Newcastle

My dearest one,
. . .

We had a good journey here and are now spending a peaceful Sunday on board. I am going to play golf this afternoon. I was really <u>quite</u> tired & slept vy soundly. It is a strain to make a speech like that[1] – so many different things to consider & keep constantly in view. I expect one must make many mistakes.

If the Germans refuse I shall have made my case for action[2] – If they accept it will be a big event in the world's affairs . . .

Here is a letter from Cornelia [Wimborne[3]]. I want you to write & accept. I have a great regard for her – & we have not too many friends. If however you don't want to go – I will go alone. Don't come with all your hackles up & your fur brushed the wrong way. – You naughty.
. . .

Your ever loving husband
W.

[1] On 18 October 1913 WSC made a major speech to a crowded meeting of Liberals in the Free Trade Hall, Manchester.
[2] One of the topics of this speech was the 'Naval Holiday', first suggested by WSC in 1912 and renewed in 1913: that both Germany and Britain should refrain from additional warship construction. The German Government refused on the grounds of the necessity of maintaining employment levels.
[3] Wife of 1st Baron Wimborne (Sir Ivor Bertie Guest; see Biographical Notes). WSC's aunt.

○ From CSC   Alderley Park[1]
[undated, 20 October 1913]   Chelford
In train to London 7 pm.

My darling Winston,

I am disgusted with the only two newspapers I have seen. The Times seems to think you are back-sliding about Ulster, & C. P. Scott[2] refuses to be lured into liking expensive ships! They are too unreasonable.

I loved coming with you & felt sad when you went away to Newcastle.

But I had such a lovely hunt this morning – We went out very early cubbing & nothing happened for a long time. Several cubs were killed just outside the coverts & about 11 o'clock Venetia [Stanley/Montagu*] & I were just going home when the hounds got away after a big cub (I believe it was an old fox!) & we had a glorious run for about half an hour ...

... The Master (Captain Higson, who was in the 14th Hussars) gave me the brush! It was a glorious moment – but the glory was a little dimmed by having to hack back 5 miles to the Motor along a very hard road.

I found your dear letter. I will write tomorrow to Aunt Cornelia. I would like to go & I will be very good I promise you, especially if you stroke my silky tail!

I had quite forgotten how nice it was to hunt – I did enjoy it ...

Goodbye my sweet darling Winston. I do hope the P.M. will say something good & advancing about Ulster on Sat. ... but he is such an old Procrastinator ...

Your loving
Clemmie

...

---

¹ The Cheshire home of Lord and Lady Sheffield (see Biographical Notes, under Stanley of Alderley).
² C. P. Scott (1846–1932). Editor of the *Manchester Guardian*, 1872–1929.

○ From WSC   H.M.S. Enchantress
22 October 1913

My lovely one,

I am so glad that you had a jolly day after the little foxes ...

To-day I was to have flown in a seaplane (like that monoplane) but it had no sooner started from the shed for the Enchantress than it 'side slipped' & is now a total wreck. The officers were lucky to get off with a ducking.

Shotley [Training Establishment] was in good condition this morning, all the boys looking clean and healthy. We have got a vy good captain there now.

My guests are I think much enjoying themselves – This afternoon I took them all out in a submarine ...

You dear bird I love you vy vy vy much indeed: & love to think of you as mine & mine only. How lucky I have been – Not vy gifted where Cats are concerned – I find by right divine the first & best.

Fondest love
Your ever devoted –
W.

○ From WSC   H.M.S. Enchantress
23 October 1913   Sheerness

Darling, We have had a vy jolly day in the air. First we all went over to Eastchurch [Isle of Sheppey Naval Air Station] where we found dozens of aeroplanes, & everyone [his staff and guests] flew ... I let the military & naval officers fly across the river with me to our other air station in the Isle of Grain – a delightful trip on wh I was conducted by the redoubtable Samson[1].

Here we found another large flock of sea planes in the highest state of activity. Just as we arrived & landed, the Astra-Torres airship wh I had sent for from Farnborough, arrived, & ... I went in her for a beautiful cruise at about 1,000 feet all round Chatham & the Medway. She is a vy satisfactory vessel, and so easy to manage that they let me steer her for a whole hour myself. Then after luncheon more sea planes, & I have finished the day by inspecting Sheerness dockyard. It has been as good as one of those old days in the S. African war, & I have lived entirely in the moment, with no care for all these tiresome party politics & searching newspapers, & awkward by-elections, & sulky Orangemen, & obnoxious Cecils & little smugs like Runciman[2].

For good luck before I started I put your locket on. It has been lying in my desk since it got bent – & as usual worked like a charm.

All the birds [pilots] are coming to dinner tonight. You may imagine how pleased the others were to have the chance of losing their aetherial virginities!

It is vy satisfactory to find such signs of progress in every branch of the Naval air service. In another year – if I am spared ministerially, there will be a gt development. When I have pumped in another million the whole thing will be alive & on the wing....

How are the chickens? The world will be a vy interesting place for them when they are grown up.

> Good night my darling
> fondest love from your devoted husband,
> W.

[1] Charles Rumney Samson (1883–1931), aviator.
[2] Walter Runciman, later 1st Viscount Runciman of Duxford (1870–1949), shipowner and Liberal MP. At this date President of the Board of Agriculture (1911–14).

○ From CSC   Blenheim Palace
Thursday [23 October 1913]

My Darling

Nellie & I came here on Tuesday & we are spending the time very pleasantly –

Sunny [Marlborough*] has got a new hard red lawn tennis court & a professional & we have lessons & practice every morning.

How splendid Lloyd George's* Swindon Speech[1] is! I think it is the greatest Speech I have ever read – Nellie read it aloud to me this morning & we were both moved to tears – Sunny is ('au fond') broad-minded about the land, but he does not let it appear on the surface & indulges in the sourness & bitterness of a crab-apple! But he works it all off at tennis –

How glorious it would be if your Naval proposal [the 'Naval Holiday'] were to bear fruit....

... Sunny was thinking of writing an answer to the Swindon Speech in the Daily Mail but has thought better of it since reading the Speech!

This morning he was cinematographed for the Empire Music Hall, seated on a new patent plough surrounded by admiring yokels! He explained that this was meant as a counter to the land campaign so that the Democracy should see that Dukes don't spend <u>all</u> their time flirting on the Riviera! I have promised to go to the Empire & to cheer the film loudly!

Your loving
Clemmie

...

[1] The Chancellor of the Exchequer, speaking at Swindon on 22 October 1913, had outlined the government's proposals for land law reforms and made particular references to rural housing; he waxed abusive of large landowners *et al.*

Early in 1913 Winston had started to take flying lessons from the instructors at the naval air stations: he found flying and the company of the brave and brilliant young aviators who were pioneering this science totally exhilarating. From his earliest days at the Admiralty Churchill had encouraged the then budding Royal Naval Air Service.

Not only Clementine, but many of Winston's friends, including Sunny Marlborough* and F. E. Smith*, tried to persuade him to give up this, then highly risky, ploy, which was certainly no part of the duty or obligation of the First Lord of the Admiralty.

O From CSC   Blenheim Palace
24 October [1913]

My Darling
    I hope my telegram will not have vexed you, but please be kind & don't fly any more just now....
    Is it very cold on the Enchantress? Do you really mean to go on to Portland after Portsmouth? Why not come to Blenheim for a few days? It is very pleasant here.

Your loving
Clemmie

...

O From CSC   Admiralty House
2 November [1913]

My Darling
    I arrived home quite safely last night....
    I found two delicious slumbering kittens, Randolph with his little arms flung out over his head looking like a sweet cherub –
    This morning my cold has gone down to my chest, but I shall be all

right if I stay in bed. I have not seen the children yet as I am afraid of giving them my cold ...

I hope you will have propitious weather for Portland....

Tender Love from
Clemmie ...

My Sweet and Dear Pig, when I am a withered old woman how miserable I shall be if I have disturbed your life & troubled your spirit by my temper. Do not cease to love me – I could not do without it. If no one loves me, instead of being a Cat with teeth & claws, but you will admit soft fur, I shall become like the prickly porcupine outside, & inside so raw & unhappy –

Good-bye my Sweet One, I want to stroke your dear Face –

I must now carry the war into Pig's country & request him not to leave the Cat's scrawls lying about. They are in the roof of writing case, Easily accessible to inquisitive folk –

O From WSC 　　　　　　　　　　　　　　　　H.M.S. Enchantress
3 November 1913 　　　　　　　　　　　　　　　　　　Portland

My dear and Precious One –

...

I loved much to read the words of your dear letter. You know so much about me, & with your intuition have measured the good & bad in my nature. Alas I have no vy good opinion of myself. At times, I think I cd conquer everything – & then again I know I am only a weak vain fool. But your love for me is the greatest glory & recognition that has or will ever befall me: & the attachment wh I feel towards you is not capable of being altered by the sort of things that happen in this world. I only wish I were more worthy of you, & more able to meet the inner needs of your soul....

Jack [Churchill*] is here – always happy in the circle of military things.

Kiss both the P.K.s for me: & telegraph to me early tomorrow that your cold is quite gone. You must take gt care if it gets on your chest. Use the thermometer, & at the slightest sign of a rise send for the Doctor – Don't forget this – it is an order, wh a good & docile cat must obey.

Always with fondest love
Your devoted husband,
W.
X X X X

O From CSC 　　　　　　　　　　　　　　　　　Admiralty House
4 November [1913] 7 a.m.

My Darling

I dined pleasantly last night with 'the Prime' & Violet [Asquith*] & her brother, Arthur[1] – The suffragette affair, on the road to Stirling was horrible & upset Violet a good deal. One of the women slashed Mr Asquith* 4 times with a crop over the head, before she was seized – Luckily his face was saved (like yours at Bristol) by the brim of his stiff hat. He never seems to defend himself on these occasions but remains calm & stolid & unwinking! About two pints of pepper were thrown into the car, but luckily no-one's eyes were injured – When arrested the 3 women gave the names of:– Violet Asquith, Frances Tennant[2], & Maud Allan[3]! And under these names they have been charged & will appear!

To-night the Prime & Violet are dining here with me, & I shall try & get Sir Edward Grey for a 4th for Bridge.

Thank-you my Darling for your dear letter – I feel <u>so</u> good now as if I never could be naughty again!

Your loving
Clemmie

. . .

[1] Arthur Asquith (1883–1939), third son of H.H. Asquith and his first wife, Helen Melland. Always known as 'Oc'.
[2] Frances Tennant, sister of Margot Asquith (d. 1925).
[3] Maud Allan (d. 1956). Dancer, actress, pianist, writer. She was the talk of London in 1908 on account of her daring dance in the *Vision of Salome*. She was invited to a Downing Street garden party, which caused a stir.

O From WSC   [Eastchurch, near Sheerness]
29 November 1913

My darling One,

I am so sorry to learn from your telegram that your Mother has to be operated upon on Monday. I fear this will be a gt anxiety to you. But do not embrace sinister conclusions, when there are still so many hopeful alternatives. . . .

I have been naughty today about flying. Down here with twenty machines in the air at once and thousands of flights made without mishap, it is not possible to look upon it as a vy serious risk. Do not be vexed with me. I shall be back tomorrow between 11 & 12 & I thought it would do us both good to play a little golf at W[alton] Heath.

Fondest love my darling one & deep sympathy with you in the cloud wh has loomed on your horizon. We must trust that it will pass in God's goodness away altogether[1]. Make any arrangement for your mother's comfort. I can perfectly well sleep in the little room & shd greatly prefer it. Don't change yourself – please – It will drive me from your side. . . .

Ever your loving husband
W.

[1] CSC's mother made a good recovery.

○ From CSC ✉[1]   Admiralty House
[undated, *c*.1913]

My darling,
I hear you want the car. But I do <u>implore</u> you not to fly this morning.
There is a high wind & it is a bad day. Quick send me back a reassuring
note.
Trembling & anxious

                                                                          . . .

[1] Admiralty House and the Admiralty building connected through internal doors.

In January 1914 there was a tussle in Cabinet over the Naval Estimates.
Churchill, demanding an increase of £3 million over the previous year's provi-
sion, was opposed by McKenna and Lloyd George*. Churchill made it clear
that for him it would be a resigning matter. Compromises were made: but
Churchill got his ships.
   The Home Rule Bill was introduced for the third time in the House of
Commons in early March. The Unionists violently rejected vital proposals on
partition. With the prospect of the Bill becoming law the troubles intensified,
both at home and in Ireland, where the Ulster Volunteers and the Nationalist
Volunteers were formed – effectively private armies.
   In a major speech at Bradford on 14 March, Churchill announced the
Government's determined policy on Home Rule and its resolve to confront
the Ulster rebellion.

○ From WSC   H.M.S. Enchantress
8 February 1914   Sheerness

My darling One,
   The weather greatly altered for the worse after I started on Saturday &
now it is raining & blowing in a detestable manner. We decided therefore
not to brave the rough seas outside the Thames estuary & have remained
here peacefully all day ... I had a little flight yesterday with Lieut. Seldon
wh was quite pleasant & not at all dangerous – tho' rather windy.
Tomorrow morning the yacht goes to Gravesend & I come up the river
from there in the green barge, arriving at the Admiralty at about 11.
Cabinet at 12. I wonder if I [Admiralty business] shall be reached & how it
will go – or whether it will all drag over for another week. The anxiety is
wearying, & I am glad to have got away from my thoughts in a change of
scene, companies, occupations & a dash of counter excitement. Anyhow
the die is cast – Acceleration or death! I have taken vy good & formidable
ground in my latest paper, wh I will show you when you return.
   The Enchantress has been vy well refitted. The forecastle deck is
finished & makes her a much better sea boat. The fore & aft bridge gives a
splendid promenade of 49 paces.... Everything is spotless.
   Perhaps this will be the last time I shall spend a week end on this vessel,
wh has been so great a feature in my life during the last 30 months....

I am becoming more & more a fatalist. There was a good verse in the Lesson today – from Revelations. 'He that overcometh shall inherit all things; & I will be his God, & he shall be my son'. I wd take it as a good augury, but I am afraid that 'overcometh' means 'overcometh oneself' – wh is a hard job when so many others are at it too.

Well – this is a most difficult and critical period for me. I am glad now to see my way so clearly on the Naval issue: but Ulster is hidden from me. I cannot tell what to do – until the time comes & the issues are plainly shaped.

Tender love to you my darling, & kisses to both those poodlings, who are so small –

Ever your devoted husband,
W.

O From CSC ✉   Admiralty House
[undated, *c.*1913]

My darling,

When your business is finished do come to bed as early as you can. You look weary from want of sleep & tomorrow you will need all your cool brain & judgment.

. . .

They spent Easter in Madrid this year. When Winston had to return home, Clementine went on to Seville, where she stayed with Sir Ernest Cassel.

O From WSC   Admiralty
23 April 1914

My darling,

I have been hampered in my writing by the lapse in time wh must necessarily intervene before the letter reaches you & by pressure here of all kinds.

The Madrid cold still hangs on to me & I croak like a frog. . . .

On my return I discovered as usual various symptoms of naughtiness among the Seals [Sea Lords]: & I have systematically laboured to reduce them to good order & discipline.

The 'Ulster Pogrom'[1] is in full swing as you will read in the papers. We have now published everything and I am confident these wild charges will become gradually discredited. Bonar Law[2] has excelled himself in rudeness to the P.M.! & feelings are on all sides bitter to a degree unknown hitherto. . . .

The kittens are extremely well and make continuous inquiries & complaints about your non-return. I do hope you are enjoying yourself and that the sights & scenes repay the exile & exertion. I am vy glad to be back: & shall be gladder when you return. . . .

Our finances are in a condition wh requires serious & prompt attention. The expense of the 1ˢᵗ quarter of 1914 with our holiday trip is astonishing. Money seems to flow away. I am seeing Cox [Cox & Co., bankers] today & propose to devote myself to this topic, unpleasant though it be, for some considerable time.

Fondest love my darling and many kisses from the babes & me,

Always your loving & devoted husband,

W

¹ In response to the risk that arms depots in Ulster might be rushed by the Ulster Volunteers, WSC, with Cabinet approval, took the precaution of moving ships to the Irish coast, in case the transport of troops from south to north became necessary. He was attacked virulently in Parliament by the Conservatives, who accused him of wishing to institute an 'Ulster Pogrom' – the term stuck.
² Andrew Bonar Law (1858–1923). Canadian born British statesman. Unionist MP from 1900 and party leader, House of Commons, from 1911. In Coalition Government, from 1915, successively Secretary of State for the Colonies, Chancellor of the Exchequer, Lord Privy Seal and Leader of House. Member of War Cabinet. Prime Minister, October 1922–May 1923.

○ From CSC   Hotel Ritz
Monday 27 [April 1914] 8.30 a.m.   Madrid

My own Darling

We have just arrived from our long 24 hour journey from Granada. It was really very comfortable, but I missed most of the lovely scenery, as I was so exhausted from sight-seeing that I slept most of the day, only waking up to eat cold chicken now & then – ! We stopped at Cordova again, & drove to a beautiful garden in the hills. . . .

It was delightful, finding your letter here – I had absolutely no news till yesterday, when at Cordova I found a copy of the Times of the 21ˢᵗ! & so heard about the revival of the 'Pogrom'. . . .

I am so sorry my Darling that you are worried over our finances. I will do all I can to help to keep down expenses. I have spent very little of the money you gave me, as Sir Ernest would not let me pay for a single thing. I hope <u>he</u> will not be ruined! . . .

I have enjoyed myself so much, but I am longing to see you my own Darling – I hope you miss me a little bit; tho' I suppose the political excitement is so great that you hardly have time –

I hope the servants are all playing up & making you comfortable.

You will see me almost as soon as this letter I shd think.

I am sorry the Seals have been bad, But do not be too harsh to the poor beasts – When the Cat's away –

I feel I know Alice Keppel¹ quite well. She is a very 'good sort' but with a strange mixture of qualities. She is <u>very</u> particular about what Violet² reads etc – & would not let me lend her a really quite harmless novel.

Goodbye my Darling Winston –

Your loving Clem

¹ Alice Keppel (born Edmonstone) (1869–1947), wife of Lt-Col. George Keppel, son of the 7th Earl of Albemarle. Long-time mistress of King Edward VII.
² Violet Keppel (1894–1972), one of the two daughters of George and Alice Keppel. Married Denys Trefusis, 1919. A bilingual (French/English) writer. She had a notorious lesbian affair with the author/poet/gardener Victoria ('Vita') Sackville-West (1892–1962), Harold Nicolson's wife.

○ From WSC   In the train
27 April 1914

My darling Clemmie,

I was delighted to get yr telegram advertising me of yr nearer approach to the domestic hearth ...

I have been spending the weekend at Portsmouth, & am now returning to a busy week. Tomorrow I am to reply to Austen Chamberlain's[1] Vote of Censure on the Pogrom. The situation has from a Parliamentary point of view been altered much in our favour by the Gun Running escapade of the Ulstermen[2]. They have put themselves entirely in the wrong, and justified to the full the modest precautions wh were taken. My line will be a vy stiff one.

Dearest – all is well at home. The kittens look forward to your return & make frequent inquiry. I think the nurse is vy good. My cold is better, but my voice is not wholly recovered. The weather is brilliant. If you don't return till the end of the week I shall go to the yacht again. I get away from my ordinary work and find much rest & refreshment on the sea. . . .

I had a long interview with Cox [& Co.] & in the result am preparing a scheme which will enable us to clear off our debts & bills and start on a clean ready money basis. We shall have to pull in our horns. The money simply drains away[3].

If you have anything left out of the £40, spend it on some little thing that you like in Paris.

Always your loving husband
W.

[1] Austen Chamberlain (1863–1937), eldest son of Joseph Chamberlain. Conservative statesman. At various dates Chancellor of the Exchequer, Secretary of State for India; Foreign Secretary, 1922–9. KG, 1925.
[2] At Larne, on 24 April, with the connivance of Sir Edward Carson MP, leader of the Ulster Unionists, and with no preventive police action, the Ulster Volunteers smuggled in 30,000 rifles and ammunition.
[3] CSC's cautious view about moving from Eccleston Square into Admiralty House, where they had now been installed for a year, was already fully justified.

○ From WSC   Admiralty [House]
29 April 1914 8.15 p.m.

My darling & Precious One,

. . .

I am so glad you are coming back tomorrow – Let me know where I shall meet you.

I asked Randolph this morning whether he wanted you to come back & why & he said 'Becos I lurve her'. So now you must come my sweet pussy & return to the domestic basket.

I have just come back from the Pogrom debate. You must read all about it. We smashed the "plot" altogether; but as you will see I yesterday at the end of my speech greatly daring & on my own account threw a sentence across the House to Carson[1] wh has revolutionised the situation, & we are all back again in full conciliation. . . .

Return my lovely one tomorrow night to your home where all who love you will salute your presence.

Give my love to your Mamma & tell her how much I hope she is progressing to good health – I am vy glad you went to see her.

Always my darling
Your loving husband
W

[1] Sir Edward Henry Carson (1854–1935), cr. Baron Carson, 1921. Irish barrister and politician, leader of the movement in Ulster to resist Home Rule. He later campaigned in Ulster in support of the Government, and was appointed Attorney-General, 1915; First Lord of the Admiralty, 1917; member of War Cabinet, 1917–18; Lord of Appeal in Ordinary, 1921–9.

Clementine was expecting her third child, but these months were darkened for her by her deep anxiety on account of Winston's flying activities, in which he persisted.

The toll of pilots and planes in these pioneering days was high: Winston himself had had a narrow escape in April, when engine failure forced the pilot of the plane in which he was flying to make an emergency descent on water near Clacton Pier.

○ From WSC
29 May 1914

H.M.S. Enchantress
Portsmouth

My darling One,

I have been at the Central Flying School for a couple of days – flying a little in good & careful hands & under perfect conditions. So I did not write you from there as I knew you wd be vexed. But now that I am back on board & am off to Portland, I hasten to tell you how much & how often you & the babies were in my thoughts during these happy & interesting days. I was delighted to get your telegram altho' I read it with an uneasy conscience: but I wd not answer from such an address! – fearing it wd make you anxious – when there was vy little occasion.

We had the false hopes of Hamel's[1] safe arrival and the sombre dispersal of them with the morning newspapers . . . it seems to have caused an immense wave of interest everywhere; & Masterton[2] tells me that the people in the streets formed little crowds round the newspaper boys in their haste to get the special editions.

I went (by air) over to see the Yeomanry in their camp eleven miles away and found them delighted to see me. We had a gt reception – the men all running out in a mob, as if they had never seen an aeroplane before . . . Goonie & Jack [Churchill*] have just arrived on board with A. Sinclair[3] – & that is all our party. . . .

Give my best love to your Mother and tell her she is to stand up for me & defend me when you say how bad I am & how unsatisfactory. Also

Nellie is to do this. Alternatively they are to abuse me like a pickpocket, & you are to vindicate me & say after all I am not so bad. This is the part I want to hear about and think about & feel is going on. Kiss also with care and earnestness Diana & Randolph on my behalf. Did you buy him a birthday toy from me & what was it? I am hoping much to come & see them next week – but some good reason for bringing the yacht must be found.

I do hope you are happy & enjoying yourself[4]. This is a scrappy & disjointed letter – but if it conveys to you the feeling of wanting much to be loved & petted by you in spite of waywardness & frowardness it will have served its purpose.

Your ever loving & devoted
W.
. . .

[1] Gustav Hamel (1889–1914), pioneer aviator. Died 23 May 1914 flying across the Channel; WSC, having invited him to give a demonstration to the Royal Naval Air Force pilots stationed near Portsmouth, was among those who had awaited his arrival.
[2] James Masterton-Smith (1878–1938), at this time Private Secretary to WSC at the Admiralty. A distinguished civil servant, he served successive First Sea Lords in this capacity, 1910–17. Later Assistant Secretary to WSC at Ministry of Munitions, 1917–19; at War Office, 1919–20. Permanent Under-Secretary of State for the Colonies, 1921–4. Knighted 1919.
[3] Sir Archibald Sinclair, 4th Bt, later 1st Viscount Thurso (1890–1970). Entered Army, 1910; adjutant to WSC, 1916. Private Secretary to WSC at War Office, 1919–21, and at Colonial Office, 1922. Liberal MP. Secretary of State for Scotland, 1931–2; Leader of Liberal Party, 1935–45. Secretary of State for Air, 1940–5. Married, 1918, Marigold Forbes.
[4] CSC was in Dieppe, staying with her mother.

○ From WSC   H.M.S. Enchantress
30 May 1914   Portland

My darling one,

We are just arrived here where there is a large fleet assembled including most of the latest ships. The Captains come to dinner to-night & Warrender[1]. Goonie has undertaken to look after him. . . .

The weather this evening has turned a little greyer, & harmonizes with my feelings – for O cat I await and long for a dear & loving letter from you. I hope one will reach me tomorrow, & until it comes I go on imagining that you are full of scoldings & reproaches against me for flying. I know this will be cleared away by what you will have written – but the worst of an evil conscience is the unamiable characteristics one attributes to those who are likely to call us to account!

Good night then my dearest. Kiss the kittens and send me your fondest love, as I do mine to you. Always your devoted

W.

[1] Vice-Admiral Sir George John Scott Warrender, 7th Bt (1860–1917). Distinguished naval officer, Commander of the 2nd Battle Squadron, 1912–16.

○ From CSC   St Antoine
30 May [1914]   16 Rue des Fontaines
                                                Dieppe

My Darling

I began writing to you, but was nipped in the bud by reading of your [flying] exploits & of your determination to repeat them the next day!...

I felt what you were doing before I read about it, but I felt too weak & tired to struggle against it – It is like beating one's head against a stone wall...

The babies are well & very happy & I think are a pleasure to Mother – She & they inhabit the large house while Nellie & I conduct our establishment in the dower house [converted coach house] opposite. Everything is minute but very comfortable – We go out every morning with a large basket & do our marketing which is very engrossing, altho' not on a large scale.

Goodbye my Dear One – Perhaps if I saw you, I could love and pet you, but you have been so naughty that I can't do it on paper – I must be 'brought round' first.

                                           Your loving
                                           Clemmie

. . .

○ From CSC   St Antoine
1 June [1914]   Dieppe

My Darling

Life here is so tame & uneventful that the days slip by without being noticed – almost too easily, for one might grow old without having felt any acute sensation of either pain or pleasure. The Daily Mail keeps me in touch with the outside world where things happen such as ghastly shipwrecks – & pigs flying & other events; when The Times arrives at 6 o'clock I am too lazy to open it – I already know the news & I don't care a bit if Mr Geoffrey Robinson [Editor of The Times] wants Ministers to spend their holidays in Ulster – I suppose he hopes they wld be lynched.

Meanwhile I have had much leisure to play with & observe the 'kittens' – You will be surprised to hear that they are getting quite fond of me – I am finding out a lot of things about them – They ask occasionally with solicitude & respect about you....

When shall I see you again??? Mother & Nellie have gadded off to the Casino to have a little flutter at Chemin de Fer, but I feel apathetic about that too.

I shall go quite to sleep unless someone takes a lot of trouble soon. I am making such good salads & coffee & I even roasted a chicken tho' the stove is so tiny here it would hardly go inside.

I shall walk out & post this letter & then I think I shall have done very well for one day –

Goodbye absent & wandering Pig!

Your loving
Clemmie

...

O From WSC   H.M.S. Enchantress
1 June 1914   Dartmouth

My darling,

...

I am planning to reach you during Wednesday on my way from Cherbourg....

This has been a day worthy of June: & this beautiful College [Royal Naval College] never looked better. The boys do not seem to be hustled as much as they used to be & my suggestions have all been in the direction of 'easing up'. There is no doubt it is the best education anyone could have.

My business proposals do not go smoothly – for the reason that the insurance companies try to charge excessive premiums on my life – political strain, short-lived parentage & of course flying ...

Well good bye my sweet one. I am looking forward so much to seeing you & the kittens – & your Mamma & Nellinita: & hope you will receive me with united welcomes....

Ever your loving & devoted
W.

O From CSC   St Antoine
4 June [1914]   Dieppe

My Darling

The Babies were sad when they found the Enchantress had sailed away in the night & that there was no 'Papa' in the Bed in the Day Nursery.

I played with them in the garden this morning for a long time. They watered the roses till the earth was mud & till they were drenched to the skin & as there was only one watering can the competition was acute & the amusement did not pall for more than an hour.

Dearest I cannot help knowing that you are going to fly as you go to Sheerness & it fills me with anxiety. I know nothing will stop you from doing it so I will not weary you with tedious entreaties, but don't forget that I am thinking about it all the time & so, do it as little, & as moderately as you can, & only with the very best Pilot. I feel very 'ears down' about it....

Your loving
Clemmie

I miss you dreadfully to-day, after seeing you –

O From CSC   St Antoine
5 June [1914]   Dieppe

My Darling

Nellie and I had a delightful day wandering about Puys[1] and sitting in
the Sun on the Beach.

... We got home very late – But after this pleasant day I have had a
miserable night haunted by hideous dreams, So this morning I am sad &
worn out.

I dreamt that I had my Baby, but the Doctor & Nurse wouldn't shew it
to me & hid it away – Finally after all my entreaties had been refused I
jumped out of bed & ran all over the house searching for it – At last I
found it in a darkened room. It looked all right & I feverishly undressed it
& counted its fingers & toes – It seemed quite normal & I ran out of the
room with it in my arms – And then in the Daylight I saw it was a gaping
idiot. And then the worst thing of all happened. I wanted the Doctor to kill
it –; but he was shocked & took it away & I was mad too. And then I
woke up & went to sleep again <u>and dreamt</u> it a second time. I feel very
nervous and unhappy & the little thing has been fluttering all the morning –

Your telegram arrived late last night, after we were in bed – Every time I
see a telegram now, I think it is to announce that you have been killed
flying – I had a fright but went to sleep relieved & reassured; but this
morning after the nightmare I looked at it again for consolation & found to
my horror it was from Sheerness & not from Dover where I thought you
were going first – So you are probably at it again at this very moment.

Goodbye Dear but Cruel One
Your loving
Clemmie

All the Sun is gone to-day & it has turned very cold & Bleak.

[1] Where Blanche Hozier and her children spent the summer of 1899, before moving into Dieppe.

O From WSC   H.M.S. Enchantress
6 June 1914

My darling One,

I will not fly any more until at any rate you have recovered from your
kitten: & by then or perhaps later the risks may have been greatly reduced.

This is a wrench, because I was on the verge of taking my pilot's
certificate. It only needed a couple of calm mornings; & I am confident of
my ability to achieve it vy respectably – I shd greatly have liked to reach
this point wh wd have made a suitable moment for breaking off. But I
must admit that the numerous fatalities of this year wd justify you in
complaining if I continued to share the risks – as I am proud to do – of
these good fellows. So I give it up decidedly for many months & perhaps
for ever. This is a gift – so stupidly am I made – wh costs me more than
anything wh cd be bought with money. So I am vy glad to lay it at your
feet, because I know it will rejoice & relieve your heart.

Anyhow I can feel I know a good deal about this fascinating new art. I can manage a machine with ease in the air, even with high winds, & only a little more practice in landings wd have enabled me to go up with reasonable safety alone. I have been up nearly 140 times, with many pilots, & all kinds of machines, so I know the difficulties the dangers & the joys of the air – well enough to appreciate them, & to understand all the questions of policy wh will arise in the near future.

It is curious that while I have been lucky, accidents have happened to others who have flown with me out of the natural proportion. This poor Lieutenant whose loss has disturbed your anxieties again, took me up only last week in this vy machine!

You will give me some kisses and forgive me for past distresses – I am sure. Though I had no need & perhaps no right to do it – it was an important part of my life during the last 7 months, & I am sure my nerve, my spirits & my virtue were all improved by it. But at your expense my poor pussy cat! I am so sorry. . . .

Always your loving & devoted
Winston

In the summer holidays the 'Winstons' and the 'Jacks' had taken nearby seaside cottages – Pear Tree Cottage and Beehive Cottage – at Overstrand, near Cromer, on the east coast.

Winston visited them as much as he could, either coming down by train or 'dropping in' from *Enchantress*.

Relieved of her gnawing anxiety by Winston's promise not to fly, these were happy sunlit weeks for Clementine personally, in the last lap of her pregnancy.

But across the sunshine scene fell the dark shadows of impending war.

O From CSC   [Pear Tree Cottage
6 July 1914   Overstrand]

My Darling

. . .

I am so happy that you did not 'disenjoy' Pear Tree. I am very happy perched among its branches – It is dear of you to have given it me; I am sure the new kitten will profit by it & be more bouncing & beautiful as the result.

Diana & Randolph observe me writing & Diana tells me to put in the letter that 'Diana and Randolph is good little children'! . . .

I am so glad you caught the train – I fear your indignation was great at having to wait 5 mins. at the station –

Your loving
Clemmie

. . .

○ From WSC   Admiralty
7 July 1914

My darling,
    . . .
    I shall sail tomorrow night and will write you later what time I arrive.
    My dearest darling I loved you so much in this last week, & to see you
in your basket surrounded by the kittens was a great joy to me. They are
good ones. Kiss them for me.

                                            Ever your loving & devoted
                                                                    W.

○ From WSC   H.M.S. Enchantress
13 July 1914

My darling,
    . . .
    It was quite forlorn leaving you last night. I don't know why a departure
to the sea seems so much more significant than going off by train. We
watched your figures slowly climbing up the zigzag & slowly fading in the
dusk: and I felt as if I were going to the other end of the world.
    The kittens were vy dear & caressing. They get more lovable every day.
Altogether Pear Tree is a vy happy, sunlit picture in my mind's eye.
    Tender love my dearest – I must try to get you a little country house 'for
always'. . . .

                                                    Your ever loving
                                                & devoted husband
                                                                    W

Tension having reached breaking point on the Irish question, the King, as a
last hope, summoned a Home Rule Conference at Buckingham Palace on 21
July; it broke up after a few days, having failed to reach agreement.
    So engrossed was the country by these domestic quarrels that the murder
of Archduke Franz Ferdinand (heir to his uncle, Emperor Franz Joseph of
Austria-Hungary) and his wife at Sarajevo on 26 June passed almost unnoticed. But it set in train a fatal sequence of events.

○ From WSC   Admiralty
22 July 1914

My darling,
    This only a line to greet you with my love tomorrow morning.
Secretissime.
    The conference is in extremis. We are preparing a partition of Tyrone
with reluctant Nationalist acquiescence. Carson absolutely refuses although

the Speaker strongly commended it. Carson & Redmond both just friendly and apparently most hopeless. But what about all of us – 40 millions!

On leaving the Palace Redmond & Dillon[1] were followed by a cheering crowd and as they passed the barracks, the soldiers of the Irish Guards ran out waving & cheering in a vy remarkable demonstration. This will make Europe take unfavourable views of the British situation – wh serious though it is – they will greatly exaggerate....

I am anxious about the political crisis: and what to do to help.

Tender love my dear one to you & the kittens
from your devoted husband
W

[1] John Dillon (1851–1927), Irish Nationalist MP.

○ From CSC   [Pear Tree Cottage]
23 July [1914]

My Darling

I was much delighted to get your letter early this morning.

The Daily Mail again seems to have received secret information of the death agony of the conference. Everything looks very black; perhaps being not on the spot makes it seem worse....

I dread to hear that the conference has broken up.

Whatever happens I hope we shall not be forced by these Ulster Rebels into an Election. I hope you will throw your influence on the side of carrying on, making just and generous offers to Ulster, and then let them rebel if they dare –

I am sure you will be of help just now – You always emerge in critical & dangerous times....

I went for a walk yesterday afternoon & suddenly felt very unwell so I hastened home & jumped into bed – To-day after a disagreeable night of anxiety I feel better but I am being careful. ...

Your loving
Clemmie
...

Both Diana & Randolph were very obstreperous this morning, so you see I have had trouble with all three of them! Much Love to you Dearest One

A test mobilization of part of the Fleet took place in July, followed by a grand review of the Fleet by the King at Spithead on 17 and 18 July. The ships were about to disperse to their home ports when Austria delivered her ultimatum to Serbia. On Sunday 26 July Churchill was at Overstrand with his family. He consulted with Prince Louis of Battenberg (First Sea Lord) by telephone, and that evening Prince Louis gave orders for the Fleet not to disperse. Winston returned to London and, after further consultation, as the crisis deepened and the likelihood of war became clearer by the hour, with the acquiescence of the Prime Minister, he ordered the First Fleet to sail from Portland to the

North Sea – its battle station. The vast concourse of warships passed safely through the Straits of Dover without lights on the night of 29 July.

Austria-Hungary had declared war on Serbia the previous day. At this point the Cabinet was split between those who saw war as inevitable and those (at least half) who were unwilling to accept the idea of war with Germany, should she attack France or Belgium; their view was supported by a large section of the Liberal Party. Churchill however continued to make all necessary preparations against the eventuality of war, both on sea and on shore.

On 1 August Germany declared war on Russia. It would not be long before she attacked Russia's ally – France.

On 2 August, after consulting the Prime Minister, Churchill ordered the full mobilization of the Fleet.

○ From WSC   Admiralty
24 July 1914

My darling One,

I have managed to put off my naval conferences and am coming to you & the kittens tomorrow by the 1 o'clock train.

I will tell you all the news then. Europe is trembling on the verge of a general war. The Austrian ultimatum to Serbia being the most insolent document of its kind ever devised. Side by side with this the Provisional govt. in Ulster wh is now imminent appears comparatively a humdrum affair. . . .

We must judge further events in Ulster when they occur. No one seems much alarmed.

Tender & fondest love
W.

. . .

○ From CSC   Pear Tree Cottage
Monday Night [27 July 1914]

My Darling

I have just come back from talking to you[1]. It is wonderful to hear your voice clearly so many miles away –

I wanted so much to put my arms round you & kiss your dear face – But now I must tell you that I am no purblind Cat! I detected a note of indulgent criticism in your voice when I said I had not seen the order to the First Fleet in the papers! I scampered home 'ears back & tail outstretched' & devoured the 'times' from cover to cover including advertisements & agony column but it wasn't there! The edition of The Times delivered in this distant spot, I suspect of being printed overnight!

Good night my Dearest One – I trust the news may be better tomorrow

– Surely every hour of delay must make the forces of peace more powerful. It would be a wicked war –

Your loving
Clemmie

¹ Pear Tree Cottage not having a telephone, kind neighbours (Sir Edgar and Lady Speyer) allowed the Churchills to use theirs.

O From WSC   Admiralty
28 July 1914 Midnight

My darling One & beautiful –

Everything trends towards catastrophe & collapse. I am interested, geared-up & happy. Is it not horrible to be built like that? The preparations have a hideous fascination for me. I pray to God to forgive me for such fearful moods of levity – Yet I wd do my best for peace, & nothing wd induce me wrongfully to strike the blow – I cannot feel that we in this island are in any serious degree responsible for the wave of madness wh has swept the mind of Christendom. No one can measure the consequences. I wondered whether those stupid Kings & Emperors cd not assemble together & revivify Kingship by saving the nations from hell, but we all drift on in a kind of dull cataleptic trance. As if it was somebody else's operation!

The two black swans on St James's Park lake have a darling cygnet – grey, fluffy, precious & unique. I watched them this evening for some time as a relief from all the plans & schemes. We are putting the whole Navy into fighting trim (bar the reserve). And all seems quite sound & thorough. The sailors are thrilled and confident. Every supply is up to the prescribed standard. Everything is ready as it has never been before. And we are awake to the tips of our fingers. But war is the Unknown & the Unexpected! God guard us and our long accumulated inheritance. You know how willingly & proudly I wd risk – or give if need be – my period of existence to keep this country great & famous & prosperous & free. But the problems are vy difficult. One has to try to measure the indefinite & weigh the imponderable – I feel sure however that if war comes we shall give them a good drubbing.

My darling one ... Ring me up at fixed times. But talk in parables – for they all listen.

Kiss those kittens & be loved for ever only by me

Your own
W.

O From WSC   Admiralty
31 July 1914

Secret.
Not to be left about –
but locked up or burned.

My darling –
    There is still hope although the clouds are blacker & blacker. Germany is realising I think how great are the forces against her, & is trying tardily to restrain her idiot ally. We are working to soothe Russia. But everybody is preparing swiftly for war and at any moment now the stroke may fall. We are ready.
    I cd not tell you all the things I have done & the responsibilities I have taken in the last few days: but all is working well: & everyone has responded. The newspapers have observed an admirable reticence ...
    Germany has sent a proposal to us to be neutral if she promises not to take French territory nor to invade Holland – She must take French colonies & she cannot promise not to invade Belgium – wh she is by treaty bound not merely to respect but to defend. Grey [Foreign Secretary] has replied that these proposals are impossible & disgraceful. Everything points therefore to a collision on these issues. Still hope is not dead.
    The city has simply broken into chaos. The world's credit system is virtually suspended. You cannot sell stocks & shares. You cannot borrow. Quite soon it will not perhaps be possible to cash a cheque. Prices of goods are rising to panic levels. Scores of poor people are made bankrupts ...
    But I expect the apprehension of war hurts these interests more or as much as war itself. I look for victory if it comes.
    I have resolved to remove Callaghan[1] & place Jellicoe[2] in supreme command, as soon as it becomes certain that War will be declared.
    I dined last night again with the P.M. Serene as ever. But he backs me well in all the necessary measures.
    All the Enchantress officers on mobilisation go en bloc to Invincible. I am forcibly detaining the 2 Turkish Dreadnoughts wh are ready [for delivery]. Ireland I think is going to be settled.
    I am perturbed at the expense for this month being £175. Please send me the bills both for Pear Tree & Admiralty [House] separately. Rigorous measures will have to be taken. I will pay the bills direct myself, & Jack [Churchill*] can check the housekeeping here in your absence.
    I am sending you the cheque for Pear Tree. I am so glad you find rest & contentment there.

Fondest love my darling one –
Your devoted husband
W

[1] Admiral of the Fleet Sir George Callaghan (1852–1920), distinguished naval commander. C.-in-C. Home Fleet, 1911–14; The Nore, 1915–18.
[2] Admiral of the Fleet John Rushworth Jellicoe, GCB, GCVO, OM (1859–1935). Entered the Navy,1872; Second Sea Lord, 1912–14; Commander of the Grand Fleet during 1914–18 war; First Sea Lord, 1916; Chief of Naval Staff, 1917. Governor-General of New Zealand, 1920–4. Cr. Viscount, 1918, and 1st Earl Jellicoe, 1925.

○ From CSC   [Pear Tree Cottage]
31 July [1914]

My Darling
    I am deeply interested by all you tell me in your letter. I much wish I
were with you during these anxious thrilling days. I know how you are
feeling – tingling with life to the tips of your fingers –
    I am astonished at the reserve of the newspapers –
    How wicked Germany is to make such a cynical proposal –
    What a frail bubble the 'city' seems to be ... I am sure you are right
about the supreme command of the Fleet. . . .
    The babies are well and blooming – They were bitterly disappointed
when they saw Jack [Churchill*] coming down the cliff towards the Beach
& found it was <u>not</u> their 'Papa' but John George's –
    Randolph asked persevering questions for 5 minutes about your
absence. He is now resigned, but not convinced of its necessity! . . .
                                        Tender love to you Darling from your
                                                                  Clemmie
                                                                      . . .

○ From WSC   Admiralty
2 August 1914 1 a.m.

Cat – dear –
    It is all up. Germany has quenched the last hopes of peace by declaring
war on Russia, & the declaration against France is momentarily expected.
    I profoundly understand your views – But the world is gone mad – &
we must look after ourselves – & our friends. It wd be good of you to
come for a day or two next week. I miss you much – Your influence when
guiding & not contrary is of the utmost use to me.
                                        Sweet Kat – my tender love –
                                                            Your devoted
                                                                      W
Kiss the Kittens

On 3 August Germany invaded Belgium. The Cabinet as a whole was now
convinced that Britain must intervene to protect Belgium's neutrality; they
had the support of all parties, and there was no division in Parliament. At
11 p.m. on 4 August, the ultimatum sent to Germany having expired, Great
Britain declared war on Germany.

Chapter V

HARVEST OF WAR

After the outbreak of war Clementine, apart from a few short visits to London, stayed on at Pear Tree Cottage with the children until the end of August.

○ From CSC   [Pear Tree Cottage]
Tuesday [probably 4 August 1914]
<u>Burn this</u>.

My Darling
    I have been cogitating for an hour or two over the 'Callico Jellatine' crisis[1] which, Thank God, is over as far as essentials are concerned.
    There only remains the deep wound in an old man's heart.
    If you put the wrong sort of poultice on it, it will fester – (Do not be vexed, when you are so occupied with vital things my writing to you about this, which, in its way, is important too). An interview with the Sovereign and a Decoration to my mind is the wrong poultice. To a proud sensitive man, at this moment a Decoration must be an insult –
    <u>Please</u> see him yourself & take him by the hand and offer him a[n] (additional) Seat on the Board, or if this is impossible give him <u>some</u> advisory position at the Admiralty – It does not matter if he 'cannot say Bo to a Goose' – His lips will then be sealed and his wife's too – Don't think this a trivial matter. At this moment you want everyone's heart & soul – You don't want even a small clique of retired people to feel bitter & to cackle. If you give him a position of honour and confidence, the whole service will feel that he has been as well treated as possible under the circumstances, & that he has not been humiliated –
    This will prevent people now at the top of the tree feeling 'In a few years <u>I</u> shall be cast off like an old shoe' – Jellicoe & Beatty & Warrender & Bayly[2] now the flower of the Service are only a few years younger than Callaghan.
    Then, don't underrate the power of women to do mischief. I don't want Lady Callaghan & Lady Bridgeman[3] to form a league of retired Officers' Cats, to abuse you. Poor old Lady Callaghan's grief will be intense but if

you are good to him now it will be softened; if he is still employed she is bound to be comparatively silent.

Anyhow I beg of you to see him –

If I were doing it – if he refused the appointment I would earnestly urge him again & again ... to accept it, saying you need his services – Then he will believe it & come round & there will not be any disagreeableness left from this difficult business.

             ...

[1] WSC had already told CSC (31 July 1914) of his intention to replace Sir George Callaghan with Sir John Jellicoe as Supreme Commander of the Home Fleet, on outbreak of war, although Callaghan was due to retire anyway in a few months. The change in command took place on 4 August. Callaghan was appointed C.-in-C., The Nore, in 1915.
[2] Vice-Admiral Lewis Bayly (1857–1938), at this time Commander of the 3rd Battle Squadron. Knighted, 1914; appointed Admiral, 1917.
[3] The wife of Admiral Sir Francis Bridgeman, who had retired prematurely as First Sea Lord in 1912, to make way for Prince Louis of Battenberg.

O From WSC   Admiralty
9 August 1914

My darling One,

The enclosed will tell you what is known officially. It is a good summary. You must not fail to burn it at once.

I am over head & ears in work & am much behindhand.

It makes me a little anxious that you shd be on the coast. It is 100 to 1 agst a raid – but still there is the chance: & Cromer has a good landing place near.

I wish you wd get the motor repaired & keep it so that you can whisk away – at the first sign of trouble. I am really in doubt whether I ought not to recall you at once à la Callaghan – 'Strike your flag & come ashore.'

Kiss the Kittens for me.

Tender love to you all
Your fondest & devoted
W

O From CSC   [Pear Tree Cottage]
9 August [1914]

My Dear One

... I have had such a good idea – Later on, in the spring when perhaps we could have afforded the motor again, let us instead have 2 chestnut horses 'with nice long tails' & ride for an hour every morning. It would be of far more value to you than a motor & I should enjoy it so much – It would not cost so much surely?

The 'Visitors' are fleeing from this place & the 'Season' is spoilt for the poor little residents who will not get any shekels this year. They are very sad & are bemoaning themselves. Yesterday the local authorities in a frantic effort to stem the ebbing tide of tourists had the following pathetic appeal flashed on the screen of the local Cinema Show – (I am not sure of the words but this is the gist)

'Visitors! Why are you leaving Cromer? Mrs Winston Churchill and her Children are in residence in the neighbourhood – If it's safe enough for her, surely it's safe enough for you!'

What a wonderful feat the taking of Mülhausen[1] must have been. It is not in the edition of the Sunday papers we get here.

I am longing to get your letter with the secret news – It shall be destroyed at once. I hope that in it, you tell me about the expeditionary force. Do I guess right that some have gone already? Be a good one & write again & feed me with tit-bits – I am being so wise & good, & sitting on the Beach & playing with my Kittens, & doing my little housekeeping, but how I long to dash up & be near you and the pulse of things.

It was thrilling to see that cheeky little Destroyer bringing the [enemy] cargo boat along – How I wish it was Bill![2] But I fear not. His present duty is patrolling the Mouth of the Wash which is a mass of sand-banks – I hope he is avoiding them neatly.

Your loving
Clemmie

Miaow

---

[1] Mülhausen, in the south of Alsace (German-held French territory since the war of 1870–1) had been re-taken by French troops in less than an hour; it was the first battle of the war.
[2] William Hozier was at this time commanding HMS *Thorn*, a torpedo destroyer.

○ From CSC   [Pear Tree Cottage]
10 August [1914]

My Darling

The secret document has been read & burnt before my eyes in the kitchen fire!

It was most interesting, but I was disappointed because I hoped you were going to tell me about the Expeditionary Force – Do send me news of it – When it is going, where it will land, which regiments are in the first batch etc –

I long for it to arrive in time to save the Liège citizens from being massacred in their houses. . . .

Another aeroplane flew over us this morning – It gives one a great feeling of not being forgotten in the scheme of defence!

Lord Abingdon is here with Goonie – He is a dear, but inconceivably bloodthirsty – He wishes all remaining Germans to be put in a compound & ill-used & mines to be laid by us in illegal places – But all the same he disapproves of the Entente & wishes we were allied with Germany!. . .

Your loving
Clemmie

. . .

O From WSC   Admiralty
11 August 1914

My dear one,
    This is only a line from a vy tired Winston. The Exped^y Force about wh
you are so inquisitive is on its road & will be all on the spot in time. I wish
I cd whisk down to you & dig a little on the beach. My work here is vy
heavy & so interesting that I cannot leave it.
    Now I am really going to knock off.

                                                    Ever your loving
                                                              W.

O From CSC   [Pear Tree Cottage]
12 August [1914]

My own Darling
    I feel such a note of fatigue in your letter.
    Now are you doing everything you can not to be too tired?
    1) Never missing your morning ride –
    2) Going to bed well <u>before</u> Midnight & sleeping well & <u>not</u> allowing
        yourself to be woken up every time a Belgian kills a German (you
        <u>must</u> have 8 hours sleep every night to be your best self)
    3) Not smoking too much & not having indigestion.
    Now shall I come up for a day or two next Monday & tease you gently
into doing all these things? or are you being a good one all by yourself –
    When the harsh & disagreeable Grimalkin is absent, I believe you
relapse into a delicious state of 'laissez faire' about details –
    The golden sands are too delicious & long to have fortifications made
on them & there is a little stream that really <u>ought</u> to be dammed – But
Alas it is too far –
    Goodbye my Sweet One. I am so proud of you & love you very much
                                                    Your loving
                                                          Clemmie

Now follows a great brouhaha! Clementine and Nellie thought it unwise for
their mother to continue living alone in Dieppe, and Nellie had been
despatched to bring Lady Blanche back to England.

O From CSC   [Pear Tree Cottage]
14 August [1914]

My Darling
    Yesterday evening Mother arrived, to my astonishment without Nellie.
She looked very feeble and was extremely tired. She brought me a letter
from Nellie in which she told me that she was going immediately with

Nancy Astor to Cliveden to help her with its conversion into a Convalescent Home after which she was going on with her to Plymouth to assist her there with Hospital arrangements.

I was not pleased at this news as I had arranged with Nellie (before she went over to Dieppe to fetch Mother) that she should accompany Mother here & help to entertain her so that I could be free to come up to London and be with you if I so wished. . . .

Imagine my surprise this morning when Mother shewed me a letter from Nellie informing us that tomorrow, Saturday, she is going to Belgium with Angela Manners[1] (who is a Nurse herself) a Surgeon, a Matron, and a party of trained Nurses. . . .

It is all cheap emotion. Nellie is not trained, she will be one more useless mouth to feed in that poor little country which in a few days will be the scene of horrible grim happenings.

Nellie's obvious and natural duty is to look after Mother whom she has brought over from Dieppe & 'dumped' down thus leaving her responsibilities without a thought to others.

I feel quite ill this morning, as I have had a very bad night & this on top of it has really upset me. I long to see you & put my arms round your neck – You are always so sane & sensible my Darling One, & you would calm my hurt and angry feelings. . . .

Angela Manners has had 3 years' hard training in the London Hospital, getting up at 5, scrubbing floors, obeying orders, working her way up from the bottom of the Nurses' profession. For this she has given up social gaieties & an easeful life – Now she has her reward – Nellie having danced herself dizzy every night thro' a hot season & done nothing for 4 months but pursue pleasure frantically, now that all that is over, must be in the heart of the next excitement[2]. . . .

But my Dear, in the midst of your work it is wrong of me to bubble over like this, but my heart is full & I can't help it.

Goonie is sweet & placid & I have confided my indignation to her. . . .

Goodbye my Darling Winston – Do you realize that perhaps in six weeks we shall have another 'P.K.' or 'Chumbolly' – We have not thought of a new name! I hope he or she will be like you my Dear Sweetheart

Your loving
Clemmie

. . .

[1] Angela Manners (1889–1970), daughter of 3rd Baron Manners.
[2] Nellie did go to Belgium with Angela Manners' nursing unit; they were taken prisoner by the Germans in the general confusion of the retreat from Mons at the end of August. At the end of November Nellie and her companions were repatriated via Norway, in high spirits, but shivering with cold in their summer uniforms.

○ From CSC   Pear Tree Cottage
14 August [1914]

My Own Darling
   I feel very worried since two hours ago, [I] have written you that long
letter full of bitterness about Nellie ...
   This place is full of minor excitements – Last night I was walking back
from Beehive Cottage with my maid at about 10.30 when suddenly a
figure sprang out from the hedge & said 'Where are you going?' I was
much startled & then saw it was a territorial armed cap à pied – I said
feebly 'Oh nowhere only home' – 'All right Miss don't be frightened' said
he patronisingly –
   Goonie arrived to luncheon at Pear Tree full of excitement – She had
seen a foreign-looking man tearing down the road as fast as he could lick,
followed by two soldiers – She and her small brother & a dog or two gave
chase too at a distance & they saw one of the soldiers nearly catch him up
& give him a small prog with his bayonette! This, tho' very exhilarating to
the pursuer had the effect of making the 'spy' run so fast that Goonie fears
he got away, tho' only for the moment I hope – He is sure to have been
stopped by someone coming the other way....
   I feel better since writing to you, my Darling ...

                                                    Your loving very tired
                                                              Clemmie

○ From CSC   [Admiralty House]
Saturday [?19 September 1914]

My Darling One & Only One
   ... Now please don't think me tiresome; but I want you to tell the P.M.
of your projected visit to Sir John French[1]. It would be very bad manners if
you do not & he will be displeased and hurt –
   Of course I know you will consult K[itchener][2] – Otherwise the journey
will savour of a week-end escapade & not of a mission – You would be
surprised & incensed if K skipped off to visit Jellicoe on his own –
   I wish my Darling you didn't crave to go – It makes me grieve to see
you gloomy & dissatisfied with the unique position you have reached thro'
years of ceaseless industry & foresight – The P.M. leans on you & listens to
you more & more. You are the only young vital person in the Cabinet. It is
really wicked of you not to be swelling with pride at being 1st Lord of the
Admiralty during the greatest War since the beginning of the World. And
there is still much to be done & only you can do it....
   You know the sailors can't do anything alone, & just becos' your
preparations are so perfect that for the moment there seems little to do,
this is not the moment to hand over the whole concern to another or to
allow the sailors who have been tutored & bent to the yoke for the last 2
years to take charge –
   Be a good one & rejoice & don't hanker. Great & glorious as have been
the achievements of our army, it is only a small one, 1/8 of the allied
forces – Whereas you rule this gigantic Navy which will in the end decide

the War. Forgive this long letter, but I have nothing to do but lie in bed &
think & your present frame of mind makes me anxious –

Your loving
Clemmie

. . .

[1] Field Marshal Sir John French (1852–1925), later 1st Earl Ypres. At this date C.in-C. Expeditionary
Forces in France.
[2] Field Marshal Lord Kitchener (see p. 1 n. 2).

○ From WSC   H.M.S. Adventure
[undated, 26 September 1914]   – at full speed –

My darling one,
    You were vy good to let me go, & I am vy grateful to you. The courage
& good sense you have shown all through these strange times in view of
yr own intense preoccupation (to whit – the kitten) are wonderful. Bill will
come up today to see you. I am so sorry I cannot see him. Lend him my
guns to shoot with.
    How right you were about telling K.

Tender love my dearest
Your ever loving
W

Sarah, their third child, was born on 7 October at Admiralty House. In the
last days before the birth Clementine had been lonely and in great anxiety
for Winston, who had been sent by the Cabinet to Antwerp to stiffen the
resistance of the beleaguered city. He arrived back a few hours after Sarah's
birth.

○ From CSC   Belcaire[1]
19 November [1914]   Lympne

My Darling
    . . . Poor Goonie is in a great state of anxiety about Jack [Churchill*][2], as
the 2d Division was in action on Tuesday & she calculates from his last
letter that Jack would that day have been in the trenches.
    Sad winter has closed in on us here; great fat snow-flakes are falling –
    I asked Band [?manservant] to send Bill your fur flying cap, as you won't
need it (I hope) for a long time. He says the cold is bitter, & he was in a
terrible gale & got into harbour in a very broken condition. How long will
it be till Jellicoe gets back his 3 big Cruisers, or one of them at any rate. I
feel anxious. The Germans are horribly powerful & cunning too; they have
devoted for years past their best intellects to the preparations for this war,
while we always think of soldiers & sailors as brave and bluff & simple not
to say <u>Stupid</u>. . . .

<u>Later</u>

Just been talking to you on the telephone[3]. Goonie is <u>so</u> happy about Jack being on the Staff. She has been so sad all day, but now she is overjoyed.

We have both been sitting completely buried by papers all the afternoon paying our bills. Outside the snow is falling thick & fast.

Tender Love to you my Darling. I hope you won't have a headache again —

Your loving
Clemmie

[1] Philip Sassoon's house in Kent, a few miles from the coast.
[2] Jack Churchill was in France with the Oxfordshire Hussars.
[3] The telephone call conveyed the good news WSC discusses in his next letter.

○ From WSC   Admiralty
19 November 1914

Most Secret

My darling,

I have got some good news for Goonie. French has taken Jack [Churchill*] on to the Staff. He has done this of his own accord and neither Jack nor I have ever asked for it. But I am vy thankful, because although there is always danger, the risk is less & the work more interesting. Jack has done a lot of hard service & is quite entitled to use his good fortune....

The swine [the German Fleet] are concentrating at Wilhelmshaven, & the situation is thoroughly 'cat & mouse'. Which will be the mouse?...

...K. has moved his army about in gt excitement for the long looked for invasion. But no such luck.

With tender love & many kisses
Ever your devoted & loving
W

As 1914 drew to a close, the war, which in the early exuberant days people had declared would be 'over by Christmas', was clamping down: the battle of Mons and the subsequent retreat, the battle of the Marne and the first battle of Ypres had given awesome warning of the sacrifice of lives to come. On the Western Front a grim pattern of trench warfare had established itself, where the armies faced each other in a grip of steel from the Channel to the Swiss frontier.

Chapter VI

THE DARDANELLES

The tragic saga of the Dardanelles is not only central to the understanding of Winston and Clementine's letters to each other at this time; it formed a sombre background to their lives for very much longer.

Looking back half a century later, Clementine could remember with stark clarity the pain and near-despair of those days in 1915–16 when Winston reached an all-time nadir in his political fortunes, and the terrible loss of life so weighed him down that she would tell Martin Gilbert, his official biographer: 'The Dardanelles haunted him for the rest of his life. He always believed in it. When he left the Admiralty, he thought he was finished ... I thought he would never get over the Dardanelles; I thought he would die of grief.'[1]

The original project adopted by the War Council (composed of senior ministers and their advisers) for the forcing of the Dardanelles Straits[2] and penetration through the Sea of Marmara to the glittering prize of Constantinople demanded, as well as the naval forces, a considerable military contingent to take and hold the Gallipoli Peninsula. Lord Kitchener, however, told the Council that no troops could be made available from the western theatre of war for a Mediterranean operation. But Vice-Admiral Carden's[3] considered opinion – that the Dardanelles could be taken by naval forces alone – decided the War Council, on 13 January 1915, that the Admiralty should prepare for a naval expedition.

It having also been resolved to send a military force to Gallipoli, the Royal Naval Division was embarked at the end of February, under the command of Major-General Sir Ian Hamilton[4]; among his officers was Jack Churchill*, now a major.

The bombardment of the outer defences of the Dardanelles began on 19 February. Churchill soon became concerned that Carden did not seem to be pressing on with sufficient vigour: Carden was in fact ill, and resigned on 16 March, his place being taken by his second-in-command, Vice-Admiral de Robeck[5]. On 18 March British and French ships entered the Straits and bombarded the Turkish forts, but after two British and one French battleships were sunk by mines, de Robeck called off the attack: it was never to be renewed. Amphibious landings on the Peninsula on 25 April cost heavy losses among the British and Anzac (Australian and New Zealand) troops; although a precarious foothold was gained along the southern tip of the Peninsula, the Turks held the higher ground, and no further advance was possible. In a tragic replication of events on the Western Front, our forces dug themselves into lines of trenches.

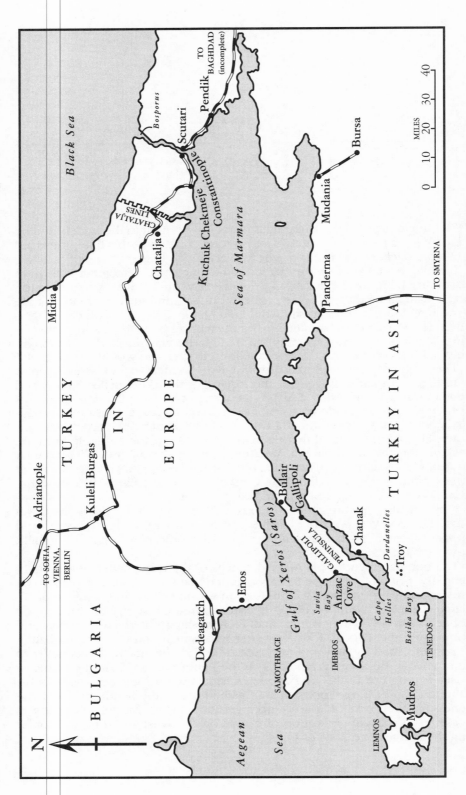

THE GALLIPOLI PENINSULA AND THE SEA OF MARMARA, AUGUST 1914

Churchill was appalled, and did everything in his power to get orders sent for the resumption of the attack. His belief in the overall strategic concept of the operation (which if successful might effectively have shortened the war) never wavered – but now there was a general reluctance at the Admiralty and at Downing Street to overrule the local commanders. Admiral of the Fleet Lord Fisher[6], initially enthusiastic in his support of the plan, obstructed all Churchill's efforts to send naval reinforcements.

When Churchill became First Lord of the Admiralty he frequently consulted Lord Fisher, then in retirement, and insisted on his reappointment as First Sea Lord to succeed Prince Louis of Battenberg in October 1914: it was an appointment Winston was to live to regret most bitterly. Wildly supportive of any plan at one moment, and as violent in his opposition to it the next, the seventy-year-old Admiral's tergiversations made him a difficult colleague – and an impossible one when events started to go awry.

But Gallipoli was not the only source of bad news at this time: at the second battle of Ypres, which began on 22 April, the Germans used poison gas for the first time – adding a grim new feature to trench warfare. Simultaneously a 'shell scandal', arising from a complaint by Sir John French of a shortage of shells, was fanned by Lord Northcliffe[7] in his newspapers, criticizing Kitchener and causing embarrassment and discredit to the Government.

On the party political front, the wartime truce started to crack: as many Conservative MPs became restive and critical of the Government, their hostility focused on the 'renegade' Winston Churchill. Now every naval disaster, his part in the siege of Antwerp, and (as the news trickled through) as chief promoter of the hourly more disastrous Dardanelles operation, made him the special object of their venom.

At this tense and crucial moment on 15 May, Lord Fisher resigned. The previous day, he had declared (to a meeting of an astonished War Council) that he 'had been against the Dardanelles operation from the beginning'.[8] Churchill, in a letter to the Prime Minister that same day, wrote: 'The First Sea Lord has agreed in writing to every executive telegram on which the operations have been conducted.' Although that evening Churchill and Fisher had had a long talk, and reached agreement on all points at issue, the following day both the Prime Minister and Churchill received letters of resignation from the First Sea Lord. Asquith*, outraged, commanded him to return to his post of duty in the name of the King. Churchill wrote him a long and moving letter. Meanwhile Fisher disappeared, and was eventually discovered lurking in the Charing Cross Hotel. He subsequently saw the Prime Minister and Lloyd George*, but obdurately refused to reconsider his decision, saying he could no longer work with Churchill, and refusing even to see him.

Rumours of Fisher's resignation filtered through to the Opposition, and on the morning of 17 May Bonar Law (Leader of the Conservative Opposition) went to Downing Street to seek confirmation of the reports. He made it clear to both Asquith and Lloyd George that the combination of the 'shell scandal' with Fisher's resignation rendered it impossible for him to restrain his party, that the political truce was at an end, that the Tories would not accept Churchill remaining as First Lord of the Admiralty, and furthermore that they were prepared to make a full-scale parliamentary challenge on the subject. After consultations together and severally, the Prime Minister, Lloyd George and Bonar Law decided upon the formation of a Coalition Government.

Bonar Law made it a condition that both Churchill and Haldane[9] should be removed from office.

The new Coalition Government was announced on 26 May. Churchill accepted the non-departmental office of Chancellor of the Duchy of Lancaster because he retained with it his seat in the Cabinet and on the War Council, and he was determined to see through events for which he bore a large responsibility, and strategic policies in which he believed wholeheartedly.

Winston and Clementine left Admiralty House as speedily as possible; and, their London home being let, Ivor Guest* (now Lord Wimborne) invited them to stay at his house in Arlington Street while they made new plans. They had already taken a house – Hoe Farm, near Godalming in Surrey – for summer weekends.

In going to the Duchy of Lancaster, Churchill's ministerial salary was more than halved: the 'Jacks' too were feeling the pinch, so the two families decided to combine households in Jack and Goonie's rather large house, No. 41 Cromwell Road in South Kensington.

Hoe Farm was to prove a true haven in the anguish of the Dardanelles crisis and the personal humiliation of Churchill's resignation. It was also the place where Winston first started to paint. Wandering in the garden and brooding miserably on events, Winston came upon Goonie painting in water-colours at her easel: she persuaded him to take a brush and try for himself. It was like waving a magic wand. Painting was to become for him a lifelong passion and occupation.

In July Lord Kitchener asked Churchill to visit the Dardanelles to give him an assessment of the situation there. The proposed visit never took place, owing to vehement opposition from Tory ministers, but this next letter was written just before Winston's planned departure for Gallipoli, where he could easily have been exposed to shell-fire.

[1] Martin Gilbert, *Winston S. Churchill*, Vol. III, 1971, p. 473.
[2] Lying between the Gallipoli Peninsula and the Turkish mainland. Turkey had entered the war on the German side in November 1914.
[3] Vice-Admiral (later Admiral Sir) S. H. Carden (1857–1930), at this time commander in the Eastern Mediterranean.
[4] Maj.-Gen. Sir Ian Hamilton (1853–1947). A personal friend from the Boer War, about whom WSC had written *Ian Hamilton's March*, published in 1900.
[5] Vice-Admiral (later Admiral Sir) John de Robeck (1862–1928), later C.-in-C. Mediterranean, 1919–22; Admiral of the Fleet, 1925.
[6] Admiral of the Fleet John Arbuthnot Fisher, OM, 1st Baron Fisher of Kilverstone (1841–1920). Born in Ceylon; entered Navy, 1854. First Sea Lord, 1904–10 and again 1914–15. Modernizer of the Royal Navy; promoter of the Dreadnought battleships.
[7] Alfred Harmsworth, 1st Viscount Northcliffe (1865–1922). Founder of the *Daily Mail* and *Daily Mirror*; proprietor of *The Times* from 1908.
[8] Gilbert, *Winston S. Churchill*, Vol. III, p. 431.
[9] The demand for the removal of Lord Haldane (Lord High Chancellor) arose from a despicable smear campaign based on Haldane's lifelong study of German philosophy and literature.

○ From WSC   Duchy of Lancaster Office
17 July 1915   Strand, W.C.

[envelope marked:]
To be sent to Mrs Churchill
in the event of my death
WSC

Darling,
   Cox holds about £1,000 worth of securities of mine (chiefly Witbank
Colliery): Jack [Churchill*] has in his name about £1,000 worth of Pretoria
Cement Shares; & Cassel has American stocks of mine wh shd exceed in
value my loans from him by about £1,000. I believe these will be found
sufficient to pay my debts & overdraft. Most of the bills were paid last
year....
   The insurance policies are all kept up & every contingency is covered.
You will receive £10,000 and £300 a year in addition until you succeed my
Mother. The £10,000 can either be used to provide interest i.e. about £450
a year or even to purchase an annuity against my Mother's life, ...
   I am anxious that you shd get hold of all my papers, especially those wh
refer to my Admiralty administration. I have appointed you my sole literary
executor. Masterton Smith will help you to secure all that is necessary for a
complete record. There is no hurry: but some day I shd like the truth to be
known. Randolph will carry on the lamp.
   Do not grieve for me too much. I am a spirit confident of my rights.
Death is only an incident, & not the most important wh happens to us in
this state of being. On the whole, especially since I met you my darling
one I have been happy, & you have taught me how noble a woman's
heart can be. If there is anywhere else I shall be on the look out for you.
Meanwhile look forward, feel free, rejoice in Life, cherish the children,
guard my memory. God bless you.

                                                         Good bye.
                                                              W.

As the summer wore on, the campaign in Gallipoli ran into yet more difficulties, culminating at the beginning of August in a disastrous attack at Suvla
Bay, the failure of which had repercussions beyond the blood-soaked
beaches, to Greece and the Balkan states. In October, Bulgaria joined forces
with Germany and Austria.
   The Coalition Government was proving to be a worse war machine than
its predecessor; the bigger Dardanelles Committee seemed too large for effective action, and in November the Cabinet decided to reduce it in numbers:
the smaller team did not include Churchill.
   His further exclusion from close and effective participation in the direction of the war made his situation even more unbearable: on 11 November
he wrote to the Prime Minister tendering his resignation, remarking that 'I do
not feel in times like these able to remain in well-paid inactivity ... I am an
officer, and I place myself unreservedly at the disposal of the military authorities, observing that my regiment is in France.'[1]

[1] A copy of this letter is in the CSCT papers at Churchill College Archives Centre, Cambridge.

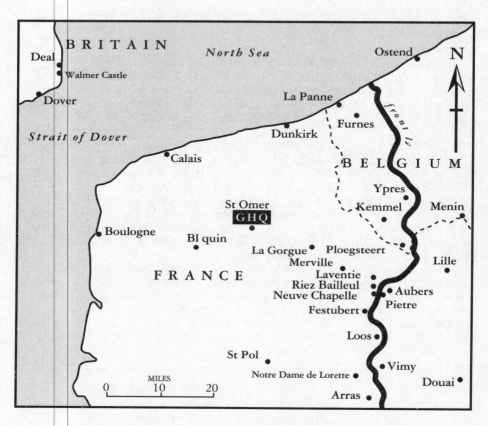

BRITAIN

Deal

Walmer Castle

Dover

Strait of Dover

North Sea

La Panne

Dunkirk

Calais

Furnes

Ostend

N

front li

BELGIUM

Ypres

Kemmel

Menin

St Omer
GHQ

Boulogne

Bl quin

La Gorgue

Merville

Ploegsteert

Lille

FRANCE

Laventie
Riez Bailleul
Neuve Chapelle

Aubers
Pietre

Festubert

Loos

St Pol

Notre Dame de Lorette

Vimy

Douai

Arras

MILES
0   10   20

THE OSTEND-TO-ARRAS SECTOR OF THE WESTERN FRONT,
NOVEMBER AND DECEMBER 1915

A week later, on 18 November, 'Major Churchill' left for France. After reporting briefly to his own Yeomanry regiment (the Queen's Own Oxfordshire Hussars), he went to GHQ at St Omer, invited by Sir John French, who welcomed him most cordially. French offered him the choice of remaining at GHQ as an ADC, or the command of a brigade: Winston unhesitatingly chose the latter, but with the request that he should serve as a regimental officer in the line before taking up such a senior appointment.

On 20 November Churchill was posted to the 2nd Battalion, Grenadier Guards, whose front-line headquarters were near Neuve Chapelle.

O From WSC
18 November 1915

General Headquarters,
British Army in the Field

My darling,

Things have fallen out vy much as I expected. I was met by a request to come to G.H.Q., wh after seeing my regt I did. French as ever an affectionate friend. He wished me to take a Brigade as soon as it could be managed. I said as I told you that beforehand I must feel myself effectively master of the conditions of trench warfare from the point of view of the regimental officer; & I suggested the Guards as the best school. This is therefore to be arranged & I expect to go into the line on Saturday for a week or two. You must not let this fret you in the least. No action is in prospect and only a vy general & ordinary risk need be contemplated. But I shall always be vy proud to have served with this famous corps: It is indeed much safer than going into the line with the Q.O.O.H. [Queen's Own Oxfordshire Hussars].

These latter were vy glad to see me in their miserable billets scattered over the countryside. I am staying tonight at G.H.Q. in a fine chateau, with hot water, beds, champagne & all the conveniences. Redmond [Irish Nationalist leader] has been dining here. Very agreeable, & admits I am absolutely right to leave the Govt. They are descending into the abyss. I am sure I am going to be entirely happy out here & at peace. I must try to win my way as a good & sincere soldier. But do not suppose I shall run any foolish risks or do anything wh is not obviously required.

I will write to you again tomorrow my dearest pet as soon as my plans are finally settled.

Always your devoted & loving
husband
Winston S.C.

P.S. New riding pants are now becoming a serious need as the fabric of these shows signs of rottenness. Please order from Tautz 2 pairs without laces or buttons at the knee – & send with all despatch to Colonel Barry, G.H.Q. who will send them on to me.

WSC

○ From CSC   41 Cromwell Road
19 November 1915

My Darling Winston

I long for news of you – I want to know where you are, what your billet
is like, whether you are comfortable, what you have had to eat, whether
you are happy my Dear One, & what you are thinking & feeling.

Yesterday I sent after you, Khaki trousers & shirts which arrived after
you departed.

Do you get the newspapers quite easily or shall I order them for you?

Altho' it's only a few miles you seem to me as far away as the stars, lost
among a million Khaki figures....

I visited my Munition Hut at Enfield Lock to-day[1] ... [and] have retreated
to my basket after a tiring day (you know I always find comfort &
consolation there). Without a motor it's harder to get to Enfield than to
France – ¼ of the day has been spent in tube, trams, train, the remainder
grappling with committees ...

Write to me Winston. I want a letter from you badly

                                                          Your loving
                                                          Clemmie
                                                              . . .

[1] In June CSC had joined the newly formed Munition Workers' Auxiliary Committee, under the
auspices of the Young Men's Christian Association (YMCA), whose purpose was to organize and
run canteens for the growing army of civilians – men and women – working day and night in the
arms factories. Her task was to organize the canteens in the north and north-eastern metropolitan area of London.

○ From WSC   G.H.Q.
Midnight 19 November 1915

My dearest soul – (this is what the gt d[uke] of Marlborough used to write
from the low countries to his cat). All is vy well arranged. I saw to-day
Lord Cavan[1] to whom after some talk I said 'I shd regard it as a vy gt
honour to go into the line with the Guards' to wh he replied – & I thought
sincerely 'we shall be proud to have you'. I therefore go tomorrow; but as
I do not know to wh battalion I am to be sent, I cannot tell the rota in wh
we shall go into the trenches. But I do hope you will realise what a vy
harmless thing this is. To my surprise I learn they only have about 15
killed & wounded each day out of 8000 men exposed! It will make me vy
sulky if I think you are allowing yourself to be made anxious by any risk
like that. You wished me to write & tell you & therefore I do – to satisfy
you, & not because I attach any importance to so ordinary & average
experience.

I went this afternoon to see my regt: also my Brigadier. They were
caressing. They highly approved of my course of action & thought it vy
right & proper. Altogether I see that the Army is willing to receive me back
as 'the prodigal son'. Anyhow I know what they think right, & mean to do
it....

I am vy happy here. I did not know what release from care meant. It is a blessed peace. How I ever cd have wasted so many months in impotent misery, wh might have been spent in war, I cannot tell.

In the intervals between going into the trenches I shall come back for hot baths etc. to G.H.Q. where I have been told to consider a place always open. French tells me he has written to you today. He is a good friend.

Always your loving husband

W.

[1] Field Marshal Frederic Rudolph Lambart, 10th Earl of Cavan (1865–1946), at this time commanding the Brigade of Guards Division.

○ From WSC   'Somewhere in France'
21 November 1915

My darling,

Here I am in the line. Except for heavy cannonading the results of wh do not come near us, everything is vy quiet. A few men are hit now & again by stray bullets skimming over the trenches, or accurate sniping. But we are able to walk right into the trenches without crawling along a sap, & even in the five trenches of the front line there is gt tranquillity. We came in last night on a 48 hours spell, then 48 hours in support, & then into the front line again up to a total of 12 days at the end of wh we are entitled to 6 days rest in Divisional reserve. I am att[d] to the 2nd Battalion of the Grenadier Guards, wh once the gt d[uke] of Marlborough served in & commanded. I get on vy well with the officers – though they were rather suspicious at first – & all the generals are most civil & kind. I am not going to be in any hurry to leave this regt while it is in the line, as its Colonel[1] is one of the vy best in the army, & his knowledge of trench warfare is complete & profound. All his comments & instructions to his men are pregnant with military wisdom; & the system of the Guards – discipline & hard work – must be seen at close quarters to be fully admired as it deserves. Altogether I look forward to an extremely profitable spell of education.

The conditions of life though hard are not unhealthy, & there is certainly nothing to complain about in them – except for cold feet. . . .

I want you to get me the following things, and send them <u>with the utmost speed</u> to GHQ.

1. A warm brown leather waistcoat
2. A pair of trench wading boots, brown leather bottoms, & waterproof canvas tops coming right up to the thigh
3. A periscope (most important)
4. A sheepskin sleeping bag; that will either carry kit or let me sleep in it Bertram[2] will advise you on all these

In addition

Please send me

5. 2 pairs of khaki trousers (wh Morris stupidly forgot to pack)
6. 1 pair of my brown buttoned boots –
7. three small face towels

Voilà tout.

Your little pillow is a boon & a pet.

The artillery fire is dying away now as the light fails; & per contra there is a certain amount of maxim & rifle fire beginning.

I am writing from a dugout a few hundred yards behind the trench where the Colonel & Adjutant are....

I am so glad to be free from worry & vexation.

With fondest love
Always yr devoted
W.

[1] Lt-Col. George Darell Jeffreys (1878–1960). Known as 'Ma' Jeffreys.
[2] Bertram Romilly (1878–1940), previously a second lieutenant in the Scots Guards, at this date a colonel attached to the Egyptian Camel Corps. Engaged to Nellie Hozier, CSC's sister, whom he married on 4 December 1915 after being invalided home with a serious head wound.

○ From WSC   [Bout Deville
23 November 1915   France]

My darling, We have finished our first 48 hours in the trenches & are now resting in billets in support. We are near enough to hear rifle fire but out of range of everything except the artillery, wh will not be likely to bother about the cottages & farms in wh we are living. I have spent the morning on my toilet & a hot bath, engineered with some difficulty. ... I have lost all interest in the outer world and no longer worry about it or its stupid newspapers. I am living with the battalion H.qrters – Colonel, 2nd in command, adjutant. When the battalion is in the trenches we live about 1000 yards behind in a dugout in rear of a shattered farm. I spent Sunday night in the trenches instead – with Grigg's[1] company: & when we go in again tomorrow night I am going to stay with them for the whole period. This gives me the opportunity of seeing & learning thoroughly. It is not more dangerous than at battalion Headquarters, because frequent walks to & from the trenches over an area where stray bullets are skimming are avoided. It is a wild scene. The line of trenches – or rather breastworks we are now holding is built along the ruins of other older lines taken from the Germans or built later by the Indians. The Guards are cleaning everything up & work night and day to strengthen the parapets & improve the shelter. The neglect & idleness of the former tenants is apparent at every step. Filth & rubbish everywhere, graves built into the defences & scattered about promiscuously, feet & clothing breaking through the soil, water & muck on all sides; & about this scene in the dazzling moonlight troops of enormous rats creep & glide, to the unceasing accompaniment of rifle & machine guns & the venomous whining & whirring of the bullets wh pass overhead. Amid these surroundings, aided by wet & cold, & every minor discomfort, I have found happiness & content such as I have not known for many months. This afternoon I rode over to see Raymond [Asquith][2] who is about 6 miles away. We had a pleasant talk & some tea. He is quite a soldier now, & much improved by the experience. I am making friends with the officers & the Colonel, and it is pleasant to see their original doubts & prejudices fading away. The discipline & organisation of this battalion are admirable. In spite of losses which have left scarcely a dozen of the original personnel remaining, and repeated refills from various sources, the tradition & the system of the Guards asserts itself in hard work, smartness & soldierly behaviour. It will always be a memorable experience to me to have served with them.

Will you send now regularly once a week a <u>small</u> box of food to supplement the rations. Sardines, chocolate, potted meats, and other things wh may strike your fancy. Begin as soon as possible....

Send me also a new Onoto pen. I have stupidly lost mine. Send me also lots of love & many kisses. Write me all about what you are doing & what plans you are making. I enclose a note to Cox in order that you may have £100 to defray any vy urgent bills wh Goonie may be troubled by. It vexes me to think she may be worried. Give my vy best love to Nellie: & tell Bertram to give me a good character to his brother officers.

Do you realise what a vy important person a Major is? 99 people out of any 100 in this gt army have to touch their hats to me. With this inspiring reflection let me sign myself

Your loving & devoted husband
W.

Kiss Randolph, Diana & that golden Sarah for me.

[1] Edward William Macleay Grigg, later 1st Baron Altrincham (1879–1955). MP (National Liberal) 1922–5 and (Conservative) 1933–45; held various government appointments; a member of WSC's wartime Coalition Government (see p. 519 n. 1, letter of 28 March 1945). Married, 1923, Joan Poynder, only child of 1st Baron Islington.
[2] Raymond Asquith (1878–1914), eldest son of H. H. Asquith and his first wife, Helen Melland. Killed in action in the battle of the Somme, 18 September 1916.

○ From CSC   41 Cromwell Road
25 November 1915 7.30 a.m.

My Darling,

I went yesterday & sent you all the things you ask for in your letter from the trenches with the exception (Alas) of the trench wading boots – London seems to be emptied of these, but I am going to make a fresh try this morning & if I fail I shall send you pro tem, a pair of rubber waders which they say is the next best thing. I wake up in the night & think of you shivering in the trenches; it makes me so miserable – (You know how warm the Kat has to be before she can sleep) – I fear I should never sleep in a trench even in a sheepskin bag. Randolph wishes to come with me to choose the wading boots – He wishes to send you as personal presents from himself a photograph of himself & a spade – He says you must have a spade 'to dig out a little sideways so if a bomb comes in the trench Papa won't be killed' – Don't you think it rather wonderful for a child of 4 to have thought of this. On Monday I dined with Venetia [Montagu*] where everyone was thrilled at your having joined the Grenadiers....

Nellie met a young soldier from a line regiment (a former partner) who said that it was common knowledge that you had refused a brigade & wished to go in the trenches – He said everyone thought this splendid as the general expectation among the rank & file of officers was that you would join your regiment for a week or a fortnight's trial, you would then be put on some staff while the regiment was given some interesting work & that you would then be given a Brigade –

I'm counting the days till you go into reserve – I calculate you will be out of the line on Dec. 2nd – Do tell me if this is right –

I have a minor anxiety which makes me unhappy – Nellie's marriage. I don't believe she loves him [Bertram Romilly] at all but is simply marrying him out of pity.... Nellie has really nothing in common with him; she is slightly physically in love with him but that's all – She vacillated (for the last week) between breaking off entirely, postponement, & immediate marriage with every hour of the day, but now she has hardened into a sort of mule-like obstinacy & says with a drawn wretched face that she loves him, is divinely happy & will marry him on the 4th. She is now furious with me for my former support of her postponing intentions, & says that if I say one word against her marriage on Dec: 4th she will leave the house & never come near me when she is married. Goonie thinks the marriage ought not to take place, but we can do no more –

My Darling I think of you constantly & I do hope that when you think of me it is not a picture of a harsh arguing scold but your loving & sad Clemmie. I love you very much more even than I thought I did – for seven years you have filled my whole life & now I feel more than half my life has vanished across the Channel – I have cut out of the Daily Mirror a delightful snap-shot of you in uniform taken just as you left the house – There was a thick fog & the figure is misty & dim & so I feel you receding into the fog & mud of Flanders & not coming back for so long....

Your loving
Clemmie
& kittens

. . .

○ From WSC   [France]
25 November 1915

My darling, I am in a dug out in the trenches. We are to be relieved tonight, thus completing our second 48-hour spell. The great & small guns are booming away on both sides but are not at the moment paying any attention to us. This morning we were shelled & I expect there will be more tonight. It has not caused us any sense of anxiety or apprehension, nor does the approach of a shell quicken my pulse or try my nerves or make me want to bob – as do so many. It is satisfactory to find that so many years of luxury have in no way impaired the tone of my system. At this game I hope I shall be as good as any. But of course we have had nothing serious yet.

Yesterday a curious thing happened. We were eating some food in the dugout (not this one) when a telegram arrived that the Corps Commander wished to see me & that a motor wd meet me at 4.30 on the main road. I thought it rather a strong order to bring me out of the trenches by daylight – a 3 miles walk across sopping fields on wh stray bullets are always falling, along tracks periodically shelled. But I assumed it was something important and anyhow I had no choice. So having made myself as clean as possible I started off just as the enemy began to shell the roads & trenches in revenge for the shelling he had been receiving from our provocative and well fed artillery. I just missed a whole bunch of shells wh fell on the track a hundred yards behind me, and arrived after an hour's walking muddy wet & sweating at the rendezvous where I was to meet the motor. No motor! Presently a Staff colonel turned up – saying he had lost the motor wh had been driven off by shells. He added that the general had wanted to have a talk with me but that it was only about things in general & that another day wd do equally well. I said that I was obeying an order, that I regretted having to leave the trenches at a moment when they were under bombardment, that if I was not wanted for any official duty I wd return at once. And this I did – another hour across the sopping fields now plunged in darkness...

You may imagine how I abused to myself the complacency of this General – though no doubt kindly meant – dragging me about in rain & mud for nothing.

I reached the trenches without mishap: & then learned that a quarter of an hour after I had left, the dugout in wh I was living had been struck by a shell which burst a few feet from where I wd have been sitting, smashing the structure & killing the mess orderly who was inside. Another orderly and an officer who were inside were shaken & rattled, & all our effects buried in mud & debris. When I saw the ruin I was not so angry with the general after all. My servant too was probably saved by the fact that I took him with me to carry my coat. Now see from this how vain it is to worry about things. It is all chance or destiny and our wayward footsteps are best planted without too much calculation. One must yield oneself simply & naturally to the mood of the game: and trust in God wh is another way of saying the same thing....

... I keep watch during part of the night so that others may sleep. Last night I found a sentry asleep on his post. I frightened him dreadfully but did not charge him with the crime. He was only a lad – & I am not an officer of the regiment. The penalty is death or at least 2 years.

Will you now send me 2 bottles of my old brandy & a bottle of peach brandy. This consignment might be repeated at intervals of ten days.

We have another spell in the trenches to do before we go into Divisional Reserve to rest. After that I shall return to G.H.Q. I feel I understand the conditions and shall not be at sea if I take a command. Nothing but direct personal experience as a company officer cd have given me the knowledge. Few generals have drawn their water from this deep spring.

With tender love to you and all my warmest wishes to our friends
Believe me
Your ever loving & devoted
W

O From WSC   [France]
27 November 1915

My darling,

I have rec'd yr letter of the 25th & others of earlier date. We are now
resting again after our second 48 hours spell. We go in again tomorrow
night 28th and come out into reserve after dark on the 30th – my birthday! I
do not mind the discomfort at all & do not think it will affect my health in
any way. . . .

We came out of the line last night without mishap, & marched in under
brilliant moonlight while the men sang 'Tipperary' & 'The Farmer's boy'
and the guns boomed applause. It is like getting to a jolly good tavern
after a long days hunting, wet & cold & hungry – but not without having
had sport. The discipline of this battalion is vy strict. For the slightest
offence – a sulky word, a single crouch under the parapet at the wrong
time, a small untidiness, men are sharply punished. But the results are
good. The spirit is admirable. The men are better than most of the officers.
The officers are quite up to the mark. A total indifference to death or
casualties prevails. What has to be done is done, & the losses accepted
without fuss or comment. . . .

What you write about Nellie makes me anxious. He is a vy nice fellow,
& all speak of him with liking & respect for him & his military conduct.
But of course Nellie is worthy of a larger mate.

Poodle darling I love yr letters and it is a delightful thought to me that
you are there at home with your 3 kittens thinking of me & feeling that I
am doing right. I do not feel the least revolt at the turn of events. Ll.G
[Lloyd George*] & McK[McKenna][1] & the old block [Asquith*] are far away
& look like the mandarins of some remote province of China. If I survive
the war I shall have no difficulty in taking my place in the House of
Commons & it must ever be a good one.

Garvin[2], [C. P.] Scott, Rothermere[3] & others shd be cultivated. They are
loyal friends of quality & power. Keep in touch with the Government.
Show complete confidence in our fortunes. Hold your head vy high. You
always do. Above all don't be worried about me. If my destiny has not
been already accomplished I shall be guarded surely. If it has been there is
nothing that Randolph will need to be ashamed of in what I have done for
the country.

I am telling Cox to put £300 to yr credit wh I want you not to touch; but
to keep as a reserve in case of accidents till thing[s] shd be settled up.

I want 2 more pairs of thick Jaeger draws, vests, & socks (soft).

2 more pairs of brown leather gloves (warm)

1 more pair of field boots (like those I had from Fortnum & Mason) only
from the fourth hole from the bottom instead of holes there shd be good
strong tags for lacing quicker. One size larger than the last.

Also one more pair of Fortnum & M's ankle boots only with tags right
up from the bottom hole (the same size these as before).

With these continual wettings and no means of drying one must have
plenty of spares. I am so sorry to be so extravagant.

Well now my darling I close with tender love to you & all the babies.
Your ever devoted husband
W

[1] At this date Lloyd George was Minister of Munitions and McKenna Chancellor of the Exchequer.
[2] James Louis Garvin (1868–1947), Editor of the *Observer*, 1908–42.
[3] Harold Sidney Harmsworth, later 1st Viscount Rothermere (1868–1940). Younger brother of Lord Northcliffe. Newspaper proprietor. President of the Air Council, 1917–18.

O From CSC   41 Cromwell Road
Sunday 28 November [1915]

My Darling

I miss you terribly – I ache to see you. When do you think you will get a little leave? Shall I come & spend it with you in Paris or will you come home?

I don't like to make any request which might worry or vex you, but it makes me very anxious to feel that you are staying longer in the trenches than your duty requires. All the other officers & the men have been hardened to the wet & cold by their training, but you have gone at one swoop from an atmosphere of hot rooms, sedentary work & Turkish baths to a life of the most cruel hardship & exposure. And besides thinking of me & the babies think of your duty to yourself & your reputation – If you were killed & you had over-exposed yourself the world might think that you had sought death out of grief for your share in the Dardanelles. It is your duty to the country to try & live (consistent with your honour as a soldier). . . .

Nellie's marriage takes place on Dec: 4th, but my heart sinks when I think of it – If it has to be I shall be glad when it is over. She does not truly care for him – I wish you had been here to speak to her & him about it. . . .

Tell me some more about your life – Have you a nice servant – What do you have to eat & do you eat it in a trench or in a farm or where? I shd mind the rats more even than the bullets – Can you kill them or wld that be wasting good ammunition?

I'm struggling on with my Y.M.C.A. canteens for the munition workers. The trains are bad & it is difficult to get to the places.

. . . Your Mother is being very generous & is contributing £40 a month to the upkeep of this establishment until she comes to live with us. This – from Dec 1st . . . .

The Daily Mail rings me up nearly every day & asks if I have had any news from 'Major Churchill'. Major Churchill has a strange sound, but I am prouder of this title than of any other. . . .

For the first time for seven years besides being parted from you I am cut off from the stream of private news & have to rely upon the newspapers & <u>rumour</u>, so that I am in a state of suspended animation. . . .

But for comfort & confidence we all look on the P.M. & McKenna both looking happy, sleek & complacent & for distraction on Violet [Asquith*]'s forthcoming marriage[1] which is turning the town topsy-turvy with excitement – But when I think of you my Dearest Darling, I forget all disappointment, bitterness or ambition & long to have you safe & warm & alive in my arms. Since you have re-become a soldier I look upon civilians of high or low degree with pity & indulgence – The wives of men over military age may be lucky but I am sorry for them being married to feeble & incompetent old men.

I think you will get this letter on your birthday & it brings you all my love & many passionate kisses – My Darling Darling Winston – I find my morning breakfast lonely without you, so Sarah fills your place & does her best to look almost exactly like you. I'm keeping the flag flying till you return by getting up early & having breakfast down-stairs.

Helen Mitford[2] dined here 2 nights ago – Her baby is 5 weeks old. She is heartbroken that it's not a boy – She is 23 & her hair is grey, which looks odd with her young face.

Goodbye my Darling. I <u>love</u> your letters. I read them again & again –

Clemmie

. . .

Am sending you foods & onoto pen.

[1] Violet Asquith married Maurice Bonham Carter (1880–1960) on 30 November 1915; Asquith's Private Secretary, he was knighted, 1916. Known as 'Bongey'.
[2] Lady Helen Mitford (see p. 56 n. 2, undated letter), CSC's first cousin, whose husband Clement Mitford was killed in action, 13 May 1915. Had her child been a son, he would have succeeded his grandfather as the 2nd Baron Redesdale.

O From CSC   41 Cromwell Road
1 December [1915] 5 a.m.

My Darling
    Your last letter was dated the 23rd of November, & I long for more news of you. . . .

Yesterday was Violet's marriage – Great thronging crowds everywhere – Randolph officiated as one of her pages & looked <u>quite</u> beautiful in a little Russian velvet suit with fur. His looks made quite a sensation & at Downing Street afterwards he was surrounded & kissed & admired by dozens of lovely women.

Nellie's marriage approaches fast; she is quite happy & now seems settled in her mind.

The great feature at yesterday's wedding was the re-appearance of K[itchener][1] who, while everyone still imagined him to be receiving the plaudits of the Italians stalked into the church & afterwards signed the register. I am told that in his absence the W.O. had begun to be swept & garnished & that his sudden return caused some dismay! . . .

– – – Later – Your letter of the 27th has just come & now that for the moment I <u>know</u> that you are comparatively safe I realize how sickening the anxiety has been – My Darling darling Winston – I would like to do a little spell with you in the trenches. I feel that if I knew exactly what it was like I should be less fearful, but perhaps the opposite would be the case! . . .

Nellie now seems quite happy & so I feel more at ease, & should be almost quite pleased about it if only poor Bertram had not been shot in the head. The excitement caused by Nellie's waverings made him ill & he has gone to Brighton for 2 days to pick up.

Dec: 2nd 6. a.m.

... Simon[2] yesterday made a long attack on Northcliffe which would certainly have been very damaging if it had not been made by a prig & a bore. ...

Randolph & Diana ask every morning anxiously after you –

I send you my Dearest many many kisses & all my love

Clemmie

...

[1] Kitchener, as Secretary of State for War, had been sent by the Cabinet to the Dardanelles in early November to report on whether the campaign should or should not continue. He had visited Italy on the way home.
[2] Sir John Simon, later 1st Viscount Simon (1873–1954), barrister and Liberal MP. At this date Home Secretary.

○ From WSC   [France]
1 December 1915

My darling,

We came out of the trenches last night, & this battalion will not return to them for 8 days. Probably indeed the Guards Division will be withdrawn from the line altogether. I am therefore going as I was told to do to G.H.Q. today & will write you later what befalls me there. It will be a blow to me if French goes; but I am strong enough to stand alone in the Army. ...

Of course I have seen vy little, but I have seen enough to be quite at my ease about all the ordinary things.

Tender love
Your devoted
W

Later

I reopen my envelope to tell you I have rec'd your dear letter of the 28th. I reciprocate intensely the feelings of love & devotion you show to me. My greatest good fortune in a life of brilliant experience has been to find you, & to lead my life with you. I don't feel far away from you out here at all. I feel vy near in my heart; & also I feel that the nearer I get to honour, the nearer I am to you. A motor is coming for me this morning to take me to G.H.Q. where I shall learn about the future. All is I fear in sad instability there; & my good friend [French] may be gone in a vy few days. ...

Yours devotedly
W

○ From WSC   G.H.Q.
Later still
[1 December 1915]

My darling,

Here I am after a glorious hot bath between the sheets in this abode of comfort resting before dinner. I sent you an 'All well' telegram wh shd for a while put an end to your anxieties. My departure from the 2ⁿᵈ Grenadiers was vy different from my arrival. Then the Colonel thought it necessary to remark 'We don't want to be inhospitable, but I think it only right to say that your coming was not a matter in wh we were given any choice'. But to-day all smiles & handwaves & pressing invitations to return whenever I liked & stay as long as I liked etc. I took of course a great deal of pains & was on my best behaviour, but certainly I succeeded – & I felt almost like leaving a place where I had been for months. Our total casualties in the battalion were 35 out of 700 in 6 days doing nothing.

My dear – where are the bi-weekly food boxes? They can be my only contribution to the messes where I lived. We eat our rations, & the officers have parcels of extras from home. So there are no mess bills. But I want to put something into the common pot. So do send me some useful & practical additions to our fare. Peach Brandy seems to me to be a hopeful feature in the liquor department.

I lunched again with Lord Cavan & had a long talk with him. He strongly advised me to take a battalion before a Brigade: & this is what I think I shall do, if it is open to me. He spoke of my having high command as if it were the natural thing, but urged the importance of going up step by step....

I am so glad my Mother has contributed to Cromwell upkeep. She has a heart of gold. I really don't think that you & Goonie shd deny yourself any reasonable comfort or convenience. Keep a good table: keep sufficient servants & your maid: entertain with discrimination, have a little amusement from time to time. I don't see any reason for undue skimping. With £140 a month there shd be sufficient. Extra bills you must write to me about. I know your probity & good sense in all these things. But I don't want you to be straitened: anyhow not for 6 months....

I don't think anything can be done about Nellie. She must make her own life. She will love him more after she has married him. He is a good man. If on the other hand she wishes postponement she shd be supported: & I will write to him if desired....

Write often & write long. Goonie may write me gossip too of Downing Strasse. Also news of Jack [Churchill*] wd be welcome.

Fondest love
Your devoted
W.

. . .

○ From CSC   41 Cromwell Road
Saturday 4 December 1915 6.30 a.m.

My Darling

Yesterday arrived a fat envelope from you containing several thrilling letters including the one written in your dug-out which you kept back. It is horrible to sit here in warmth & luxury while danger & suffering are so close to you – That dreadful walk across the fields there & back among falling shells was on Nov: 24th & now it is 10 days later & Heaven knows what narrow escapes you may have had since –

My Darling, altho' I ache for you to have a brigade so that you may be in less danger I admire you so very much for taking a battalion first – I am sure it is the right & wise thing –

General Bridges[1] came to see me last night; (what a tremendous fellow he is to look at). He told me he had seen you & that you were then in high spirits – He said 'I suppose Winston is going to get a brigade'. I said I thought you would rather take a battalion first – His face lighted up & he said 'I am *so* glad' – It is nectar to me to feel & see generous admiration & appreciation of you, which for so long have been denied unjustly –

General B also spoke of your eventually coming to high command as the natural expected thing, but <u>he</u> also urged step by step – like Lord Cavan.

I am so glad that you & Lord Cavan are friends – He seems to be a fine soldier & one of the few unblighted generals in the general mildew.

What you tell me of Sir John F[rench] grieves me but not really for your sake, for I prefer you to win your way than to be thought a favourite of the C. in C. I <u>feel</u> confidence in your star – my Dearest & I know all soldiers who meet you will love you – Till I got your letter I had no idea that a change in France was more imminent than for instance a month ago. General Bridges confirmed what you said, but it seems nothing is settled? He said there was dismay at K's return as even in one week without a Chief the circulation of the W.O. had improved – Ah! if all these weary months a good man had been there –

Margot [Asquith] & Elizabeth [her daughter] came here yesterday to tea & were very friendly. The 'Block' [H. H. Asquith*] I have seen only at Downing Street after Violet's wedding; he ran across me <u>&</u> Lord Haldane(!) together in the hall, muttered a few civil words & shuffled off sniffing nervously – Goonie & I have been bidden for luncheon there on Sunday which is most unusual as they are generally away; I don't expect the old boy will be there. . . .

To-day is Nellie's marriage, but the whole house is still asleep – For the last few days the rooms have looked very odd, full of Nellie's presents & cardboard boxes & new clothes & tissue paper – She & Bertram have taken a little furnished cottage at Taplow (practically lent by Nancy & Waldorf [Astor]) & they go there after the honeymoon at Avon Tyrrel.

– – –

I see in your postscript you are more hopeful about Sir J [John French]. But I fear it is only a momentary pick-up – I think the P.M. is slowly & undecidedly wobbling towards a change.

I saw poor Clare Sheridan[2] the other day – My Darling I don't know how one bears such things. I feel I could not weather such a blow – She has a beautiful little son 8 weeks old, but her poor 'black puss' sleeps in Flanders – You <u>must</u> come back to me my dear one – (You are now my orange pug again, trotting away happily to fight with his 'panache' in the air & his ears to the wind)....

I hear lots of little bits of indirect news of you –

I will write to you again to-night & tell you about the wedding. Randolph Diana & Johnny are terribly excited as they are to carry Nellie's train arrayed in white satin.

My dearest love to you –
Clemmie

. . .

. . .

[1] Lt-Gen. (later Sir) G. T. M. Bridges (1871–1939). Lt-Col. 4th Hussars, 1914; Head of British Military Mission, Belgian Field Army, 1914–16.
[2] Clare Sheridan (born Frewen) (1885–1970), WSC's first cousin. Her husband, William Sheridan, was killed in action at the battle of Loos, 25 September 1915. She was a gifted and successful sculptor.

O From WSC   G.H.Q.
4 December 1915

My darling,

. . .

[in margin against next two paras: 'vy vy secret']
French returned last night & we dined with two or three faithful slaves and discussed anxiously the situation. Asquith* clearly wants him to go, & go without any kind of friction. French wants to stay but also to behave with dignity. Asquith has so left the case that French is free to stay & is all the time tortured by the sense of utter insecurity. For three weeks no one has thought of the enemy. Tis secret. Anyhow I don't expect any immediate change.

I proposed to French that I shd take a battalion; but he rejected it, & said 'no a brigade at once' & that he would settle it quickly in case any accident shd happen to him. I have acquiesced. The 2nd Grenadiers do not go into the trenches till the 8th – if then –

If my affairs are still unsettled then I shall go with them. It is the right thing to do – Meanwhile I live here in gt comfort. I have just got back from a vy long walk with French – talking about all things in heaven & earth. I am so sorry for him. No man can sustain two different kinds of separate worries – a tremendous army in the face of the enemy: a gnawing intrigue at the back. He seems to have told a good many people of my refusal of a Brigade and insistence on going to the trenches. He said the P.M. spoke with emotion about me. But Asquith's sentiments are always governed by his interests. They are vy hearty & warm within limits wh cost nothing.

Tomorrow I go to the French 10th army under the chaperonage of Spiers[1]. It will be vy interesting to see the scene of these terrible Arras battles & I shall learn a good deal of their system in the trenches.

My bird – no letter from you has yet arrived today: & I am much hoping that a later post will bring me one. No food box has arrived yet. Where did you send it. I want particularly to take one back with me to the Grenadiers if I return to take pot luck with them.

Also send me a big bath towel. I now have to wipe myself all over with things that resemble pocket handkerchiefs. I shall be able to keep all my accumulating kit in a portmanteau here or elsewhere in St. Omer, & it will be a comfort to me.

. . .

They all say I look 5 years younger: & certainly I have never been in better health & spirits. Christmas in Paris – I think for you & me. I shall probably be in the collar then; but 2 or 3 days shd not be an impossibility.

Tender love my darling from
Your devoted
W.

[1] Capt. (later Maj.-Gen. Sir) Edward Louis Spiers (1886–1974), later 1st Bt. At this time Liaison Officer with French 10th Army, 1915–16. He changed the spelling of his name to Spears in 1918. Married, first, 1918, the American author Mary Borden (d. 1968); secondly, in 1969, Nancy Maurice.

○ From CSC   41 Cromwell Road
Monday 6 December [1915] 7.30 a.m.

My Darling,

Nellie was married on Saturday –

I feel much happier now about her, as from several people I have heard good reports of Bertram in Egypt.

I wish you could have been here – Nellie looked really lovely; her long train was carried by Diana, Johnny & Randolph – After the wedding we all went to Aunt Mary [Lady St Helier]'s house in Portland Place & many people came there to see the last of her as Miss Nellie Hozier! It is 7 years & nearly 3 months since you & I drove away from there to Blenheim.

Yesterday Goonie & I lunched at Downing Street, having first gone to St Paul's. No 'Block' (he had gone down to Munstead[1] after attending a conference at Calais on Saturday.) But Violet [Asquith*] & Bongey [Bonham Carter] appeared from their honeymoon on their way to the Italian Riviera where they are to spend a month – They both looked rather dreary & 'blue-stockingy'.

I long for more news from G.H.Q. where you have now been for 6 days.

. . . The post will be here in a few minutes & I eagerly await a letter from you.

Later

Your two long letters of the 3rd & 4th have now come –

I hope so much my Darling that you may still decide to take a battalion first, much as I long for you to be not so much in the trenches. I am absolutely certain that whoever is C in C, you will rise to high command. I'm sure everyone feels that anything else would be wasting a valuable instrument – But everyone who really loves you & has your interest at heart wants you to go step by step whereas I notice the Downing Street tone is 'of course Winston will have a brigade in a fortnight' – Thus do they hope to ease their conscience from the wrong they have done you & then hope to hear no more of you. I have the fear that if you are now suddenly given a brigade & Sir John shortly afterwards goes, you might perhaps stick there as his successor might feel stodgy & that enough had been done for you. Sir John loves you & wants <u>himself</u> to have the joy of doing something for you, but I believe in Lord Cavan's' advice – You & he should make a very strong combination & if he gets a corps I feel sure you wld soon get a division under him. Do get a battalion <u>now</u> & a brigade later.

I am so distressed about the food, & to-day I have despatched a big box to G.H.Q. My previous one I sent to 2ⁿᵈ batt. Grenadier Guards as I thought it was for <u>their</u> mess you wanted it. It must have reached there after you left there. I have also sent boots (3 pairs), vests, pants, socks, gloves, sleeping cap, onoto pen....

I feel so grieved for Sir J [French]'s anxieties, but I am sure a change is inevitable & tho' I am sure he is a good soldier if I were Prime Minister I would make the change; but I hope swiftly & with decision not wavering towards it in the way he does about everything – Do not my dear be shocked & angry with me for saying this – I know he is your friend & I too feel much warmth & affection & gratitude towards him, but with the 2 disasters impending in the East, I would like a fresh untortured mind in the West –

Goodbye my Darling – I feel sad to-day & as if we could not win the war. But perhaps this is becos' I long for you very much & I feel the reaction after Nellie's wedding & rain is falling in buckets – But in your star I have confidence.

Your loving
Clemmie

...

Do Majors or Colonels command battalions?

¹ Munstead House, Godalming, Surrey, home of Col. Sir Herbert Jekyll KCMG, whose daughter Pamela married Reginald McKenna, 1908.

○ From WSC   [France]
8 December 1915

My darling,

I am still in uncertainty as to my immediate employment. Whether a battalion or a brigade – nothing is settled. French is away in Paris & general instability is in command.... I shall therefore return tomorrow to the Grenadiers for another cycle in the trenches. I shall be quite happy with them.

I send you a letter from Curzon [Lord Privy Seal] wh arrived with enclosures last night. I have a feeling that the decision has been taken to renew the naval attack. You see how well Rosie Wemyss¹ comes out of it all. It wd not have been any good my joining in these discussions. A fresh uncompromised champion like Curzon had a better chance than I cd ever have had: & he has stated the case as well as I cd have done. Please lock up all these papers after reading them, & never say you have seen them. Also keep in touch with Curzon & others. Don't fail to keep the threads in yr fingers. Let me know who you see. Curzon's letter & enclosures have of course revived distressing thoughts. My scorn for Kitchener is intense. If they evacuate [Gallipoli] in disaster – all the facts shall come out. They will be incredible to the world. The reckoning will be heavy & I shall make sure it is exacted.

Yesterday I went to La Panne to see General Bridges & the positions there. Captain Spiers came with me. We passed an interesting morning and saw long stretches of the line both from the trenches & from ruined church towers. A little shelling. On the way back I looked in on Maxine [Elliott*] in her barge², & Spiers & I stayed to dinner. Such a jolly place, & Spiers after so many months of war weariness & danger found it quite hard to climb the ladder wh led out into the night. I like him vy much: & he is entirely captivated.

I have been given a fine steel helmet by the French wh I am going to wear, as it looks so nice & will perhaps protect my valuable cranium. Maxine was absolutely alone – & vy lonely. She has done good work & is a really fine woman – tho' she must be judged by special standards.

... My darling one – I love you so much and think often & often of you with yr kittens gathered round.

With tenderest sentiments
Your ever devoted
W

P.S. ...

Ching – keep yr eye fixed on Parigi [Paris], some day or other we will meet there & drink a generous red wine & buy some clothes of taste and jauntiness, ...

Good night my darling
W.

¹ Rear-Admiral Rosslyn Wemyss (1864–1933), Acting Vice-Admiral at the Dardanelles, November–December 1915. Knighted, 1916; cr. Baron Wester Wemyss, 1919.
² Maxine Elliott organized a Belgian Relief Barge from which she gave food and clothing to large numbers of refugees.

O From WSC   [G.H.Q.]
10 December 1915

<u>Secret</u>

My darling,

I am to be given the command of the 56th Brigade in the 19th Division. Bridges will command the Division ..., & the Bde I shall command comprises 4 Lancashire Battalions. The division has a good reputation, has been out here some time, & is now in the line, next to the Guards. ...

I hope to get Spiers as Brigade Major & Archie [Sinclair] as Staff Captain.

Of course there will be criticism & carping. But it is no good paying any attention to that. If I had taken a battalion for a few weeks, it wd equally have been said 'he has used it merely as a stepping stone etc'. I am satisfied this is the right thing to do in the circumstances, & for the rest my attention will concentrate upon the Germans.

The Grenadiers are now holding a vy much better line than before – with good dry communication trenches & comfortable dugouts. I visited them yesterday and they offered to make me acting second in command – wh considering all things is a gt compliment. I intend to go on with them until I actually go to the Brigade. French has asked me to stay here at G.H.Q. for the next day or two as the political situation & his own affairs are so uncertain....

Salonika is vy bad – the 10th Division routed with loss of guns: the French right exposed: their retreat compromised. All has fallen out as I predicted 6 weeks ago. I am inclined to think a disaster here & at Baghdad[1] may make the Government still less inclined to engineer a third smash at Gallipoli: & that they will at any rate resolve to 'Wait & see'[2].

I found the first food box at the Grenadiers H.Q. No boots have yet reached me; but I can wait for a few days. Now that I shall be starting a mess of my own I shall want regular bi-weekly supplies & I will give you full directions later. None of this expense is to come out of yr housekeeping, as my pay is meant for this among other things.

Please order another khaki tunic for me as a Brigadier General. Let the pockets be less baggy than the other 2, & let the material be stouter....

With tenderest love
Your devoted
W

. . .

[1] The British Expeditionary Force had failed in its mission to capture Baghdad. After a great victory at Kut-el-Amara on 29 September, the force had advanced to within 13 miles of Baghdad but was defeated on 24 November, one-tenth of its men killed or wounded, and retreated to Kut.
[2] A favourite maxim of Asquith.

O From CSC   41 Cromwell Road
12 December [1915]

My Darling

Your letter of the 8th containing Lord Curzon's & the papers threw me into a state of agitation & wild hope that at last for the first time since you left the Admiralty a courageous & bold decision was going to be taken or had already been taken. How clear & able Lord C's 2 papers are – I wish he could be Sec^y of State for War instead of that cowardly & base old K [Kitchener].

I got hold of Eddie [Marsh*][1] & have heard the sad news about Suvla & Anzac[2] & also about Sir John [French] ...

I cannot understand the unearthly calm that has come over Parliament & the Press – Is it torpor or an ominous lull before an explosion of wrath? The government seem quite complacent about the Baghdad fiasco. Lord

Crewe [Lord President of the Council] was quite naïf about it in the Lords [saying] – Things did not go as well as the Government had expected that was all – It's a pity but it's not anybody's fault – A complete surprise to everyone.

My Darling I am so distressed about your parcels of clothes & boots. None was over 7 lbs, & nearly all your letters go thro' Mr Creedy[3]. I trust boots etc have now arrived....

Sarah has been ill for a week which makes me unhappy – Acute bouts of neuralgia in her head – She becomes rigid & screams with agony for about 20 minutes & when the pain ceases she is quite done & exhausted & falls asleep. She has lost her lovely pink cheeks & is losing weight. [Dr] Parkinson has been called in & has prescribed (as the last resort) bromide, but we have not yet opened the bottle. It is on the mantelpiece & I'm putting it off as long as I can. To-day she is a little better.

We have no gossip from Downing Street. I think the P.M. looks on me like Banquo's ghost! To-day I feel easier as you are not (I calculate) in the trenches. But return there Alas! on Monday night. On all sides I hear how the young officers in the Grenadiers like & appreciate you. Be careful too my Darling what you say – That disagreeable young Philip Kerr[4] (R. Table) said to me that he had heard from an officer that he was afraid of talking freely as he was chock-full of Cabinet secrets which you had told him....

Meanwhile I toil away at my working-men's restaurants. After Christmas I am opening 2 to seat 400 men each[5].

Tell me when you think you will have leave. Christmas?...

It is snowing hard & it makes me fear that you are wet & cold. Write & tell me what everyone thinks about Sir John's retirement. I fear you will perhaps not go to G.H.Q. so often now? Do you know Haig[6] & is he a friend?

Your own
Clemmie

...

[1] At this date Assistant Private Secretary to the Prime Minister (Asquith).
[2] On the N.E. coast of Gallipoli Peninsula (see map p. 108). The evacuation was completed on 20 December 1915.
[3] Herbert James Creedy (1878–1973), Private Secretary to successive Secretaries of State for War, 1913–20. Knighted 1919.
[4] Philip Kerr (1882–1940). Editor, *The Round Table*, 1916–21; Secretary to Prime Minister, 1916–21. Succeeded his cousin as 11th Marquess of Lothian, 1930. British Ambassador at Washington, 1939 until his death.
[5] During the ensuing months CSC was responsible for opening, staffing and running nine canteens each feeding 400–500 munitions workers.
[6] Sir Douglas Haig (1861–1928), later 1st Earl Haig KT, OM. Commander of 1st Army Corps, 1914–15. Succeeded Sir John French as C.-in-C, British Expeditionary Force, 19 December 1915; appointed Field Marshal, 1917.

O From WSC   [France]
12 December 1915

My darling,

I am out here now with the Guards again in a shell torn township whose name need not be mentioned. We go into the trenches tomorrow,

& I shall continue doing duty with them till I get other directions. I saw Cavan today & told him what was settled. He seemed quite pleased & has arranged for me to study the supply system tomorrow morning – what they call the Q [Quartermaster] side of the work – I am to follow the course of a biscuit from the base to the trenches etc. He has written a long memo. on my 'Variants of the Offensive'[1] generally in cordial agreement & urging action. If only French were staying – all these thoughts wd take shape and have their fruition in some fine event. That odious Asquith*, & his pack of incompetents & intriguers ruin everything.

I am now quite cut off from information and am content to be. I thought it more seemly to come out here, than to wait about at G.H.Q. – comfortable as it was, & civil as was everyone. Really they are nice to me here, & delighted to see me....

My Darling the most divine & glorious sleeping bag has arrived, & I spent last night in it in one long 11 hours purr. Also food boxes are now flowing steadily; & I get daily evidences of the Cat's untiring zeal on my behalf. The periscope ... was the exact type I wanted. How clever of you to hit it off.

My [French] steel helmet is the cause of much envy. I look most martial in it – like a Cromwellian – I always intend to wear it under fire – but chiefly for the appearance.

My dearest one – I have your little photograph up here now – and kiss it each night before I go to bed.

Love to the children and all others near & dear

Always yr devoted
W

Reassure Curzon that his letters are all safe & encourage him to write more. I think F.E. [Smith*] is coming out to see me here one day this week. He will bring any letters & parcels for me. Get into touch with him.

[1] 'Variants of the Offensive', memorandum by WSC dated General Headquarters BEF, 3 December 1915. Churchill Papers, CHAR 2/73; published in full in Martin Gilbert, *Winston S. Churchill, Companion Vol. III*, 1972, part 2, pp. 1303–8.

O From WSC   [G.H.Q.]
15 December 1915

My darling One,

I am back here at G.H.Q. to see the last of my poor friend who returns to pack up tomorrow. I don't know what effect this change of command will produce upon my local fortunes: possibly it will throw everything into the melting pot again. Believe me I am superior to anything that can happen to me out here. My conviction that the greatest of my work is still to be done is strong within me: & I ride reposefully along the gale – I expect it will be my duty in the early months of next year – if I am all right – to stand up in my place in Parliament and endeavour to procure the dismissal of Asquith* & Kitchener: & when I am sure that the hour has come I shall not flinch from any exertion or strife. I feel a gt assurance of my power: & now – naked – nothing can assail me.

After Monday or Tuesday there will be no more G.H.Q. for me: but I will let you know where to write & how letters can be safely conveyed. F. E. [Smith*] comes over on Saturday morning & shd bring anything you have to send me. . . .

We had a quiet time in the trenches. I finished another 48 hour spell last night. The artillery on both sides shelled each other's infantry a good deal, but all the shells came over the front line and burst behind us on the communications or on houses etc in rear. 10 grenadiers under a kid went across by night to the German Trench wh they found largely deserted or waterlogged. They fell upon a picket of Germans, beat the brains out of two of them with clubs & dragged a third home triumphantly as a prisoner. The young officer by accident let off his pistol & shot one of his own Grenadiers dead: but the others kept this secret and pretended it was done by the enemy – do likewise. Such men you never saw. The scene in the little dugout when the prisoner was brought in surrounded by these terrific warriors, in jerkins & steel helmets with their bloody clubs in hand – looking pictures of ruthless war – was one to stay in the memory. C'est très bon. They petted the prisoner and gave him cigarettes & tried to cheer him up. He was not vy unhappy to be taken & to know he wd be safe & well fed till the end of the war.

. . . In the Grenadiers the opinion is that I am to have a division. This they seemed to consider quite reasonable. I shd be happy to take a company: but I do not want much to go under fire again – except with a definite responsibility however small. . . .

The hour of Asquith's punishment & K[itchener]'s exposure draws nearer. The wretched men have nearly wrecked our chances. It may fall to me to strike the blow. I shall do it without compunction.

I have only had one letter from my Darling in 5 days & shd like vy much to receive one every day. Perhaps the later post will bring me one.

Tender love. I see photos of Diana & Randolph in all the papers. They will be getting quite vain. Kiss them.

Your ever devoted,
W

Later
My darling,

I reopen my letter to say that French has telephoned from London that the P.M. has written to him that I am not to have a Brigade but a battalion. I hope however to secure one that is now going into the line. You shd cancel the order for the tunic!

Do not allow the P.M. to discuss my affairs with you. Be vy cool & detached and avoid any sign of acquiescence in anything he may say.

Your devoted
W.

O From CSC   41 Cromwell Road.
15 December [1915]

My Darling
I am thrilled to hear that you are to have a Brigade[1], but I should rejoice
more if I thought that in that position you would be in less danger than
you are now. I suppose the danger from rifle fire will be less & that from
shells greater....
Eddie [Marsh*] told me in the 'strictest confidence' that Sir John [French]'s
resignation would appear in to-day's papers – But not a word. Can it be
that there is some change again?...

– – –

Later. Goonie has just returned from lunching at Downing Street where
she sat between the P.M. & K[itchener]. She reports that K looked very
thin; he told her that he had seen your paper on Trench Warfare which he
thought very good & he is having it circulated to the Staffs. The P.M.
snuffled & asked after you & asked if you were happy to which Goonie
replied, acting according to consultation (for we had discussed it
beforehand) that you said in all your letters that you were very happy –
The old Boy looked rather uncomfortable & then passed on to me – 'Why
don't I see Clemmie, why doesn't she come here?' Goonie enquired if I
had ever been invited to which he replied that I ought to propose myself.
I think he feels thoroughly sheepish & uneasy, or perhaps he just pretends
to be cos' he thinks it good taste....
I'm so relieved that at last the things I ordered are beginning to arrive –
Now Christmas congestion is beginning, so if there is anything very special
you want, let me know quickly & I will send it out by F.E. [Smith*]. I
spoke to him this morning on the telephone & he said he would come
and see me before starting.
The Government attitude is that everything is now going splendidly at
Salonika – Rumours of the Dardanelles evacuation are of course all over
London (the usual W.O. leakage I suppose) but the rumours differ.
The latest Society canard is that the Government will fall this week &
that for the duration of the war the Speaker will be made P.M.! This is the
very newest – last week it was Lord Derby –
Christmas is coming very soon – Shall we meet then?
Goodbye my Darling Winston – I think of you constantly especially at
night – I hope you are not very cold

                                                                    Your
                                                                    Clemmie

                                                                    . . .

[1] CSC had not yet received WSC's letter of 15 December.

O From CSC   41 Cromwell Road
17 December [1915]

My Darling Winston
Yesterday's official communiqué said that on Wednesday S.W. of Ypres
the enemy sprang a mine under one of our trenches, but that our men

rushed in, seized the crater & repelled the Germans – I feel that this is your mine, & I feel so relieved that as far as you are concerned this particular danger is over – Mr Steel[1] rang me up to say he had spoken to you on the telephone & that you were well.

I met Lord Esher[2] at a restaurant yesterday fresh from France – He said you looked like a boy, all the lines of care gone from your face.

He seemed to think there was going to be a row over your Brigade. I pointed out to him that if you had had a Battalion first & then a Brigade there would have been 2 rows instead of one.

Jack Tennant[3] denied knowledge of it in the House yesterday –

When will it be announced? I feel very anxious & long for a sight of you.... Do you know Sir Douglas Haig? Did he agree to your appointment or was it finally settled before he supervened? He looks a superior man, but his expression is cold & prejudiced, & I fear he is narrow....

Randolph asks every day about you & also asks every day when the war will be over. I fear he's a peace crank. I feel like that too!

Your loving
Clemmie

[1] Gerald Arthur Steel, who had been WSC's Private Secretary at the Admiralty.
[2] Reginald Baliol Brett, 2nd Viscount Esher (1852–1930). Member of Committee of Imperial Defence, 1905–18; head of British Mission in Paris throughout First World War.
[3] Harold John Tennant (1865-1935), Parliamentary Under-Secretary of State for War, 1912–16. (Margot Asquith's brother.) He was answering a question tabled by the Conservative MP Maj. Sir Charles Hunter.

○ From CSC   41 Cromwell Road
17 December [1915]

My Darling

Since writing to you I have been wondering whether I ought not to have told you exactly what Lord Esher said – I did not do so becos' I thought your appointment was absolutely fixed; but now I hear from Eddie [Marsh*] that you say that the recall of Sir John [French] may affect your private fortunes. So I will tell you (for what it is worth) what Lord E[sher] said – Of course you will know better than I can whether he is in touch with feeling in the Army or not & whether to attach importance & weight to his opinion. He said 'Of course you know Winston is taking a Brigade & as a personal friend of his I am very sorry about it; as I think he is making a great mistake. Of course it's not his fault, Sir John forced it upon him – All W's friends are very distressed about it as they hoped he would take a battalion first.'

He said how tremendously popular & respected you had become in the short time you had been there & repeated to me the story you told me of the Colonel of the Grenadiers receiving you so disagreeably & then being entirely won over. This interview took place in the crowded grill room of the Berkeley – I preserved a calm & composed demeanour, but I was astonished & hurt at his blurting all this out to me. He repeated again & again that the thing was a mistake; I tried at last to lead him off by asking him personal questions about you, how you were looking, if you were well – He then launched forth again, saying that you had been in the greatest danger, in more than was necessary etc – & that French had determined to give you this Brigade as he was convinced you wld otherwise be killed – After this I crawled home quite stunned & heartbroken.

My Darling Love – I live from day to day in suspense and anguish – At night when I lie down I say to myself Thank God he is still alive. The 4 weeks of your absence seem to me like 4 years –

If only my Dear you had no military ambitions. If only you would stay with the Oxfordshire Hussars in their billets –

I can just bear it – feeling that you are really happy. I have ceased to have ambitions for you – Just come back to me alive that's all –

Your loving
Clemmie

O From CSC   41 Cromwell Road
18 December [1915] 1 a.m.

My Darling

Late in the evening I had a telephone message from F.E. [Smith*] saying he was going to see you tomorrow – I would like to have sent you some delicacies but the shops were closed so all this letter brings is my tender love.

My Dear – Your letter has just come telling me that your hopes of a Brigade have vanished – I do trust that Haig will give you one later – If he does it may be all for the best – but if not it is cruel that the change at G.H.Q. came before all was fixed.

You will receive later by King's messenger 2 letters written earlier in the afternoon – Do not pay any attention to No 2 written at a moment of sadness uncertainty & agitation. Your letter with its firm & confident tone has restored me.

I telephoned to F.E. where he was dining & he very good naturedly came round & saw me. He is your true & faithful friend & I feel so glad you will now see each other. . . .

I must say I am astounded at the P.M. not backing you for a brigade but I cannot help hoping that he has asked Haig to give you one later on after you have commanded a battalion for a little while.

My own Darling I feel such absolute confidence in your future – it is your present which causes me agony – I feel as if I had a tight band of pain round my heart –

It fills me with great pride to think that you have won the love & respect of those splendid Grenadiers & their austere Colonel. In happier times you must let me see them all.

Perhaps if any of them come home on leave they would come & see me –

Your loving
Clemmie

. . .

○ From WSC
18 December 1915

General Headquarters,
British Army in the Field.

My darling

French has returned. The position is as follows. He saw Asquith*, told him that he had given me a Brigade & Asquith said he was delighted. A few hours later, being I suppose frightened by the question in the House, Asquith wrote a note to French, (wh French showed me <u>vy privately</u>) saying that 'with regard to our conversation about our friend – the appointment might cause some criticism' & shd not therefore be made – adding 'Perhaps you might give him a battalion'. The almost contemptuous indifference of this note was a revelation to me. French was astonished; but in his weak position he cd do nothing, & now he is no longer C. in C. Meanwhile he had told everyone that he had given me a Brigade & is of course deeply distressed at the turn of events.

To measure Asquith's performance one has to remember that on my leaving the Admiralty he offered me a Brigade: & that when I told him three months ago of the offers that French had made to me if I came out to the front, he advised me to go & assured me that any advancement wh was thought fitting by the C. in C. wd have his hearty concurrence. One has to remember all the rest too of a long story of my work & connexion with him. Altogether I am inclined to think that his conduct reached the limit of meanness & ungenerousness. Sentiments of friendship expressed in extravagant terms, coupled with a resolve not to incur the slightest criticism or encounter the smallest opposition – even from the most unworthy quarter. Personally I feel that every link is severed: & while I do not wish to decide in a hurry – my feeling is that all relationship shd cease. I will write again about this....

This afternoon French is to see Haig & intends to tell him the whole story. My action will necessarily depend on the new man's view & disposition. Unless he is inclined to make himself responsible for the decision to wh French had come and takes clearly a favourable & friendly view. I shall remain with the Grenadier Guards as a company officer. I think they will be willing to make an exception to their rule about only Guards commanding Guards & will let me do the work in a regular way. This at any rate is the place of honour and as they will be continuously in the line till the 25th Jan[y] I shd find the service of great interest.

Meanwhile I do not think any difficulty wd be placed in my way, if I required to return home for Parliamentary duties and the situation needed my presence.

Darling I want you to burn those two letters I sent you yesterday[1]. I was depressed & my thought was not organised. It is now quite clear & good again & I see plainly the steps to take. You will do this to please me. Everyone has hours of reaction; & there is no reason why written record shd remain.

F.E. [Smith*] comes here tonight & I shall be vy glad to talk the whole position over with him.

Always yr devoted
W

Later.

Haig came to see French who told him the whole position. I was called in and had an interview with Haig. He treated me with the utmost kindness of manner & consideration, assured me that nothing wd give him greater pleasure than to give me a Brigade, that his only wish was that able men shd come to the front, & that I might count on his sympathy in every way. He had heard from Cavan of the 'excellent work' I had done in the trenches. Altogether it was quite clear that he will give me a fair chance. In these circumstances I consented to take a battalion – wh one is not yet settled – but it will be one going in the line. I asked for an officer – Archie [Sinclair] or Spiers – and he went off and arranged at once that I was to have what I wanted. It is possible even that I shall get the two in a short time. The need of a few competent professionals is really vy great, and every step I take is watched by curious eyes. I must be well supported.

I was greatly reassured by his manner wh was affectionate almost. He took me by the arm and made the greatest fuss. I used to know him pretty well in [the] old days when he was a Major & I a young M.P. But I am bound to say the warmth of his greeting surprised me.

I asked him if he wd like to see 'Variants of the Offensive' & he said he wd be 'honoured' – ! So I am back on my perch again with my feathers stroked down. French was much relieved to know I was satisfied. He is a dear friend. I want you & Goonie to get him to come & dine with you and cherish him properly: & write him a nice letter. My heart bled for him in this wrench. We motored out today together & picnicked in a little cottage & had long talks on the way home about every sort of thing.

As for Asquith – make no change except a greater reserve about me & my affairs. The incident is best ignored; but it need not be forgotten. Don't you tell me he was quite right – or let him persuade you. Esher talks foolishly. It wd not have been a great mistake for me to take a Brigade. There was something to be said either way. But on the whole it was worth taking. As for my having been in 'the greatest danger' etc, it is all nonsense. Only one officer in the whole division of Guards has been hit while I have been with them: & he was out raiding the German trench. . . .

What lovely letters you write me. These two today gave me the greatest pleasure. (Send me all the press cuttings; also my Cabinet papers I asked for). . . .

Your devoted & everloving
W

[1] The two letters of 17 December referred to have not survived.

O From WSC   [St Omer]
20 December 1915

My darling,

Your 1 a.m. 18th letter has just arrived, & stimulates me to add a little to what I wrote this morning. I have now moved into Max Aitken's[1] house – a sort of Canadian War Office – where I am comfortable and well looked after. I am simply waiting d'un pied à l'autre for orders. It is odd to pass these days of absolute idleness – waiting 3 or 4 hours together in tranquil vegetation, when one looks back to the long years of unceasing labour & hustle through wh I have passed. It does not fret me. In war one takes every thing as it comes & I seem to have quite different standards to measure by. As one's fortunes are reduced, one's spirit must expand to fill the void.

I think of all the things that are being left undone & of my own energies & capacities to do them & drive them along all wasted – without any real pain. I watch – as far as I can – the weak irresolute & incompetent drift of government policy and turn over what ought to be done in my mind, & then let it all slide away without a wrench. I shall be profoundly absorbed in the tremendous little tasks wh my new work will give me & I hope to come to these men like a breeze. I hope they will rejoice to be led by me, & fall back with real confidence into my hands. I shall give them my vy best.

French's departure was affecting. He saw a long succession of generals etc & then opened his door & said 'Winston it is fitting that my last quarter of an hour here shd be spent with you.' Then off he went with a guard of honour, saluting officers, cheering soldiers & townsfolk – stepping swiftly from the stage of history into the dull humdrum of ordinary life. I felt deeply his departure on every ground – public & private. It was not I think necessary or right. The French are rather unhappy about it: The army has no real opinion. But Asquith* will throw anyone to the wolves to keep himself in office. . . .

Dearest & sweetest – I love you so much.

Your devoted
W

---

[1] Sir Max Aitken – later Lord Beaverbrook; see Biographical Notes – was acting as a Canadian eye-witness at the front and had a house at St Omer, near General Headquarters.

Chapter VII

'PLUG STREET'

Winston had a short period of leave from 24 to 27 December – so he was home for Christmas. During this brief spell he saw Asquith*, Lloyd George* and Garvin.

O From CSC   [41 Cromwell Road]
28 December [1915]

My Darling,
    Your letter from Dover just arrived & I am sending it on at once to Ll.G [Lloyd George*] coupled with an invitation to luncheon. It seems centuries ago since you left & a thick pall of fog has settled round me thro' which I can neither hear nor see the conflict. Something good must come of it. If as I fear the P.M. keeps his pledge, at any rate we get conscription[1].
    Tomorrow I go to Alderley till Monday. I am absolutely worn out with emotions & the excitement of seeing you & I must have a few days' rest. I can't sleep for anxiety.
    I send you one or two letters & a cutting. I know nothing, but I feel the break-up is not yet; this futile government will fumble on for a few more months.
    I could not tell you how much I wanted you at the station. I was so out of breath with running for the train.

Your loving
Clemmie
(With such a headache)
. . .

[1] Shortage of manpower for the services had made conscription (compulsion) a running controversy. WSC and Lloyd George had both, reluctantly, become convinced it was necessary. The Cabinet was sharply divided, with Asquith still supporting voluntary recruitment, although finally he changed his stance. In January 1916 the Government brought in the first measures of compulsion.

◇ From CSC   [41 Cromwell Road]
29 December [1915]

My Darling,
   The newspapers announce that the 'crisis' is over and that we are to
have compulsion straight away. It looks as if this were true as most of the
Ministers have returned to the country to finish their holidays. I sent your
letter round to Ll.G [Lloyd George*] but he had departed to Walton Heath
– He is lunching with me to-day; so I hope to send you some <u>real</u> news
presently. . . .
   <u>Later</u> Ll.G has been & gone. As I feared the crisis is over with 'no
change' except the extremely unlikely resignations of Runciman [President
of the Board of Trade] & Simon[1]. The P.M. appeared at the Cabinet
yesterday & did <u>all</u> the fighting <u>for</u> compulsion – Ll.G & Curzon hardly
opened their mouths. Runciman and McKenna argued against it on the
ground of injuring the trade of [the] country, but finally all agreed with
exception of Simon & Runciman who are 're-considering' their positions. I
asked Ll.G if he & the other die hards had tried to break the government;
he said there wasn't a chance as the P.M. had come right over on to their
side. He expressed great distress at you not being in the Government – He
said repeatedly 'We must get Winston back' – He asked me if you would
come back & manage the heavy gun department of the Munitions
Office. . . .
   Ll.G is a strange man. He was very polite & civil & most friendly, but for
the moment the chance of working with you is gone & so his fire is gone
and he is more detached than the other day. . . . Write me a love letter. I
can't write you nice things till I get one, But I do love you.

                                                      Your loving
                                                      Clem

[1] Sir John Simon, Home Secretary, was the only government minister to resign on the issue of
compulsion. See p. 123 n. 2.

◇ From CSC   Alderley Park
30 December [1915]

My Darling,
   I came here last night & intend to stay till Monday. I hope the change
will cure the melancholia which was dispelled by your return, but which
has now settled on me again! . . .
   I forgot to tell you in yesterday's letter that McKenna absented himself
from the War Council and sulked down at Munstead which caused a mild
flutter, but Ll.G [Lloyd George*] said that a little flattery & cajolery from the
P.M. would bring him round. I suppose that if compulsion is carried
without a single resignation (which seems likely) it will be a feather in the
P.M.'s cap & a vindication of his slow state-craft. I am very much afraid
this is going to be a 'personal triumph' for him.
   I think my Darling you will have to be very patient – Do not burn any
boats – The P.M. has not treated you worse than Ll.G has done, in fact not

so badly for he is not as much in your debt as the other man, (i.e. Marconi[1]). On the other hand are the Dardanelles.

I feel sure that if the choice were equal you would prefer to work with the P.M. than with Ll.G – It's true that when association ceases with the P.M. he cools & congeals visibly, but all the time you were at the Admiralty he was loyal & steadfast while the other would barter you away at any time in any place – I assure you he is the direct descendant of Judas Iscariot. At this moment altho' I hate the P.M., if he held out his hand I could take it, (tho' I would give it a nasty twist) but before taking Ll.G's I would have to safeguard myself with charms, touchwoods, exorcisms & by crossing myself –

I always can get on with him, & yesterday I had a good talk, but you can't hold his eyes, they shift away –

You know I'm not good at pretending, but I am going to put my pride in my pocket and reconnoitre Downing Street.

Even this one night in the country has done me good & I feel able to sit up and take an interest in life – Yesterday I was bitterly dejected & could not quench an endless flow of tears.

McKenna's & Runciman's arguments that if more men are taken the machinery of the country will not function, seemed to me yesterday rather true on my journey. Not a porter to be seen for miles even at the big stations like Crewe & the one or two gray-haired ones who eventually were produced wore khaki armlets[2] – This being the 'Derby County' the men wear the armlets instead of keeping them in their pockets....

Your loving
Clemmie

. . .

Your little grey pocket-book has vanished which is very vexing – But please get enough morphia to soothe <u>one</u> man, not enough to kill 500 – Seriously you might so easily make a mistake if wounded.

Many kisses my own darling.

[1] WSC had done much to help Lloyd George during the Marconi scandal of 1912–13, when the latter failed to reveal to the House of Commons that he owned shares in the American Marconi Company.
[2] Under the 'Derby scheme' introduced in 1915 khaki armlets were worn by those who had attested their willingness to serve in the Army or Navy but had not yet been 'called up', on the basis that young single men would be called up before older married men. A stepping stone between the voluntary system and conscription, the scheme was intended to protect the wearer from zealous recruiting officers and ladies issuing white feathers. Its failure paved the way to the introduction of conscription early in 1916.

O From WSC   [France]
1 January 1916

My darling,

All my tenderest wishes for a Happy New Year. I think it will be better for us than the last – wh after all was not so bad. At any rate our fortunes have more room to expand & less to decline than in Jan[y] last. We must expect a year of war. I do not see how any end will be reached in 1916: and the probability is that 1917 will dawn like this new year in world wide bloodshed & devastation. We must be unyielding & unflinching. We must do more than we have ever done before. We must find a way to win.

Of course I cannot help feeling the lack of scope for my thought & will power. I see so much that ought to be done, that cd easily be done, that will never be done or only half done: and I can't help longing for the power to give those wide directions wh occupied my Admiralty days. There seems such want of drive & fresh thought in the military world. As for the Navy – it has dozed off under that old tabby [Balfour]. All the Allied plans are flowing down into a vast offensive for wh no one has yet found the method.

Well – a battalion is now in the offing, & several others show their sails above the horizon. I expect in a day or two to hoist my pennant in one of them. The most likely is the 6th Royal Scots Fusiliers, in the IXth Division. . . . The general of the Division (I do not know him) Furse[1] is said to be vy capable, & is anxious to have me. The Chief of Staff is that good looking Tom Holland[2] – who you know – a vy old friend of mine, & I think he is busying himself in the matter. So I hope soon to be at work. Our place in the line wd be a few miles to the left of where I was before. (I must not give you a more precise direction.) But I shall be in the same neighbourhood & I don't think it is particularly unhealthy.

I saw Haig yesterday. He was vy polite & friendly: but listless & careworn. G.H.Q. is a desert now – only Philip [Sassoon*][3] sits like a wakeful spaniel outside the door; . . .

I am vy glad you had Ll.G. [Lloyd George*] to lunch. Do this again: & keep in touch. It really is most important. A situation may develop at any time, wh wd throw us inevitably together. Our relations are now good – & shd be kept so.

Of course I cd not leave the Army in the field for any position wh did not give me an effective share in the direction of the war.

Tender love to you & the kittens. Kiss them all often for me. I am writing Diana an answer to her beautiful letter.

Your ever loving
W

[1] Brig.-Gen. (later Sir) William Furse (1865–1953), at this time commanding the 9th (Scottish) Division.
[2] Maj.-Gen. (later Lt-Gen. Sir) Arthur E. A. Holland (1862–1927), known as 'Tom'. Commander of the 1st Division, 1915–16.
[3] Philip Sassoon was now Private Secretary to Sir Douglas Haig.

◇ From CSC   Alderley Park
New Year's Day 1916

My Darling
The only letter I have received from you was the note covering your letter to Lloyd George* written from Dover & I hunger for news of you. The household here . . . is very subdued in spite of seven grand-children – Three daughters of the house, Margaret Goodenough & Blanche Serocold[1] & Sylvia Henley* look patient but war worn. Margaret has seen her Admiral 4 times since the beginning of the war (he is still cruising around

in the Southampton). Blanche is going to have her 3rd child & her husband recovered from his serious wound has his Brigade in the line somewhere – Anthony Henley[2] is moderately safe on a Divisional Staff – Venetia [Montagu*] the prosperous and the happy[3], arrives this evening to enliven us & to lift us out of the Doldrums – We expect to hear from her 'the latest' concerning the crisis – She entertained the P.M. on New Year's Eve to Beer & Skittles – Harold Baker[4] is here and he says that at Thursday's Cabinet McKenna [Chancellor of the Exchequer] opened his case for a 'moderate' sized army (the discussion having shifted from conscription which is 'agreed', to the number of Divisions we are to have in the field) with a slashing attack on Lloyd George's stewardship while at the Exchequer – This onslaught tho' very personal & vindictive & in the best McKenna style was also very damaging –

The gossips say that if McKenna had resigned & Ll.G [Minister of Munitions] had tried to get back to the Exchequer there would have been wholesale resignations of Treasury permanent officials!

McKenna & Runciman may have since given up objecting to conscription – They agree that the Cabinet is bound to redeem the P.M.'s hastily-given pledge. But they have revived the subject of the size of the army & Sir William Robertson[5] is being asked how much he wants; so that Kitchener's 70 Divisions are by no means certainties. I suppose if the numbers are reduced K. will really & truly have to resign, and if he goes with the Die Hards [against conscription] they will be saddled with him. These are my own speculations and I hope you are getting news also from some other source! . . .

. . . Goodbye my Darling – Where are you? I suspect you of having returned to the Guards, but why don't you write?

Clemmie

. . .

[1] Blanche Serocold (1885–1968), daughter of 4th Baron Stanley of Alderley and cousin of CSC. Married 1912 Brig.-Gen. Eric Pearce-Serocold.
[2] Brig.-Gen. Anthony Henley (1873–1925), husband of Sylvia Henley.
[3] Venetia Stanley had married Edwin Montagu on 26 July 1915.
[4] Harold Baker (1877–1960), member of HM Army Council, 1914; Inspector of Quartermaster-General Services, 1916. Known as 'Blue Tooth' or 'Bluey'.
[5] Maj.-Gen. Sir William Robertson (1860–1933), cr. 1st Bt, 1919. Entered Army as private soldier, 1877, and rose from ranks to become Field Marshal, 1920. At this date (1915–18) Chief of Imperial General Staff.

○ From WSC   [France]
2 January 1916

My darling,

I went to see the IXth Division H.Q. last night and was welcomed warmly by Tom Holland & his general. I dined with them & found we were all in full agreement about military matters. They evidently wd like vy much to have me. The general – Furse – is extremely well thought of here and is a thoroughly frank & broadminded man. . . . Most of the staff had met me soldiering somewhere or other, & we had a pleasant evening.

I made careful inquiries about the battalion. Like all the rest of this Scottish division it fought with the greatest gallantry in the big battle[1] & was torn to pieces. More than half the men, & ¾s of the officers were shot, & these terrible gaps have been filled up by recruits of good quality, and quite young inexperienced officers. I shd therefore be able to bring in my two good officers, Spiers & Archie [Sinclair] & put them where I liked. They will be sorely needed. In spite of its crippled condition the regiment has been for two months in the worst part of the line; but now they are resting & do not go in again till the 20th: & then to an easier part. Thus I shd have at least a fortnight to pull them together and get them into my hand. On all these facts I think I shall take them – & I expect to have it settled tomorrow. . . .

You are a vy sapient cat to write as you do in yr last letter [30 December 1915]. But I feel that my work with Asquith* has come to an end. I have found him a weak and disloyal chief. I hope I shall not ever have to serve under him again. After the 'Perhaps he might have a battalion' letter I cannot feel the slightest regard for him any more. Ll.G. [Lloyd George*] is no doubt all you say: but his interests are not divorced from mine and in those circumstances we can work together – if occasion arises. After all he always disagreed about D'Iles [Dardanelles]. He was not like H.H.A. [Asquith], a co-adventurer – approving & agreeing at every stage. And he had the power to put things right both as regards my policy & myself. But his slothfulness & procrastination ruined the policy, & his political nippiness squandered his agmt [argument]. However there is no reason why ordinary relations shd not be preserved.

My dearest one – I will write again tomorrow. I am vexed not to recover the pocket book wh had some pencil notes in it, under the morphia! . . .

With fondest love
Your ever devoted
W

PS It was quite an odd sensation writing to Diana – & signing myself for the first time 'your loving father'!

[1] The Battle of Loos (25 September–8 October 1915), in which the Germans were driven back towards Lens and Loos but their line remained intact; more than 15,000 British soldiers were killed in the first two days of the offensive.

◇ From CSC   41 Cromwell Road
Wednesday 5 January 1916 5 a.m.

My Darling,

When I got home late on Monday night I found your first letter, & another one arrived yesterday morning so I feel revived, but not yet nourished.

I do hope you will take the battalion under General Furse – I have always heard nice things about him. His wife is a nice woman, & when I hear it is all settled I will go and pay my respects to her – . . .

When Ll.G [Lloyd George*] lunched here he had just returned from his Christmas visit to Glasgow – He told me that he had not been very well

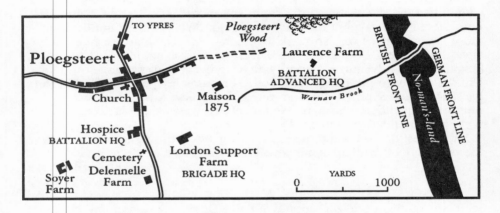

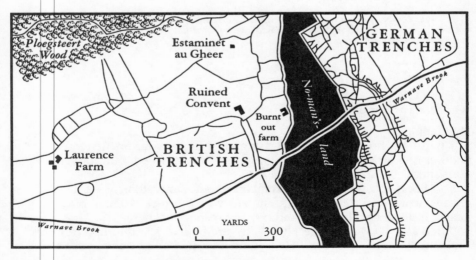

THE PLOEGSTEERT SECTOR OF THE WESTERN FRONT, 1916

received by 'some of the men' who 'interrupted' him – Now it is all leaking out that he very nearly had to do the Birmingham trick[1] again! I believe he never delivered the speech at all, but merely gave it to the press.... The account of the meeting & his whole visit was censored by his order, but the Forward, a Glasgow Socialist rag, has printed a perfectly accurate account of what took place & has now been suspended. I will try & get you a copy. ...

I expect after the Glasgow incident you will find Ll.G more affectionate than ever – He is a barometer, but not a really useful one as he is always measuring his own temperature not yours! ...

– – – Later. The post has come bringing 2 letters from you – Like my food-boxes, they were delayed. So forgive my 'corker' from Alderley –

I will write you more news later in the day. Be sure and let me know when I can address my letters Lt.-Col. and tell me where to send them as G.H.Q. surely makes a delay.

Your very loving
Clemmie
Many kisses to you my Darling.

[1] On 18 December 1901 Lloyd George had been due to speak at the Town Hall in Birmingham: he had aroused hostility particularly among supporters of Joseph Chamberlain (whose fiefdom Birmingham was) by his outspoken criticism of the latter, and by his stance against the Boer War. Unable to make his speech because of the riotous and threatening behaviour of the 7,000-strong audience, Lloyd George dictated the speech and had it distributed to the press as if he had delivered it: he then departed from the Town Hall, disguised as a policeman.

Churchill joined the 6th Battalion Royal Scots Fusiliers at Meteren on 5 January; he and his small staff were billeted in the village of Moolenacker for nearly three weeks. The battalion's task was to hold a thousand yards of the front line centred on the Belgian village of Ploegsteert ('Plug Street' as it became known instantly by the soldiers). As Battalion Commander, Churchill was based alternatively at the hospice in the village belonging to the Sisters of Zion, which was Support Battalion Headquarters, or at Laurence Farm, the Advanced Battalion Headquarters, much nearer the front line.

○ From WSC   France
6 January 1916

My beloved,

I have been a most faithful & regular correspondent since I returned, & every day a long letter has started on its voyage to you. I send them always by the G.H.Q. bag....

I am now deeply immersed in the vy small things wh fall to my lot. I do all I can with zest: but I must confess to many spells of emptiness & despondency at the narrow sphere in wh I work & the severely restricted horizon. When we get into the line this will pass: because war is always war & well worth living through. But a fortnight at least intervenes between us and that experience.

This regiment is pathetic. The young officers are all small middle class Scotsmen – vy brave & willing & intelligent: but of course all quite new to soldiering. All the seniors & all the professionals have fallen. I have spent the morning watching each company in turn drill & handle their arms. They are vy good. The mess also is well managed – much better than with the Grenadiers. The regiment is full of life & strength, & I believe I shall be a help to them. Archie [Sinclair] is vy happy, & I hope he will be made a Major.

Seely[1] decided to return to England for the compulsion Bill & he will I expect have been with you this morning. He will give you all my news. I keep turning things over in my mind without doing much good. But broadly my conclusion is that nothing but a complete change of regime will require me to return – or be of any use. Asquith* will never face the certain elements of opposition hostile to me. Only <u>need</u> will count. Meanwhile I feel vy much the departure of my friend [Sir John French]. Haig tho' civil & I daresay friendly is quite out of my sphere: & I do not think he takes any active interest in my affairs one way or the other –

This is a disorganised sort of letter; but you must make allowances! My strong natural vitality will carry me along.

Always yr devoted
W

[1] Maj.-Gen. John ('Jack') Seely (1868–1947), cr. 1st Baron Mottistone, 1933. Secretary of State for War, 1912–14; Commander of the Canadian Cavalry Brigade, 1915–18.

O From WSC   6 Royal Scots Fusiliers
7 January 1916   France

My darling,

I expect I have missed the post.... Meanwhile my removal from H.Q. has interposed a new delay in my own incoming mail, & I must just wait without news at a time when it wd be specially interesting & welcome. I watch in The Times (6th inst) the movement of political things & I must confess it excites & disturbs my mind. I try however not to look back too much, having not only put my hand but fettered it to the plough. I must rely on you to keep constant touch with the friends & pseudo-friends I have. I do not like to feel forgotten & déconsidéré out here – especially when I am not in the trenches, but only waiting in reserve billets – i.e. squalid little French farms rising from a sea of sopping fields & muddy lanes.

I made my battalion parade this morning & drilled them myself all together. They have not done this before and I am anxious to make them feel their corporate identity & the sense of my personal control. A colonel within his own sphere is an autocrat who punishes & promotes & displaces at his discretion. The Brigadier[1] is leaving me to myself for these first days in order that I may get all the threads in my hand. It is not hard to me to give orders as you know and I do not feel at all overweighted. Archie [Sinclair] does a vast amount of household work, & the young officers are also made to do their full share.

... I feel vy much bound on the wheel of things out here, and when politics calm down again, I shall yield myself to the inexorable motion with suppleness and placidity. But peace here & crisis at home make a disturbing combination for my mind.

You cannot write to me too often or too long – my dearest & sweetest. The beauty & strength of your character, & the sagacity of yr judgment are more realised by me every day. I ought to have followed yr counsels in my days of prosperity. Only sometimes they are too negative. I shd have made nothing if I had not made mistakes. Ungrateful country!

Tenderest love to you & the kittens.
Your devoted husband W.

[1] Brig.-Gen. Henry Walshe (1866–1947), Commander of 27th Infantry Brigade, Sept. 1915–April 1916.

◇ From CSC   41 Cromwell Road
Sunday 9 January 1916

My Darling,

To-day, I lunched at Downing Street & for the first time since you resigned talked to the P.M. He talked a great deal about you and asked a great many questions. I was perfectly natural (except perhaps that I was a little too buoyant) & he tried to be natural too, but it was an effort. I think it is a good thing to keep up civil relations & it is always interesting to follow the Block's train of thought. He seemed very much pleased at the <u>Parliamentary</u> situation, but I expect things must still be very uncertain judging from the fact that this is the 2nd Sunday he has spent in London. The new pet is Robertson, poor old K[itchener] has not a friend left. Violet [Asquith*/Bonham Carter]'s sharp tongue has been playing round him!... she & Bongey have returned from their Italian honeymoon.... Randolph wishes you to write to him & is very insistent about it....

No letter from you yesterday and no post to-day becos' it's Sunday & I'm longing for news of your regiment & of you.

Tender love and many kisses from
Clemmie

. . .

○ From WSC   6th Royal Scots Fusiliers
10 January 1916   In the field

My darling,

Your two letters of the 5th & 6th have at last reached me & will I hope be the heralds of a stream.

I continue to work at the details of my battalion wh is officered entirely by quite young boys ... they yield implicit loyalty & obedience &

endeavour to meet or forestall every wish. I am fairly confident of being able to help them to do well, in spite of the woefully attentuated state of the regiment's officers.

The guns boom away in the distance, & at night the sky to the Northward blinks & flickers with the wicked lights of war. But otherwise we are lapped in profound tranquillity. This little farm house is quite comfortable, though my bedroom is large enough only to hold a bed.

I think it is rather hard lines on Ll.G. [Lloyd George*] to be mocked at for going and facing those ill-conditioned Glasgow syndicalists. He has not played a loyal or a clever game. But still keep in touch with him. I cannot see any way in wh Asquith's* interests can stand in need of me. However friendly his feelings, his interests are best served by my effacement. If I were killed he wd be sorry: but it wd suit his political hand. Ll.G. on the other hand wd not be sorry, but it wd not suit his political hand. It is this factor that alone counts in the cruel politics of to-day. I can feel no sense of loyalty or friendship for Asquith after the revelation of his utter indifference shown by his letter to French. Still here again there is no occasion for a personal breach.

Whenever my mind is not occupied by war, I feel deeply the injustice with wh my work at the Admiralty has been treated. I cannot help it – tho' I try. Then the damnable mismanagement wh has ruined the Dardanelles enterprise & squandered vainly so much life & opportunity cries aloud for retribution: & if I survive, the day will come when I will claim it publicly. . . .

> Tender love my dearest one
> Your ever devoted
> W

P.S. I do not ever show anything but a smiling face to the military world: a proper complete detachment & contentment. But so it is a relief to write one's heart out to you. Bear with me.

◇ From CSC   41 Cromwell Road
11 January [1916]

My Darling

Yesterday a batch of 3 letters arrived simultaneously. I think the field post is probably as good as a 'bag'; . . .

I knew my Darling that you would be feeling the political excitement of the last 10 days.

Everybody here seemed rather thrilled, but I could not get worked up over it as it seemed impossible to me that the anti-compulsionists would face the racket. I'm afraid I can't agree that the P.M.'s position is only temporarily strengthened – He will always in the end tip down on the side of strong measures after delaying them & devitalising them so as to try and keep everybody together.

His method of defeating the enemy is not by well planned lightning strokes, but by presenting to him a large stolid gelatinous mass which he (the enemy) is supposed to pommel in vain.

I am afraid the war will drag slowly to its end with him & K[itchener] still at the helm. No one trusts Ll.G [Lloyd George*] & Bonar [Law] is light metal. These are only my own reflections as I have seen no-one of consequence for some days – yesterday I was very sad, the end of Gallipoli & a fine battleship gone down[1].

If you ask the P.M. to publish the Dardanelles papers let me know what happens. If he refuses or delays I beg you not to do anything without telling me first & giving me time to give you my valuable (!) opinion on it. It is an unequal match between the P.M. & an officer in the field in war-time....

... Are you quite certain however that this is the best time for publication, when you are away and not able to speak in the debate which is bound to take place? I am very anxious that you should not blunt this precious weapon prematurely....

Tender love to you and kisses my darling,
from
Clemmie.

[1] In mid-January the last of our troops were evacuated from Gallipoli. The battleship *King Edward VII* struck a mine in the Pentland Firth and sank on 6 January 1916; no lives were lost.

◇ From CSC   41 Cromwell Road
12 January 1916

My own Darling,

I long so to be able to comfort you. Later on when you are in danger in the trenches you will be equable and contented, while I, who am now comparatively at ease will be in mortal anxiety. Try not to brood too much; I would be so unhappy if your naturally open and unsuspicious nature became embittered. Patience is the only grace you need. If you are not killed, as sure as day follows night you will come into your own again – I know you don't fear death, it is I who dread that. But I am almost glad to be suffering now, becos' I am sure no single soul will be allowed to live thro' this time without sorrow, so perhaps what we are enduring now will be counted and we shall be spared the greatest pain of all.

I remember quite well when we were at the Admiralty during those wonderful opening weeks of the war we were both so happy, you with the success of the Naval preparations & with the excitement of swiftly moving events and I with pride at the glamour surrounding you & the Navy – I remember feeling guilty and ashamed that the terrible casualties of those first battles did not sadden me more. I wondered how long we should continue to tread on air –

When it is all over we shall be proud that you were a soldier & not a politician for the greater part of the war – soldiers and soldiers' wives seem to me now the only real people.

I am glad you tell me all you feel my Darling, I want to know it all. I too shew a detached and smiling face to the world.

I have Goonie for a safety-valve & you must make use of Archie [Sinclair] who is safe and loyal – Do not tell curious acquaintances of your opinion of the P.M.'s character or policy....

We hope now that Cape Helles has been evacuated that Jack [Churchill*] may come home on leave, but we have had no news....

I will try and see Lloyd George* again –

I wish I had some interesting news for you.

Goodbye my Darling. I send you many kisses –

Your letters are very precious.

Your loving
Clemmie

...

Do you want any more cigars yet?

O From WSC   6 RSF [Royal Scots Fusiliers]
13 January 1916   In the field

My darling,

I have got behindhand in my letters – not because much has been happening – but little! The days slip away quickly enough, & tho' I run in and out of good spirits, on the whole they pass pleasantly. The Brigadier-General [Walshe] has left me quite alone, tho' vy civil – He has not meddled at all in my affairs wh I am conducting with confidence....
Yesterday I spent seeing all the officers & NCO's, company by company & explaining to them how I wish things to be done. It was odd to see these politicians of a year ago – Glasgow grocers, fitters, miners – all Trade Unionists probably, who I have harangued in bygone days in the St Andrews Hall – now all transformed into Sergeants & corporals stiffened by discipline and hardened by war into a fine set of warriors.

In the morning Archie [Sinclair] & I practised bomb-throwing. It is a job to be approached gingerly. You pull out the safety pin, & then as long as you hold the bomb in your hand nothing happens.... As soon as you have thrown it, you bob down behind the parapet, until the explosion has occurred.... Everyone has to learn. It is perfectly simple & safe as long as you do it right....

Ll.G. [Lloyd George*] by all accounts is isolated. He has been vy foolish in his relations with me, Bonar Law, F.E. [Smith*] & Curzon. He might have combined us all. As it is he has earned the deep distrust of each, & I who was his friend and had worked with him so long, have now largely by his action been rendered quite powerless for the time being.

You do not tell me in yr letter what the PM said. You only say he said a lot. But I shd like a verbatim report of the Kat's conversation with the old ruffian. He has handspiked compulsion as long as he cd, & long after it was needed; & only adopted it in the end, against his deepest convictions, to keep his office – or what is perhaps truer – to keep Ll.G. out of his office; and for this 'statecraft' at the expense of our arms & treasure – he is acclaimed as the saviour of the Nation....

Thank God they got off Helles all right. I expect the Turks were as exhausted as our men, & only too glad to let them get away. Also perhaps a little money changed hands: & rendered this scuttle of 'imperishable memory' less dangerous than it looked. Well as the Lokalanzeiger [Berlin newspaper] joyfully remarks – 'Churchill's dream of a victorious march to Constantinople is at an end.' I am going to take my battalion for a route march this morning instead.

At last all of a sudden your big Christmas hamper has arrived. I never saw such dainties & profusion. We shall eat them sparingly keeping the best for the trenches....

I am looking forward keenly to having these boys in the line. Another week of rest wd be more welcome after our 12 days' spell than before it....

I am going to write to Randolph. Give him & all the kittens my fondest love & many kisses.

Accept the same yourself my darling one

Your ever devoted
W.

○ From WSC   6th Royal Scots Fusiliers
16 January 1916   In the field

My beloved,

Your letter of 12th is splendid. I run in & out of moods; but I do not doubt the wisdom & necessity of my coming out here: nor do I repent at all my decision. I cd not have agreed to the Dardanelles-Salonika policy & to resign on such an issue wd have been most difficult. Neither cd I have sat still in England – painting to keep my mind quiet & waiting for the wind to change. Here I have to sit still; but somehow dullness does not fret me. The days slip quickly by & soon the work will become more interesting. Even a month out of the line sets the generals' minds onto parade smartness, & all the little points of peace time soldiering. This battalion is the weakest in the brigade & makes the least good appearance.... Up to the present however I have been entirely occupied with practical points – gas helmets, rifles in good order, trench discipline & routine etc. As we are going to be a week more out of the line, I shall give them some vy precise drill & marching. It is all helpful.

I pause for <u>Bath</u> – a bi-weekly event. A large tub – hot water getting cold. I will resume later....

This afternoon, the sports I have arranged are to come off & in the evening after dark we have a regimental concert, to wh Jack Seely & possibly the Chief of Staff – Holland are coming. The officers & men have taken a lively interest in both affairs. It is odd no one has got any up for them before. We have got hold of a piano – & much practising has been going on.... I will let you know how it goes off. I think they want nursing & encouraging, more than drill-sergeanting; but we must follow the fashion.

Always your loving & devoted
W.

◇ From CSC   41 Cromwell Road
16 January 1916

My Darling

Nellie & Bertram have arrived from their country retreat & are spending a few days in London at 56 Eccleston Square which belongs to Bertram's father. I dropped them there last night after a play & it felt like old days when we were first married driving round that secluded enclosure with its handsome trees and grimy laurels – They look very happy & cannot be parted for one moment. . . .

If you received the impression from my letter that the P.M. 'said a lot' about politics and the situation I gave you a wrong impression – He talked a great deal about trivialities and femininities which you know he adores and he asked a good many questions about you & about the detail of your life out there – He <u>wanted</u> the answers to be reassuring, and my good manners as a guest forbade me making him uncomfortable which of course I could easily have done. He seemed grateful to me for sparing him – ! He is a sensualist & if I had depicted you in a tragic & sinister light it would have ruined his meal & I should probably not be bidden again! Darling I do not like you even to write (becos' if you write it I fear you say it) that the P.M. has acted against his 'deepest convictions' '<u>to keep his office</u>.' I always assume that all (first-class) politicians act from high motives, becos' I am the wife of a politician! I object to people saying 'Politics are a dirty game' and other things like that. I expect in a year or two to see you in high office, so you mustn't debase the currency! . . .

I'm told that the P.M. remarked the other day, with satisfaction, that there was not a single large town where Ll[oyd]-George* could address a Meeting without a row from the working-men – . . .

Tender Love from
Clemmie

Later

. . .

My canteens are increasing every day – There is a big new Government factory in the Hackney Marshes opening in six weeks. . . . It will employ 3,000 men, half working by day & half by night – I have been asked to undertake the feeding arrangements . . . 1,000 men must be fed at one sitting & the canteen is to be open day & night. . . .

Aunt Cornelia must be a proud woman – A son Viceroy of Ireland and a son-in-law Vice-roy of India![1]

If I came to Dieppe could you get 2 days' leave? I do long to see you. I'm very very lonely –

. . .

---

[1] Refers to her son Ivor, who had succeeded his father as 2nd Baron Wimborne and was Lord Lieutenant of Ireland, 1915–18; and to her son-in-law, Frederick Thesiger, 3rd Baron (later 1st Viscount) Chelmsford (1868–1933), appointed Viceroy of India in 1916, whose wife was Frances Guest, her daughter.

O From WSC   [France]
17 January 1916

My darling,
   The sports were highly successful & the men were really delighted. They
were most amusing sports – mule races, pillow fights, obstacle races etc.
All well organised, & supported by gt keenness & interest. After dark we
had our first concert in a big barn. Such singing you never heard. People
sang with the greatest courage who had no idea either of words or tune.
Jack Seely ... presented the prizes for the sports, & called for three cheers
for me & an extra one for you, wh were most heartily given. We had quite
a banquet in the evening – ... Quite a cheery day. The men enjoyed
themselves immensely. Poor fellows – nothing like this had ever been
done for them before. They do not get much to brighten their lives – short
though these may be....
   Air fights have been going on overhead this morning, & I think there
has been an air raid on some of the neighbouring townships, as a lot of
our machines are up. There is no excuse for our not having command of
the air.
   Since I left the Admiralty, the whole naval wing has been let down: & all
our previous ascendancy has been dissipated. If they had given me control
of this service when I left the Admiralty, we shd have supremacy today.
Asquith* wanted this, but in contact with the slightest difficulty &
resistance, he as usual shut up....

                                        Tender love
                                        Your devoted
                                               W.

...

O From WSC   R.S.F.
18 January 1916   In the field

My darling,
   Orders have now come in that we march nearer the line on 24th, go into
support 26th & actually take over the trenches 27th. Where we go I must
not write – but it is at present a vy quiet part of the line – much quieter
than that wh the Guards used to hold. I will tell you more about its
character when I have seen it, as I hope to do on Thursday.
   All goes well with the battalion & I think they are coming well into
hand. But I am sorry to detect a distinctly hostile tone in the Brigade
Staff....
   On the other hand the Divisional people are genuinely friendly. Furse
came round yesterday morning to see us, & I took him into [the] Orderly
room & introduced him to all my officers. Tom Holland too – who is the
brain of this Division and its most accomplished soldier – is of course a
thoroughly trustworthy friend....
   Bath, bi-weekly is now clamouring for me.
   I rode into – – – [Hazebrouck] (the town) yesterday to attend Tom
Holland's lecture on the Battle of Loos. The theatre was crowded with

generals & officers.... Tom spoke vy well but his tale was one of hopeless failure, of sublime heroism utterly wasted & of splendid Scottish soldiers shorn away in vain – with never the ghost of a chance of success. 6,000 k[illed] & w[ounded] out of 10,000 in this Scottish division alone. Alas alas. Afterwards they asked what was the lesson of the lecture. I restrained an impulse to reply 'Don't do it again'. But they will – I have no doubt.

Your ever devoted
W.

○ From WSC   St Omer
19 January 1916   [G.H.Q.]

My beloved,

I am in here for an hour or two. All the day I have been at the Machine gun school, with scores of Colonels listening to not vy illuminating lectures....

My precious – I don't take back a word of what I wrote about Asquith*. He has cruelly & needlessly wronged me; & even in his power & prosperity has had the meanness to strike at me. No – if I survive – my political life will be apart from him. He passes from my regard. My mind is now filling up with ideas & opinions in many military & war matters. But I have no means of expression. I am impotent to give what is there to be given – of truth & value & urgency. I must wait in silence the sombre movement of events. Still it is better to be gagged than give unheeded counsel....

I had a nice letter from Rothermere – saying that 'I had emerged unscathed from Gallipoli'. Do I beseech you keep in touch with him; & also through Aitken [Beaverbrook*] with Bonar Law. Don't neglect these matters – I have no one but you to act for me. I shd like you to make the seeing of my friends a regular business – like your canteens wh are going so well. It is fatal to let the threads drop. Curzon, FE [Smith*]; B.L [Bonar Law]; Carson; Garvin; Rothermere; Goulding; Alick M[1], all these you shd keep in touch with. There is nothing to ask of them – only represent me in their circle....

Well this is a moody letter. 6 o'clock is a bad hour for me. I feel the need of power as an outlet worst then; & the energy of mind & body is strong within me –

Fisher suffers too – alas he ruined us both. No, Kitchener with his muddles did that....

... Tell Randolph I am going to write him a letter tomorrow.

Tender love my sweet bird – I shd indeed be homeless without you.

Your devoted
W

[1] Alexander Murray, Baron Murray of Elibank (1870–1920), Under-Secretary of State for India, 1909; Chief Liberal Whip, 1909–12. At this date Director of Recruiting for Munition Works.

◇ From CSC   41 Cromwell Road
20 January [1916]

My own Darling

I have just sent you (via Creedy & King's Messenger) your Colonel's
tunic, . . .

My Darling, thro' all your moods, never regret resigning at the moment
you did – You would as you say have been practically forced to do so
later, on the Dardanelles evacuation, which as it has turned out to be
completely successful would not have left you in nearly so good a
position.

You would have been miserable doing nothing in England –

It makes me terribly anxious to feel that your battalion is so weak. It will
be a great credit to you if you improve it & bring it up to the mark. Do not
think me over-cautious, but don't be too ambitious at first or try your men
too high – I wish you were not going so soon with these untried men into
the line. . . . Randolph clamours for a letter – He is getting very grown-up
[four+ years] and expects a lot of attention. Later – – – Important & please
answer this by return. Rosie [Ridley] is going over to Paris to help her
sister, Lady Chelmsford to buy her vice-regal trousseau – She suggested I
should accompany her if you could get a few days' leave to come to Parigi
[Paris]. Tell me if you could. I shall not go unless you are sure you could
come as it will be very expensive anyhow (going with Rosie more so).
Rosie wants to know if you can shew her any battlefields – I told her I
feared you could not in your present position leave your new raw men. . . .
                              Tenderest Love to you my Darling from
                                                             Clemmie

I hope you love me very much Darling – I long for you often – I wake up
in the night and think of you in your squalid billet & of all the women in
Europe who are lying awake praying for safety for their men.

○ From WSC   6th Royal Scots Fusiliers
20 January 1916   In the Field

My beloved,

I wrote a miauling letter yesterday, & I expect the Kat will be flustered
by my directives to her to keep in touch with so many people. Do only
just what comes easily & naturally to you my darling. On the other hand
don't simply vanish out of the political circle & plunge into bed &
canteens. Do what you can.

I have just come back from the line, having had a jolly day. I examined
the whole of our front & all its approaches thoroughly. It is much the best
bit of line I have yet seen all along the front. Incomparably better on every
score than the sector where the Guards were. It is dry – the trenches are
boarded & drained. The parapets are thick & bullet-proof. The wire is
good. The field of fire clear. . . . I think we cd stand a pretty good
pounding here with comparatively little loss. . . . The battalion H.Q. (where
I live) is about 500 yards only from the trenches in a farmhouse [Laurence

Farm]. This is often good quarters. I have a small room to myself with a little cellar underneath where Archie [Sinclair] thinks of establishing himself. . . .

I am rather attracted by the cellars of a ruined convent right up in the firing line, & if they can be drained & made comfortable they wd be a better and safer H.Q. especially for fighting purposes than this commodious but conspicuous farm. . . .

There was a little shelling to-day. The weather beautiful in the morning. I shall like this line vy much & shall feel vy proud to take charge of 1,000 yards of 'the frontier between right & wrong'. . . .

It was vy odd your putting in your letter yesterday about Dieppe. The same idea was in my mind when I received your letter before I opened it. It cd be arranged I think, but not till we have had a spell or two in the line & all is running smoothly. I will try to fix a date in about 3 weeks. I wd love to see you, & Dieppe is quiet – no spiteful newspapers or gossiping people. It wd be divine – this is a khaki world – My dearest soul I shd like to do this so much.

The following is important: Buy <u>at once</u> from the Army & Navy Stores a small 'Corona' typewriter & send it out here by the tamest King's Messenger or the best route open to you. I want it to instil more order & style into my official correspondence. At present we scribble in pencil, & it all looks vy slipshod. My new tunic has not yet arrived. I fear it has got on to that bloody Havre route.

Your ever loving & devoted
W

. . .

◇ From CSC   41 Cromwell Road
21 January [1916]

My Darling

Three letters from you reached me in a batch this morning – one of them describing the sports and the concert written in good spirits, the others in a sombre mood. I never long to be with you so much as when you are sad – (Jan 22). . . .

The plan of going with Rosie to Paris to see you is no use as you tell me that from the 24th you begin to approach the trenches. Oh my dearest I can't get used to the idea –

I will try & see your friends, but everyone 'in office' seems to be unbelievably smug – Were we like that when you were in power? There is an atmospheric non-conductive barrier between those whose men are in danger & those whose men are in powerful security at home. The Treasury now contemplate withdrawing M.P.'s pay from soldiers in the field on the ground they cannot perform both duties at once[1]. Last night Edwin Montagu reminded me how long ago when the idea was mooted how angry you were with him. . . . Everyone not in office is much disturbed at the gradual ascendancy of the German aeroplane. If only, when you left the Admiralty you had been given the 'air'! – I believe if you had really tried for it you might have got it, as in the press there was a movement in that direction – Do you think there is a chance even now tho' 'too late'?

The P.M. has alarmed people by announcing that there is a serious shortage of Munition Workers for the new National Factories. I hope this is not the prelude of future disclosures revealing want of foresight & muddle. I think it will take Ll[oyd] George* (even allowing for his marvellous recuperative powers) a long time to recover – If tomorrow the P.M. disappeared Bonar Law would be the successor. He has made a great impression in the House during these last weeks by his skilful handling of delicate topics & this impression will spread to the country – Myself I think Bonar is not a big man, but he is a very skilful one & does not miss his markets. I think Ll.George will remain 'perdu' for a bit & then gradually slide away from his 'compulsion' attitude towards the working men.

Montagu after an absence of 6 months from the Cabinet[2] finds very little change except a greater disinclination to action, the only Warrior is Curzon.

God bless you my Darling & keep you safe
Your loving
Clemmie

[1] On 17 February the Prime Minister recommended that no MP should receive both a parliamentary salary and soldier's pay. This controversial motion was withdrawn in April.
[2] With the change of government in May 1915 Edwin Montagu had left the Cabinet, relinquishing his Chancellorship of the Duchy of Lancaster, and returned to the Treasury as Financial Secretary. He re-entered the Cabinet in January 1916 as a member of the War Committee, Financial Secretary to the Treasury, and was restored to the Duchy of Lancaster.

○ From WSC   6th Royal Scots Fusiliers
23 January 1916   In the Field

My darling,

... Today I lunched with Tom Holland at the Division H.Q. & Archie [Sinclair] & I have just cantered back across the fields. Holland completely reassured me about the Brigade Staff. The Brigadier [Walshe] had been he said much perturbed at the idea of my coming; but was now content, & had said that it had been a vy gt advantage to the battalion wh had sensibly improved. Furse also had been full of praise. So at any rate we go into the line with a good backing.

Last night Archie & I entertained all the officers at a Regimental dinner in the neighbouring town. We sat down 20 & had an elaborate feast beginning with oysters & lots of champagne.... I made the officers a little speech, & the Bde Major told them all about the regiment in the battle: & the pipes played doleful dirges; & we sang Auld Lang Syne and generally there was a scene of much enjoyment. This is the first time they had ever been brought together around a table. Poor lads, they were really delighted.

Altogether things here have now gone vy well. I put it to Holland & the General (Furse) not to hustle us into raids etc till we had really got a full knowledge of the terrain & the enemy; ...

I am going to establish meanwhile a duplicate Headquarters in the cellars of the convent – wh I shall call 'The Conning Tower' where all my telephones will be installed so that if they tease us too much at the Farm [Laurence] I shall have a second string to my bow.

... I am enchanted at the idea of F.E. [Smith*] coming out. Tell him to keep it secret so as to give no handle for political & newspaper gossip. I told him to come to see you & bring everything that you give him. Brandy & cigars wd be welcome....

I do not think I cd get to Paris easily – or get away at all just yet. Dieppe in about 3 weeks is most promising. O my beautiful darling it is a wonderful thing to possess your sweet love. Don't worry about my safety – the Fates have decided that. I do not think this will be particularly dangerous. Women & children are still living in the farms & houses near where we shall be. It is against the rules for a commanding officer to take part personally in minor enterprises. He has to remain at a telephone in a bomb proof (more or less) dugout....

Your ever loving & devoted
W

P.S.... I get Archie to frank & sign these letters for me in order not to excite the curiosity of some censor. Then I take my chance with the best, 100 to 1. Besides I am vy discreet.

◇ From CSC   41 Cromwell Road
24 January [1916]

My Darling,

I have ordered your Brandy, Stilton, raisins etc, ...

I have also purchased your type-writer (11 guineas) and will find a tame messenger, but he will have to be very extra tame as it is a heavy parcel.

To-day I lunched with Lloyd George* & had easy & pleasant talk with him – He is very anxious to be amiable – He talked about current events; just now he is quite out of it – I brought in Bonar Law's name & said how well he had led the House. He didn't like that much & said that he had estranged more Tories than he had conciliated Liberals – He is going to France next week & says he means to seek you out.... He is going to open a big new canteen for me & I have promised to produce 1000 friendly Munition Workers to listen to him!...

Now don't scold your Kat too much for being a hermit. Here in two days I have hob-nobbed with Montagu, Birrell[1], Lloyd George and a South African potentate! Tomorrow night I am dining with Cassel. Please send me home the Distinguished Conduct Medal at once & much praise – A long letter has at last arrived from Jack [Churchill*] – Still at Mudros [in Egypt] with Birdwood[2] with whom he is staying. The French have given him (Jack) the Légion d'Honneur which excites us very much....

Lloyd George expressed a great wish for a long talk with you – I get on so well with him & I know he likes me, but he is a sneak – I would never like you to be intimately connected becos tho' he seems to recover again

& again from his muddles and mistakes I am not sure his partner would; he would instead be saddled with the whole lot while Ll.G skipped off laughing.

Your conspicuous farm makes me nervous – I prefer the cellars of the convent. Do ask Archie to get some hand-pumps and bail them out.

Tender love to you my own
Your loving
Clemmie

Have put salt on King's Messenger's Tail – He is taking type-writer

[1] Augustine Birrell (1850–1933), barrister, writer and Liberal MP. President, Board of Education, 1905–7; Chief Secretary to the Lord Lieutenant of Ireland, 1907–16.
[2] Lt-Gen. Sir William Birdwood (1865–1951), Field Marshal, 1925; cr. 1st Baron Birdwood, 1938. GOC Australian and New Zealand Army Corps, 1914–18; commanded Anzac Corps in Gallipoli landings. Jack Churchill had joined Birdwood's staff in October 1915.

○ From WSC   6th Royal Scots Fusiliers
24 January 1916   In the Field

My darling,

... Your letter of the 22nd has just arrived, also one from Goonie – the first I have had. My new tunic & Glengarry reached here as we marched in, ... The battalion has now got 500 steel helmets & looked vy imposing on the line of march. I spent the afternoon walking round the farmhouses & barns where the men are billeted & discussed the war with the French women who carry on the business in the absence of all but old men & children....

Of course I wd take an Air Ministry – if it were offered me <u>provided</u> it carried with it a seat on the War Council. But the P.M. will never face the minor difficulties of such a departure, & I am sure he knows that his interests are best served by my political or other extinction. I think over a gt many plans; but it is better to go on simply here for a while....

It is splendid having you at home to think about me & love me & share my inmost fancies. What shd I find to hold on to without you. All my gt political estate seems to have vanished away – all my friends are mute – all my own moyens are in abeyance. But there is the Kat with her kittens, supplied I trust adequately with cream & occasional mice. That is all my world in England.

Most tender love & many many kisses –
from your ever loving & devoted
W.

○ From WSC   6th Royal Scots Fusiliers
26 January 1916   In the Field

My Beloved,

I am extremely well lodged here [at the Hospice] – with a fine bedroom looking out across the fields to the German lines 3,000 yards away. Two nuns remain here and keep up the little chapel which is a part of the building. They received me most graciously when I marched in this morning, saying that we had saved this little piece of Belgium from the Germans, who were actually here for a week before being driven out. I have made the women at all the billets where I have stayed make their excellent soup for us – wh they do most gladly – ... On the right & left the guns are booming, & behind us a British field piece barks like a spaniel at frequent intervals. But the women & children still inhabit the little town & laugh at the shells wh occasionally buff into its old Church.... The trenches are good, well wired, with a broad interval between the lines. The houses have been little damaged. Some of the men of the battalion we are relieving call it 'The Convalescent Home'. I think instead of being anxious you ought to set your mind gratefully at peace. The Btn we are relieving has lost 70 men only in 4 months: whereas in one day where I was before the Grenadiers lost 20 – doing nothing.

We take over the trenches before daylight tomorrow. You must not suppose that they will not be adequately defended. Although we have only 700 men instead of 900 wh our predecessors have, 1,050 wh we ought to have, we have more machine guns – so important. Rest assured there will be no part of the line from the Alps to the sea better guarded. It will be watched with the vigilance that mobilised the Fleet.

This morning marching in in the half light a soldier from another regiment shouted out 'We wish you were back with the Navy Sir – Good old Enchantress' I wonder where he came from....

I am sorry for what you tell me about Ll.G. [Lloyd George*]. He has been vy faithless & is now friendless. Still he has been more on the true trail than anyone else in this war.

I shd find it vy difficult to write anything for print here. The days pass quickly, & my daily letter to you makes an inroad on my time equal to the pleasure & relief it gives me to write. I had almost lost the art of writing at the Admiralty. I am gradually regaining it through my missives to you – My darling One....

There are 2 bright red pigs rooting about among the shell holes of the meadow in front of this house. I think they must be Belgian Tamworths[1].

Your own – ever & forever
W

[1] A breed of English pig.

◇ From CSC   41 Cromwell Road
27 January 1916

My Darling

A telephone message came this morning from F.E. [Smith*] saying that he is going to France tomorrow & asking me to dinner – So I am sending this by him & also the type-writer ... Cigars, Brandy & periscope I hope to send also....

The opening of my canteen by Ll.G [Lloyd George*] is assuming rather formidable proportions! It is developing into a public meeting & the Manager of the Works is arranging for him to speak to the day & night shifts at the same time ..., so he will be speaking to about 2,000 men. I am in complete charge of the arrangements & feel like a Chief Whip! He will get a very good reception I hope, a pleasant change from the Clyde. I went to see Ll.George[1] at the Ministry of Munitions & he received me in his palatial apartment, where he was sitting in solitary grandeur....

A letter just came from you my Darling with tender messages of affection for me. Do not fear, your political Estate has not vanished, it is all waiting for you when the right moment comes, which (Alas for the country) may not be till after the war – If only you come safely thro'.

To-day is your first day in the trenches & how I pray you may be protected. I hope you wear a steel helmet always & not the Glengarry....

It seems so hard that I cannot come & see you – It wld be so easy & I cld live with the poor French women in a ruined cottage & hoe turnips. Randolph was overjoyed with your letter.

> My love & many tender kisses
> from
> Clemmie
>
> . . .

[1] At this date Minister of Munitions.

○ From WSC   6th Royal Scots Fusiliers
27 January 1916   In the Field

My darling –

The relief was accomplished this morning before daylight with the utmost precision in under 2 hours. I don't think the Grenadiers ever did better. We now hold about 1,000 yards of trenches & I am responsible for this whatever happens. We have so far had no losses – though there has been shelling & sniping & our parapet has at one place been blown in. All is proceeding regularly & the day has been quiet & normal in spite of being the Emperor's birthday. I spent three hours in the trenches this morning deciding on all the improvements I am going to make in them, & looking into the arrangements of the company commanders. It is now dark, & we are able to light our fire without being betrayed by the smoke, so that we shall get a hot dinner as usual. Archie [Sinclair] is now going round the trenches, & I shall go again after dinner. It takes nearly 2 hours to traverse this labyrinth of mud....

I talked to all the officers for an hour last night, & gave them my ideas & directions & various hints. 'Don't be careless about yourselves – on the other hand not too careful. Keep a special pair of boots to sleep in & only get them muddy in a real emergency. Use alcohol in moderation but don't have a great parade of bottles in yr dugouts. Live well but do not flaunt it. Laugh a little, & teach your men to laugh – gt good humour under fire – war is a game that is played with a smile. If you can't smile grin. If you can't grin keep out of the way till you can.' Since Polonius' advice to Laertes there had been nothing like it – I trust they were edified. . . .

I am delighted Ll.G [Lloyd George*] is coming to France and I hope we shall meet. I have much to say to him. You have indeed been active seeing all those people. It is so important to be there & not there at the same time. Persevere. The D.C.M. is yours. . . .

About food – the sort of things I want you to send me are these – large slabs of corned beef: stilton cheeses: cream: hams: sardines – dried fruits: you might almost try a big beef steak pie: but not tinned grouse or fancy tinned things. The simpler the better: & substantial too; for our ration meat is tough & tasteless: & here we cannot use a fire by daylight. I fear you find me vy expensive to keep. Mind you bill me for all these apart from your housekeeping. . . .

With fondest love my own darling, your ever loving & devoted – greedy though I fear you will say

W.

P.S. I see a new tone in some of the press cuttings about my work at the Admiralty. The atmosphere is less spiteful. . . .

◇ From CSC   41 Cromwell Road
30 January [1916]

My darling

Today the newspapers contain very alarming news of a German attack – I wish I knew for certain that it was nowhere in your neighbourhood – No letters from you lately, the last is dated Jan: 24th. . . .

The atmosphere here is very bleak & gloomy & chills my heart in the spare moments of my work – The Government people are unbelievably smug – I am seeing them occasionally to please you my Darling but I cannot take any interest in these soul-less cold-blooded tortoises & I have ceased to feel any curiosity about them. I feel that is the attitude of the general public towards them, just bored with them, but not hostile becos' our obvious substitute is not on the horizon and the country must be governed by somebody. I shall be seeing Lloyd George* again this week & will then do a little prospecting in the Bonar Law area & then in the Curzon district. None of these potentates seem to be working together or forming any sort of combination – . . .

I fear this trivial letter will be no good to you my Darling; I am rather in the rut to-day & can see only miles & miles of uphill road – Are your men & officers religious? Tell me if being near danger makes you think of Christ. Being unhappy brings Him to my thoughts but only, I fear, becos' I want to be comforted not becos' I want Him for Himself. I copy a little poem out which I sometimes think about[1] – I keep sending you the press-cuttings – It is quite out of the common to come across a sentence that is not ignorant & prejudiced. But all this does not really influence the public agst you becos' the public is very fond of your personality.

Goodbye my Dearest Love – I send you tender kisses and fervent wishes for your safety.

Your loving
Clemmie

> Does the road wind uphill all the way?
>   Yes, to the very end.
> Will the day's journey take the whole long day?
>   From morn to night, my friend.
>
> But is there for the night a resting-place?
>   A roof for when the slow, dark hours begin.
> May not the darkness hide it from my face?
>   You cannot miss that inn.
>
> Shall I meet other wayfarers at night?
>   Those who have gone before.
> Then must I knock, or call when just in sight?
>   They will not keep you waiting at that door.
>
> Shall I find comfort, travel-sore and weak?
>   Of labour you shall find the sum.
> Will there be beds for me and all who seek?
>   Yea, beds for all who come.

[1] 'Up-hill' by Christina Rossetti (1830–94).

○ From WSC   [France]
31 January 1916

My beloved,

F.E. [Smith*] will give you all the news from here, ...

I highly approve of your Ll.G. [Lloyd George*] meeting. You shd praise each other well, & find some crumbs for me besides. I am sure his set back is only temporary. Bonar Law & he & I have been driving about all the morning, & I am now quite au fait. I expect we shall be working together someday – if no accident intervenes. They are rather inclined to air [ministry] for me. <u>Yes</u> – if the conditions were satisfactory.

We go into the line tomorrow for 6 days, & as you know I like this sort of work vy much. It occupies me & I hope to be able to do it well. I don't think there is much difference in safety between the trenches & our 'rest billets'. Both my H.Q^{rs} advanced and support are registered & shelled. But it takes an awful lot of shells to do much harm; apart from bad luck. On the whole I prefer the trenches where there is always something going on, & where one really is fighting in this gt war for the triumph of right & reason. No doubt about it – one is doing the real thing – wh has to be done by someone.

Various good foods have arrived & the typewriter – & cigars & brandy. So we are well provided.

I must say I felt vy strong & self reliant meeting these two men today:

& did not envy their situation or regret at all my decision to quit them. If I come through all right my strength will be greater than it ever was. I wd much rather go back to the trenches tonight, than go home in any position of mediocre authority. But I <u>shd</u> like to see my beloved pussy cat.

Your own devoted
W.

○ From WSC   6th Royal Scots Fusiliers
[undated, ?1 February 1916]   In the Field

My darling,

F.E. [Smith*] & Ll.G. [Lloyd George*] will have told you of the comical & scandalous incident wh marked their visit[1]. The satisfaction extorted from the Adjutant-General's Branch was so complete that I rather feared they might owe me a grudge. So after the Ministers had departed I went in to see the A.G. [Adjutant General] & his faithful 'Fido' Childs (who sends letters for me etc). I was received with almost suspicious cordiality. General Macready[2] (AG, my man of Tonypandy days) said he was about to write to me to express his regret that a friend of mine shd have been inconvenienced & while my guest; that I was entirely blameless; his only reproach was that I had not asked him to arrange it all for me beforehand – he wd have gladly done it – . . .

But I still have not been able to make out what actually happened. I am sure they had it in their minds that F.E. was trying to break their rules & they wished to obstruct his movements & make him come to heel. (Of course he ought to have had proper papers.) In doing this (according to my surmise) their underlings sustained the impression that he was hostilely viewed, & immediately began to act crudely. . . . However the contrary impulse from on high has now been so unmistakeable that I fancy such a piece of cheek & folly will go long without a repetition. . . .

I write all this trivial stuff, as it may amuse you. . . . Some of these potentates get more upset about an 'incident' of this kind than about sending 1,000 men to their deaths.

We came into our trenches again this morning & I have passed practically the whole day in them arranging work & studying their intricacies. . . . I am much interested in your lunch with McKenna. . . . The group I want to work with & form into an effective governing instrument is Ll.G [Lloyd George]: F.E [Smith]: B.L [Bonar Law]: Carson: & Curzon. Keep that steadily in mind. It is the alternative Government, when 'wait & see' is over.

Tender love my dearest soul to you & the kittens.

Send me another box of squeezer pens. I have been inoculated for tetanus, as I progged my hand showing how easy it was to climb barbed wire, & every scratch here needs attention. A cold is threatening me & I am keeping it at bay with quinine. The weather is bright & chilly – but no actual frost. We are vy comfortable & well supplied, & I have plenty of clothes & boots. . . .

> Good night my dear one,
> Your devoted
> W.

¹ F. E. Smith, at this time Attorney-General, had dined with WSC at The Hospice on 29 January. In the early hours of 30 January he had been arrested by the Provost Marshal for being in a war zone without a pass; he was held under arrest for the rest of the night, before being allowed to rejoin his friends and colleagues, Lloyd George, Bonar Law and WSC. There was a great furore about the incident in which the military authorities did not come out too well, and had to apologize abjectly.
² Gen. Sir Nevil Macready, later 1st Bt (1862–1946), Adj.-Gen., British Expeditionary Force, 1914–16. During the riots at Tonypandy in November 1910, WSC, then Home Secretary, had sent the Metropolitan Police to the scene, putting Macready in command of any troops which might have been required in support.

○ From WSC   6ᵗʰ Royal Scots Fusiliers
2 February 1916   In the Field

My darling,

. . . We have had profound peace here to-day – Not a shell or a casualty – hardly a bullet. . . . I am inclined to think no serious operations will take place for the present. . . . So don't be anxious. . . .

Tender love my dearest one. Give my fondest messages to Diana & Randolph & kiss repeatedly that moon faced Sarah for me.

No I don't think the road will be always uphill for us [referring to the poem CSC had sent him] – if it runs on far enough, it will lead along a high plateau – with a commanding view of the country on either side, the air will be vy clear, & my eye will be rested & practised, & I shall sweep in my glance over spacious regions. I daresay I shall be no happier than in the mud of the Flanders trenches –

I want to see you, poodle – I am resolving the Dieppe scheme. But I must stay here longer first.

> Your ever devoted
> W.

◇ From CSC   [41 Cromwell Road]
Friday 4 February 1916

My Darling

The great meeting¹ is over & the whole thing went off brilliantly – Ll-G [Lloyd George*] made a quite undistinguished speech and the shabby little tike altho' he said he had just returned from the Front never mentioned your name. On the way home he said quite casually 'I'm so surprised, Curzon wants the "Air" [Ministry], I thought perhaps Winston might have done it – Do you think he would have liked it?' I said 'Winston would do it better than anyone else.' He did not reply – I don't hate him, but I feel contempt & almost pity for him. This ungenerous cautious streak in his nature will in his old age which is fast approaching leave him lonely &

friendless – Ishmael! I do not think you will ever need him, he will need you when he is on the down gradient – & of course you will help him & he knows it. As we drove home silently in the dark he was very white, shabby & tired & I felt young, strong & vital & felt you out there young & strong & vital & I thought & I know he felt me thinking 'If only Winston is not killed you will need us both – Meanwhile you won't strike a blow or speak a word for him becos' you know it won't make any difference to his attitude later – You can always rely on him in any "Marconi" affair' – He is very civil to me – But I must tell you about the meeting. First of all there was a little reception in the Canteen, ... the tables all laid for 500 ready for the men's suppers – ... There was my Head Cook, Mr. Quinlan resplendent in white coat & hat, the paid staff in brown holland overalls & my voluntary workers (about 150) looking like blue & white angels. There was a great crowd of people from the neighbourhood & some from London and all the Y.M.C.A. swells ... I took Ll.G round the kitchens, larders etc. and introduced him to lots of people & then we all proceeded to the new workshops for the Meeting where the really important people were assembled – the men 2,000 of them packed like sardines standing very silently. They did not cheer when they saw Ll.G but looked at him with interest & curiosity, (but don't say I said so) they gave me a beautiful cheer.... Some of the men had planned to give Ll.G some sleeve links made in the pattern of [a] 6-inch shell, but yesterday they changed their mind & decided that this gift was to be sent out to you in Flanders! Ll.G knows this as I had previously told him he was to receive a present. He was very well received but not enthusiastically. I was simply deluged with presents, a bouquet, a cheque from the Directors of the firm for 100 guineas, (not for myself! but to spend as I like on the canteens), sleeve-links for you from the men and a little brooch in the shape of a shell from the men enclosed in a really lovely gold box studded with turquoises, pearls & diamonds for me[2]. I nearly fainted with emotion & my speech was wrecked as I had not expected these gifts – (except the cheque). But I just read out your message & the men were delighted – Don't tell anyone about all this as it sounds vain, but I want you to know about my small success. I really have worked hard but now I shall have to redouble my efforts to deserve all this. I feel I must give the men fat chickens every day to eat!...

My Darling Dear One, to-day I feel happy & hopeful about you & your future. I know (D.V.) that you will come back rejuvenated & strengthened from the War & dominate all these decrepit exhausted politicians. Don't close your mind to the P.M. entirely. He is lazy but (or perhaps therefore) healthy & anyhow he is not a skunk tho' a wily old tortoise. I must meet him this week & tweak his ear – I feel full of beans as if you were commander in chief & not merely Lt. Colonel....

I long for a letter.

God bless you & I send you a thousand kisses

Clemmie

...

---

[1] Ponders End Canteen was opened by Lloyd George, 3 February 1916.
[2] I have the little box now – a treasured possession.

○ From WSC   6th Royal Scots Fusiliers
4 [February] 1916[1]   In the Field

My darling One,

Yesterday (3rd) we had a lucky escape. We had just finished an excellent lunch and were all seated round the table at coffee & port wine, when a shell burst at no gt distance making the window jump. Archie [Sinclair] said that at the next one we wd go into our dugout in the barn just opposite & we were discussing this when there was a tremendous crash, dust & splinters came flying through the room, plates were smashed, chairs broken. Everyone was covered with debris and the Adjutant (he is only 18) hit on the finger[2]. . . . The wonderful good luck is that this shell (a 4.2) did not – cd not have – burst properly. Otherwise we shd have had the wall thrown in on us – & some wd surely have been hurt.

I have made them put up another still stronger dugout – quite close, on wh they are now hard at work. I slept peacefully in my tiny war-scarred room last night, after a prolonged tour of the trenches. To-day we have been let alone, but our 'rest' H.Q. (where FE [Smith*] visited us) have been much harried; also the Bde H.Q^{rs}. . . .

. . . The cellars of the convent, 'The Conning Tower' I call them, are now clear of water, & will make a splendid battle H.Q^{rs}.[3] Everyone continues extremely civil: & the battalion is working admirably. . . .

Your devoted & loving husband,
W.

[1] This and twelve succeeding WSC letters, of which nine are quoted in this volume, are all dated *January* 1916. Reading them in conjunction with CSC's letters, it is quite clear that they were written in *February* 1916; I have amended the dates accordingly, as in Martin Gilbert, *Winston S. Churchill, Companion Vol. III*, 1972.
[2] Lt Jock McDavid (1897–), appointed Acting Adjutant 6th Royal Scots Fusiliers, December 1915. Gassed 1918.
[3] But not for long, owing to heavy waterlogging from the overflow from Warnave Brook.

○ From WSC   6th Royal Scots Fusiliers
6 [February] 1916   In the Field

My beloved,

This morning a telegram arrived telling me to take over command of the Brigade, & so I came on to Brigade Headquarters & am now in command of 5 battalions & 4,000 yards of front. I thought at first that the change meant something effective: but it turns out that I am for the moment actually the senior commanding officer, & the Brigadier – Walshe – is expected back tomorrow. . . . Tomorrow at daylight the whole Brigade is relieved in the line and comes out into reserve. I expect to be back with my battalion tomorrow night.

On arrival here [Brigade HQ] I found an invitation to lunch with the Division & there I met George Curzon [Lord Privy Seal], who with much persistency had demanded to see me & was duly brought out. I took him out to my shattered farm & along my own trenches; & he told me all the news & his view of men & politics in his usual sprightly style. It is clear he wd like Air – as I think from what he said that the P.M. has discussed it with him. 'Napou' as the soldiers here say meaning 'Il n'y a plus'.

I got yr long letter about the meeting & I am really delighted it was such a splendid success for you & that your work has made a deep impression. I read & re-read yr account and also the report in the Times. I am invigorated by yr optimism. My darling one, what shd I do without you?

Young Mr McDavid the Adjutant – 18! – goes home tonight on leave & he will come to see you tomorrow. He is a nice boy & will tell you all about our life out here. I have had a letter from my mother giving an interesting account of her talk with Asquith* at the Cassel dinner. Also one from Masterton Smith – telling me my 'caterpillar'[1] was tried before the old tabby [Balfour, First Lord of Admiralty] and performed miracles. Foolish slugs & dawdlers. . . .

Well my dearest bird – good night.

With tender love
Your devoted
W

[1] 'Caterpillars' were prototype tanks. While at the Admiralty WSC had instigated research and development of what came to be known as 'tanks'. After he left the Admiralty the project was continued but lacked his energizing 'push'.

◇ From CSC   41 Cromwell Road
Monday 7 February [1916] 6 a.m.

My Darling

. . . I went to see F.E. [Smith*] on Friday & heard from him the whole of the amazing story of his arrest & subsequent turning of the tables – Ll.G [Lloyd George*] never said a word about it, cautious secretive little fellow. Of course garbled versions are all over London –

Before this letter reaches you, you will have seen Garvin's appeal in the Observer for you & Lord Fisher to return – You as Air Minister, Fisher as First Sea Lord. If only you had been given the 'air' last May something substantial might by now have been accomplished – Oh my Darling I long so for it to happen, & I feel that it would, except for the competition for the post inside the Cabinet – There are, Alas, 12 Ministers with minor offices who probably all think themselves competent. I have been invited to stay at Walmer[1] next Sunday. How wonderful if would be if by then you had returned.

Goonie has come back from a round of gaiety at the Vice-regal Court[2] & finds London rather dull, I fear –

You will be surprised when you see Diana – I have cut off her hair & she now looks like Peter Pan – A great improvement! Sarah is on the verge of voluble speech & is only waiting for some teeth – . . .

Tender love to you my darling
from
Clemmie

[1] Walmer Castle in Kent, official residence of the Lord Warden of the Cinque Ports. Lord

Beauchamp, then holder of this ancient office, had lent the castle to the Asquiths as a weekend retreat.
² She had been staying in Dublin with Lord and Lady Wimborne (Ivor and Alice Guest; see Biographical Notes). Lord Wimborne was Lord Lieutenant of Ireland.

◇ From CSC   41 Cromwell Road
8 February [1916]

My Darling

Last night arrived such a delightful youth, Mr McDavid, bringing with him the nose of the shell which shattered your bedroom, your oiler lamp and photographs of you, also very exciting news, i.e. that for the present you are a Brigadier – I wonder if you are to be one for good? Also that you have received a visit from Lord Curzon* – ...

Rothermere does not seem to be of much use as a manipulator of the Northcliffe press. Its malice is quite extraordinary – I cannot make out why Northcliffe does not wish you to be air minister. I have written to Rothermere and asked him to visit me – Next Sunday I spend with the P.M. at Walmer. I cannot gauge the Fisher danger – He is certainly very active & has a good press, but neither Asquith* nor Balfour can possibly want him back. I expect however that some fancy post will be found for him to satisfy the ignorant and famishing public. Write quickly and tell me that you have arranged a safer headquarters – I fear so that the Germans in front of you may know you are there.

I have asked Mr McDavid to dine here next week on his way back to you. ...

Goodbye my Sweetheart, be of good cheer & write to me every day to keep me swimming well above water.

from
Clemmie

P.S. Kisses from your 3 Babies.

○ From WSC   6th Royal Scots Fusiliers
8 [February] 1916   In the Field

My darling,

The General did not return yesterday as was expected and no one seems to know when he will turn up. ... So I remain here in command. It is not a vy satisfactory arrangement, as of course I am only a caretaker and cannot attempt to take a grip of the whole machine. I do the office work and have prepared myself to meet any emergency; but otherwise I wait about from hour to hour. The whole Brigade is now out of the line & in rest billets, so there is nothing going on. Archie [Sinclair] however has just telephoned that they have been shelling one of the company farms & have wounded 3 men. They are getting spiteful & fire 5 or 6 shells at once without any warning – then wait 20 minutes or so and have another go.

I had tea with General Tudor¹ yesterday. He commands all the artillery

of the Division, & is quite young – my age about. He & I were friends at
Bangalore as lieutenants – & much good polo did we play together. We
were vy pleased to meet again after so many years – I had not seen him
since S. Africa – My dear what mistakes they made at Loos. You simply
cannot believe them possible. But there is a gt lack of 'drive' throughout
the administration of the Army. Take the telephone system for instance. It
is grotesque. You cannot get through. When you do you cannot hear.
There is always a dog fight going on on the wires. They have stuck in the
main to the same little field instruments that an army on the move uses,
instead of making a perfect system wh cd so easily be done. And how
vitally important it might be in a battle! If we had been content at the
Admiralty to paddle along at that feeble pace, we shd never have mastered
the German submarines. Then of course there ought to be 10 times (at
least) as many light railways on the front. This war is one of mechanics &
brains & mere sacrifice of brave & devoted infantry is no substitute &
never will be. By God I wd make them skip if I had the power – even for
a month.

The cutting from Zukunft, wh I enclose is curious. I suppose that in
Germany they realise I was a dangerous war criminal. While I never doubt
the wisdom of my decision to quit office, I writhe daily at the lack of
power to make things work. And so I am sure does the old Malay[2]. The
time may come when I shall feel it is my duty to go home & make an
effective opposition. But not yet. I have now been out here 3 months. It
has passed vy quickly, & not unpleasantly. . . .

The lull in military operations everywhere has enabled the Govt. to turn
over for a good snooze. The control of the war has passed into the hands
of the War Council: and the War Council hardly ever meet. I asked some
of my late colleagues who was running the war. I was told 'It runs itself'!
Yet there is not one minute in the 24 hours when steps cd not be taken
wh wd save life & treasure and hasten the conclusion of the conflict. . . .

. . . Send me a small tiny edition of Shakespeare – & the Burns – as I
asked for. Also <u>regularly</u> boxes of those big cigars of my own, &
brandy. . . .

When is that truant Goonie going to return? Nellie & Bertram will be
interested to see the little lamp. Give them all my best love – & give the
children many kisses. I am so glad you have so much important work to
do. You cannot be too active both on my account & yr own.

Your ever loving & devoted
W.

[1] Henry Hugh Tudor (1871–1965), Royal Artillery Brig.-Gen. commanding the 9th Division
Artillery, 1916–18. Knighted, 1923. He had served with WSC in India and South Africa.
[2] Lord Fisher was known as 'the old Malay' because of his oriental cast of countenance.

○ From WSC   6th Royal Scots Fusiliers
10 [February] 1916   In the Field

My darling,
     . . . I have returned to the Fusiliers. It was vy unsatisfactory commanding

the Brigade from hour to hour as a caretaker; ... We are established in a farm[1] further back than our old reserve H.Qrs and believed to be perfectly safe from shelling. But as we are crowded & uncomfortable I move back after dark each night into the old H.Qrs to dine & sleep. This is a convenient arrangement. From our farm I watched yesterday afternoon the shelling of the little town [Ploegsteert] whose name I cannot mention.... Three of our men who were strolling in the town were hit – one fatally, & another sustained a shock from being near a shell from wh he immediately died. In the last 2 days of 'rest' I have lost 8 men, or more than in 6 days in the front line. I am now reduced to under 680 men instead of 1000. There are many other battalions like this; & it is one of the fruits of 'wait & see' & that admirable political tactfulness & craft for wh the Prime Minister is so justly renowned.

I do not think they will want me for Air. The view I take of my duty, renders me powerless at present as a critic of the Government, & consequently Asquith* can afford to let me alone. He knows this & will act quite naturally upon it. Garvin's article[2] was vy friendly & I am touched by his loyalty: but it will not count in the decision. Neither do I expect any speedy promotion here.... Haig will no doubt eventually – if I survive – give me a Brigade. But he will be chiefly concerned at the impression such an appointment wd produce in the army: & he will certainly run no risks on my account. Can you blame him? We are only acquaintances. The soldiers are of course impressed with my position & vy respectful & friendly about it; but at the same time they are naturally rather embarrassed at having a kind of large fish in a vy small puddle....

I told G. Curzon to go & see you on his return. He will give you all the news of me....

Your ever loving & devoted
W

[1] Soyer Farm. WSC used it as a Battalion HQ for a few weeks.
[2] In the *Observer*, 6 February 1916. Referred to by CSC in her letter of 7 February.

◇ From CSC   '41 Cromwell'
11 February [1916]

My Darling

No letter from you since the one written on the 4th describing the wrecking of your farm by the shell – I know that since then you have had an interesting time, being made a temp[ry] Brigadier & seeing Lord Curzon – & I am longing to hear all about it from your pen. I shall hear news of you to-day as I am lunching with Lord Curzon for that purpose!...

... Half an hour now till the post comes. Will wait & see if there is a letter for me

– – –

(Feb: 12th 5 a.m.) There was a nice fat letter for me, but I could not continue mine yesterday.... Till I got your letter yesterday I had not realized that you were now in rest-billets. The relief I feel is quite extraordinary. One doesn't realize how high the tension is until it is suddenly lowered. How long do you rest & are you safe from shell-fire while resting – ?...

Yesterday Goonie & I lunched with Lord Curzon at his handsome Mansion which (to indicate war economy even among the highest in the land) was swaddled with dust sheets – He was very affable & talked a great deal about you & also & especially a great deal about himself & his experiences in Flanders! He told me you were well & in high spirits and said he thought you would soon be a Brigadier. But he did not as I should have liked express indignation & surprise that you should be commanding a battalion, but seemed to think it very natural, suitable and proper – What short memories these people have – !... Altogether he was most superior & patronizing tho' genuinely friendly, & Goonie & I laughed at him a good deal as we drove home in his motor which he kindly lent us for the afternoon – He gave me 3 bottles of brandy for you which I will despatch by a tame messenger.

It is heart-breaking to hear of the terrible mistakes at Loos – there is I suppose no reason why they should not be made again.... Your remark that 'Victory is not yet out of the grasp of our enemies' makes me shudder. Surely you must be wrong about this, surely in spite of everything, muddles, errors, slackness, we must be going to win – ... I laughed so much at what you said about the government 'turning over for a good snooze' – Their slumbers however are slightly disturbed by old Fisher & his press who are rampaging about like anything – ... Perhaps he will be given an honour! I don't suppose I shall find anything out at Walmer – But I don't think I should have been invited there on the verge of your enemy being restored to power.

Tender love to you Darling
from
Clemmie

◇ From CSC   Walmer Castle
Sunday 13 February [1916]

My Darling,

The journey here yesterday was terribly long & tedious; we took four hours & the train stopped at each station.

But I am glad to have come as I think it is useful & also I am having a pleasant Sunday. A perfect day, glorious sunshine, the sea blue and without a ripple & no wind. I sat in the garden most of the morning & found growing out of doors a pink rose, a white violet & a sprig of cherry pie! I have just returned from playing a round of golf with the Prime [Asquith*] who was very pleasant & mellow. I have not touched a club for 18 months but I missed only 2 drives & at one moment I thought I was going to give the old boy a good beating (which I shd have relished) but Alas! I fell off towards the end & he won by a short length. However I won the bye.

If only you had been here my Darling it would have been delicious. Venetia [Montagu*] & Montagu are here, the Gladstones[1], Jack Pease & a pale brainy young man, Lord Eustace Cecil who is I think courting Elizabeth [Asquith] or rather allowing himself to be courted by her!... This morning sitting on the bastion we could distinctly hear the rumble of heavy guns – I think it must have been our ships shelling Dixmunde....

> Tender Love to you my Darling from
> Clemmie

[1] 1st Viscount Gladstone (1854–1930), son of William Ewart Gladstone. Married Dorothy, born Paget.

○ From WSC   In the trenches
13 [February] 1916

My beloved,

It is odd thinking of you at Walmer now. I remember so well being there at the end of February last, when all was hope at the Dardanelles & I looked forward to a vy wide sphere of triumphant activity. Everything is changed now – only the old block [Asquith*] continues solid & supine.

I am now in the line again and am living in the farm I told you of [Laurence Farm]. I am protecting it in various ways by sandbags etc against a renewed incursion of shells; & I have now 2 vy substantial dugouts – sandbags over steel cupolas – wh will at a pinch accommodate our whole population at H.Qrs. – 35 or 40.

This afternoon many aeroplanes overhead, & much shooting at them. I was disgusted to watch 1 German aeroplane sailing about scornfully in the midst of <u>14</u> British – ... As for our guns they fired hundreds of shells without lifting a feather of this hostile bird.

I send you some copies of the photo of Archie [Sinclair] & I taken at Armentières....

Kiss the kittens. I think a gt deal about you all. I never expected to be so completely involved in the military machine. It almost seems to me as if my life in the gt world was a dream, & I have been moving slowly forward in the army all these years from subaltern to colonel. Good night my dearest soul

> Your ever devoted
> W

○ From WSC   [6th Royal Scots Fusiliers
14 [February] 1916   In the Field]

My darling,

I take up my pen to send you my daily note. Another long day in the trenches has closed, & I sit in a battered wicker chair within this shot-scarred dwelling by the glowing coals of a brazier in the light of an acetylene lamp. At 6 I went round my trenches, just as day was breaking and was saluted on my doorstep by a vy sulky bullet. All the morning I laboured in the small business of the battalion, & dealt with my company

commanders & sent off the numerous reports for wh our superiors
clamour – ... Then at lunch came General Tudor who had organised
another artillery 'sträfe' – this time on our front – ... After half an hour of
this we (Tudor & I) returned to join the others in the dugout: to receive
your letter & read it with eager appetite & to browse about among
ungrateful press cuttings & the unfriendly newspapers....

And so here – darkness has fallen & dinner is almost ready. I shall go
round the trenches again tonight, & on the whole when sleep comes I
think I shall have earned my 25 shillings.

I see Garvin has had a hint that George Curzon is to be Air Minister.
Well I do not care. I cd have done it well....

Well my darling & dearest companion, here is my screed tonight & it
bears with it my fondest love to you & the babies –

Ever your loving & devoted
W

○ From WSC   [6th Royal Scots Fusiliers
15 [February] 1916   In the Field]

My darling,

This day has slipped quickly by & almost without incident.... There has
been a good deal of fighting to the North of Ypres & our trenches on a
front of 3 divisions have been much knocked about. We cd hear the
cannonades splintering & snarling away all through the night....

Last night after writing & after dinner, I had a splendid walk with Archie
[Sinclair] all over the top of the ground. We left the trenches altogether &
made a thorough examination of all the fields, tracks, ruins etc
immediately behind our line. You cannot show yourself here by day, but
in the bright moonlight it is possible to move about without danger
(except from random bullets) & to gain a vy clear impression. Archie was
a vy good guide. We also went out in front of our own parapet into the
No man's land & prowled about looking at our wire & visiting our
listening posts. This is always exciting. Last night two of my officer patrols
went right up to the German wire & cut large strands of it as trophies. One
was foolish enough however to leave a Union Jack fastened on to it in
bravado. This will only make them more vigilant. Can you imagine such a
silly thing.

My leave plans are shaping like this: – ... I shall try to leave on 2nd &
travel via Dunkirk & destroyer – reaching you the same night. I shall have
seven clear days at home – i.e. till 9th. This is the only leave I shall get for
another 3 months. It will therefore be important for me to see various
people: and I shall take decisions about my future plans....

Goodnight my darling – tender love & many kisses.

Your devoted
W

◇ From CSC   41 Cromwell Road
Wednesday 16 February [1916] 5 a.m.

My Darling
Three letters from you arrived in a covey, ...
My Walmer visit ended very pleasantly except that owing to a canteen
engagement I had to travel up to London by a dreadful train leaving
Walmer at 8.30 & reaching Victoria at 12! Margot was very nice to me but
seemed very wretched – I heard afterwards that she & Violet
[Asquith*/Bonham Carter] have had a real bad row – I thought that now V
was married the friction would be diminished instead of which there has
been a big explosion. ...
Darling, one of the letters I received yesterday was written in a sombre
mood. Do not I pray of you let this mood deepen & permanently tinge
your heart & mind.
There are only two things that can prevent you from again being the
heart of action in this country – I mean your death or a serious wound.
But I <u>will</u> not believe that either of these terrible things are going to
happen. I am sure you will return to power after the war with increased
prestige. There will be 2 million khaki votes for Churchill. ...
Last night, I mean Monday, that nice boy Mr McDavid dined with
Goonie & me & we took him to a Music Hall. He is very small & young &
rather lovable. I feel sorry for his Mamma, ...
The children are becoming so grown up & intelligent. They will be very
sweet companions & I look forward with longing to the time when you
come back to me & we will have a little country basket & in the intervals
of your work we will all curl up together in it & be so happy. Only you
must not become too famous or you won't have time for these pastoral
joys! You will have to promise me that in future however full of work &
ideas you are you will keep out of every day an hour & every week a day
& every year 6 weeks for the small things of life. Things like painting,
playing grizzly bear, sitting on the grass with me & generally Leisure with
a big L. ...

> Tender love to you my Darling
> from
> Clemmie

○ From WSC   [6th Royal Scots Fusiliers
16 [February] 1916   In the Field]

My darling,
Archie [Sinclair] & I were out late in the trenches last night, where it is
vy difficult to maintain that high and continuous vigilance on wh honour &
safety depend, & we did not get to bed till 1.30 having made ourselves
thoroughly disagreeable. We had only just finished dressing this morning
when shells began to arrive in the neighbourhood. ... Archie & I
persevered in our breakfast – till a tremendous bang, clouds of debris &
the whizzing of splinters proclaimed our house hit again – this time our
dining room was pierced on the other side, & our joint bedroom

penetrated in 5 or 6 places – the signal office in the next room completely shattered. (Mercifully I had just ordered the signallers to take refuge in the dugout). The signal officer Lieut. Kemp – down with 5 wounds (not dangerous) & another man hit. Without knowing all that had happened, we hastily seized our eggs & bacon, bread & marmalade, & took refuge in our dugout. . . . Then the 'sträfe' being over we emerged and went about our business. I have now had 2 officers hit out of 5 in my H.Q. mess: & there is no doubt that we are rather a target. But I do not intend to change these H.Qrs as they are convenient & it is difficult to find others. Instead I am piling sandbags inside all the walls & on the upper floor & trying to make it proof against the 30 pr [pounder] shells. . . .

It was odd gobbling bacon & marmalade in the dugout, while the doctor bandaged the gt raw wounds of our poor officer a foot or two away! Archie is vy good – cool, methodical careful – yet quite fearless. I do not think I mind it vy much. At any rate it does not affect my spirits or my temper. But it is a vy curious life to live.

The enclosed[1] wh speaks for itself arrived last night from that faithful d'Eyncourt[2]. You see this idea is bearing fruit. . . .

Your ever loving & devoted
W.

P.S. Read the enclosed, seal it & send it on to Asquith* if you like – in an envelope of yours[3] – The matter is so important that I feel bound to shove it under his nose. Then I have done my part. . . .

W.S.C.

. . .

[1] A letter about the first trial of the 'tank'.
[2] Eustace Tennyson d'Eyncourt (1868–1951). Naval architect, at this time Director of Naval Construction and Chief Technical Adviser at the Admiralty. Knighted 1917; created 1st Bt, 1930.
[3] Asquith returned the letter to CSC, writing that it had interested him very much.

○ From WSC   6th Royal Scots Fusiliers
18 [February] 1916   In the Field

My darling,

The rain & mist today prevented the enemy from shelling us, so no opportunity of testing our new sandbag defences occurred. . . .

We are relieved at daybreak tomorrow having completed six days. Casualties 10 men & 1 officer. Last night a vy good N.C.O. was killed & another seriously wounded. Otherwise most of the casualties have been at Headquarters. I organised a little sträfe last night of wh I enclose my report. I had to sit at the end of a telephone, so that I did not get much fun out of it. But it worked vy well. . . .

I am disappointed not to hear any account from you of yr conversations at Walmer to wh I was looking forward with some interest. . . .

I am in a sombre mood tonight – so I will put down my pen before I darken the paper.

Your ever loving & devoted
W.

○ From WSC   6th Royal Scots Fusiliers
22 February 1916   In the Field

My darling,

I have every hope of coming home on the 2nd. I propose to come to
Dover by destroyer & that you meet me at the Lord Warden Hotel where
we can lunch & go up to London together. You must parcel out the days
as well as possible. I will have one dinner at my mother's, at least 3 at
home, 2 plays alone with you & one man's dinner out somewhere. Make
up a programme on these lines. Also lunches & try to work in all my
friends. You can let people know that I am coming home for a week. I
leave it all to you. . . . I will be vy good & keep all my engagements
punctually. Time is so short. Mind you have a servant ready to look after
me, & let him come in time to have everything ready on arrival. I put it all
in your hands my dearest soul. Arrange whatever you like to amuse us
both the most. I much prefer people coming to dine with me than dining
out with them. I want to have at least one day's painting in Lavery's studio.
Do you know I think that [painting] will be a gt pleasure & resource to me
– if I come through all right.

We had a quiet day yesterday – not a shell came near us, though to the
Southward there was a vy heavy & prolonged cannonade. To-day it is
snowing and they cannot see to shoot. This unusual interlude is
welcome. . . .

I am suddenly beginning to look forward vy much to coming home.

That old grey tabby [Balfour] is going to abolish the Naval Division[1].
How easy to destroy. How hard to build. How easy to evacuate. How hard
to capture. How easy to do nothing. How hard to achieve anything. War is
action, energy, & hazard. These sheep only want to browse among the
daisies. . . .

                                        Your devoted & ever loving
                                                             W

[1] The Royal Naval Division had been established by WSC on 16 August 1914, when he was First
Lord of the Admiralty. Balfour in fact did not abolish the Division: it sustained heavy losses at
Gallipoli, but was made up to strength from various battalions and sent to France in May 1916.

◇ From CSC   41 Cromwell Road
23 February [1916]

My Own Darling

I was distressed this morning by receiving from you two rather sad
letters complaining that I had not written & especially that I had not
reported conversations at Walmer.

My letters must be delayed becos' really I have written nearly every day
and as for 'conversations' at Walmer, except that of the most frivolous &
trivial nature they were non-existent. You know what the P.M. is – He
loathes talking about the War or work of any sort. He asked anxiously if
you were happy –

Lulu[1] told me that the P.M. had fished your letter (the one about the caterpillar I sent) out of his pocket and read him short extracts from it, & seemed pleased to have heard from you.

I think if you could do it, you might write to him occasionally private interesting friendly letters. With him it is so much out of sight out of mind – I am sure that he feels affection for you & that he would like you to be in the Government again, if it could be done without a row. This sounds very cowardly, but few Prime Ministers would do more. Anyhow nothing is gained by letting him see that you consider he has behaved badly; he only waddles off as quickly as possible and avoids you in future – ...

After scolding me for not being more communicative about Walmer in one of your letters there is a passage crossed out ending 'Well well' – I tried to read it but couldn't. I fear you are cross with me. Please don't be my Darling – What is it?

These constant hair breadth escapes freeze me into terror – ...

Good-bye my Dear One write & tell me that you love me.

Clemmie

Rothermere has been rather a broken reed over the Daily Mail – It's no use I fear trying to influence the capricious press. One day when you no longer need it they will fawn on you....

Verdun[2] again looks very threatening – I do trust your part of the line will not be involved in any counter-offensive.

I tried yesterday to pick up again the threads of my canteen work & found that during the last 10 days all sorts of little things had gone awry – One of the cooks had been drunk & had used bad language! The tea had been weak at a meal in another canteen – grave dissatisfaction in consequence!!

Goodbye my Darling Winston – I await news of you eagerly and will write again then.

Your loving
Clemmie

[1] Lewis Harcourt; see p. 12 n. 1. First Commissioner of Works, 1915–17.
[2] On 21 February the Germans had launched an attack on forts surrounding Verdun. Four months of fierce fighting were to follow, but Verdun, and the inner ring of forts, remained in French hands.

○ From WSC   6th Royal Scots Fusiliers
[undated, probably 24 February 1916]   In the Field

My beloved one – The blow has fallen. All leave is stopped except in vy special circumstances till further orders. It seems that the Germans are expected to develop a gt offensive against this Western front quite soon....

I am really vy disappointed not to come home & see you all. I had begun so much to look forward to it. It is only when one thinks of going home that one measures the strain & severity of this life.

I will write again tomorrow when I get into the line.

Ever your loving & devoted
W.

◇ From CSC   41 Cromwell Road
Friday 25 February [1916] 6 a.m

My Darling
  A very thick fall of snow here & no-one to clean the streets &
pavements, so people paddle about in snow-boots – I wonder if you have
had it too & how it affects you. I fear your trenches must be running
streams. Will it hamper the Germans in front of Verdun? I do hope so....
  Well my Darling the P.M. & Margot are dining here to-night & I have
had to work like a beaver to get together the 8 indispensable bridge
players which are necessary for their comfort & happiness. Everyone was
engaged – However the party is: – P.M. Margot, Ivor Wimborne [Guest*],
Lady Mainwaring, Bogey Harris, Goonie, Mr Cazalet[1], myself, Sir E. Cassel.
Nine people becos' Lady Mainwaring refuses to play bridge as she always
bunny-hugs & fox-trots after her meals. You will wish to know who she is
– She is an extremely beautiful dashing young woman ... We invited her
as we thought the P.M. would like something quite new! Bogey Harris is
an intimate of Alice Keppel's & a good bridge player – Mr Cazalet is barely
19, is in the Life Guards & will have £100,000 a year!...
  Your Mamma has nearly sold her house or let it – It is rather sad to part
with such a lovely possession, but I think she will be happier when she
has done it –

God bless you my Darling
Clemmie

. . .

[1] Victor Cazalet (1896–1943), at whose home, Fairlawne, in Kent, CSC used to stay before her
marriage. Brilliant squash and tennis player. Served Life Guards, 1916–18. Unionist MP from 1924.
In Second World War was Political Liaison Officer to the Polish General Sikorski (then Prime
Minister of the Polish government-in-exile), with whom he died in an aircraft crash at Gibraltar,
4 July 1943.

○ From WSC   6th Royal Scots Fusiliers
26 February 1916   In the Field

My darling,
  Here we are back in the line. Our farm is now much more protected
and it wd take 5.9" guns to smash it up....
  Colonel Holland came to say good bye yesterday. He is to be G.S.O.I.
[General Staff Officer I] to the 3rd Army, ... He told me that General Furse
had spontaneously sent in an official recommendation that I shd be
selected for a Brigade command; & that he (Holland) was going to impress
this upon G.H.Q. where he stays tonight. It is satisfactory anyhow that my
immediate superiors have confidence in my work.

Snow covers the ground and we do our scouting in calico gowns – almost invisible at 20 yards. I was up till 1.30 in the trenches, as the night was so dark & 'the price of safety is eternal vigilance.' ...

I like this farm [Laurence] so much better than the one I am in at 'rest'. Archie [Sinclair] & I have a nice little square room together, the ceiling is propped up by timber, & there are 3 layers of sand bags & brick bags on the top, and all the sides are heavily protected.... Inside we have a glowing brazier & two comfortable canvas beds, on wh I spread the W of the R.H.P.B. [Womb of the Red Hot Polar Bear, his sleeping bag] & Archie the Bosom of the Amorous Pole Cats [ditto] – in wh we sleep warm and peaceful....

Your ever loving & devoted
W.

◇ From CSC   41 Cromwell Road
Sunday Morning 27 February 1916, 5.30 a.m.

My Darling,

To-day I am going to map out your short leave[1] to, I hope, the pleasantest & best advantage. It is thrilling that you are coming home & I can't quite realize it yet.... I wonder if I shall hear from you more exactly the time of your arrival at Dover? If not I will go there by an early train & wait for you in the Lord Warden Hotel....

You will be interested to hear that the dinner for the P.M. was a great success & that the old sybarite thoroughly enjoyed himself – Sunny [Marlborough*] turned up at the last minute & made himself very agreeable & as Ivor [Guest*, now Wimborne] was there too, the Churchill family presented a solid & prosperous appearance. The food was good & afterwards there were 2 tables of bridge – I sat between the P.M. and Sir Ernest Cassel – The P.M. won a little money & went home in high good humour. Ivor remained behind & philosophised & moralised....

I feel so terribly anxious lest in these last few days before you come home, something may happen to you. I do hope you are careful not to expose yourself more than you need.

Tender love my Darling – I shall see you very soon after you get this.

Your loving
Clemmie

[1] CSC had obviously not yet received WSC's letter of 24 February, announcing that all leave had been cancelled.

◇ From CSC   41 Cromwell Road
28th [February 1916] 4.30 a.m.

My Darling,

I'm heartbroken at your not coming home. I was counting the days. Alas! When shall I see you now. I had planned such lovely dinners for you my Dearest Love – I'm so disappointed I won't write more now, but will wait for tomorrow.

All your friends will be sad. They were all looking forward to seeing you.

Tender love and a thousand kisses from
Clemmie

In the event the expected German attack which had caused the cancellation of all leave never developed, so all leave arrangements were restored; Winston and Clementine met as planned at the Lord Warden Hotel at Dover on 2 March.

Chapter VIII

HIS TRUE PLACE

As soon as Winston arrived in London he learned that the following week (Tuesday and Wednesday, 7–8 March 1916) there would be a debate in the House of Commons on the Naval Estimates; he resolved to take part, and to attack the Government for the ineffectual prosecution of the naval war, and for the inadequacy of their shipbuilding programme. Throughout the ensuing days, he conferred with political confidants who were eager for him not only to take part in the debate, but to return to the home political front and form an effective opposition to what they regarded as the sluggish and inept conduct of the war.

Among those Churchill saw were J. L. Garvin of the *Observer* and C. P. Scott of the *Manchester Guardian*, who for some time had been promoting the idea of repairing the rift between Churchill and Fisher; and calling for Fisher's return to the Admiralty to galvanize the naval chiefs into more effective activity. He also saw F. E. Smith* and Max Aitken (Beaverbrook*); the latter particularly was urging Winston to return. Clementine already viewed with unease Winston's growing friendship with the dynamic Canadian; her life-long mistrust of him may well date from this time, when she knew Aitken was advising her husband on a course of which she deeply disapproved.

These were days of great anxiety to her: once more, as in the matter of the 'Brigade', she found herself taking an opposing opinion to Winston – but against all her heart's instincts – and she viewed with dismay the possible re-emergence of Lord Fisher on the scene.

On the evening before the debate the Asquiths dined with the Churchills. In a private conversation after dinner the Prime Minister tried to dissuade Winston from what he judged to be a most unwise and personally injurious course[1]: but Winston's mind was made up.

Churchill spoke from the Opposition front bench late on the Tuesday afternoon. He made a powerful case, and his unrivalled knowledge commanded the serious attention of the House: but his last few sentences – when he urged the First Lord of the Admiralty to recall Lord Fisher – changed the whole scene, 'turning what had been to that moment one of the most serious and skilful speeches he had ever made into an object of derision'.[2]

The following day Balfour delivered a scathing reply, to which Churchill responded briefly and with dignity; but he had lost the ear and the sympathy of the House: he was stunned and humiliated by the reaction he had provoked. The only newspaper to support his speech was the *Manchester Guardian*.

Churchill had also been wrestling with the question as to whether he should now return home. On 8 March he wrote to Lord Kitchener (Secretary of State for War) asking to be relieved of his command as soon as this could be done without disadvantage to the service. Despite the hostile reception of his Naval Estimates speech, Churchill was now determined also to speak in the Army Estimates debate the following week; Kitchener, at his request, extended his leave (due to expire the next day).

On Thursday 9 March Churchill went to No. 10 Downing Street to see the Prime Minister. Asquith* knew of his request to Kitchener, and had approved it, but he earnestly besought him not to follow the example of his father, Lord Randolph Churchill*, who 'had committed political suicide through one impulsive action'.[3] The next day Churchill wrote to the Prime Minister saying that he had decided to return to his battalion.

During his days in England he saw Fisher more than once; on 12 March he also saw Sir Henry Dalziel[4], one of his few supporters in the House of Commons. He was also in touch with Aitken. All these counsellors urged him to stay in London.

He had already prepared a speech for the Army Estimates debate, but he remained undecided: Clementine's strongly held view that he should return to his battalion (if only in the short term) weighed with him, but Churchill requested and received from the Prime Minister a written assurance that no obstacle would be placed in his way should he decide thereafter to return to political life[5]. He left London on Sunday 12 March, rejoining his battalion in their forward trenches the following day.

Although he had now returned to France, Winston still held to his case for coming back to England sooner rather than later to lead a strong Opposition group. Clementine took a less sanguine but infinitely more realistic view of the support he would command. But when she waved him farewell on Dover pier, she had in her possession his letter to the Prime Minister (for immediate despatch), asking to be relieved of his military duties so that he could return home to take part in political affairs. She also bore a statement for the Press Association, and instructions to contact various people who would need to be apprised of these developments.

The letters take up the tale.

[1] Violet Bonham Carter, *Winston Churchill as I Knew Him*, 1965, p. 445.
[2] Martin Gilbert, *Winston S. Churchill*, Vol. III, 1971, p. 722.
[3] Bonham Carter, *Winston Churchill as I Knew Him*, p. 454.
[4] Sir Henry Dalziel (1868–1935), Liberal MP and newspaper proprietor. Cr. Baron Dalziel of Kirkcaldy, 1921.
[5] H. H. Asquith to WSC, 11 March 1916, CHAR 1/124. Quoted in Gilbert, *Winston S. Churchill*, Companion Vol. III, 1972, p. 1450.

○ From WSC   6 R.S.F.
13 March 1916   In the Field

My darling,

I felt the need of a few more days' reflection in this vy different atmosphere and I therefore telegraphed to Asquith* to delay action on my letter of yesterday [12 March] until he heard again from me. I cannot conceive I shall change my decision, but I needed rest sorely – my dearest & so must you. Just do absolutely nothing – so far as press & friends are concerned. . . .

My dearest soul – you have seen me vy weak & foolish & mentally infirm this week. Dual obligations, both honourable both weighty have rent me.

But I am sure my true war station is in the H. of C [House of Commons]. There I can help the movement of events.

I cannot tell you how much I love & honour you and how sweet & steadfast you have been through all my hesitations & perplexity.

I am not going to write to anyone – or ask anyone for his advice or opinion.

My fondest love my own darling. I was so grieved to think of you tired & lonely on the pier as my destroyer swept off into a choppy sea.

Don't we live in a strange world – full of wonderful pictures & intricate affairs. Across the troubled waters one can only steer by compass – not to do anything that is not honourable & manly, & subject to that to use my vital force to the utmost effect to win the war – there is the test I am going to try my decision by.

Always your devoted & loving
W.

Many, many kisses to the kittens.

◇ From CSC   41 Cromwell Road
13 March [1916] 7 o'clock p.m.

My Darling

I have just returned home and found this note from 'Bongie'[1] – Of course I do not yet know what it means & I am anxiously waiting to hear further, but in the meanwhile if it means you are taking more time for consideration, I am sure my Darling that you are wise.

I had a long talk with Sir Edward Carson this morning & altho' he was personally very friendly towards you & wanted much to see you he told me frankly that he thought your return just now would be a mistake as the circumstances were 'inauspicious' ... When he realized that your decision (as I then thought) was final he said that he thought you would have to observe the greatest restraint if you wished to really do good & to be very careful & accurate. He liked the Fisher part of your speech, (I mean the idea of reconciliation) but of course thought its tone dictatorial!

I must tomorrow my Dearest write you a long letter about everything & of my love & tenderness towards you. This is just a hasty line to catch the 'Bag' just to let you see the 'trend' of the Carson interview (a sort of bird's eye view). I am very very tired as the car broke down several times. . . . I was 2 hours at the Carsons. My Darling I wish now I were near you. I feel that perhaps now you are in France you may revise your judgement. I long for you to come back, but I want you to come back welcomed & acclaimed by all, as you ought to be and as I know you will be very soon. Whatever you finally decide I loyally agree to.

– – – A dreadful anxiety has just seized me. I have just recollected that you said that the only thing that would make you pause would be the knowledge that we were going to attack. Please God it is not the reason. Surely we are not going to make a counter-offensive? Let me know quickly the truth.

My Dearest own Winston, thro' these tumultuous days we have been together I have never been able to tell you or shew you how deep & true my love is for you and how I know that ultimately what you decide will be right & good.

God Bless you
Clemmie

---

[1] Maurice Bonham Carter, Asquith's Private Secretary; married to Violet Asquith. See p. 122 n. 1. His letter no doubt apprised CSC of WSC's telegram to Asquith.

◇ From CSC   41 Cromwell Road
14 March [1916] 6 a.m.

My Darling

Last night I was able only to send you a hurried scribble to catch the bag –

I saw the little destroyer with its big white ensign steam away & then went back to my hotel[1] ... I felt very exhausted & wished to be alone to try and think everything out clearly. I wrote

(1) to the P.M. enclosing the notice to the Press Association & asking for sanction to publish –

(2) to Sir Frederick Cawley[2], a private letter briefly explaining developments & sending him for private perusal your letter to him on the Admiralty....

I then crept into bed & thought about you & prayed for happier days & calm waters.

Yesterday morning [13th] I got up early & by 9.30 was on my way to Birchington which turned out to be over 20 miles away by very bad turning roads, ... [which] I reached about 11, but then another half hour was spent searching for the 'Carson Chateau' ... There I was received by Lady Carson, surprised but very friendly – At first she said I could not see Sir Edward as he was sleeping....

Presently I was asked to come upstairs & there in a narrow little bed looking very weak, but very intelligent lay poor Carson. (Do not repeat anything about his health as they are both very sensitive about it). He was very pale & one eye was slightly larger than the other – He first enquired if your letter to the P.M. (asking to be relieved) had actually been sent & when I said 'yes' he looked grave & said it was a very serious step & he hoped you had not made a mistake – I told him you had weighed the matter most carefully & that you considered it your duty to be in Parliament – He agreed that it was most desirable that you should be there & said he had always disapproved of you leaving the Cabinet, ... But he went on to say that if you returned in these not very favourable circumstances he feared that for the present your position would not be a good one & that therefore your usefulness would be temporarily impaired

– He said – 'Winston has probably done the country and the government a service by his intervention last Tuesday, but he has not done himself any good.' He spoke with great admiration of your qualities.... He asked me when I thought you would be returning & I said I thought about a week & he said he would <u>very</u> much like to see you then. He cannot write to you as this is not yet allowed. He hopes to be recovered in a fortnight....

I wish so much that we had planned things better & that you had seen him before sending the P.M. your letter – I am sure that tremendous decisions require <u>time</u> to resolve & a quiet atmosphere. The inferno of last week was not a favourable atmosphere. I hope I have not given the impression that Carson does not think you would be an asset here – He does, but would like the asset in an undamaged condition. I feel sure that nothing will be lost by waiting – My Darling if the telegram [to Asquith*] had not come last night I would have thought your decision irrevocable & would not have put you off your stroke by telling you all this – I would have drawn the picture in fainter colours.... I then said good-bye & Lady Carson gave me a little lunch before speeding me on my way. She has beautiful eyes & is I feel a true good cat but with a very violent disposition! I think we have a friend in her.

It was half past one by the time I started again on my way. The rain was blinding, the roads bad & the car went even more slowly than the day before.

Finally at 4.15 at Gravesend we punctured....

At 6.30 I crept into 'Cromwell' to find numberless telephone questions from the press which Goonie had answered by: – 'Col. Churchill is in France.' – 'I don't know' etc. etc....

I quickly wrote you [her letter of 13 March] my impressions of the Carson visit in case they might be any guide & that's all I have done since we parted – Now I feel helpless & can only wait & pray. God bless you & keep you and guide & inspire you my Darling & bring you peace of heart.

Your loving and devoted
Clemmie

¹ WSC had left on Sunday night, 12 March. CSC had gone to Dover with him and spent the night at the Lord Warden Hotel.
² Sir Frederick Cawley (1850–1937), cr. 1st Baron Cawley of Prestwich, 1918. Liberal MP, at this date Chairman of the Liberal War Committee.

◇ From CSC   41 Cromwell Road
16 March [1916] 5.30 a.m.

My Darling

Every time the post came yesterday I ran down to the hall for the letter explaining your telegram to the P.M.

Every time I was disappointed – Late in the afternoon I retired to bed as my cold had gone down to my chest – I fell into a deep sleep & woke up only a few minutes ago – I immediately realized that while I had been sleeping, the best post of all (10 p.m.) for letters from the front, had been and gone – I crept downstairs thro' the sleeping house & there on the hall table was the much wished-for blue envelope, ...

I am so thankful that you were inspired to send the telegram to the Prime Minister as this very grave decision needs quiet & concentrated thought which in the turmoil here it could not possibly receive – I do wish you could have seen Sir Edward Carson – I tried to give you a faithful picture in my two letters –

I think there are some solid qualities which English men & women value very highly – virtues such as steadfastness & stability – After your speech in the House of C [15 November 1915] in which you placed yourself 'unreservedly at the disposal of the Military Authorities' it seems to me that more than your <u>own</u> conviction is needed that it is your duty to return to Parliament –

I am convinced that sooner or later the demand will be made & that once made it will become insistent – Your speech has certainly animated & vivified the Admiralty but it has done you personally harm – I mean if you had been silent or put it differently, the demand for your return wld perhaps come sooner – But come it will – It must.

I pray therefore my Darling Love that you may decide to bide the time – We are living on such a gigantic scale that I am sure everything ought to be simplified – our actions too, so that without explanation or justification they & their motives can be understood and grasped by all. You have assumed the yoke of your own free will like many other men, tho' none of them are in your situation. The others, having assumed the yoke cannot dis-engage themselves. You, owing to your exceptional circumstances have received the written promise of the head of the Government that, on your speaking the word you shall be free. But that word must be spoken by others, if when free you are to be effective as an instrument to help the movement of events. Please forgive me my Darling if I express myself clumsily – ...

I have seen no-one in the official world – The last 3 days have been spent in getting back into the routine of my canteen work – ...

I long for more news of you. Write often my own Winston – I love you dearly –

Your loving
Clemmie

. . .

○ From WSC
16 [March] 1916[1]

6 R.S.F.
In the field

My darling dearest

Yr two most interesting letters arrived this morning.

I am still considering my course, & I cannot think that anything will be lost by the delay – now that the Army debates are beyond my reach. Carson is a most important factor & I am impressed by his misgivings. That it is right for me to come home is certain. What is not clear is when & on what grounds. It is worth while studying this a little longer – & here the days slip by calmly and quietly without excitement or distracting counsels. In a few more days I will settle whether (a) to write to Asquith* to act on my letter of the 12th or (b) to stop out here definitely for at least another 2 months ... General Furse to whom I talked openly had no doubts that my duty was at home – 'although it may be easier for you here with a battalion or a brigade & pleasanter, you have no right to think of that.' All talk about changeability etc – he regarded as irrelevant. 'The thing is much larger than that.'

Meanwhile the unfortunate Walshe – the Brigadier – has been 'Stellenbosched'[2] & has gone home precipitately, so that this Brigade is vacant; & no doubt my claims – if such there be – will be balanced now at G.H.Q. Although this matter cd in no way <u>determine</u> my action, I may as well have its decision before me before I settle. It will only take a day or two I expect.

Archie [Sinclair] is a strong advocate of my staying here – till there is some definite reason for a break. He is a gt comfort to me out here. It is odd how similar are the standpoints from wh you & he both view my tiresome affairs.

Meanwhile we have moved from that dirty crowded Soyer Farm into a new farm[3] only 700 yards behind my Advanced H.Q[rs]. This is well protected. The House is heavily sandbagged, & the ceilings are all propped up with tree trunks so that they carry a really effective load of brick & earth.... We are therefore as safe and much more comfortable than at Soyer farm – tho' the roads & approaches are subject to shelling.

All day the Germans have been shelling the little town [Ploegsteert). The hospice (where I entertained F.E. [Smith*]) has been hit repeatedly, & the little chapel wrecked & all the houses around hit. Great clouds of pink brick dust mingled with the black & white smoke of the shells, the gaping holes in the buildings, the soldiers & people running about to escape, the loud detonations following the continual whirring of the projectiles as they passed overhead made a vivid impression on the mind. We were just 100 or 150 yards in front of it all; & from the doorway of my dugout I watched the whole scene....

... On Sunday night I am going to give the men a concert, & have secured the Divisional band for the occasion. Perhaps by then I shall have come to a decision. If not another spell in the trenches! 'Yield thyself willingly to Clotho[4]– – –' ...

Tender love my dearest soul – I cannot tell you how much I treasure & count on yr aid & counsel. It was vy hard on you to set you such exhausting tasks. You discharged them famously.

Now mind you keep in touch with Garvin, Scott & Dalziel & don't let them drift off or think I have resigned the game. Tell them I am taking time to consider, method & occasion, but that in principle I have decided. Also I think you might have a talk with Cawley – & even with the Fiend [Lord Fisher] himself.

Your devoted & loving
W

Squeezer nibs are a necessity. This is the <u>last</u>. Send some in an envelope.

---

[1] This and several other letters dated by WSC as 'January', but their context clearly places them in March. Re-dated here, as in Martin Gilbert, *Winston S. Churchill, Companion Vol. III*, pp. 1454–7.

² Term from Boer War. Stellenbosch was a military base camp in Cape Colony to which misfits and incompetents were relegated.
³ 'Maison 1875', which would be Churchill's Reserve Headquarters for the rest of his time in France. See map p. 146.
⁴ One of the three Fates in Classical mythology, Clotho was the spinner of the web of life.

○ From WSC   6 R.S.F.
17 [March] 1916   In the Field

My darling,

A quiet day – not a shell near us. I have remained in & around my farm. Newspapers arrived telling of the Army debate. How different I cd have made it! My conviction strengthens & deepens each day that my place is there, & that I cd fill it with credit & public advantage. Meanwhile however the actual step seems so easy to put off – so irrevocable when taken, that I continue to pause on the brink, not undecided but dilatory....

This evening Archie [Sinclair] & I took a stroll up the lines on our right & went to the H.Q^{rs} of the battalion there. The same conditions & features reproduce themselves in every section – shattered buildings, sandbag habitations, trenches heavily wired, shell holes, frequent graveyards with thickets of little crosses, wild rank growing grass, muddy roads, khaki soldiers, – & so on for hundreds & hundreds of miles – on both sides. Miserable Europe. Only a few rifle shots & the occasional bang of a gun broke the stillness of the evening. One wondered whether the nations were getting their money's worth out of the brooding armies.

Cd I help to a victorious peace more in H. of C. than here? That is the sole question. Believe me if my life cd materially aid our fortunes I wd not grudge it.

Always your devoted & loving
W.

○ From WSC   6 R.S.F.
19 March 1916   In the Field

My darling One,

Leave is reopened, and Archie [Sinclair] who is much run down starts for home on 21st for 7 days. I want him to stay at Cromwell & you & Goonie to cherish & nourish him. He is all alone in the world, & vy precious as a friend to me. I am telling him to come straight to you on arrival – so get my room ready for him in good time. He will tell you all about our life out here, & my disturbing moods....

Archie will explain himself to Asquith* how the matter stands.

G. Trotter – late Col. of the Coldstream – a vy old acquaintance of mine & a first rate soldier has been given the Brigade. This will be vy nice, & a gt improvement on our last man. But the appointment clearly shows that I have no prospects. I do not mind this a bit. If I were to stay out here, I cd hardly be better suited than where I am. A Brigade wd give me no more scope & less personal interest. There is no doubt at all in my mind as to what I ought to do, & it is this conviction that overrides the arguments of your letter, present though they are in my mind. . . .

We go into the trenches again tomorrow morning for six days. Not a shell has fallen at Laurence Farm in my absence. Curious! But I am sure they do not know my movements or whereabouts. . . .

Tender love my dearest one. You must write to me every day. I shall be vy much alone while Archie is away. Your letter is always to me the event of the day. . . .

Always your devoted & ever loving
W.

◇ From CSC   41 Cromwell Road
22 March [1916]

My Darling,

Your letter announcing Archie [Sinclair]'s immediate arrival has just come and I have been hastily arranging things for his reception – I am so glad he is coming here especially as he will bring more immediate news of you– – –. I was interrupted by the visit of Mr C. P. Scott [Editor of *Manchester Guardian*] – While he was here Archie arrived & was therefore able to deliver your letter in person.

Mr Scott is glad that you still feel that your proper sphere is the House of Commons, but is very anxious that your return should not make an unfavourable impression – He thinks the right opportunity shd be waited for and then seized at once. . . .

I am struck by Archie's appearance – He looks pale and careworn. He cares for you much & takes your affairs to heart I think.

He seems to me to need rest and distraction.

He has gone to have a 'Turkey' [Turkish bath] & is returning to dinner – I will write again later – Keep a level mind my Darling & a stout heart.

Your loving,
Clemmie

. . .

○ From WSC   6 R.S.F.
22 [March] 1916   In the Field

My beloved,

Archie [Sinclair] will be with you now & will have given you full tidings of me. I have told him to see various people on my account and am looking forward to his reports. . . . The broad facts may with confidence be submitted to the public. Let us see what they are. 1. I resigned my office & gave up a salary of £4,300 a year rather than hold a sinecure at this time. 2. I shall have served for nearly five months at the front, almost always in the front line, certainly without discredit – discharging arduous & difficult duties to the full satisfaction of my superiors & to the advantage of my

officers & men. 3. I have a recognised position in British politics acquired
by years of public work, enabling me to command the attention (at any
rate) of my fellow countrymen in a manner not exceeded by more than 3
or 4 living men. 4. The period of our national fortunes is critical & grave:
and almost every question both affecting war & peace conditions, with wh
I have always been prominently connected, is now raised. I cannot
exclude myself from these discussions or divest myself of responsibilities
concerning them.

Surely these facts may stand by themselves as an answer to sneers &
cavillings. At any rate I feel I can rest upon them with a sure & easy
conscience. Do not my darling one underrate the contribution I have made
to the public cause, or the solidity of a political position acquired by so
many years of work & power. Gusts of ill feeling & newspaper attack
sweep by. But public men who really are known by the mass of the
nation, do not lose their place in public counsels except for something wh
touches their private character & honour. My command of the 6th R.S.F.
[Royal Scots Fusiliers] will certainly not unfavourably affect these general
conclusions.

> Your ever loving & devoted
> W

◇ From CSC   41 Cromwell Road
Friday 24 March [1916] 4 a.m.

[cover page, in CSC's handwriting:
'No. 1 written in the night']

My Darling,
Yesterday morning I received another visit from Mr C. P. Scott – He had
been thinking over the letter he received from you – He told me that he
was going to write & urge you to return as soon as possible. I have a great
admiration for his character & integrity, but I do not think he is a good
judge of what is _effective_ political action – You remember his
championship of _militant_ suffragism. Garvin is the same, tho' a dear &
faithful friend not a sound counsellor. . . .
Sir Ian Hamilton came to tea yesterday & was very pleasant. I told him
you were almost certainly coming home – He asked when? I said 'I think
as soon as possible; perhaps when his regiment comes out of the line' –
He looked serious & said 'Tell him on no account to come home _before_
that' –
My Dearest Love you know that you can rely upon my steadfastness &
loyalty, but the anxiety & grief at the step you are about to take sinks
deeper into my heart day by day. It seems to me such an awful risk to
take – to come back just _now_ so lonely & unprotected with no following
in the House & no backing in the country – Please do not be angry with
me for writing plainly –
I think I know you very well & it seems to me that you are actuated by
2 motives – 1) You want to be in the place where your powers for

helping to win the War will have fullest scope 2) You have a devouring thirst for 'War Direction' – Now I do beg you to reflect on this 2nd point – The war is (D.V.) ¾ over, the corner is nearly turned – (Perhaps you will disagree). The end is a long way off but still I think we are going to win in spite of slowness & hesitation – In your present weakened condition, shall you recover prestige & the necessary power in time to be of real use? I think perhaps you may if you <u>wait</u> a little longer – But it is a great risk – It is <u>indeed</u> a gamble – If you do not succeed you may gradually decline in the public opinion (tho' a speech would always attract attention).

If that happened then your return from the battlefield in the middle of the War might be a serious handicap to you in the future – The Government is nerveless & helpless but it represents all there is practically in public life – If you come back & attack them they are bound to defend themselves & try to down you – And just <u>now</u> you are very defenceless. The Government may not wage War very vigorously but when on the defensive they are very strong.

Do not be anxious about my attitude – I do not tell my thoughts to any but you. When you were here last week I did not feel that there were any great or good elements of strength surrounding you. Fisher a powerful but malevolent engine; you think him unimpaired by age but when the break-up comes, as soon it must, it will come with a damaging explosion to all near him – Garvin & Scott, good time men & personal friends, but often wrong-headed, Dalziel curious & interested but corrupt & time-serving. <u>In</u> the Cabinet that Judas Lloyd-George* never staunch in times of trial, always ready to injure secretly those with whom he is publicly associated (e.g. the sending you of those secret documents on the Naval situation was a base act of treachery to the Government, of whom he is a member. If he were honest, he would resign). Could you have the courage & the self denial if you returned to see <u>no one</u>, to help & not merely to criticize to refrain <u>absolutely</u> from personal attack. (You are vulnerable & your enemies would hope that you would indulge in this), to refrain also from <u>all</u> recriminations and attacks upon the <u>past</u> but only to apply your mind to the future – ...

I reflect upon you my Dear for hours together & lately I have had the time as I have had a little attack of bronchitis of which I have had to take care.

I was going away to the country for 3 days to try & shake it off when Archie was announced & so I put it off. I am not much fun for him as I can't go out –

The atmosphere here is wicked & stifling. Out where you are it is clean & clear – I fear very much that you will be very sad and unhappy here.

You must forgive me for this letter. If I did not tell you my thoughts I could not write at all –

The War is a terrible searcher of character. One must try to plod & persevere & absolutely stamp self out. If at the end one is found grimly holding on to one's simple daily round one can't have failed utterly....

Jack [Churchill*] is announced for leave at the beginning of May which will be very delightful – Birdwood[1] will then be in France I suppose and Jack will stay on with him. . . .

> God bless you my Darling
> Clemmie

[1] Gen. Birdwood returned from Egypt and established his Anzac corps headquarters near Hazebrouck in April 1916.

◇ From CSC   [41 Cromwell Road]
25 March [1916]

My Dearest,

Your letter [of 22 March] has just come & raised my spirits – Your silence had begun to depress them seriously –

The facts you mention in support of your immediate return are weighty & well expressed, but it would be better if they were stated by others than yourself (in public of course I mean). I cannot but think that they would be if you were seriously attacked. . . .

Archie [Sinclair] needs a rest badly; he looked pale & thin when he arrived. I think he is altered & improved –

My Darling these grave public anxieties are very wearing – When next I see you I hope there will be a little time for us both alone – We are still young, but Time flies stealing love away & leaving only friendship which is very peaceful but not stimulating or warming –

> Clemmie

. . .

○ From WSC   6 R.S.F.
26 March 1916   In the Field

My darling,

All your letters arrived together. I enclose you my reply to Carson. Send it to the address wh finds him soonest. . . . Of course if C. [Carson] chooses he can make my path smooth; but smooth or rough I mean to tread it. I am absolutely sure it is the right thing to do – & all these fears of taunts & criticisms shd be treated as if they were enemy's shells – i.e. they shd not deter one from any action wh is necessary in the general interest. . . . Have a good confidence & do not easily lend yourself to the estimates formed by those who will never be satisfied till the breath is out of my body. All this dawdling is wrong. Manoeuvring for position is only a minor part of war; a strong army & a good cause & plenty of ammunition drives ahead all right.

Meanwhile I am extremely well, & am getting quite inured to the ordinary hazards of the day. Nothing will now turn me from my intention. The more I feel myself cool & indifferent in danger here, the more I feel strong for the work that lies before me. I have been generous in regard to risks lately. If I thought that were a real reason at the back of my mind, I

shd never dare to face the tests of home politics at this time. But sure of
myself I am prepared to follow my instinct. If Carson & his whole
Committee[1] advised against my return – protested even – still I shd come –
& at once

Tender love my darling one
Your devoted loving
W

[1] Carson's Unionist War Committee, consisting of over 150 Conservative and Unionist MPs, had
been set up at the beginning of 1916, to press for greater state control of shipping, coal and food
distribution and more efficient war management.

○ From WSC   6th Royal Scots Fusiliers
28 March 1916   In the Field

My Beloved and darling Clemmie,
    I dined last night with General Lipsett[1] – the originator of the raids....
He has gone out of his way to be helpful to me out here, even coming out
with me on a prowl into No man's land to see if there were any
possibilities of bringing off an enterprise agst the German trenches....
    Oh my darling do not write of 'friendship' to me – I love you more each
month that passes and feel the need of you & all your beauty. My precious
charming Clemmie – I too feel sometimes the longing for rest & peace. So
much effort, so many years of ceaseless fighting & worry, so much
excitement & now this rough fierce life here under the hammer of Thor,
makes my older mind turn – for the first time I think – to other things than
action.... But wd it not be delicious to go for a few weeks to some lovely
spot, in Italy or Spain & just paint & wander about together in bright warm
sunlight far from the clash of arms or bray of Parliaments? We know each
other so well now & cd play better than we ever could.
    Sometimes also I think I wd not mind stopping living vy much – I am so
devoured by egoism that I wd like to have another soul in another world
& meet you in another setting, & pay you all the love & honour of the gt
romances....

Tenderest love my darling
Ever your devoted
W

P.S. The two red Tamworths [pigs] I wrote to you about two months ago
having survived all the perils of these shot swept fields, & the risks
incidental to their profession, have just turned up at the mouth of my
dugout on a visit of ceremony – for wh I am grateful in default of other
callers.
    What is this bronchitis my darling? I am distressed to hear you complain
of it. Mind you see Parky [Dr Parkinson]: & then go to Brighton for a few
quiet days ... Do take care of yourself, & don't do too much
canteening....
    More love – & kisses for Diana & Randolph.

[top left corner of front page of letter:]
P.P.S. I must reopen my letter to tell you that quite a good mouse has also paid me a visit just now. I have been watching the little beast reconnoitring the floor of this cave with the utmost skill daring & composure.

[1] Brig.-Gen. Louis James Lipsett (1874–1918) of the Royal Irish Regiment; attached to the Canadian Expeditionary Force, 1914–16.

◇ From CSC   41 Cromwell Road
1 April 1916

My own Darling,
     Your delicious loving letter arrived last night and warmed and comforted me. To-day is my birth-day and it is like the 1st of May in a poetry-book – so blue and sunshiny – This afternoon I go to Bournemouth to stay with Sir Ernest Cassel.
     Yesterday I read all the accounts of the deeds for which soldiers have been given the V.C. and other rewards. There was a long list of wonderful actions chronicled in the Times. What a heroic age – …
     I am so glad your Tamworths have escaped the shells – Please do not let your men kill them for bacon!
     I will write from the sea-side. Goodbye just now my sweet Winston – I am 31, but if the war were nearly won and you were safe and had peace of heart I should not feel more than 20 –

                                                   Your loving
                                                   Clemmie

◇ From CSC   [41 Cromwell Road]
6 April 1916

My own Darling,
     I have returned from salubrious Bournemouth & done 2 days' canteening & feel fit to drop so tomorrow I must write you a proper letter; this just brings you my love – On my return I found four letters from you, (one dated March 26th containing various letters …) … I have dispatched all letters you sent me to forward with the exception of one that reached me this morning for Lord Northcliffe (which you said I might hold up for a couple of days) & which I earnestly beg you not to ask me to post, but to destroy. If it goes it will form part of your biography in after times, & after the way Lord N has flouted you I cannot bear that you should write to him in that vein. Besides I do not think it is as well expressed as some of your letters.
     I am sure it is no use writing private letters to great journalists – Even if they do, in consequence decide to run you, they feel patronising and protective about it & the support then lacks in genuine ardour.
     My Darling own Dear Winston I am so torn & lacerated over you. If I

say 'stay where you are' a wicked bullet may find you which you might but for me escape – When I think with joy of your speedy return, my heart sinks a little at the idea you expressed in your last letter that you may lose your soldier's halo, which if you keep it is unique & different from all others – It was a wonderful thing your going out as you did; it made my heart (& many others less intimate) thrill with pride and I cannot bear that your enemies should try to kill this clean daring with bathos.

If I were sure that you wld come thro' unscathed I would say: 'wait, wait, have patience, don't pluck the fruit before it is ripe – Everything will come to you if you don't snatch at it' – To be great one's actions must be able to be understood by simple people. Your motive for going to the Front was easy to understand – Your motive for coming back requires explanation.

That is why your Fisher speech was not a success – people could not understand it. It required another speech to make it clear. I do long to see you so terribly – Your last visit was no help to me personally – I must see you soon –

Meanwhile your poor Mama is ill – She has had a toe (which was much inflamed) cut off & she is in great pain. Do write and comfort her. Also burglars have stolen all her pretty trinkets, valuable and personal things she had collected all her life. It is cruel.

Darling don't be vexed for me for writing so crudely – If to help you or make you great or happy I could give up my life it wld be easy for me to do it. I love you very much – By doing nothing you risk your life, by taking the action you contemplate you risk a life-long rankling regret which you might never admit even to yourself, & on which you would brood & spend much time in arguing to yourself that it <u>was</u> the right thing to do – And you would rehearse all the past events over & over again & gradually live in the past instead of in the present & in the great future – ...

If you will only listen a tiny bit to me I know (barring all tragic accidents) that you will prevail & that some day perhaps soon, perhaps not for 5 years, you will have a great & commanding position in this country. You will be held in the people's hearts & in their respect. I have no originality or brilliancy but I feel within me the power to help you now if you will let me. Just becos' I am ordinary & love you I know what is right for you & good for you in the end.

Your devoted loving
Clemmie

O From WSC   6 R.S.F.

10 April 1916   In the field

My darling,

You shd read the enclosed, if you like, seal them and send them all on with the exception of the one to Asquith*. This last I write to replace the former one now out of date, & I wish you to keep it by you ready to send on whenever I telegraph 'Forward letter'. I must be ready to act at any moment & cannot trust these uncertain posts. You can fill in the date wh shd be 2 days earlier than you send it. All these come to you by Mr McDavid who is having another trip home....

You are deluded if you think that by remaining here & doing nothing, I shall recover my influence on affairs – On the other hand I must be vy careful in all I do & how I do it.

If the Coalition breaks up under Asquith, I think it vy likely that Lloyd George's* necessities, the good will of B.L. [Bonar Law] & Carson, & F.E. [Smith*]'s active partisanship may draw me back into the war-direction. But of course I may be wrong, & then if a new Government is formed without me, I shall have to fight it out here – as I am quite prepared to do if no wider opportunities of aiding the war are open to me.

On the other hand if Asquith keeps on, I shall return as soon as I see a good chance – & await a further development quietly & patiently at home.

It is vy trying to have to watch this vital business from a distance: but provided the forces on wh I count are available, it may turn out to be the soundest policy. I see far more objections to hurrying home on the eve of a crisis, than to a deliberate & cool decision to return to Parliament taken solely on general grounds....

Now mind in these critical days you keep in touch with my circle. You may find [it] in yr power to help more than you wd believe....

It is a beautiful day.

> Fondest love
> Your devoted
> W

◇ From CSC   41 Cromwell Road
12 April 1916

My Darling,

Mr McDavid found Goonie & me dining with Lord French[1]. He delivered your letter & is coming to dinner on his way back to the Front when I will send you a letter by him –

I have read your letter carefully & am following out your instructions i.e. I have sent on all the letters to their destination with the exception of the one to the Prime Minister which I am putting under lock & key. Your previous letter to him I am destroying.

I hope you will consider carefully before sending the releasing telegram, as once this letter is received there is no going back. On 2nd thoughts I am sending you back your first letter to the P.M. together with a copy of the present one for you to compare. The 2nd letter is not so courteously worded – I do not know if this is intentional? It seems to me a pity....

I understand that your present position is
a) If the Government is reconstructed under new leadership you remain where you are unless you are included in the new Government. In that case no letter is needed, certainly not one to Mr Asquith* –
b) If the P.M. yields to pressure and the crisis passes over as before leaving a slightly lowered temperature you intend to return – In that case

there is no <u>immediate</u> hurry about the letter & it would be better to write a fresh one rather than release one written perhaps a fortnight sooner, the wording of which you do not quite remember.

I entirely approve of (a) I mean the first proposition – As to (b) you know my anxieties. The present Government may not be strong enough to beat the Germans, but I think they are powerful enough to do you in, & I pray God you do not give the heartless brutes the chance –

You say in your letter to me: 'You are deluded if you think that by remaining here & doing nothing, I shall regain my influence on affairs.' That is not what I do think.

What I do think is that remaining there you are in an honourable, <u>comprehensible</u> position until such time as a portion at least of the country demand your services for the State. If you come back before the call you may blunt yourself – People will always try to deny power if they think you are looking for it. To gain a share of War direction you are contemplating a terrible risk, the risk of life-long disappointment & bitterness. My Darling Love – <u>For once only</u> I pray be patient. It will come if you wait. Don't tear off the unripe fruit which is maturing tho' slowly or check its growth by the frost of a premature return –

I could not bear you to lose your military halo. I have had cause during the 8 years we have lived together to be proud and glad for you so often, but it is this I cherish most of all. And it is this phase which when all is known will strike the imagination of the people – The man who prepared & mobilized the Fleet, who really won the war for England in the trenches as a simple Colonel. It would be a great romance –

You say you want to be where you can help the War most. If you come home & your return is not generally accepted as correct soldier-like conduct you will not be really able to help the war. You <u>are</u> helping it now by example. You are always an interesting figure, be a great one my Darling – You have the opportunity.

Oh Winston I do not like all these letters I have to forward. I prefer Charlotte Corday[2] – Shall I do it for you?

Do not be alienated from me by what I write – If I hide what I feel from you the constraint wld be unbearable.

Your loving
Clemmie

[1] Sir John French, cr. Viscount, 1916; 1st Earl of Ypres, 1922. (See p. 105 n. 1.)
[2] Charlotte Corday (1768–93), right-wing republican during French Revolution, who stabbed the Jacobin leader, Jean Paul Marat to death in his bath, July 1793, and was guillotined four days later.

◇ From CSC   41 Cromwell Road
14 April [1916]

My Darling,

It is a long while since I have had real news of you – Your last letter contained only instructions & enclosures. Keep me going with something more. These last weeks since you returned to France have been sad & cruel & I have not been well which always makes anxiety harder to bear.

Sometimes when I have been out all day canteening I dread coming home to find a telegram with terrible news. And now if the telephone rings it may be the War Office to say that you have been killed. And yet in spite of this I keep on writing urging you not to leave the scene of these awful dangers. . . .

I saw Rufus Isaacs[1] the other day at a party after dinner at Downing Street – He was very friendly & I had a long talk to him. He fears coming back unless sent for would be injurious to your reputation. Nearly all the Ministers were there. Grey terribly aged & worn-looking, Kitchener thinner & sad, A.J.B. [Balfour] wan and white, but still purring away.

Goonie hopes for Jack [Churchill*]'s return any moment now.

Your poor Mama is better now & can just put her foot to the ground. She is very plucky.

Nellie is going to have a Baby & is feeling rather ill poor Darling. They have taken a tiny little house quite close to Eccleston Square & will soon be moving in. . . .

Oh my dear I would spare one of your arms or legs to get you safely home.

To-night I dine at Downing Street – I will see if I can discover any news. . . .

My bronchitis has returned – I have given up fighting against it!

Your loving
Clemmie

[1] Rufus Isaacs, later 1st Marquess of Reading (1860–1935), Lord Chief Justice of England, 1913–21.

A Secret Session of Parliament to debate the question of conscription[1] was called by the Prime Minister for 25–6 April. Learning of this, Churchill applied for leave, which was granted on condition he returned immediately the debate was over. He arrived in London on 19 April, and applied for a further two weeks' leave to grapple with the complicated situation which would arise from the debate: this too was granted.

On 25 April Churchill spoke in the Secret Session, and was preparing to take part in the open session on Friday 27th, when he received a telegram recalling him immediately as his battalion was in the trenches: he left at once for France.

[1] The Military Service Act (February 1916) had provided for partial conscription, but in May that year conscription was to be introduced for all males aged 18–41.

◇ From CSC   [41 Cromwell Road]
Friday [28] April 1916

My own Darling

I was relieved when I heard that you had caught the destroyer, but only for a very short while – This morning's news shews why you were so insistently recalled – Heavy fighting all along our Front – How I pray Ploegsteert may be spared. . . .

My Darling I am in an agony about you. But I cannot believe that after living thro' these dangerous months unscathed these last few days will be fatal to you. . . .

If only your speech [in Secret Session] had been reported I feel the Press would urge your recall. . . .

God bless you & keep you.
Clemmie

Winston had always hoped that a 'natural break' might provide an acceptable moment for him to leave his battalion and return home – for it was upon this course that he had now decided. Because of heavy losses in the Scottish regiments, several battalions were to be amalgamated: in the reorganization a senior colonel had prior claims, and so Churchill's command of the 6th Battalion came to its end.

○ From WSC   6 R.S.F.
2 May 1916

My darling,

. . . I shall go into G.H.Q. tomorrow to arrange about leave & the future of various officers. I apprehend no difficulty: & I expect to return (D.V.) Saturday or Sunday. The battalion will by then have ceased to exist. It is really a most fortunate and natural conclusion: & well worth having waited for.

Wd it not be vy nice to go to Blenheim for the Sunday. If you arrange this, please get me 3 large tubes of <u>thin</u> White (not stiff) from Robersons: also 3 more canvasses: and a bottle of that poisonous solution wh cleans the paint off old canvasses.

I shall address my constituents at Dundee on the following Saturday: but this need not be settled till I return.

The Germans have just fired 30 shells at our farm hitting it 4 times: but no one has been hurt. This is I trust a parting salute.

Your ever loving & devoted
W

On 6 May Churchill gave his officers a farewell luncheon at Armentières and, after taking leave of his men the following day, he returned home.

Chapter IX

LAST HEAVE

On his return from France Churchill took his seat in the House of Commons on the Opposition benches. But hanging over him, weakening both his role in opposition and his chances of inclusion in any government, was the dark shadow of the Dardanelles. Winston was determined to clear his name and pressed vehemently for the publication of the official Dardanelles papers. On 1 June 1916 it was announced that these papers would be laid before Parliament, but Asquith* subsequently decided against their publication on grounds of security, and that it was not in the public interest to do so. Many MPs as well as Churchill, angered by this change of mind, pressed for a full-scale debate (18 July), as a result of which the Government proposed to set up a select committee 'to inquire into the conduct of the Dardanelles operations'.

The Commission of Inquiry on the Dardanelles started its sittings in August 1916, and published its interim report in March 1917. Although the whole story was not told, Churchill's reputation was publicly cleared of the damaging charges which had previously been voiced without contradiction; and the Report clearly demonstrated that he had not acted alone in the decisions taken throughout the operation.

In December 1916, general discontent within and outside the Government, fuelled by the long-drawn-out slaughter of the Battle of the Somme (July–November), enabled Lloyd George* to manoeuvre Asquith from power. On 5 December five ministers, including Bonar Law, Curzon and Lloyd George, resigned: this powerful defection precipitated Asquith's resignation that same evening. Winston confidently hoped to be included in the new administration, but the Dardanelles Commission's final report was not yet published, and Lloyd George did not feel secure enough to ignore the bitter opposition of certain powerful Tories to Churchill's being given a post.

Towards the end of 1916 Winston and Clementine moved back into 33 Eccleston Square; they also started looking around for a country house, and the following spring they found Lullenden, a charming house and small farm near East Grinstead, Sussex.

Between May 1916, when Winston finally left France and his life as a soldier to re-enter politics, and the end of the following May there is only one letter extant between him and Clementine: now they were mostly together, and his life was once more centred round the House of Commons. Clementine was fully occupied with her family life, the newly acquired

Lullenden and her continuing canteen work – for which in January 1918 she would be appointed a CBE.

In some ways 1917 would prove to be the hardest year of the war: scarcely a family in the land had escaped bereavement; universal conscription and the demands of the war effort weighed upon people's lives; Zeppelin raids were an added strain; and the stranglehold of the U-boats on supplies brought price controls and rationing of food and materials.

In the early summer Lloyd George began confiding in Winston a good deal, making no secret that he greatly wished for him to be in the Government, and on 17 July Churchill was appointed Minister of Munitions: this received much adverse criticism. As all newly appointed ministers had to seek re-election, there was forthwith a by-election in his parliamentary seat of Dundee. It was quite a stormy campaign, and Clementine took her full part, addressing meetings when Winston was kept in London by ministerial duties. The result, declared on 29 July, gave Churchill a majority of 5,226.

As Minister of Munitions, Winston often visited the military commanders in France to study their requirements at first hand.

O From WSC   Tramecourt
17 February 1918

My darling
This vy clear weather & the state of the moon will certainly expose you to danger. I do wish you wd not delay to send the children out of town & of course I shd greatly desire your not sleeping in London during the raid period except when absolutely necessary. It made me feel vy anxious last night to see how bright & quiet the night was. The motor is ready any time you like to go....

I am just getting up at Tramecourt – near the field of Agincourt – to begin a fairly long day on ammunition, tanks & gas with the different people who we supply.... Tomorrow I shall probably move down Southwards to the Cavalry Corps. I shall not go to Paris this time. I will let you know if anything shd occur to delay my return.

Darling one I send you my fondest love. It is vy nice getting out here – without a care – except that I do not like to think of you & the kittens in London[1]. Better be sure than sorry....

With tender thoughts & vy best love
Yr devoted
W.

[1] On account of Zeppelin raids it was decided that the three children (aged eight, six and three) should from now on be country-based; they were joined at Lullenden by Jack and Goonie's boys, Johnnie and Peregrine (aged eight and three).

○ From WSC   [France]
23 February 1918

My darling One – I have been enjoying myself so much, & have had such
vy interesting days & pleasant evenings. I spent one day with General
Lipsett as I told you, & the next I came on here to General Barnes[1] where
we were vy warmly welcomed. I went all round my old trenches at
Plugstreet. Everything has been torn to pieces & the shelling is still at
times severe. The British line has moved forward about a mile, but all my
old farms are mere heaps of brick & mouldering sandbags. The little
graveyard has been filled & then smashed up by the shells. I missed
Plugstreet church. We ran past the place where it had stood without
recognising it! My strong dugout however wh I built at Laurence farm has
stood out the whole two years of battering, & is still in use. So also are the
cellars of the convent wh I drained & called the 'conning tower'.
Otherwise utter ruin.

Jack [Churchill*] came with us on this expedition & we lunched at
Birdwood's HQ before starting. Birdwood told me that he expected &
hoped every day to see Jack's name in the Gazette for a D.S.O. He is
much appreciated where he is, & seems to have a lot of varied &
interesting things to manage....

Yesterday ... we went out to see the Ypres salient. I had not been in
Ypres for 3 years. It has largely ceased to exist. As for the country round &
towards the enemy – there is absolutely nothing except a few tree stumps
in acres of brown soil pockmarked with shell holes touching one another.
This continues in every direction for 7 or 8 miles. Across this scene of
desolation wind duckboard tracks many of them in full view of the
enemy; ...

Then we walked for miles (I have walked five hours at least each day)
over these duckboards till finally we got to Glencorse Wood & Polygon
Wood. These consist of a few score of torn & splintered stumps only. But
the view of the battle field is remarkable. Desolation reigns on every side.
Litter, mud, rusty wire & the pock marked ground – Very few soldiers to
be seen, mostly in 'pill boxes' captured from the industrious Hun.
Overhead aeroplanes constantly fired at. The Passchendaele ridge was too
far for us to reach but the whole immense arena of slaughter was visible.
Nearly 800,000 of our British men have shed their blood or lost their lives
here during 3½ years of unceasing conflict! Many of our friends & my
contemporaries all perished here. Death seems as commonplace & as little
alarming as the undertaker. Quite a natural ordinary event, wh may
happen to anyone at any moment, as it has happened to all these scores
of thousands who lie together in this vast cemetery, ennobled & rendered
forever glorious by their brave memory.

One vy odd thing is the way in wh you can now walk about in full view
of the enemy & in close rifle shot.... Yesterday in fact the duckboard track
led us to within 500 yards of a vy strongly held Hun position at
Polderhoek Chateau. It was like walking along a street – not a scrap of
cover or even camouflage. Still people kept coming and going & not a
shot was fired. In my days at Plugstreet it wd have been certain death. But

I suppose they are all so bored with the war, that they cannot be bothered to kill a few passers by. We on the other hand shoot every man we can see.

On the way back we passed the lunatic asylum blown to pieces by the sane folk outside! ...

Now my sweet one – I must really finish. ... I reach Paris if all goes smoothly Tuesday ... I hope to cross by a destroyer and reach you lateish on Thursday, I hope for dinner. ...

Your ever loving & devoted
W.

...

[1] Maj.-Gen. (later Sir) Reginald Barnes (1871–1946), one of WSC's closest army friends since Cuba days (1895); at this time commanding the 57th Division.

○ From WSC   Ritz, Paris
31 March 1918

My darling,

I hope Ll.G. [Lloyd George*] will show you my telegrams wh give the best account of my activities.

Yesterday was vy interesting, for I saw with Clemenceau[1] all the commanders – Haig, Foch[2], Pétain[3], Weygand[4], Rawlinson[5] etc; & heard from each the position explained. The old man [Clemenceau] is vy gracious to me & talks in the most confidential way. He is younger even than I am! and insisted on being taken into the outskirts of the action wh was proceeding N of Moreuil. Seely's Brigade had just stormed the wood above the village & were being attacked by the Huns there. Stragglers, wounded horses, blood & explosives gave a grim picture of war. I finally persuaded the old tiger to come away from what he called 'un moment délicieux'.

We dined with Pétain in his sumptuous train and I was much entertained by Clemenceau. He is an extraordinary character, every word he says – particularly general observations on life & morals is worth listening to. His spirit & energy indomitable. 15 hours yesterday over rough roads at high speed in motor cars. I was tired out – & he is 76!

He makes rather the same impression on me as Fisher: but much more efficient, & just as ready to turn round & bite! I shall be vy wary.

'This battle fares like to the morning's war,
When gathering clouds contend with growing light'

(You shd read the passage in Henry VIth part III). I think we ought to hold them for the time being, but a most formidable prolonged tremendous struggle is before us – if we are to save our souls alive. ...

Beloved, it is yr birthday tomorrow. ... I send you my fondest love and my dearest wishes for long & happy years. Do write to me & let me know all about our affairs. ...

Go on with all the plans for evacuating Eccleston Square.[6] ...
Tender love

Your devoted
W.

[1] Georges Clemenceau (1841–1929), Prime Minister of France, 1906–9 and 1917–20; presided over the Paris Peace Conference, 1919. Known as 'the Tiger'.
[2] Gen. Ferdinand Foch (1851–1929), C.-in-C. Allied armies in France, March 1918. Marshal of France, August 1918.
[3] Gen. Philippe Pétain (1856–1951), Marshal of France, 1916. French military commander and national hero following his defence of Verdun, 1916; C.-in-C., May 1917–November 1918. In Second World War, as Prime Minister (June 1940) he negotiated an armistice with Germany and became Chief of State of Vichy Government, 1940–4; subsequently sentenced to death for treason, the sentence being commuted to life imprisonment.
[4] Gen. Maxime Weygand (1867–1965), Chief of Staff to General Foch, 1914–23. Briefly, 1940, Supreme Allied Commander. Served under Pétain in Vichy Government; arrested and imprisoned in Germany, 1942. After the war charged with treason, but acquitted.
[5] Gen. Sir Henry (later Baron) Rawlinson (1864–1925), commander of the Fourth Army, 1916–18.
[6] The lease on 33 Eccleston Square expired this year, and they did not renew it.

○ From WSC   Paris
6 June 1918

Beloved darling,
    An Air Raid is in progress & I am due & overdue for bed. So these lines will be few but to the point. Much work has come upon me here & I have found the days all too short – I have seen vy many interesting & influential people & transacted a good deal of business satisfactorily.
    You can judge the general situation for yrself. On the whole I am hopeful. But the fate of the capital hangs in the balance – only 45 miles away[1]. Next time I come here (if there is a 'next time') you must really try to accompany me. You must prepare a good cause under the shelter of the Y.M.C.A.[2] (Y'a Moyens Coucher Avec) (as Loucheur[3] calls it) & spend a few jolly days in this menaced but always delightful city....
    D.V. Weather permitting & the rest of it, I purpose to fly to Kenley Aerodrome[4] Wed. or Thursday. I will send you notice. Try to be at Lullenden so that we can be together....
    Tender love to you & all dear & dearest ones

Yr devoted
W.

[1] The Germans had launched a great spring offensive, and by 3 June their front line was at one place less than fifty miles from Paris. On 11 June the French counter-attacked and staved off further enemy advances towards the capital.
[2] CSC's canteens were under the auspices of the Young Men's Christian Association.
[3] Louis Loucheur (1872–1931), French Minister of Munitions, 1917–20.
[4] A few miles south of Croydon, Surrey.

○ From WSC   Paris
Midnight 10 June [1918]

My darling One,
    The vy critical and deadly battle on the Montdidier–Noyon front has
raged all day, & the latest accounts (5.30 p.m.) are apparently satisfactory:
There is no surprise here, but a blunt trial of strength – the line strongly
held with troops & good reserves at hand. If the French cannot hold them
back on this sector, it is not easy to see what the next step on our part shd
be. I am hopeful. . . .
    I have bought you a little present in Paris, wh I shall shew you when I
arrive –
    The young flying officer[1] has won my heart. His wife was there the
other day when we started. He is vy gallant, & vy <u>battered</u>.
    Tender love my dearest soul to you & all yr chicks. . . .
                                                        Your always loving
                                                                    W.

[1] Lt (later Maj.) Cyril Patteson of the Royal Engineers, who had won the MC at Suvla Bay. Seconded
to the Royal Flying Corps, 1917. At this time serving with the No. 7 Aircraft Acceptance Park,
Kenley. Known as 'The Canary', he often piloted WSC.

◇ From CSC   Lullenden
23 July [1918]

My Darling
    1) Is Cassel coming down this Sunday or are you going to France?
    2) If not going to France I hope you are coming down <u>Friday</u>?
    <u>Please telephone</u> re these two points
    On Saturday I want you to take me to Crawley in the motor (about 10
miles) to see Cheal's Nursery Gardens. I want to buy some little rock plants
to put in the chinks everywhere – This cannot be done before the autumn
but the <u>point</u> is to see them all in bloom before they fade for the effect.
    I have not seen papers yet to-day as [the] pony cart is broken but they
are coming presently. I have done a lot of weeding on the lawn plantains
etc. I got a new tool in E. Grinstead which fishes them out beautifully
roots & all.

                                                            Love from Cat
                                                                    . . .

○ From WSC [typewritten][1]   Château Verchocq[2]
10 August 1918

My darling,
    We had a very pleasant fly over and passed fairly close to Lullenden. I
could follow the road through Croydon and Caterham quite easily. . . . We
landed here in good time for dinner. The chateau is very comfortable –
simple but clean. I have a charming room, filled with a sort of ancient

wood-carved furniture that you admire, and which seems to me to be very fine and old. The grounds contain avenues of the most beautiful trees, beech and pine, grown to an enormous height and making broad walks like the aisles of cathedrals. One of these must be nearly half a mile long. The gardens are very pretty, though of course there are not many flowers. I am sitting now in the open air on a glorious evening writing this to you.

Yesterday we went to the battle-field, motoring through Amiens and Villers Bretonneux ... This was about 5,000 yards inside the lines which the Germans had held the day before[3]. As they were shelling the village and trying to shell the road, we moved the car down a side road about half a mile where we found a safe place for it, and then we walked about on the battle-field, picking our way with discretion. The actual battle front had rolled on nearly four miles from where we were, and all our heavy batteries in this neighbourhood had just received the order to move forward again. Jack [Churchill*], who is with Birdwood in the neighbourhood of Verchocq, came with us and acted as escort and guide. The ground everywhere was ploughed up by shells, but nothing to the same extent as the Somme and Ypres battle-fields. The tracks of the Tanks[4] were everywhere apparent....

On our way to the battle-field we passed nearly 5,000 German prisoners, penned up in cages or resting under escort in long columns along the roadside.... I went into the cages and looked at them carefully. They looked a fairly sturdy lot, though some of them were very young. I could not help feeling very sorry for them in their miserable plight and dejection, having marched all those miles from the battle-field without food or rest, and having been through all the horrors of the fight before that. Still, I was very glad to see them where they were.

To-day I have been working at G.H.Q. on shells. The German shells have false noses which make them go much further than ours, and the question is, Why have we not developed these earlier? There is no doubt we have fallen behind, and great efforts will have to be made in this class of supply if we are to catch up next year.... Tomorrow I think of going again to the battle-field if I can get horses. It will be very interesting to see the armies moving forward. The events which have taken place in the last 3 days are among the most important that have happened in the war, and, taken in conjunction with the German defeats on the Marne and at Rheims, entitle us to believe that the tide has turned. Up to the present there must be at least 30,000 prisoners in our hands, with several hundred guns. In addition, Montdidier is surrounded and the troops holding it are cut off.... On the front of three armies, the fourth British and the first and third French, several hundred thousand men have been marching forward for several days through liberated territory. Our cavalry are still out in front, and in some parts of the line there are at the moment no Germans left. The Australian armoured cars rushed through the moment the front was broken and attacked the headquarters of the transport and everything they could find in rear.... I am so glad about this great and fine victory of the British Army. It is our victory, won chiefly by our troops under a British Commander, and largely through the invincible Tank which British brains have invented and developed. Haig has done very well, and it does not follow that we are at the end of our good fortune yet.... One

American regiment has taken part on our front in this battle. Would you believe it – only three American Divisions were in the line at any one moment between Rheims and Soissons[5]. They certainly had a good press. That is one reason why I rejoice that we should have won a great success which no one can take from us. . . .

I send you a copy of an extremely appreciative telegram which I had from Haig in answer to my congratulations. It is certainly very satisfactory to have succeeded in gaining the confidence and good-will of the extremely difficult and to some extent prejudiced authorities out here. There is no doubt that they have felt themselves abundantly supplied.

Tender love my darling one
Your ever loving
W

[1] This appears to be the first typewritten letter from WSC to CSC.
[2] Lord Haig had placed Château Verchocq, near St Omer, at WSC's disposal to facilitate his visits to France.
[3] The Allied counter-offensive had been launched on 8 August near Amiens.
[4] Tanks had been used for the first time in September 1916, in the battle of the Somme.
[5] The USA had declared war on Germany, 2 April 1917. The first American troops arrived in Europe in June 1917.

◇ From CSC   Brookside
Sunday 11 August [1918]   Sutton Courtenay

My Darling
I arrived here on Friday night to stay with Goonie and find her in a haven of dreamy peace lapped by the waters of the Thames – . . .

Johnny [nine] & Peregrine [five] are charming; 'Pebbin' has dropped his churlish manners & is most gracious keeping however a shy & dignified reserve. John is very happy at school & is a dear little boy. . . .

Tomorrow I go to Mells to stay with Frances Horner[1] for 2 days, then a day in London for Canteens, then Lullenden & next Sunday I shall be at St Margaret's Bay with the Children. . . .

I have been reading (lent by Goonie) Married Love[2]. It is a most remarkable pamphlet really meant for Husbands not for Wives – Goonie says the opposite point of view is in Ovid.

I can't think why this pamphlet was not written years ago – It is the book which you told me was being discussed at the 'Other Club' a little time ago –

I hope it will not be jeered at by middle aged, plain cynical men over their wine. It is meant for beautiful god-like young men ardently pursuing tender & lovely nymphs. It is 'Dedicated to young Husbands & all those who are betrothed in Love'.

It has an introductory letter from a Roman Catholic Priest who agrees with the Author about everything except 'Birth Control' – He has to make a stand over this I suppose or the Pope would punish him –

I would so much like to see you again soon – Let me know your plans –
Love from
Clemmie

. . .

[1] Lady Horner, Frances, born Graham (1858–1940), wife of Sir John Horner KCVO (1842–1927), barrister.
[2] By Marie Stopes (1880–1958), pioneer birth-control campaigner; published 1918.

◇ From CSC   The Manor House
Tuesday 13 August [1918]   Mells[1]

My Darling

I am progressing with my round of Country House visits & arrived here yesterday.

I had not remembered the charm & beauty of this place. Perhaps having a delicious little home of one's own makes one more observant. The garden is enclosed in 3 beautiful old pink brick walls, the south front of the house forming the 4th side. In the evening the house is full of the heavenly fragrance of stocks, tobacco plants, lavender & roses....

Alas I could not bathe[2] but I watched Lady Horner & her Grandchildren (Katharine Asquith's daughters[3]) disport themselves.... This morning she drove me round the village & shewed me the remains of Mells Park, a tragic spectacle.

You remember it was gutted by fire a little time ago. It looked like one of the palaces at Messina after the earthquake, the almost perfect front but with staring windows – inside unspeakable havoc & ruin....

Then I was shewn the home Farm with a big dairy ... They have their own private bull ... I am gleaning all the farming tips I can, you see!...

Paying visits in War time in August must be what visits were like in Miss [Jane] Austen's time. No bustle, no motors, very few fellow guests, walks in the shrubbery, village tittle-tattle....

Should you be returning home next Tuesday or Wednesday you might land near Dover in your aeroplane & come & see the children & take me back in your motor.

The War news continues good but it seems to me that 'the Victory' is now complete & that for the present nothing more is to be expected?...

I hope to get a letter from you –

This one is very long & leisurely I fear. I have forgotten the Canteens –

Your loving
Clemmie

[1] Ancestral home of the Horner family, near Frome, Somerset.
[2] CSC was expecting her fourth child in November.
[3] Katharine Horner, widow of Raymond Asquith (see p. 117 n. 2); they had two daughters. He had been killed in action in September 1916.

○ From WSC   [Paris]
15 August 1918

My darling One,

I never saw anything like the tropical brilliancy of the weather here. Each day is more perfect than the other. It was provoking to be cooped up in a conference hour after hour[1].... It is quite an impressive gathering – the 4 great nations assembled along the tables with their ministers & generals etc. We arranged that each gt power shd represent one of the little powers (so as to restrict members). France took Greece, Italy was given Serbia, the U.S. Belgium, & we look after the Portuguese; so we are like four kangaroos each with an infant in the pouch. Ours is rather a dirty brat I am afraid....

Dearest & best beloved let me know what plans you make for Lullenden next Sunday....

Always yr devoted
W.

[1] WSC was attending a series of meetings on munitions problems.

◇ From CSC [written in pencil]   The Manor House
15 August [1918]   Mells

My Darling

Thank-you for a most interesting account of what is going on in France – How much better you describe things than the most brilliant Newspaper Correspondent. But I forget. You were one once – but that was before I knew you....

This is a delicious place to rest and dream & I feel my new little baby likes it – Full of comfort, beautiful things, sweet smelling flowers, peaches ripening on old walls gentle flittings & hummings & pretty grandchildren. But under all this the sadness & melancholy of it all – Both the sons dead, one lying in the little Churchyard next to the House, carried away at sixteen by Scarlet Fever, the other sleeping in France[1] as does the Husband of the best loved daughter of the House Katharine Asquith – Both their swords are hanging in the beautiful little Gothic Church beside long inscriptions commemorating long dead Horners who died in their beds –

Mr Birrell has arrived, dilapidated & frail but full of wit & fun – He says he has been demoralized by staying with Venetia [Montagu*] & Edwin at Breccles, their Norfolk Lullenden, in company with Diana Manners [later Cooper*] & Scatters Wilson[2].

We all go to Bath to hear him speak to-day & then I go home over the week-end – On Monday I shall escort Sarah to her sea-side Residence near Dover, where if you do not tarry in France too long I will await your return....

I hope I shall get another letter

Your loving
Clemmie

[1] Edward Horner, killed in action 1917.
[2] Lt-Col. Sir Mathew Wilson, 4th Bt (1875–1958), soldier and Unionist MP. Known as 'Scatters'. He was very much in the Asquith–Montagu set.

○ From WSC   Verchocq
8 September 1918

My Beloved,
    We sailed across the Channel through a fierce storm and were over the
other side in about 11 minutes.... I am going to lunch with Haig today
and am spending the morning in bed with my papers....
    It was so nice yesterday on the beach [St Margaret's Bay] with you & the
kittens. They all looked 'in the pink'. I do hope you were not cold going
back in the car, or were not worried at my method of travel [flying]. It
gives me a feeling of tremendous conquest over space, & I know you wd
love it yourself. The Canary [his pilot, Cyril Patteson] is much alarmed by
motor cars & thinks them far more dangerous than aeroplanes.
    I am looking forward to receive a long loving delightful letter to wh I
will endeavour to send a suitable reply. I am vy happy to be married to
you my darling one, & as the years pass I feel more & more dependent
on you & all you give me.

                                                        With tender love
                                                            Your own
                                                                W

...

○ From WSC   Verchocq
10 September 1918

My darling,
    I was out all yesterday on the battlefield & went over the celebrated
Drocourt-Queant lines under the guidance of General Lipsett. I will not
weary you with the military lessons wh emerged, but they were vy
interesting & instructive. Everywhere the soldiers received me with the
broadest of grins & many a friendly shout or hand wave. I think I value
the spontaneous & unmerited goodwill of these heroic men more than the
Garron Tower estates[1]. But do not be alarmed. I am not going to renounce
them....
    My darling one – I remember that this letter shd reach you on the 12th
September. Ten years ago my beautiful white pussy cat you came to me.
They have certainly been the happiest years of my life, & never at any
moment did I feel more profoundly & eternally attached to you. I do hope
& pray that looking back you will not feel regrets. If you do it [is] my fault
& the fault of those that made me. I am grateful beyond words to you for
all you have given me. My sweet darling I love you vy dearly.

                                                   Your own unsatisfactory
                                                                W
                                                               ...

[1] In Co. Antrim. Part of WSC's eventual inheritance through his great-grandmother Frances, wife
of the 7th Duke of Marlborough, born Lady Frances Vane-Tempest-Stewart, daughter of the 3rd
Marquess of Londonderry.

○ From WSC   Hotel Ritz
12 September 1918   Paris

My darling,

Loucheur wants to spend a night with me at Verchocq & proposes to
come Sunday. I fear therefore I shall not be able to return this week-end
as I had hoped. I shall try to be back in London on Tuesday morning
early. Let me know through Eddie [Marsh*][1] where you will be that day &
what yr plans for the week are.

I motored on here yesterday as the weather was too bad for the Canary.
I was alone & took the road by Montdidier in order to see the ruin the war
had brought on this unlucky town.... But bad as it is, it does not reach the
utter destruction of Bailleul & Meteren in the North. Here the British
artillery has been at work – regardless of expense – & nothing but red
smears of brick bats mark the site of what were once in the spring thriving
townships....

Who shd I meet in the foyer of the Ritz, but Muriel[2] & her husband! He
is a vy average specimen. But she seems quite happy with him. I did not
discern any signs of kittens. She looked vy handsome & is over here on
'husband's leave'. The Ritz is chock-full again....

I am trying also to arrange to give the Germans a good first dose of the
Mustard gas[3] before the end of the month. Haig is vy keen on it & we shall
I think have enough to produce a decided effect. Their whining in defeat
is vy gratifying to hear.

Ten years ago my dearest one we were sliding down to Blenheim in our
special train. Do you remember? It is a long stage on life's road. Do you
think we have been less happy or more happy than the average married
couple? I reproach myself vy much for not having been more to you. But
at any rate in these ten years the sun has never yet gone down on our
wrath. Never once have we closed our eyes in slumber with an
unappeased difference. My dearest sweet I hope & pray that future years
may bring you serene & smiling days, & full & fruitful occupation. I think
that you will find real scope in the new world opening out to women, &
find interests wh will enrich yr life. And always at yr side in true & tender
friendship as long as he breathes will be your ever devoted, if only
partially satisfactory, W

                                                                        ...

Many kisses.

[1] Eddie Marsh had returned to WSC as Private Secretary in 1917.
[2] Muriel Wilson, WSC's old flame, who in 1917 had married Maj. Richard Warde.
[3] Mustard gas had been used for the first time by the Germans at Ypres, July 1917. The first significant use of the gas by the British was on the night of 26–7 September 1918. Chlorine gas had
been used by the Germans at the start of the Second Battle of Ypres, April 1915, and by the British
for the first time at the start of the Battle of Loos, 25 September 1915.

○ From WSC   [Château Verchocq]
15 September 1918

My darling,

Eddie [Marsh*] received my instructions to convey to you my reproaches yesterday. Up to this moment I have not had a single letter. Really it is unkind. Mails have reached me with gt regularity & swiftness by aeroplane or messengers. They have comprised all manner of communications, but never one line from the Cat. The Canary on the other hand receives each day through my bag a bulky screed from his mate. You have certainly given me no chance to <u>answer</u> yr letters. You have deprived yourself of any opportunity for accusing me of not having read them – When I reflect on the many and various forms which yr naughtiness takes, I am astonished at its completeness & its versatility. So there!

Having put down my barrage on yr trenches, let me explain further why I have not returned home. Loucheur has to visit Dunkirk today & on his way back proposes to bring his party (six) to dinner here. I have asked also Jack [Churchill*] & [Sir John] Simon, & the owner of the Chateau (he is a Count) was likewise tactfully invited to the feast by me. Tomorrow I must return to Paris, where Mr Ryan[1] (Air) has at last arrived....

My days here have been fruitful in business & I have got a lot of things moving wh were otherwise stuck. The hamper of mustard gas is on its way. This hellish poison will I trust be discharged on the Huns to the extent of nearly 100 tons by the end of this month – in one dose. I find each day lots to do, & lots to see. Indeed I have not done half the things I wanted to do yet. In the mornings or afternoons I sit here quietly working at my papers – or I can sally out in my car to some friend up in the line. Or I can get someone I want to talk shop to, to come & dine here. Meanwhile the work arrives in steady consignments, & the telephone & aeroplane keep me in the closest touch. It is just the sort of life I like – Coming out here makes me thoroughly contented with my office. I do not chafe at adverse political combinations, or at not being able to direct general policy. I am content to be associated with the splendid machines of the British army, & to feel how many ways there are open to me to serve them....

Darling one – I do not expect I shall be home before Wednesday. Saturday we go to Edwin [Montagu] – do we not? All this makes me desirous of Lullenden news – Do write me by pouch all about it....

My lovely one I will now close with fondest love & many kisses from

Your ever devoted
though vilely neglected
Pig

[1] John Dennis Ryan (1864–1933), Director of the (US) Bureau of Aircraft Production, May–July 1918; Assistant Secretary of War and Chairman of Aircraft Board, August–November 1918.

Having moved out of 33 Eccleston Square, the Churchills for a period had no London home; they therefore perched in various lent or leased houses. Winston, owing to the pressures of his work, and during this 'homeless' interlude, often stayed in rooms in his ministry – the Hotel Metropole, commandeered by the Government, in Northumberland Avenue, off Trafalgar Square.

○ From CSC   16 Lower Berkeley Street[1]
17 September 1918

My Darling Winston

You have been away such a long time & I have not written to you once, & you have sent me two lovely letters.

It seems ages since that evening when you disappeared like a swallow into the twilight over the sea – You started too late in the evening; it was getting dark & cold & 5 minutes after you had left the ground, that horrible thunder-storm [see WSC's letter of 8 September] burst out – I was really very uneasy & stayed awake all night thinking & dreading some message would come. You seemed to fly right into the storm.

I'm much looking forward to your return –

Don't forget next Friday we go to Breccles [in Norfolk] to stay with Edwin & Venetia [Montagu*]....

Do come home soon – You have been away for nearly a month with your 2 visits – you bad Vagrant. Next time I shall trip over to America & back. I shall just have time to be found dozing on the hearth at Lullenden when you return from your Château or Paris –

Love from
Clemmie

[1] The Horners' town house, lent to the Churchills for the last two months of CSC's pregnancy.

○ From CSC   3 Tenterden Street[1]
29 October [1918]

My Darling

I hear that a pouch is about to fly over to you so I write a few hasty lines.

I do not know where to picture you during these last days: – witnessing triumphal British troops in re-captured Flemish cities in company with Millie[2] & Rosemary[3] ... or sitting on the Dais at Lille behind the red Tabs [high ranking military] or in Paris assisting at inter Allied Councils – I hope the last picture is the correct one –

It is a rather awful spectacle, two great Empires cracking, swaying & on the verge of toppling into ruins – If only these things could happen gradually & tidily....

Meanwhile my Darling do come home and look after what is to be done with the Munition Workers when fighting really does stop. Even if the fighting is not over yet, your share of it must be, & I would like you to be praised as a reconstructive genius as well as for a Mustard Gas Fiend, a Tank juggernaut & a flying Terror. Besides the credit for all these Bogey parts will be given to subordinates and not to my Tamworth [pig] –

I have got a plan – Can't the men Munition Workers build lovely garden cities & pull down slums in places like Bethnal Green, Newcastle, Glasgow, Leeds etc., & can't the women munition workers make all the lovely furniture for them – Baby's cradles, cupboards etc.?...

Do come home & arrange all this....

Tender Love from
Clemmie.

I <u>would</u> have enjoyed a letter from you these last days, but I am not fretting or pining for you, but I just think you are a little pig. 'What can you expect from a pig but a grunt?' says the adage – But I haven't even had a grunt from mine –

...

[1] Lady Wimborne (Aunt Cornelia)'s house, lent to WSC and CSC for CSC's confinement.
[2] Millicent, Duchess of Sutherland (1867–1955), widow of 4th Duke of Sutherland (d. 1913); she subsequently married again twice. Directed a Red Cross front-line ambulance, 1914–18, and later made her home in France.
[3] Lady Rosemary Leveson-Gower (1893–1930), daughter of the 4th Duke of Sutherland and Millicent, Duchess of Sutherland. Served in the Red Cross. Married, 1919, Viscount Ednam (Eric Ward), later 3rd Earl of Dudley (1894–1969).

Victory came at last. On 11 November 1918 London went wild with relief and joy. Four days later, on 15 November, Clementine gave birth to their fourth child – another red-headed girl – Marigold Frances.

Two weeks after the Armistice, Parliament was dissolved, and there was a General Election – the first since December 1910. Lloyd George* sought to keep the Coalition Government in being, supported by his own wing of the Liberal Party. He went to the country in what became known as the 'coupon election' because he and Bonar Law (leader of the Conservative Party) issued a joint coalition programme and sent signed letters – 'coupons' – to candidates supporting the Coalition. ('Coupons' were not issued to Asquith* and his 106 supporters.)

The campaign was conducted in an hysterical atmosphere of patriotic fervour and demands for 'Hang the Kaiser' and vengeance against Germany. Churchill campaigned as a strong supporter of maintaining the Coalition, and was one of a small number of candidates who opposed enforcing a harsh peace on Germany; he also warned in the strongest terms against the dangers of Bolshevism.

The election result, on 28 December, was a triumph for the Coalition.[1]

[1] The Coalition won more than 5 million votes (47.6% of the total vote). The Liberals won only 28 seats (Asquith himself being defeated); Labour, 63 seats; and Sinn Fein (their first appearance), 73 seats.

Chapter X

PIPING IN PEACE

In the new Government Winston Churchill was appointed Secretary of State for War and Air. As such he had immediately to grapple with the demobilization of nearly 3,500,000 soldiers. There was already mounting disaffection in the army, and a near-mutiny took place in London on 8 January. Shortly after his appointment Churchill announced a new scheme, which was seen as being essentially fair. But Britain's military strength had to be equal to the tasks of peace (e.g. maintaining the Army of Occupation of the Rhine), and a million men had to be conscripted in peacetime: a necessary but not popular measure.

In Ireland the scene was sinister and increasingly violent. The seventy-three newly elected Sinn Fein MPs refused to take their seats in Westminster, and set up their own Parliament – the Dail – in Dublin, demanding immediate independence and proclaiming the Republic of Ireland. Following on this the IRA (Irish Republican Army) launched a campaign of terrorism against the police and the Government. In February 1920 the new Home Rule Bill, envisaging partition between North and South Ireland, was fiercely denounced by Sinn Fein. Churchill, as Secretary of State for War, was directly responsible for increasing the number of troops sent to Ireland to cope with the violence and the slide towards civil war.

In November 1920 intelligence reports revealed that Sinn Fein planned to kidnap a number of ministers, including the Prime Minister and Churchill; consequently a Special Branch officer was allotted to him as a bodyguard – Detective Constable Walter Thompson[1], who would be with him whenever he travelled for many years to come.

The Peace Conference was convened at Versailles in January 1919. The three dominating figures were: Lloyd George*; Clemenceau, for France; and President Wilson[2] of the United States of America.

[1] Walter H. Thompson, bodyguard to Churchill, 1920–32 and 1939–45.
[2] Thomas Woodrow Wilson (1856–1924), Democrat; 28th President of the USA, 1912–21; champion of the League of Nations.

○ From CSC   1 Dean Trench Street[1]
9 March 1919

My Darling Winston

I hope that some sensible and wise decisions are being arrived at in Paris this week. People here don't seem to care 2d. about what is happening in Germany or indeed anywhere in Eastern Europe.

I had a pleasant evening with Philip Sassoon* on Friday – Consuelo [Marlborough/Balsan*] was there fresh from her election Victory[2]....

Darling really don't you think it would be better to give up the Air & continue <u>concentrating</u> as you are doing on the War Office? It would be a sign of real strength to do so, & people would admire it very much. It is weak to hang on to 2 offices – You really are only doing the one. Or again if you swallow the 2 you will have violent indigestion! It would be a tour de force to do the 2, like keeping a lot of balls in the air at the same time. After all, you want to be a Statesman, not a juggler....

You are being so splendid at the W.O. & I don't want there to be one weak spot in the armour – The Observer has a delightful paragraph about you saying that last week was <u>your</u> week in the Commons & that you were like a super Dreadnought manoeuvring about among pre-Dreadnoughts!...

My Dear, our new gardener Bailiff seems a most energetic man – I fear he may turn out a Super Holden [a previous bailiff] in the wish to have his own way. However I've engaged him, but I wish you could have seen him first. He insists on grubbing the 2 wild fields at once & turning a motor plough on to them – & sowing corn! He is engaging 3 labourers for about 3 months for this job – He is moving the garden up at once to the top & shifting the greenhouse with his own hands.... He says unless these things are done the place will always be a dead weight of expense, but that afterwards it will certainly pay....

If we sell Lullenden we can pass this tyrant on with the place!... He is quite different to the type I have interviewed so far – Great decision & apparent knowledge....

What I feel about him is that either he will save Lullenden for us or we shall be positively forced to sell. But it's no use going on in this moribund condition – I'm sure he will get a tremendous move on....

Goodbye my dear.

I feel very anxious about our private affairs – It's clear we are far too much extended –

I'm sending this in a W.O. bag. I hope it will reach you quickly.

Your loving
Clemmie

[1] House rented by the Churchills from early 1919 to early 1920.
[2] She had won a seat on London County Council for North Southwark Ward, standing as a Progressive.

Later in the year Winston and Clementine reluctantly decided that they must sell Lullenden. The buyers were old friends, Sir Ian and Lady Hamilton.

During 1918 and 1919 a virulent influenza epidemic swept across the world: more than 150,000 people died of it in England alone, and in the Churchill household a most tragic event took place. Winston was away in France when Isabelle, their charming Scottish nannie, who had been with them for several years, was seized by this deadly illness; becoming delirious, she took Marigold from her cot into her own bed. Clementine tried to get a doctor, but so many people were ill she did not succeed; she took Marigold into her bed, and spent a fearful night going up and downstairs between the dying Isabelle and her frightened child.

Clementine herself had influenza, but fortunately not of the virulent strain; and for several days there was great anxiety lest Marigold might be infected, but she too escaped the scourge.

○ From CSC   1 Dean Trench Street
[undated, March 1919]

My darling
    Isabelle died this morning at half past Five after a most terrible night. I long to see you – I am unhappy. She talked fast & loud in an unearthly voice like a chant for several hours. I could hear Everything. I'm afraid I am in for influenza. My temperature this morning is 102, but perhaps it's the sleepless night.

Tender Love from
Clemmie

○ From WSC   [Paris]
11 September 1919

My darling One,
    Only these few lines to mark the eleventh time we have seen the 12th Sept. together. How I rejoice to think of my gt good fortune on that day! Then came to me the greatest happiness & the greatest honour of my life. My dear it is a rock of comfort to have yr love & companionship at my side. Every year we have formed more bonds of deep affection. I can never express my gratitude to you for all you have done for me & for all you have been to me.

Yr ever loving & devoted
W.

Enclosed [cheque] will assist in minor matters.

○ From CSC   Lullenden
14 September 1919

My Darling Winston
    At Wynyard[1] early in the morning of Sept 12th I woke up & remembered suddenly the importance of the day, & I had not written to you! And then

your dear letter appeared upon my breakfast tray. It made me very happy and illumined my day.

I love to feel that I am a comfort in your rather tumultuous life – My Darling, you have been the great event in mine. You took me from the straitened little by-path I was treading and took me with you into the life & colour & jostle of the high-way. But how sad it is that Time slips along so fast – Eleven years more & we shall be quite middle-aged. But I have been happier every year since we started.

Thank you <u>very</u> much for the cheque – £10 I keep for frivolity and the rest will be distributed fairly among the shops....

Nellie has arrived from Palestine[2] & is at present at Dieppe with Mother.

God bless you Darling – Perhaps you will be back by the time this letter reaches the W.O.

Your loving
Clemmie
...

[1] Wynyard, Co. Durham. Home of the Marquess of Londonderry and the Castlereaghs (see p. 325 n. 4).
[2] Bertram Romilly was Military Governor of the Province of Galilee, 1919–20.

After they moved out of Lullenden the Churchills were again homeless. During the winter to spring months of 1920, the family stayed with Freddie and Amy Guest* at Templeton, Roehampton, on the outskirts of London, sharing living expenses.

Clementine continued her house-hunting, and found No. 2 Sussex Square, a high, handsome house (destroyed in the Blitz) north of Hyde Park, into which they moved in April. It was admirably suited to their family's needs – and additionally they would make a spacious studio for Winston in a mews building which they also acquired behind the house.

While Clementine grappled with the move, Winston went off for a holiday, combining boar hunting and painting at the Duke of Westminster's* estate at Mimizan in Les Landes (south-west France).

○ From WSC [typewritten]   [The Woolsack
26 March 1920   Mimizan, Les Landes]

My darling One,

It is very sad that Bendor is laid up on his yacht at Toulon with diphtheria [quinsy, in fact]. We have had a pathetic telegram from him saying that he is very ill and cannot possibly join us.... To-day we have received no news, although we telegraphed particularly for it ... so that no news may I think be taken as good news.

We had a smooth crossing and an uneventful journey. I dined at the Embassy, ... Before dinner I had a visit from the French Minister of War (Lefèvre), and for an hour and a quarter he poured out his griefs against England. You never heard such a tale. One really would have thought that we were worse than the Germans. Beginning with 'charbon' and ending with Constantinople, he traversed the whole world and found no single subject in which France had not been unfairly or wrongly treated by every other nation in the world. Unlucky country!...

His principal demand was to march into Germany and seize Frankfurt and Darmstadt and hold them as further guarantees; for charbon, an indemnity ... I warned him very plainly that we would have nothing to do with a policy of crushing Germany. He seemed a very foolish inexperienced man; spoke with great scorn of Clemenceau, as much as to say how much better he was doing – I don't think!...

To-day we[1] have been out hunting. We did not succeed in securing a pen-wiper[2], though we were within two minutes of one and the hounds yelped like mad. We were riding pretty hard for more than five hours, but I am not at all tired. We got back here in time to paint a nice picture. There are some lovely views here; now that the gorse is out the whole of these dark pine-woods have an underwing of the most brilliant yellow and really look most beautiful. ✐The weather is bright – but none too warm.... We are just going out riding to the sea shore.

With tenderest love my darling to you & to all yr dear kittens

Believe me
Your devoted & loving
W.

---

[1] WSC's fellow guest was Gen. Lord Rawlinson (see p. 207 n. 5), whom he already knew from Western Front days.
[2] WSC's name for wild boar: they reminded him of dirty 'penwipers'.

○ From WSC [typewritten]   [Mimizan]
27 March 1920

My darling One,

I have just had good news from Bendor. He has telegraphed that he is much better and is going to bring the yacht round by sea.... He wants us to go on hunting here until he can join us....

The General and I are entirely alone here and we lead a very simple life divided entirely between riding, painting and eating!...

As the hounds will not be fit for hunting till Monday, we went out for a long ride this morning down to the sea; over two hours at a pretty good pace. I had a splendid horse – a different one to the one I hunted yesterday; an enormous black English hunter with a head and shoulder which made you feel as if you were on the bridge of a battle cruiser....

Three quarters of an hour's ride brought us to the sea. Most lovely sands are spread out for miles. There was, as is usual here, a fine display of breakers; seven or eight great walls of foam advancing, one on top of the other, ... We rode our horses into the surf up to their hocks, and so for a couple of miles along the beach and then back to lunch....

I have been reading Phillip Gibbs' book about the war[1] – very impressive and terrible, also extremely well written. If it is monotonous in its tale of horror, it is because it is full of inexhaustible horrors. We shall certainly never see the like again. The wars of the future will be civil and social wars, with a complete outfit of terrors of their own....

Tonight we painted by the lake at a new place, from which we returned by water. The General paints in water colours and does it very well. With all my enormous paraphernalia, I have so far produced very indifferent results here. The trees are very difficult to do and there is great monotony in their foliage; also, water has many traps of its own. How I wish Lavery* were here to give me a few hints; it would bring me on like one o'clock....

&Tender love my darling from yr devoted & loving

W.

...

P.S. I have not done one scrap of work or thought about any thing. This is the first time such a thing has happened to me. I am evidently 'growing up' at last. Pouches are however expected today.

WSC

[1] Philip Gibbs, *The Realities of War*, 1920.

○ From WSC   The Woolsack
30 March 1920

My darling One,

This is a line & only a line (as the sun is shining bright) to wish you many many happy returns of the day. Twelve times now I have seen yr birthday come, & each time yr gracious beauty & loving charm have made a deeper impression on my heart. God bless you my darling in the year that now opens & give you happinesses wh fill yr life. Always yr devoted loving husband

W.

◇ From CSC   Templeton
31 March 1920   Roehampton

My Darling Winston

Mr Brindley [a former canteen colleague] is dead. I can hardly believe it – He had influenza followed by pneumonia –

I think it is a great pity – He was a very good man – I went & saw him & his new wife only 3 days before he was taken ill....

The Canteens – I sometimes wonder now if it was all a dream. One thing is certain, I couldn't manage them again – I began to think I had real organising ability, but it died with the War – if there ever was any!...

This week has been occupied in taking Randolph to have his school clothes fitted. He looks such a thin shrimp in trousers and an Eton collar![1]

Your loving
Clem

...

I hope you will get a penwiper or two – Please bring me back their gleaming tusks.

. . .

[1] This summer term Randolph, aged nine, started at Sandroyd Preparatory School, near Cobham in Surrey.

On New Year's Day 1921, Lloyd George* offered Churchill the post of Colonial Secretary, and to take charge also of a new Middle East Department incorporating responsibility for the British Mandates of Iraq and Palestine; the appointment would not take effect until 13 February, but Winston started straight away to fix his mind on the problems of his new office. Meanwhile there was time for a holiday in the sunshine; he and Clementine were the guests of Sir Ernest Cassel in the Excelsior Hotel Regina at Nice from 13 January.

On 22 January Winston had to return home to business, but Clementine stayed on. She was in an exhausted state both mentally and physically. Marigold's birth immediately after the strains of the war had depleted her. Living in a series of temporary London houses, house-hunting, and the big move out of Lullenden and into 2 Sussex Square had all made their heavy demands. Now sunshine, agreeable company and tennis provided just the holiday she so badly needed.

O From WSC
27 January 1921   [Colonial Office]

My darling One,
    I hope you found my telegram on arrival to welcome you. I envy you the brilliant sunshine. Here all is well – but hardly ever have I had such pressure of big work. Ireland, the Army Navy & Air fortunes, speeches agreements Cabinet work have kept me at the fullest strain. It is all I can do. But I can do it. . . .
    Work is proceeding here [2 Sussex Square] rapidly & the studio etc will soon be ready. We had the coldest day ever known in these latitudes on Wednesday, & of course it synchronised with the hot water pipes being out of action! Now it is warmer & the pipes are gurgling full again.
    Nellie has found suitable premises [for a shop] & I have promised to lend her £500 to carry on with, . . . I thought you wd wish this.
    I am glad the book[1] is so nearly ready. The influx will be welcome. I am paying all sorts of bills – nearly £3,000 in all. We must try to live within our income. . . .
    10.30 a.m. my Cte meetg. – so I must rush to my bath.
    Darling one – Do take care not to get overtired & do try to get the fullest value out of the beautiful Riviera. You will want to be fit for the political fights that are drawing near.
                                              Always yr devoted & loving husband
                                                                                              W.

P.S. I finished The Prince and the Pauper[2] to Randolph before he left. He is a sweet.

[1] The first volume of *The World Crisis*, published in 1923.
[2] Mark Twain, *The Prince and the Pauper*, 1881. A Victorian classic.

○ From WSC   Chequers[1]
6 February 1921

My darling,
    Here I am. You wd like to see this place – Perhaps you will some day! It is just the kind of house you admire – a panelled museum full of history, full of treasures – but insufficiently warmed – Anyhow a wonderful possession.
    The so-called Duckadilly [Marigold] marched in to my room this morning, apparently in blooming health. It was a formal visit & she had no special communication to make. But the feeling was good. I have not yet received reports about the Broadstairs party – except that they are all right[2]. Nor any news from Randolph. . . .
    I am to take over the Colonial Office seals tomorrow at 7. Thus for a week I shall hold the seals of three separate Secretaryships of State – I expect a record [Colonies, War and Air]. . . .
    The Strand Magazine accept my terms & will pay £1,000 for two articles with pictures reproduced in colour. As this will not be subject to Income Tax, it is really worth £1,600. So the painting has paid for itself, & a handsome profit over[3].
    Great news (but not for circulation) from the Berkeley Square front. My mother has sold her house for £35,000 – a clear profit of £15,000. She has already taken a little house in Charles St. No need to go abroad. All is well. I am so glad.

                                                    Tender love my darling one,
                                                              from yr devoted
                                                                        W.

. . .

[1] Large Elizabethan house and surrounding land near Princes Risborough, Buckinghamshire, presented to the nation by Lord and Lady Lee of Fareham 'as a place of rest and recreation' for her Prime Ministers for ever. The Chequers Estate Bill (1917) ratified the gift and set up the Trust, but it was not until early 1921 that Lloyd George formally took it over from the Lees (8 January 1921), so WSC was an early guest. See Norma Major, *Chequers: The Prime Minister's Country House and its History*, 1996.
[2] Diana (twelve) and Sarah (seven) had started at Notting Hill High School as day pupils in the autumn of 1920. But after a winter of coughs and colds they had been sent, although it was term-time, to lodgings at the seaside in Broadstairs, Kent, with Annie (a long-serving and reliable maid).
[3] These articles, published in the *Strand Magazine* in December 1921, were eventually to become the enchanting small volume, *Painting as a Pastime*, 1948.

Clementine next stayed with the Countess of Essex[1] at St Jean Cap-Ferrat, and in her first letter from there she writes about a most important event in the Churchills' lives – the inheritance which came to Winston on the death of his kinsman Lord Henry Vane-Tempest[2], who died in a railway accident in Wales on 26 January. The Garron Towers Estate was worth around £4,000 a year; some jewellery and other chattels were also involved in the will.

[1] Adèle (born Grant), Countess of Essex (1859–1922). American second wife of 7th Earl of Essex, who died 1916.
[2] Lord Henry Vane-Tempest (1862–1921), brother of 6th Marquess of Londonderry. Died unmarried. On the Garron Tower Estates, see pp. 213 n. 1 and 233).

◇ From CSC   Lou Mas
7 February 1921   St Jean Cap-Ferrat

My Darling Winston
    ... I can imagine that all the various things which are filling your mind, i.e. your new post, your inheritance, the painting, Chequers, the P.M., the re-arrangement of the Government, the Emeralds[1], the Book, the poor old worn out War Office – make this little peninsula seem a pin point in the sea, while you are soaring in an aeroplane above the great Corniche of life. ... this last month so many things have happened to us that it makes me quite dizzy. And strangely enough the change of Office, which when it has happened before has always been of intense interest & sometimes thrilling excitement – takes rather a back seat. But this won't be for long becos I do think it is the best office just now & if you are able to 'feature' the Empire once more it will make all English people happy, at peace with each other (more or less) & able to resume our lofty but unconscious contempt of the Foreigner – I wish I were with you spinning round & round instead of sitting lazily here in the Sun. ...
    Yesterday (on my small scale) I had a disastrous day in Monte Carlo. First of all in the Salons Privés a bad old lady pinched 2 Louis which I had just won & which I was leaving on to accumulate.
    Being somewhat inexperienced I did not protest loud or long enough for justice to be done – So shaking the dust from my feet I proceeded to the more select atmosphere of the Sporting Club where I lost all the money I had made ...
    I am longing for news of you my Darling one & what about those Emeralds?

                                                                Your very loving
                                                                         Clem

...

[1] Part of the Garron Towers inheritance.

○ From WSC   War Office
9 February 1921

My darling,
    ... This morning a long letter has arrived from you. ... Nellie is vy worried about her affairs & hopes to retrieve them by her hat shop

venture. I have told her I will help her through. She gave many reasons agst leaving England now. She was distressed at not being able to come to yr aid[1].

I sent for Gomez [CSC's doctor] yesterday morning & had a talk with him about the Cat. He still takes a serious view of the need of extreme care, in wh case he is confident a complete recovery will be made. Please my darling think of nothing but this, subordinate every thing in yr life to regaining yr nervous energy & recharging yr batteries. Don't throw away yr gains as you make them.

Don't play in any tournament. If you play tennis – play for pleasure – not to excel. . . .

I have been interrupted by the so-called Duckadilly [Marigold] who pays me her morning visit. She really seems 'in the pink'. I told Miss Elgie [nursery-governess] to write to Annie & say that if the two children were doing vy well at Broadstairs they might stay there a third week. Miss Elgie visited Randolph yesterday & gives a vy good report of him. So all the kittens are for the moment blooming.

The Laverys* do not come out [to the Riviera] till 17th. They gave a vy amusing party on Tuesday to the P. of W. [Prince of Wales]. We danced in the studio & had an entertainment. Last night Philip [Sassoon*] renewed the party – reinforced by Ll.G. [Lloyd George*]. Unhappily in dancing . . . I trod with my heel upon the P. of W. toe & made him yelp. But he bore it vy well – & no malice. The little lady[2] was vy much to the fore. I am booked almost every night for one of these tiny parties. . . .

The new cook has arrived. I think she will do the dinners all right. . . .

F.E. [Smith*][3] has gone absolute Pussyfoot [teetotal] for a year. He drinks cider & ginger pop & looks ten years younger. Don't make a mock of this, as he is quite sensitive about it. He looks sad. Not for Pig.

Your devoted & loving
W.

[1] Nellie had hoped to join CSC in France and keep her company after WSC had returned home.
[2] Freda Dudley Ward, born Winifred Birkin (1894–1983), who in 1913 had married William Dudley Ward, Liberal MP and Vice-Chamberlain to the Royal Household; divorced, 1932. The Prince of Wales met her in 1918, and was devotedly in love with her for sixteen years. In 1937 she married, secondly, the Marqués de Casa Maury; divorced, 1954 (he died 1968).
[3] Now 1st Baron Birkenhead (1919), Lord Chancellor.

◇ From CSC   Lou Mas
10 February [1921]

My Darling
I have been meditating still further on the Strand Magazine offer & this is what now suggests itself to me: –

Would it not be possible to reproduce your pictures <u>but</u> for someone else to write the Article –

Because if <u>you</u> write the Article what are you going to write about.
1) Art in General?
    I expect the professionals would be vexed & say you do not yet
    know enough about Art –

2) Your own pictures in particular – ?

The danger there seems to me that either it may be thought naïf or conceited –

I am as anxious as you are to snooker that £1,000, & as proud as you can be that you have had the offer; but just now I do not think it would be wise to do anything which will cause you to be discussed trivially as it were. If there is to be an argument let it be as to whether you are going to be a good 'Imperial Minister' or not – Also the Colonies & Dominions might think that you ought to be concentrating on them –

Also remember that M. Charles Morin[1] still exists. You have not publicly repudiated him. I have a sort of feeling that the 'All Highest' [Curzon][2] rejoices every time you write an Article & thinks it brings him nearer the Premiership, tho' I think that a man who has had to bolster himself up with two rich wives to keep himself going is not so likely to keep the Empire going as you, who for 12 years have been a Cabinet Minister & have besides kept a fortuneless Cat & four hungry Kittens.

I think one of the reasons that your friends rejoice in your new fortune is that it frees you from the necessity of earning money from Writing at inconvenient moments....

I wonder when you go to Egypt?[3]

Tender Love from
Clemmie

. . .

[1] In January 1921 WSC had exhibited a number of his paintings in the Galerie Druet, Rue Royale, Paris, under the pseudonym of Charles Morin. Six paintings were sold, but we do not know the prices paid. Naturally WSC was greatly gratified to be accepted as a 'selling' artist.
[2] Curzon was at this time Foreign Secretary (1919–24) and Leader of the House of Lords.
[3] A Middle East Conference was to be held in Cairo in March.

◇ From CSC   Lou Mas
13 February 1921

My Darling

. . . I am a little disappointed that the emeralds or their present-day equivalent in money are gone beyond recall, but on the other hand this avoids what might have been almost a feud & would certainly have been a distinct coolness with a branch of your family.

I am so glad you are looking into Mother's affairs for her.

I do hope you will be able to improve matters for her, & anyhow I would like her to have £100 a year out of the increased allowance you are so kindly making me....

Mr Garvin [Editor of the *Observer*] came to luncheon yesterday; Adèle very kindly asked him at my request.

He has a great belief in you. He was as voluble as ever & his eyes seemed to be starting out of his head, but he could not get really going at lunch as Adèle & Jean Hamilton kept the conversation in pleasant but shallow depths – However I took him out in the garden afterwards & he released about 1/3 of an Observer Article on me. He also told me that Northcliffe was full of curiosity both about your painting & your inheritance – He wanted particularly to know what M. Morin had received in payment for the picture sold at Druet's – ... He was also inquisitive as to the amount of the heritage ...

Ashmead Bartlett[1] is at Beaulieu – I saw him playing tennis & could not remember whether his conduct merited 'the cut direct' – While I was revolving this he came up & nodded so I bowed coldly & as there was a rabbit wire fence between us I did not have to shake hands. He has a mean odious face & is the sort of creature who would haunt the Riviera.

I went into Monte Carlo to the Salons Privés yesterday armed with a Chinese system for Roulette. It did not work at all well but I think it is better than playing without a system as one certainly loses one's money more slowly....

Your loving Cat

...

[1] Ellis Ashmead-Bartlett (1881–1931), soldier, war correspondent and Conservative MP, who represented the London press throughout the Dardanelles expedition, 1915, and was hostile to WSC.

○ From WSC [typewritten]   War Office
14 February 1921

My darling,

I went to see Randolph yesterday at Sandroyd and found him very well and very sprightly. The Headmaster described him as very combative, and said that on any pretext or excuse he mixes himself up in fights and quarrels; but they seemed quite pleased with him all the same....

He declared himself perfectly happy and said he did not want anything. Most of the boys have got colds, and he is a happy exception....

All that you say about the article on painting I will carefully consider. There is nearly a year before it will appear and it will be the only one I shall write. It is quite unconnected with politics and therefore not open to any of the objections which have been urged against others. An article by Mr Balfour on golf or philosophy, or by Mr Bonar Law on chess would be considered entirely proper. I think I can make it very light and amusing without in any way offending the professional painters. On the contrary, I hope to encourage other people to make an effort and experiment with the brush and see whether they cannot derive some portion of the pleasure which I have gained in amateur painting....

You will see that I delivered an oration at the banquet of the English Speaking Union to Lord Reading which has been well reported in the Times. I have been elected the new [Chairman] of the English Speaking Union. It was uphill work to make an enthusiastic speech about the United States at a time when so many hard things are said about us over there and when they are wringing the last penny out of their unfortunate allies. All the same there is only one road for us to tread, and that is to keep as friendly with them as possible, to be overwhelmingly patient and to wait for the growth of better feelings which will certainly come when the Irish question ceases to be in its present terrible condition. If anything it has been getting more grave in the last few weeks, and the confident assertions of Hamar Greenwood[1] and the military do not seem to be borne out by events. I am feeling my way for a plan for submitting the cases both of Ireland and Egypt to the Imperial Cabinet, which meets in June, where all the Prime Ministers will be assembled. . . .

A day of intense bustle & pressure. I will write again tomorrow – Tender love. Let me know how much more money if any you want.

Yr devoted & loving
W

[1] Hamar Greenwood (1870–1948), cr. Viscount, 1937. Canadian-born Liberal MP, 1906–22; Conservative MP, 1924–9. At this date Chief Secretary, Ireland, 1920–2.

○ From WSC   War Office
16 February 1921

Beloved one,

Yr beautiful letter of 13th has just come in. I read them all with delight. You write such sprightly letters with a real literary touch and all glowing with love. . . .

What an odd thing about Haldane's slanderous malice[1]: & that it shd come to my notice in this form when the P.M. has been pressing me to get rid of him, & I have been holding him – for the present – in his position. I have known for years of his attitude – but have always prided myself on feeling so much his superior in every way as to be able not merely not to feel revengeful, but even to take a kind of pity upon him. That was why I gave him his present appointment wh was so vital to him: & when in due course I change him for a junior man (as the troops go) it will be solely on public grounds. I do not harbour malice.

Perhaps I wd be a stronger character if I did. But it is too much trouble, in a life so full of interesting work & movement & so happy & comfortable – with so many to care for.

I went to a jolly little dance at Freda [Dudley Ward]'s on Monday night (in my uniform) & danced indefatigably till 2 a.m. . . . I got on all right. It is quite amusing. The little prince [of Wales] was there – idolizing as usual. People are getting quite bored with it. They think that a door shd be open or shut. . . .

Yesterday & today no Duckadilly [Marigold]. She has another cold. . . . She is better today & I am going up to see her. The others ought to come back soon. Then I shall indeed feel myself in charge. . . .

I was busy all yesterday forming my new Middle Eastern department. I have got Lawrence[2] to put on a bridle & collar. Curzon [Foreign Secretary] will give me lots of trouble & have to be half flattered & half overborne. We overlap horribly. I do not think he is much good. Anyhow I have the burden on my back. We are quite on good terms personally. I shall take lots of trouble to bring him along. . . .

I am to meet Cox[3] in Cairo on Mar. 8. I have to take the Air Estimates through the Commons Mar. 1. One day between these two dates look out for me. . . .

Dear darling pussy cat. Are you really making steady progress to health

& nerve strength. I am so counting on this. It is such a chance. I expect yr weather will be getting lovely now.

> With tender love
> Yr devoted
> W.

---

[1] Lt -Gen. (later Gen.) Sir James Aylmer Haldane; see p. 2 n. 5. At this time C.-in-C. Mesopotamia. During the Boer War he had been taken prisoner with WSC.

[2] Thomas Edward Lawrence ('Lawrence of Arabia') (1888–1935), soldier, Classical scholar and writer, who in 1916 had helped to reorganize the Arab army and rode with them into Damascus. Member of British delegation, Peace Conference, 1919; Adviser on Arab Affairs, Colonial Office, 1921–2. Joined the RAF, 1922, as an aircraftman under the name of Ross, and in 1927 changed his name to Shaw. Lawrence's Arabian exploits were recorded in his celebrated book, *Seven Pillars of Wisdom*, 1935. He visited Chartwell on a number of occasions. Killed in a motorcycle accident.

[3] Maj.-Gen. Sir Percy Cox (1864–1937), at this time High Commissioner, Mesopotamia, 1920–3.

◇ From CSC
18 February 1921

Hotel Bristol
Beaulieu-s-Mer

My Darling Winston

Here I am feeling rather lonely in this vast hotel full of middle-class English people. But I have made the acquaintance of your formidable foe Lieut[nt] Colonel J. B. Maclean[1]. . . .

I told Colonel Maclean that I had heard that he was a strong Imperialist & that you were one also, & that being so he ought to 'wait & see' before attacking you. He then talked a lot about F.E. [Smith*] & said that a lot of his prejudice against you was owing to the fact that you were his friend – I asked him why he did not like F.E. & he said that his visit to America & Canada during the War was a series of blunders & insolences. That at every public dinner he was drunk, that every speech he made was tactless, patronising & in bad taste that at one town when he arrived some pretty women were asked to meet him at dinner & that he made a bet he would kiss all seven of them before the evening was out etc – etc – etc –

I told Colonel Maclean that since all these happenings F.E. had become Lord Chancellor & that he was said to be one of the greatest Lord Chancellors that had ever been, that he couldn't have been nearly as drunk as he seemed, that he was a tremendous sportsman (hunting, tennis etc), that his wish to kiss the seven ladies only indicated his general admiration of transatlantic women & that anyhow you weren't in the least like him. . . .

I then encouraged him to talk about Canada & himself which he did at enormous length. He is naïf, vain, touchy, kindhearted, horribly energetic & vital . . .

You say in your letter that perhaps you would be a 'stronger character' if you harboured malice. I do not think so – I always think that the fact that you don't altho' you are very ambitious sweetens & strengthens your nature. . . .

How clever of you to get Lawrence, & you will get great Kudos if you manage to wheedle the 'All Highest' [Curzon].

I am a little bit anxious about your keeping the Air Ministry up your sleeve – Wouldn't it be better to persuade the P.M. to give it to some capable young man & you could always speak up for it in counsel? . . .

– – –

Just as I write these words your telegram saying Conference in Egypt is 13th handed in. I have just had a flash of inspiration. As I am here could I not sail with you to Egypt. The sea voyage in the <u>warmth</u> would do me good & I should love it. . . .

If not suitable for me to do so on so official & serious an occasion could I not go to an Hotel incognito?

I read both your Speeches & liked them especially your farewell to the W. Office. I'm sure the soldiers will miss you very much. . . .

Do my Darling use your influence <u>now</u> for some sort of moderation or at any rate justice in Ireland – Put yourself in the place of the Irish – If you were their leader, you would not be cowed by severity & certainly not by reprisals which fall like the rain from Heaven upon the Just & upon the Unjust –

You say (in a recent letter) that the confident assertions of Hamar [Greenwood] do not seem to be borne out by events. It makes me blush to think that men of the calibre of yourself & the P.M. should have listened to a man of the stamp of Hamar who is nothing but a blaspheming, hearty, vulgar, brave Knock-a-bout Colonial – I think he has done his executive part pluckily & efficiently (tho' considering he has had the whole resources of Scotland Yard for his protection I don't see why he should be much alarmed). He has probably got a good digestion which keeps his conscience robust.

It always makes me unhappy & disappointed when I see you <u>inclined</u> to take for granted that the rough iron-fisted 'hunnish' way will prevail. . . .

I am lunching with the newly arrived Laverys* tomorrow. They arrive in a blaze of glory for the whole Riviera is ringing with their Party to the Little Prince, & all the Party Lovers are bewailing the fact that they are <u>here</u> & not in London.

I have not been <u>quite</u> so well these last 3 days so I am taking it easy & having my favourite poached egg in bed instead of going down to dinner –

Don't be alarmed – I am taking every care of myself.

Your loving
Clemmie

I miss you very much my Dear & it 'joys' me to think that soon we shall meet again. If you can't take me in your waistcoat pocket to Egypt try & spend more than 2 days hereabouts.

. . .

[1] Lt-Col. John Bayne Maclean (1862–1950), Scottish-Canadian journalist and publisher.

○ From WSC
19 February 1921   [Secretary of State for War writing paper]

My darling,

I had a blow yesterday when I found that the [Garron Towers] Estate is about £7,000 less than I thought....

The work is vy heavy indeed. Many gt thorny questions pressing for solution in Cabinet & in my various departments. No time for painting or book. All work – but vy interesting.

Tender love my darling – I have looked in vain for a letter these 3 mornings. I do love yr letters so. Do write. I have written Adèle [Essex] –
x x x x x x x x x x x   Your ever loving
                                                                      W.

◇ From CSC   Hotel Bristol
21 February 1921   Beaulieu-s-mer

My Darling Love

I have just got your letter which ends in a complaint that I have not written & which says 'I do love your letters so' –

It warms my lonely heart to read these words, for I am very solitary in this big rather dreary hotel but very happy as I am living in blissful contemplation of our smooth and care-free future; (I mean from a money point of view) & I am laying up stores of health by staying a lot in bed. The last two days I have been thinking chiefly of the great pleasure and excitement of going with you to Egypt & Palestine. I am thrilled by the idea & so so longing to see you....

I am so sorry my Dearest that you have had a deception as to the amount of the inheritance – It is certainly very disappointing after you had worked it out so carefully & thought about how to lay it out to the best advantage; but don't let a 'crumpled rose leaf' like this spoil the really glorious fact which rushed on us so suddenly a little time ago – that haunting care had vanished for ever from our lives –

It's so delicious to be easy – I hope I shall never take it for granted but always feel like a cork bobbing on a sunny sea....

Do I take Bessie [her maid] to Egypt & Palestine? She would be a great comfort if not too expensive, & not in the way – Please telegraph this as I shall have to arrange my wardrobe a little differently if she isn't going[1].

Shall I propose myself to the Hamiltons & meet you at Marseilles from their house 2 hours from there?...
                                        Tender Love to you my Darling – Your loving
                                                                            Clemmie

                                                                                ...

[1] Bessie did accompany CSC on this journey.

◇ From CSC   Hotel Bristol
26 February 1921   Beaulieu-s-mer

My Darling Winston

I must write at once & tell you of a most exciting event which happened yesterday & that is that in the Open Women's Doubles Miss Greenwood (Hamar's sister who plays about the same as I do) & I actually got 4 games out of a sett playing against Mrs Lambert Chambers[1] & Miss Gosse – (the runner-up for the American Women's Championship)....

... Of course we thought we should not get a single game & determined just to hit hard & try not to look foolish or nervous ... The audience were most sympathetic & clapped us & urged us on. Mrs Lambert Chambers was very nice & kind to us, but I don't think she liked it as Mlle Lenglen[2] was looking on mockingly.

Well I suppose it never can happen again but I feel as you would if you shot 4 goals at Polo playing with 3 other players [of] your own strength against Lord Dalmeny, Jack Wodehouse, Captain Lockett etc. [all polo champions].

Of course it was an accident & will never occur again but we are both dizzy with the glory & suffering from swelled head. Our friends heaped congratulations on us as we left the court....

Your loving
Clemmie

[1] Dorothea Katherine Douglass (1878–1960), married R. L. Chambers, 1907. Wimbledon ladies' singles champion seven times, 1903–14.
[2] Mlle Suzanne Lenglen (1899–1938), Wimbledon ladies' singles champion six times, 1919–23 and 1925.

○ From WSC   Colonial Office
27 February 1921 7.30 a.m.
Hard work at Air Estimates all to-day

My darling Clemmie,
    ...
Yr letter vy sweet. I am looking forward eagerly to seeing you again. We shall have a beautiful cabin together – if only it is not rough – then I shall hide in any old dog hole far from yr sight.... If it is fine, it will be lovely & I shall write & paint: & we will talk over all our affairs.

The Broadstairs detachment arrived home yesterday. They were in the pink. I brought them home two days earlier in order to catch a glimpse of them before I left. The Duckadilly [Marigold] received them with joy & is quite free from cold. Indeed she is to go out today....

We are going down to see Randolph today. I gave the children the choice of Randolph or the Zoo. They screamed for Randolph in most loyal & gallant fashion. So we arranged for the Zoo too.... They were vy loving & ate enormously....

F.E. [Smith*] dined last night. Only cider! He is becoming vy fierce &

calm – a formidable figure – rather morose – vy ambitious. Terrible results of intemperate self restraint.

Yr ever loving
W

Winston left London on 2 March 1921, collecting Clementine *en route* for Cairo at Marseilles the following day.

After the Cairo Conference ended, on 22 March, they went on to Jerusalem for a few days, where Winston was deeply involved with deputations and discussions with both Arab and Jewish organizations, and with the Emir Abdullah of Transjordan.

They finally returned home via Alexandria, Naples and Syracuse, arriving back in London on 10 April.

Chapter XI

DARK YEAR

Winston and Clementine had been back from their travels less than a week when they received tragic news.

Bill Hozier, aged thirty-three, Clementine's beloved brother, had been found dead in his hotel room in Paris on 15 April: he had shot himself. After the war Bill had retired from the Navy and gone into business; unfortunately, like his mother and twin sister Nellie, he was a gambler, which led him into financial difficulties. But no evidence was ever found to indicate that he was at the time of his death in financial straits. Clementine and Nellie travelled at once to Dieppe to be with their mother.

◇ From CSC   Hotel Metropole
Sunday [17 April 1921]   Dieppe

My Darling Winston
   Your beautiful letter has come –
   My poor Mamma is so brave and dignified, but I do not think that she will recover from the shock & the grief. She sits in her chair shrunk and small. When we saw her she did not yet know that Bill had killed himself, but I saw by the look of agony & fear that she half guessed – Then she said 'No one must ever know – Winston will keep it out of the newspapers won't he?' Later she said: – 'Our Clergyman here won't bury him I am sure – If he refuses I shall not mind, but then Bill must be buried in the garden of my house under the elm tree.' . . .
   We hoped the coffin would be taken to the church & lie there till the Service, but that cannot be allowed & it is in the Hearse which brought it from Paris in the Coach House, waiting to be transferred to the other hearse which will take it to the Cemetery – Oh Winston my Dear do come tomorrow & dignify by your presence Bill's poor Suicide's Funeral. In case you can manage it I have had the burial put off till 4 but no one will know that you are coming in case you can't do it – The train leaves Victoria at 10 & the boat gets in just before three[1]. . . .
   – – –

Later

Nellie has just seen Mr Hodgson the Clergyman & he has been very kind & now says Bill's body may be in the Church from tomorrow morning – The funeral will therefore start from the Church at 3.30 & take place at the Cemetery at 4 – I sent your letter for him to see as I wanted him to realize what we all felt for Bill, & that he was not a mere scapegrace disowned by his family.

... Bill left no message. His pass book shewed that 10,000 francs had just been paid into his account – Nothing is known of any losses in Paris. Race cards were found on him with very small bets registered on them, 200 francs or so –

Mother will not I fear be able to go to the Funeral. Everyone at Dieppe is startled & grieved as Mother is so well known & much liked.

Yesterday when we arrived at Newhaven I saw the Conductor of the Pullman Car run after Nellie & wring her hand. Tears were in his eyes. He knew Bill who often travelled on that line & who had given him some money once when he was hard up....

Later. I shall come back Tuesday....

Your loving tired
Clemmie

[1] WSC excused himself from important public business and travelled to Dieppe for Bill's funeral: he had always been devoted to him.

At the end of May Lady Randolph [Churchill*], wearing predictably high heels, tripped and fell down a staircase, severely fracturing her ankle: gangrene developed, and her leg had to be amputated. She faced the operation and its aftermath with characteristic pluck, and seemed to be making good progress at her London home in Westbourne Street; indeed on 23 June Winston had telegraphed her husband, Montagu Porch[1], who was in Africa on business, to give him a good report. But on 29 June Jennie had a sudden and violent haemorrhage: Winston, urgently summoned, ran from nearby Sussex Square, but his mother was dead when he arrived. She was sixty-seven.

Jennie had been a great beauty, a great charmer and a great character. Her worldliness and extravagance were counter-balanced by her vitality and her courage. On her death tributes and letters poured in: she had come to be a legend in her own lifetime.

It had become increasingly clear that the policy of coercion in Ireland had failed, but the Government was strongly divided: Churchill advocated negotiation and conciliation and strongly supported Lloyd George in his efforts to achieve a truce. At the end of May elections were held in both Southern Ireland and Ulster[2]. In the South, Sinn Feiners were overwhelmingly returned, while in Northern Ireland Unionists carried the day by a large majority over the Nationalists and Sinn Fein.

King George V opened the first Parliament of Northern Ireland on 22 June, and made a strong appeal to all sides for peace. On 8 July the Truce was signed: months of negotiation lay ahead, and acts of violence continued, but finally on 6 December a Treaty between Great Britain and Ireland would be signed (Churchill being one of the signatories) giving Southern Ireland Dominion status. Ireland (as a Dominion) was now part of the Colonial Secretary's responsibility. Churchill became an IRA target for assassination, and measures for his security increased: for many months he slept with a revolver at hand.

[1] Montagu Porch (1877–1964), a member of the Nigerian Civil Service. Younger than Jennie by 23 years, he had married her in June 1918.
[2] Under the Government of Ireland Act 1920, Ireland had been partitioned, with one Parliament in Dublin and another in Belfast for the six counties of Ulster.

◇ From CSC   Menabilly[1]
11 July [1921]   Par Station, Cornwall

My Darling
    I am much interested to hear that you are going to see 'Peelings'[2]....
    ... Darling let us beware of risking our newly come fortune in operations which we do not understand & have not the time to learn & to practise when learnt. Politics are absolutely engrossing to you really, or should be, & now you have Painting for your Leisure & Polo for excitement & danger.
    I long for a country home but I would like it to be a rest & joy Bunny not a fresh pre-occupation.
    I do think that if we really lived in the country it would be the greatest fun & also a life occupation ... & just now I am for relaxation –
    I want to lie in the sun & blink & wake up now & then to eat a mouse caught by some one else, & drink a little cream & doze off again –
    But now I do wish my Dear one that you were in this Irish Settlement [Truce of 8 July]. Would you have been if you had not been 'en froid' with Ll.G. [Lloyd George*][3]? I do feel that as long as he is P.M. it would be better to hunt with him than to lie in the bushes & watch him careering along with a jaundiced eye – This household is of course very anti-government & it is rather amusing to see their disgust & terror at the idea that the present Régime is going to bring off this wonderful thing – It will keep Ll-G in power for another good lap –
    How are you? I have not been favoured with much news from the Home Front – have I?
    I return home at Cock Crow on Thursday morning & will breakfast with you & hear your news....
    To-day is Diana's birthday – 12 years old.
    Please lock up my letters or burn them.
    Do you love me? Please do – I cannot do it actively alone....
                                                                    Your loving
                                                                    Clemmie

[1] Menabilly, a very old beautiful house close to the sea, was leased at this time to the Horner family.
[2] A seaside property in Sussex belonging to the Duke of Devonshire.
[3] There had been a chilly atmosphere between WSC and Lloyd George since the Government reconstruction in March. WSC had been away at the Cairo Conference when the Cabinet changes

were being made; he aspired to the Chancellorship of the Exchequer. But by the time he got back to London, Sir Robert Horne (later 1st Viscount Horn of Slamannan (1871–1940); Conservative MP, 1918–37; President of the Board of Trade, 1920–1; Chancellor of the Exchequer, 1921–2) had already been Chancellor for 12 days. WSC remained deeply offended with Lloyd George for some time.

Now we have the first glimpse of Chartwell. Clementine was writing from Fairlawne, near Tonbridge, Kent, belonging to the Cazalet family, where she was staying for a tennis party. Earlier in July Winston had been captivated by a nearby property, Chartwell Manor, near Westerham; Clementine now took this opportunity to inspect it.

◇ From CSC   Fairlawne
Wednesday [20 or 27 July 1921]

My Darling

I can think of nothing but that heavenly tree-crowned Hill – It is like a view from an aeroplane being up there –

I do hope we shall get it – If we do I feel we shall live there a great deal & be very very happy –

To-day Randolph arrives – I hope looking well – Sarah's report has just arrived & is excellent – She is said however 'to talk too much in Class'!

About the house on the Tree crowned hill.

Don't you think that if the Estate [Garron Towers] will pay for it it would be wise to add at once a corresponding wing on left side of house? . . .

. . . (One of the delicious things about having a country home will be to be able to have Jack [Churchill*] & Goonie & their children) If we built the wing we could have 3 nice sunny extra bed-rooms & a good tall room looking north with a <u>high</u> window. . . .

Tender Love

. . .

The plans for the summer holidays seemed most agreeable: for the first half of August, all four children in charge of a young French nursery governess, Mlle Rose, would stay in lodgings at Broadstairs, on the Kent coast. About the middle of the month the elder children were to join their parents in Scotland.

Meanwhile Clementine set off ahead of Winston on 8 August to stay at Eaton Hall, Chester, with the Westminsters*, to play some tennis.

◇ From CSC   Eaton[1]
Tuesday the 9th [August 1921]

My Darling

I arrived here last night about 11.30 & found dancing in full swing, so I changed quickly & joined them. There are about 36 people in the house; the tournament has begun & I won my first round of handicap singles this morning against an American called Mrs Burden.

I have asked Bennie [Westminster*] & the Duchess[2] about when they will be at Lochmore[3]; they seem rather vague but I gather that she will not be there till Sept: 1st & he there only a few days earlier – Dunrobin[4] it appears is quite close to Kylestrome[5] so you could either come there first & we could go together to Dunrobin ...

My Darling – My thoughts are much with you as I know you will miss Walden[6] very much. He understood all your ways so well & was so devoted & faithful.

My tender love to you
Your loving
Clemmie

[1] Eaton Hall, Chester, the north country seat of the Duke of Westminster. Rebuilt in the 1870s by Waterhouse – a vast Gothic fantasia reminiscent of St Pancras Station. It was demolished in the 1960s.
[2] Bendor's second wife, Violet Rowley (born Nelson), whom he married in 1920; they divorced in 1926.
[3] Lochmore, the principal lodge on the Westminster estate on the Forest of Reay, in Sutherland. From Loch More runs the beautiful Laxford river, famous for its salmon fishing.
[4] Dunrobin Castle, seat of the Duke of Sutherland near Golspie on the north-east coast.
[5] Kylestrome, another large lodge on the Westminster estate.
[6] Thomas Walden, WSC's faithful manservant, who had just died. He had worked for Lord Randolph in the 1890s and for WSC during and since the Boer War.

O From WSC   Colonial Office
10 August 1921

Splendid letters from the children
from Randolph especially....

My darling Clemmie,
    ...
    Jack [Churchill*] came up, we both went to poor Walden's funeral. The wreaths arrived punctually – I fastened yr card on mine & laid it in the grave. There was no singing & the clergyman mumbled through the service in an unceremonious fashion, but there were beautiful flowers & about 40 mourners including all our household who wept bitterly. Alas my dearest I grieve to have lost this humble friend devoted & true whom I have known since I was a youth in my father's house....

    The books have arrived and are disposed according to yr imperious will. 'She-whose-commands-must-be-obeyed'.

    They do not take up too much room....

    Porch [Lady Randolph's widower] comes home tomorrow. Poor fellow – to a denuded house & lonely land. Jack is waiting to receive him....

I have much Colonial Office work to clear up....

Tender love my darling. Dance & dream – but keep a corner for

Yr devoted
W.

Letters from the children at Broadstairs recounted usual seaside holiday events: sunburned legs; expeditions in rowing boats; and shrimping. Marigold had had a bad cold, but then was reported to be much better; perhaps because during the previous months she had suffered quite frequently from sore throats and coughs, not enough attention was paid initially to what in retrospect one sees was the early stages of her fatal illness. Tragically for the darling 'Duckadilly' the day of antibiotics had not dawned, and her painful sore throat progressed into septicaemia. She became really ill about 14 August, but it was a day or two before Mlle Rose (urged by the anxious landlady) sent for her mother. Clementine left Eaton at once and rushed to Broadstairs; the three elder children travelled up to Scotland as planned, in the care of their mother's maid, Bessie.

Marigold's condition deteriorated swiftly: Winston came down from London, and a specialist was called – but to no avail. She died on the evening of 23 August, aged two years and nine months; her parents were with her. She was buried at Kensal Green Cemetery on 26 August, and that evening Winston and Clementine, stupefied by grief, took the sleeper train north to join the other children in Scotland.

They all stayed at Lochmore for nearly a fortnight, and then Clementine took the children back to London to get ready for school. Winston went on to Dunrobin to stay with the Duke and Duchess of Sutherland.

For many years Clementine suffered bitter remorse that she had been away when Marigold became ill; she also felt she had entrusted the children to an inexperienced young nannie. But all such tragedies bring their unanswerable questions.

◇ From WSC [typewritten]   Dunrobin Castle
19 [18] September 1921

My darling,

We are here an enormous party, 25 or 30, mostly extremely young. I wish you could have come as there is constant lawn tennis and many pleasant things to do. But you would have found it much too large....

To-day a most glorious, cloudless sky; the weather brilliant but cool....

In the afternoon I went out and painted a beautiful river in the afternoon light with crimson and golden hills in the background. I hope to make it much better to-morrow. Geordie [Duke of Sutherland] wants me to shoot grouse to-morrow. They have a number to be killed, but I think I shall beg off if the weather is fine and go back to my stream....

I have been thinking out the headings of my speech for Saturday [in Dundee]. Three main topics – first, the reasons why the Government have had to go slow over their social programme.... Second, Ireland, on which you know my views; but of course I must be guided by developments meanwhile. Third and last: peace, disarmament and the Washington Conference[1]. I do hope I shall be given a quiet and patient hearing, as I intend to make a very careful and thoughtful speech.

The Prince of Wales is here and his brother, and Dudley Ward[2] and his wife, and boys and girls galore....

I am looking forward greatly to coming back to London – East-West, home's best!

X X X X X X

✍︎19th.

It is another splendid day: & I am off to the river to catch pictures – much better fun than salmon.

Many tender thoughts my darling one of you & yr sweet kittens. Alas I keep on feeling the hurt of the Duckadilly – I expect you will all have made a pilgrimage yesterday....

Fondest love my sweet kat,
from yr devoted loving
W.

P.S. I am reading Fielding's Amelia. It is saltly written[3].

[1] Washington Conference on disarmament, 12 November 1921–6 February 1922.
[2] William Dudley Ward (1877–1946), barrister and MP. Treasurer of the Royal Household, 1909–12; Vice-Chamberlain, 1917–22. Married, 1913, Winifred (Freda) Birkin (see p. 227 n. 2).
[3] Henry Fielding, *Amelia*, published 1752.

◇ From CSC   2, Sussex Square
22 September 1921

My Darling Winston

I am ashamed not to have written a word before, but there was so much to do for the children that I have hardly sat down for a minute –

I was startled this morning to hear about Sir Ernest [Cassell]. His Secretary rang me up early this morning & told me, and asked me to let you know. I have been through so much lately that I thought I had little feeling left, but I wept for our dear old friend; he was a feature in our lives and he cared deeply for you....

... I went round to Brook House this afternoon & took some flowers from us both. They took me up to his great empty bed-room – There he lay, already in his coffin – he looked serene & as tho' only lightly asleep – I feel the poorer becos' he is gone – He was a true & loyal friend & a good man.

I took the children on Sunday to Marigold's grave and as we knelt round it ... a little white butterfly ... fluttered down & settled on the flowers which are now growing on it – We took some little bunches. The children were very silent all the way home.

Yesterday we hired a Car ... & we all escorted Randolph in triumph back to School. Miss Elgie [governess] who has visited us every day came too.

We stopped on the road and had a splendid pic-nic & hide & seek & arrived torn & dishevelled at Sandroyds.... To-day was Diana & Sarah's turn & now I can lean back with a sigh – But I still have arrears of clothes to send after them!...

I wish so much I could be in Dundee to hear you Saturday night.

I much want to see you....

Your loving
Clemmie

...

After Christmassing *en famille*, Winston went to Cannes with Lloyd George*; it being school holiday time, Clementine remained at home, planning to join him later.

Scarcely had Winston left the house on Monday 26 December than No. 2 Sussex Square was smitten by the influenza epidemic then rife in London.

On Tuesday 27 December Clementine wrote an enormously long hour-by-hour account of the ensuing events, of which I summarize the salient facts:

Bessie and Gertrude (the maids), Randolph, and subsequently Diana, fell victim to the 'plague'; and all had high fever for several days.

Cousin Moppet (Maryott Whyte*), who had recently arrived to be in charge of the children, became rather more seriously ill with pneumonia.

Dr Hartigan[1] was sent for and two nurses engaged (there was a drama about one of them, who had to be summarily dismissed and replaced). The entire house was turned over to the care of the patients; and extra domestic help taken on.

Having organized the arrangements (and pounded up and down the tall staircases innumerable times) Clementine herself succumbed to 'nervous exhaustion' and was sent to bed by Dr Hartigan with strict instructions to stay there for a week: from where she sent her 'report' to Winston, writing in debonair mode: 'Am thinking of advertising "2 empty beds for rich patients at 2 Sussex Square, 50 guineas a week" – this would pay for the whole thing!'

She ended her account:

There is nothing to be anxious about Darling Winston – Yesterday for a few hours I did feel as if I was in a hail storm with no cover in sight, but now everything is arranged & comfortable.

I am only disappointed that it is of course out of the question for me to join you.... I do hope you are having a delicious time. I shall long to hear all about it. It is providential you went away as it would have been most annoying if you had caught it, & your room is most useful as with 2 extra Nurses etc we are very full. The Bumble Bee [Sarah] is still with Aunt

Maudie[2] & I do hope she will escape, but if she gets it we are well
equipped now to deal with it....

Tender Love my Darling from
Clemmie

... 6.30 Nurse has just come in with evening report. Both children are 100
– Moppet is only 99 bad neuralgia – Bessie & Gertrude both coughing &
100 are going on satisfactorily.

[1] Dr Thomas Hartigan (d. 1941), the Churchills' London GP for many years.
[2] Lady Maude Whyte (born Ogilvy) (1859–1933), daughter of the 10th Earl of Airlie; Cousin
Moppet's mother.

○ From WSC   Cannes
29 December 1921

My darling One,

I am so relieved to get yr telegram saying 'Everybody better' I do hope it
includes yrself. What a cataclysm! Poor darling I expect you have had an
awful time. But as usual you have risen to the occasion, & yr letter about it
all is Napoleonic.

I am also vy glad you have gone to bed. A week on yr back will do you
all the good in [the] world. Then come out here to recuperate in this
delicious sunshine and let me mount guard in yr place over the Kittens....

Ll.G. [Lloyd George*] read two of my chapters[1] in the train & was well
content with the references to himself. He praised the style and made
several pregnant suggestions wh I am embodying. I cannot help getting vy
interested in the book. It is a gt chance to put my whole case in an
agreeable form to an attentive audience. And the pelf will make us feel vy
comfortable. Therefore when darkness falls, behold me in my bunny [bed],
writing, dictating & sifting papers like the Editor of a ha'penny paper. Far
away in the distance I can see you – also in yr bunny (I trust) and just
about to have dinner with a little 'panya' [champagne] to keep yr spirits
up. Far beyond that again in outer circles of darkness ranges the wide
colonial Empire and the Emerald Isle. In ten days it will all be on top of
me again....

Freddie [Guest*] is pursuing the beautiful Miss Gellibrand who is here
staying with a minor French Royalty. He even talked to me of matrimony –
after disposing of the Amy [his wife] problem – I replied sepulchrally that
she was young enough to be his daughter, & that ten years wd carry us
both to the brink of the sixties. Also that he wd lose his office[2] if he lost
his Amy. So there's a problem! Don't make chaff about it.

Goodnight my sweet Clemmie.

With fondest love from yr devoted but fainéant [idle, lazy] pig
W.

...

[1] *The World Crisis*, published in 4 vols, 1923–9.
[2] Freddie Guest was at this time Secretary of State for Air.

○ From WSC   Lou Mas[1]
1 January 1922

My darling Clemmie,
    I moved here yesterday & return to Cannes tomorrow. . . .
    I hope to see yr Mama in Monte C[arlo] this afternoon when darkness
falls. She has made herself quite well known there. The Sporting Club
people mentioned her name to me with the utmost appreciation & granted
me my ticket of admission sans phrase. Evidently she has taken possession
of this gambling resort[2]. . . .
    . . . From my room (you know it) I can see the Cap d'Ail Hotel: so linked
in my mind with those last few days I saw my poor Mamma. What
changes in a year! What gaps! What a sense of fleeting shadows! But your
sweet love & comradeship is a light that burns the stronger as our brief
years pass.

                                            Tender love my darling
                                            Yours devotedly,
                                                        W.

. . .

[1] WSC was staying with the Countess of Essex (Adèle).
[2] In the wake of his legacy, WSC had made a generous present to Lady Blanche, and he and CSC
had hoped this would enable her to live more comfortably: but no! She preferred to stay in a
cheap hotel at Monte Carlo and merrily gamble the rest away!

◇ From CSC   2 Sussex Square
4 January 1922

My Darling Winston,
    You will have been puzzled at receiving a telegram from me asking
you not to open a certain letter. I hope you obeyed the instructions and
did not behave like Pandora – Please burn that letter without opening it –
I know that there are no fires on the Riviera, only Central Heating, but put
a match to it in the empty grate.
    Because, there are two letters in that envelope written on Black Monday
No 2 [2 January], a day of deep misery & depression –
    Your letter promised for that morning on the previous Friday did not
arrive & I was very disappointed – Later in the day arrived the typed letter
[not to hand] – This was piling Pelian on Ossa coming after one of the
most dreary & haunted weeks I have ever lived through – So I wrote
bitterly & miserably to my poor Pig – Late Monday night came at last a real
letter in his own paw, followed yesterday by another, telling me all I
longed to know.
    My Own Darling – I am glad that you are having these few sunny care-
free days – I only wish I were with you basking in the sun.
    But we have really escaped luckily at home – All our patients are
recovering well, tho' Diana is slow. There have been a great many cases
which have turned to pneumonia & a good many deaths in Marylebone,
mostly poor people who did not go to bed in time & who were not
properly nursed.

Sarah & I have escaped, but the week that I was in bed I wandered in the miserable valley too tired to read much & all the sad events of last year culminating in Marigold passing & re-passing like a stage Army thro' my sad heart. But now that I am up – I feel better & more rested. It is so vexing, always collapsing from fatigue for no reason at all. I wish I could accumulate a store of strength. But my battery holds only enough electricity for about half a day & then it needs re-charging. . . .

Randolph is up to-day, looking rather weak & weedy poor boy.

Tender Love
Clemmie

○ From WSC   [Cannes]
4 January 1922

My darling Clemmie,

Last night I gave a dinner party at Ciro's! Yr Mamma, Consuelo & Balsan*[1], Adèle [Essex] & Philip [Sassoon*], vy pleasant. . . . Afterwards we went to the Sporting Club and yr Mamma won 400 francs. I think she enjoyed her evening. She is such a dear. . . .

I have been working vy hard morning & evenings at the book: & have done more than twenty thousand words. . . .

Yesterday Monday & today I have painted or am about to paint at Consuelo's villa. I have done a beautiful picture of Eze – wh I know you will want, but wh I cannot give you – because Consuelo & Balsan praised it so much I gave it to them. . . .

Today I move to the Negresco Nice to stay with Max [Beaverbrook*] for a couple of days & we then return together on Saturday. My dear he was furious with me for urging him to come out here & then not being at the Mont-Fleury [Cannes] when he arrived! Such a to-do. The P.M. [Lloyd George*] anxiously pacifying him. Bonar [Law] stroking him. Freddie [Guest*] almost in tears. (I did behave rather badly). So I said I was sorry – As he continued to sulk I said I had done all I could & said all I cd, & that if that was not enough he cd go to hell. He showed some inclination to take me at my word: but eventually we were reunited! So much for that.

The P.M. is singularly tame. I have never seen him quite like this. Vy pleased to have me with him again. He is piling a gt deal on to me now. Next week will be vy heavy. He seems to me to have much less vitality than formerly. But his manner is vy sprightly & his conversation most amusing. . . .

Tender love my sweet Clemmie
from yr ever loving & devoted
Pig . . .
W.

---

[1] Lt-Col. Jacques Balsan, who had recently married Consuelo, Duchess of Marlborough.

O From WSC [Hôtel Mont-Fleury
4 January 1922 Cannes]

My darling,
I cd not bear not opening yr letter in the cream coloured envelope, in
spite of yr telegram. In law it was my property once it was delivered to
me, & any letter from you is better than none at all. My poor sweet I can
see exactly what happened. My 'supplement' arrived in advance of my
own letter. I am so sorry you had such a churlish message. I do so love &
value yr being pleased to hear from me, & even the shadow cast by that
pleasure to have disappointed is dear to me.
I have been thinking so much about you & worrying over yr health.
Adèle [Essex] has been charming – praising you so much. I have returned
to the Mont-Fleury to the exigeant Max [Beaverbrook*]. . . .
I must confess to you that I have lost some money here – though
nothing like so much as last year. It excites me so much to play – foolish
moth. But I have earned many times what I have lost by the work I have
done here at my book: & also our shares at home have done well. Still I
am vexed with myself. Max highly disapproved on every ground. As I was
punished by the Cat when I was not at fault, you must now pardon me
when I am!
This letter shd reach you Saturday, & I shd reach you myself on Sunday.
I am looking forward to coming home. My work will be vy important next
week, ... But how barren these things wd be, & how precarious my
pleasures & interests if I had not a real home to come back to & a real
sweet to await me there –

Goodnight my darling one
Your ever devoted,
W.

Winston returned from the Riviera on 7 January, and towards the end of the
month Clementine, who by now badly needed a holiday, went off to Cannes,
where she stayed at the Hôtel Mont-Fleury; for a companion she had Venetia
Montagu*, who also much enjoyed playing tennis.

O From WSC In the train.
27 January 1922

My Beloved darling Clemmie,
I am on my way to Lympne [Sir Philip Sassoon's*]. This has been a really
hard worked week for me. Continual speeches & discussions on one grave
subject after another. A foretaste perhaps of what will some day come
upon me. I have completely succeeded in carrying all my views on the
Financial Geddes Report[1] etc. But the fighting with the Army, Navy &
Air on the one hand, & agst Ll.G. [Lloyd George*] & Geddes & the Stunt
Press on the other has been very stiff.
I don't feel the slightest confidence in Ll.G.'s judgment or care for our

rational naval position. Anything that serves the mood of the moment & the clatter of the ignorant & pliable newspapers is good enough for him. But I try – however feebly – to think for England. Then on the other hand I have to turn and squeeze Beatty[2] most cruelly to get rid of naval 'fat' as opposed to brain & bone & muscle. It is a vy peculiar ordeal & the vulgar have no idea of it at all.

You will no doubt have seen the newspaper speeches.... Everything here is working up to a shindy. That is as it shd be. The sooner the election comes the better now that controversy is definitely engaged....

The children are vy sweet. Diana is shaping into a vy beautiful being. Sarah full of life & human qualities – & with her wonderful hair. The Rabbit [Randolph] has got removes in 3 subjects.

I am troubled a bit with poor Porch. We guaranteed his overdraft to £4,500 & it looks as if £1,000 wd fall on me. I do the best I can.

I don't see much chance of getting away. The political situation grows more lively evy day. The gt attack is on Ll.G., his character, his record, his baffling elusive policy, his cosy opportunism. Still I have not quite given up hope of escaping for a few days....

I do hope you are having some fun & tennis, & <u>above all</u> recharging yr accumulators. Remember you have another task my sweetest of wh only we two know, wh will require all yr best energies[3].

Do write & tell me all you do. Don't get overtired: & don't worry.

Always yr loving & devoted husband
W.

He has been quite well fed lately!

[1] In response to parliamentary and newspaper clamour for greater economy in government expenditure, a committee had been set up under Sir Eric Geddes which in December 1921 had recommended, among other savings, drastic cuts in the manpower and pay of the armed services. As a result of his strong protests, Lloyd George appointed WSC Chairman of a Cabinet Committee of Defence Estimates. The policy of retrenchment was known as the 'Geddes Axe'.
[2] David Beatty (1871–1936), cr. 1st Earl Beatty, 1919. WSC's Naval Secretary, 1912. C.-in-C. Grand Fleet, 1916–18, and hero of the Battle of Jutland (1916). First Sea Lord, 1919–27.
[3] CSC was in the early stages of pregnancy.

◇ From CSC   Hôtel Mont-Fleury
Saturday [28 January 1922]

My Darling
What Weather! Icy cold and rain, sometimes pelting, sometimes an icy drizzle –

To-day we are going over to Monte Carlo to see Mother. I read your speech[1], which was well reported in the Times – with delight. I thought it <u>very</u> good.... The only thing I didn't quite agree with was when you said that most Liberals (leaders as well as rank & file) stood aside from the burden & heat of the day in Peace as well as in <u>War</u>. The Cat does not think this is quite fair becos' the Liberals (nearly all) behaved splendidly in the War, which is more credit to them than it is to Tories who revel in slaughter & the Army etc – Think of Raymond & Oc Asquith. Perhaps it was not quite rightly reported?

Last night we dined at the Casino & danced & I played a little Chemin de Fer cautiously & brought away 15 Louis profit! – Venetia [Montagu*] played on a grander scale & I fear lost a bit. Sarah Wilson[2] is here, in attendance on H.R.H. Princess Christopher of Greece[3], who poor dear remains hidden in her villa for fear of not being properly curtsied to.

Tender Love
from
'Pawser'

[1] At a dinner of the 1920 Club, at Hotel Victoria, London, on 25 January 1922.
[2] Lady Sarah Wilson, WSC's war-widowed aunt (d. 1929). She was a sister of Lord Randolph Churchill.
[3] Nancy May (Anastasia) Leeds (born Steward of Cleveland, Ohio), first wife of Prince Christopher of Greece (1888–1940), whom she married in 1920; she died, 1923. He was the fifth son of King George I of Greece, and an uncle of Prince Philip, Duke of Edinburgh.

○ From WSC   [no address]
3 February 1922

My Beloved,

I send you a dictated account [dated 4 February] of some of my affairs. The Irish situation is in the fire again & the reactions of Ulster hostility upon the growing party crisis may be vy serious. I have only just finished my report upon Geddes. These tasks & the Arabs & the Kenya folk & the Ishmaelis for Iraq & Palestine have kept me busy from morning to night. I have carried the load well. It is better to have a few big burdens than lots of little packages – so long as you can stand the weight.

I dined with Jack [Churchill*] & Goonie the night before last, but usually (3 nights out of the last 4) the P.M., F.E, Max[1] & I dine together. They all think the situation vy critical. I think the clouds will break, & we shall get through....

Darling I have not heard from you for three days – Do please send yr daily telegram. I do hope you are benefitting from yr rest & change.

The Children are well and vy sweet.

Yr devoted loving
W.

[1] Lloyd George; Lord Birkenhead (Lord Chancellor); Lord Beaverbrook. See Biographical Notes.

○ From WSC [typewritten]   2 Sussex Square
4 February 1922

My dearest Clemmie,

I expect you will have been reading the papers and have realised that the political temperature is rising steadily here. F.E. [Smith*/Birkenhead] made a very successful speech, which gained great publicity and was entirely along the lines I wished....

You were quite right in fastening on that unfortunately turned sentence in my speech about Asquith* and the Wee Frees[1]. Goonie tells me the old man is very upset and in fact, in accepting her invitation to dinner next week, stipulated that he should not meet me. I certainly did not mean to reflect upon his personal contribution in the days when he was Prime Minister. But there is no doubt that once he was removed from that position he stood aside, gave no help, and was ready to profit by any disadvantage that occurred to the Government.... And therefore I think what I said was fully justified, although I am sorry that it should appear to be capable of a construction which reflects on his war effort. I do not think any withdrawal or explanation is to be considered. Everything is going to get more disagreeable, and not less disagreeable, up to the time the Election takes place. I have always been very courteous and considerate to the old man.... All the same, I cannot forget the way he deserted me over the Dardanelles, calmly leaving me to pay the sole forfeit of the policy which at every stage he had actively approved. Still less can I forget his intervention after I had left the Government to prevent Bonar Law giving me the East African command and to deprive me of the Brigade to which French had already appointed me. Lastly, there was the vacancy in 1916 at the Ministry of Munitions, when he could quite easily have brought me back, as Lloyd George* urged him to.... As you know, I am not in the least vindictive; on the contrary, very much the other way. All the same I do not think there can be any doubt on which side the account of injury shows a balance.

... Ireland is sure to bring us every form of difficulty and embarrassment, and I expect I shall have to bear the brunt of it in the House of Commons. Still I am very glad to have this task in my hands, and hope to be able to steer a good course through all the storms and rocks....

I am going to settle another large batch of bills for Miss Street[2]. She tells me the books were quite moderate last week.

I am just off to Sutton [Place][3]. I shall hope to see Randolph, perhaps on the way down to-night, perhaps on my way back on Monday....

Long talks with Thornton Butterworth [publishers] about the size of the book. He is clear that the first volume must be one volume only and not two, but his reader thinks all the stuff so good that it is a pity to cut any of it out. I am not at all sure. I think much pruning is desirable, ...

We have summoned Arthur Griffith[4] and Michael Collins[5] over here immediately in order to try to restore the threatened Irish position. But will they come? Aye, there's the rub. If they do, I shall have to come up from Sutton to-morrow....

The Palestine Arabs came to see me this morning and received a draft Constitution which they have taken off to mumble over....

Allenby[6] is on his way home from Egypt, though not this time quite as the Conqueror of the East. All the jingo papers are praising the great, strong military giant, and deriding the poor, weak, feeble, surrendering Government. Little do they know the actual facts....

I have agreed with Mr Hunt to the construction of the bookshelves and the wine and coal cellars. I have continued to deny myself a parquet floor in my bedroom. There are at least eight very large tintacs sticking out of the oilcloth in ambush for my unsuspecting paw.

Alas, I see no prospect of the Sun and the South, unless of course the gloomy prophets are right and we are released from our duties by a Parliamentary bombshell. In that event I shall lose no time in joining you.

Much Love

Yr loving husband

W

[1] 'Wee Frees' was the name given to the minority of the Free Church of Scotland which stood apart when the main body amalgamated with the United Presbyterian Church to form the United Free Church in 1900; it became the nickname for the Asquithian Liberals.
[2] Margery Street, Australian Private Secretary who came in April 1921 to help out for a few months but stayed with the family until 1933, when she returned to Australia. Affectionately called 'Streetie'. We always kept in touch with her.
[3] Sutton Place, near Guildford, one of the Duke of Sutherland's houses; later home of J. Paul Getty, US oil billionaire and art collector.
[4] Arthur Griffith (1872–1922), President of the Sinn Fein Party, 1917, and leader of the representatives who had signed the Irish Treaty in December 1921; President of the Dail.
[5] Michael Collins (1890–1922), Irish nationalist and Sinn Fein leader.
[6] Field Marshal Sir Edmund Allenby, 1st Viscount Allenby (1861–1936), at this time High Commissioner for Egypt (1919–25).

◇ From CSC   Hôtel Mont-Fleury
3 February 1922

My Darling Winston

Do not worry about my health – I am <u>really</u> very well considering. . . .

Lovely Sunshine for the last 3 days but to-day Mistral but Sunshine too – I am playing a little tennis – There is a mild Club Tournament going on here & I am playing in it but only in 'doubles'. . . . Don't think I am doing too much. On the contrary since the sun has come out & I have been playing I feel better & after playing I go to my Bunny & eschew the Casino & its heat & tobacco smoke, not to speak of its financial dangers. The poor Cat has lost £10 at Chemin de Fer & is much annoyed –

This hotel is so comfy & they are very kind to me. . . .

I read F.E.'s [Smith*/Birkenhead] speech – Quite good I thought. I must say I don't like this Genoa business. Ll.G. [Lloyd George*] will be rubbing noses with all this Bolshevik riff raff & playing off the Germans agst the Poor French[1].

I don't think we ought to meet Lenin until he has had a General Election – The French Politicians are a tiresome set of people, but the French people themselves are so brave & hard-working I don't think we ought to allow them to quarrel with us. . . .

I do love getting your letters. . . .

I had a long talk with Lord Derby[2] in the rooms the other night – We held a Committee Meeting over Lady Curzon's[3] Grand Cross of the British Empire & we both agreed it was disgraceful, a scandal & so forth – He then told me he was hurrying home to be a thorn in Lord Curzon's side over Egypt – I said I thought his side was like a hedgehog with other people's thorns & there wouldn't be any room for his final dart! What a contemptible slave he is – arriving always in full cry to give the coup de grace to the dying victim –

People think he is bluff & independent & honest & John Bullish but he is really a fat sneak –
Venetia [Montagu*] stays up late & plays like fun....
Oh my Darling Sweet Pig I do long for you to be here....
Goodbye Darling – Kiss the two red-haired Kittens for me. I wonder if the new one will have red hair. Shall we have a bet about it: 'Rouge ou Noir'?

Your loving
Clemmie

[1] The Genoa Conference, 1922, called to agree on re-scheduling of German reparations (which were in arrears), to persuade the USA to remit or reduce the war debts owed to her by the Allies, and to encourage Russia to trade with other countries. In the event the Americans did not attend, the French refused to make any concessions over reparations, and the Russians and Germans made a private agreement.
[2] Edward George Villiers Stanley, 17th Earl of Derby (1865–1948), at this date Secretary of State for War, 1922–4.
[3] Grace Duggan, second wife of 1st Marquess Curzon of Kedleston, whom she married in 1917. Cr. GBE, 1922.

O From WSC   House of Commons
7 February 1922   [from the Front Bench]

My darling,
I am listening to Sir Donald Maclean![1] The session comes in like a lamb – & vy likely will go out like a donkey.
Archie [Sinclair] returned this morning and gave vivid & glowing accounts of you. He described yr prowess & agility at tennis ... in terms wh caused me much pleasure – but also some anxiety (having regard to certain circumstances known only to us both).... But also he cheered me up enormously by the picture wh he painted of yr gt restoration to health & spirits. I am so glad. Do stay until you are really re-equipped to fight. I shall need you vy much. The situation is steadily approaching a crisis & you can render me enormous help in the battle....
I am quite in agreement with you about Genoa. I hate all that orientation. It is not a national British policy but only a purely personal Ll.G. [Lloyd George*] affair. Still we are all tied up together! (Sir Donald is still labouring; & the P.M. bridling to reply.)...
Tender love my sweet one – Shall I send you some more money – You have only to express yr gracious pleasure. You have been away a fortnight today. I know what a conomical [an economical] cat it is, but the Riviera is a frightfully expensive place....
Above all don't get overtired....
... So now Sir Donald has finished his tame oration & Ll.G. is on his legs. Once more my fondest love & I wish I cd kiss yr dear lips

Goodbye my beloved
Here ends this fragmentary & discursive scribble from
your faithful & churlish Pig
W

[1] Sir Donald Maclean (1864–1932), Liberal MP. Chairman of Liberal Parliamentary Party, 1919–22.

◇ From CSC   Hôtel Mont-Fleury
7 February 1922

My Darling

Two delightful and engrossing letters from you....

I am a little sad about the Asquith* episode (I mean that sentence in your speech). All you say about the cold & detached way he treated you on the occasions you mention is more than true –

Still it seems to me that as you did <u>not</u> mean to reflect upon his war effort & that it <u>was</u> merely the way the sentence was turned that gave it that construction, it would be handsome and sensible & generous to say so.

Everyone is conscious of his limitations & I daresay that in his dreams & lonely thoughts the old man goes over his war days & tries to prove to himself that he could not have been more energetic – He was as energetic as he could be, but he is not energetic by Nature – He was more energetic then than he is now to get himself back into office.

It is quite a different thing to criticize his unhelpfulness to the Government after the War; but really he would be inhuman if he did not now & then rouse up & try & put a snag in their path – Oh Darling do be a Dove & put it right – to please me & to please yourself. People will only say 'Look how nice Winston is'.

I do not mind hard hitting (at least much) but I do think it is so cruel to say anything about a man's war record – And he has suffered more than we have by the War, by Death....

Oh I must tell you that Mr Scovell & I won the Mixed Doubles (handicap) in the Cannes Lawn tennis tournament! This is a great event in my lawn tennis life as I have never carried off a trophy in a Public Event. It makes me feel so well playing, & the tiny Kitten inside loves it too – He [She – in fact!] says 'well played' quite loud now & then....

I do long to see you my own Darling Winston.

I am looking very pink & well everyone says, or as Bessie [her maid] puts it uncomplimentarily, 'less graylike than you looked when we came'....

                                                        Tender Love from
                                                              Clemmie

                                                                . . .

○ From WSC [typewritten]   Colonial Office
10 February 1922

My darling,
    . . .
The Session opened very tamely. Parliament seems more dead than alive, and one cannot escape the feeling that its usefulness and its mission are exhausted.

The full brunt of the Irish business has now come on to me, ... It is going to be very difficult to keep the goodwill of the Ulstermen while carrying out the Government policy. At present, oddly enough, they seem much more friendly to me than to any of the regular Conservative leaders. . . .

Late the night before last I made a speech replying generally on the Debate and in particular to Master Oswald Mosley[1]. I determined that I would not prepare this in any way, so I went out and dined with Edie [Marchioness of Londonderry] at Londonderry House. . . . I then came back to the House of Commons three-quarters of an hour before speaking, listened to what was said, and let myself fly on what F.E. [Smith*/Birkenhead] calls 'the unpinioned wing'. It really was a great success; no worry, no work, but quite an agreeable experience. . . . I think I have really got my full freedom now in debate, and I propose to make far less use of notes than ever before. . . .

I am thrilled by your tennis triumphs. You seem to be playing in the very pink of the form out there, and it must be delightful to shine in a game you love so well. . . .

I have been feeling my throat a good deal lately and have passed the last four nights with cold water compresses. I must try to reduce the smoking a little.

✍I sat up too late last night at Edwin [Montagu]'s birthday dinner – only 8 men – but much jaw.

With tender love my dearest Clemmie
Your loving
W.

[1] Oswald Mosley (later 6th Bt Mosley) (1896–1980), at this time Conservative MP. In 1920 he had married Lady Cynthia Curzon, daughter of Lord Curzon; she died in 1933, and in 1936 he married Diana Mitford, daughter of the 2nd Baron Redesdale. Briefly an Independent. Sat as Labour MP, 1924–31; Chancellor of the Duchy of Lancaster, 1929–30. Founded British Union of Fascists, 1932. He and his wife were both imprisoned in the Second World War under Regulation 18B.

◇ From CSC   Hôtel Mont-Fleury
13 February 1922

My Darling

. . .

I am so much thrilled by your brilliant debating reply last week – It's of course more dangerous to speak without notes in case one should make a slip, but how much more fun –

Master Oswald Mosley is a very cheeky young Cub & wants keeping in his place, but of course it is rather an honour to have one of the leading figures in the Country holding you down in it.

I am very happy to think that your views on so many big topics are prevailing. . . .

In the Nice Tournament we had fun but did not get so far as there were so many crack players. . . .

Shall I come home for [the] Royal wedding[1] or stay till 1st week in March? I am rather home sick & need stroking by my Pig. To-day the first really warm day & I am sitting on my balcony writing to you.

Goodbye my Darling Love. Venetia [Montagu*] has left me & will bring you all my news.

> Your loving
> Clemmie

[1] The marriage of Princess Mary, the only daughter of King George V and Queen Mary, to Viscount Lascelles, later 6th Earl of Harewood, on 28 February 1922.

In July Clementine (who was expecting her baby in September) and Goonie took a seaside house in Devonshire for a few weeks.

◇ From CSC
Friday 14 July [1922]

> Preston House
> Saunton Sands
> Barnstaple

My Darling Winston

This house is on the right hand side of a beautiful bay. As I look out of the window I see four or five miles of hard golden sands & Westward Ho! on the other side of the bay.... Yesterday we explored Barnstaple which is a pretty old town. We found a delightful antique shop & Goonie & I both made some advantageous purchases!...

... The arrival of the newspapers at about eleven o'clock is a great event & I settle down to them for a good hour with far more attention than I give to them in London, where I expect to hear the news personally from you! Is Northcliffe dying?[1] The paragraph today sounds ominous – How queer if he & Lenin[2] drop off the globe about the same time like sort of mental Siamese twins....

How are you my Darling. I hope not too tired & the indigestion better.

> Tender Love from your Pussy
>
> ...

Please send me the Coué book[3] by return.
I hope you are having poor Jack [Churchill*] to dinner – He has only a policeman's wife to look after him who nourishes him exclusively on salt haddock!

> Give him my love.
> Clemmie

[1] Lord Northcliffe (see p. 110 n. 7) died on 14 August 1922.
[2] Vladimir Ilyich Lenin (1870–1924), Russian revolutionary and leader of Soviet Union from 1917, d. 21 January 1924.
[3] Dr Emile Coué (1857–1926), French doctor from Nancy, whose system of cures by 'auto-suggestion' (Couéism) became famous worldwide.

○ From WSC   Colonial Office
15 July 1922

My darling,
  A lovely letter arrived from you this morning – thus putting me on an
equality with yr Mamma who had received hers overnight!... I trust you &
Goonie will amuse each other & be happy together; & that you will collect
strength in peace & quietness....
  I have had a vy tiring week with late sittings in the Commons, & last
night a dance at Philip [Sassoon*]'s at wh I stayed till 2. All my partners
were there & I danced 8 times running. Good exercise. I bought this
morning a copy of Milton bound by 'Cobcore'¹ for Edwina². I am sending
it to her with a note explaining that 'Paradise Lost' is not the message I
mean to convey. She was dancing all last night in rapture with the sailor
boy. Very pleasant to watch. I hope they will be happy. They surely will
only have themselves to blame if they are not.
  The dinner to the Prince is expanding & will I think attain 16 or even
18. Don't be alarmed. I will organise it all with yr excellent staff.
  Ireland labours in the rough sea, & now all the Army Navy & Air Force
Estimates are coming on top of me to criticise, & many many other toils as
well. However I have accepted these burdens & must carry them. I can!
  Goodbye my darling one. My love to Goonie & a thousand kisses to
yourself from

                                          Yr ever loving husband
                                                          W

¹ John Milton, *Paradise Lost*, printed and bound at the Doves Press, Hammersmith (Cobden
Sanderson), 1902. Now worth £1,000.
² Edwina Ashley, Sir Ernest Cassel's grand-daughter, married Lt the Lord Louis Mountbatten RN
(later Earl Mountbatten of Burma) on 18 July 1922.

○ From WSC   Gunnersbury Park¹,
Sunday 16 July 1922   Acton, W.3.

Darling,
  I don't quite know why I came down here. There were several strange
people indoors, & outside a total lack of sunshine....
  I meant to tell you yesterday about Northcliffe. He has streptococcus
infection in his blood & no one has ever got well from this particular
disease. His brother² is my informant. 'Sic transit gloria mundi.' I cannot
help feeling sorry – altho' God knows how cruel he was to me in those
evil days of 1916.
  Our revered leader [Lloyd George*] is no doubt greatly relieved on this
score, but on the subject of Honours or rather Dishonours he is as timid as
a hare³.... He has consented to a Royal Commission to see what steps shd
be taken to prevent a Prime Minister from committing abuses of the
Prerogative. An awful humiliation out of wh he hopes to slide & slither in
a fairly cheap way.
  Tender love my dearest one. I do not easily habituate myself to yr

absence. Let me know when you will return from yr Devonian excursion....
Your devoted
W.

P.S. The old boy [Asquith*] turned up at Philip [Sassoon*]'s party vy heavily
loaded. The P.M. accompanied him up the stairs & was chivalrous enough
to cede him the banister. It was a wounding sight. He kissed a great many
people affectionately. I presume they were all relations.

Really this letter consists in telling 'sad stories of the deaths of Kings'.

I shall go & dance at V. Rutland's[4] tomorrow night – after the Division.
WSC.

[1] Gunnersbury Park, a home of Mrs Leopold Rothschild.
[2] Harold Sidney Harmsworth, 1st Viscount Rothermere; see p. 121 n. 3.
[3] Lloyd George allowed the sale of knighthoods and other honours to unsuitable candidates: this was eventually to contribute to his downfall.
[4] Violet, Duchess of Rutland (born Lindsay) (d. 1937), wife of the 8th Duke of Rutland (1852–1925). An artist. Mother of Lady Diana Cooper (see Biographical Notes).

◇ From CSC
17 July 1922
Preston House
Saunton Sands

Darling Winston

Your letter reached me this morning also the Coué book which is
remarkable but very short considering its stupendous subject.

Philip [Sassoon*]'s dance must have been great fun – He is a wonderful
entertainer –

I am afraid my poor little tablecloth will not stretch to 18 guests. But I
providently bought a brace in case you entertained Royalty two weeks
running! (one never knows but that it might become a habit)....

Yesterday we motored to Ilfracombe which is the principal health resort
in these parts & according to the meteorological reports published in the
local guide book it possesses the most equable winter climate in the
British Isles.... We are both glad to have seen Ilfracombe as now we need
never go there any more. It seemed to be composed of boarding houses
and a great variety of 'places of worship'....

I hope the Government will scrape thro' the 'Honours' Debate to-day – I
expect they will as the House of Commons seem quite inept & incapable
of driving any point really home....

I see that Lady Beatty thinks one of her ball guests pinched her £2,000
Brooch! Did you go to her Ball?!!

I have always had a great fancy for pink & gray pearls –

Your loving

'who every day in every respect is getting' rounder & rounder[1]

[1] A reference to Couéism, which required those practising it to repeat constantly the mantra:
'Every day, and in every way, I am becoming better and better.'

○ From WSC   Colonial Office
18 July 1921[22]

XX for Goonie.
Jack dines with me tonight.

Darling,
   I got such a jump on Sunday when [Dr] Hartigan telephoned about
Sarah. I was quite relieved to hear it was measles. That school certainly
purveys diseases with inexhaustible capacity. This morning Sarah was
normal & Hartigan pronounced her convalescent. But we must take gt care
not to let her get about too soon. So far Diana seems all right.
   I was so glad you were out of the way. On no account must you come
back. . . .
   My dinner had to be put off. The prince never having had measles –
feared to jeopardise his holiday – hard earned. He will come in October
instead.
   The debate on honours was squalid in the extreme & will do nothing
but harm to the Govt in the country, & to the country in the Empire. The
P.M. [Lloyd George*] was lamentable & is universally pronounced to have
made the worst speech of his career. It is indeed a decline. All this year
we have suffered from his personal contradictions . . . & now lastly the
Honours Gaffe. But for these – things have gone pretty well.
   My darling one I do hope you are enjoying yrself and not worrying in
any way. . . .
   Things are good in the City. Enormous crowds at the Cassel wedding. I
cd not go.

                                                            Tender love
                                                            Yr devoted
                                                            W.

○ From WSC   Colonial Office
20 July 1922

My darling,
   I strongly recommend yr going to the Ritz[1] & pigging it there while
passing thro' London. You ought not to come in contact with Diana as if
she developed measles & you caught it it wd be a vy gt disadvantage to
you & to yr kitten. I think we must obey Hartigan in this matter. . . .
   I hope Parlt will rise on Aug 4. & before that date I shall try to join you
at Frinton [-on-Sea]. . . .
   I send you a couple of notes[2] I dictated while dressing. Perpend
[ponder, consider].
   Tender love my darling Clemmie. I am much looking forward to another
letter & still more to seeing you again.

                                                       Always yr devoted
                                                            W

[1] One of my father's favourite aphorisms used to be: 'It's cheaper at the Ritz in the end.'
[2] Only one of which is to hand (see below).

◇ From WSC [typewritten]
[undated]

DISSERTATION ON DINING ROOM CHAIRS

There should not be less than twenty of these chairs in the house. They should be of a kind of which those not required for the Dining Room could be used in the Drawing Room or Studio.

The Dining Room chair has certain very marked requisites. First, it should be comfortable and give support to the body when sitting up straight; it should certainly have arms, which are an enormous comfort when sitting at meals. Second, it should be compact. One does not want the Dining Room chair spreading itself, or its legs, or its arms, as if it were a plant, but an essentially upright structure with the arms and the back almost perpendicularly over the legs. This enables the chairs to be put close together if need be, which is often more sociable, while at the same time the arms prevent undue crowding and elbowing.

If these reasonings seem well founded, I suggest that in the next three or four months we should sell our present Dining Room chairs and eight or ten other chairs of different kinds, and should buy with the proceeds twenty chairs conforming to the conditions above. . . .

◇ From CSC   Saunton Sands
21 July [1922]

My Darling

Thank you for your letter. I have digested your dissertation on Dining Room Chairs & I will begin searching for a comfortable model as soon as possible. . . .

I am longing to see you. Shall we dine together somewhere Monday night? Ritz?

I arrive at Waterloo 3.50 on Monday & shall go straight to my hotel which I hope will be quite close to Sussex Square. This will be much nicer than staying at the Ritz as Miss Street can come round & see me, & if I want any clothes etc one of the maids can bring them round. . . .

Tender love my Darling from
Clemmie

Clementine, who all her life loved being at the seaside, was blissfully happy in these last weeks of her pregnancy with her nursery world at Frinton-on-Sea. She was quite content that Winston should have his own plans, before coming to join them all in the last lap before they returned to London for the birth of their fifth child.

◇ From CSC   Maryland
8 August 1922   Frinton-on-Sea

My Darling Winston
. . .
   Victor Cazalet & his sister[1] arrive here to-day & Nellie is here. Her
children are such darlings & Sarah is enamoured of them. . . . Lord
Northcliffe seems to be dying by inches. What will happen to all his
papers? On the other hand Lenin seems to be perking up again. Poor Pig –
No luck!! I hope my own Darling you are being wise & wary & not
Singeing your poor whiskers at the Tables. Just think last year in one night
you lost nearly the rent of this lovely house. I am so happy here – It's so
comfortable & delicious. I hardly ever go outside the garden but just bask.
The children scamper all over the place but I am not (just now) nimble
enough to chase after them. . . . I am reading Shakespeare to Diana &
Randolph & they love it which pleases, but rather surprises me.
   We are just finishing The Merchant of Venice & are going on to
Henry V. I am making them learn some speeches by heart. . . .
   I feel quite excited at the approach of a new Kitten – Only 5 weeks now
& a new being – perhaps a genius – anyhow very precious to us – will
make its appearance & demand our attention. Darling I hope it will be like
you –
   Three days from now, August the 11th, our Marigold began to fade; she
died on the 23rd. . . .

                                                    Your very loving
                                                         Clemmie

[1] Thelma Cazalet (1899–1989), campaigning feminist and art collector. Conservative MP, 1931–45;
held junior office briefly in WSC caretaker Government, May–July 1945. In 1939 she married David
Keir (d. 1969); changed her name to Cazalet-Keir.

O From WSC   In the train
9 August 1922

My darling Clemmie
   I am on my road to Paris. The weather at Deauville was vy
disappointing – cloudy, cold, floods of rain. I got a little fitful sunshine in
the afternoons & painted a small picture & daubed a few canvases.
   Yesterday Max [Beaverbrook*] got a temperature from a chill through
bathing; & in the night he was pretty poorly 102° or more. Today he is
better & the doctor (frog) declares he will be all right tomorrow. . . . I rode
each day with Jack W[odehouse][1]: & am really much better so far as
Indygestion is concerned – & indeed generally. Deauville improved on
acquaintance as one got a circle of friends. . . .
   The King of Spain arrives this afternoon. His advance guard in the shape
of a beautiful actress has already installed herself in a sumptuous villa: &
many ponies have also arrived.
   What a parcel of gossip! But the whole place is full of this sort of thing.
I am not sorry to get away – tho' I wd have liked to see Max fully restored
before departing. . . .

Max gave me a most sombre account of Northcliffe's closing scenes. Violent resistance to treatment, 2 male nurses, gt constitutional strength fighting with a fell poison, few friends, no children, mania, depression, frenzies. . . . Poor wretch – his worst enemies cd not but grieve for him. Max professed gt sympathy & sorrow & generally maintained a most correct attitude about the fate of his formidable rival. It cannot be long now.

My darling sweet I am being frightfully lazy. Literally doing nothing at all. Bed every night before 12. No gambling – I lost my 300 francs & was frankly bored by it. I refrained from the sea (after one shivering plunge) & have escaped the evil consequences that have befallen Max.

I shall look forward to seeing you all on 20th.

Tender love
Your ever devoted
W.

P.S.
Among other notorieties in the rooms I perceived the Shah of Persia also parting with his subjects' cash, handed to him packet by packet by his Prime Minister. Really we are well out of it with our own gracious Monarch!

[1] John ('Jack') Wodehouse, later 3rd Earl of Kimberley (1883–1941), polo-playing friend of WSC and his personal political secretary, 1922–5.

○ From WSC
14 August 1922

The Woolsack
[Mimizan, Les Landes]

My darling One,

The days have passed like lightning. I ride from 7.30 to 9. Work at my book[1] till lunch 12.30. Sally out in the motor with Ferdinand to paint till Dinner. Then bed. Tomorrow we[2] go to Biarritz & St John of Lice [St Jean de Luz] for two or three days. I daresay we shall not stay so long. The weather has not been specially good. . . . tho' I have painted every day. This is really a wonderful part of the world. The people are prosperously poor. Happy, friendly & with lots of vy pretty children. The scenery is not only rich but varied. I find it full of beauty & charm. . . .

I am losing nothing by being away so far as politics are concerned & perhaps for some reasons it is just as well to be out of them for a bit.

The Irish situation ripens steadily & there shd be a chance of advancing to unity before long. Arthur Griffith's[3] death is a serious blow. But I think we are strong enough now to survive. Poor fellow – he was a man of good faith & goodwill. I wish he had not died. . . .

My darling I have thought vy often of you all & most of all of you. Yes I pass through again those sad scenes of last year when we lost our dear duckadilly. Poor lamb – it is a gaping wound, whenever one touches it & removes the bandages & plasters of daily life. I do hope & pray all is well with you. No letter came by the messenger – but no news is I am sure good news.

Your own adventure is vy near now & I look forward so much to seeing you safe & well with a new darling kitten to cherish ...

With tender fondest love to you & Diana, Randolph & Sarah X X X

I remain

Your ever loving husband

W.

P.S. I have polished up, polished off & completed the 3 remaining chapters of the book & sent them off to the printer.

[1] The first volume of *The World Crisis*, published 1923.
[2] WSC was accompanied by Eddie Marsh as Private Secretary on duty.
[3] Following Griffith's death on 12 August 1922, Michael Collins took over as head of state; he was murdered by fellow Irishmen ten days later (22 August).

Winston, as planned, headed for home and Frinton, where the whole family were together for about ten days, after which Winston and Clementine returned to London.

Early on the morning of 15 September Clementine was delivered safely of her fifth and last child – a daughter – Mary.

This September saw another important event in the family: Winston bought Chartwell Manor, near Westerham in Kent, which he had seen and fallen in love with the previous year. We know Clementine's first impression on seeing the property had been highly favourable: however, after further visits, her enthusiasm rapidly waned. To counter-balance the beautiful situation overlooking the Weald of Kent, the Victorian mansion built round a much older house was damp, dilapidated and infected with dry rot: these inconveniences could only be overcome, she realistically perceived, by virtually rebuilding the house. Her growing objections to buying Chartwell seemed at first to have won the day with Winston: but he was enamoured of the place, and while they looked at a number of other properties, its charms lurked in his heart and mind. He did not tell Clementine when, very shortly before my birth, he made an offer for Chartwell, and later in the month his offer of the asking price of £5,500, for the house and eighty acres, was accepted.

My mother told me that, in all their fifty-seven years of marriage, this was the only time she felt my father had acted with lack of candour towards her. 'Winston was not indifferent to Clementine's feelings in this matter – on the contrary, he longed for her approval over this major step in their life. But he never doubted that he could bring her to share his enthusiasm for the place which had so captivated him, and which he was sure would make a perfect home for them all.'[1]

[1] Mary Soames, *Clementine Churchill*, 1979, p. 219.

Chapter XII

NO SEAT, NO PARTY, NO APPENDIX

Although the result of the General Election in 1918 had been a decisive victory for the Coalition, and a triumph personally for Lloyd George*, his position was fragile, the Government being dependent on Conservative support; and as time went on, tension increased between the Liberals and Conservatives. At the election the Labour Party had become the largest of the opposition parties, and in succeeding years working-class support for Lloyd George and the Liberals ebbed away. The blatant sale of honours by Lloyd George, and finally the Chanak Incident in the Graeco-Turkish war[1] in the early autumn of 1922, exacerbated the demand for the break-up of the Coalition. At the famous meeting at the Carlton Club on 19 October 1922, attended by a large majority of the parliamentary Conservative Party, Stanley Baldwin[2], supported by Bonar Law, in a forceful speech called for the end of the Coalition; Churchill, who had tried to dissuade Baldwin from attacking the Coalition, was not himself present, having been taken ill three days before with acute appendicitis.

At the Carlton Club a large majority voted to withdraw from the Coalition; this precipitated the fall of the Government. Bonar Law formed a Conservative administration, and a General Election ensued.

In those days appendicitis was a dangerous condition: on 17 October Winston successfully underwent an appendectomy in hospital, but he was too ill to travel or to take part in the election campaign in Dundee until the last days. Clementine, however, taking her seven-week-old baby with her, gallantly set out on 6 November to join the fray in the North.

A loyal and enthusiastic band of supporters and friends such as General Spears (Winston's friend since Western Front days) and Lord Wodehouse rallied round in Dundee, but it was hardly a cheering omen that the house where Clementine stayed was in Dudhope Terrace.

---

[1] In August 1922, when the Turkish army advanced on the Greeks towards Chanak, on the Asiatic side of the Dardanelles (a neutral zone imposed under the Treaty of Sèvres, 1920), Lloyd George, supported by Churchill, had taken a strong stance, making it clear to Turkey that any violation of the Treaty would result in war with the British Empire. Through independent action by the local commander, and Lloyd George's determined stance, war was avoided. At home Lloyd George was much criticized; the Conservatives were particularly angered by his failure to consult the Dominion leaders. Churchill also was blamed.

[2] Stanley Baldwin (1867–1947), later 1st Earl Baldwin of Bewdley. At this time Chancellor of the Exchequer, 1922. Would serve three terms as Prime Minister, 1923–4, 1924–9 and 1935–7.

○ From WSC [typewritten]   2 Sussex Square
6 November 1922

My darling,
    [Dr] Hartigan examined Sarah this morning and said she had had a little
cold behind the nose which would naturally cause a certain irritation in
the ear, and that there was no connection whatever between this and the
glands[1]. Her temperature is normal and she is quite all right. We are,
however, keeping her indoors for a day or two as a precautionary
measure....
    I do hope you were not too tired by your long journey. I felt it was a
great effort for you to cart yourself and your kitten all that way last night.
Jack W[odehouse] telephoned this morning that you were all right and
were addressing a meeting this evening. Do take it easy. The mere fact of
your presence will I am sure be highly beneficial....
    The doctors were quite content this morning with my progress and seem
to think there is no doubt I shall be able to keep my engagement at
Dundee.
    Tender love my darling darling – many kisses to you & the sweet kitten
                                          from yr devoted loving
                                                                W.

[1] Sarah suffered from tubercular glands in her neck about this time, and during her childhood
underwent several operations which were ultimately successful.

Clementine flung herself into the front line, making spirited speeches at
packed rowdy meetings. General Spears reported to Winston on the bitterness and violence of the campaign: at one meeting Clementine, wearing a
string of pearls, had been spat upon by women. Spears commented admiringly: 'Clemmie's bearing was magnificent – like an aristocrat going to the
guillotine in a tumbril.'[1]

[1] Recounted in Martin Gilbert, *Winston S. Churchill*, Vol. IV, 1972, p. 878.

◇ From CSC   10 Dudhope Terrace
Thursday afternoon [possibly 9 November 1922]

My Darling,
    I have seen F.E [Smith*/Birkenhead] & he gave me your letter – I do
rejoice that you are to be a 'Companion of Honour'[1]. I think that is a
distinction to be proud of.
    The situation here is an anxious one .... Of course I feel the minute you
arrive the atmosphere will change & the people will be roused – If you
bring Sergeant Thompson [detective] etc tell him to conceal himself
tactfully, as it would not do if the populace thought you were afraid of
them. The papers are so vile, they would misrepresent it, & say you had
brought detectives becos you were afraid of the rowdy element – They are
capable of anything. If you feel strong enough, I think besides the Drill

Hall Meeting which is pretty sure to be broken up, you should address one or two small open meetings. Every rowdy meeting rouses sympathy & brings votes & will especially as you have been so ill. Even in the rowdiest foulest place of all the people tho' abusive were really good-natured. . . .

I am longing to see you & so is Dundee – I shall be heartbroken if you don't get in – I find what the people like best is the settlement of the Irish Question. So I trot that out & also your share in giving the Boers self government. The idea against you seems to be that you are a 'War Monger'[2], but I am exhibiting you as a Cherub Peace Maker with little fluffy wings round your chubby face. I think the line is not so much 'Smash the Socialists' as to try with your great abilities to help in finding solution of the Capital & Labour problem & I tell them that now that you are free from the cares & labours of office you will have time to think that out & work for it in the next Parliament.

My Darling, the misery here is appalling – Some of the people look absolutely starving – Morel's Election address [Labour candidate] just out <u>very moderate</u> & in favour of only constitutional methods. So one cannot compare him with Gallacher[3] –

Your loving
Clemmie

[1] WSC had been appointed a Companion of Honour in the Resignation Honours List.
[2] A tag to which WSC's role in the Chanak Incident had added much colour.
[3] William Gallacher (1881–1965), the Communist Party candidate, would hold a seat in Fife, 1935–50; he was one of two Communists in the 1945–50 parliament, the last (to date) in the House of Commons.

Despite gallant efforts, the tide was flowing inexorably against Churchill, who arrived in Dundee on 11 November; still very weak, he had to deliver the greater part of his speeches sitting down. The hostility of the meetings grew ever more violent as the campaign drew to its end: when the result was declared his massive 1918 majority (15,365 votes) had been swept away.[1]

Nationally the Conservatives won a strong majority. In the Liberal Party there was a decisive verdict against Lloyd George*. But – most significantly – the Labour Party had polled over 4 million votes to the Conservatives' 5.5 million.

Defeated and utterly exhausted, Winston and Clementine returned home to lick their wounds. Winston had not been out of Parliament for twenty-two years, and now, freed from both ministerial and parliamentary ties, they decided to winter abroad. No. 2 Sussex Square was let, and in early December the family moved to Cannes, where they rented the Villa Rêve d'Or for six months.

As 1923 dawned Winston was, as he wryly wrote of himself much later: 'without an office, without a seat, without a party, and without an appendix'.[2] But this was a pleasant time: Clementine played tennis; Winston continued writing his war memoirs (*The World Crisis*) and, while painting in the winter sunshine, he had time to reflect upon his situation.

In the last months of the Lloyd George Government Winston had striven without success to foster the Coalition spirit in the formation of a centre grouping which would invite liberal/radical opinion to form an effective bulwark against the rising menace of socialism. Now he found himself wandering in a political 'no man's land', between diehard Toryism and a divided and much enfeebled Liberal Party.

During these months he returned home only on three occasions, escorting Randolph and the other children to and from their schools, attending to his literary affairs, and supervising the extensive works in progress at Chartwell.

Clementine remained at Cannes, celebrating her thirty-seventh birthday on 1 April – when Winston gave her a beautiful diamond brooch.

[1] The victors (it was a two-seat constituency) were E. D. Morel (Lab.) and Edwin Scrymgeour (Prohibitionist).
[2] Winston S. Churchill, 'Election Memories', in *Thoughts and Adventures*, 1932, p. 213.

○ From WSC [typewritten]   Ritz Hotel
27 January 1923   London

My darling,

We arrived after a quite easy and comfortable journey, and Randolph was not a bit overtired. The next day I took him and Pebbin [Peregrine Churchill] down to Chartwell, where Tilden[1] met us. I went most carefully into the whole question of the new wing at the back of the house. . . .

First. . . . The library ceiling is now exposed and is really a very fine oak roofed ceiling like Blois. . . . It can therefore be made into an additional reception room with an oak ceiling, in the direct line of the drawing room and the boudoir. When the doors are opened all through the length of these three rooms will be over 80 feet. Tilden is very keen on this. It undoubtedly makes a very fine sweep. . . .

I will get everything forward into a condition in which we can discuss the whole question as soon as I come out, . . . Goonie and Jack [Churchill*] are coming down with me to see it to-morrow. . . . All the work on the garden is going forward steadily.

I have been working continuously at the book and there are many things I can settle here which it is quite impossible to do by correspondence. I think it will be finally off my hands by the time I leave on Sunday week. . . .

. . . Grey[2] and Garvin lunched with me yesterday and we had a long interesting talk. They are very pessimistic about the state of Europe and seem to think that some awful thing is going to happen quite soon. I do not believe it. I think the awful thing has happened.

I went to see Sir Hugh Fraser, the counsel whom my solicitors recommended, about the Evening News libel. There is no doubt it is a gross libel unprotected by privilege. I am therefore issuing a writ in the course of the next few days against the Evening News and am scrutinising other papers which repeated the offence.[3] . . .

Such is my report.

✍Tender love my darling one to you & to yr kittens. Randolph was sad at going back, but bore up manly.

I am longing to get back again to the sunshine....

Your ever loving
W

¹ Philip Armstrong Tilden (1887–1956), architect, decorator in murals and bookplate designer. As well as the Churchills, his clients included Lloyd George and Philip Sassoon.
² Sir Edward Grey, now 1st Viscount Grey of Fallodon; see p. 48 n. 3.
³ The *Evening News* of 12 January 1923, followed by the *Daily Herald* the next day, had alleged extravagant expenditure of public funds on WSC's trip to Egypt in March 1921. WSC brought and won a libel action against both papers, which was heard in the High Court of Justice in July 1923.

○ From CSC   Villa Rêve d'Or
Tuesday 29 January [1923]

My darling,

Thank you for both your letters....

The Chartwell plans sound charming. I hope in the new Tower arrangement, the 'sewing-room' has not been eliminated? This is distinct from the 'linen room'.... Tell Mr Tilden. The Sewing-room should be as large & nice as the Lingerie here, as 2 or 3 maids will sit & sew there every day.

The extra Reception room making a vista of 80 feet sounds very lovely & grand. We must have a State Festival there!

I do hope we catch that dirty Rothermere out & make him grovel¹.

I won the Tournament with Mr Scovel! Great excitement. I enjoyed it very much. My Mama has been here & to-day I conduct her back to Monte Carlo in our car....

Mama has patronised the Casino 2 or 3 times. She goes from 3 to 7[p.m.]. I have not put my foot in it since your departure except for the purpose of raiding it & removing Mother forcibly. She won 7,000 francs laboriously & then flung it all away in 10 minutes. I cannot understand such folly....

... I am now going to have four quiet days like Diogenes in his tub, sallying forth now and then for a little tennis – Do visit the rabbit [Randolph] before coming back. The weather is heavenly.

Your loving
Clemmie
...

¹ A reference to the libel suit against the *Evening News*, which was owned by Lord Rothermere.

○ From WSC [typewritten]   Ritz Hotel
29 January 1923

My darling,

I send this by Archie [Sinclair], who is just starting for Cannes. I have no news beyond what I wrote you two days ago. I have been working steadily at the book and there is practically nothing now to do except to read the final page proofs. All the outstanding points are settled.... It has been a tremendous hustle.... We are still in doubt about the title, which is to be settled finally on Tuesday. 'The World Crisis', 'The Meteor Flag' and 'Within the Storm' are the best suggestions we have up to date. They are none of them very satisfactory....

Jack [Churchill*] and I went to a play together last night. To-morrow I dine with the Wodehouses; Tuesday with Haldane[1]. Garvin is reading my proofs now and comes to lunch on Tuesday to tell me his impression. It will be very interesting to learn if he is pleased.

✍Tender love my sweet – a vy nice photo in the Times yesterday of your netting a back hander.

I am much looking forward to coming out again –

Your loving devoted
W

[1] 1st Viscount Haldane, a former Lord Chancellor; see p. 51 n. 3.

○ From WSC [typewritten]   Ritz Hotel
30 January 1923

My darling one,

The week is passing very rapidly away and I am so busy that I hardly ever leave the Ritz except for meals.

... To-morrow I lunch at New Court [N. M. Rothschild's, Bankers] to do business in the city. I am going to visit Jack's office[1] for the first time. On Thursday the Prince [of Wales] is lunching with me at Bucks Club with Freddie Guest* and Jack Wodehouse to talk polo and politics....

The Evening News, confronted with the writ, have sent round wishing to apologise and protesting that they never meant any harm. I find many of the other papers issued even worse libels, and my idea is to deal with them altogether and make them all come up in court and tender their apologies....

Commander Hilton Young, the new Chief Whip of the Lloyd George Liberals, asked to come to see me. He seems very anxious to find me another seat. He will no doubt look about, but it is what Asquith* called 'A dark and difficult adventure'.

I am practically through the book now and have nothing more to do except to read finally through the page proofs and alter commas and odd words. We have reached the moment when one must say 'As the tree falls, so shall it lie'.

...

I see in my press cuttings very nice photographs of Sarah and Diana in the Battle of Flowers; ...

I am much looking forward to getting away again. I do hope we are going to have some pleasant sunshine in which I can paint to my heart's content.

> Au revoir my darling
> Tender love for all
> Your devoted
> W

[1] Jack Churchill had joined the firm of stockbrokers Vickers Da Costa.

Chartwell was not nearly ready for occupation, so they took a charming house, Hosey Rigge, on Hosey Common above Westerham, from where they could constantly visit the property; already the older children could enjoy the garden. Needless to say, Hosey Rigge soon became the 'Cosy Pigge' or the 'Rosy Pigge'.

In August, Clementine stayed in a guest house in Cromer, on the Norfolk coast, taking part in a tennis tournament.

The next letter is difficult to date precisely, but it clearly belongs to this period when Winston was a political wanderer: it shows how closely Clementine followed, and shrewdly appraised, political matters.

O From CSC   2 Sussex Square
Saturday [probably summer 1923]

My Darling Winston

I want to appeal to you to think again before you go to Max [Beaverbrook*]'s this evening. Ll.G. [Lloyd George*] is not in the same position as you – He is in not out [of the House of Commons], & he shares or practically shares the throne with Asquith*.

Now I am sure the old <u>real</u> Liberals will want you back, but of course there <u>is</u> the shyness of a long estrangement. Do not give them cause (quite wrongly I know) for thinking that you would like a new Tory Liberal Coalition – That might cool them off.

Instinctively, one of the reasons I wanted Rusholme[1] was that if you were to lose a seat I felt it would be better for you to be beaten by a Tory (which would rouse Liberal sympathy) than by a Socialist.

My Darling it is important –, I shall say <u>nothing</u> if you go, but consider the imprudence of losing the offer of a good Wee Free seat (as opposed to extinct Nat. Liberal) for the sake of a pleasant evening.

> Your loving & sympathetic Pawser
> . . .

[1] Rusholme (now in Greater Manchester), one of several seats in which WSC had been interested around this time.

○ From WSC [typewritten]   2 Sussex Square
13 August 1923

My darling Clemmie,
    I have been toiling for three hours at proofs so that I hope you will excuse typescript.
    We had a pleasant Sunday at Philip [Sassoon*]'s.... I worked nearly all day.
    I took Fowler [chauffeur] with me on Saturday in the little car, and drove all the way there. I sent him back by train to get the big car in order. This morning I drove the Car back myself alone. It is exactly 50 miles, and we did it in an hour and 55 minutes, ... I can drive the car quite easily now, which will be a great help in our arrangements. It goes vy nicely at 35 miles p.h. & will do 40 easily....
    I am to see Baldwin[1] at 3 o'clock tomorrow, so I shall go up and work at Sussex Square tomorrow morning.
    ✍I will send the proofs tomorrow.
    Tender love my darling one. I am just going to Chartwell, having finished my toil, in order to examine the progress....

                         With many many kisses, from me & Mary
                                 Your ever loving husband
                                         W

[1] Stanley Baldwin had become Prime Minister on 22 May, in succession to Bonar Law, who had resigned due to ill-health.

○ From CSC   Newhaven Court Guest House
15 August 1923   Cromer

My Darling,
    The lovely weather has Alas broken & this morning we woke to gray skies & torrents of rain, which has now degenerated into a fine drizzle almost like a Scotch mist. However the British do not allow anything so trivial as the Climate to interfere with their Summer Sports & I understand we are to play through the thick of it – ... I have not played yet & am discreetly remaining in my room until my non-attendance is noticed & I am sent for – I have meanwhile sent down the Town for nets to wear over my shoes, a contrivance to minimize the slipping – ... As I write the summons has come – so more anon
– – –
    A false alarm –
    How clever of you to manage the little car so quickly – I must, on my return, resume my lessons....

                                         Your loving
                                       Clemmie

O From WSC   2 Sussex Square
15 August 1923

<u>Secret</u>
My darling Clemmie,
   My interview with the P.M. was most agreeable. He professed
unbounded leisure & rec^d me with the utmost cordiality. We talked Ruhr,
Oil, Admiralty & Air, Reparations, the American Debt & general politics. I
found him thoroughly in favour of The Oil Settlement on the lines
proposed. Indeed he might have been Waley Cohen[1] from the way he
talked. I am sure it will come off. The only thing I am puzzled about is my
own affair[2]. However I am to see Cohen on Friday. It is a question of how
to arrange it so as to leave no just ground of criticism. My talk with the
P.M. was quite general & I did not raise the personal aspect at all at this
preliminary & non-committal stage. Masterton[3] in whom I confided was vy
shy of it on large political grounds. However I shall proceed further before
making up my mind.
   I entered Downing Street by the Treasury entrance [in Whitehall] to
avoid comment. This much amused Baldwin. However Max [Beaverbrook*]
rang up this morning to say he hoped I had had a pleasant interview, &
that I had greatly heartened the P.M. about the Ruhr! He is a little ferret.
He has to go to Scotland tonight so I am going to dine at the Vineyard[4]
instead of his coming here.
   Keyes[5] came down [to Chartwell] last night & we had long jolly talks
about the war & what they killed each other for. I purchased in London
two delicious young lady grouses wh were the feature of dinner....
   ... I have 8 articles to write as soon as the book is finished £500, 400, &
200 = 1100. We shall not starve.
   I do hope you are enjoying yrself my beloved & not tiring yrself out.
The happy mean.

                                                    With tender & fondest love,
                                                        Your ever devoted
                                                                W

---

[1] Sir Robert Waley Cohen (1877–1952), Managing Director, Shell Transport & Trading Co. Ltd.
[2] WSC had been invited by the Royal Dutch Shell and Burmah Oil companies to represent them
in their application for a merger with the Anglo-Persian Oil Company. Following consultation
with the Prime Minister, a scheme was drawn up under WSC's guidance, but before it could be
examined Baldwin made a declaration in favour of Protection and called a General Election; WSC,
considering it his duty to return to public life and oppose this policy, in November 1923 withdrew from the oil merger negotiations and renounced his personal interest in the matter.
[3] James Masterton-Smith, see p. 88 n. 2. At this time Permanent Under-Secretary of State, Colonial
Office.
[4] The Vineyard, Lord Beaverbrook's house in Fulham, south-west London.
[5] Sir Roger Keyes, later Admiral of the Fleet 1st Baron Keyes of Zeebrugge GCB, KCVO, DSO
(1872–1945). At this time Deputy Chief of Naval Staff, 1921–5.

O From WSC [typewritten]   2 Sussex Square
16 August 1923

Secret
My darling,
    Tilden has sent the enclosed plans which are a variation upon the
original. I think they are an improvement, ... We shall have to take a final
decision Tuesday at the latest. Meanwhile I am agreeing to everything up
to the eaves.
    The progress is really quite good.... The water will be connected in a
few days with the cisterns, and all the baths, taps, kitchens, etc., all over
the house will flow....
    I dined with Max last night. After much beating about the bush the
mystery of his learning of my visit to Baldwin was explained. He had
visited him afterwards, at B's request and found him delighted....
    The children come back tomorrow, and I have had a delightful letter
from Diana. I am going to amuse them on Saturday and Sunday by making
them an aerial house in the lime tree. You may be sure I will take the
greatest precautions to guard against them tumbling down. The
undergrowth of the tree is so thick it will be perfectly safe, and I will not
let them go up except under my personal charge.
                                                        Your ever loving devoted
                                                                          W
    ...

Clearly Clementine had expressed her growing anxieties about the ever-
mounting cost of the works in progress at Chartwell, and the future expense
of living there (about which she had long taken a pessimistic view). Winston's
attempt to reassure her, by outlining in detail what he expected to receive
for his writings, highlights the extent to which now – and indeed always –
he kept his family by his pen and ceaseless industry.

O From WSC   Flying Cloud[1]
2 September 1923

My darling,
    This is a most attractive yacht. Imagine a large four-masted cargo boat,
fitted up in carved oak like a little country house, with front doors,
staircases, & lovely pictures. She can sail 12 knots & motor 8, &
accommodate 16 guests.... We lie in the harbour of Bayonne, today under
bright skies, & awaiting my brush & paint box from the poop.... Benny
[Duke of Westminster*] very charming & Violet [his wife] too. They are vy
glad to have me; but wd much like you. It is absolute quiet & peace. One
need not do anything or see anybody. The polo ground is reported
excellent, & the first game is to-day. There are numerous frogs, who do
not play too well, Ivor W [Guest*/Wimborne] is coming with his cracks, &
Alfonso the Toreador (Spaghoni)[2]. We have got quite a good team, bearing
in mind the handicap....

The fares for the ponies from Boulogne to Bayonne are only £6 <u>each</u> and this by special arrangement includes the return journey. I shall make them walk to Folkestone. So it is not vy expensive....

My beloved – I do beg you not to worry about money, or to feel insecure. On the contrary the policy we are pursuing aims above all at <u>stability</u>. (Like Bonar Law!) Chartwell is to be our <u>home</u>. It will have cost us £20,000 and will be worth at least £15,000 apart from a fancy price. We must endeavour to live there for many years & hand it on to Randolph afterwards. We must make it in every way charming & as far as possible economically self contained. It will be cheaper than London.

Eventually – though there is no hurry – we must sell Sussex [2 Sussex Square] & find a small flat for you & me ... Then with the motors we shall be well equipped for business or pleasure. If we go into office we will live in Downing Street!

The estate [Garron Towers, his inheritance] at this moment is at least as large as it was when I succeeded, but part is invested in Chartwell instead of in shares. You must think of it in this light....

Add to this my darling yr courage & good will and I am certain that we can make ourselves a permanent resting place, so far as the money side of this uncertain & transitory world is concerned. But if you set yourself against Chartwell, or lose heart, or bite your bread & butter & yr pig then it only means further instability, recasting of plans & further expense & worry....

... When we return from Mimizan & Bayonne, we shall I trust be clear of Tilden, Browne Mott & Jeff & Co. for ever. And the spring of 1924 will cover with its verdure the stains and blemishes with wh they have disfigured our gardens. You must push ahead with the plans for these – modest but complete; so that we can discuss them on my return – Meanwhile I will prepare the sinews of war with three or four hours writing a day....

My darling one – my heart is full of love for you & your dear kittens, & my keenest wish is to see you happy & prosperous & safe. For this I will indeed work my utmost and avoid imprudence of all kinds.

Do write & tell me yr. news & also telegraph each day.

Your devoted
W

P.S. I have had a long morning writing & now I am going to paint.

[1] The Duke of Westminster's yacht.
[2] King Alfonso XIII of Spain. 'Spaghoni' was a WSC/CSC joke originating in an Edwardian music hall song about a Toreador – Spaghoni.

○ From CSC
3 September 1923

Hosey Rigge
Westerham

Darling Winston,

This is my first day up & about –

The throat is much better[1]. No pain – only stiffness & a certain ache after talking – I wonder if I shall ever get my normal voice back again? It is hopelessly broken & croaky at present. I asked the doctor & he opined it would be all right in a month or two, but that it is lucky I am not a singer.... I feel much better but rather knocked about & very vulnerable.

I went over to Chartwell this morning & was much disappointed to find they have not made the slightest attempt at starting the new [Nursery] Wing; not even a gesture such as pegging something out – It is now 10 days since I have seen the place & the only notable advance is the removal of the laurels!...

Goonie & Jack [Churchill*] & the 2 boys spent yesterday here – It was a lovely day & I think they all enjoyed it. I was very glad to see them.

I hope you will have good painting weather.

The poor League of Nations[2] is on its trial. I hope it prevails & is not made a laughing stock of – I couldn't bear that overbearing Devil Mussolini[3] to have it all his own way. But how can the L of N accomplish anything without a Navy & an Army behind it?

Your loving
Clemmie

[1] CSC had been afflicted by a 'quinsy' (an abscess in the region of the tonsils), which had to be lanced by the local doctor.
[2] The principle of a League of Nations had been adopted by the Allied Powers at the Peace Conference in 1919; it came into being formally on 10 January 1920, and in October that year transferred its headquarters to Geneva, Switzerland.
[3] Benito Mussolini (1883–1945), Italian dictator and founder of the Fascist Movement; Prime Minister of Italy from 1922. Known as 'Il Duce'.

O From CSC   Hosey Rigge
Tuesday 4 September [1923]

My Darling Winston

Torrents of rain to-day – Diana & Randolph have nevertheless gone riding – I have finished Vanity Fair & am consuming a very inferior book of [H. A.] Vachell's, The Face of Clay. Tilden is by way of coming this afternoon but he may be put off by the weather –

Poor little Japs – The Kaiser & Mussolini seem quite benevolent & humane compared to the Almighty when He lays about Him[1]. He is so quick too – In one day He kills as many people as in six months of the Great War. Somewhere in the Psalms it says 'One Day in Thy Courts are as a Thousand Years'!!![2]

What fun the Japanese Tildens (if there are any left) will have putting all the Pagodas up again – I shall suggest to our Tilden that he hurries up with Chartwell & then emigrates to Tokyo[3]....

I hope your weather is holding up....

Your loving
Clemmie

[1] More than 100,000 people had been killed in an earthquake in Japan, 1 September 1923.
[2] CSC had got her (not very relevant) quote somewhat muddled. Psalm 84, v. 10 reads: 'For one day in thy courts: is better than a thousand.'
[3] By this time both the Churchills were considerably irritated by their architect, Mr Tilden (a familiar syndrome).

○ From WSC   Flying Cloud
5 September 1923

My darling,

We have been vy successful at the tables. Benny [Westminster*] with persistent luck & without playing vy high has won over half a million francs. I pursuing a most small & conservative game am nearly 30,000 [francs] to the good. We are now off by sea to San Sebastian. The weather has turned vy dull today & it is raining hard. But tomorrow perhaps the sun will let me paint again....

It continues to be vy pleasant here. I write & work in bed all the morning as usual. If the sun shines I paint, & thereafter go down to the 'Office' [Casino]. This séance usually lasts till about 3.30 a.m: but last night we got to bed at 4!

I am looking forward greatly to coming back and seeing you all again. I hope the progress of Chartwell continues under yr supervision to be rapid – or comparatively rapid.

What a swine this Mussolini is. I see Rothermere is supporting him! I am all for the League of Nations. Poor devil it is life or death for it now....

Tender love my dearest. No letter has reached me yet from you; but I suppose they will overtake me soon.

In a few days I will turn homewards....

Your devoted ever loving
W

Although the Conservatives had won a clear victory in the General Election in November 1922, the new Government did not last long. In October Stanley Baldwin pledged the Conservative Party to the reintroduction of tariffs as a remedy for unemployment. The revival of the Protection issue had a divisive effect on the Tory party, but brought together the two wings of the Liberal Party under Asquith's* leadership, who united with the Labour Party in campaigning for Free Trade.

Parliament was dissolved on 16 November 1923. The General Election took place on 6 December, the results showing a clear defeat for Protection. Although the Conservatives were still, with 258 seats, the largest single party, Labour (191) and the Liberals (159) denied them an overall majority.

Ramsay MacDonald[1] formed the first Labour Government in January 1924. When Asquith decided to support this new Government Churchill, who had stood as a Liberal Free Trader at West Leicester (where he had been defeated), came to breaking point with the Liberal Party.

In the New Year of 1924 the Churchills spent a week together in Paris, staying in Lord Derby's flat. Afterwards Winston went to hunt boar with Bendor Westminster* at Mimizan, and Clementine visited Consuelo and Jacques Balsan* at their house, Lou Sueil, at Eze, near Cannes, where Winston hoped to join her.

[1] James Ramsay MacDonald (1866–1937), first Labour Prime Minister, January–November 1924. He had been the first Secretary of the newly born Labour Party, 1900, and was elected to Parliament in 1906; Leader of the Labour Party, 1911–14, and from 1922. Served a second term as Prime Minister, 1929–35.

○ From CSC   Lou Sueil
16 February 1924

My Darling Winston

I have just written to Lord Derby to thank him for our visit to his flat. I expect you have too, but you may have been too busy chasing the pig! I hope you caught him & that he was a monster.

Yesterday we descended from our mountain fastness & lunched with the Wards at Villa Rosemary[1] – Afterwards I played a little mild but pleasant tennis. It is bright & glistening here but piercingly cold & to-day I could not accompany Consuelo & Mary & Blandford[2] on an expedition to Cannes as I spent the day in bed with a sore throat.... I really spent a most thrilling day, reading Mrs Spears' book Jane, our Stranger[3] – It is thrilling & I think brilliantly written....

The character of your friend the Imbroglio[4] is dissected under a magnifying glass with a white hot needle....

I hope you will find great progress at Chartwell. Do write at once.

Poincaré[5] is an idol in this household – I rather gather he is in all French milieux which are not actively in politics.

The ladies we saw at Ciro's & who I believe accompanied you to Mimizan were here, & were considered queer fish – I am afraid the behaviour here has been outrageous.

People are very cool about Benny & sorry for her in a detached way[6].

Your loving
Clemmie

. . .

[1] South of France home of Viscount and Viscountess Ednam (Eric and Rosemary Ward); see p. 217 n. 3.

[2] John Albert ('Bert') Spencer-Churchill, Marquess of Blandford, later 10th Duke of Marlborough (1897–1972); married, 1920, Mary Cadogan (1900–61), daughter of Viscount Chelsea.

[3] *Jane, Our Stranger* by Mary Borden, the American wife of Maj.-Gen. Sir Louis Spears; see p. 127 n. 1.

[4] Mrs Reginald Fellowes (1890–1962). Born Marguerite, daughter of the 4th Duc Decazes and de Glücksbjerg, and always known as 'Daisy'. The nickname 'Imbroglio' derived from her marriage in 1910 to Prince Jean de Broglie (d. 1918). In 1919 she married WSC's first cousin, Reginald Fellowes, whose mother was Lady Rosamond Spencer-Churchill. In the 1930s WSC would often stay at Daisy Fellowes' South of France villa, Les Zoraïdes. CSC disliked her.

[5] Raymond Poincaré (1860–1934), French Prime Minister and Minister of Foreign Affairs, January 1922–June 1924.

[6] The marriage between Bendor and Violet Westminster was falling apart; they were divorced in 1926.

○ From WSC   The Woolsack
17 February 1924

My darling,

We had two good hunts, but no pig. Four hours galloping made me tired, stiff & well. We shall try again tomorrow.

Yesterday we motored to Biarritz & raided the Casino. Play was meagre, but after some vicissitudes I collected five milles [5,000 francs] & levanted with them....

My sweet one – I am so glad you are in such a downy basket. Do not over exert yrself at tennis. Doubles not Singles <u>please</u>....

Poodle I love you. I feel quite lonely & sometimes frightened without you to give me a kiss or a prog [WSC/CSC-speak for nudge or prod].

I will visit Chartwell on Wed (D.V.) & will report to you at length the progress of the toil –

Tender love my sweet Clemmie –
Your own ever devoted
W

...

○ From WSC   [2 Sussex Square]
Thursday 21 February 1924

My dearest One,
Enclosed you will find some account of our affairs.

I have been busy all the morning dictating my article, & am now off to Chartwell....

I telegraphed to you about Randolph & the baby. All is going well.

Last night I dined at the Vineyard. Max [Beaverbrook*], Ll.G. [Lloyd George*], Rothermere – You will exclaim 'Lamppost'.[1] Still it was pleasant – & we had a most amusing film.

Tender love, my darling
Your devoted
W

[1] Private joke: when WSC consorted with cronies such as these, CSC always said they were like 'dogs round a lamp-post'.

○ From WSC [typewritten]   2 Sussex Square
20 February 1924 [enclosed with
his of 21 February]

I have just come back from Chartwell. There is considerable progress all along the line. The drawing room has two coats of plaster, and the cornice is up. The dining room has one coat of plaster, and all the French windows are in with their glass. They are lovely and add enormously to the appearance of the wing....

<u>Out of doors</u>. The roadway wall is finished with the exception of the outer curves, and so are the palings....

The pigs, ponies and cows are doing well. The new pig is getting very near her time, and I hope soon to report a large family. Twenty-four new chickens have been hatched, and more are expected shortly....

I found the children very well, with the exception of Mary who, as you know, has had slight influenza. She is getting on all right, ... Influenza has also broken out at Sandroyds, and Randolph is a victim....

Tomorrow I shall have to do my second article (*done), and on Friday and Saturday I have two short speeches to prepare; but I shall hope to get to Chartwell in the afternoons all the same.

We had a very good hunt the last day at Mimizan. There were no less than eleven pigs: embarras de choix. I saw seven all together, including one quite big one, and two others separately galloping through the woods. After a long chase we finally slew a sow. She ran for twenty minutes as fast as the horses could gallop. The two young persons did not make a particularly good impression, and I think Benny [Westminster*] had quite enough of them before they departed. I enjoyed myself so much at Mimizan.... I continue to read a great deal about the war, consuming on the average a book a day. I think I shall stay here till you come back, as I am pretty full now of ideas which should be set down.

Although Winston was now estranged from the Liberals, he was not ready to re-join the Conservative Party, and when a by-election arose in March 1924 in the Abbey Division of Westminster, he stood as an Independent Anti-Socialist; there was also an official Tory candidate.

Clementine was away when Winston decided to fight the seat, but she was home by the end of February and was active in his campaign. The by-election aroused much interest and excitement, and several prominent Conservatives supported Churchill: but he was defeated on 20 March by forty-three votes.

Determined to get back into Parliament, Winston immediately was on the look-out for possible seats, and several approaches were made to him in the ensuing months.

In June, Baldwin (Leader of the Conservative Party) publicly renounced his Party's pledge to introduce Protective Tariffs – thus removing for Churchill the last serious obstacle to his reconciliation with the Conservatives.

O From CSC   Lou Sueil
24 February 1924

My Darling –

Your telegram about the Abbey Division excited me a good deal. I hope all may happen as you wish. – I notice in to-day's Continental Daily Mail a 'one inch long' report of your Shirley Kellogg speech[1] in which you widen the existing breach between yourself & official Liberalism.

Do not however let the Tories get you too cheap – They have treated you so badly in the past & they ought to be made to feel it – I must wait for Times for complete report.

The advance at Chartwell seems considerable & I am longing to see it.

I am distressed that after her measles Mary should have influenza & our poor little Randolph too in his chilly school. . . .

I have visited the Sporting Club 3 times & have lost nearly 3,000 francs, 1,000 francs each time with admirable regularity, so now I shall not play any more. Mary Blandford has won – She is a dashing & optimistic gambler – rather like you. . . .

We play a great deal of Mah Jongg[2] here –

Nothing could be kinder & more charming than Consuelo [Balsan*] & Balsan – They love each other very much & it is a most peaceful & restful atmosphere. . . .

In the French non political world Poincaré is still an idol – They love him & venerate him. . . . In the Political Notes I see The Times impartially advocates the Abbey Division being given to Sir George Lloyd[3], Pretyman & Jack Hills – What fools the people who direct The Times are to imagine that any of these men can help the Tory Party out of the quagmire of inefficiency & stupidity in which they are up to their necks –

My Darling do not stand unless you are reasonably sure of getting in – The movement inside the Tory Party to try & get you back is only just born & requires nursing & nourishing & educating to bring it to full strength – And there are of course counter influences, as none of the Tory Leaders want you back as they see you would leap over their heads – The Times I feel sure is against you at present, or at any rate not helping – Couldn't we cultivate John Astor[4] gradually? I feel that though no genius he would be quite as much help as Beaverbrook*. The Times can really do more than the Daily Express. . . .

I feel very anxious about it all – I am sure with patience all will come right; but these silly Tories are probably now so pleased with Ramsay [MacDonald] over the 5 Cruisers[5] that they will not yet feel the need of your help in fighting Labour –

Perhaps your hour will come only after Labour has a big independent Majority & shews itself in its true colours – I fear these ruminations may not seem very intelligent as I am cut off from knowing what really is going on.

Tender Love,
Clemmie

[1] On 22 February WSC presided at a dinner given by the English-Speaking Union in honour of the US Ambassador Mr Frank Kellogg and his wife. Mr Kellogg was Ambassador in London 1923–5.
[2] A Chinese game played with 'tiles' like dominoes, introduced into the USA about 1919 and very fashionable at this time.
[3] Sir George (later 1st Baron) Lloyd (1879–1941), Conservative MP, 1910–18 and 1924–5. Governor of Bombay, 1918–23. High Commissioner for Egypt and the Sudan, 1925–9.
[4] John Jacob Astor, later Baron Astor of Hever (1886–1971). Younger brother of Waldorf, 2nd Viscount Astor (see p. 68 n. 1). Conservative MP, 1922–45. Chief Proprietor of *The Times*, President of the Press Club, the Newspaper Press Fund and the Commonwealth Press Union. Renowned for his public and charitable activities. Married (1916) Lady Violet Mercer Nairne, a war widow; they lived at Hever Castle, a few miles from Chartwell.
[5] On 21 February 1924 the House of Commons was informed that, in view of serious unemployment, especially in the shipbuilding industry, the Government had decided to proceed with the earlier Conservative programme of laying down five new cruisers.

○ From WSC   2 Sussex Square
24 February 1924

My Darling,

This Westminster Abbey by-election swooped down upon me like a
thunderstorm. Rothermere & Max [Beaverbrook*] offered the full support
of their press; & it was necessary for me to let it be known straight away
that my cap was in the ring. It is an amazing constituency comprising –
Eccleston Sq., Victoria Station, Smith Sq., Westminster Abbey, Whitehall,
Pall Mall, Carlton House Terrace – part of Soho, the south side of Oxford
Street, Drury Lane theatre & Covent Garden! It is of course one of the
choicest preserves of the Tory Party. . . .

There must be at least a hundred MP resident voters in the division, & I
shall have no difficulty in securing a vy fine & representative platform. [Sir
Edward] Grigg, L. Spears & other Liberal M.P.'s will fight for me, & it is
possible E[dward] Grey (a resident) will give me his support. [Reginald]
McKenna too – I think. Then I hope to get a letter from AJB [Balfour], also
a resident – Altogether it is an exceedingly promising Opportunity, & if it
comes off I shd hold the seat for a long time. . . .

At Baldwin's suggestion I had a long talk with him yesterday of the
friendliest character. He evidently wants vy much to secure my return &
cooperation. Their eyes are fully open to the dangers that lie ahead.
MacDonald is making a gt impression on the country, & there is no doubt
that he is gaining numerous adherents – mostly at the expense of the
Liberals.

I informed Ll.G. [Lloyd George*] of my resolves. He said I was only
acting in accordance with my convictions & made no reproaches of any
kinds . . . .

Of course if I stood as a Cons. it wd almost certainly be a walk over. But
I cannot do this, & it is far better for all the interests we are safeguarding
that I shd carry with me moderate Liberals.

I do not think there is any need for you to alter yr plans. If you are here
by the third or fourth of March you will be in time for the fight – if there is
one. . . .

Tender love my sweet Cat – Enjoy yourself & get fit for the fray.

                                                           Your devoted
                                                                 W
. . .

After the effort of the election Clementine was exhausted, and in mid-April
she went with her sister Nellie and Bertram Romilly to stay with their mother
in Dieppe for Easter.

While she was away, Winston made the move into Chartwell. I think it is
most significant that Clementine was not there at a moment when most
women would feel their presence to be absolutely necessary – and indeed

would be unable to bear missing the emotion and the excitement of the move into a new home.

She had worked hard supervising and chivvying the operations at Chartwell – and no doubt this also had contributed to her fatigue – but somewhere deep down her basic disbelief in the 'Chartwell Dream' must have contributed to her absence at this time.

○ From WSC   Chartwell
17 April 1924

My Darling,

This is the first letter I have ever written from this place, & it is right that it shd be to you. I am in bed in your bedroom (wh I have annexed temporarily) & wh is sparsely but comfortably furnished with the pick of yr two van loads. We have had two glorious days. The children have worked like blacks; & Sergeant Thompson [detective], Aley[1], Waterhouse[2], one gardener & 6 men have formed a powerful labour corps. The weather has been delicious, & we are out all day toiling in dirty clothes & only bathing before dinner. I have just had my bath in your de luxe bathroom. I hope you have no amour propre about it! The household consists of the nursery party reinforced by Lily – the K[n] [Kitchen] maid. I drink champagne at all meals & buckets of claret & soda in between, & the cuisine tho' simple is excellent. In the evenings we play the gramophone (of wh we have deprived Mary) & Mah Jongg with yr gimcrack set.

All yesterday & today we have been turfing & levelling the plateau [the main lawn]. The motor mower acts as a roller.... I hope to finish tomorrow.

Your steps are nearly made in the centre of the bank. The front basement windows go on apace.... The drawing room floor is finished & half planed....

Everything is budding now that this gleam of deferred genial weather has come.

　　　Only one thing lack these banks of green –
　　　The Pussy Cat who is their Queen.

I do hope my darling that you are all enjoying yourselves & that you are really recuperating. How I wish you were here.... You cannot imagine the size of these rooms till you put furniture into them. This bedroom of yours is a magnificent aerial bower. Come as soon as you feel well enough to share it. Don't go to London. I will send the motor to meet you at Newhaven: & if you telegraph one day in advance everything will be ready for you.

I had a satisfactory conversation with Jackson [Conservative Chief Whip]. He is going to try to fix up St George's[3] for me. The Liberal Party is in a stew. They are disgusted with the position into wh they have been led & then left without leading. There is an intensely bitter feeling agst Labour, wh everywhere is cutting Liberal throats in the constituencies. How often I find myself called wrong, for warning people of follies in time. Perhaps you have the same experience in the domestic sphere!

Tender love my sweet Clemmie. Please keep wiring, & think sometimes of yr devoted

paterfamilias porcus
Yr ever loving
W

. . .

¹ WSC's chauffeur until 1928, when he went to Brendan Bracken, with whom he stayed until the latter's death in 1958.
² Edmund Waterhouse, retired gardener of Chartwell's previous owner, Col. Campbell-Colquhoun; WSC kept him on in his cottage, and when the Churchills moved in to Chartwell he became Head Gardener, from 1924 to September 1926, when he finally retired.
³ St George's, Westminster, the next-door constituency to Westminster Abbey.

In reply to Winston's exuberant description of his first days at Chartwell, Clementine wrote rather wistfully: she knew she was missing something. But even this letter is tinged with doubt, and, despite a touching pledge of personal endeavour, one feels her lack of real enthusiasm.

Yet whatever her deeper doubts and anxieties, on her return home in early May she was to throw herself wholeheartedly into decorating and arranging the house, and making it the charming and delightful home it was to live in.

O From CSC   16 Rue des Fontaines
21 April 1924   Dieppe

My Darling Winston

I was so much delighted to get your long letter describing all that you are doing at Chartwell. I read it again & again & it made me long to be with you there.

If we are able in the future to live happily & peacefully there it will make up for all the effort you have poured out for it –

I have had sweet letters from all the children – They are blissfully happy. They will get to love it very much & it would be sad to have to part with it. I will do everything I can to help you to keep it –

This is a sad old place & to me it is extraordinary that Mother should make it her home. To me it is haunted & decayed & melancholy. My sister Kitty died here of typhoid fever, & Bill is buried here in the cemetery at the top of the hill.

I remember we came here quite suddenly the summer that I was thirteen years old – We were living at Seaford near Newhaven & Mother was afraid that my Father was going to try & get Kitty & myself back under his guardianship. . . .

It is extraordinary to reflect that if Mother had not on that first occasion come to Dieppe both Kitty & Bill might be alive today –

I say Bill as well as Kitty, because it is here that Mother first began her regular gambling habits & it is here that Bill saw gambling from his

childhood, & used to come after he was grown up when on leave from his
ship on week end gambling expeditions –

I went with Nellie to the Casino the other night & I was astounded at
the reckless manner in which both Mother & Nellie gambled. Nellie very
intelligently & dashingly, Mother in a superstitious & groping manner. It
made me feel quite ill & ashamed to watch them & I went home to bed....
I had no idea what a grip this cursed chemin-de-fer has on both of
them.... Bill's grim & lonely end has not made the slightest difference – I
don't feel I ought to criticize because gambling is not a temptation to me.
It just seems to me a morbid mania –

Nellie has not been again since that night. I didn't say anything but she
saw it was a shock to me.

Mother who is getting very old & very feeble totters down every
afternoon & plays – I believe only for an hour – But Bancos 2,000 francs
again & again without turning a hair – I have observed her way of life & I
calculate that her income being £800 a year she lives on £300 & has the
rest for play. She lives in a most modest pension instead of in either of her
nice little houses at 26 francs a day! which covers everything.

I am not enjoying this but I am resting – I find I am enormously &
unbelievably tired & the strong air makes me drunk with sleep.

I will come home on <u>Friday</u> & come straight to Chartwell as you
suggest....

Your loving
Clem

Once more the 'Jagoons' and Clementine and her children spent part of the
summer holidays together – this time in the 'Wilds of Wales' (so described
by Clementine), where Jack Churchill* and Goonie had taken a house.

○ From WSC [typewritten]   Chartwell Manor
19 August 1924

My darling,

...

Since you left we have had visitors, to wit, Freddie Guest*, Ll.G. [Lloyd
George*] and [Sir Roger] Keyes. Each has stayed one night in Henry VIII
[principal visitors' bedroom]. I had a long and very satisfactory talk with
Ll.G., and we were closer together politically than we have been since he
took part in putting in the Socialists....

My lunch with Rosebery[1] was delightful.... He is thoroughly au fait, and
in very much better health than he was two years ago. He wants us to stay
with him for the Edinburgh meeting (at Dalmeny[2]), and perhaps on the
whole it would be as well to have a Liberal headquarters, especially as it is
Liberal Imperialist.

Everyone is working frantically at your room. The whitewashers, the
oakstainers, the carpenters and the plasterers are hard at work from morn

till night. I hope that all will be to your liking when you return. They are allowing nothing to stand in the way of this.

Work on the dam[3] is progressing . . . the water has been rising steadily. We have this evening seven feet. . . .

Meanwhile the old lake is practically dry. There is an average of a foot of mud, and I am going to go at it hard with my railway to clear it out. The men are now reinforced to nine all told. Thompson [detective] and I have been wallowing in the most filthy black mud you ever saw, with the vilest odour, getting the beastly stuff to drain away. The moor hens and dab chicks have migrated in a body to the new lake and taken up their quarters in the bushes at the upper end. . . .

A formal offer has arrived from Mr Blain, the head Conservative Agent of the West Essex [Epping] Division. I am getting him down here to lunch. . . . It looks one of the safest seats in the country. But you never can tell[4]. . . .

Rosebery has just wired saying that he will be delighted to 'welcome the fourth generation'. . . .

My beloved – it will be jolly having you back on Monday. The house seems vy empty without you. With tender love,

Your devoted
W.

. . .

[1] 5th Earl of Rosebery (see p. 28 n. 1), a former Liberal Prime Minister and Foreign Secretary.
[2] Dalmeny House, South Queensferry, West Lothian, property of the Earl of Rosebery near Edinburgh, overlooking the Firth of Forth.
[3] The dam in construction in the valley below the house created two lakes fed by the Chart well.
[4] WSC was formally adopted by the Epping Conservative Association on 22 September 1924.

O From CSC   Tan-y-Graig
20 August 1924   Pentraeth, Anglesea

My Darling Winston
. . . I am longing for news of home – However I shall soon be back now – I wonder how everything is getting on? Whether my mantelpiece is arrived whether the dining room chimney is being improved & whether your 'Lake' is filling satisfactorily. I ought to have asked Miss Fisher[1] to keep me posted. . . .

I have written to Moppet [Whyte*] to ask her to arrange about Randolph meeting me in London on Monday so that we can see about his 'trousseau'[2].

Your loving
Clemmie

. . .

[1] Lettice Fisher, WSC's Private Secretary, 1923–9.
[2] In September 1924 Randolph, aged 13, went to Eton College, Windsor, in Mr Sheepshanks's house. Arthur Charles Sheepshanks (1884–1961) was Assistant Master (Classics) at Eton College, 1918–38; Headmaster, 1922–38.

○ From WSC [typewritten]   Chartwell Manor
22 August 1924

My darling,

I took Randolph over to the Durdans[1], and we had another very pleasant lunch with Lord Rosebery. He took the trouble to find in his library a most interesting book called 'Paradoxes and Puzzles' by Paget[2], published some forty-five years ago, in which there is the most effective vindication of the Duke of Marlborough in regard to the Brest Expedition charge that I have yet seen. Paget ridicules the accuracy of Macaulay[3], and convicts him repeatedly not merely of mistakes but of deliberate misrepresentations of facts, etc. This has turned my mind very seriously to the great literary project which so many people are inclined to saddle me with[4]. . . .

Everything is progressing in your room; . . . . They are fixing the new mantelpiece. I do not know whether it will be ready by Monday.

There are 7 feet 6 inches of water in the dam, and it is rising steadily. . . .

We are all looking forward much to your return on Monday. My dearest – it will be a comfort to have you back again. I do hope you have enjoyed yourself.

My fondest love –

Your devoted
W
. . .

[1] Home of Lord Rosebery at Epsom, Surrey.
[2] John Paget, *Paradoxes and Puzzles, Historical, Judicial and Literary*, Edinburgh, 1874.
[3] The historian Thomas Babington Macaulay (1st Baron Macaulay) (1800–59), who was very hostile to Marlborough.
[4] The biography of his famous ancestor John Churchill, 1st Duke of Marlborough (1650–1722), which WSC would undertake in the 1930s.

On 25 September Winston made a speech of major importance to a packed and enthusiastic meeting of Scottish Conservatives in the Usher Hall, Edinburgh, in which he declared 'no gulf of principle' existed between Conservatives and Liberals – Socialism was the threat.

Clementine must have been bitterly disappointed not to be with Winston, but she was not well.

○ From CSC   Chartwell
Thursday. 5 p.m. [25 September 1924]

My Darling Winston

I am in imagination following all your movements & in a little over 2 hours you will all be assembled for your great Meeting, which I pray may be a brilliant success for you – and may assist you in the new road on which you are setting out –

I have retired to bed & am having a four days' 'rest cure'! I sent for

Doctor Ward this morning & he took my blood pressure which he found very low....

I look forward to the papers tomorrow morning....

Mary sends Papa a 'tiss'.

Your loving
Clemmie

In October 1924, following the fall of Ramsay MacDonald's Government, there was another General Election – the third in three years. The result (29 October) was a decisive Conservative majority, with 419 seats to Labour's 151 (a big drop), and the Liberals dwindling to 42 seats. Stanley Baldwin formed his second administration.

Churchill, while fully supporting, and supported by the Conservative Party, stood as a Constitutionalist, and won Epping by a majority of 9,763. He would represent this seat uninterruptedly for the remaining forty years of his parliamentary life[1].

In forming his new Government, Baldwin invited Churchill to become Chancellor of the Exchequer.

On 30 November Winston celebrated his fiftieth birthday.

[1] The seat was later re-named the Wanstead and Woodford Division of Essex.

Chapter XIII

NUMBER ELEVEN

Winston and Clementine spent their first Christmas and New Year at Chartwell with all their children, the 'Jagoons' and the Romillys.

They moved into No. 11 Downing Street (the official residence of the Chancellor of the Exchequer) during the latter half of January. No. 2 Sussex Square was sold.

In the first week of January, Winston went to Paris to take part in the negotiations over international war debts; after intensive parleyings, it was agreed he achieved a remarkable settlement.

On 28 April he presented his first Budget, putting Britain back on the Gold Standard. He himself had initial doubts about this policy, but it had already been agreed in principle by the Treasury, supported by the Labour Chancellor. Churchill was criticized then and in the future for the 1925 Budget, but the doctrine of return to the Gold Standard was widely accepted at the time.

◇ From CSC   2 Sussex Square
8 January [1925]

My Darling Winston

The newspapers are full of you & Mr Sutcliffe[1]!

Your departure from Victoria, illustrated by snapshots of a débonnair Pig, your arrival with lists of those who met you.... Altogether you are the Pet of the moment – I do not see how you <u>can</u> fulfil <u>all</u> the expectations that are entertained....

I am busy making lists of furniture to be moved from here to Downing Street.

Yesterday Moppet [Whyte*] brought the children up & I took them to the big circus at Olympia[2]....

I gave Venetia [Montagu*] luncheon at Claridges on Tuesday – She starts on her travels tomorrow. She looked so white & shattered. If you have five minutes do write & thank her for that lovely jade & enamel box of Edwin's[3] which she sent you with that charming letter. I remember always seeing it on his Table....

                                                                 Your loving
                                                                 Clemmie

...

Important.
Would you like to go & stay with Bee [Pembroke][4] at Wilton on Saturday the 23rd over Sunday? Please telegraph Yes or No.

[1] Herbert Sutcliffe (1894–1978), famous cricketer.
[2] Bertram Mills' Circus. This was to be an annual outing for us children – and later for *our* children. WSC always came if business permitted.
[3] Her husband Edwin Montagu (see p. 74 n. 1) had died on 15 November 1924. The beautiful box is now in my possession.
[4] Countess of Pembroke (born Lady Beatrice Paget), wife of the 15th Earl of Pembroke (1880–1960). WSC and CSC often stayed at their home, Wilton House, near Salisbury, at Whitsun, which was then labelled in the Wilton visitors' book as 'Winstontide'.

O From WSC   British Embassy
10 January 1925 Evening   Paris

My darling Clemmie,
    At last I have a quarter of an hour to myself! We have made vy good progress, & tonight after arduous wranglings on subjects as complicated as the rules of Mah Jongg when first you hear them, we have reached practically unanimous agreements on every important issue. Tomorrow and Monday the experts will draft in accordance with our agreements; on Tuesday we shall present our work to the plenary conference supported by all the six gt powers & on Wed[y]. at noon (bar accidents) I start for home....
    I have scarcely moved outside the Embassy except to the series of conferences & conciliabules[1] & interviews wh have occupied the day. Even meal times have been devoted to meeting people of consequence. I had an interview with Herriot[2] in his sick room. Poor man – he seemed vy seedy & worn with worry & phlebitis. We got on well. Tomorrow I am to see President Doumergue[3] in the morning; lunch with the Imbroglio [Daisy Fellowes] – watch the 'All Blacks' play France in the afternoon, & visit Clemenceau in the evening & dine with Loucheur. Last night & tonight big dinners at the Embassy....
    I have had tremendous battles with the Yanks & have beaten them down inch by inch to a reasonable figure. In the end we were fighting over trifles like £100,000! However there was never any ill will & I have now made quite a good arrangement with them wh will be announced on Tuesday with the rest. I think on the whole I have succeeded. Certainly I have had plenty of compliments. But that is not a vy trustworthy test.
    I do not want to go to Wilton – nor anywhere else but Chartwell. I expect to see a lot of progress on my return. The cottage, the book cases, the woodshed, the Loggia: I shall be glad to prowl about them again. Give my fondest love to all the kittens. I hope they are good & well. And you my darling – yr letter was a gt treat. I wish I cd have written earlier. But I know you will understand.

With tender love & many kisses
Your ever devoted
W.
...

P.S. I will write to Venetia [Montagu*] when I return.

[1] French word (also used in English) meaning secret meeting; confabulation.
[2] Edouard Herriot (1872–1957), at this date Prime Minister of France (June 1924–April 1925 and July 1926). President of the Radical Party, 1919–40.
[3] Gaston Doumergue (1863–1937), at this time the first Protestant President of France, 1924–31.

◇ From CSC   Lou Sueil[1]
Sunday Morning [probably 8 March 1925]

My Darling I am writing to you in bed in this marvellous scented nest – It is really almost too beautiful & too comfortable. One simply wallows. How I wish you were here to wallow with me, & to paint.

Consuelo [Balsan*] looks younger & more ethereal every year. Her hair is more silvery but on the other hand her cheeks are pinker & her eyes brighter. Her Jacques surrounds her with petits soins – ... The garden is a dream – carpets of purple gold & cream flowers on the emerald green grass....

George Curzon has been staying here – Consuelo says he was so changed & sad & <u>humble</u>! The Fairy Queen [Grace Duggan, his second wife] flouts him & laughs at him now he is no longer the 'All Highest'[2] – He is more unhappy than King Lear, for of his 3 daughters [of his first marriage][3] not one of them is a Cordelia – The lovely Baba ever so gently admonished (not to cheapen herself with Fruity Metcalfe for instance) threatens on her 21ˢᵗ birthday (which is approaching) to remove herself & her £10,000 a year for ever from the Paternal Roof – The Duggan brood are equally harsh & mercenary so that poor Lord Curzon is threatened with the Workhouse in his old age –

Consuelo says he was a charming guest & entertained them with witty anecdotes & conversation for a whole fortnight & when he departed he shed tears & said he had not had so happy a holiday since he was a young man.... He told Consuelo that he constantly thought of Mary, his first wife, & was sure she was waiting to welcome him on the Other side. I hope she will have got a comfortable & noble Mansion ready for him & precedence all arranged with the Authorities....

Well – Goodbye my Darling – Forgive this trashy gossip – The air up here is exhilarating.

Your loving
Clemmie

...

Do not write my Darling if you are very busy & tired.

[1] *Chez* the Balsans, where CSC was paying another visit.
[2] He had resigned as President of the Council, his last office, on 6 November 1924.
[3] Curzon's only children (by his first wife) were: (1) Irene, 2nd Baroness Ravensdale of Kedleston (1896–1966), who succeeded to the barony in her own right, and was made a life peeress in October 1958; (2) Cynthia (1898–1933), who in 1920 married, as his first wife, Sir Oswald Mosley; (3) Alexandra ('Baba') (1904–94), who in 1925 married Major Edward Dudley ('Fruity') Metcalfe (d. 1957), sometime ADC and Equerry to the Prince of Wales; later ADC to him as Duke of Windsor in France; divorced, 1955.

○ From WSC
8 March 1925

Treasury Chambers
Whitehall

My darling,

We have just returned from the Zoo, where I took Diana and Sarah. The new aquarium is wonderful. Have you seen it? There are some new fish just arrived from Java, about three inches long and painted entirely with most brilliant yellow and white belts.... Many other things, including the Mappin terraces, amused us very much. We saw quantities of bears, two of them wrestling quite beautifully for a long time. I think the children enjoyed it very much.

Yesterday I paid my weekly visit to Chartwell.... The second arch of the Palanquin [loggia] is completed. I hope another fortnight will see this finished.... I brought back fourteen dozen eggs, and twenty dozen have been put in pickle. Great advance by the crocuses and snowdrops. All the other work is progressing, but very slowly, Alack!... It will take us all our time to be ready by Easter.

Baldwin achieved a most remarkable success on Friday. He made about the only speech which could have restored the situation, and made it in exactly the right way.... A strong Conservative Party with an overwhelming majority and a moderate and even progressive leadership is a combination which has never been really tested before....

The revenue is coming in well; and if only I can win my battle with the Admiralty, I shall not be left penniless. In a fortnight they will be able to give me definite figures to work upon, instead of the vague forecasts which are all that are yet available....

We are all anxious about poor George Curzon, who has haemorrhage of the bladder and is to have a serious operation tomorrow morning. I telephoned to enquire, and he sent his secretary round to give me rather a grave tale[1].

The work gets heavier every day. All this week I am to have a stream of deputations, and every morning my boxes are full of stiff papers about the Budget. I have decided not to try the third volume[2] and to retire from the literary arena, at any rate for some time to come. I could not do justice to it and my other commitments. Moreover the taxes ate it nearly all.

Philip [Sassoon*] came here last night and fell into raptures over the Sargent drawing. I was hard put to it to reconcile truth and politeness. I wanted to point out the awful concavity of my right cheek. However, one must not look a gift portrait in the mouth[3].

The children declared they were writing to you today, but they may be frauds. ✍No – Sarah has just weighed in.

Tender love my darling one. I hope & pray you will have sunshine, peace & joy.

Your ever loving & devoted
W.

[1] Lord Curzon died 20 March 1925. They obviously had no idea he was terminally ill when CSC wrote the preceding letter.
[2] Volume III of *The World Crisis*, entitled *1916–1918*, Parts I and II, were both published in 1927.
[3] This drawing, now in the Lobby at Chartwell, portrays WSC in the ceremonial robes of the Chancellor of the Exchequer.

◇ From CSC   Lou Sueil
Wednesday 11 March [1925]

My Darling

I was delighted to get your letter –

No I have never seen the new Aquarium at the Zoo – It sounds lovely – How sweet of you to take the children there.

I had gathered from the papers that Mr Baldwin had achieved a personal triumph over the Levy Bill –

I think he has a genuine feeling for the working people of the Country –

Now my lovely one – stand up to the Admiralty & don't be fascinated or flattered or cajoled by Beatty [First Sea Lord]. I assure you the country doesn't care two pins about him. This may be very unfair to our only War Hero, but it's a fact. Consuelo [Balsan*] tells me that he lunched here a little time ago (when he came out to see Lady B[eatty] who is quite queer & mad) & that he said 'I'm on my way home to fight my big battle with Churchill' – Consuelo said 'Oh I expect Winston will win all right' – to which Beatty retorted 'I'm not so sure' – Of course I think it would be not good to score a sensational Winstonian triumph over your former love, but do not get sentimental & too soft hearted. Beatty is a tight little screw & he will bargain with you & cheat you as tho' he were selling you a dud horse which is I fear what the Navy is....

Much Love to you Darling
Clemmie

○ From WSC   11 Downing Street
15 March 1925

My darling – .... I am tired & have rather a head at the end of a long week. I do hope you are having rest, peace & sunshine & that you will return really refreshed. I have polished off two more articles to help pay the Income Tax: & perhaps I may get another one out of myself this afternoon or tomorrow morning.

Mary is flourishing. She comes & sits with me in the mornings & is sometimes most gracious. Diana is just back from school & we are all planning to go to see Randolph [at Eton] this afternoon.

When do you think you will return my dear one. Do not abridge yr holiday if it is doing you good – But of course I feel far safer from worry and depression when you are with me & when I can confide in yr sweet soul. It has given me so much joy to see you becoming stronger & settling down in this new abode. Health & nerves are the first requisites of happiness. I <u>do</u> think you have made great progress since the year began, in spite of all the work & burdens I have put on you. The most precious thing I have in life is yr love for me. I reproach myself for many shortcomings. You are a rock & I depend on you & rest on you. Come back to me therefore as soon as you can.

Your ever loving & devoted
W

. . .

Clementine had planned to return home on Monday 23 March, but was summoned to Dieppe, where her mother had become seriously ill.

○ From WSC   11 Downing Street
22 March 1925

My dearest darling,

I have just got yr telegram. I feel for you so much – & poor Nellie too. Yr Mamma is a gt woman: & her life has been a noble life. When I think of all the courage & tenacity & self denial that she showed during the long hard years when she was fighting to bring up you & Nellie & Bill, I feel what a true mother & grand woman she proved herself, & I am the more glad & proud to think her blood flows in the veins of our children.

My darling I grieve for you. An old & failing life going out on the tide [she was seventy-three], after the allotted space has been spent & after most joys have faded is not a case for human pity. It is only a part of the immense tragedy of our existence here below against wh both hope & faith have rebelled – It is only what we all expect & await – unless cut off untimely. But the loss of a mother severs a chord in the heart and makes life seem lonely & its duration fleeting. I know the sense of amputation from my own experience three years ago. I deeply sorrow for yr pain.

I greatly admired & liked yr Mother. She was an ideal mother-in-law. Never shall I allow that relationship to be spoken of with mockery – for her sake. I am pleased to think that perhaps she wd also have given me a good character. At any rate I am sure our marriage & life together were one of the gt satisfactions of her life. My darling sweet I kiss you.

I have been working all day (Sunday) at pensions & am vy tired. Please telegraph me how events develop & whether there is anything that I can do.

Good night my dearest,
Your devoted husband
W

15

Board of Trade,
Whitehall Gardens,
S.W.

My beloved – Get up! I want
to come & see you. Let
us go for a walk before
lunch. I slept till 10.3
Several interesting letters have
arrived wh I will show
you. The sun shines
bright, & my heart
throbs to see you again.
Sweet & precious —
Your devoted
W.

1. Note to Clementine from Winston, on his office writing paper, mid-August 1908. They were staying with his mother, Lady Randolph Churchill, at her home, Salisbury Hall, near St Albans.

3

Before Marriage

TELEGRAMS: WEST LONDON COLNEY.
TELEPHONE 5 PO. ST. ALBANS.

SALISBURY HALL,
ST ALBANS.

Darling – I am
surrounded by
millions of letters
which I am
trying to answer —
I will be down
in about an hour
a little more —
I love you
Clementine

2. Note from Clementine to Winston at Salisbury Hall, obviously a reply to 1.

3. The engaged couple, photographed by Mrs F. E. Smith in August 1908.

4. Winston's mother, Lady Randolph Churchill (Jennie) in her late fifties, *c.*1915.

5. Jack and Goonie on their wedding day, 7 August 1908.

6. The sisters-in-law at Blenheim Palace, 1909. Clementine facing the camera.

7. Churchill, at German army manoeuvres in August 1909, is greeted by Kaiser Wilhelm II.

8. Sir Ernest Cassel, a great figure in Edwardian society, pictured here wearing the insignia and robes of the Order of St Michael and St George. He was a generous and hospitable friend to Winston and Clementine.

9. Drawing in the *Manchester Evening News* of the attack on Churchill by a militant suffragette, Miss Theresa Garnett, at Bristol railway station on 14 November 1909.

10. In 1910, Winston (now Home Secretary) and Clementine escorted the Prime Minister, H. H. Asquith, on a tour of Labour Exchanges, which were pioneered by Churchill while President of the Board of Trade.

11. Churchill (Home Secretary) with the Earl of Crewe (Secretary of State for India) and, left, Sir Edward Grey (Foreign Secretary) in London, 1910.

12. Clementine with Diana aged two years, at Seaford, June/July 1911.

13. Venetia Stanley, Clementine's cousin, *c.*1914. A close friend of H. H. Asquith, she was soon to be married to Edwin Montagu.

14. Winston Churchill and Lloyd George driving away from Downing Street, 1911.

15. The Blenheim Palace house party watches a tense moment in the Yeomanry sports at their summer camp, May 1911. WSC, to right, in pale suit and bow tie.

16. A powerful press family: the brothers Lord Northcliffe and Lord Rothermere, with Esmond Harmsworth, the latter's son and heir to both the title and the newspapers, *c.*1920. Lord Northcliffe was now chief proprietor of *The Times*. Between them, at this date, the brothers controlled the *Evening News, Daily Mail, Daily Mirror, Sunday Pictorial* and *Glasgow Record*.

17. Photograph in the *Daily Sketch*, May 1913, showing the nannie and nurserymaid with their charges under police protection after the Churchills had received letters from militant suffragettes threatening to kidnap the children.

18. Clementine taking part in the Ladies' Parliamentary Golf Tournament at Ranelagh, 1913.

19. Winston and Clementine at military manoeuvres near Daventry, October 1913.

20. A fatal friendship. Churchill with Admiral of the Fleet Lord Fisher, whom he had recalled from retirement to be First Sea Lord in October 1914.

21. Churchill was thrilled and impressed by the growing possibilities of air power. During his time as First Lord of the Admiralty he frequently flew with naval air pilots. Here he is seen boarding a seaplane in Portsmouth harbour to view the Fleet from the air, April 1914.

22. During an inspection of the Grand Fleet in 1914, in Scotland, Churchill goes aboard a naval launch, followed by Field Marshal Sir John French, C.-in.-C. designate of the British Expeditionary Force in France: a firm friend.

23. Nellie Hozier, Clementine's younger sister, aged twenty-six, in 1914. She joined a nursing unit which was captured by the Germans during the retreat from Mons.

24. Bill Hozier, Nellie's twin, aboard HMS *Thorn*, a torpedo destroyer, which he commanded, *c.*1914.

25. Clementine speaking at the opening of the first YMCA hut canteen for women munition workers in Edmonton, north London, in August 1915.

26. Major Churchill leaves for the Western Front, 18 November 1915, after resigning from the Government.

27. Nellie Hozier and Bertram Romilly were married at the Guards' Chapel, 4 December 1915, attended by Diana, Randolph and Johnnie (Jack and Goonie's elder son).

28. Lt-Col. Winston Churchill, Commanding Officer of 6th Battalion, the Royal Scots Fusiliers, in the 'Plug Street' sector, early 1916.

29. Lt-Col. Churchill (wearing the *poilu*'s steel helmet given him when he visited a French regiment) with his second-in-command, Major Sir Archibald Sinclair, 1916.

30. Lloyd George (Chancellor of the Exchequer) opened a large canteen for men and women munition workers at Ponders End (near London) on 3 February 1916. Here he is seen with Clementine (the organizing Chairman) and, left, Violet Asquith.

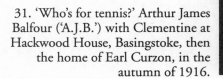

31. 'Who's for tennis?' Arthur James Balfour ('A.J.B.') with Clementine at Hackwood House, Basingstoke, then the home of Earl Curzon, in the autumn of 1916.

32. In June 1918 Jennie Cornwallis-West (Lady Randolph Churchill), aged sixty-three, married for the third time: her bridegroom, Montagu Porch, was over twenty years younger than herself. It was to be a happy marriage. Jennie now reverted to calling herself Lady Randolph Churchill.

33. Churchill in conversation with the Prince of Wales (later the Duke of Windsor) in 1919. Winston had known the Prince since he was a boy, and admired his manifest qualities.

34. Winston, Clementine and Sylvia Henley (*back right*) take Sarah, aged nearly five years, to watch a march past of the Guards' Brigade at Buckingham Palace in 1919.

35. During the Cairo Conference in March 1921, Winston (then Colonial Secretary) and some friends did some sightseeing. *Centre group, left to right*: CSC; WSC; Gertrude Bell (traveller, writer and Orientalist); Col. T. E. Lawrence ('Lawrence of Arabia'); and behind him, Detective-Sergeant Thompson.

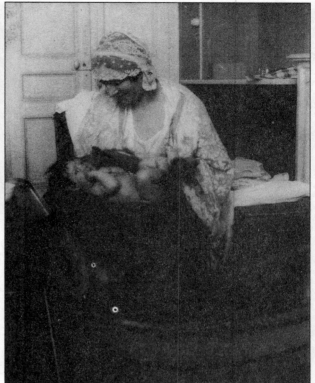

36. Marigold, the darling 'Duckadilly', at Broadstairs, shortly before she became ill; she died on 23 August 1921, aged two years nine months.

37. Bath-time. Clementine with Mary, born 15 September 1922.

38. Three colleagues leaving Downing Street in 1922, before the October election which put the Coalition Government out of power. Left to right: David Lloyd George (Prime Minister), Lord Birkenhead ('F.E.', Lord Chancellor) and WSC (Secretary of State for the Colonies).

39. After visiting the private view of the Royal Academy Summer Exhibition at Burlington House in May 1922: Clementine with 'Eddie' (later Sir Edward) Marsh, Private Secretary to WSC, and lifetime friend of both.

40. Summer 1923: Sarah and Randolph with their first cousins Giles and Esmond Romilly at Hosey Rigge, near Westerham, where the Churchill family lived pending the move into nearby Chartwell.

41. The Duke of Westminster ('Bendor') with Clementine at Epsom on Derby Day, June 1923.

42. Rained off the courts at Regent's Park, June 1923. *Left to right*: Mrs Lionel Guest; Sir Neville Pearson; CSC; Lionel Guest (WSC's cousin).

43. Winston, the Independent Anti-Socialist candidate in the Abbey Division of Westminster by-election, with Clementine: they are listening to a question at a meeting of brewery employees he addressed, 14 March 1924.

44. The 'anti-sosh' Independent candidate acknowledges cheers from his supporters. Churchill was narrowly defeated.

45. Winston playing polo at a match on the old Ranelagh ground, c.1923. The photograph clearly shows the connecting strap on his right arm which he had to wear whenever playing polo after dislocating his shoulder severely while disembarking from a boat at Bombay on his arrival in India with the 4th Hussars on 1 October 1896.

46. Chartwell Manor (from the south-east) before the Churchills bought it in 1922.

47. September 1928. Winston at work on what would be Wellstreet Cottage at Chartwell. Intended to house a married butler, Wellstreet Cottage was our core family winter refuge in the 'slump' years 1929 and 1930.

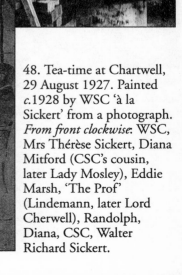

48. Tea-time at Chartwell, 29 August 1927. Painted *c.*1928 by WSC 'à la Sickert' from a photograph. *From front clockwise*: WSC, Mrs Thérèse Sickert, Diana Mitford (CSC's cousin, later Lady Mosley), Eddie Marsh, 'The Prof' (Lindemann, later Lord Cherwell), Randolph, Diana, CSC, Walter Richard Sickert.

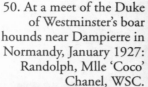

49. Clementine's mother, Lady Blanche Hozier, aged seventy-one. She died in 1925.

50. At a meet of the Duke of Westminster's boar hounds near Dampierre in Normandy, January 1927: Randolph, Mlle 'Coco' Chanel, WSC.

51. On the way to the House of Commons from No. 11 Downing Street to hear WSC present his last Budget, April 1929. *Left to right*: Detective-Sergeant Thompson, Robert Boothby MP (WSC's Parliamentary Private Secretary), WSC, CSC, Sarah, Randolph.

52. The Duke of Marlborough ('Sunny', WSC's cousin) with Clementine at Aintree for the Grand National, 1930. They were staying with the Duke of Westminster ('Bendor') at Eaton Hall, Chester. On right, Lady Seely, Jack Seely's (later Lord Mottistone's) wife.

53. Out of office after the defeat of the Conservative Government in May 1929, WSC embarked in August for a three-month tour of Canada and the United States. Here is the travelling 'Churchill troupe' (WSC's expression): WSC and Jack Churchill, his brother, with their sons Randolph (*left front*) and Johnnie.

54. The big one that *didn't* get away! WSC caught this 188lb swordfish off Catalina Island, California, 22 September 1929.

55. After staying with William Randolph Hearst at his famed 'citadel' San Simeon, the Churchills went to Los Angeles, where WSC was guest of honour at a luncheon on 18 September 1929 at the Metro-Goldwyn-Mayer studios in Hollywood. *Left to right*: William Randolph Hearst, WSC, Louis B. Mayer.

56. Desmond Morton. A vital source of information to WSC on Germany's warlike preparations in the thirties.

57. A line-up after luncheon at Chartwell, 19 September 1931. *Left to right:* 'Mr Pug', Tom Mitford, Freddie Birkenhead (F. E.'s son), WSC, CSC, Diana, Randolph, Charlie Chaplin.

58. Clementine and Winston campaigning in the rain in the thirties, in the West Essex (Epping) constituency (later renamed the Wanstead and Woodford Division of Essex). WSC won the seat in 1924 and would be its Member of Parliament for forty more years.

59. Winston (P: Pug/Pig) supervises major operations at Chartwell, winter to spring 1934–5, during Clementine's absence on Lord Moyne's yacht *Rosaura* in the far Pacific. In this photograph the peninsula on the lower lake was being transformed into an island.

60. Terence Philip and Clementine on board MY *Rosaura* at Madras, early January 1935.

61. A local inhabitant engages Lord Moyne in lively conversation. Photograph taken by Lady Broughton off the coast of Papua, New Guinea, January 1935.

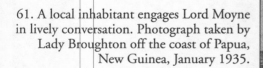

62. The handsome and intrepid Vera Broughton, Walter Moyne's great friend and companion.

63. View on the island of Komodo, one of the Sunda Islands in the Dutch East Indies (now Indonesia).

64. Preparing the trap for the dragon lizards, March 1935.

65. Two of the dragon-like 'monitor' lizards which were the objectives of Lord Moyne's expedition in MY *Rosaura*, winter to spring 1934–5.

66. During the celebrations for the Silver Jubilee of King George V and Queen Mary, my parents took me to witness the King and Queen receiving loyal addresses from both Houses of Parliament in Westminster Hall, 9 May 1935. On the left is Nana (Cousin Moppet), the guardian angel of my childhood.

67. Vic Oliver. In many ways a charming, sensitive and talented man; he and Sarah were very much in love, but their marriage could not stay the course of wartime separation and deep dissimilarities.

68. 'Mr Cochran's Young Ladies' rehearsing (in November 1935) for the revue *Follow the Sun*. Sarah is third from left.

69. Winston painting at the Moulin de Montreuil at St Georges Motel, where he and Clementine were staying with Jacques and Consuelo Balsan in August 1939, in the last weeks of peace.

70. All in an afternoon's work for a Member of Parliament's wife. CSC opens the bowling for the 'Lyons Girls' cricket team, who were playing the Woodford Police Athletic Club, 3 September 1936.

71. '. . . Don't I look big in front of the Alps? I wish I could really master them!' (CSC, 29 January 1937).

72. Maxine Elliott in 1937, aged sixty-nine.

73. Published in the *Sunday Pictorial*, 23 April 1939, this cartoon reflects the widespread disillusion after the post-Munich agreement in September 1938, and the public's awakening realization that WSC's warnings about the necessity for Britain's urgent rearmament were indeed valid.

"BRING HIM BACK—IT'S YOUR LAST CHANCE"

74. Max Beaverbrook and WSC walking in the garden at No.10 Downing Street during the Second World War.

75. Churchill leaving No.10 Downing Street with Brendan Bracken to go to the House of Commons on 20 August 1940. In his speech, Churchill paid his famous tribute to the Battle of Britain RAF pilots: 'Never in the field of human conflict was so much owed by so many to so few.'

76. This innocent picture showing Winston in London buying a 'flag' from Clementine in support of her Red Cross Aid to Russia Fund, supposedly on 16 December 1941 – the official Flag Day – was in fact taken several days earlier. By the time it appeared in the newspapers Winston was at sea in HMS *Duke of York*, on his way to the United States.

77. Winston at the White House, Washington, during his Christmas 1941–January 1942 visit (Arcadia Conference); with him are Harry Hopkins and Harry's daughter Diana, who is in charge of President Roosevelt's dog, the celebrated 'Fala'.

78. A picnic luncheon hosted by 'Monty' on 4 February 1943 after the Victory Parade in Tripoli, when Churchill took the march past of the 51st Division. During luncheon puffs of shellfire burst high overhead as a German reconnaissance aircraft was chased away. *Left to right*: General Sir Alan Brooke, Randolph, Lt-Gen. Sir Oliver Leese, WSC, General Sir Bernard Montgomery ('Monty').

79. Pamela Churchill in 1943 with 'baby' Winston (nearly three years old) striding out.

80. FDR, WSC and UJ (Uncle Jo) at Winston's sixty-ninth birthday dinner, 30 November 1943, at the British Legation in Tehran, where the first Big Three Conference was being held.

81. Churchill with his Private Office team, 29 September 1941. *Front, left to right*: John Colville, WSC, John Martin, Anthony Bevir. *Back, left to right*: Leslie Rowan, John Peck, Miss Watson, Cdr Thompson, Charles Barker.

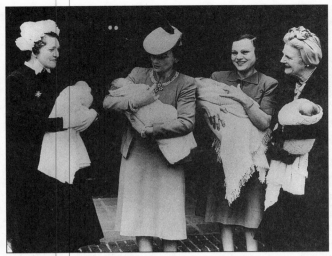

82. A line-up of VIPs and babies at the Fulmer Chase Maternity Home for the wives of serving officers, near Gerrards Cross, Buckinghamshire, on the occasion of a royal visit. Clementine, Chairman of the House Committee from November 1939, took a detailed interest in the running of the Home. *Left to right*: Matron, HRH The Duchess of Gloucester, Lady Baron (who owned the house), CSC.

83. On 18 January 1944, within a few hours of returning from his hazardous journeyings and his serious illness in November–December 1943 in Tunisia, Churchill went to the House of Commons. Clementine and her two 'service' daughters went to witness Winston's heartwarming welcome home.

84. On 14 February 1945 Churchill, on his second visit to Athens within seven weeks, drove in an open car with the Regent of Greece, Archbishop Damaskinos, and was on this occasion ecstatically cheered by a 40,000-strong crowd in Constitution Square. Here he congratulates Sergeant Rose who conducted the British military band.

85. In August 1944 Churchill spent several days with Gen. Alexander and his army in northern Italy, and observed action at close quarters. Here Gen. Alexander, WSC, Gen. Sir Oliver Leese (in shorts) and, extreme right, Sir Rupert Clarke (ADC to Alexander) scan a valley at Arezzo.

86. Sovereign and servant. During the strains and stresses of the war a strong bond of trust and friendship developed between King George VI and his Prime Minister, photographed here at Buckingham Palace, 4 August 1944.

87. For five weeks in April–May 1945, Clementine travelled in the Soviet Union, on behalf of her Red Cross Aid to Russia Fund, which had supplied enormous quantities of medical and surgical supplies to Russian hospitals. Here she is surrounded by children recovering from the effects of starvation during the blockade of Leningrad.

88. The 'new' Big Three meet informally before the Conference at Potsdam, Germany (17 July–2 August 1945). *Left*: Marshal Stalin; *centre*: President Truman (who had succeeded to the US Presidency on Roosevelt's death, 12 April 1945; *right*: WSC.

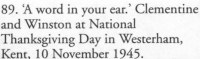

89. 'A word in your ear.' Clementine and Winston at National Thanksgiving Day in Westerham, Kent, 10 November 1945.

90. Nellie Romilly, Clementine's younger sister, at Chartwell, c.1948. She died of cancer, 1 February 1956.

91. Off to the races, May 1949. After the war, inspired by his son-in-law Christopher Soames, Winston acquired several racehorses. Clementine did not share this new interest, but nevertheless sometimes accompanied Winston to see his horses run.

92. Winston's first, and most famous, racehorse was his French-bred grey colt, Colonist II, who was a great favourite with the racing public – as was his owner! Here Winston and Clementine watch Colonist parading in the paddock before going on to win the Lime Tree Stakes, September 1949.

93. In his later years, painting continued to be one of Winston's principal occupations. In the New Year of 1950 he, Clementine and Diana visited Madeira. Here Winston is settled into painting the harbour scene at Camara de Lobos, near Funchal, on 9 January 1950. His detective (*left*) adjusts the umbrella.

94. In the February 1950 General Election Winston, as well as defending his own seat, helped Randolph, who was standing in Devonport against the socialist Michael Foot. Here WSC is with RSC and June (Randolph's second wife, whom he had married in 1948). After a stalwart fight, Randolph was defeated.

95. In Winston's Woodford constituency, Clementine discusses election posters with the Conservative agent, Mr Mummery, 7 February 1950.

96. Christopher and Mary Soames' third child, Jeremy, was christened at St Mary's, Westerham, in the summer of 1952. *From the left*: CSC; Emma Soames (aged nearly three), in front of her father Christopher; Mary, holding Jeremy; WSC; 'Monty' (Viscount Montgomery of Alamein), a godfather; *in front*: Nicholas Soames (aged four and a half).

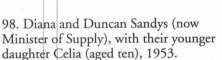

97. Holidaying in Capri, August 1952: Clementine (*right*), with Sarah and her husband Antony Beauchamp, whom she had married in 1949.

98. Diana and Duncan Sandys (now Minister of Supply), with their younger daughter Celia (aged ten), 1953.

99. In the New Year of 1952, Churchill, again Prime Minister, visited the United States. While in New York he stayed with his old friend, the elder statesman Bernard Baruch ('Bernie'). He is seen here in conversation with his host and (*right*) Gen. Dwight D. Eisenhower ('Ike'), now President-elect, 5 January 1952.

100. The Conservative Party Conference at Margate, in October 1953, was the first public occasion for Winston after his severe stroke in the summer. He made a brilliant address, and confounded the scrutiny of suspicious and curious eyes in the audience and world media. To WSC's right is CSC, and on her right, Anthony Eden (Foreign Secretary).

101. In 1953 Winston was awarded the Nobel Prize for Literature. At the time of the annual presentations in Stockholm, he was attending the Bermuda Conference. Clementine therefore received this notable prize on his behalf from King Gustav VI of Sweden, on 10 December.

102. During the 1950s Clementine suffered much from neuritis. Here she is leaving to undergo a cure at Aix-les-Bains, France; with her is Grace Hamblin, her Private Secretary for many years.

103. Winston resigned as Prime Minister on 5 April 1954. The previous evening he and Clementine entertained the Queen and the Duke of Edinburgh to dinner at No. 10 Downing Street. The Queen is greeted on her arrival by her hosts.

104. Throughout his life Winston enjoyed visiting his cousins at Blenheim Palace near Oxford. This snapshot shows him playing bezique, a game to which he was much addicted, with Mary, Duchess of Marlborough (wife of the 10th Duke), some time in the fifties.

105. While staying with Emery and Wendy Reves at Roquebrune, in February 1957, Winston lunched with Aristotle and Tina Onassis on board his yacht SY *Christina* in Monte Carlo harbour. Later Winston and Clementine would go on a number of cruises aboard the fabulous boat. Here Wendy Reves is talking to WSC; behind right, Emery Reves almost conceals Aristotle Onassis; top back are Tina Onassis and Anthony Montague Browne.

106. From May 1940 until Winston's death, Sir Charles Wilson (Lord Moran from 1943) was his physician, accompanying him on nearly all his wartime journeys. Lord Moran, ever vigilant, is photographed leaving London to go to Winston, who had become ill while staying with the Reves at Roquebrune in February 1958.

107. Many, including Clementine, disapproved of Winston's long-time friendship with Lord Beaverbrook (Max), and their friendship survived some serious disagreements. However, in old age all was harmony, and Winston and Clementine greatly enjoyed staying at Max's beautiful villa, La Capponcina, at Cap d'Ail. Here WSC and Max are driving from Nice airport to stay at La Capponcina, 31 July 1958.

108. On 12 September 1958 Winston and Clementine celebrated their Golden Wedding at La Capponcina. Randolph and his daughter Arabella (aged eight) were with them.

109. Clementine playing croquet with her granddaughter Celia Sandys (aged fifteen) at Chartwell in July 1958. After the war the tennis court had been converted into a croquet lawn; CSC loved playing this congenial game, and WSC enjoyed watching keen contests of family and guests.

110. Late evening sunshine: the last summer for him. Winston, on the lawn at Chartwell, takes pleasure in the company of two Soames grandchildren, Charlotte (ten years old) and Rupert (aged five, wearing his father's hat). Left, Miss Hilda King, the Soames nannie.

WESTERHAM 3344

July the 4ᵗʰ 1963

CHARTWELL,
WESTERHAM,
KENT.

My Darling,
The Time has seemed long without Zou —
I shall be on the door-step to wel-come Zou Home.
Zour devoted
Clemmie

111. CSC to WSC, 4 July 1963. A note sent to the airport on Winston's return from Monte Carlo.

112. WSC to CSC, 8 April 1963.

My darling one,
This is only to give you my fondest love and kisses a hundred times repeated

I am a pretty dull & pretty scribbler; but my such as it write carries my heart along with it.

Your ever & always,
W

April the 8ᵗʰ 1963

113. This picture says it all. Winston and Clementine at La Pausa in the 1950s.

○ From WSC [London]
25 March 1925

My darling –
The telephone talks are a comfort – in spite of the clippings & clickings & cuttings off.

I had rather hoped from what you said that if yr Mamma got through these two or three critical days, her lungs wd clear & she might recover. I am grieved that the doctor will not encourage this hope.

I marched in poor G. Curzon's cortège this morning. The service was chill and dreary. He faced his end with fortitude & philosophy. I am vy sorry he is gone. I did not think the tributes were vy generous. I wd not have been grateful for such stuff. But he did not inspire affection, nor represent gt causes. Baba[1] looked a dream in crape – Much the best memorial. . . .

Ll.G. [Lloyd George*] has returned – washed out to Westminster – I had a pleasant talk with him. He is going to the Canaries for a cruise. He said he ought not to come to the House – but it was like not being able to keep away from the 'pub'. He made a speech on foreign affairs full of truth & knowledge – but lacking any clear purpose. Austen [Chamberlain, Foreign Secretary] did the heavy father in rebuke: & Baldwin professed to be much scandalized. It is now a convention that foreign affairs are only to be treated in unctuous platitudes wh bear no relation to what is really going on. This is called 'Open diplomacy'.

Really the offer about the house[2] wh I enclose is exhilarating. I expect I cd get 80 guineas a week for 17 weeks – nearly £1400. But where shd we go? It is like offering a snail a fine rent for his shell. He wd like to take it: but what the hell is he to do without the shell?

Think it over – we cd go to Dinard or some beautiful place for the Children's holidays & have Chartwell for nothing for the whole year.

On the whole I am for living there ourselves.

Tender love my sweet
Yr ever devoted
W

. . .

My dearest – I just add this line to say how I am thinking of yr dear Mamma & of all her goodness & rare qualities – I always felt what a gt lady she was, how instinct with dignity, how dowered with amiability. She knew I had a deep regard for her.

[1] Lady Alexandra ('Baba'), Curzon's youngest daughter; see p. 289 n. 3.
[2] They were considering letting Chartwell.

◇ From CSC [Dieppe]
Thursday 26 [March 1925]

My Darling
Half an hour after we had finished talking on the telephone your letter with enclosure about Chartwell arrived. . . .

We could establish the children in a comfortable but economical hotel near Dinard, go there ourselves for part of the time & travel about, painting for you, sightseeing for me – Or we could go to Tours & do the 'Chateaux' again – And we could go to Florence & Venice[1].

Poor Mother is fading but very very slowly – Sometimes she is stationary – But since the marvellous rally she made on Monday when we were full of hope she has not shewn any flick of strength. She has now been unconscious since Monday night at 11 o'clock –

I thought Ll.G. [Lloyd George*]'s Foreign speech clever but it was mere 'thinking aloud' which I suppose in a man who has held such great positions is unusual! Austen [Chamberlain] was very ponderous I thought. Has he done well abroad? & is his stock therefore high just now?

Tender Love from
Clemmie

[1] It seems extraordinary now – the suggestion that Chartwell should be let, and that WSC/CSC could go to a hotel (with four children, a nannie, a valet and a lady's maid), plus the extra hotel bills and fares if WSC/CSC travelled, and that this could possibly be a saving. However, the idea did not materialize – perhaps for this reason.

◇ From CSC   [Dieppe]
Sunday Night [29 March 1925]

My Darling
Mother died to-night just before nine o'clock. A change took place suddenly at half past eight o'clock, but the Nurse thought she would not go till tomorrow morning – And then she slipped away from us in a few minutes – It has been an agonising struggle & twice we thought she would surmount the cruel illness –

Nellie sends you her love. Your very loving

Clemmie

Please give Moppet [Whyte*] the enclosed. It is about sending me some black clothes.

In March 1926 Clementine and Goonie spent two weeks in Rome with the British Ambassador, Sir Ronald and Lady Sybil Graham[1], who were friends.

[1] Sir Ronald Graham (1870–1949), diplomat. Ambassador at Rome, 1921–33. He married (1912) Lady Sybil Brodrick (d. 1934), daughter of the 1st Earl of Midleton; she was a grand-daughter of CSC's great-aunt Mary, Lady St Helier (see Introduction).

○ From CSC   British Embassy
Saturday 20 March [1926]   Rome

My Darling
Since we arrived on Wednesday evening we have been living in such a turmoil of excitement over Ancient Medieval & Modern Rome that this is the first moment that I have had to myself....

To begin with Modern Rome; I have seen Mussolini[1] – He came very privately to tea with Sybil the day after we arrived – He is most impressive – quite simple & <u>natural</u>, very dignified, has a charming smile & the most beautiful golden brown piercing eyes which you see but can't look at – When he came in everyone (women too) got up as if he were a King – You couldn't help doing it. It seemed the natural thing to do – He fills you with a sort of pleasurable awe –

You feel at once you would like to do something for him, or at least quickly carry out his wishes.

He loves music & plays the violin himself. Sybil had arranged a lovely little concert for him – I had a few minutes talk with him – He sent you friendly messages & said he would like to meet you. I am sure he is a very great person – I do hope nothing happens to him. He looked pale & thin but not I thought ill – It is certain that he inspires fanatical devotion in his followers – He is speaking next week to 50,000 people in the open air – It will be the 5th anniversary of 'Fascismo' –

Goonie & I are going to hear him – We shan't understand a word, but it will be interesting all the same – He seems to like the Grahams very much.

Then as to Ancient Rome – we have been to the Baths of Caracalla – an astounding sight. 40,000 people could use them at one time. They are larger than Olympia – Then we spent a thrilling afternoon in the Forum. How I wish you had been there – You would have loved it. Then we climbed the Palatine & looked down on it all lying below.

This morning we went to the Vatican but could not get further than the Sistine Chapel. It quite surpasses in glorious but sombre beauty all my expectations.... I have also glanced at St Peter's but have not grappled with it yet.

Last night we dined with the Volpis[2]. Very pleasant. Tomorrow they are taking us to Tivoli to see Hadrian's Villa.

News trickles thro' to me slowly owing to my not being able to read the Italian newspapers. Mussolini said he had heard a rumour that <u>you</u> were going to the Foreign Office! –

Tender love. Kiss the Kittens for me.

Clemmie

[1] See p. 274 n. 3, letter of 3 September 1923. Now leader of the Italian Fascist Government, and in November of this year would become absolute ruler of Italy.
[2] Count Guiseppe Volpi (1877–1947), Italian Minister of Finance, 1925–8.

The ensuing letters feature what Winston called 'the Kershaw incident'. On her return from France, after her usual visit to the Balsans, Clementine had obviously had a misunderstanding with HM Customs about a silk dress. 'Misunderstanding' I am sure it was, because my Mother was meticulous in such matters. Whatever occurred with the Customs officials at the port was observed (and possibly misconstrued) by a Mr Kershaw, who recognized her, and had evidently made a fuss, on the assumption that the wife of the Chancellor of the Exchequer was being shown favours. It would appear that Clementine wrote him an explanatory letter, which was perhaps unwise.

Kershaw did not publish any letter or pursue the matter further, and no doubt all was settled correctly with the Customs.

○ From WSC   Treasury Chambers
20 March 1926   [Chartwell]

My darling Clemmie,

The enclosures will show you the latest phase of the Kershaw incident. I am not myself sure that he really will be such a cad as to publish yr letter without at least asking yr permission. It is possible he is only girding at the Customs. They are now making inquiries, & it is probable that you will be required to pay the Duty on the dress.... There is nothing else that can be done. Don't worry about it.

I have had a vy laborious but quite successful week: & am now at Chartwell with Jack [Churchill*]. Nellie came down to lunch & to see her offspring [Giles (nine) and Esmond (seven)], with whose condition she appeared content. She is off to Egypt next week, as Bertram[1] has been clamouring for her....

All is well here. Mary [three] breakfasted & Sarah [eleven] dined with me. Diana [sixteen] talked quite intelligently about politics & seemed to have a lot of information derived from the newspapers. They are all vy sweet & it is a joy to have them down here. They love every minute of it. I don't know wh I love most. But Diana is going to be a gt feature in our lives in the next few years. Nature is mysteriously arming her for the ancient conflict. She has a wonderful charm & grace, wh grows now perceptibly from month to month.

I have heard nothing of Randolph [fourteen] since you saw him. I am inquiring today & will give you news in my next letter.

It is frigid here, with icy blasts of snow & hail hurled in the North wind & occasional gleams of Arctic sunshine. I worked at the cement stones all day & have finished all in the 'water garden'. The effect is quite good. In a vy little while you will not be able to tell them from stone....

Poor Austen [Chamberlain, Foreign Secretary] has returned – the Manchester Guardian unkindly suggesting that this time he shd receive the Thistle![2] And on Wednesday we are all to go to the Guildhall to see him made a free man [of the City of London]. As a matter of fact both the Locarno triumph[3] & the Geneva disaster[4] are impostors. Things have improved a gt deal & he has done a lot to help. But when praise & rewards are excessive at one moment, the reaction has a certain justice in it. Anyhow it is rather ridiculous....

I got yr telegram with gt delight on Friday. I am sure you will have a lovely time. I shd so like to be with you. Both politics & painting are specially exciting in Rome. I expect they are making a lot of the Cat. But not more than she deserves when she is good. Give my love to Goonie. And darling one think now and again of your loving devoted

W
...

[1] Bertram Romilly was Chief Instructor at Cairo Military School, Egyptian Army, 1925–8.

[2] The 'Most Ancient' Order of the Thistle, a Scottish order of knighthood ranking second to the Order of the Garter, founded 1687. Austen Chamberlain had been made a Knight of the Garter on 1 December 1925. He was also awarded the Nobel Peace Prize.

[3] WSC had been the moving spirit behind the concept of Locarno: a guarantee of frontiers in which Germany would be a signatory and equal partner. Negotiations leading to the signature of the Locarno Treaties in London on 1 December 1925 had been largely the work of Austen Chamberlain and had been hailed with wild enthusiasm throughout Europe; it was the crown of his career. Under the Treaties the signatories (Britain, France, Germany, Italy, Belgium and Czechoslovakia) formed a pact of non-aggression; Germany's western frontiers were guaranteed; the Rhineland demilitarized; and Germany entered the League of Nations.

[4] The Geneva Protocol (for the Settlement of International Disputes), laid before the League of Nations Assembly in October 1924 and supported by the Labour Government, had been stillborn; the new Conservative Government, with Chamberlain as Foreign Secretary, in March 1925 made it clear that Britain would not ratify the Protocol.

○ From CSC   British Embassy
25 March [1926]   Rome

My Darling
    Your letter, to my great delight arrived this morning. Amid all these new & strange scenes it was delicious to hear from Home.
    I am so sorry about the 'Kershaw incident'. But I feel robust about it as I behaved quite properly.... Let him 'Publish & be damned'!...
<u>Friday the 26th</u> –
    I have just received a beautiful signed photograph from Mussolini!

<u>A la Signora Winston Churchill</u>
<u>Devotamente</u>
<u>B. Mussolini</u>
<u>Roma 25 marzo 1926</u>

is inscribed on it.[1]
    All the Embassy ladies are dying of jealousy!
    We are going to hear him speak at a large open air Meeting on Sunday to celebrate the 7th Anniversary of 'militant Fascismo'. There will be 50,000 people there....
    Goonie & I arrive at <u>Folkestone Wednesday</u> evening the 7th of April rather late.... Would you send the big car & we will come straight to Chartwell.

                                                               Tender Love
                                                                  Clemmie

[1] No doubt Il Duce was charmed by CSC, but no harm could be done in paying marked courtesy to the visiting wife of a prominent British politician and Cabinet minister. The photograph was displayed in the drawing room at Chartwell as a trophy of her Roman holiday; but it was removed to obscurity within a short period of time. It remains, however, in CSC's papers.

○ From WSC   Treasury Chambers
25 March [1926]

My darling,
    I have two of yr dear letters. The description of Mussolini is vy vivid. No doubt he is one of the most wonderful men of our time. I am glad you

have met him & been able to form a personal impression.... I am so glad you are steeping yrself in Ancient Rome. The middle ages & the Renaissance are vy small topics beside the long Imperial splendour. All my interest is with the ancients. If only they had paid a little more attention to mechanics & science they might have survived all the barbarian shocks....

Austen is a goose & to-day I go to the city to see him cooked. We had a debate yesterday on Debts. You shd read my speech. It all went vy well. There is a vy hard feeling agst the U.S....

Darling Clemmie I shall be so glad when you are back. Altho' my days are occupied every minute from waking to sleeping, I feel lonesome in yr absence. The empty bunny [bed] is melancholy. Still, enjoy yr excursion & return with health strength & new fields of interest to your ever loving

W

O From WSC   Treasury Chambers
28 March 1926

My Best Beloved & Darling Clemmie. This ought to reach you on yr Birthday & it carries with it my fondest love and dearest wishes for many happy returns of the day & many happy intervening years. The Kittens are all writing. Mary says she has already written. She also observed to Jack 'Mummie is bored with me so she has gone to Rome.' She is a wonder....

What a picture you draw of Mussolini! I feel sure you are right in regarding him as a prodigy. But as old [Augustine] Birrell says 'It is better to read about a world figure, than to live under his rule.' ...

Tender love my dearest darling – Enjoy yrself in a new & I am sure delightful world, but do not forget that we are all eagerly looking forward to yr return to yr basket, after so many prowlings over classical, mediaeval & ecclesiastical tiles.

Yr ever loving & devoted
W

X X X

The General Strike in May 1926 lasted for nine days and brought the country to the brink of civil strife. The reasons for the Strike were rooted in the post-war economic depression which had brought falling exports and mass unemployment: heaviest hit of all was the coal industry, with pit owners and miners at loggerheads.

Beginning on 4 May, there was a complete nationwide stoppage in transport, heavy industry, the docks, printing, gas and electricity. Thousands of mainly middle-class volunteers assisted the Government in keeping essential services running and supplies delivered. There was amazingly little violence, but the Strike shook the country to the core.

Churchill and a small team headed by himself and J. C. C. Davidson[1], a junior minister, produced and printed an emergency newspaper, *The British Gazette*. By 11 May more than 2 million copies were being distributed throughout the country. Clementine and a group of friends organized canteen arrangements for the volunteers producing and printing the paper.

By 11 May, when the Government showed no sign of giving way, Sir Herbert Samuel[2] offered to mediate, and produced a package of terms acceptable to the TUC, who had at first supported the miners, but who called off the Strike on 13 May. The miners felt betrayed by the TUC and refused to go back to work; the owners refused to compromise, and so the coal strike dragged on until December, when the miners conceded, and returned to work with longer hours and less pay.

[1] J. C. C. (later 1st Viscount) Davidson (1889–1970). At this date Parliamentary Secretary to the Admiralty, 1924–7.
[2] Sir Herbert Samuel, later 1st Viscount Samuel (1870–1963). Statesman and philosopher, one of the first Jewish members of British Cabinet. Liberal MP. Secretary of State for Home Affairs, 1916 and 1931–2; first British High Commissioner, Palestine, 1920–5; Leader of Liberal Parliamentary Party, 1931–5.

O From CSC   Grantully Castle[1]
Monday [6 September 1926]   [Aberfeldy, Perthshire]

My Darling
News reaches here late – I see that you have had to bring the Mine Owners to heel[2].

I fear however that the men have left it too late to get any amelioration from them. How I do hope your mediation will prosper –

Yesterday after lunching with the Wards[3] at their lodge we motored on to Cortachy, as Consuelo [Balsan*] is thinking of taking it next year.

The Airlies[4] were there. I shewed her [Consuelo] everything & she seemed to like it very much – They (the Airlies) have spent mints of money on the place & are I fear feeling rather impoverished –

Private
Consuelo tells me that her marriage to Sunny [Marlborough*] has been annulled by the Pope!

I was so staggered that I lost the chance of cross-examining her about it.

It reminds me of the opening lines of the hymn: 'God moves in a mysterious way his wonders to perform' – However after I had recovered from my embarrassment I asked her on what grounds she had suggested to His Holiness that He should operate the miracle – And she replied 'Coercion, being under age at the time'[5] –

She says Sunny is enchanted as rumour has it that he is to be received into the Church of Rome & will then be able to marry Gladys[6] properly – I suppose Jacques' family suggested it [the annulment] as they are strict Catholics & consider him to be living in sin with Consuelo[7] –

Burn this letter becos' of 'les domestiques'....

... I shall be home on Monday the 13th. How is your Lake proceeding?

And is my chicken run (No 1) completely de-weeded? And will Chicken run No 2 be regularly cleared & purified?

Give my love to Diana & Sarah & Mary....

Your loving
Clemmie

[1] CSC was staying with Consuelo and Jacques Balsan, who for several summer seasons rented Grantully Castle.
[2] When Baldwin went abroad in August/September he had left WSC in charge of the negotiations between the coal owners and miners. WSC had much sympathy with the miners' case, and (unsuccessfully) put considerable pressure on the owners to concede various points.
[3] Eric Ward, Viscount Ednam (1894–1969), and his first wife, born Lady Rosemary Leveson-Gower (d. 1930) (see p. 217 n. 3). He succeeded his father as 3rd Earl of Dudley, 1932.
[4] David Ogilvy, 12th Earl of Airlie (1893–1968), CSC's cousin. He succeeded his father in 1900 and in 1917 married Lady Bridget Coke, daughter of the 3rd Earl of Leicester.
[5] This was true; she had been coerced into the marriage by her mother and forced to give up a man she loved.
[6] Gladys Deacon (1881–1977) of Boston, Mass.; she was a Roman Catholic.
[7] Consuelo and Jacques Balsan had been married according to both British and French civil law in 1921, but following the annulment of Sunny Marlborough and Consuelo's marriage in 1926 they were married according to Roman Catholic rites, after which the Balsan family consented to receive her.

◇ From CSC   Grantully Castle
Friday 10 September [1926]

My Darling
I am anxiously awaiting further news after your telegram saying that Owners' action involves 'serious collision, with political reaction next week'....

There is a nice tennis court & when there is no shooting we disport ourselves there. I have also taken to golf[1] – !...

I am looking forward so much to seeing you again my Darling – You are having an anxious but a thrilling & engrossing time with power & scope which is what the Pig likes....

I hope your 'lamp-post' Party on Sunday will be pleasant –

Please do not allow any very low conversation before the Children. I don't necessarily mean 'improper', but Lord B[eaverbrook*] does manage to defile any subject he touches, & I hope the relationship between him & Mrs Norton[2] will not be apparent to Randolph & Diana's inquisitive marmoset-like eyes & ears.....

Tender Love
from
Clemmie

[1] This was a *reprise* as in their early married years WSC/CSC played quite a lot.
[2] Jean Norton (d. 1945). Close friend of Lord Beaverbrook for many years.

In the late summer Clementine was away in Scotland and France. Parliament being in recess, Winston stayed at Chartwell, fully occupied with his outdoor works, his painting and his writing, and receiving company at weekends.

However, the expense of running Chartwell as well as London obviously weighed heavily upon him; and as we know Clementine had for some time been voicing similar anxieties.

During these weeks he drafted the following memorandum.

O From WSC [typewritten]   [Chartwell]
[late summer 1926]

1. It is proposed first of all to put Chartwell in the Agents' hands for letting from the New Year onwards....

All the following assumptions are based on a short let next year, and a long let, perhaps, later on, if it is found necessary: –

2. Martin [Farm Manager] leaves at Michaelmas, (September 29th).

3. All the red poll cattle will be sold at Reading in October. Estimate – say – £150.

4. All the chickens and pigs, except Diana's, will be disposed of at the end of December.

5. All the ponies, except Energy [the last of the polo ponies] and her foal, will be sold as soon as any reasonable offer can be got....

7. During the next three months the household to remain at Chartwell, and no books of any kind will be opened in London, i.e. till November 15th. During these three months the big car should be used as little as possible, i.e. practically laid up. Aley must be got to work the electric light so as to take over from Martin at the end of September, ...

10. Whatever happens about the let, neither Chartwell, nor Downing Street, must ever be opened for less than a month at a time. We must keep to this rule however inconvenient.

11. We had better spend the Christmas holidays in London, and only come down here for picnics with hampers....

13. The groom will leave as soon as the ponies go, or these holidays end, whichever is the earlier.

14. BILLS.

Miss Street will prepare a list of £1500 of bills most urgent for payment in the next fortnight....

No further bills must be added to this list. Every new bill as it occurs is to be shown to me.

All small bills are to be paid monthly.

Nothing expensive should be bought, by either of us, without talking it over.

HOUSEHOLD EXPENSES.

The Household expenses (food, wages, maintenance and car) for the last six months have averaged – say – £300, but the last two months have averaged – say – £477. We cannot afford to average more than £250 a month on these four heads....

The following should be tried at once: –

a. No more champagne is to be bought. Unless special directions are given only the white or red wine, or whisky and soda will be offered at luncheon, or dinner. The Wine Book to be shown to me every week. No more port is to be opened without special instructions.

   b. Cigars must be reduced to four a day. None should be put on the table; but only produced out of my case. It is quite usual to offer only cigarettes.

   c. No fruit should be ordered through the household account; but only bought and paid for by you and me on special occasions.

   d. No cream unless specially sanctioned.

   e. When alone we do not need fish. Two courses and a sweet should suffice for dinner and one for luncheon, ...

   The fact that we are making these economies should make it possible to enforce a stricter regime in the Servants' Hall.

   f. We must only invite visitors very rarely, if at all, other than Jack and Goonie, in September.

   The question of reducing the household by three on our return to London must be studied, when the results of these economies are apparent.

   The cost of washing can surely be reduced, i.e. two white shirts a week should be quite enough for me for dinner in the country. Dimmer [WSC's valet] must make a plan to reduce my washing by one third, which I will go into with him. I will, also, go into boot polish and other things said to be used on my account....

   There are, no doubt, many aspects of household expenses which you would like to discuss with me. I am quite ready to agree to anything that is necessary, ...

   NEW WORK.

   The chicken-houses and cow-houses should be pulled down, but not re-erected – ... The clearance of trees and bushes between the house and the lake, and the replanting of certain apple trees should be all we can attempt....

Like many draconian pronouncements which fly in the face of personal convenience or natural desires, this ruthless document was considerably modified: Chartwell was not let; and I do not remember shortage of food or drink; or my father wearing dirty, crumpled shirts. The family spent the greater part of that winter in London; and the Christmas holidays were spent at Chartwell, where over Christmas and New Year eleven people signed the Visitors' Book.

   However no more was heard of dairy cattle, and the groom and ponies disappeared; the pigs were reduced in number (subject to natural increase) and farming activities were henceforward on a more modest scale.

   In the New Year of 1927 Winston, accompanied by his brother Jack and Randolph (now fifteen and a half), set out for a holiday-cum-business tour: he took his 'home work' – *The World Crisis* – with him.

   The party set out on 4 January 1927 by train (via Paris) for Genoa, there boarding the *Esperia*, which conveyed them to Malta, where they were the guests of Winston's old friend and colleague, Admiral of the Fleet Sir Roger Keyes[1]. From Malta they went briefly to Athens and on 14 January arrived in

Rome, where they stayed with Sir Ronald and Lady Sybil Graham at the British Embassy. During this visit Winston had discussions with the Italian Finance Minister, Count Volpi, and two short meetings with Mussolini. Both Winston and Randolph were also received by the Pope.

[1] C.-in-C., Mediterranean Station, 1925–8; see p. 271 n. 5.

○ From WSC   Esperia
6 January 1927

My darling One,
    We are just off & I send you this line by the Fascisti[1]. They have been saluting in their impressive manner all over the place, & the Esperia staff gave us a most cordial welcome[2].
    I worked till 2.30 this morning & again from 8 till now at the proofs. They have all been left with the Hotel to post tomorrow (everything is shut today): under threats of vengeance from Mussolini if anything goes wrong. It is now off my hands for good or ill for ever. It will I hope secure us an easy two years without having to derange our Chartwell plans: & by that time I will think of something else....
    ... Tomorrow Naples. I wish you were here....
    This country gives the impression of discipline, order, good will, smiling faces – A happy strict school – & no talking among the pupils. Great changes have taken place since you & I disembarked from this ship now nearly 6 years ago....
    I will write again from Naples.

                                                                          Your ever devoted
                                                                                    W

[1] Members of the PNS (Fascist Party); they were not necessarily uniformed, some wore badges.
[2] The Churchills had travelled in *Esperia* on their return from the Middle East in 1921.

○ From WSC   Esperia
7 January 1927   Off Naples

My darling, I had literally to work till the last minute yesterday in order to get the proofs off before the ship sailed. But it is all done now, & I trust I shall not see its face again....
    The voyage has been quite smooth & we are now approaching Naples. The Rabbit [Randolph] is a vy good travelling companion. He curls up in the cabin most silently & tidily. We have played a great deal of chess in wh I give him either a Queen, or two castles, or even castle, bishop & knight – & still wallop him. I am shocked to see him wear nothing under his little linen shirt, & go about without a coat on every occasion. He is <u>hardy</u>, but surely a vest is a necessity to white people. I am going to buy him some....

As soon as yr garden[1] is done two of the extra men shd be got rid of, ...
& the others can stay till I come back.

Tender love my darling pussy cat
from yr ever devoted
W.

Jack [Churchill*] is clamouring for me to come and look at Vesuvius. It is
erupting mildly.

[1] The grey-walled garden, just in the making, near the house. It was later planted with roses and
was known as the Rose Garden. It was always very much CSC's special garden.

O From CSC   Chartwell Manor
10 January 1927

My Darling

It is a week to-day since you vanished from Chartwell – I miss you very
much – But I am glad you are having a change tho' I fear not really a rest
as until 3 days ago the Book (that Old Man of the Sea) was still (like the
Albatross[1] to thoroughly mix my metaphors!) hanging round your poor
neck.

You cannot be having better weather than we are enjoying at Chartwell.
To-day I was out all day without hat or coat till a quarter to 5 – The sunset
was quite glorious orange, striped with aquamarine, and all day soft faint
silver sunshine, & not a breath of wind. ...

Nellie & her children arrived here last Tuesday; but she deserted me
very soon to go to Cliveden for one of Nancy [Astor]'s parties! She is by
way of returning tomorrow.

I was alarmed by the rumour that she intends after all to publish her
hair-raising auto-biography – for that is what it really is – I was told that
she is sending it to America – I asked her about it, but she brushed the
topic aside[2]. Her boys are really brilliantly clever, & much improved – I
think & hope they are happy here.

Last Wednesday I motored to Woodford & attended a Meeting of the
Junior Imperial League presided over by Hawkey[3]. It was rather dreary & I
thought not worth the long motor drive there & back, but I daresay it was
a good thing to do. ...

... On Saturday I took Diana & Sarah to see a thrilling Detective
Melodrama called The Ringer[4] – The children were properly frightened &
harrowed & loved it. ...

... Work is proceeding in the garden. I do my best to spur things on.

I think I have now given you a complete account of my doings.

Tender Love my Darling

Your dear letter just came & 2 from Randolph whom kiss for me

Your loving
Clemmie

[1] A reference to Samuel Taylor Coleridge's poem, 'The Ancient Mariner'.
[2] In 1932 Nellie, under the name Anna Gerstein, published a novel, *Misdeal*, which was largely
autobiographical.
[3] Sir James Hawkey (1877–1952), Deputy Chairman, Epping Conservative Association, 1922–6,

and Chairman, 1927–52. Mayor of Wanstead and Woodford, 1937–8 and 1943–5. Cr. Bt, 1945. He was a staunch and faithful supporter of WSC throughout all weathers. His wife and family also became enduring friends.
⁴ *The Ringer*, play by Edgar Wallace, 1926.

○ From WSC   Admiralty House
10 January 1927   Malta

My darling –

We had a calm voyage here & all was pleasant. The Professor who presides over the excavations of Pompei showed & explained us everything.... He translated all the inscriptions painted on the houses. An election for the Aedileship¹ was in progress when the volcano intervened. The candidates' appeals remained uncancelled & unanswered for two thousand years!

It is a new pleasure to me to show the world to Randolph. He is vy well, vy good mannered & seems to take things in. It is or ought to be a wonderful experience for him. Every day something entirely novel & of fascinating interest....

I got through the polo without shame or distinction & enjoyed it so much.² ...

The house is full of the Keyes children & midshipmen & all yesterday they played 'Bear' in wh pursuit R. was an active figure. I have seen more of him in these few days than all the rest of the holidays. Evidently he is a gt success with the others.

I am planning to join Bendor [Westminster*] at Dieppe on the 26 for a couple of days after the pig [wild boar] before the Cabinets begin....

Anyway we shall meet 21 at Eze [staying with the Balsans*]....

Tender love my darling & I am wondering vy much whether it will be Purra! or only Wow! However it may be I long to see you again & kiss your dear face my sweet pussy cat.

Your devoted
W

¹ The *aediles* were originally two plebeian magistrates at Rome, who had charge of temples, buildings, markets and games.
² This was to prove the last time WSC played polo.

○ From WSC   In the train
25 January 1927   [between Eze and Paris]

My darling Clemmie,

Only a line to tell you how sad I feel at leaving you & how lonely: & to send you back a kiss of deep & true love. It was sweet to hear you say I was 'the wine of yr life'. Well I know how unworthy I am to play that part & how many are my shortcomings. You must make many allowances my darling & above all do not lose heart over trifles. At the present moment our affairs are by no means in an unsatisfactory state. Indeed I am hoping that with care & prudence we may have a couple of peaceful years, & consolidate our Chartwell position. Try to rest & recuperate at Lou Sueil & come back reinvigorated.

I will send you a full report of the progress of yr garden & of other Chartwell projects; & will also tell you about the hunting at Eu.

With tender love,
Yr ever devoted
W.

O From WSC   Grand Hotel
28 January 1927   Dieppe

My darling –

Benny [Westminster*] came with me this afternoon when I laid two wreaths on yr Mama's grave, & Bill's. Both were well kept – tho of course at this bleak season the plants do not grow.... The military graves close by are now all finished, with their orderly lines of tombstones & the high Cross of Sacrifice. We wandered among them reading the inscriptions wh recall the history we know so well.

Loucheur's luncheon in Paris was a considerable affair. Briand[1], Peret, Vincent Auriol[2], about 15 MPs representing leading elements in all parties – & vy advanced politicians. I conducted a general conversation in my best French, & defended Debt demands & Mussolini interviews with some spirit. All vy friendly. I saw Crewe[3] beforehand & did some business with him. . . .

Yesterday we hunted the penwiper [wild boar]. A dramatic moment occurred when he appeared from a lake where he had refreshed himself & galloped into our midst. The wire netting round a covert prevented his escape. He turned to bay. Colonel Hunter fired repeatedly & missed. Benny advanced pistol in hand – but luckily on horseback – to fire the final shot. The pistol in bad order wd not cock. The penwiper charged – grazed the horse, scattered the company & eventually made good his retreat & escape into the depths of the forest. Tomorrow we hunt again. . . .

The famous Coco [Chanel][4] turned up & I took a gt fancy to her – A most capable & agreeable woman – much the strongest personality Bennie has yet been up against. She hunted vigorously all day, motored to Paris after dinner, & is today engaged in passing & improving dresses on endless streams of mannequins. Altogether 200 models have to be settled in about 3 weeks. Some have to be altered ten times. She does it with her own fingers, pinning, cutting, looping etc. . . .

I am going back by the night boat tomorrow night, so as to have all Sunday at Chartwell. The speeches are 'peser'ing [weighing] on me. Why do I ever agree to make any? I shall bring Diana down to Chartwell to keep me company & will send her early to school Monday. . . .

Tender love my sweet Clemmie. Think kindly of yr ever loving & devoted

W.

Write London.

[1] Aristide Briand (1862–1932), French socialist statesman. Eleven times Prime Minister; Foreign Minister, 1925–32.
[2] Vincent Auriol (1884–1966), French socialist statesman. Principal financial expert of the French Socialist Party; General Secretary of Socialist group in the Chamber, 1919–36. Later first President of the Fourth Republic, 1947–54.
[3] Robert Crewe-Milnes, 1st Marquess of Crewe. British Ambassador in Paris, 1922–8.
[4] Gabrielle ('Coco') Chanel (1883–1971), French *couturière*, who revolutionized women's fashions in the 1920s, liberating them from the restriction of corsets, and designing simple comfortable clothes and costume jewellery; also famous for her 'Chanel No. 5' scent. Mistress of the Duke of Westminster, 1925–30.

○ From CSC   Lou Sueil
Saturday 29 January [1927]

My Darling Winston

I long to hear how you are & all about your hunting adventures, also if Mlle 'Coco' Chanel was at Dieppe & what she is like!...

There has been a consistent 'va et vient' in this house, very agreeable French people succeeding each other....

There is no doubt they are far more agreeable & more witty than English people but it is all fireworks & nothing is left afterwards....

My Dearest Love I hope you have forgiven me for being such a scold when you were here. When I arrived & saw you a flood of happiness spread through my being. It is a great fault in me that small things should have the power to harass & agonise me. I do not think Voronoff's[1] monkey glands would do me any good! What I need is to be inoculated with vegetable marrow or cucumber juice!...

                                                      Your loving
                                                      Clemmie
                                                          ...

[1] Dr Serge Voronoff, a Russian-born physiologist, specializing in the grafting of animal glands into the human body and the effect of gland secretions on senility. His book, *The Study of Old Age and My Method of Gland Grafting*, was published in 1927.

○ From CSC   Lou Sueil
1 February 1927

My Darling

I did enjoy your Dieppe letter so much.

Your description of the penwiper chase is thrilling. He seems to have got the best of you all. In future revolvers will hold no terrors for me....

But more exciting than the 'penwiper' is your account of 'Coco'. I must say I should like to know her. She must be a genius....

It was good of you to remember my Mama and Bill....

... Margot [Asquith] is causing a commotion on the Riviera by proposing herself to unwilling & nervous hostesses & not taking 'No' for an answer or standing any nonsense! Consuelo [Balsan*] is flying to Paris to avoid a too prolonged visitation. Don't make a joke of this as it might get round to the said Margot. My Darling I wish you had not the fatigue of these 3 speeches. But I know they will be good. C. P. Scott [of *Manchester Guardian*] is I see vexed over your partiality to 'Pussolini'.

Your loving

She is getting sleek & placid.

○ From CSC   Lou Sueil
Monday [7 February 1927]

My Darling

I hope that after your labours in the Midlands you had a pleasant & restful week-end at Chartwell....

The Oxfords[1] have been here since last Thursday – The old boy is most friendly but getting very very old. His surly, disagreeable manner to you at our dinner party must be purely his bad manners as he has spoken of you most affectionately & admiringly. He told me that his contribution (during the General Strike) to the British Gazette was prompted solely by his penchant for you!...

... Margot is as sprightly as a grasshopper, very amusing but most fatiguing.

I have enjoyed my holiday but I now long for England Home and – Winston –

Your most loving
Clemmie

[1] H. H. Asquith had been created 1st Earl of Oxford and Asquith in 1925. He died in 1928, aged 75.

On 15 June Clementine was knocked down by a bus while crossing the Brompton Road; she was not badly injured, but suffered severe bruising and shock. The accident was reported in the press, and as a result the painter Walter Sickert[1], who had known Clementine and her family at the turn of the century in Dieppe, marched up to No. 11 and enquired about his friend of long ago.

Clementine was delighted to see him again and introduced him to Winston: the two men got on very well, and Sickert came both to Chartwell and Downing Street; the long painting sessions they had together strongly influenced Winston's style and technique.

The shock of her accident was more severe than had at first been realized, and Clementine's doctor recommended that she should go away for a full six weeks to re-establish herself thoroughly. Accompanied by Diana (now eighteen), she left for Venice in the third week of September.

[1] Walter Richard Sickert (1860–1942), British painter. Spent three years on the stage; theatrical subjects would be among his best works. At the Slade School he studied under Whistler. Spent much time in France and was greatly influenced by Degas. Leader of Camden Town Group formed in 1920. Royal Academician 1934 (resigned 1935). Married, thirdly (1926), Thérèse Lessore.

○ From CSC   Grand Hotel des Bains
Monday [26 September 1927]   Lido-Venise

My Darling
    It is divine here. You must come. Please do. . . .
    No more now. This is first to catch the post – Such a vile hotel pen –
The Schneider Cup[1] (put off from yesterday becos' of wind) is being flown
to-day –

                              Tender Love – from Clemmie

    We have bathed twice. Delicious warm sea. Great breakers.
    I would like to go with you in a Gondola. You remember we never did
on our honeymoon.

[1] International seaplane competition founded in 1916, the trophy being awarded for top speed in a 'free-for-all' class. Britain won the Cup in 1927, defeating the Italians on 26 September.

○ From WSC [typewritten]   Chartwell Manor
26 September 1927

Chartwell Bulletin[1]
Published weekly – or bi-weekly.
    . . .
    Sickert arrived on Friday night and we worked very hard at various
paintings and had many discussions. I am really thrilled by the field he is
opening to me. I see my way to paint far better pictures than I ever
thought possible before. He is really giving me a new lease of life as a
painter.
    Jack [Churchill*] proposed himself for the week-end, Abe [Bailey] came
to lunch on the Sunday. So I had plenty of company. Jack brought with
him his portable wireless and we had a wonderful concert each night. I
had no idea that they could produce such results; no blare, no clack, just
quiet, fine music. We turned out the lights and listened by the hour
together. These sets cost £30, but there are better ones and by fixing even
this one to an aerial you get an enormous increase of choice. . . .
    Hill[2] has three extra men, including the two old fellows, who have all
accepted at 35/- a week though they think the wage a very low one. The
first thing is to get the kitchen garden properly weeded and the new
garden completed, and one man will dedockulate [*sic*]. I think the privet
hedge must rank after these.
    The pig-stys are finished and three Middle White sows have arrived and

will enter on occupation tomorrow. A new calf was born this morning. Twenty-five sheep are also busy on nibbling duty in the orchard....

The dam continues to progress and the water rises a steady inch a day, even when it does not rain. I hope to be really through with it this week. I have only four men now.

The Prime Minister [Stanley Baldwin] returns tonight and I shall probably go up to see him tomorrow. I will then find out what his plans are for Cabinets, etc. and will wire you definitely whether I can come or not. I am enormously attracted by the idea of joining you on the Lido and of painting in Venice by my new method[3]. On the other hand every minute of my day here passes delightfully. There are an enormous amount of things I want to do – and there is of course also the expense to consider. Nevertheless I am poising....

I look forward much to a letter from you telling me all about the Lido and the Schneider Cup. I am so glad we won!

[1] The first of the 'Chartwell Bulletins', of which there are over 100; all appear in the *Companion Volumes* to Martin Gilbert, *Winston S. Churchill*.
[2] Albert Hill, head gardener at Chartwell from 1926 until his death in 1944.
[3] Sickert, apart from long sessions with WSC, wrote him two 'teaching' letters (autumn 1927) instructing his new pupil principally in the technique of preparing canvases. He also taught WSC how to make use of photographs as *aides-mémoires* and guides to constructing paintings.

O From CSC   Grand Hotel des Bains
Wednesday 28 September [1927]   Lido-Venise

My Darling Winston,

Up to this moment I have written you only one scribble as I thought perhaps you might have started for Venice before a letter could reach you. Now your telegram saying that, perhaps you will join us next week has come – I do hope you really will. First of all it would be a joy to me and then I believe you would have a delicious holiday with sunshine.... To-day we have hired a hut & 2 canvas beds & we are spending the whole day on the beach! The Schneider Cup crowds have vanished (thank God) as tho' by magic. The poor Italians were beaten to blazes. They took it very good-humouredly – They seem to like the English – We watched the Race from our bedroom windows....

Do you know I am sure I can get you a local Italian valet (who can speak English) & then you could come with just Sergeant Thompson & not even Furber [her maid] –

I am quite comfortable without a maid & I am teaching Diana (gradually) how to keep her room tidy & how to darn her stockings & generally to keep herself neat & like a lady without having to be waited on – She & I are very happy together....

We have not done much sightseeing so far as we have been taking life very easily – Yesterday afternoon we spent in a Gondola – We went out into the lagoons – The sunset was quite lovely.... We are waiting for a dull day to go & look at the pictures – So far we have mostly walked about out of doors. It is delicious to feel there is no hurry & that all these marvellous things are still waiting for us.

I must say that my culte for Mussolini is somewhat diminished by the almost ferocious poster Campaign which goes on everywhere – You might think there was an Election on, tho' that is the last thing which he would allow. His photograph is everywhere, sometimes in very ludicrous attitudes. That sinister stencilled face appears in the most unexpected places – on the walls of lavatories & on the porphyry pillars of the most ancient churches.

You never hear his name mentioned either by Foreigner or Native. . . .

Goodbye Darling Tender Love to Sarah & Mary –
Write please & telegraph that you are coming
Your loving
Clemmie

. . .

○ From WSC   Chartwell Manor
27 September [1927] <u>midnight</u>

My darling,

. . . I will start for Venice on Thursday (or at the latest Friday) arriving 7th or 8th. Meanwhile (you will think it odd of me) I am going up to Bendor [Westminster*] for three or four days. The dam is quiescent & slowly filling up; & he promises unparalleled salmon & stags. So I shall fill the interval by a northern flight. . . . My sweet one I was deeply touched by yr letter. It warmed my heart. Yr love for me is so much more than I deserve. . . .

Dearest Clemmie take a full six weeks' break. All will be well here: but let yr rest be a rest, & recharge yr batteries.

Baldwin came to lunch & was treated with much ceremony by Mary. How women admire power! The P.M. was most friendly. It was nice of him to come down to me. . . .

Good night my sweet Clemmie – I am tired with a long day . . . & the dam is vy exacting –

So I send my fondest love to you – & dear Diana –

ever yr devoted
W

. . .

○ From CSC   Grand Hotel des Bains
Friday 30 September [1927]   Lido-Venise

My Darling

You said the other day that you were tired of being a 'Pig' & that you wished to become a 'Lion' –

Well this is the very place for the Transfiguration. Saint Mark <u>and</u> his Lion are the Patron Saints of Venice & effigies in stone, bronze, marble, alabaster & pigment are seen everywhere of this noble beast. And no two are alike

311

to look at in form or countenance so you will have plenty of models to choose from, or you could even strike out a line of your own....

Your letter arrived this morning & gave me pleasure....

I will write again – There is nothing to paint on the Lido – But it is delicious for bathing –

Your loving
Clemmie

. . .

○ From WSC   Stack Lodge[1]
1 October 1927   Lairg

My darling,

Here I am at the North Pole! Last night the fishing was unexpectedly vy good. I had connexion with 5 fish in 3 hours, & killed 3 viz 16, 14 & 12½ lbs.

'Coco' is here in place of Violet [the Duchess]. She fishes from morn till night, & in 2 months has killed 50 salmon. She is vy agreeable – really a gt & strong being fit to rule a man or an Empire. Bennie vy well, & I think extremely happy to be mated with an <u>equal</u> – her ability balancing his power. We are only 3 on the river & have all the plums [best pools]. To-day the river was 'in perfect order': & of course after 6 hours grinding toil (wh has nearly broken my back) not a fish wd bite. Curious creatures of caprice, these salmon! If they don't choose to be killed, nothing will persuade them.

Just as I was starting from Chartwell the Prof [Lindemann*] blew in in his motor, arriving from Aix. I thought it wd be nice for him to come out with us. We shall fly to Parigi [Paris], if the weather is practicable.

I am delighted by Maurois' Disraeli[2]. I hope Randolph will not imitate him & lose us £7,000 at 20 years of age. More than cd be borne by yr ever devoted

loving husband
W.

. . .

[1] At the head of the Laxford River, on the Duke of Westminster's Reay Forest estate.
[2] André Maurois, *Disraeli*, 1927.

The plans worked out: Winston left England with 'the Prof' (Lindemann*) on 7 October and joined Clementine and Diana in Venice for about ten days, after which the men had to return home, duty calling. Clementine and Diana went to Florence a day or two later.

○ From WSC [typewritten]   [Chartwell]
19 October 1927

Our journey was uneventful and the time passed smoothly and swiftly in the Prof's agreeable and always instructive company. All was well when we reached here. Moppet [Whyte*] and Mary in the best of spirits gave a royal welcome. . . .

Arnold[1] has achieved wonders with his men during the ten days. It is extraordinary the amount he manages to do. . . . The lake is slowly filling – 4½ inches rise during my absence. . . .

The weather continues mild and dry. But I have developed a most frightful cold in my head and throat. Fancy after all these months of perfect health to have this affliction with an endless crop of speeches and going in and out of hot meetings looming down upon me. I have retired to bed tonight to take the most strenuous measures possible to shake it off, and in this posture after a long and tiring day must now try to whip up a speech for Nottingham on Friday.

[1] Farm manager at Chartwell, 1927–37.

○ From WSC   Chartwell
22 October 1927

Darling,

No letter yet from you! I wonder whether you are still at the hotel or whether you have been rescued by Alice K[eppel]. . . . I have a vy hard week in front of me, & I want to know that things are well with you, & that you are improving in spirits & health. So I sent a wire this evening asking for a reply.

What a delightful postcard correspondence you carried on with Mary! She showed them all to me with gt pride. . . .

In my 'Bulletin' [hereafter] I have told you of my journey to Nottingham[1]. It was quite pathetic to see the Prince [of Wales] & F[reda Dudley Ward]. His love is so obvious & undisguisable. But his manners were of the highest quality. . . . You have undervalued him I think in some ways. . . .

How odd the Birkins shd have produced this delightful little Sèvres porcelain shepherdess. The atmosphere of manufacturing prosperity & taste of their mansions are with me still. . . .

My dearest one I do trust you are aiding yr recovery of poise & strength in every way. Not doing <u>too</u> much Art treasures – & trapesing to show Diana galleries – not fretting about troubles wh will never come to pass – & above all not feeling too dissatisfied with

Your ever loving
W

He has been reading Ludwig's Bismarck[2] (sent to us by the author) & he has taken a vow tonight to be Valiant.
Goodnight my darling.
(Bulletin enclosed)

[1] On Friday 21 October WSC made an important speech in Nottingham; he stayed with Freda Dudley Ward's family, the Birkins. Lt-Col. Charles and Mrs Birkin (an American) lived at Radcliffe-on-Trent, Nottinghamshire; their family business was lace-making, for which Nottingham is famous. As usual the Prince of Wales was in close attendance on his best-loved Freda. See also p. 227 n. 2.
[2] Emil Ludwig, *Bismarck: The Story of a Fighter*, published in London, October 1927.

O From WSC [typewritten]   Chartwell Manor
22 October 1927

CHARTWELL BULLETIN

A minor catastrophe has occurred in the pig world. Our best new sow, irritated by the noise of a pick-axe breaking the ground near the pig sty, killed six of a new litter of eight little pigs. She was condemned to be fattened and to die, but to-day she has received the remaining two and proposes to bring them up in a sensible manner. She is therefore reprieved on probation.

I have been vigorously treating my cold. Dover's powders every night, and every kind of spray, etc. I got through Nottingham all right and my voice held out quite well. The day before the Prince telephoned that he and F[reda Dudley Ward] would come down by the same train.... The Prince was staying with the other sister Vera, (who lives half a mile away) inspecting his horses before the hunting season. I left as soon as possible this morning as I thought the animation of the Birkin household would not amuse me so much as solitude at Chartwell....

Moppet [Whyte*] and Maria have shifted their headquarters to London. I looked in upon them on my way through and was very graciously received.... Yesterday she [Mary] encountered Mrs B[aldwin] in the garden[1] and was taken by her into the Cabinet room and introduced together with the pug to a number of people. I said to Moppet 'Was she dressed all right?' meaning, was she [Mary] tidy? to which Mary replied 'Oh, yes, she (Mrs B) was wearing a nice grey frock.'!

It is pouring with rain to-day and my lake has risen one inch and a quarter in 24 hours.

Hawkey[2] is coming over to lunch tomorrow, Sunday. He was in a great state to see me about the campaign and made a long story about the state of the division [constituency]. At one end the farmers are furious because they are not given more money, and at the other the women & Wanstead & Woodford are furious because the flappers are to have votes[3]. Generally one would have thought from his manner that the whole place was in rebellion. I am sure it is all nonsense and I am really quite glad to be going among them to inculcate a higher standard of loyalty and discipline. I will let you know how I get on. It will be a pretty stiff week.... However I expect I shall crash through somehow or other. I am going to support the Flappers' Vote on the well known principle of making a virtue of necessity. I think it will turn out all right, but anyhow it has now become inevitable.

Freda was very nice about Diana and praised her greatly....

I have opened my new controversy with the Admiralty demanding no cruisers this year or next.... I am almost certain that the Cabinet Committee and the Cabinet will endorse my views. There may be a very stiff tension before it is settled, and really I think I am bound to fight this pretty hard.... It looks as if I am going to get through all right but this must not be proclaimed. I have to talk beggary and bankruptcy for the next few months.... Luckily however there are windfalls and what we lose on the swings we shall perhaps more than recover on the roundabouts. It is really very like our private affairs though on a larger scale....

✍Orders have been given to begin yr new Pantry on Monday.

[1] No. 10 and No. 11 share the large walled garden at the back of Downing Street.
[2] Sir James Hawkey, WSC's Constituency Chairman; see p. 304 n. 3.
[3] A reference to the Representation of the People (Equal Franchise) Bill, first reading. The Bill gave the vote to 1,800,000 women over thirty, 2,200,000 women under thirty who were married or earned their own living, and 216,000 'unoccupied spinsters', who opprobiously came to be dubbed 'flappers'.

○ From WSC [typewritten]   Chartwell Manor
30 October 1927

Except for two meetings in the Wanstead district on Monday the Epping week is over. I have done nine meetings this week in addition to Nottingham on the previous Friday, so I have had quite enough. It has not been so bad as I apprehended, in fact I have hardly minded it at all. Punctuality was quite all right throughout though I expect you would have had some uneasy journeys had you been here.

The meetings were without exception the best attended and the most friendly I have ever had since the election. Hawkey had taken enormous pains, spent a good deal of money on advertising and provided Community Singing throughout (I cannot get the 'Land of Hope and Glory' out of my head. I have been trying all day to drive it out by humming 'Pack up your trouble in your old kit bag', and now that is taking root.)

Hawkey was staggered at the meetings. He had been deeply disturbed by half a dozen resignations of individuals from various committees, mostly on the ground of the Flappers' Vote, but one because he did not think I subscribed enough to the funds of the Association....

I dined with the old General [Colvin][1] and with Lady Lloyd[2], and supped with Goschen[3] who produced a distinguished company, local, and who put two cock pheasants in the car on which we are subsisting during the weekend. Arnold [farm manager] has also shot one in the demesne so that we are really 'living on the country' and 'making war support war' as the great Napoleon always inculcated. Generally speaking I may say of Epping 'Order reigns in Warsaw'. The very strong support from the general mass of the electorate had an instantaneous effect on individuals....

The battle is joined on the estimates. No more airships, half the cavalry, and only one-third of the cruisers. I think it will be all right as the Admirals are showing signs of far more reasonableness than ever before. I do not miss Beatty[4] as much as I thought I should! Neville [Chamberlain][5] costing £2½ millions more and Lord 'Useless' Percy[6] the same figure and we are opening a heavy battery against them this week. It is really intolerable the way these civil departments browse onwards like a horde of injurious locusts. . . .

Chartwell Bulletin this week records very little. The lake is practically finished and is rising a few inches every week. . . .

The remaining new sow has had seven piggies, so all our four are now heads of households. We got rid of three more cows and calves just paying expenses. The twelve apostles (the black pigs) are rootling most industriously and there is no doubt they will eradicate the blackberry bushes in a few months. . . .

Although Tuesday is the 1st November the roses are thrusting out as hopefully as in May, . . . the Dahlias and Chrysanthemums make a fine show. . . . Hill [head gardener] would like to take them up but they are so beautiful that he has not the heart.

. . . Pray let me know what your date of return is likely to be and whether I cannot count on you for the Lord Mayor's feast. . . .

[1] Brig.-Gen. (later Sir) Richard Colvin (1856–1936), Lord Lieutenant of Essex from 1924 until his death.
[2] Lady Lloyd (born Mary Leckie), widow of General Lloyd.
[3] Sir Harry Goschen (1865–1945), Chairman of the Executive Committee of West Essex (Epping) Division. He and Lady Goschen were indefatigable supporters of WSC.
[4] Admiral of the Fleet Earl Beatty (1871–1936), who had just retired as First Sea Lord.
[5] Neville Chamberlain (1869–1940). Son of Joseph Chamberlain and half-brother of Austen Chamberlain. Married (1911) Annie Vere, daughter of Major W. U. Cole. Lord Mayor of Birmingham, 1915–16. Conservative MP from 1918. Minister of Health, 1923, 1924–9 and 1931; Chancellor of the Exchequer, 1923–4 and 1931–7; Leader of Conservative Party, 1937. Prime Minister, 1937–May 1940; Lord President of the Council, May–November 1940.
[6] Lord Eustace Percy (1887–1958), seventh son of the 7th Duke of Northumberland, created 1st Baron Percy, 1953. At this date President of the Board of Education (1924–9).

◇ From CSC
31 October [1927]

Hotel Royal Grande Bretagne & Arno
Florence

My Darling Winston

I am so delighted that the meetings have been successful – In fact the Campaign has been a brilliant one which repays all your trouble & fatigue – I have just received from Lady Lloyd a long letter, describing the enthusiasm roused by your speeches – She is a dear kind woman –

Diana & I day by day are getting through the regular Florentine programme of Museums & Churches. . . .

Yesterday we lunched with the Actons[1] – He is the kind fat man who helped you with your painting when you were here 2 years ago & he lent you his studio. This time, the 2 sons were at home – They are unpleasant creepy young men with over-developed artistic sensibilities[2] – The garden where you painted was lovely in the autumn sun-shine. . . .

Yesterday was the 5th anniversary of the March on Rome & there was a grand Fascist display on the Piazza in front of the Palazzo Vecchio (the great old building, in the courtyard of which you painted the fountain).

Volpi arrived & read a message from the Duce. I should think there must have been 30,000 people in the Square. We had tickets & saw it all from a window high up in the Palazzo Vecchio – It's wonderful how Mussolini holds not only his power, but the public imagination & interest – And he never seems to play for popularity – He always does the hard cruel thing.

I do hope he lasts & does not get killed. They had 2 armoured cars, bristling with machine guns in the middle of the Square! Imagine doing that in England to keep order at a public meeting! When the Square got crowded women & children climbed on the top of them to get a better view.

There is great excitement, speculation, dismay & alarm at some new laws which Mussolini is <u>said</u> to be drafting & which will be (so it is said) presented to an obsequious Parliament next year. The first one is directed against motorists & inflicts 10 years imprisonment for killing a pedestrian & 5 years for injuring him. All the rich people's chauffeurs have sent in their caps & jackets as from the day it operates – Then there are a series of new laws the object of which is to make people moral by Act of Parliament. The gossip is that Mussolini wants to keep in with the Pope, ... & that these laws (besides being pleasing to the Duce's drastic nature) are to propitiate the Pontiff & to lead to co-operation with him. They are so ridiculous that I cannot think the rumour is well founded, but it is current everywhere –

1) Love is forbidden except between husband & wife – Lovers if found out will be punished, even if both unmarried
2) A man may not live with his wife except for the purpose of having a child
3) The sale of Contraceptives is forbidden.

They say there will be a general exodus from Italy!

I suppose you will soon be in residence at Downing Street? In fact I am sending this there.

Your loving
Clemmie

[1] Arthur Mario Acton and his wife Hortense (born Mitchell), of La Pietra, Florence. Well-known figures in literary, artistic and Florentine society.
[2] One of the 'creepy young men' was Harold Acton (1904–94), who inherited La Pietra. Writer and aesthete; prominent figure in cosmopolitan society and host to countless visitors. Knighted, 1974. Author of several books on Italian history; also *Memoirs of an Aesthete*, 1948; *More Memoirs of an Aesthete*, 1970; *Nancy Mitford: A Memoir*, 1975.

Christmas and New Year were spent at Chartwell; and early in January 1928 Winston took Randolph to Normandy to hunt boar in the Forêt d'Eu with the Duke of Westminster*.

In February Clementine was gravely ill with mastoid: on 12 February she underwent two operations within ten hours of each other (carried out at home, No. 11, as was then the custom). Winston wrote to Randolph at Eton on 13 February: 'We had a very trying day yesterday. Two separate operations at 2.30 and midnight! Your mother astonished the hardened doctors by her wonderful courage. If you should turn out – as I do not doubt – to be a fearless man, you will know where you got it from.'[1]

Clementine was ill for several weeks, and at times low in spirit. Winston spent much time with her, and she later told me he used to read passages from the Psalms to her: her illness brought them very close.

Consuelo Balsan* had telegraphed at once that Clementine must go to Lou Sueil to convalesce. But it was not until the end of March that she was strong enough to travel; she took Diana with her.

During Clementine's absence Winston was grappling with the last stages of the de-rating scheme which he proposed to introduce in his next Budget, abolishing the existing system of local rates. The object of de-regulation was chiefly to ease the burden on British industry and agriculture, and to alleviate unemployment, which stood at one million. Cabinet and other colleagues were strongly divided, but on 4 April the full Cabinet agreed to proceed with the measure. A delighted and triumphant Winston telegraphed his good news to her.

[1] Quoted from W. S. Churchill, *His Father's Son: The Life of Randolph S. Churchill*, 1966, p. 50.

○ From CSC   Lou Sueil
4 April 1928

My Darling

Your telegram saying 'finally complete agreement' has just come & I do rejoice with you & congratulate you. It must have been a strenuous week with constant meetings & I fear you must be very tired – But not so tired perhaps as the other people – I expect you were like the Widow with the Unjust Judge!'[1] ...

Yesterday (except the day of our arrival) was the first warm day – It really has been surprisingly cold & bleak & one needs all one's winter clothes – I do not think you would have been able to paint....

On Wednesday I push on to Florence ... [staying with Alice Keppel]....

By the way presently Joan Bull and her Mama will require an explanation of your abstention in the Flappers' Vote Division![2] The Continental Daily Mail are making a great 'song & dance' over it ... But really as it was bound to go thro' it was naughty of you not to vote – I fear it may cool off some of the Epping Women – young and old –

Tender Love from
Clemmie

...

[1] Gospel According to Luke, 18: 1–8.
[2] The second reading in the Commons of the Representation of the People (Equal Franchise) Bill (see p. 315 n. 3) took place on 29 March. WSC took no part in the debate and abstained from voting. The second reading was carried by 387 to 10.

○ From WSC   Treasury Chambers
4 April [1928]

My darling one,
  I am ashamed not to have written before. These last days have been one
continuous strain of Cabinets, Committees & personal discussions. But all
is settled now: complete agreement [on de-regulation] and at any rate ¾ of
what I was aiming at. Now I have chucked work & am off to Chartwell for
a change. You know all of a sudden you feel you do not want to stay any
longer in the same place.
  Two of yr letters have reached me – I loved to read what you wrote in
yr first. I am always 'there'; but I am afraid that vy often my business & my
toys have made me a poor companion. Anyhow my darling I care for no
one in the world but you – & the kittens; & in spite of the anxiety of yr
illness I was glad to feel that you relied on me & that I cd help & comfort
you a little. I trust you are taking care of yrself: not getting tired; lying
down a great deal; bed early etc. Don't let external things fret yr mind. . . .
  From Chartwell to-night I will send you a 'Bulletin'. . . .
                                          Your ever loving devoted
                                                        W
                                                        . . .

○ From WSC [typewritten]   Chartwell Manor
5 April 1928

Beloved Clemmie,
                      CHARTWELL BULLETIN
Here we are reunited, so far as our broken circle goes. All are well. Mary
is a picture of health and enchanted to get back to the country. Sarah
looks very well too. Randolph has grown gigantically. I am sending him to
play golf with the Professional tomorrow, and on Saturday Johnny
[Churchill] is coming down for the week-end. I am also going to teach him
Rubicon Bezique[1].
  Forty-eight new chickens, out of 49, have been safely incubated. . . . Two
sittings of turkey's eggs are under hens. One sheep has lambed. . . . The
ram is quite cheeky now, swollen with pride at his fertile harem. We are
taking all necessary precautions not to be butted or chased by him.
  The swans are very sweet. The white ones have begun their nest and
laid three eggs so far. They take it in turns to sit. I found Jupiter doing this
work last night. He was most affable and tried to explain to me exactly
what he was doing. Juno has been reduced to law and order by the black
swans. . . . This morning the news is that the black swans* have been seen
carrying bullrushes and reeds in their beaks with the presumed intention
of constructing a nest. Every care will be taken to protect them from
intrusion. [in margin ✍:]* Ils font l'amour chaque matin. . . .
  How idiotic the Daily Mail is about the Flapper vote division. Nobody
expected there would be a division, as only about ten people were known
to have the courage of their convictions. The whole episode shows how
completely Rothermere is devoid of even the slightest influence upon the

House of Commons. I expect in your Riviera retreat his silly headlines may have given you a wrong sense of proportion. No one has paid the slightest attention, and I think Ministers are ceasing to read his paper. At any rate the subject has not been mentioned at any of the numerous Cabinets in which our days have been passed.

I am becoming a Film fan, and last week I went to see The Last Command, a very fine anti-Bolshevik film, and Wings which is all about aeroplane fighting and perfectly marvellous. . . .

The Cabinets on my big policy [de-regulation] were very lengthy and difficult. Neville [Chamberlain] most obstinate and, I thought, unreasonable. But he made his point a matter of amour propre and, as I cared about the scheme much more than he, I had to give way. It was not a very important point, and substantially my plan is intact. The great advantage is that we are completely united and the whole Cabinet is keen. . . .

                         🖋Always yr ever loving & devoted
                                               W

P.S. I hope you are not punishing me for my neglect to write, by not writing yrself. Every post I ask for a letter – but for two days – none. This is not fair, because I have really been hunted – & you are basking. . . .

[1] Bézique, the card game which supplanted Mah Jongg, and which remained a favourite game with WSC/CSC for evermore. The card table in the Drawing Room at Chartwell is set in preparation for a game.

○ From WSC   Chartwell
8 April 1928

My darling Clemmie,

Very satisfactory reports have arrived about Randolph. I enclose the letters of Sheepshanks[1], Birley[2], & Routh[3]. There is no doubt he is developing fast, & in those directions wh will enable him to make his way in the world – by writing & speaking – in politics, at the bar, or in journalism. There are some vy strange & even formidable traits in his character. His mind is free & growing more powerful every day. It is quite startling to hear him argue. His present phase is rabid Agnosticism, & last night in argument with Grigg[4] he more than defended his dismal position – The logical strength of his mind, the courage of his thought, & the brutal & sometimes repulsive character of his rejoinders impressed me vy forcibly. He is far more advanced than I was at his age, & quite out of the common – for good or ill.

Today we all went to the Links[5] & I played 18 holes with Grigg in most delicious spring sunshine. When we came to the big drive over the valley, I did miss you so much. I remembered all the strokes of our game – the one before you got ill – & wished indeed we had been playing together again. I have bought myself a set of clubs & a bag – so that all is ready for you – my darling. . . .

Everything is vy comfortable in the house & seems to go with the utmost smoothness. Butterworth has sent the extra £1,500 advance on The

Aftermath [Volume IV of *The World Crisis*]: & I have sent my first 2 articles
(£1,000) to America – so that we can jog along. But August Sept. & Oct.
will be months of hard work at the book.

The Budget speech is half done. I do hope you will be back to hear
it. . . .

. . . my dearest one I think so often & so tenderly of you & of the glory
& comfort you have been to me in my life & of your sweet nature wh I
love so much, & your unchanging beauty wh is my delight.

With my fondest love
Your ever devoted
W
X X X X

P.S. I wish you were coming nearer & not going further away.

[1] Arthur Charles Sheepshanks; see p. 284 n. 2.
[2] Robert Birley (1903–82), distinguished future Headmaster of Eton College, 1949–63; knighted
1967.
[3] C. R. N. Routh (1896–1976), History and Classics Master at Eton College, 1923–57, and House
Master, 1933–49. Known as 'Dick'.
[4] Percy James Grigg (1890–1961), Principal Private Secretary to successive Chancellors of the
Exchequer, 1921–30. Knighted 1932. Secretary of State for War in Coalition Government, 1942–5.
[5] Tandridge Golf Course, about six miles from Chartwell.

O From CSC   Villa dell' Ombrellino[1]
13 April 1928   Bellosguardo, Florence

My Darling,

Your delightful letter (with Randolph's report) arrived to-day & I read it
with joy – I am so glad about Randolph. He is certainly going to be an
interest, an anxiety & an excitement in our lives. I do hope he will always
care for us. . . .

Alice [Keppel] is well & sweet & amiable as ever & sends you her love. I
am really beginning a pick up – These last 2 days I feel stronger & I am so
thankful –

Your loving & tender
Clemmie –

I am so glad you missed me at the 'Valley' hole. . . .

Tender Love
Clemmie

[1] Home in Italy of Mrs Keppel.

O From WSC [typewritten]   Chartwell Manor
15 April 1928

My darling Clemmie,

All day long I am grappling with the Budget Speech. It will be 15,000 or
16,000 words long and at the rate of the articles would be worth a lot. It is
about three-quarters done. But the number of difficult questions that have

to be settled precisely – Yes or No is very large; one keeps on balancing and hesitating and turning and twisting for a comfortable place in the bed up to the last few days before the event. But I have now reached the stage where final answers have to be given of great importance. This is tiring and anxious although there is some exhilaration about it.

All is arranged for the seats and you have nothing to do but to come back and walk into your pew. At the end of the week I go up to Newcastle for a big public meeting in order to ram home the policy in a great industrial centre. I am taking Randolph with me but we shall arrive back at Chartwell on the Sunday morning.

The fields look lovely. The daffodils are all in full bloom, the sheep having carefully avoided nibbling them. A veritable shower of lambs descended upon us last Sunday, no fewer than five being born between lunch and dinner. We have now eight lambs, ... They look very pretty in the orchard and I am sure you will be delighted when you see them. They are now couched in front of my windows among the daffodils....

I shall not go up to London until Tuesday as I can work down here much better than in that centre of effervescence and unrest called Westminster.

I shall put the Budget to the Cabinet on Thursday but everything of consequence is settled, there only remains to fire the gun. Please God it hits the bull's eye.

Give suitable messages to Alice from me. I trust you have some sunshine....

... The white swans have now laid nine eggs. They not only sit on these alternately but together, side by side. I never knew that they did this....

The garden is coming well forward and May should see it very bright. The pink and crimson rhodies in the water garden are at their best....

Tender love my dearest soul and forgive my dictated bulletin.

Your ever devoted
W

In the event, Clementine felt she should complete her convalescence in Italy: she came home at the end of April.

Diana accompanied her father to the House of Commons and heard him present his Budget, which earned him praise in high quarters.

Now follows a 'corker' from Clementine.

◇ From CSC   11 Downing Street
Monday 25 June [1928]

My Darling

I am writing to you as I know how busy you are, & a conversation would take longer & might degenerate into a long & tedious argument.

I want you to re-consider your decision about not lunching here on Thursday when Edie Londonderry[1] is coming.

These are the facts which I would like you to realize. Last week, Edie wrote to me from Ulster saying she much wanted to see <u>you</u> & telling me she would be in London this week for three days only –

I asked you thro' Eddie Marsh* which day I should arrange & you replied (thro' Eddie) 'Luncheon Tuesday or Thursday, <u>preferably</u> Thursday' – I sent Edie a reply paid telegram & she chose Thursday. (luckily, as I then foolishly thought).

Now, because you very naturally want to be at Chartwell as long as possible you propose chucking.

Now, may I point out that
1) I myself want to go to Chartwell on Thursday, & would have been going <u>before</u> luncheon had it not been for this engagement
2) that by going before luncheon you gain 2 or 3 hours more, at most –
3) that you really are having a very nice long week-end rest – Thursday to Monday, altho' it is not all being spent at Chartwell
4) that you wished to accept the Winchilseas' invitation; <u>I</u> suggested refusing it & spending the week-end at Chartwell
5) that it is really rather unkind & very rude if you chuck your guest and not very helpful to Diana and me, who are going to spend a week as the guests of the Londonderrys in August.

I feel sure that when you have reflected upon all these points that you will consent to honour your invitation –

Please let me know – If you decide against being present, I shall put Edie off, as the point of the little luncheon will have disappeared. . . .

Of course I should not let you down with Edie – I should invent a lie about a forgotten public engagement. But If you will oblige me (and yourself) this time, I promise <u>never</u> again, even with your consent, to make any engagement in which you have a share.

Yours affect^{ly}
Clementine S.C.

[1] The Marchioness of Londonderry (born Edith Chaplin, daughter of 1st Viscount Chaplin); her husband, the 7th Marquess, was a kinsman of WSC.

I do not know the outcome of this scenario: I suspect Winston would have lunched with his guests as planned.

As mentioned in her ferocious letter, Clementine and Diana stayed with the Londonderrys at Mountstewart, Co. Down, later that summer, and it would seem there were no 'ruffled feathers'.

O From CSC	Mountstewart
6 August 1928	Newtownards, Co. Down

My Darling

When we arrived here Saturday morning we were greeted by the most lovely golden sun-shine – The place looked like Paradise & so Edie & I were moved to send you an urging telegram. But perhaps it is as well you

323

could not come, becos' to-day all is gray & damp & clammy & poor Lord Berners'[1] gay & brilliant little vista of the garden has become like an inferior Corot looking like fog and sea-weed.

The Laverys* are here with Hazel's delightful & beautiful daughter by her first marriage[2]. She is never allowed to be seen in London for fear of Hazel's approximate age being guessed at!... Hazel has had a 'froideur' with the McNeills[3], & is much displeased with them. She tells me (& everybody else) that Mrs McNeill asked her (Hazel) to bring over a party of 'suitable' English people to stay at the Vice Regal Lodge for the Horse Show – Hazel thinking it would be a good idea to bring over one or two who would subsequently give, in Royal circles at home, a good impression of Sinn Fein Ireland, suggested Lord Gage[4] among a varied selection (very well chosen) – She thereupon received a long & pompous letter from Mrs McN explaining that anyone however humble & unknown who had any connection with the King would not be persona grata, not of course on personal grounds, but for high political reasons! The letter was otherwise rather patronising in its tone to Hazel, who as you know had (& still has) Vice-Regal aspirations herself – Hazel, encouraged by the Londonderrys, wrote to say that in view of Mrs McNeill's anti-English views neither herself nor John nor any of the other suggested guests would come! So Hazel & John are here, very grand & dignified, but not having so much fun as if they had gone to Dublin.

I must interrupt my gossip as the post is leaving – A further instalment will follow in next!

Your loving
Clemmie

[1] Gerald Hugh Tyrwhitt-Wilson, 14th Baron Berners (1883–1950), diplomat, musician, composer of opera and ballets, painter, writer and grand dilettante. The model for Lord Merlin in Nancy Mitford's *Love in a Cold Climate*, 1949.
[2] Alice Trudeau, Lady Lavery's daughter by her first husband, Dr E. L. Trudeau of New York; she married, 1930, Peter McEnery, an Irish farmer.
[3] James McNeill (1869–1938). At this time Governor-General of the Irish Free State, 1928–32. His wife was Josephine Aherne of Fermoy, Co. Cork.
[4] Henry Rainald Gage, 6th Viscount Gage (1895–1932), Lord-in-Waiting to King George V, 1924–9.

O From CSC   Mountstewart
6 August [1928]

My Darling
    2nd Instalment of Irish Tittle Tattle!
    Hazel is particularly annoyed at Mrs McNeill's conduct as she (Hazel) 'made' her – That is to say that when she first came to London Hazel took her up, encouraged her, told her she was pretty, arranged her hair for her, took her to an expensive dress maker – and now forsooth, Mrs McNeill, tho' a Red Republican expects Hazel as well as all other women to curtsey to the ground!
    The Horse Show is being ostracised by the North by order of the Abercorns[1] & poor little Brenda Dufferin[2] who was innocently going there to buy a pony was told not to go, and isn't going – John Lavery* is here

sweet & gentle as usual.... He is a very friendly & beneficent influence between the North & the South. Lord Berners is here & a charming artist called Brock who has painted all the Londonderry family many times – The Wimbornes [Ivor and Alice Guest*] are here with their daughter Cynthia – at least they were, but Ivor & Cynthia have left to-day for a Moor they have taken in Scotland....

Poor Ivor is suffering from mortal boredom which he tries quite ineffectually to conceal. His one interest in Life (pursuing ladies) has practically disappeared over the horizon – He sits dismally about & looks at the pictures of 'Bathing Beauties' in the Bank Holiday picture papers.

Robin Castlereagh³ is here & I like him & find him congenial – But he has a reputation as a 'girl hater' – Consequently Cynthia & Diana are timid with him – Cynthia is the pluckier of the two having a thicker skin than our sweet Diana.

Edie confided to me (somewhat naïvely I thought!) that she was inviting a few girls in a panic, hoping Robin would not be too rude to them....

Charley & Edie [Londonderry]⁴ are both amiable but I must say I think they are each in their different way absolutely puerile & futile, & much as I desire (as every Mother should & must!) that her daughter should make a good marriage, I must say the prospect of a succession of visits here would fill me with gloom, not to say consternation – They are completely wrapped up in themselves & their own importance & cannot see anything further than the Stewart family, & perhaps the Royal Family....

Charlie by the way is cross because you (i.e. your Secretary) have not replied to a letter of his complaining about super tax being charged on some money which was used by him to diminish un-employment.... He told me he was practically ruined & really his sorrows almost brought tears to my eyes. I nearly offered to lend him £100 – In a fortnight they leave this place & proceed to a deer forest which they rent from the Sutherlands. He said he did not know how he should find the money to pay for it!...

If ever you are made P.M. I think you will incur great displeasure here if Charlie is not included in the Cabinet, as a Secretary of State of course, none of your Board of Trades or Local Government Boards or Ministry of Healths!

Unless you can put this scrawl under lock & key, perhaps better burn it –

I long for my Pig meanwhile. I am used to him, odious as he sometimes is, & cannot do with these inbred effete sprigs of the ancien régime!

I hope you are happy & comfy at Chartwell & that your Lake is behaving –

Tender Love from
Your Pussy (not in her basket).

¹ James Hamilton, 3rd Duke of Abercorn (1869–1953) and his wife, born Lady Rosalind Bingham. Conservative MP for Londonderry (1900–13); Lord Lieutenant of Tyrone from 1917; Governor of N. Ireland, 1922–45.
² Marchioness of Dufferin and Ava (born Brenda Woodhouse) wife of 3rd Marquess (1875–1930).
³ Robert ('Robin') Vane-Tempest-Stewart, Viscount Castlereagh (1902–55), elder son of 7th Marquess of Londonderry, whom he succeeded in 1949. In 1931 he married Romaine Combe (d. 1951).
⁴ Charles Vane-Tempest-Stewart, 7th Marquess of Londonderry (1878–1949). WSC's cousin.

Entered Parliament, 1906, and subsequently held various government appointments including that of Secretary of State for Air, 1931–5. Lord Privy Seal and Leader of House of Lords, 1935.

○ From WSC [typewritten]   Chartwell Manor
7 August 1928

My darling,

Everything has been progressing here, and the zoo has been full of incidents. The black swans have laid two eggs and are sitting stolidly upon them. The horse and foal and the sow both got second prizes at the Show. There was only one other horse and foal, which makes the event resemble Randolph's boxing feats! Still Arnold [farm manager] brought home £3. Five new cows have arrived. They are as big as elephants, and one immediately had a beautiful white calf. Twelve little pigs have been born, and more are expected. Work has started on the children's house, and I hope to have some results to show you when you come.

The Prof [Lindemann*] and I motored over to see Randolph in Camp [Eton Officers' Training Corps] on Sunday, and the General commanding the Division invited us and him to lunch. Alas, when we arrived we were informed with much embarrassment that he was confined to Camp for having gone out with some other boys the night before on to the top of a hill to watch the Tattoo from afar. So we had rather a wild goose chase in every sense of the word. However, we saw Randolph in his camp in a state of considerable indignation against the authorities.... He looked very nice in his uniform, ... He arrives home tomorrow with, I expect, only a small amount of military ardour left. He puts himself into opposition to all the prevailing acceptances and heartinesses, and was this time very much disappointed at the result.

I have been working fairly hard, and so has Miss Fisher!... Nearly 3,000 words in the last two days! I have to keep this rate up continuously, if we are to finish by October 31; and I do not conceal from you that it is a task. But it is not more than I can do.... Certainly nothing will suit me better than to be quiet here and have hardly any visitors. I am entirely with you in this....

Tender love my dearest
Your own
W

...

○ From CSC   Vaynol[1]
10 August [1928]   Bangor

My Darling Winston

I was glad on my arrival here to find your chronicle of Chartwell events – Moppet [Whyte*] had meanwhile very kindly written to me twice to keep me 'au courant'. But it is always nice to get a chit from G.H.Q....

The 'party' for Michael's[2] Coming of Age has not yet arrived – But by to-night the young people who are converging upon us from London, Scotland & Ireland will all be assembled.

On our way here yesterday we stopped & lunched with Leonie [Leslie][3] at Glaslough. It is really rather a lovely place & below the house is a lake which would make your mouth water. It is a mile long ¼ of a mile broad & in places is 80 foot deep. It is beautiful & rather melancholy. The house is ugly outside but comfortable & as pretty as Leonie's good taste can make it within – But she is obviously a fish out of water there – Jack [Leslie][4] on the other hand is in his element – He loves every acre, farms 1,000 himself & is respected & beloved. I think they look upon Leonie as an amiable foreigner....

Your loving
Clemmie

[1] Vaynol Park, on the Menai Straits, home of Lady Juliet Duff (1881–1965), widow of Sir Robert Duff, 2nd Bt (killed in action, 1914). She was a friend of WSC and CSC for many years.
[2] Sir Michael Duff (1907–80), who had succeeded his father as 3rd Bt in 1914.
[3] Lady Randolph's sister; see p. 13 n. 1.
[4] Colonel Sir John ('Jack') Leslie, 2nd Bt (1857–1944).

○ From WSC [typewritten]   Chartwell Manor
10 August 1928

My darling Clemmie,

All your delightful letters have reached me. I hope you will have found mine awaiting you at Vaynol.

Everything is very peaceful here. Randolph duly returned and his reports are not bad. He and the Prof. [Lindemann*] play golf and tennis. I have persuaded the Prof. to stay on until Monday. He is a great companion both for me and for Randolph.

Baruch[1] lunched yesterday and sent you ceremonious messages. I gave him my slogan for the Democratic Party. 'AL for all, and all for AL.'[2] ... These American Presidential Elections are extraordinary games in which with the greatest zest and party bitterness the whole nation takes part, although there is no real difference between the parties except that of 'ins and outs'....

I have got eight men clearing the site of the new cottage[3]. The work is proceeding very rapidly and we are to start laying it out on Monday. You will be surprised to see what a fine broad plateau we have made. The oak tree comes down this afternoon. (✍Since down – a wollop! We are going out to burn it & hack it up.)

Mary's house[4] is growing and I hope to have a treat for you when you come.... Mary has taken the greatest interest in the work and laid the foundation stone with great ceremony....

You will see by the papers that the P.M. did not think it expedient to do what I am sure he wished to do – to leave me in charge, so Hogg[5] has been made to give up his Canadian tour. All this reveals how serious is the handicap I have had to carry in the party by warning them off the Protectionist question[6]. I do not at all regret the steps I took which are only for their good; but of course all the powerful interests who would make money out of Protection keep up a steady pressure and half the Tory party are religiously convinced about tariff. [In margin:] ✍Really I feel vy independent of them all. ...

Tender love my dearest one
from yr loving
W
...

✍P.S. What cheek of Mrs McNeill to make people curtsey to her in the name of a sovereign she repudiates! The thing is to let them stew.

¹ Bernard M. Baruch (1870–1965), American financier and elder statesman (Democrat). He met WSC when the latter was Minister of Munitions in 1918 and Baruch a Commissioner on the American War Industries Board: they became, and remained, very great friends.
² Albert Smith, Democratic candidate in 1928 US Presidential Elections; he was defeated by Herbert Hoover (1874–1964), who became the 31st President (until 1933).
³ This new cottage (Wellstreet) was intended for a married butler.
⁴ My father built for Sarah and me a one-roomed cottage in the kitchen garden brick wall. It was completely equipped and furnished. WSC painted a picture of the foundation stone ceremony, which is now in the Studio at Chartwell.
⁵ Sir Douglas Hogg, later Viscount Hailsham (1872–1950), at this time Lord Chancellor, and Acting Prime Minister for August/September 1928 in Baldwin's absence abroad.
⁶ In the summer of 1928 the question of a return to Protection was once more being canvassed in the Tory party: this put WSC, a long-time Free Trader, at cross-purposes with some of his colleagues.

O From WSC   Balmoral Castle¹
25 September 1928

My darling One,

Here I am – not at all tired by a racketting journey. The meeting² went off well, there was gt enthusiasm and the prospects of the poll seemed healthy. I caught the Scottish Express at 12.45 a.m. at Rugby, & motored on here this morning from Perth – a beautiful drive. There is no one here at all except the Family, the Household & Queen [sic; Princess] Elizabeth³ – aged 2. The last is a character. She has an air of authority & reflectiveness astonishing in an infant. ...

The King is well – but ageing. He no longer stalks but goes out on the hill where the deer are 'moved about for him', & it may be that some loyal stag will do his duty. He & the Q asked much after you.

Miss F[isher; secretary] does not arrive till late this evening with the heavy luggage. I am much looking forward to my release on Saturday from this honourable & luxurious captivity.

Mind you rest, & do not worry about household matters. Let them crash if they will. All will be well. Servants exist to save one trouble, & shd never be allowed to disturb one's inner peace. There will always be food to eat, & sleep will come even if the beds are not made. Nothing is worse than worrying about trifles. The big things do not chafe as much: & if they are rightly settled the rest will fall in its place.

I trust all is well with the cygnets. The cold will try them hard. However God is responsible both for the cygnets & the change in the weather, & he must settle the problem. Our contribution must be to keep the Fox away by finishing the wire fence. The rest falls in a sphere with wh it wd be impious to meddle too much....

With tender love
Your devoted
W

[1] WSC was on his statutory ministerial visit to Balmoral.
[2] WSC had spoken the previous evening, 24 September, at Cheltenham, where a by-election was in progress.
[3] HRH Princess Elizabeth (b. 1926), the future Queen Elizabeth II, whose first Prime Minister (1952–5) Winston Churchill would be.

O From CSC   Chartwell
25 September [1928]

My Darling
    Rather a meagre account of your speech in the Times, but what was reported I thought good – I <u>do</u> hope you are not overtired by the effort....
    I cannot tell you how perfectly sweet the black swans & cygnets were this evening parading about on the big lake among all the other water fowl & letting me come quite close – I tried to feed them but they refused bread. I expect they thought it unwholesome for the children!...

Tender Love
Clemmie

. . .

O From WSC   Balmoral Castle
27 September 1928

My darling,
    . . .
    I am just back from a vy hardworking day's stalking 10 till 5.30 always on the move. I killed a good stag 10 pointer – but missed another thro' being out of breath.
    Tomorrow we are to shoot grouse. Luckily I brought my guns & cartridges. The K[ing] is really vy kind to me & gives me every day the best of his sport. Yesterday we had a most interesting talk after picnic lunch about Guarantees, Baldwin's Dissolution in 1923, Curzon's chagrin at not being P.M. etc. The King is a strong advocate of his Government and highly approves of my criticism of Ll.G. [Lloyd George*]. I defended him a certain amount. H.M. also shares my views about the Yankees & expressed the same in picturesque language.
    Cheltenham is splendid[1]. I enclose a vy nice telegram from the new member.
    I am healthily tired out.

With tender love my darling one
from yr ever devoted
W

[1] In the Cheltenham by-election, 26 September 1928, the seat was retained by the Conservative candidate, Sir Walter Preston, with a majority of 3,760.

In the late autumn Clementine was afflicted with blood poisoning, which derived from infected tonsils; she went to a nursing home, Preston Deanery Hall at Northampton, to undergo a strict curative regime. She was really quite ill.

○ From WSC   Treasury Chambers
7 November 1928

My darling One,

I sent you a telegram this morning & hope you have found comfortable quarters. I expect to hear from you tomorrow about it all. I am sure the dullness & tiresome treatment will be a vy small price to pay for a reasonable share of health....

The session opens super-tame. The P.M. almost mute – a sort of Coolidge[1] or Hoover[2]. It is astonishing what goes down in these days of mass politics. One thing is as good as another. All the old Parliamentary drama & personal clashes are gone – perhaps for ever.

So Hoover has swept the board – I feel this is not good for us. Poor old England – she is being slowly but surely forced into the shade. I have a fairly good speech for tomorrow. Perhaps you will read it.

I am taking no end of pains.

Your ever loving
W

[1] Calvin Coolidge (1872–1933), Republican, 30th President of the USA, 1923–9; declined to run in the 1928 presidential election, and supported Herbert Hoover.
[2] Herbert Hoover, Republican, had been elected 31st President of the USA on 7 November, with 444 electoral votes against Albert Smith, Democrat, 87. He held the office until 1932.

○ From CSC   Preston Deanery Hall
8 November [1928]   Northampton

My Darling

I was so glad to see your handwriting.

This seems to be a beautifully run place –

The treatment is tiresome & very lowering as one gets nothing to eat or drink but orange juice & 2 cups of tea a day! Apparently poison cannot be thoroughly eliminated from the system while one is eating.... There is the most delicious smell of onions & roast mutton coming in thro' my key-hole & under the crack of my door & I am inhaling it with longing....

So far I have been kept in bed – There is a very good masseuse who comes every morning.

I shall think of you this evening speaking in the house & read you eagerly in the Times tomorrow....

Tender Love
from
Clemmie

I am thinking of all the delicious food I shall eat when I get home....

○ From CSC   Preston Deanery Hall
12 November [1928]

My Darling
Tho' gradually becoming weaker from continued starvation (I was
weighed to-day & have lost 6 lbs in 5 days! 8 stone 6 lbs in a nightgown is
my <u>present</u> weight) – I must put pen to paper to ask you what you think
of Coolidge's Armistice Speech[1]. Its coldness, smugness, self sufficiency,
boastfulness, Pharisaicalness & cant make me boil & freeze alternately – It
ought to be learnt by heart by every one over here so that we shall
thoroughly grasp what the Swine think & mean. It looks as tho' they mean
to do us in, & it will take great coolness & vigilance on our part to keep
our heads above water....
Darling I did enjoy your visit yesterday. It was good of you to come.
I hope there are no spelling mistakes in this letter – I'm told a shaky
handwriting & forgetting how to spell supervene about the 5th or 6th day of
orange juice.
Do not forget your Birthday Dinner & rope Streetie [Margery Street,
secretary] into the preparations for it.

Tender Love from
Your attenuated
Powser

Oh my Darling I am so melancholy – Shall I ever taste a chop again?

[1] Calvin Coolidge, the outgoing Republican American President, had spoken in Washington on
11 November about the US contribution to the war, and its policy and generous attitude to post-
war reparations and settlements.

○ From WSC [typewritten]   Treasury Chambers
14 November 1928

My darling one,
My blood boiled too at Coolidge's proclamation. Why can't they let us
alone? They have exacted every penny owing from Europe; they say they
are not going to help; surely they might leave us to manage our own
affairs. I absolutely agree with what you write.
I have had very busy days, trying to push the book forward and at the
same time with heaps of engagements and politics....
Rothermere, having ordered his organs to smash up the De-rating Bill[1],
has gone off to luxuriate in Egypt. The wretched papers loathe doing this
sort of work which is against their convictions and sympathies but to
which they are forced by an imperious, ill-informed, restless and sore
proprietor.... We shall drive the Bill through. It is a great piece of social

reform and well worth fighting for amid the shallow chatter of these days. . . .

✍You saw no doubt about Diana Mitford[2]. I suitably congratulated Walter[3].

Dearest I grieve to think of yr austerities: & what you tell me of yr weight and strength distresses me. However it is half over now – & you are in vy skilled hands. . . .

With my fondest love
Yr ever devoted
W

Don't worry about anything: but send for me if you feel the need.

[1] In two parts: The Rating and Valuation (Apportionment) Act, 3 August 1928, and the Local Government Act, 27 March 1929. Under these Acts agriculture was to be free of rates from October 1929 and industry relieved by 75%.

[2] Diana Mitford (1910–), daughter of 2nd Lord Redesdale and CSC's cousin. In 1929 she married Bryan Guinness, son of Walter Guinness (see below); they were divorced in 1934. In 1936 she married Sir Oswald Mosley (see p. 254 n. 1).

[3] Walter Guinness (1880–1944), cr. 1st Baron Moyne, 1932. He married (1903) Lady Evelyn Erskine (d. 1939). Held various government appointments; at this date Minister of Agriculture and Fisheries (1925–9). Deputy Minister of State, Cairo, 1942–4, when assassinated by Jewish terrorists.

O From CSC   Preston Deanery Hall
Wednesday [14 November 1928]

My Darling

Yesterday after Diana had returned to London I had a very disagreeable & frightening experience . . . I felt giddy & prickly & had a sort of fainting fit or heart attack. . . . Luckily the Nurse was in the room & succoured me as well as she could & then fetched the Matron –

When I recovered sufficiently I was given Brandy. . . . The Cat was very miserable & if she had not been completely immobilized would have rushed home. But when Dr Cameron arrived he did not seem a bit concerned – He said it frequently happened & did not do any harm. . . .

Now do not be alarmed as it is all over & he has sworn to me that I shall not have another attack.

I expect you are too busy but I should like some one to come down & see me for a couple of hours & hold my paw. . . .

Did you hear Ll[oyd] George* yesterday – He is a little 'Swob' isn't he? All right in War, but in Peace always taking sides against his own country – I suppose this 'Pact' affair[1] is a most awful floater. I think it would be a good idea if you went to the Foreign Office – But I am afraid your known hostility to America might stand in the way – You would have to try & understand & master America & make her like you. Its no use grovelling or even being civil to her – But I think you could do it. . . .

I see old Cushendun[2] is ill again – Now why doesn't the P.M. promote someone young. That nice Captain Eden* who I see has made a good speech. . . .

Thank-you for the lovely flowers my Darling

Your loving
Clemmie

[1] The Kellogg–Briand Pact, signed in Paris on 27 August 1928, a multilateral agreement which attempted to renounce war as an instrument of national policy. It was to prove useless as it did not provide for sanctions against any state which broke the pledge – although such sanctions were provided for under the League Covenant, with which the Pact was associated.

[2] 1st Baron Cushendun, formerly Ronald McNeill (1861–1936), had been appointed Acting Secretary of State for Foreign Affairs in August on account of Sir Austen Chamberlain's illness; he held the office until December 1928.

On 15 April 1929 Winston delivered his fifth (and last) Budget.

A General Election took place on 30 May, after a singularly undramatic campaign. Despite solid achievements at home and in foreign affairs, the Conservatives were soundly defeated: unemployment at over a million and the shadow of the General Strike were powerful elements in their undoing. The Labour Party won 288 seats, the Conservatives 260 and the Liberals 59. Ramsay MacDonald formed his second Government, although again without an overall majority: the new Labour administration was dependent on Liberal support.

At Epping Churchill was victorious, with a 4,967 majority over the Liberal candidate – but he also failed to achieve an overall majority.

Chapter XIV

'WESTWARD, LOOK, THE LAND IS BRIGHT!'[1]

O ut of office, Winston was certainly not out of work: he plunged at once into his new and major literary project – the life of his great ancestor, John, 1st Duke of Marlborough. He also determined to take a three-month journey to Canada and the United States: part holiday and part a programme of speeches and lectures in major cities. Planned to go with him were Clementine and Randolph; Jack, his brother; and Jack's son, Johnnie Churchill.

However, to her bitter disappointment, Clementine was prevented from going on this exciting journey: her tonsils once again flared up, and on 4 July she underwent an operation in hospital for their removal; her recovery was slow, and there was no question of her being able to travel.

[1] From 'Say not the struggle nought availeth', 1855, by Arthur Hugh Clough (1819–61).

O From WSC	Canadian Pacific
3 [August] 1929	S.S. Empress of Australia

My darling one,

It was not without some melancholy twinges that I watched the figures of Diana & Sarah disappearing on the quay. All departures from home – even on pleasure are sad. The vessel drifts away from the shore & an ever-widening gulf opens between one and the citadel of one's life and soul. But most of all I was distressed to think of you being lonely & unhappy & left behind. My dearest it wd have been madness for you to face this rocketing journey until you had regained full normal strength. This I trust & pray may be the result of 6 or 7 weeks of real quietness & calm. You are quite right not to make plans till you feel yrself again. But <u>then</u> surely there are lots of delightful alternatives. Do let me know as soon as any form themselves attractively in yr mind. Do not exclude USA. Do not hesitate to telegraph often & fully about yr plans & fortunes. . . .

We are plodding across a calm Channel & this goes to you from Cherbourg. I expect to do a lot of work – Certainly 2 articles before landing: & to read copiously into Marlbro [Marlborough].

I think of you at each hour, where you will be and how you will look. I long to see you smiling & sedate – taking things coolly & gathering strength. Send me a wireless to mid-ocean to tell me how you are getting on.

With tender love
Your devoted
W

x   x   x   x   x

○ From CSC   Admiralty House[1]
8 August [1929]   Portsmouth

My Darling Winston
    I think, by now your voyage may be ended. I hope it has been pleasant & sufficiently calm for you to enjoy the luxuries of the ship –
    Diana & Sarah report that your personal suite on board is so magnificent that it will be necessary to build on another wing to Chartwell to satisfy your enlarged ideas & those of Randolph on personal comfort!...
    To-night we go to the Tidworth Tattoo.
    A Turkish General comes to luncheon in a few minutes & is to be shewn, such portions of the Dockyard as are good for him to see & realize. I went & paid my homage to the Victory[2] this morning....
    Thank-you & Randolph for letters from Cherbourg –

Tender Love
from
Clemmie

Oh – I went all over the Enchantress[3] – She was looking rather shabby but just the same.

[1] CSC and Diana were staying with Admiral Sir Roger Keyes (see p. 271 n. 5), at this date C.-in-C., Portsmouth.
[2] Nelson's flagship, now preserved in Portsmouth harbour.
[3] The Admiralty yacht in which WSC (chiefly) and CSC spent so much time during his first tenure as First Lord (1911–15).

○ From WSC [typewritten]   On Board 'EMPRESS OF AUSTRALIA'
8 [9] August 1929   ✍ Rimouski [on St Lawrence river]
noon 9 Aug.

My darling,
    We have had a wonderfully good passage with only one day of unpleasant motion. The ship is comfortable and well-found, and we have splendid cabins....
    We have just passed the Straits of Belle Isle, and tomorrow night will arrive at Quebec. It was pleasing this morning to see the green shores of Labrador after six days of grey sky and sea.... The boys were called by the Captain at 6.30 a.m. to see a large iceberg – 150 ft. high – which we

passed at no great distance. They did not, however, wake me, which was a pity. . . .

We are now in the great inland sea between Newfoundland and the mouth of the St. Lawrence. It is calm and bright, and getting steadily warmer.

I have found no difficulty in amusing myself as you may imagine. I have written an article on John Morley[1], with which I am quite satisfied; . . . When it is paid for, everything will be provided satisfactorily up to the end of October, when the big payments for the 'aftermath' [*The World Crisis*, vol. IV] come in. . . . For the rest I have played a great deal of Bezique with Jack [Churchill*], and have inflicted most cruel defeats upon him, . . . I have been trying to enforce discipline upon Randolph, and get him up and to bed at reasonable hours, and to secure a certain amount of reading being done. I have met with partial success. There is a fine swimming pool on board where the youth of both sexes play water polo. . . . I stick to the hot water. . . .

I have been reading a good deal on 'Marlborough'. It is a wonderful thing to have all these contracts satisfactorily settled, and to feel that two or three years agreeable work is mapped out and, if completed, will certainly be rewarded. . . .

I have done nothing so far about preparing speeches. It will be better to see what the atmosphere is on landing, and I shall have all Sunday and Monday morning before my luncheon speech at Montreal. I have, of course, got some ideas already formed. . . .

✍ My darling I have been rather sad at times thinking of you in low spirits at home. Do send me some messages. I love you so much & it grieves me to feel you are lonely. I should greatly like to make a fine plan for October. But you must get fit & well. Tender love my sweet Clemmie, from yr devoted loving husband

W.

. . .

[1] 1st Viscount Morley of Blackburn (1838–1923), barrister, Liberal MP and writer, twice Chief Secretary for Ireland, 1886 and 1892–5; Secretary for India, 1905–10; Lord President of the Council, 1910–14.

O From WSC [typewritten]   CANADIAN PACIFIC RAILWAY
12 August 1929   At Quebec, Mount Royal Car. In the train

My darling,

We arrived to Quebec punctually and were met by the C.P.R. and by Mr Beauchesne who represents the British Empire Parliamentary Association and to some extent Mr MacKenzie King, the Premier[1]. We stayed at the Château Frontenac, a tremendous hotel on the most modern lines. Saturday we saw all the sights, the Citadel, Wolfe's Cove and the Plains of Abraham, where the battle which decided the fate of Canada was fought. . . .

Sunday we lunched with the Lieutenant-Governor, a charming French Canadian who had been a distinguished Judge. He had read my war books and was very complimentary. A number of the elite of Quebec were present and made themselves very agreeable....

... Considerable state & formality attaches to the representative of the Crown and we were in our Sunday best for the occasion.

Late in the afternoon ... we took an open motor car and went off twenty miles into the blue. I wanted to see the country at close quarters and nibble the grass and champ the branches. We saw hills and forests scarcely trodden by the foot of man, every kind of tree growing in primeval confusion and loveliest Scotch burns splashing down to rivers....

Our first morning there arrived a Mr Larkin, a great swell in the Bethlehem Steel Corporation, sent specially on a twenty-four hours' journey by Mr Schwab[2] with the most cordial messages. Mr Schwab places his [railway] car at our disposal during the whole of our tour in the United States! This solves all problems. We timidly suggested paying the haulage, but this was brushed aside with pained looks. It will certainly be an enormous convenience and comfort....

✍ The Vice P. of the C.P.R. has lent me his Stenographer [Secretary] for the trip. This is a gt boon as I don't know how I shd deal with correspondence, telephones etc without this help.

Randolph is behaving vy well. He 'studies' for several hours daily. I keep him up to the mark & try to get him down to breakfast. However even if he goes to sleep before midnight he sleeps till 10. No harm in this. The others send their love.

I will write again from Toronto, but this mail leaves tonight.

Always my darling one, with fondest love,

Yr devoted

W.

...

X X many kisses X X to you
& to Diana X X to Sarah X X
to Maria.

P.S. We are now in our [Canadian Pacific Railway] car on the way to Montreal through vast lush country following more or less the course of the St Lawrence. This car is to be our home for three weeks so we have been unpacking all our clothes and arranging them afresh. When we leave the car we shall only take a tiny suitcase each. The car is a wonderful habitation. Jack [Churchill*] and I have large cabins with big double beds and private bath rooms. Randolph and Johnnie have something like an ordinary sleeping car compartment. There is a fine parlour with an observation room at the end and a large dining room which I use as the office and in which I am now dictating....

W

---

[1] William Lyon MacKenzie King (1874–1950), Leader of the Liberal Party of Canada, 1919–48; Prime Minister of Canada, 1921–6, 1926–30 and 1935–8.
[2] Charles Michael Schwab (1862–1939), US steel magnate. Chairman, Bethlehem Steel Corporation, 1903–39. WSC had had dealings with him when at the Admiralty during the 1914–18 war: as Director-General of the Emergency Fleet Corporation, he had built 495 ships for the Allies.

O From WSC [typewritten]   CANADIAN PACIFIC RAILWAY
15 August 1929   At Ottawa

My darling

Our journey continues most interesting and stimulating, but it is also, as I cabled you, extremely strenuous. I have made two full dress speeches, one at Montreal and today here in Ottawa. I took a great deal of time and trouble over them on account of the unfamiliar atmosphere and also because of the delicacy of the topic[1]. The audiences were very large and overflowing and most enthusiastic. I have been every where welcomed in the warmest manner. Men whom I have not seen for thirty years, but whom I ran across in my wanderings, have come up in twos and threes at every place to shake hands. Today a former Sergeant of the Engineers, who helped me in '98 ... make my plans for the battle of Omdurman for the 'River War', held me up in the street, introduced himself and presented me with a box of excellent cigars for use on my journey. He was in quite humble circumstances and I was greatly touched....

... I am gradually developing information and acquiring a line of arguments and ideas. This will make the later speeches easier. I have had to take on three more speeches, namely, Regina, Edmonton and Calgary, but I do not expect to have to prepare for them.

The immense size and progress of this country impresses itself upon one more every day.... The sentimental feeling towards England is wonderful. The United States are stretching their tentacles out in all directions, but the Canadian National Spirit and personality is becoming so powerful and self-contained that I do not think we need fear the future.

We are staying here in great comfort with the Willingdons[2]. The beautiful 'Blossom'[3] is here with her husband, and all is extremely pleasant. The Prime Minister, MacKenzie King, has been most kind and cordial. We all went out and lunched at his small country place about fifteen miles from Ottawa. It is just the sort of place you would like to buy for me, a tiny bungalow, three hundred acres of hills and forests with a large lake and Scotch Burn, all just the right size for me....

Randolph has conducted himself in a most dutiful manner and is an admirable companion. I think he has made a good impression on everybody. He is taking a most intelligent interest in everything, and is a remarkable critic and appreciator of the speeches I make and the people we meet. Jack and Johnnie are enjoying themselves thoroughly. I am a little tired this evening after the speech and worry of preparing it. We travel tonight after dinner to Toronto which we reach at seven A.M. tomorrow....

✍ 16th

I have just come back from the Toronto Meeting – A tremendous affair. I made my best speech so far. Tonight we go to Niagara, see the falls tomorrow at 7 a.m., then back here for a large luncheon – then off for 36 hours run to Winnipeg. More speeches – too much!

My darling – my tender love – I think often of you & the Kittens & hope you are all happy & well. Do write & wire, & forgive me using short hand [typewritten letters], I cd not possibly tell you about things otherwise.

Always your loving husband
W ...

P.S. Montreal bought 600 copies of my W/Cr [*World Crisis*] and in my rights I get 1 dollar for each. If this keeps up we shall make an unexpected profit.

¹ In his Canadian speeches WSC dealt with imperial and international affairs, including the controversial subject of Empire Free Trade, but avoiding mention of local political matters.
² Freeman Freeman-Thomas, 1st Viscount Willingdon, later 1st Earl and 1st Marquess (1866–1941), Governor-General of Canada, 1926–31; Viceroy and Governor-General of India, 1931–6. Married (1892) Lady Marie Adelaide Brassey.
³ Maxine Forbes-Robertson, their daughter-in-law. A niece of Maxine Elliott; in 1924 she married Inigo Brassey Freeman-Thomas, later 2nd Marquess of Willingdon; they were divorced, 1932.

○ From CSC   Chartwell
20 August [1929]

My Darling Winston

I was glad to get your letter describing your voyage. It sounded most comfortable for the elders & uproarious fun (in the swimming bath) for the boys.

Diana & I have been to Lympne where everything was as luxurious & beautiful as ever – The Auxiliary Airmen ... were swooping about everywhere, (flying rather low I thought) & being hospitably entertained by Philip [Sassoon*]....

Now you will want to hear the Chartwell news. The portion of the wall to the road is finished & looks really beautiful & not a bit too high....

... [Arnold, farm manager] is very civil & obliging, & in your absence I am getting on very well with him! I expect that as Christ explained he cannot serve 'God and Mammon'¹. Now that you are away I have become God which is pleasant, & is a slight compensation for your absence.

Our French lady, Madame L'Honoré² has arrived – She is a most stimulating person & keeps us all in fits of laughter. She is going for the next 4 weeks to give Diana, Sarah & Mary a lesson every day – Besides this she chatters lovely Parisian French all day & corrects one's mistakes....

Tomorrow I go to Dieppe to see Nellie – I stay at an Hotel as her little house³ is full with her boys, home for the holidays – My conscience was pricking me about her & I must see how she is poor Darling –

Your very loving
Clemmie

¹ Gospel According to Matthew, 6: 24; Gospel According to Luke, 16: 13.
² Madame Gabrielle L'Honoré, a most charming and gifted Frenchwoman who came to Chartwell for three or four years, usually in the summer holidays, to teach (principally me) French.
³ Nellie Romilly had inherited Lady Blanche's house.

○ From WSC [typewritten]   Canadian Pacific Railway
22 August 1929   (Montreal)

My darling Clemmie,

I intended to begin this letter while we were still running along the north shores of Lake Superior, but we have been travelling so incessantly, I have had to speak so often, & have had to meet so many people, that five days have slipped away.

First of all we traversed the more populated and well cultivated regions of Quebec and Ontario. Then, leaving Toronto on our long forward bound course of twelve hundred miles to Winnipeg, we passed through an enormous region of rocky hills covered with birch and pine and interdispersed with innumerable lakes of every size....

At Winnipeg begins the corn belt and thence westerly and northward stretches about five thousand square miles (a square mile is eight times as large as Chartwell!).... Thenceforward we are in an ocean of green fields as far as the eye can reach, on every side nothing but waving corn with tiny farmsteads dotted about salutes the eye. They have a new machine called the 'Combine' [introduced 1928] which not only cuts the corn, but threshes it, ...

Tomorrow we arrive at Edmonton, the Capital of Alberta, and thereafter leave the corn belt for the rising slopes of the Rocky mountains. This region, twenty Switzerlands rolled into one, alone stands between us and the beautiful and luxuriant Pacific Coast.

I have had to consent to no fewer than ten public speeches, six of which are over, ... The meetings have all been crammed to overflowing and everyone of consequence of all parties, classes and religions have attended.... I took a great deal of trouble about my earlier speeches, but am now working over old ground as in an election campaign.

At Winnipeg we were taken charge of by a Mr Richardson, who is the leading grain merchant. A very good specimen of a new world business man, ... We saw the Winnipeg Wheat Exchange where frantic dealers screamed and gesticulated as the telegrams from all the world recorded the ceaseless fluctuations of wheat prices....

I had almost forgotten to tell you that we spent the morning at Niagara Falls now two thousand miles behind, that the river was exceptionally full, that the falls were magnificent and at their very best, ... and we went across the great whirl pool in a frail aerial car borne by wires six hundred yards long. This looked alarming but was really quite safe.

This is now our seventh successive night in the train and tomorrow will make an eighth. The car is very comfortable. Although the baths are very short, by lying on one's back with one's paws in the air, a good dip can be obtained....

Tender love my darling,
from your somewhat harassed
but ever devoted
W.

○ From WSC   Banff Springs Hotel
27 August [1929]   Banff, Alberta

My darling, I have longed again & again for you to be here. There have
been days wh you wd have enjoyed beyond measure, & sights to see &
people to please the Cat. But then there have been many more days wh
wd simply have flattened you out. We have never ceased travelling,
starting, stopping, packing, unpacking, scarcely ever two nights in any one
bed except the train; & eight nights running in that. Racket of train, racket
of motor, racket of people, racket of speeches! I have made 9 & have 2
more. It has been a whirl: & on arriving here last night after two motor
drives of 80 miles with a long speech at Calgary between them, I decreed
a halt. So we stay here 36 hours in this magnificent hotel with ev^y comfort
– an outdoor swimming pool kept at 90°, & riding – & I am going for the
first time to try to paint a picture. I went to bed at 10 utterly tired out: &
have just wakened at 7.30!

I have been wonderfully received in Canada. Never in my whole life
have I been welcomed with so much genuine interest & admiration as
throughout this vast country. All parties & classes have mingled in the
welcome ... I am profoundly touched; ...

... I am greatly attracted to this country. Immense developments are
going forward. There are fortunes to be made in many directions. The tide
is flowing strongly. I have made up my mind that if N.Ch. [Neville
Chamberlain] is made leader of the C.P. [Conservative Party] or anyone
else of that kind, I clear out of politics & see if I cannot make you & the
kittens a little more comfortable before I die. Only one goal still attracts
me, & if that were barred I shd quit the dreary field for pastures new. As
Daniel Peggotty[1] says 'There's mighty lands beyond the seas'. However the
time to take decision is not yet....

I long to hear Chartwell news; & I am expecting another letter from my
darling in a day or two.

Randolph is growing into a vy strong man. His neck [and] his thighs are
vy noticeable: I think he will be quite big & solidly built. He speaks so
well. So dexterous, cool & finished.... He sleeps ten & sometimes 12
hours a day – deep oblivion. I suppose it is his mind & body growing at
the same time. I love him vy much. A sweet letter from Sarah, & a pet
from Mary have duly arrived.

                         Most tender love my darling one from your
                                              loving & devoted
                                                           W

Kisses to all   XXX   XXX   XXX   XXX

[1] Yarmouth fisherman in Charles Dickens' *David Copperfield*.

O From CSC   Chartwell
31 August 1929

My Darling
   Mary's Birthday is approaching & great secret preparations are going
forward in connection with it –
   I hope you will send her a cable to reach her on the magic day ...
   Life is very peaceful & uneventful here. The weather is glorious –
Madame L'Honoré is the most tremendous success. She looks like Madame
de Pompadour, takes away all Diana's young men from her & would lure
a deaf & dumb orang-outang to speak French –

September 1.
   To-day is Sunday & we have that nice tall young man Alan Lennox
Boyd[1] staying with us & Nancy Mitford[2] (Diana Guinness's tall beautiful
elder sister). Major [Desmond] Morton* dined with us last night & helped
to keep in countenance Mr Lennox Boyd who was surrounded by a
'clowder of (6) cats'....
   On Friday I took Sarah to London for the day in order to replenish her
wardrobe. We lunched at Selfridges & afterwards ... we went up on to the
roof.... It is a wonderful & really lovely sight – The whole of the vast
expanse is laid out in the most charming gardens with grass & fountains &
pillars & awnings.... If you want to see the wonderful panorama of
London you climb a little tower & then you behold an extraordinary sight.
The Crystal Palace is the most noticeable Landmark – Nearer, the tower of
the Roman Catholic Cathedral is more prominent than Big Ben & the
Victoria Tavern.... Everywhere great cranes pointing their skeleton fingers
to the sky & if you looked at their base you saw the old fashioned houses
being pulled down & great tall square biscuit tin buildings going up, a
new London in poor little old England – The new Grosvenor House flats
dominate the foreground. The same day driving by in a taxi I saw
Dorchester House[3] being demolished – the glorious cornice carved
garlands of fruit & flowers was coming down in sections. By the time you
are back every trace will have gone. 'Sic transit etc...... '
                                                              Your loving
                                                              Clemmie
...

[1] Alan Lennox-Boyd, later 1st Viscount Boyd of Merton (1904–83). Conservative MP, 1931–60.
Married (1938) Lady Patricia Guinness, daughter of the 2nd Earl of Iveagh. Served RNVR, 1940–3;
later held various government appointments.
[2] Nancy Mitford (1904–73), eldest of the six daughters of 2nd Baron Redesdale, CSC's cousin.
Married (1933) Peter Rodd; divorced 1958. Best-selling author (novels and historical biographies).
Légion d'honneur, 1972;. CBE, 1972.
[3] Dorchester House, Park Lane, designed by Lewis Vulliamy for the millionaire R. S. Holford and
completed in 1857. Demolished 1929 to make way for the Dorchester Hotel.

○ From WSC [typewritten]   CANADIAN PACIFIC RAILWAY COMPANY
1 September 1929   En route to Vancouver

My darling Clemmie,

I have some news which will interest Mary. First of all we have encountered <u>bears</u>. We were motoring along when suddenly at a turn in the road, bears were seen approaching at no great distance. It was in fact a she-bear attended by two large cubs. We stopped the motor alongside of them. The she-bear reared up on her hind legs in what looked at first a menacing attitude, but it turned out that she was not at all hostile, but was in fact only begging for biscuits, for which purpose she was accustomed to waylay travellers passing along this road. Alas we had no biscuits. . . .

Two days later Jack [Churchill*], riding out near Lake Louise, saw a much larger bear and one far less accustomed to human beings, but after rearing up on his hind legs he turned and galloped off at great speed, much to Jack's relief. . . .

After the meeting at Calgary, which was a great success, we motored eighty miles to Banff, . . . Here we rested for a day and then started on a three day motor tour of about three hundred miles. The first night we spent at Radium Hot Springs. . . . It is the same sort of water as that recently prescribed for you. We bathed night and morning in the open air swimming bath, which was about as hot as a real hot bath. . . . The second night we slept at Lake Emerald, after a fine drive along the sides of precipitous hills, across foaming torrents and through magnificent gorges. Lake Emerald has an extraordinary colour, more Turquoise or Jade than Emerald. . . . I painted three pictures which give a very inadequate idea of the great beauty of this spot.

The third day we went on to Lake Louise visiting en route the Yoho Valley. The scenery was most grand and awe inspiring. . . . In the evening we reached Lake Louise, where there is another enormous hotel. . . . Another green Lake of wide expanse surrounded by enormous precipices and with a wonderful line of snowclad peaks and glaciers in the centre. . . . That day . . . I spent in painting a picture which gives some idea of the colouring, and thereafter we all rode up to the glaciers. . . . No more perfect Alpine scene exists than this though it is but two hours' ride from a Ritz hotel. No wonder Lake Louise is becoming one of the most famous pleasure resorts on this continent!

Today we are making our last railway journey in the car. We are running at this moment along the Fraser River, a broad and winding torrent of clear Green water rolling, like us, down to the Pacific ocean. Tonight we reach Vancouver where alas I have to open an Exhibition and make a speech, . . . I have reluctantly consented to make another speech at Victoria [on Vancouver Island], as it is said to be the most English of all Canadian towns, with a large colony of retired officers of the Army and Navy whose pensions apparently go further here than at home. . . .

✍ Good bye my darling till Victoria when I will write again. I have just returned from opening the Exhibition – 2 speeches – 20,000 people touching loyalty & friendship. . . .

Always yr ever loving & devoted

W

. . .

○ From WSC [typewritten]
12 September 1929

New Place
Burlingame, California

My darling Clemmie,
  Since last I wrote we have been so constantly in movement that I have fallen behindhand in my account. Now there is so much to tell you that it would take almost a volume. . . .
  We reached Victoria in Vancouver Island (which is as big as England) by a beautiful voyage in a perfectly appointed ship through an archipelago of delicious islets. Victoria is English with a splendid climate thrown in. Sentiment, vegetation, manners, all revive the best in England.
  A splendid old Scotsman, Mr Randolph Bruce, who landed forty years ago with £1 in his pocket and is now very wealthy, is Lieutenant-Governor. He entertained us in royal state. We were played into and through dinner by a Highland Piper and were much petted by all parties. I addressed an enormous luncheon, 700 or 800 men, the cream of Victoria, for an hour. Thanks were proposed to me by the Dean – a foolish Cleric with Socialist leanings, who asked a number of cheeky questions and maundered on unduly, so I put up Randolph to reply and he, in a brief, admirably turned debating speech of five minutes completely turned the tables upon the Dean, to the delight of the audience and also to their amazement. . . . I could not have done it so neatly myself.

◇ From CSC
12 September 1929

Westerham

I WAS GLAD TO HEAR YOUR VOICE. I HOPE WE WILL HAVE MANY HAPPY RETURNS OF TODAY. [12 SEPTEMBER WAS THEIR WEDDING ANNIVERSARY.] PROF [LINDEMANN*] SEEMS ANXIOUS ABOUT RANDOLPH'S OXFORD CAREER IF HE DOES NOT RETURN IN TIME FOR TERM. TENDER LOVE.

CLEMMIE

○ From WSC
19 September [1929]

Santa Barbara

All vy Secret

My darling,
  I have tried to keep my tale up to date but we have moved far – continually and my account will have to follow this.

It was delightful hearing your voice at S. Francisco. I could picture you all gathered in the pantry? – & Maria – I heard her best of all. I wished I cd have leaned forward & kissed your dear lips – Alas 7,000 miles!

I am vy glad you are taking Venetia [Montagu*]'s house for the session. Do not hesitate to engage one or two extra servants. Now that we are in Opposition we must gather colleagues & M.P.s together a little at lunch & dinner. Also I have now a few business people who are of importance. We ought to be able to have lunches of 8–10 often, & dinners of the same size about twice a week. You shd have a staff equal to this.

Now my darling I must tell you that vy gt & extraordinary good fortune has attended me lately in finances. Sir Harry McGowan[1] asked me – rather earnestly – before I sailed whether he might if an opportunity came buy shares on my account without previous consultation. I replied that I could always find 2 or 3,000 £. I meant this as an investment limit i.e. buying the shares outright. He evidently took it as the limit to wh I was prepared to go in a <u>speculative</u> purchase on margin. Thus he operated on about ten times my usual scale, & as I told you made a profit on our joint account of £2,000 in Electric Bonds & Shares. With my approval he reinvested this in Columbia Gas & Electric & sold at a further profit of £3,000. He thus has £5,000 in hand on my account, & as he has profound sources of information about this vast American market, something else may crop up. Since I left office the following have come to hand as the fruits of fortune & labour; –

	£
Advance on £20,000 Marlborough	6,000
Profits by American investment before sailing	1,300
" " since	900
McGowan's profits	5,000
Rise of Sherwoods from 17/6 to 22/6	2,000
Article for Answers	225
" Jewish Papers	300
3 articles on Rosebery, Morley & Trotsky for Nash	1,350
Butterworth advance payment on Royalties due Oct. 30	1,700
Contract for articles on American tour (not yet done)	2,750
Proposed address to Economic Club of Worcester Massachusetts	300
	£21,825

So here we have really recovered in a few weeks a small fortune.... This 'mass of manoeuvre' is of the utmost importance, & must not be frittered away.

But apart from this there is money enough to make us comfortable & well-mounted in London this autumn, & you shd be able to do the nursery wing all right. Go on with yr plans & have it all ready for us to settle finally when I get back. Tender love my darling one – It is a relief to me to feel something behind me, & behind you all.

I will write later to you about our visit to Hearst[2].... As the result of a week's intimacy I like Hearst. He is a vy serious sure spoken man – & a trained politician of broad democratic & pacifist convictions. His papers sell 15 million copies a day, & his income is 4 million £ a year. His house is rudely described as Monte Carlo Casino on the top of the rock of Gibraltar – but it is better than this.

Mrs Hearst was there. I got on vy well with her. She was pleased with her visit to us[3]: [and] praised you a gt deal.... She altered all her plans in order to receive us. She has not got an easy rôle to play: but with 5 sons & a separate establishment some sort of arrangement is necessary & not impossible....

On Tuesd 17 we left the mountain ranch & Hearst took us all to Los Angeles – Here he runs the film world, has another palace & an unofficial wife, Marion Davies[4]. I thought 5 days of Hollywood wd be a little too much: so I accepted Mr McAdoo's invitation to stay at his house at <u>Santa Barbara</u> (<u>here</u>) for 2 days. He was the democratic candidate for the Presidency against Coolidge in 1925, & S[ecretary] of S[tate] during the war under Wilson. His wife – a charming woman – is President Wilson's daughter.... They mounted their country house especially for us <u>for two days</u> or two weeks if we had the time – and then disappeared. So we are all alone. Tomorrow we return to Los Angeles. I could write for hours – but must close now – with tenderest love my darling one from your devoted

W

...

[1] Sir Harry McGowan (1874–1961), cr. 1st Baron McGowan, 1937. Industrialist. Later Chairman of Imperial Chemical Industries (1930–50).
[2] William Randolph Hearst (1863–1951), US newspaper proprietor and art collector. Renowned for his introduction of banner headlines, lavish use of illustrations, and sensationalist journalism. His ranch at San Simeon, California, housed a collection of medieval and Renaissance art and furniture. He was said to be the model for Citizen Kane in Orson Welles's film (*Citizen Kane*, 1941).
[3] The Hearsts had visited Chartwell in September 1928.
[4] Marion Davies (1900–61), long-time mistress of Hearst. Started her professional dancing career with the Ziegfeld Follies in 1918. Subsequently appeared in many films.

O From WSC   Barstow
29 September [1929]

My darling Clemmie,

... We are travelling across the Californian desert in Mr Schwab's [railway] car, & we have stopped for 2 hours at this oasis. We have left the train for a bath in the hotel, & as it is so nice & cool I will write you a few of the things it is wiser not to dictate.

Hearst was most interesting to meet, & I got to like him – a grave simple child – with no doubt a nasty temper – playing with the most costly toys. A vast income always overspent: Ceaseless building & collecting not vy discriminatingly works of art: two magnificent establishments, two charming wives; complete indifference to public opinion, a strong liberal & democratic outlook, a 15 million daily circulation, oriental hospitalities, extreme personal courtesy (to us at any rate) & the appearance of a Quaker elder – or perhaps better Mormon elder.

I told you about Mrs H. (the official) & how agreeable she made herself. She is going to give me a dinner in N.Y. & look after the boys on their way through. At Los Angeles (hard g) we passed into the domain of Marion Davies; & were all charmed by her. She is not strikingly beautiful nor impressive in any way. But her personality is most attractive; naive childlike, bon enfant. She works all day at her films & retires to her palace on the ocean to bathe & entertain in the evenings. She asked us to use her house as if it was our own. But we tasted its comforts & luxuries only sparingly, spending two nights there after enormous dinner parties in our honour. We lunched frequently at her bungalow in the film works – a little Italian chapel sort of building vy elegant where Hearst spends the day directing his newspapers on the telephone, & wrestling with his private Ch. of the Excheq – a harassed functionary who is constantly compelled to find money & threatens resignation daily.

We made gt friends with Charlie Chaplin[1]. You cd not help liking him. The boys were fascinated by him. He is a marvellous comedian – bolshy in politics – delightful in conversation. He acted his new film for us in a wonderful way. It is to be his gt attempt to prove that the silent drama or pantomime is superior to the new talkies. Certainly if pathos & wit still count for anything it ought to win an easy victory.

I stayed in the main at the Biltmore hotel – wh is the last word in hotels ... Mr Page who obtained 'the honour' of entertaining us – a hearty Banker – refused to allow us to pay anything.... I met all the leading people & have heard on every side that my speech & talks (to circles of ten or twelve) have given much pleasure.... I gave a dinner & a lunch to the leading men I liked the best, mostly British born, & all keenly pro-England. (With much difficulty I succeeded in extracting the cost of these meals from the Bill & paying them myself.)... These Californian swells do not of course know Hearst. He dwells apart. The first time they had ever come in contact with him or the film world was at the luncheon he gave to me. They regard him as the Devil. But when they heard him speak in friendly terms about England, they all said how right I had been to stay with him & praised the good work....

We went on Sunday in a yacht to Catalina island 25 miles away. We had only one hour there. People go for weeks & months without catching a swordfish – so they all said it was quite useless my going out in the fishing boat wh had been provided. However I went out & of course I caught a monster in 20 minutes!

I have also made friends with Mr Van Antwerp & his wife. He is ... a gt friend of England [and] a reader of all my books – quite an old fashioned figure – He is going to look after some of my money for me. His [stockbroking] firm have the best information about the American Market & I have opened an account with them in wh I have placed £3,000. He will manipulate it with the best possible chances of success. All this looks vy confiding – but I am sure it will prove wise.

Now I have to rush for my train wh is just off.

Goodbye my sweetest Clemmie
With tender love from your devoted
W

---

[1] Charlie Chaplin (1899–1977), British-born film actor and director, who became world-famous in silent films as a tramp with clipped moustache, bowler hat and cane. In 1943 married as his fourth wife Oona O'Neill, daughter of Eugene O'Neill, Irish playwright. Politically suspect in USA under McCarthy anti-Communist witch-hunt of the 1950s, he settled in Switzerland. Knighted, 1975. The film referred to by WSC was probably *City Lights* (1931).

○ From CSC   Chartwell
30 September [1929]

My darling

This afternoon, Mr Vickers[1] rang me up to tell me that on Saturday he sails for New York & that he expects to see you very soon after his arrival; so I am entrusting him with this letter.

I was thrilled last week to see that you had landed a gigantic fish. How you must have enjoyed the excitement of it....

Here all has been very peaceful and quiet – The weather has been glorious. One perfect sunny day after another. Goonie has been here & her pretty little Clarissa [nine], also Peregrine [sixteen] – (he & Sarah [nearly fifteen] seem more wrapped up in each other than ever). Mr Buchan Hepburn[2] came down for one night.

I think he is rather a remarkable young man & very agreeable. Horatia Seymour[3] came for 10 days – She is a charming & restful guest. Lord Berners came for a week-end & also 'the Nellinita' – I do hope she is not up to any more mischief....

At the end of this week Diana & I start for Italy, first to stay with Alice Keppel & then with the Grahams in Rome. We had intended to start sooner, but the weather has been so glorious that I could not tear myself away....

Mary has become a school-girl! Every morning, arrayed in a Blue tunic, white shirt & scarlet girdle Moppet [Whyte*] motors her to a little local school[4] where she is being taught to read & count....

Tender Love my Darling. The political situation here seems to me unpromising, not to say bleak – Poor Mrs Neville Chamberlain has had her tonsils out. She wrote me a nervous letter before, asking innumerable questions.

Your loving
Clemmie

[1] Horace Cecil Vickers (1882–1944), WSC's stockbroker. Founder and senior partner of Vickers Da Costa, in which Jack Churchill was a partner.
[2] Patrick Buchan-Hepburn, later 1st Baron Hailes (1901–74). WSC's Private Secretary, 1929–30. Conservative MP, 1931–57; Government Chief Whip, 1951–5; Minister of Works, 1955–7. Governor-General of the West Indies, 1958–62.
[3] Horatia Seymour, daughter of Horace Seymour (Gladstone's Private Secretary, 1880–5). A little older than CSC, with whom her lifelong friendship began in the early 1900s. She was one of CSC's bridesmaids. Very beautiful and intelligent; a strong Liberal; she never married. Died 1966.
[4] Irwin House, Limpsfield, Surrey. I seem to have been very late in starting formal education at seven years old.

The 'Churchill Troupe', as Winston referred to them, arrived in New York on 6 October, and stayed with Bernard Baruch. Winston was constantly occupied with business matters and literary plans. Randolph and Johnnie left on 9 October to return to Oxford. On 18 October Winston cabled Clementine just before setting out for a tour of some of the most famous battlefields of the American Civil War.

◇ From WSC   New York
18 October 1929

AM VERY REMISS WRITING. MUCH PRESSED BUSINESS. EVERYTHING CONTINUES SATISFACTORY.
ARRANGED TWENTY-TWO NEW ARTICLES IN WEEKLIES ALL MATURING BEFORE JUNE ON USUAL
TERMS. MONTHLIES IN ADDITION ALL INVOLVING HEAVY WORK ON RETURN. GOOD TALK
MACDONALD[1]. THANK DIANA CHARMING LETTER. HOPE ITALY AGREEABLE. LOOKING FORWARD MUCH
TO RETURN NOVEMBER FIFTH. WE WILL PLAN WING TOGETHER. ... START TONIGHT WASHINGTON,
RICHMOND, PHILADELPHIA, RETURNING NOVEMBER TWENTY-FOURTH. CABLE FULL WEEKEND
LETTER. TENDER LOVE. ADDRESS BARUCH NEW YORK

                                                                        W

[1] The Prime Minister, Ramsay MacDonald (see p. 275 n. 1), celebrated his 63rd birthday while in
New York. WSC called to congratulate him.

Winston returned to New York on 24 October – the day which came to be known as 'Black Thursday', when the New York stock market collapsed, precipitating the 'great crash' of 29 October.

During his Canadian–American journeyings Winston had speculated in the New York stock market (we have had glimpses in his letters): in the débâcle his losses were over £10,000 (£200,000 in 1990 values).

On 30 October he sailed for home. Clementine met him off the boat train on 5 November; there and then, on the platform, he blurted out his bad news.

As they had made firm arrangements to rent Venetia Montagu's* house (62 Onslow Gardens, SW7) in November and December, they stuck to plans. But for the next year or two they often stayed at the Goring Hotel off Grosvenor Gardens, SW1, or rented furnished houses for a few months at a time.

That winter of 1929 Chartwell was run down to a low ebb: the big house was dust-sheeted, only the study being left open so that Winston could work there. The charming small house, Wellstreet Cottage (which he had been building, and had been intended for a butler), now became our 'slump' haven. Nana Whyte* and I took up our residence there, and my parents came down at weekends: I remember it all being very cosy.

Chapter XV

'NOT WANTED ON VOYAGE'

Nineteen-thirty was largely a stay-at-home year for Winston and Clementine, and there are no letters between them to hand.

In 1930 and 1931 the political question which loomed largest was India. While Winston was still in America in 1929, Baldwin and the Conservative Shadow Cabinet agreed to support the Labour Government policy – to grant Dominion status to India[1]. Churchill strongly disagreed with this policy. A further cause for his growing alienation from the Tory party was the raising once more, as a result of the economic situation, of the thorny question of Protection – the very issue over which he had left the Tories and joined the Liberals some twenty-five years before. It was, however, on the Indian question that Churchill resigned from Baldwin's 'Business Committee' (Shadow Cabinet) on 27 January 1931, thereby sundering his association with the Conservative Front Bench.

Randolph, now nineteen, and about halfway through his time at Oxford, received a tempting offer to make a lecture tour in the United States, which he accepted – despite earnest attempts by his father and his Oxford mentors to dissuade him. In October 1930 he had left Oxford, having been given a term's leave: in the event he never returned to his university studies.

On 21 December, Clementine wrote to him:

I have had an inspiration. Papa very kindly has offered me a tiny car as a combined Christmas & Birthday present. But I thought if you liked it I would spend the money on paying you & New York a flying visit?

Shall I hop on to a boat one day at the end of January or beginning of February & come to New York for a week? . . . I should enjoy it so much.

. . . I should love to come and hear you lecture. I feel very nervous & excited about the idea. Papa is amused & rather outraged at the idea of me going to America without him! But I think I should prefer to go alone & not as the appendage of a distinguished man![2]

On receiving her son's enthusiastic reply Clementine duly made her arrangements, and on 8 February she embarked on the SS *Europa*, a German liner bound for New York.

[1] Under which Britain would continue to appoint a Viceroy and control military and defence matters. Indians at both national and provincial levels would, in the space of a few years, run their own affairs.
[2] Quoted from Winston S. Churchill, *His Father's Son: The Life of Randolph S. Churchill*, 1996, p. 75.

○ From CSC   D. 'EUROPA'
12 February 1931

My Darling Winston

We are 24 hours late owing to fogs & gale – But everyone says it is a comfort to have a careful Captain who goes slow when there is a fog – I thought I saw an iceberg just now but was unable to get expert opinion on the subject. If this was a smaller ship I might have been ill, but this beautiful monster ploughs thro' everything. . . .

I really do not think we must ever fight the Germans again – I'm sure they would win – Really we didn't beat them in 1918 – They were just stifled by numbers. This ship is just a huge piece of propaganda – The Captain is a tremendous fellow with a beard & whiskers, rather Tirpitz[1] like – I wonder what <u>he</u> did in the Great War? Sank the Lusitania[2] perhaps? I sit next to him at his Table, but I don't dare to ask him – There is a Baroness Hindenburg on his other side (a cousin of the great man) on her way to lecture in America on Hindenburg[3] & modern Germany. . . .

You must forgive this bad writing but the ship is rocking like fun.

Feb: 13<u>th</u> Friday. . . . There is the most lovely music every day 3 times, after luncheon, at tea time & after dinner – I have now had time to examine my fellow passengers – They are nearly all German American Jews of the most porcine description like Hoggenheimer who you remember remarked 'I'm not rude, I'm rich' – I now understand American anti-semitic prejudice – I have never seen Jews like this in England. . . .

. . . Yesterday Baroness Hindenburg delivered her lecture (accompanied by a film) on pre-war, war, & Modern Germany – It was dreary & monotonous & I crept out in the dark – the first sign of German incompetence I have seen – But perhaps it's on purpose to lull us into security. It certainly put everyone to sleep who sat it out – It ends up shewing Hindenburg feeding his chickens! . . .

Soon I shall be seeing Randolph. The idea thrills me & excites me more than I can say. I will cable you & write as soon as I have had a long talk with him.

Darling Winston I love you very much – I hope you are well and happy but that you miss me a little – I hope political matters will gradually shape themselves as you wish. I believe they will – I am completely starved for news. The little Daily Gazette they issue every day on board has only German & American news. The only English events they have published in one week is Lord Bessborough's[4] appointment to Canada & the birth of twins in Holloway Gaol to Mrs Wise the Murderess.

My Dear Love to all & will you let Mrs Pearman[5] copy suitable portions of this letter & send them to Sarah[6] at Broadstairs & Diana[7] in London. Kiss my only stay at Home child Mary tenderly for me.

Your devoted
Clemmie

---

[1] Alfred Friedrich von Tirpitz (1849–1930), German admiral; planner of the First World War U-boat campaign.
[2] The British liner *Lusitania*, sunk by the Germans off the south coast of Ireland, 7 May 1915, with a loss of 1,198 lives.
[3] Field Marshal Paul von Hindenburg (1847–1934), German soldier and statesman. Supreme commander during First World War; President of Germany, 1925–33.

[4] Vere Brabazon Ponsonby, 9th Earl of Bessborough (1880–1956), who had just been appointed Governor-General of Canada.
[5] Violet Pearman (1901–41), WSC's Principal Private Secretary from November 1929 until 1938, when she was forced to retire through ill-health; although she continued to work part-time. She died March 1941, aged 40.
[6] Sarah (16) was in her last year at North Foreland Lodge, Broadstairs, Kent.
[7] Diana (21) was studying at the Royal Academy of Dramatic Art (RADA) in London.

The next letter from Clementine reveals what had been at least part of her reason for proposing her visit to Randolph: they had evidently heard rumours concerning Randolph's attachment to 'a young lady from Cleveland, Ohio'.

O From CSC   FLORIDA SPECIAL
Tuesday 17 February [1931]   New York–Palm Beach–Miami
                                             In the train on the way to Palm Beach

My Darling – I have much to tell you.
    The Europa docked early on Saturday & before 8 Randolph was on board looking splendid and beaming – His joy at seeing me was really sweet & I felt much moved – You were right in your conjecture that lecturing had not during these last 4 months completely monopolised his thoughts. Before we had been together 2 hours Randolph told me that he loved a young lady from Cleveland Ohio, & that he intends to marry her if he can persuade her to do so. He has already asked her several times & been put off, but last week she became more favourable to the idea & said that if she liked me & I liked her & she liked you, & you liked her, she might consider the question –
    I have met her & she approves of me ... She is coming to England in June when you & she will have the opportunity of sizing each other up.
    I will now tell you what she is like to look at & what I have been able ... to discover about her & her antecedents – She is Miss Katharine [Kay] Halle* & she is 27 years of age. Her Father is a Jew – (but not Mrs Halle). He owns a big Department Store in Cleveland, & is a rich man – He has one son & 4 daughters of whom Katharine is the eldest. Last night Mr Baruch rang me up & said that as a result of his secret enquiries he found that the Halles were a solid respectable family & that the children had been well brought up – Now her appearance. She is tall with a beautiful figure, a sensible intelligent face, not pretty – A clear & lovely complexion fair hair, good hands. She is (unlike the Americans one usually meets) not at all cosmopolitan. She seems earnest in her outlook & a little provincial in her manner.... I have had several long talks with Randolph about it all. I pointed out the great difference of age – 8 years – He said a younger woman would bore him & that he felt the need of a wife who would not allow him to bully her & overbear her – I asked him how he was going to keep her & he said that he supposed you would be willing to continue his allowance of £400 a year, that he was sure he could make at least £1,000 a year & that he thought she had some money of her own say £1,000 a

year – I pointed out that in 4 months since he has left home he has consumed <u>alone</u> £1,000, which is at the rate of £3,000 a year for one person – He replied that he was sure he could earn enough to keep 2 people & that being married would be an incentive to trying hard. I said I thought he was too young to marry – He said he couldn't live without women in his life, that he objected to prostitutes, that affairs with married women might land him in the Divorce Court, & that affairs with young girls might land him on the altar steps with the wrong one, that he was desperately lonely, that he must have a companion & that if he could wear down Miss Halle's objections he would certainly marry her. I said 'When?' – And he said 'next October'.

It seems strange, but I do not think if she is really a nice woman that it would be entirely a bad thing – Anyhow it would be madness to go against the idea as I think he might try & rush into it. Much may happen before next October & Miss Halle may not come up to the scratch. She is I think very fond of Randolph but rather flustered & worried.[1]

The newspapers have got hold of the rumour. But I have managed to avoid the reporters. Several paragraphs have appeared saying that I have arrived from England to put a stop to the whole thing – It <u>is</u> an odd coincidence that I should have arrived the very day the report got into all the papers.

Now my other information will be flat after this startling piece of news – I heard Randolph lecture on Sunday to a crowded & thrilled audience – Frankly it was not at <u>all</u> good, & it is <u>very naughty</u> of him, becos' if he would only take a little trouble it could be very good indeed. But he finds it will go down with the majority, so he won't take pains & this is a great pity.... He delivers the same lecture everywhere, so he really ought to have got it good by now. There are some extremely funny and even witty things in it, & he has a most fascinating manner & delivery & the audience seemed spell-bound – but I think it was his looks & his colossal cheek chiefly!

He is a darling – He has quite captivated me – He is a most sweet companion & he seems to enjoy my company quite as much as that of Miss Halle. I am enjoying myself enormously – It is quite like a honeymoon. When Randolph asked the negro attendant to open the communicating door between his compartment & 'my Mother's' he grinned & said – 'All right I'll open the door & then you can go & sleep in there or she can come & sleep in here' –

Randolph is impatient & hungry for luncheon so no more –

Tender Love
Clemmie
& also from Randolph

[1] In the event Randolph and Kay Halle never married, but they remained devoted friends.

○ From WSC [typewritten]   Chartwell
26 February 1931

My darling One,
    Your letter from the ship reached me last Saturday.... I am looking
forward greatly to hearing what happened when you landed, and all about
Randolph, his lectures, his finances, his alleged engagement....
    Since I last wrote I met the constituency in full force at Winchester
House. It was loving, ardent and unanimous. I will send you the report
from the Daily Mail verbatim of the speech. There is no doubt that the
whole spirit of the Conservative party is with me, and that much of their
dissatisfaction with S.B. [Stanley Baldwin] turns itself into favour with me.
The next day I strolled into the quarterly Meeting of the National Union [of
the Conservative Party]. I have never hitherto ventured onto this highly
orthodox Central Office ground, and expect six weeks ago[1] I should have
had a very cool welcome. As it was they received me with unequalled
acclamation, suspending their standing orders and altered their luncheon
hour so as to pass unanimously a motion calling for firm government in
India.... Rothermere has now, I think, definitely settled down to a solid
campaign in my interest. All his papers in every part of the country are
writing eulogistic articles and friendly paragraphs, and the Daily Mail and
Evening News are overdoing their support....
    Last night we had Charlie Chaplin to dinner. Jack [Churchill*] and
Johnnie came from London and slept the night. Bracken* and Boothby[2]
motored down for dinner. Mary [nine and a half] stayed up by special
arrangement and seemed absolutely thrilled by Charlie. He has been
wonderfully received in this country and treated with far more honour
than any Royalty. He made himself most agreeable, and with much good
nature performed various droll tricks. I am sorry not to be able to go to his
première [*City Lights*] on Friday, but the Speaker has commanded me to
his levée. Diana also came to dinner looking very pretty, and got on very
well with the great man....
    It is astonishing looking back over the last six weeks what a change has
been brought in my position. Every speech that I have made, and step that
I have taken has been well received beyond all expectation. The turning
points were the first Indian speech and my separation from the Shadow
Cabinet. Anything may happen now if opinion has time to develop. If not
I shall be quite happy.
    ✍ I am hoping to get another letter from you vy soon my darling. I am
well here & happy – but of course the articles & speeches make gt
demands on one's mind. There is always the need for exertion. Perhaps it
is healthy. Markets are a little better. The taxes are awful. Tender love & a
thousand kisses.

                                        Ever your loving & devoted
                                                    W
                                                    . . .

[1] Before his resignation from the Shadow Cabinet.
[2] Robert Boothby (1900–86), cr. life peer, 1958. Conservative MP, 1924–58; Principal Private
Secretary to WSC (as Chancellor of Exchequer), 1926–9.

O From CSC   Carlton Hotel
Sunday 1 March [1931]   Washington

My Darling

I find I have not written to you for a whole week but while at Palm Beach there was really very little to tell you.

The weather there was most disappointing – cold windy & the last 2 days deluges of tropical but nevertheless chilly rain. . . .

Yesterday we lunched at the British Embassy, a beautiful red brick building by Lutyens which you had to pay for when you were at the Exchequer – I remember you were rather annoyed at the expense. . . .

To-day we lunch with Mrs Longworth (Alice Roosevelt that was)[1]. I am looking forward to this as I'm told she is extremely amusing. . . .

Later in the day

We have just returned from lunching with Mrs Longworth. She is a most delightful woman & was very nice to us both – It was an enormous luncheon party & I found it difficult to identify the people. Viola Tree[2] was there. She is acting here to-night & we are going to see her & sup with her afterwards . . .

Private I think there is a froideur on Mr Baruch's part towards Randolph, caused I imagine by the Rabbit having a flirtation with a lady whom Mr Baruch considers as his property – Randolph thinks Mr Baruch had them followed!! Anyhow he knows all that happened – He never shewed the flicker of an eyelid to Randolph or me but he complained to the Lady who reported the matter to Randolph – She had been very indiscreet, not to say disloyal, & described in minute detail all her transactions physical & financial with Mr B. I will tell you the rest when we meet, meanwhile please burn this portion of my letter & please do not, unless the Rabbit confides in you, tell him that I have told you –

Mr Baruch promised to meet us here & make our visit pleasant but he did not turn up – in fact he rather let us down – He is a curious old Boy rather revengeful – Randolph describes him in Yankee slang as a 'cagey old Bird'. . . .

Tender Love from
Clemmie

[1] Mrs Alice Longworth (1884–1980), daughter of Theodore Roosevelt, 26th President of the USA (d. 1919). Married Nicholas Longworth, 1906. Columnist, *Ladies' Home Journal*; member of Republican National Committee, 1932.
[2] Viola Tree (1844–1938), actress daughter of actor-manager Sir Herbert Beerbohm Tree (1853–1917). In 1912 she married Alan Parsons (1887–1933), civil servant, and later dramatic critic and columnist.

O From CSC   The Ambassador
Monday [Thursday] 5 March [1931]   New York

My Darling, Here we are (since the day before yesterday) back in New York which is Randolph's spiritual home! I must say I love it too – We are most comfortable in this sumptuous hotel, & we have been taken in by the kind proprietor at half price becos' the Scotch Kat wanted to go to a cheaper hotel, & he said he could not bear to lose us!...

... Food is unbelievably expensive & incredibly nasty except at one or two cafés, but luckily we are asked out. I have been lent a sumptuous Rolls Royce by a Mr Mortimer Schiff whom I'm afraid I do not terribly like – However it is very obliging of him....

I wrote to you last from Washington – We spent another day there & lunched again with Mrs Longworth this time at the Senate – She is almost the only woman with a marked personality I have met so far; the others I've seen are just clothes pegs & painted masks, <u>very</u> lovely, but rather inane & dull....

On arriving Tuesday we went to the most entertaining & most improper play called 'The Greeks had a word for it'. The word is <u>hetaira</u>. Is that how you spell it? Any how it's the Greek word for tart. The acting over here is I think supreme in comedy & Revues – Yesterday we went to 'City Lights' – I wish I knew Charlie Chaplin. He is a great man, more of a tragedian than a comedian. What a condemnation too of the 'Talkies'!

Last night I dined with Mrs Cornelius Vanderbilt & went to the Opera – She talked about F.E. [Smith*/Birkenhead][1] She seemed to have been very fond of him.

My Darling I was so glad to get your dear letter ... It sent a warm thrill thro' my heart – I'm bird happy here, but I wish I was at your side to enjoy with you enjoying watching your Barometer steadily rise – I watch it all from here every shoot up, every flicker –

Tender Love from
Your
Clemmie

I can see 18 sky-scrapers from my windows – They ought not to be called by such an ugly name – I think they are quite beautiful

[1] F. E. Smith, 1st Earl of Birkenhead, had died on 30 September 1930, aged 58. His death was a great grief to WSC.

Clementine returned home in early April 1931.

The American Great Crash of 1929 had long-term effects: in Britain, by May 1931 unemployment had risen to 2.5 million, and by July the situation was so dire that foreign investors panicked and there was a run on gold. Ramsay MacDonald's Government resigned in August, but MacDonald immediately formed a National Government of Labour, Conservative and Liberal ministers. Emergency measures were introduced, and the General Election of 27 October 1931 resulted in a landslide majority for the Conservatives, who won 473 seats: MacDonald remained as Prime Minister.

At Epping Churchill nearly doubled his majority, but his resignation from Stanley Baldwin's Shadow Cabinet (in January 1931) precluded his inclusion in the new Government.

Winston now therefore addressed himself to his own affairs. On 2 November the last volume of his war memoirs, *The World Crisis, The Eastern Front*, was published, and a month later he set out for the United States to undertake a strenuous tour of forty lectures, with the intention of recouping some of his 1929 financial losses.

Winston, Clementine and Diana embarked in the *Europa* on 5 December, reaching New York on the eleventh. Two evenings later, Winston was knocked down by a car while crossing Fifth Avenue on his way to visit Bernard Baruch. He suffered severe shock and bruising, and developed pleurisy; but for the fact that he had been wearing a heavy fur-lined over-coat, he might well have been killed. He was in hospital, or in bed at his hotel, until after Christmas, when Clementine and Diana took him to Nassau, in the Bahamas, to convalesce.

This was a low moment for Winston: still suffering from severe pain in his arms and shoulders from the accident, he brooded over his losses in the Great Crash, and over the diminution of his political power.

Nevertheless he soon galvanized himself into action, and, returning to New York at the end of January 1932, resumed his lecture tour. During February he travelled widely in the United States, speaking every day in a different place.

Once Clementine was confident Winston could sustain the pace and strain of the tour, she embarked in RMS *Berengaria* for home.

○ From CSC   Cunard RMS 'BERENGARIA'
Thursday 18 February [1932]

My Darling
    This is a very nice boat – old but comfortable & with most kind & attentive stewards.
    Yesterday I was moved from my very comfortable cabin to a 'sumptuous suite'. At first I was not sure that I did not prefer my original cosy quarters – But as it was meant as a compliment, I migrated, & now my paws are re-buttered.... All I need is a little company as this splendour is a little lonely....
    I have made some inroad into the book on Stonewall Jackson[1] lent me by Sir Ronald Lindsay[2]. It is extremely long, some 800 pages & not very human, being chiefly about military strategy....
    You will soon be sailing [for home] when you get this letter which is going to be terribly long!

Friday the 19th
    ... I am getting on with Stonewall Jackson – How I should like to see the Shenandoah Valley[3]. Is it, I wonder, as beautiful as its name. The book is full of abuse of politicians who try to interfere with Generals in the field – (Ahem!) The author is very cross with Lincoln & also with the Southern President, a Mr Davis, also Mr Benjamin the Secretary of State for War for the South.
    By the way – no more type-written letters please or I shall have to copy Martha Washington & destroy them![4]

Saturday the 20 th
We are well over the half-way line now – I have telegraphed to Moppet [Whyte*] to ask her to bring Mary to Southampton to meet me on Tuesday.

We have got $60.000.000 worth of gold on board in little barrels. It is being met at Cherbourg by officials of the Banque de France & being conveyed to Paris under an armed guard (I wonder if I could abstract one very small barrel?)...

We are also carrying poor Edgar Wallace[5] home – He died in California – The crew are much upset that there will be no more thrillers from his pen. ...

Monday the 22 nd
My solitary voyage is nearly over – It is beautifully calm now but we have had 2 rough days & 2 rougher nights. I have found a good back-gammon opponent in Major Courtauld[6] –

Tender Love my Darling to you both – I hope for news of you

Your
Clemmie

This will be posted at Cherbourg.

[1] Thomas Jonathan ('Stonewall') Jackson (1824–63), Confederate general in the American Civil War. The book was G. F. R. Henderson, *Stonewall Jackson and the American Civil War*, 1898.
[2] Sir Ronald Lindsay (1877–1945), diplomat. Ambassador at Washington, 1930–9.
[3] The scene of some of Jackson's greatest military exploits (1862).
[4] Martha Washington (1732–1802), widow of George Washington (1732–99), secretly burned all his letters to her shortly before her own death.
[5] Edgar Wallace (1875–1932), English author famed for his prolific output of crime novels and plays. He died on 10 February 1932.
[6] Maj. John Sewell Courtauld (1880–1942), Unionist MP for Chichester since 1924.

Clementine arrived back in England on 23 February 1932, and nearly a month later Winston followed her, having completed his lecture tour.

There is now a gap of nearly two years in their correspondence: Winston and Clementine were leading their busy lives, between London[1] and Chartwell, and holidaying together.

Diana completed five terms at the Royal Academy of Dramatic Art (RADA), but her acting career never 'took off'. In December 1932 she married John Bailey[2], son of Winston's old South African friend, Sir Abe Bailey. The marriage was fated not to last: they would be divorced in 1935. Randolph had become a journalist and was contracted to write a series of articles for the *Sunday Graphic* and a regular weekly column for the *Sunday Dispatch* (both Rothermere papers). In 1931 and 1932 Sarah was at a 'finishing school' in Paris run by les mesdemoiselles Ozanne. She made her official debut, and was presented at Court in 1933. I was a day girl at the Manor House School, Limpsfield.

The India controversy was still at its height, but now a darker cloud was gathering – and on a nearer horizon. In March 1932, in the Presidential Election in Germany, Adolf Hitler[3] and his National Socialist Party polled 40 per cent of the total vote. A second election in April was needed to confirm the re-election of Field Marshal von Hindenburg. In July, elections for the

Reichstag made the National Socialists the largest political party in Germany.

At Westminster in May, despite the meteoric rise of Hitler, who vociferously urged revision of treaties and German rearmament, the Foreign Secretary, Sir John Simon, pressed the case for speedy and comprehensive disarmament.[4] In the debate, Churchill sounded a note of caution.

January 1933 opened on a gloomy economic and social note: unemployment in Britain peaked at three million. On 30 January Hitler came to power as Chancellor of the German Reich. On 14 October Germany withdrew from the re-convened Disarmament Conference, and on 21 October she left the League of Nations. Since March Churchill had been attacking disarmament proposals which would give Germany parity with France, and warning of Britain's inadequate defences.

For the first 'leg' of the 1934 summer holidays, Winston and Clementine had different plans. In August Winston went to stay with their old friend Maxine Elliott* on the Riviera[5]. Clementine preferred to make a Scottish plan, taking Sarah and myself with her, while Winston had Randolph for company. He was working hard on the third volume of *Marlborough* (the second volume was published in October 1934).

On 12 September 1933 Winston and Clementine celebrated their Silver Wedding.

[1] In 1932 the Churchills acquired a long lease on a top-floor maisonette, No. 11 Morpeth Mansions, near Victoria. This would be their London home until the outbreak of war in 1939.
[2] Later Sir John Milner Bailey, 2nd Bt (1900–46).
[3] Adolf Hitler (1889–1945), German Nazi dictator, born in Austria. Leader (Führer) of Nazi party from 1921. Wrote his 'credo', *Mein Kampf*, 2 vols, 1925, 1927. Chancellor of German Reich from 30 January 1933. Succeeded Hindenburg as head of state, 2 August 1934.
[4] The World Disarmament Conference had convened in Geneva in February 1932.
[5] After selling Hartsbourne, where the Churchills had often stayed, in 1923 Maxine had moved to Paris. In 1930 she built the Château de l'Horizon, near Cannes, where she lived and entertained lavishly for the last ten years of her life.

○ From WSC   Château de l'Horizon
22 August 1934   Golfe-Juan (A.M.)

Darling Clemmie,

A week yesterday I started. It is incredible how long it seems compared with Chartwell. I have enjoyed it vy much & have painted a gt deal, & now finally finished with all my proofs of Vol. II. I hope Miss Hamblin* has been sending them to you. We are still a tiny party.... Randolph has been a gt success. His manners are the subject of highly favourable comment, and he has been vy nice to everyone. Diana comes here on the 25th. Maxine was delighted to have her as well as R & me. The Prof [Lindemann*] arrives the 28th & we shall then motor by 5 stages to Paris, I painting on the way as occasion serves.

You will by now have made your proposals to Walter [Lord Moyne][1] – I expect. We seemed from your letter to be in perfect accord upon the arrangements....

I was disgusted by the D.M. [*Daily Mail*]'s boosting of Hitler. R[othermere] is sincerely pacifist. He wants us to be vy strongly armed and frightfully obsequious at the same time. Thus he hopes to avoid seeing another war. Anyhow it is a more practical attitude than our socialist politicians. They wish us to remain disarmed & exceedingly abusive.

I was glad that so many had the courage to vote against making that gangster [Hitler] autocrat for life.[2]

Tender love my sweetest pussy from your ever devoted husband

W

...

[1] CSC had received an invitation for them both from Lord Moyne (Walter Guinness: see p. 332 n. 3) to go on one of two cruises in his steam yacht *Rosaura*. WSC/CSC's joint choice was for the Eastern Mediterranean voyage.
[2] In a vote taken in Germany on 19 August 1934 to regularize Hitler's position both as Chancellor and (following Hindenburg's death on 2 August) as President, 7 million out of 45.5 million votes had been cast against Hitler.

○ From CSC
22 August [1934]

Gosford House[1]
Longniddry, East Lothian

My Darling Winston

First I must tell you how engrossed & thrilled I am with your Book.

I have read but eleven chapters (I am a slow & laborious but painstaking reader!) but although the great events are still to come, you prepare the reader for them by the statue you are chiselling of Marlborough –

I feel I know him now – No wonder Sarah [his wife] loved him & him alone. He really is Olympian – One marvels at his patience & understanding. . . .

I am very happy here, & so I think is Sarah. Her little dog is sweet & not much 'Trouble'![2]

I love to think of you painting sparkling sun-lit scenes – Are you keeping them cool & pale à la [William] Nicholson*? . . .

Give my love to the Rabbit. I hope he is well. . . .

Your loving
Clemmie

[1] One of the homes of the 11th Earl of Wemyss (1857–1937) and his wife Mary Wyndham (m. 1883); they had turned Gosford House into a 'country hotel'.
[2] Sarah's dog, given her by a beau, was a chocolate spaniel called (not without reason) Trouble.

○ From WSC
25 August 1934

Château de l'Horizon

My darling,

If the first week seemed long the second has flown. In a few days we start our journey home. I have painted four pictures and begun another. I think you will be surprised by them. I have done a new one of the Notre Dame de Vie, à la [William] Nicholson* – vy luminous. If you like it, it shall be for yr bedroom at the Flat instead of another. It is the best I think I have yet done. . . .

Yesterday I had a most satisfactory proposal from George Riddell[1] – to write 30–35,000 words of my Life to date for the News of the World: price £3,000–3,500. This will be vy easy to do, and it makes next year as good as this. . . .

I hope to pay off a good many bills at the end of this year, & next we really ought to be able to save a substantial sum.

But there is a frightful lot of work ahead. . . .

I shall bring my section of the family home to you on the 4th. Till then we shall be thinking of you Sarah & Mary – the junior half with tender love.

I am so glad it is fixed up with Walter [Moyne]. It wd be terrible to see the D'Iles [Dardanelles]. God never meant to allow that, or let the human race off so cheaply.

Always yr ever loving & devoted husband
W

[1] George Riddell (1865-1934), Chairman, *News of the World*, from 1903. Knighted, 1909; cr. Baron, 1920.

O From CSC   Gosford House
26 August [1934]

My Darling

I have now read XXI Chapters of the Book & am well past Blenheim.

I really think it surpasses the 1st Volume. I hope you are very happy & proud about it. . . .

I have also been reading Randolph in the [Sunday] Dispatch!! . . .

The Sunday Papers are full of the Churchills & their works. Your instalments of Marlborough, Randolph's Searchlight, news that you & he are playing roulette (you did not tell your poor Pussy Cat!), you 'intensely' he in 'an effervescent manner'! Gladys Marlborough[1] according to one rag now calls herself 'Mrs Spencer' & keeps 80 Blenheim Spaniels in a small farm in Oxfordshire – My doings are not chronicled, but for your information I have been playing golf indifferently (once with Margot [Asquith]), have done a lot of 'sight seeing' which I love, & have heard all the conflicting gossip which rages round this establishment & its management. . . .

Tender Love to you & to Diana & Randolph
Your Clemmie

. . .

[1] Widow of 9th Duke of Marlborough. See Biographical Notes.

○ From WSC   Château de l'Horizon
[undated, probably 27 August 1934]

My darling,
I am so glad you have been reading M. [*Marlborough*] II with pleasure,
and all you say about it is deeply interesting. . . .
I have indeed been playing at the Casino, though at Chemin de Fer, and
have lost uniformly, but not on a large scale. Randolph too has lost & has
stopped playing. I wrote an article today on Philip Snowden's
Autobiography[1] wh will pay expenses: & the stocks & shares have done
well in my absence.
Tomorrow at nine we start in two cars – one the Prof [Lindemann*]'s –
for Grenoble along Napoleon's route[2]. I have read the story again in
Houssaye[3]. It was an amazing episode. 'Jusqu'à Grenoble j'étais aventurier.
A Grenoble [je suis] devenu prince.' I really must try to write a Napoleon
before I die. But the work piles up ahead & I wonder whether I shall have
the time & strength. . . .
Although on pleasure & holiday I have done a good deal of work. . . .
And the book proof readings have been laborious. But it has been a jolly
change, & I hope to come again next year if all's well. . . .
I send this letter by Mrs P [Violet Pearman, secretary] with my fondest
love.
Looking forward to coming home and reuniting the entire family
                                        I am your devoted loving husband
                                                                    W

[1] Philip Snowden (1st Viscount Snowden, 1864–1937), *An Autobiography*, 2 vols, 1934.
[2] The road along which Napoleon had travelled to Paris after his escape from Elba in 1815.
[3] Henri Houssaye (1848–1911), French historian, author of several books on Napoleonic era. The
work referred to here is probably *The Return of Napoleon*, part 2 of *1815* (3 vols, 1893–1905),
translated into English and published in London, 1934.

Towards the end of September Winston and Clementine went, as planned,
for a cruise with Lord Moyne in his yacht *Rosaura*, visiting Lebanon, Syria
and Palestine; flying to Cairo (where Winston painted the Pyramids);
returning via Alexandria; and disembarking at Naples. They arrived home on
21 October.

Chapter XVI

'BUT THERE'S AN ISLAND YONDER . . .'[1]

Lord Moyne, Winston and Clementine's host for their Mediterranean summer cruise, was planning a very much longer expedition, and one with a specific scientific purpose: he had undertaken to capture alive for the London Zoo some specimens of the dragon-like monitor lizards which inhabit the island of Komodo, one of the Lesser Sunda Islands in the Dutch East Indies (now Indonesia). He invited both Winston and Clementine to go with him in the *Rosaura* on this four-month journey.

Apart from the fact that Winston would not have enjoyed being cooped up in a boat for such a lengthy sea voyage, he could not have even contemplated being so far removed from the political scene. Moreover he was deeply engrossed in working on his life of Marlborough.

Although he viewed such a separation with considerable dismay, Winston perhaps recognized that in their life together, Clementine's preferences and plans had nearly always been subordinated to his, and so – somewhat ruefully – he agreed that she should accept Walter Moyne's invitation.

Clementine left London by train to travel overland to Messina, where she would join MY *Rosaura*.

[1] From a poem by William Paton Ker (1855–1923), Professor of Poetry at Oxford from 1920.

○ From CSC In the Train
Tuesday 18 December [1934] Excuse wobble

1ˢᵗ Instalment of Diary

My darling,
. . .
As my train steamed away from Victoria & I saw you all collected on the platform, I thought how much I love you all, & above & more than all you my sweet and Darling Winston. You all looked so sweet & beautiful standing there, & I thought how fortunate I am to have such a family – Do not be vexed with your vagabond Cat. She has gone off towards the jungle with her tail in the air, but she will return presently to her basket & curl down comfortably. . . .

Tender love from your travelling Pussy.

. . .

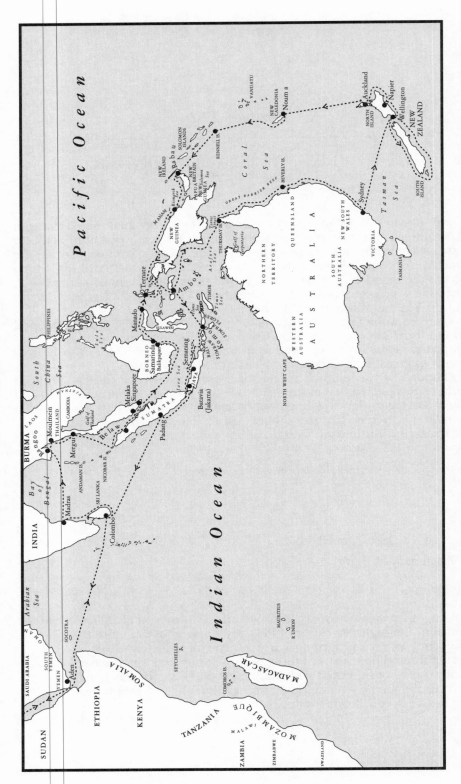

VOYAGE OF MY ROSAURA TO THE EAST INDIES AND AUSTRALASIA, 1934–1935

O From CSC   M.Y. Rosaura
Saturday 22 December 1934   R.Y.S.

My Dearest Darling

... As I lie in bed I contemplate the photographs of my family erected on the chest of drawers against the opposite wall. I don't generally take photographs away with me but this time is such a long absence I felt I could not do without them. ...

Mr & Mrs Lee Guinness[1] [fellow guests] are both ill – Not in bed, but they have come on the trip just for the sea voyage & if they find the tropics too much they will take a big liner home from Singapore. He is an inventor (K & G sparking plugs etc) & has a large factory – I think I shall like him – Very simple & quiet – interested in machinery & in his wife, 'Posy' – Isn't that a pretty name? She is amusing, sharp-tongued, witty, scandalous & extremely intelligent –

When I got your telegram yesterday saying 'Beaten Lords 238 to 62', I thought at first you had won – I read it that you had beaten (the Government in the) Lords by 238 to 62!

I dashed off a telegram to you saying 'Long live the House of Lords' – Then I read it again & saw that it Alas was the other way round[2] – So I stopped my answer in the nick of time, but not before I had told the Guinnesses that we had had a 'famous victory' –

I can't think how I read it wrong – I suppose the wish being father to the thought, & also you saying you wouldn't telegraph unless we won. Ah well. I felt very dunched.

It's really very rough, but I am up & about – 'Posy' is prostrate, so are the maids, & Mr Guinness can't face a square meal. ...

I am ... beginning an enormous piece of needlework which Venetia [Montagu*] made me bring. I have got 144 reels of silk with which to quilt it, & I calculate that even if I sew all day & never catch a butterfly or a dragon, I could not finish it before I return! However I must see what I can do before Rangoon[3]. ...

Wow – You are now all assembling at Blenheim[4] & I wish I were there too. I hope I shall receive all the news & a lot of gossip from everyone.

                                          Tender love from your

    Clemmie

                                          Wow & <u>re</u>wow

---

[1] Kenelm Lee Guinness was a cousin of Walter Moyne.
[2] WSC had cabled CSC (19 December 1934) the result of an anti-Government amendment to the Report of Government of India Act, moved by Lord Salisbury in the House of Lords on 15 December.
[3] It was never finished!
[4] It was the beginning of a new reign: the 9th Duke of Marlborough (Sunny) had died on 30 June 1934, and had been succeeded by his elder son, the Marquess of Blandford (Bert). He and his wife Mary (born Cadogan) hospitably 'took in' the Chartwell party for Christmas at Blenheim: WSC; all four children; the 'Jagoons'; and the 'Prof' (Lindemann).

○ From CSC   M.Y. Rosaura
Saturday 29 December 1934   Gulf of Aden

My Darling

Yesterday we spent at Aden. It was a day full of 'alarums & excursions'
culminating, after several days' uncertainty as to whether or no to land in
Ceylon. . . .

According to one source of information, besides the Malaria, there is
also influenza of a very virulent type. . . . The Lee Guinnesses are both
invalids; & they have both come merely for the sea voyage. They intended
to land at Colombo, spend a few days visiting the interior of the island, &
while the yacht with Mr Philip[1] & myself on board pushed on to Rangoon,
to our rendez-vous with Walter[2], take a big liner home, where both of
them poor things have to undergo operations. . . .

So that is why we stopped at Aden – They [the Lee Guinnesses] decided
to get off there & wait for a ship . . . . We went ashore & enquired at the
Shipping Office – A big ship was due that very afternoon. . . . And then –
literally at the last minute of the last half hour they announced that they
were staying in the yacht after all, & would trans-ship homeward at
Rangoon or Singapore! All this sounds as if they were unwilling &
uncomfortable travelling companions, but really they are a charming, tho'
rather queer couple.

I'm very glad they are coming on becos', altho' I like what I have seen
of Mr Philip, I don't know him at all well, & 10 days' tête à tête with a
stranger is more trying (I expect, for I have never tried it) than complete
solitude –

While all this was going on we managed to see the sights of Aden. . . . I
was amazed by the beauty of the native population & their gloriously
coloured robes. They are very black. The blackest of all are however
Somalis from across the Gulf.

Sunday Dec: 30th.

I have just seen the last sight of land – Sokotra – till 5 days ahead we
sight Minikir, a small island (Latitude 8 Longitude 73). . . . I had no idea the
distances were so enormous. 3 days from Port Said to Aden – 36 hours
from Aden to the opening of the Gulf of Aden & yesterday at Noon we
were 3000 miles from our next stop Rangoon. . . . I'm enjoying sea life very
much – Far from being monotonous there seems such a lot to do – I'm
reading a lovely book called 'The Dragon Lizards of Komodo' by an
American Explorer W. Douglas Burden – Do get it. . . . we bathe & play
Water Polo in the Sail Bath, & I play a little backgammon with Posy who is
a demon at it. . . .

New Year's Eve, Indian Ocean.

There is a monsoon blowing which is rather trying. It began yesterday
morning & has got worse since. I have not succumbed, but sleeping is
difficult owing to the motion & the tearing noise of wind & wave. . . .
Last night I took a sleeping draught, & achieved 5 hours' sleep – So this
morning I feel as fresh as a daisy & have just had breakfast on deck
with the spray blowing about & occasionally great splashes on the
deck. . . .

<u>New Year's Day 1935</u>
The Monsoon has gone, the Sky is blue flecked with tiny fleecy clouds – there is still a swell, but the Captain thinks it may subside.

Oh my Darling I'm thinking so much of you & of how you have enriched & broadened my life. I have loved you very much, but I wish I had been a more amusing wife to you. How nice it would be if we were both young again....

<u>Wednesday January 2</u>
The swell has subsided it is now lovely again. But we are all rather disappointed with the Indian Ocean. At its best so far it is like the English Channel on a fine Summer day....

Now the Red Sea on the other hand with the arid & jagged mountains of Arabia as a coast line gives one quite a different feeling – Lots of flying fish yesterday & 2 steamers a long way off.... No British Wireless News since the 27th – that's 7 days ago – I can't bear not to know what Ramsay [MacDonald] is doing! By the way will you <u>ever</u> have time to read this endless letter. I fear you will have to imitate your Father & give Mary half-a-crown to finish it[3]. Please don't – becos' there are some nice little private bits for you alone.

I'm jealous of the yellow cat. Is he dozing on your bed?...

<u>Thursday Jan: 3rd</u>
. . .
There are a good many British ships in these waters who fly the Dutch flag & employ Dutch crews becos' the rate of pay is less. Rather shabby?... We are now heading for Madras where we deposit the Lee Guinnesses. We reach there (D.V) on Saturday the 5th at 1 p.m.; oil, & go on to our rendez-vous at Rangoon the same night....

<u>Saturday January 5</u>
We reach Madras to-day at lunch-time – All yesterday we were skirting Ceylon which has a fairy like mountainous coast line – At 22 miles from shore a mosquito blew in thro' the Captain's port hole borne by a strong land wind! He was executed under suspicion of being a malaria carrier....

I've just had your cable about Hazel[4]- It saddens me to think of that bright, gay, beautiful affectionate being who brought so much pleasure & animation wherever she went, lying stark & cold. I will write to John [Lavery*]. I feel he will not last long now.

Do what you can to comfort him. Do you remember how good he was in the War to us when we were in the Cromwell Road? I used sometimes to go & sit with him in the evenings when I was anxious about you, & when you came back from Flanders you used to paint in his Studio....

I'm very sorry the Guinnesses are leaving. When Posy gets home she is going to write or telephone to you & tell you my news. I'm sure you will like her. She's full of life & fun tho' often rather wrongheaded. I wonder if you will think her pretty? I believe she has a devastating effect upon the male heart – So beware!...

Tender Love to all from
Clemmie

[1] Terence Philip (*c.*1892-194?), a 42-year-old bachelor who was Director of the London branch of

Knoedler's, the New York art dealers. Born in Russia, where his father was a merchant, and much of his early life had been spent there; he spoke fluent Russian. In the late 1930s he went to New York and worked at Wildenstein's gallery, until his early death during the Second World War.
[2] Their host, Lord Moyne, and Lady Broughton (see p. 384 n. 2) were flying out to join *Rosaura* in Rangoon.
[3] A reference to Lord Randolph Churchill who, it is related, being much bored by a long story a neighbour at a men's dinner was telling him, gave the waiter a sovereign and said: 'Be a good fellow, sit down and listen to the rest of this story for me.'
[4] Hazel Lavery, wife of Sir John Lavery, had died on 3 January 1935. Her husband died in 1941.

O From WSC   Chartwell
31 December 1934

My darling Clemmie,

... It is only prudent to avoid Ceylon as this epidemic of malaria is most serious and dangerous. If you touch at the Andaman Islands, the convicts shd be avoided. Lord Mayo, a Viceroy, was murdered by one of them in the last century. I wirelessed to you about this today.

So now I suppose you right in the middle of the Indian Ocean, 'so bright, so calm, so blooming blue' as Kipling has it; & paddling along, chug, chug, chug, through its placid waters. Or is there the monsoon? . . .

Blenheim passed off vy well. I played a lot of Bezique with B & M [Bert and Mary Marlborough] & actually emerged a small winner. The children enjoyed themselves – especially Mary [Churchill]. Blandford [Bert] showed himself more serious & urbane than I have seen him. We were all invited to 'come again' next year, & B stressed how you must come then. Personally I spent most of the time in my suite – the one you know – reading Marlborough letters, & dictating 'episodes' for the film[1]. All our tummies were a little disordered, & the weather outside cold raw & wet. . . .

Diana was vy sweet & demure. She has greatly improved in dignity & charm. I am vy fond of her. It is arranged that Moppet [Whyte*] accompanies her to the Court in January[2]. I would gladly go, but they all agree that would mean flash light photos etc, whereas otherwise it will probably all pass off unnoticed.

Sarah has now gone off for a round of visits. She was much admired at Blenheim. Randolph has just returned here after three days hunting with Bendor [Westminster*] wh I fixed for him, tho' I cd not go myself. He leaves today and I shall be quite alone. But I am getting absorbed in the campaign of Ramillies, & am going on building the wall towards Hill's cottage[3], so I shall not be idle.

My darling one I felt so sad when I got home the other day after seeing the last wave of your dear white hand out of the carriage window. It will be 4 months before we meet again, and to see you vanishing away like that was a melancholy thing. I miss you vy much & feel vy unprotected. But I did not feel I ought to try to do you out of a wonderful trip on wh you had evidently set yr heart. . . .

... Tomorrow I am going to send you a 'Chartwell Bulletin' which will tell you some local & political news.

Tender love my sweet darling pussy cat from yr ever devoted loving

W

...

[1] In September 1934 the film producer Alexander Korda (see p. 374 n. 1) had asked WSC to write the script for a film on the reign of King George V, in time for the Silver Jubilee in 1935.
[2] When her divorce suit from John Bailey would be heard. (See p. 375 n. 1.)
[3] Head gardener's cottage at the top of Chartwell property, by the road.

○ From WSC [typewritten]   Chartwell
1 January 1935

My darling One,

I send you Chartwell bulletin No. 1[1] which will conclude, like Napoleon's famous bulletin after his Russian catastrophe, 'The health of the Emperor is excellent.'

The pool has now been raised another fifteen inches. It is filling gradually from the spring through the old filter and is absolutely clear and limpid owing to the algae being asleep for the winter.

I have arranged to have one of those great mechanical diggers which is working close by to come here in a few days at a cost of £25 a week. In this one week he will do more than forty men do. There is no difficulty about bringing him in as he is a caterpillar and can walk over the most sloppy fields without doing any harm. His first task will be to make your 'ha-ha'....

After this the digger will make the peninsula [on the bottom lake] into an island by cutting a channel about as broad as my bedroom is long. The earth from this will be carried by the small railway into the big hole behind Mr Pilbrow's[2] oasthouses which he is filling up, and which he said I was welcome to fill. The digger is believed to be capable of doing all this in a week....

I have begun to lengthen the brick wall with the balled pillars to Hill's cottage, and am already a quarter through the first bay. I am cutting down all the scrub and rubbish and making it into a nice clear grass area with only the most presentable trees left standing. I think you will like this when you see it.

I have told Southon [builder] to put another bookcase in my bedroom....

The film folk came down last Thursday and we spent many hours jawing and seeking inspiration. I have no doubt that the film will be a commercial success and that I shall get at least my £10,000 out of it. I am far more anxious about whether it will be worthy of the subject [King George V] and worthy of the reputed author [WSC]. It is a very difficult task indeed, but several very fertile practised minds are working continuously upon it, and I have given them a whole flood of ideas....

I have paid another £800 of bills and our total indebtedness stands now only at £1,500.... Anyhow we have finished up the year better than we have ever done and the financial prospects of this coming year are very much more favourable than anything we have known. If we avoid all large new capital expenditure and save money wherever we can, we ought to be in a good position by this time next year. This would be important for you if anything happened to me or to my earning power....

Mrs Donkey Jack[3] will very likely never be able to walk again as it is unlikely her fractured ankle will knit together at her age. She was knocked down by a workman on a push bicycle and no compensation of any kind can be obtained for her in this desperate misfortune. Should the worst be realised I shall try and get her into a decent home for the rest of her days at some small cost.

Meanwhile her savage dog (the little one) still stands a faithful sentry over her belongings. He allows Arnold to bring food at a respectable distance, and consents to eat it, but otherwise he remains like the seraph Abdiel[4] in Paradise Lost.

'Among innumerable false, unmoved,
Unshaken, unseduced, unterrified;
His loyalty he kept, his love, his zeal.'

A fine moral lesson to the baser breed of man!

I was sitting down last night to eat my New Year's Eve dinner as I thought in solitude, when I noticed an extra place at the table, and in marched Diana looking absolutely lovely. She had come down on her own to keep me company, which I thought was nice of her....

I have made some progress in spite of many interruptions with the opening chapters of Marlborough, volume III. What a downy bird he was. He will always stoop to conquer. His long apprenticeship as a courtier had taught him to bow and scrape and to put up with the second or third best if he could get no better. He had far less pride than the average man. This greatly helped his world schemes and in raising England to the heights she has never since lost. But when he fell into evil days and was stripped of power, it is rather pitiful to find him asking the sovereigns he had defeated and well nigh ruined to help him keep his private property. There never has been anyone so perfectly shaped for the purpose for which he was required than this valiant, proud, benignant, patient and if necessary grovelling, daredevil and hero. It is only on the field of battle and in his love for Sarah that he rises to the sublime. Still Mars and Venus are two of the most important deities in the classical heaven.

I expect you will now not be far from the toe of the great Indian peninsula. I am very glad you are not going to Ceylon. Owing to their rash experiment in Home Rule they have let down all their sanitary arrangements and so have this plague. Imagine what will happen to India when sagacious, scientific, uncorruptible direction is withdrawn!

Tender love my darling one from yr
ever loving & devoted husband
W

---

[1] This particular series of Chartwell Bulletins, numbered 1–12 and dated between 1 January and 13 April 1935, was published in single-volume form (annotated by Martin Gilbert) by the International Churchill Society in 1989.

[2] Mr Pilbrow was the owner of Chartwell Farm (over 300 acres) in the valley adjoining Chartwell.

[3] Mr and Mrs 'Donkey' Jack were gypsies who lived in a shack on the common land above

Chartwell; they had a donkey. When Mr 'Donkey' Jack died in 1933, WSC paid for his funeral to save him from a pauper's grave. In October 1934 Mrs 'Donkey' Jack received notice of eviction by the local council: WSC gave her permission to move her encampment into Chartwell wood-land, where she lived until her death a few years later.
[4] The seraph Abdiel, in John Milton's *Paradise Lost* (1667), was the only one of Satan's cohorts who refused to revolt against the Almighty.

O From CSC
Sunday 6 January 1935

M.Y. Rosaura
Bay of Bengal

My Darling
    Yesterday we reached Madras – As soon as we docked, an avalanche of natives invaded the yacht....
    We drove about the town & visited the Native Bazaar, the Aquarium, the food Markets an enormous Temple (we were not allowed inside) the Post Office (to get your letter off by Air Mail) & finally wrote our names in Their Excellencies' Book at Government House....
    At the local Roxy Cinema they were showing a Film called 'One Hundred % Pure' featuring Jean Harlow, who is the most ultra Blond & voluptuous type of American film Star. The film I'm told is indecent – I can't imagine anything likely to do more harm to British prestige than allowing these sort of films to be shewn.... We walked all over the Native Bazaars for over 2 hours & never saw a single white person. The poor people seem to have beautiful manners & <u>looked</u> contented....
    We all four dined at 'Spencer's' ... Then Terence Philip & I returned alone to the yacht leaving the Guinnesses to wend their way home across India, taking ship at Bombay....
    You must forgive my shocking writing; but the weather is shocking. Very rough & also torrents of rain – To look at like the North Sea, but stuffy & hot – I hope it won't be like this all the way to Rangoon....
    <u>Wednesday January the 9th 7.30 A.M. Rangoon.</u>
    Here we are at last – Yesterday afternoon the weather changed – The sea flattened out into almost oily calm – It was lovely & a rest after all the knocking about & staggering about. We have only just anchored so we are only just in time for our Rendez Vous.... So in a few minutes as soon as I can get Terence Philip up we are going to <u>do</u> Rangoon & then drive to the aerodrome 15 miles off & meet the flyers....
    Later.
    The plane was 1½ hours late. They seem to have had a perfect trip – They stepped out looking as fresh as paint. I've not seen my letters yet – Terence Philip & I, while awaiting Walter, visited the big golden Pagoda – Later – We are sailing in ½ an hour so I must post this letter.

Tender Love
Clemmie

◇ From CSC   [MY *Rosaura*]
[13 January 1935]

CAUGHT SEVEN LOVELY BUTTERFLIES ON DESERT ISLAND. SUMATRA TOMORROW. LOVE

CLEMMIE

◇ From WSC   [Chartwell]
14 January 1935

CAUGHT THREE LOVELY FILMS HERE. DELIGHTED ABOUT BUTTERFLIES. ALL WELL HERE.
FILM PROSPERING. BIG MAIL LEAVES 20ᵀᴴ. RADIO FREELY. FONDEST LOVE

WINSTON

○ From CSC   M.Y. Rosaura
Thursday 17 January 1935
6.30 am. Nearing Singapore

My Darling Winston
    Sumatra is a 'Wow'.... We landed in the north at Port Belawan &
motored 150 miles into the interior to Lake Toba which is 3,000 feet up in
the hills.... We drove thro' a bewildering variety of scenery: the densest
jungle with glorious orchidlike flowers in great clusters; the most intense &
minute cultivation, forests of palm & rubber, & as we neared the lake great
rolling moors & highlands like Yorkshire & Scotland. We saw rice, tapioca,
tea coffee tobacco growing in neat plantations & thro' all this is cut the
most beautifully engineered road perfectly tarred & kept with a velvet
surface. Along all those miles the road had wide grass verges kept closely
mown by mowing machines; the contrast between the wild jungle on
either side & these exquisitely kept strips on each side of the road is very
remarkable.... The natives are Malays, friendly, but really repulsively ugly;
quite unlike the Burmans, where the women are so graceful & pretty with
little heart-shaped faces.
    ... We saw a man walking on the verge with 6 or 7 dogs on a string – I
thought they were part of the local pack being 'walked'. They were going
to the 'Dog market' to be killed for food – The natives think them a great
delicacy....
    Yesterday we landed at Malacca, (which belongs to us) and Oh the
contrast to Dutch Sumatra – All the houses (except those lived in by rich
Chinese) wanted painting, untidy rubbish everywhere, everything was
down at heel & shabby. We were much depressed....
    We are now drawing close to Singapore & I'm going up on the bridge to
see the approach –
    My Darling I do love you so much & I constantly think of you & of all

you do and are. I will leave this open in case I can add anything after I have seen my mail. In case it has to go as it is I send you my Heart's Love
Clemmie

Later
Miaow – Letters from faithful Mary & Moppet [Whyte*] but no Pig's paw. . . .

O From WSC [typewritten]   Chartwell
18 January 1935

Darling,
CHARTWELL BULLETIN NO. 2
While I was working on the new wall today Mrs Donkey Jack came walking along having trudged all the way from Westerham upon her injured ankle. She was proposing to walk down there again tonight to get her pensions arrears which have accumulated while she was in hospital. I stopped this, and we supplied her with food till Monday. I went with her to see the dogs' welcome. It was most touching. The brown dog leaped at least three feet into the air repeatedly, but the little savage dog on the other hand seemed quite overcome and crept up to her with his tail between his legs. I suppose he thought she had returned from the dead. . . .

I have finished two new bays of the wall on the road and mounted two new balls upon them. Half the third bay is also done. There are only two more.

The mechanical digger has arrived. He moves about on his caterpillars only with the greatest difficulty on this wet ground. But when he gets to work he is simply marvellous. He did not begin to dig your haha till noon yesterday and by noon today it was finished. . . . He lifts nearly a ton in one mouthful and puts it wherever he wishes in a circle of about thirty feet. He also pushes great heaps of earth sideways or forwards like an elephant with his trunk, and pulls great rocks out of the ground as if they were walnuts. Tomorrow he is going to begin making the peninsula into an island. For this I have hired a railway for £6 as I thought it better to have a broader gauge and strong[er] rails than my little skips. . . .

We had a demonstration last Sunday of the Photophone [cinema] down here. All the servants and some of the neighbours attended. We had three films including Henry VIII and Catherine the Great. . . .

Meanwhile I have been working very hard at my own poor film. I produced a great number of incidents and dialogues, and I am sure that as soon as I know the kind of thing they actually want I can make an effective contribution. . . . Korda[1] dined with me last night at the flat, and said that while I had contributed a great quantity of material, he was not at all satisfied with the way it had been handled by the technical people. In other words, it would not do at all. . . . He told me that every film he has produced has gone through its moment of despair. In fact Henry VIII was rewritten twelve times. . . .

Randolph has plunged into the Wavertree Election[2] as a candidate. . . . This is a most rash and unconsidered plunge. At the moment Randolph and his three or four Manchester friends . . . are sitting in the Adelphi Hotel at Liverpool without one single supporter in the constituency whom they know of – high or low. Randolph is to hold his first meeting to-morrow. Of course with the powerful support of the local Daily Mail and the Sunday Dispatch and with the cause, which is a good one, and with his personality and political flair he will undoubtedly make a stir. But in all probability all that he will do is to take enough votes from the Conservative to let the Socialist in. All together I am vexed and worried about it. . . . Randolph has no experience of electioneering and does not seem to want advice, and the whole thing is amateurish in the last degree. To have a hurroosh in the streets and publicity in the newspapers for three weeks and then to have a miserable vote and lose the election to the Socialist will do no end of harm. . . .

¹ Alexander Korda (1893–1956), Hungarian-born film producer who became a British subject, 1936. In 1939 he married the film star Merle Oberon (1911–79); the marriage was dissolved, 1945. Korda made 112 films and was knighted, 1942.
² One of the Liverpool seats. The by-election was occasioned by the sitting Conservative Member's elevation to the peerage. Randolph decided to stand as an Independent anti-India Bill Conservative, despite there being already an official Conservative candidate.

○ From CSC   [MY *Rosaura*]
Sunday 20 January 1935   South East Coast of Borneo

My Darling Winston

We arrived at Singapore on the morning of Thursday the 17ᵗʰ – It is a most prosperous & imposing looking place – After shopping & calling for our letters (none for 'Poor Pussy whose coat is so warm' etc) we were taken round the dock yard by Commodore Mark-Wardlaw – a very nice capable practical sailor. . . . The dry dock is a magnificent sight – Over 1,000 feet long – Its cement walls are 30 feet thick & so also is its floor! There were to have been <u>six</u> of these docks in a row – This has been cut down to this single one. A basin for small craft, destroyers etc, when half built, was finished on one side with a slope instead of with a cement wall so that it holds only half the ships it was intended to accommodate. I believe only £100,000 was saved by this cheese paring economy. . . .

The Straits between Singapore Island & the Mainland can accommodate our whole fleet & are deep & do not need dredging. I think it might interest you to get a plan of the Dock Yard from the Admiralty so as to really see what is being done. I was thrilled & could have stayed many more hours in spite of a temperature of 92°. But I was saddened to see how everything has been cut down. . . .

I asked the principal bookshop in Singapore if there was a brisk demand for your books – They said the compressed World Crisis had gone very well. The second volume of Marlborough was doing better than the first. They had sold 12 sets of Marlborough & had 5 more on order. I think that is rather good when you realize how expensive it is.

Walter bought 2 baby 'honey bears' at Singapore – They are very droll little animals. Clumsy but rather charming. They follow one all over the deck. . . . The monkey hates them & is violently jealous. . . .

I had a letter from Moppet [Whyte*] at Singapore dated the 4th of January, saying Diana's case[1] would be coming on 'the week after next'; ... Poor little girl. We must pray for some great happiness for her to make up for the rough time she has been through.

Tender love my Darling....
from Clemmie

[1] Diana was granted a divorce decree nisi from John Bailey on 12 February 1935.

O From WSC [typewritten]   [Chartwell]
21 January 1935

CHARTWELL BULLETIN NO. 3

The mechanical digger began work on the isthmus this morning and has done about one third. I expect it will be finished at lunch time on Wednesday. We should get on much quicker if the big skips did not repeatedly tumble off the line, causing delay and vexation.

I have decided to rebuild Howes' [the chauffeur's] cottage for him on the old site, but standing a little further away from the existing buildings so as to improve their lighting.... The kind of cottage we are going to build would cost £700 in the ordinary way. Goodwin [local architect] estimates it can be built ... for £340....

Randolph's campaign opens tonight. He has taken the Wavertree Town Hall, which only holds four hundred people. It will certainly be crowded out, the reporters alone taking a good slice. He has no friends or supporters in the division on whom he can count at present, but Rothermere[1] is giving tremendous support through all his papers, which are very powerful in the district. Bendor [Westminster*][2] has issued a statement on his behalf, and has promised to take the chair at one of his meetings, and has subscribed £500 to his campaign. Mr Watts, the Manchester man, has given £200. I am producing £200. I do not doubt Rothermere will provide the rest. The total expenditure is limited to £1,200, so that is all right. Much depends on whether this meeting goes well tonight and the impression Randolph makes. Of course in action of this kind he has a commanding and dominating personality, and there is great feeling that Lancashire needs someone of vigour and quality. Already the election has become a national fight. I shall know at ten o'clock tonight how he gets on.... I have not yet decided whether I shall intervene myself. The India Defence League is holding an executive meeting tomorrow afternoon to decide their line of action. I do not expect they will do more than express sympathy and leave their members to take what action they think fit. But of course if they support him actively I shall probably go north myself....

We have had a great blow about the film. It appears that an Act of Parliament says that a film which does not consist wholly or mainly of topical news reels, and which is longer than two reels, must be provisionally released six months before it can be finally released ... , when of course it would be much too late for the Jubilee [in early May] and not worth doing.... I am of opinion that this plan will fall to the ground, and all my labours, which have been most arduous, will be wasted. . . .

All the black swans are mating, not only the father and mother, but both brothers and both sisters have paired off. The Ptolemys always did this and Cleopatra was the result. At any rate I have not thought it my duty to interfere.

Sarah has already gone up to work for Randolph, and Diana follows tonight, so at any rate he has two supporters, . . .

[1] Lord Rothermere, newspaper proprietor (see p. 121 n. 3). At this date his Associated Newspapers controlled the *Daily Mail, Sunday Dispatch*, and *Evening News*. He was also owner of the *Daily Mirror* and founder of the *Sunday Pictorial* and the *Glasgow Daily Record*.
[2] Whose home at Eaton Hall, Chester, was nearby.

O From WSC   Chartwell
23 January 1935

My darling Clemmie,
   In your letter from Madras [not to hand] you wrote some words, vy dear to me, about my having enriched yr life. I cannot tell you what pleasure this gave me, because I always feel so overwhelmingly in yr debt, if there can be accounts in love. It was sweet of you to write thus to me, & I hope & pray I shall be able to make you happy & secure during my remaining years, and cherish you my darling one as you deserve, & leave you in comfort when my race is run. What it has been to me to live all these years in yr heart & companionship no phrases can convey. Time passes swiftly, but is it not joyous to see how great & growing is the treasure we have gathered together, amid the storms & stresses of so many eventful, & to millions tragic & terrible years?
   I have sent you vy full accounts of all that has passed here, & of Randolph's spirited adventure. It is easier for me to tell you at length about all these things by dictation than to write them out long hand. I have almost lost the art of thinking with a pen in my hand. So please do not be vexed with this habit of mine where news only is concerned. . . .
   Poor old Clara [Frewen][1] died at 82 last Friday. Advised in time by Oswald [her son] I wrote her a letter of affection which reached her on her last day. . . .
   Give my love to Walter & commend me to yr companions. You have now been gone 5 weeks, and it seems a vy long time. In another three weeks it will be half over, & we shall all be counting the days for yr return. . . .
   I am now about to begin my vy hard fight in the House about India. The odds are vy heavy against us. But I feel a strong sense that I am doing my duty, & expressing my sincere convictions. . . .

With my fondest love & many many kisses & constant thoughts for yr well being & safety

> Your ever loving & devoted
> husband
> W
>
> . . .

¹ Clara Frewen (1850–1935), the eldest of the three Jerome sisters, and WSC's aunt. She married Moreton Frewen (1853–1924).

O From WSC   [Chartwell]
23 January 1935

[CHARTWELL] BULLETIN NO. 4

Randolph had a great success at his opening meeting. He took the local Wavertree Town Hall holding about five hundred. He did not know half an hour beforehand whether he would have a large or small attendance, ... However when he got there the hall was packed and the streets outside crowded. The platform also was blocked by enthusiastic people standing there to support him. He made a brilliant speech. Then he went to an overflow almost as packed as the first, and finally more than a hundred walked a mile and a half to the committee rooms to give in their names as helpers.

The Daily Mail and the Morning Post played this up in their front pages and even the enemy papers admitted the enthusiasm shown and the reality of the candidature. On this the India Defence League Executive decided on Tuesday to go all out for Randolph.... This is the first time we have definitely opposed a Government candidate at a bye-election, and it may be we shall lose some of our members for the decision. They even seemed to think that perhaps the Government would refuse the Whip¹ to all members of the League. I do not believe they dare do that. Anyhow all were resolved to go forth, so Randolph will have all our circus at his disposal ... I have promised him to wind up his campaign in the Sun Hall on February 5.

Needless to say this election will cause much heat and bitterness. On the other hand it arouses enthusiasm and will be a national fight.... A first-rate agent and many very experienced people have now been concentrated on the scene and all the committee rooms are reported to be open.... There will be no difficulty about a shoal of meetings, and Randolph will have a couple of M.P.s to support him every night. I told him to have a meeting for business men in the centre of the city which he will do on Wednesday.... Of course the other side will turn on all their forces; but the Liverpool [Tory] caucus has long been unpopular ... and their candidate Mr James Platt is a thoroughly unattractive nonentity, with no knowledge of politics, but a socially ambitious wife and a large fortune, which no doubt weighed with the caucus committee which chose him....

Well, there it lies tonight, and it must run its course. You will see that I am much more easy in my mind about it than I was at first sight. Randolph of course is in the seventh heaven. This is exactly the kind of thing that he revels in and for which his gifts are particularly suited. . . .

My going to Liverpool on the 5th has altered my plans for the debate in Parliament. . . . So I shall move the rejection of the Bill in a considerable speech and then travel by the Tuesday night train to Liverpool, where I shall stay for the poll and declaration. How nice it would be if I could bring Randolph back to Westminster with me. Alas, such day-dreams must not deceive us. That he will emerge a new public figure of indisputable political force is certain.

Tender love
W

. . .

[1] Depriving a Member of Parliament of the Whip is the extreme method of party discipline and leaves the member without official party assistance or support.

◇ From CSC   [MY *Rosaura*]
[25 January 1935]

ANXIOUS FOR NEWS DIANA'S CASE. YESTERDAY MENADO. TOMORROW AMBOINA.
TENDER LOVE AND THOUGHTS FARAWAY.

CLEMMIE

○ From CSC [continuation of diary]   [MY *Rosaura*]
Saturday 2 February 1935   Eastern Coast of Australia

Darling Ever since the afternoon of Wednesday January the 30th we have been steaming hard, just pausing at Thursday Island to pick up the pilot who is guiding us between the coral reef & the Eastern Coast of Australia – The reef stretches (I think) all the way from the north to Sydney about 1,700 miles – It varies from 1 to 3 miles from the shore. . . .

The coast seems forlorn & deserted – not a town, not a village, not a house, not a soul. We have just been passing the reef where Captain Cook[1] got stuck in the Endeavour – All the geographical points were named by him after his experiences – Hope Islands – Tribulation Bay – Weary Bay –
Sunday February 3.
This morning at 9 o'clock we were 1,000 miles from Sydney – The barrier reef is now much further from the shore (about 25 miles) & all day we have been threading our way thro' the most lovely islets between it & the coast. . . . It is very hot, 86º in the shade on the ship & inland it is said to be 120º in the shade! In the sun on the ship it is about 115°. . . . Tomorrow we reach Brisbane about 350 miles from Sydney. . . .
Evening of Wednesday the 6th [February]
I have just been spending the day with Streetie[2] – Her Sister whom she has been nursing devotedly died last week – So she is very sad.

Sydney is the most lovely place –
We are just sailing to New Zealand –

Tender Love
Clemmie

[1] Captain James Cook (1728–79), British naval explorer, who in 1768 was given the command of an expedition to the South Pacific. Sailing in *Endeavour*, with Joseph Banks and other scientists on board, he reached Tahiti; then found and charted New Zealand and sailed on to make a detailed survey of the east coast of Australia. After negotiating the Great Barrier Reef, *Endeavour* was grounded off the Queensland coast, but Cook had her repaired and sailed her home, reaching England in June 1771.

[2] Margery Street (see p. 251 n. 2). Former Private Secretary who had returned to Australia in 1933 to care for her sick sister, after eleven years with the Churchills. Much beloved by us all.

○ From WSC   11, Morpeth Mansions
30 January 1935   Westminster, S.W.1.

My Beloved Clemmie,
    My heart was pierced by yr radio 'Faraway Clemmie'. Indeed it makes me gasp to look at the map & see what enormous distances you have covered since I saw the last of your dear waving hand at Victoria Station: and it depresses me to feel the <u>weight</u> of all that space pressing down upon us both. How glad I shall be when you turn homewards, & when the mails will be closing up together, instead of lagging & widening apart! I do hope you are not dispirited or homesick: but I know the feeling of being so far off from all one loves. . . .
    Here are some vy nice lines which Ch. James Fox[1] composed on his 50th birthday to his wife (a reformed harlot who had reformed him) which I found in this new book about him.
        'Of years I have now half a century passed,
        And none of the fifty so blest as the last,
        How it happens my troubles thus daily shd cease,
        And my happiness thus with my years shd increase,
        This defiance of Nature's more general laws
        You alone can explain, who alone are the cause.'
Substitute sixty for fifty, & darling Clemmie for Mrs Fox, & come back home yourself, and these lines would admirably fit
                                    Your ever loving & devoted
                                                        W

                                                        . . .

[1] Charles James Fox (1749–1806), English Whig statesman, leader of the opposition to Pitt the Younger. As Foreign Secretary (1806), he brought about the abolition of the slave trade.

○ From WSC [typewritten]   Chartwell
31 January 1935

CHARTWELL BULLETIN NO. 5

Darling,

I send you some photographs which I have had taken to show you
what the digger is doing. . . .

Making the island has proved a bigger and longer business than I
expected. It will take a fortnight in all. But the results will be pleasing, as I
am making all the slopes gentle so that you will see the new strip of water
from the dining room. . . .

The whole family with the exception of Mary have gone up to Liverpool
for the election, including Moppet [Whyte*]. Mary is 'parked' at the Fox's[1]
where she is quite happy, but I am going to make her come back here for
the Sunday.

I delivered my broadcast on India on Tuesday night, and it is judged a
great success. It came off very opportunely for the election, as all the
Wavertree electors were told to listen in.

. . . The important decision was taken by the India Defence League
executive to support Randolph. . . . Rumours that the Government would
deprive all Members who supported Randolph of the Whip did not deter
anyone from going to Wavertree. . . . About twenty-five Members have
already sent assurances of their sympathy to Randolph and he has all the
speakers that he wants. . . . Whatever resources we can command are being
used. . . . The weak point is the canvassers, of whom there [are] only about
eighty when we ought to have two hundred at least. . . . He [Randolph] has
made a wonderful impression and excites tremendous enthusiasm. All his
meetings are crowded out. He has at least five a day. . . . The Daily Mail
rampages away behind him, covering the constituency with placards and
making every possible point in his favour. I believe he will beat Platt, in
which case the responsibility for losing the seat is thrown upon the
weaker candidate. . . . More than that I dare not hope, . . . There is no doubt
he will emerge from this election a public figure of unquestioned
importance, . . .

. . . I go up on Monday to Eaton[2] for dinner and to sleep. Randolph
comes for supper and I probably will speak at the Constitutional Club in
Manchester at luncheon on Tuesday the 5th, and then go to the big
meeting in the evening. Five thousand electors have received tickets for
the Sun Hall and another two thousand five hundred for a big hall actually
in the constituency. The demand is extraordinary and there is no doubt
both these 'Father and Son' meetings will be crowded out. I am carefully
keeping away till then. All the underlings of the Government have been
up, but last night the Attorney-General Inskip[3] had his second meeting
only half filled. But they have crowded in agents from every part of the
north country. . . . Long before you get this letter you will have heard the
news. If Randolph polls eight or nine thousand, we shall not have suffered
a rebuff. If he beats Platt, it is a victory. If he is elected, it is a portent.

. . . Ramsay [MacDonald][4] sinks lower and lower in the mud, and I do
not think the poor devil can last much longer. Buchanan[5], the Clydesider
in the House of Commons, called him a 'cur', a 'swine' and 'one who

should be horsewhipped'. These brutal insults were allowed to pass by the Chair and no single member of this great majority – no Minister on the Treasury Bench, no Whip rose to claim a breach of order. Buchanan got off without withdrawing. If I had been there I would certainly have risen to protect this wretched man from such a Parliamentary outrage. What utterly demoralised worms his colleagues and their hangers-on must be to allow their Prime Minister to be insulted in this way in breach of every Parliamentary rule without one daring to stir on his behalf!

Oddly enough, in spite of all this fighting (perhaps because of it) Ministers are extremely civil. I am dining tomorrow night at the Foreign Office to meet Flandin[6] and Co. for whom there is a banquet, and last night I gave a dinner at Claridges' for the Portuguese Ambassador at which Cunliffe-Lister[7] and others were present. You would never have supposed there was the slightest difference between us. They see the terrible difficulties into which they are plunging.

... There is a certain amount of distress in the constituency at our fighting a Government candidate, and Hawkey and Co. are very active and agitated to defend the fort. But there is no doubt we have the Association at least ten to one on our side....

The new cook has learned to make Madrilène[8] quite well and so has Margaret[9]. I miss the old Hungarian, but we are getting along all right in this respect....

Always your loving devoted

W

...

[1] Hospitable neighbours.
[2] Eaton Hall, Duke of Westminster's home near Chester.
[3] Sir Thomas Inskip, later 1st Viscount Caldecote (1876–1947). Barrister and Conservative MP. Former Solicitor-General. Attorney-General, 1928–9 and 1932–6. See also p. 427.
[4] Ramsay MacDonald (see p. 275 n. 1). He was deemed by the Labour left to have 'sold out' by forming the National Government.
[5] George Buchanan (1889–1958), Member of Independent Labour Party. Labour MP for the Gorbals, Glasgow, 1922–48. Held ministerial office in Labour Government, 1945.
[6] Pierre Etienne Flandin (1889–1958). Member of the French Chamber of Deputies since 1914. At this date Prime Minister of France (November 1934–June 1935).
[7] Sir Philip Cunliffe-Lister, later 1st Earl of Swinton (1884–1972). Secretary of State for the Colonies, 1931–5. Appointed Secretary of State for Air, June 1935.
[8] WSC liked only clear soups. *Madrilène* is a chicken *consommé* flavoured with tomato.
[9] Margaret was the cook-housekeeper at Morpeth Mansions (the Churchills' London flat).

◇ From WSC   [Chartwell]
7 February 1935

RANDOLPH BEATEN AFTER MAGNIFICENT BATTLE[1]. NO HARM DONE. HAVE YOU SEEN FIGURES. SEND HIM A MESSAGE. TENDER LOVE FROM ALL. WOW.

[1] The Wavertree results, announced late on the night of 6 February, were: Labour, 15,611; National Conservative (Platt), 13,771; Independent Conservative (R. Churchill), 10,575; Liberal, 4,208. Labour majority, 1,840. Randolph had split the Conservative vote, thus ensuring a Labour victory.

◇ From CSC   Edgecliff, New South Wales
[8 February 1935]

JUST SPENT DELIGHTFUL DAY WITH STREETIE. PURCHASED PAIR BLACK SWANS AT ZOO. TWO
WALLABIES AND OPOSSUM. SAILING TONIGHT NEW ZEALAND. LOVE.

                                                                CLEMMIE

◇ From WSC   [Chartwell]
9 February 1935

MENAGERIE WELCOME

                                                                WINSTON

O From CSC   M.Y. Rosaura
Friday 22 February 1935   Deep Water Cove – Bay of Islands N.Z.

My Darling Winston,
    I can't describe to you my relief & joy when on arriving at Auckland,
two days ago I found your dear letters, also Sarah's, Diana's, Mary's &
Moppet [Whyte*]'s & a whole budget of news awaiting me.... How
anxious & agonising & thrilling Wavertree must have been. I wish I had
been there to help – Darling Winston – I hope it has not queered the pitch
at Epping. I do think the Rabbit ought to have consulted you before
rushing into the fray. However he seems to have done very well....
    Now I must resume the account of my travels –
    After our visit to the Mountains & Sounds of the South Island we
returned to Wellington for a day & a night before starting our exploration
of the North Island....
    We had intended to sail the next day but were stormbound by a horrible
gale. So altho' we felt we had exhausted the charms of Wellington we had
to spend another day there. We drove all round the great natural harbour,
visited the Zoo in search of aboriginal animals (very poor after Sydney) & I
went & played tennis at Government House with Lady Bledisloe[1], ...
    By nightfall the gale was still raging, but the Captain said it was 'safe but
very uncomfortable', so a vote was taken, & it was unanimous i.e. to put
to sea at once – It was absolutely frightful! The propellor was several times
right out of the water & the poor ship quivered from prow to stern – But
in the morning the sun was shining & we found ourselves anchored
outside Napier which, four years ago, almost to the day, was laid
completely flat by the most terrible earthquake. Every building except <u>one</u>
whole street fell down. – About 300 people were killed....
    Here at Napier we left the yacht for a three day motor expedition thro'
the island – She [Rosaura] went on to Auckland to await us. The first day
we drove thro' very arid mountainous country ... & in the afternoon
reached what is known as the 'Thermal Region'. This is most extraordinary
& wonderful, but rather a monstrosity of Nature – There the earth's crust is

extremely thin & the boiling centre explodes thro' the crust in geysers, boiling pools, 'fumarols' & 'blow holes'....

... If you poke your stick into the ground only 4 inches a thin curl of steam comes out – The cold streams are full of trout, & you can catch one & without taking it off the line flick it into a boiling pool & cook it! All round great rocks with strange red & greenish streaks – The sun was setting & we were alone in the valley – I sat on the hot ground & felt that underneath there was a heaving Titanic monster insecurely imprisoned....

That night we pushed on & reached Rotorua, which is a watering place with hot baths & mineral springs & is the headquarters of the Maoris where they live in a 'reserve' – This is another valley rather like the one I have described but gentler & less infernal – The boiling water here is used to warm the native huts & cook suet pudding, ... They do not take the water into their huts to cook, but just stand the saucepans & kettles in a boiling stream....

The next day we reached a place called Waitomo where there are the most weird & enchanting caves – You wander thro' stalagmites & under stalactites drip drip dripping – It takes 300 years to make one square inch of stalactite & some of them are 20 foot long....

We spent the night at Waitomo & were very glad to get to Auckland & the yacht & Oh joy – news from home next day....

We then put to sea again & reached this wild & lonely stretch of coast 2 days ago. This is the headquarters for catching the Master Fishes Sword Fish, Mako Shark, Marlin & so on. Lady Broughton[2] I should tell you came here immediately on her arrival in N.Z., as she is a noted 'rod' & that's what she's come for. We found her plucky, but damped in every sense of the word. For 10 days it had rained & rained & rained – except for one day when she caught 2 fish, a Sword & a Mako, but only 260 lbs & 330 lbs, which it appears is nothing. Her bed-room, a lonely hut on the hill side was infested with rats, there was no lock on her door & she kept hearing 'stealthy footsteps' – She was very glad to re-join the yacht – I must say she is a plucky & determined woman but it seems to me rather misdirected energy!

Yesterday I & Terence Philip were sent out to catch a sword fish – I know you understand how it's done as I remember you caught a monster in California....

We started out in a heavy launch taking with us an ample luncheon.... When we got 'outside' my heart sank into my boots or rather rose & stuck in my throat. But with Vera Broughton's example & with the sea under the rocking pitching launch stiff with sea monsters I was not going to give in.... In 2 other launches on the gray heaving sea were Walter in one & Vera Broughton in the other – After 3 hours I said I felt faint & wanted food. So we left the fishing grounds for an hour & got into a little bay & had luncheon – But I felt so sick I could only drink claret & suck some very strong peppermints – Afterwards we tried again. But no good. Torrents of rain – We got home at 4 drenched & exhausted. This morning Vera & Walter are at it again.

Now this enormously long letter must come to an end because a launch is waiting to take it into Russell, the nearest town. It brings you all my love. . . .

Tender love & kisses
from
Clemmie

. . .

[1] Wife of Charles Bathurst, 1st Viscount Bledisloe (1867–1958), Governor-General of New Zealand, 1930–5.
[2] Vera Broughton, wife of Sir Delves Broughton (1888–1942), from whom she was divorced in 1940. The close friend of Walter Moyne, she was handsome, an intrepid voyager and deep-sea fisherwoman. She died in 1968, in her early seventies.

O From WSC   Chartwell
23 February 1935

My darling One,

. . .

Randolph has plunged into this Norwood[1] contest with a candidate of his own. He has acted entirely against my wishes and left my table three days ago in violent anger. The weak point of the Norwood contest is that as there is no Liberal standing, the Liberals (who polled 7000 in 1929) will vote for the Baldwin candidate[2], and against Randolph's man[3]. This has not I think occurred to R. But he is quite beyond reason or even parley; and I am leaving him alone.

The 2 black swans have mated, built a nest on the new island, & have laid several eggs. They sing to each other vy sweetly every morning. I wonder how they will take to yr two new ones from Sydney. And will the wallabies concur with the goats [Mary's]! It will be almost as complicated as politics. . . .

. . . There is a brilliant film on here called Maskerade, . . . You would like it vy much. Diana – our Diana, took me to it & I thought it charming. She has greatly improved & is so gentle & sweet. She turns up every now and again to accompany me to Epping: & generally manifests affection for her Papa. She has learned a lot.

Mary has just been in to see me. She is gone out hunting – Her Saturday treat. She is tremendously keen, & a veritable she-Nimrod[4]. . . .

. . . But now you will be approaching the Dragons. Mind you telegraph about them, & do not get eaten by them. I shd be too far away to play Perseus[5]. . . .

A thousand kisses my sweetest pussy-cat & tender love from
Your ever loving & devoted husband
W
. . .

[1] There was a by-election pending at Norwood, in south London, almost immediately after Wavertree, and, at the height of the committee stage debates on India, Randolph announced his intention of putting forward a candidate to challenge yet again the Government's policy on India.
[2] The official Conservative candidate was Duncan Sandys (see Biographical Notes), who later met Diana; they fell in love, and were married on 16 September 1935.
[3] Richard J. Findlay, who had served in the RAF, 1918. He had briefly been a member of the British Union of Fascists in 1934.

⁴ 'Nimrod', pseudonym of C. S. Apperley (1777–1843), an English sporting writer who devoted much of his life to hunting.
⁵ In Greek mythology, the son of Zeus (Jupiter) and Danaë. Perseus among other marvellous feats rescued Andromeda, who had been chained to a rock and was about to be devoured by a monster. (Perseus afterwards married Andromeda.)

O From WSC [typewritten]   11 Morpeth Mansions
23 February 1935

My darling,
CHARTWELL BULLETIN NO. 6
The new bookcases sunk in the new walls of the drawing room and my bedroom are finished. They look extremely nice and will relieve the congestion of books. I have arranged to have the drawing and dining rooms thoroughly redecorated as I understand you would like to have this done.

The digger has taken a great deal longer than I expected in making the peninsula into an island. Indeed for the last three weeks it has done nothing as its works broke, and further, it got itself into a hole from which the greatest efforts have been necessary to extricate it. However this is not at my expense and it will be able to act tomorrow.... The engineers of the firm owning the digger were so anxious to get it out of its hole that they worked for forty hours at a stretch without sleep or rest....

The ha-ha and the he-he are being very nicely finished. All you will see is a gentle slope of grass.... [✍ I have bought 2 goats for £1 each, & they are on nibbling duty around the pool. They are nannies & will have kids in April. They are vy friendly.]

Three new bays of the wall with the balls on it are completed and I hope to do the other three before your return....

The repercussions of Randolph's exploits at Wavertree have been very far-reaching. They did not prevent our increasing our strength in the division on the second reading . . . On the other hand much perturbation has been caused to many of our best friends in our constituencies. Hawkey [Constituency Chairman] has been very worried about the Epping division.... Against this Chigwell and Harlow have passed strong resolutions of support and encouragement, and the great voting masses of Woodford and Wanstead seem quite solid....

... However the great thing is to let things simmer down. This may be difficult for Randolph is quite uncontrollable.... He does not seem to wish to consider any other interests but his own and we have had sharp words upon the subject. If he should run the candidate at Norwood I expect the India Defence League will decline to support him, and I shall certainly consider myself bound by any decision which they take. I doubt even if Rothermere will support him and his man may come a dreadful flop. Perhaps this will be the best way out of it. I still think he will defer to my advice. If not events must take their course.

We began the Committee stage in the House two days ago and we have thirty-four more days of India debates ahead of us. We do very well in the debate but the Government have mobilised two hundred and fifty of their followers who do not trouble to listen to the debates but march in solidly and vote us down, by large majorities, usually swelled by the Socialists and always by the Liberals. It is going to be a long wearing business. . . .

○ From CSC   M.Y. Rosaura
Tuesday 26 February 1935   At Sea Between N.Z. & the
                                                                Loyalty Islands

My Darling Winston,
    It is 3 days since I sent my last budget – This one will be a long time on its way as I don't think it is any use posting this at the Loyalties or the Solomons.
    The weather at Bay of Islands was atrocious which was sad. . . .
    However Vera Broughton caught 2 more fish, bringing her total to 4. Two swordfish & 2 sharks. Poor Walter caught 1 shark only. But <u>he</u> did not mind – He is the most unselfish man in the world, & thinks the whole time of making pleasure & fun for his guests.
    Terence & I gave up fishing after our one rough unsuccessful day, & we managed one picnic on a desert island on the one day when the sun gleamed fitfully. We bathed & looked for shells and read & it was pleasant. . . .
    Yesterday we spent the day hunting for 'Tuataras'. They are beautiful lizards about 2 foot long, very rare, to be found only here on one small uninhabited island – It is forbidden to export them; but Walter got permission . . . to get a pair for our Zoo. . . .
    The island is a great rock with sheer sides, except in one spot where you can climb up one by one single file holding on to roots & jutting stones. Halfway up (about 100 feet) it becomes a jungle covered slope & the top is flat densely covered with jungle. The lizards live under stones & in holes in the undergrowth. I enjoyed the first part as I love rock climbing; & you know I always start with zest on any excursion or expedition – Where I fall short is that I soon get physically exhausted. Scrambling on hands & knees thro' the bush soon tired me out & I thought I would go back & wait in the dinghy at the foot of the cliff . . . I was <u>sure</u> I could retrace my steps – But presently I realized that I was hopelessly lost. I shouted but there was no answer. I then tried to retrace my steps to where I had left the exploring party & found I was struggling helplessly & that I was very tired. I sat down & reflected & rested. Meanwhile a great tropical thunder storm had been approaching – It burst upon the island & soon I was soaked in spite of the fact that I could hardly see the sky thro' the tangled & enmeshed branches. . . . The storm passed & I started wandering & creeping on hands & knees again – Suddenly I saw one of the lizards, quite close looking at me with his agate eyes – He was motionless – I sat down near him & we watched each other – Then I started shouting again & thought: Now the lizard will scuttle off, but he did not move. They are stone deaf. But my voice did not carry far – . . .
    Presently the lizard moved off & left me. Suddenly I heard Walter's voice

far far away – I could not tell in what direction. I called back but I felt he could not hear – Still I felt comforted – Presently I heard a loud crackling of branches & there was the second officer – I almost kissed him.

He blew a whistle, which was the signal Walter had arranged for whichever found me first. There were about 8 looking for me by now. Presently Walter appeared white with anxiety – I was really lost for only 1 hour, but it felt like much more in that dense enchanted wood – Of course there was no danger really, I suppose, but I thought of lying there & dying of hunger as far away from you as I can be on this earth.

Meanwhile several tuataras had been bagged. We looked them over, kept the best brace & liberated the remainder[1]....

Feb: 28th

Darling – Here we are at Nouméa, in New Caledonia. It belongs to the French; they pinched it from us.

A messagerie Maritime boat leaves in ½ an hour for Sydney so you may get this letter sooner than I thought.

Tender Love
Clemmie

[1] Of the several tuataras that were captured, only one survived the voyage home. It was presented to the London Zoo by Lord Moyne, but lived only five or six months.

○ From WSC [typewritten]   Chartwell
2 March 1935

My darling,

CHARTWELL BULLETIN NO. 7

The digger has involved me in a chapter of accidents and I doubt if I shall get out of it under £150, as it broke down at the critical moment through its cogwheels tearing. It was more than a week before it was repaired.... Meanwhile the weather changed and downpours of rain occurred. The digger sunk deeper into the mud and finally wallowed himself into an awful pit. It became necessary to bring four hydraulic jacks, ... Then railways sleepers had to be sunk in the ground under the digger to make a foundation for these jacks, and as the jacks hoisted the digger, of course the sleepers sunk deeper. However after nearly a week the animal emerged from his hole and practically finished the job, though there is still a fortnight's tidying up for five men. This animal is very strong with his hands but very feeble with his caterpillar legs, and as the fields are sopping, they had the greatest difficulty in taking him away. They will have to lay down sleepers all the way from the lake to the gate over which he will waddle on Monday. I shall be glad to see the last of him.

However the island is made and the ground gradually sloped towards it....

All this has delayed the re-turfing and finishing of your 'ha-ha'. But I hope to get the whole thing settled by the end of March, so that it should all be okay clean and green when you get home. Indeed I am glad you do not see it now, for there is an awful mess....

In the animal world a casualty has occurred. One of the five 'flying fools' [geese] was devoured by the foxes. There have been three or four about and it is a mercy that nothing more valuable has suffered. The black swan is now sitting on four, probably five, eggs. She has very prudently established herself upon the island ... , and her husband passes his days in harrying every other bird, including his own children, who though they practise incest have so far shown no signs of fertility.... The cat treats me very graciously and always wishes to sleep on my bed (which I resent). When I dine alone, and only then, she[1] awaits me on the table.

The Norwood by election, of which I wrote you in my last letter, has absorbed all the children except Mary. Randolph seems to have got a considerable fund through Lady Houston[2] and appears disposed to form an organisation to run candidates not only at by elections, but against Government supporters at the general election. His programme seems to be to put Socialists in everywhere he can in order to smash up MacDonald and Baldwin. I need not enlarge upon the fury this will cause and its unfavourable reactions upon my affairs..... He has for his candidate at Norwood nothing of the powerful support I was able to bring him at Wavertree. Not a single Member of Parliament will, I expect, appear on his platform. The India Defence League will leave him severely alone, and now the Evening News whose aid Rothermere had promised him, has made it clear that they will go no further....

Randolph's party consists of half a dozen of his Wavertree friends, ... together with Diana (whose principal occupation now is fighting by elections), Sarah (half-time with dancing)[3] and Moppet [Whyte*] (indefatigable).... Randolph has, I believe, plenty of money, but nothing else. Now that the Rothermere press has deserted him, it seems to me that he is in for a thoroughly bad flop which will strip him of any prestige he gained at Wavertree. This will probably do him a lot of good and reduce his pretensions to some kind of reason. In every other direction, especially in mine, it will do harm.

... Great efforts have been made to try to induce him to withdraw his candidate who is an ex-Fascist airman, Findlay by name (not much good).... Baldwin said to me in the Lobby two days ago that Mrs B had said to him 'One's children are like a lot of live bombs. One never knows when they will go off, or in what direction.' I suppose this must be the attitude of parents towards the new generation, who will make the world as they choose and not as we choose.

The India Bill is now in Committee and I am in the House all day long two or three days a week speaking three or four times a day. I have been making short speeches of five, ten and fifteen minutes, sometimes half an hour, always without notes, and I have I think got the House fairly subordinate. I am acquiring a freedom and facility I never before possessed, and I seem to be able to hold my own and indeed knock the Government about to almost any extent.... I have led the opposition with considerable success so far as the debates are concerned. The divisions go the other way, but we mock at them [government supporters] for being lackeys and slaves....

... They are a really bad government in spite of their able members. The reason is there is no head and commanding mind ranging over the whole field of public affairs. You cannot run the British Cabinet system without an effective Prime Minister. The wretched Ramsay [MacDonald] is almost a mental case – 'he'd be far better off in a Home'. Baldwin is crafty, patient and also amazingly lazy, sterile and inefficient where public business is concerned. Almost wherever they put their foot they blunder. Cabinet Ministers can only hold a meeting in any part of the country with elaborate police arrangements and party caucus arrangements to secure them an uninterrupted hearing. It is quite certain that things cannot last. Lloyd George* of course would like to come in and join them and reconstitute a kind of War Cabinet Government, in which I daresay I should be offered a place. But I am very disinclined to associate myself with any administration this side of the General Election....

I am very disappointed of course at the way in which film prospects have all narrowed down, but I have made some other contracts, including one with Colliers [American magazine], which will make us quite comfortable this year.

> Your loving
> W

[1] It is curious that my father habitually endowed the beautiful marmalade neutered male cat, called Tango, with the feminine gender.
[2] Lady Houston, Fanny Lucy (born Radmall) (1857–1936), widow of Sir Robert Houston (her second husband, d. 1926). Keen suffragist. Helped finance experiments in aircraft development. Gave £100,000 for the Schneider Cup Air Trophy Conquest.
[3] Sarah, in pursuit of a stage career, was studying at the De Vos School of Dancing.

○ From CSC   M.Y. Rosaura
7 March 1935   The Pacific Ocean

My Darling – It is exactly a week since I posted my last letter to you at Nouméa, one of the New Caledonia group.... Since Nouméa we have been crossing the trackless Ocean calling at various islands – We are quite out of touch, the waters round some of these islands are uncharted, they are surrounded by cruel coral reefs & often no bottom can be found. Captain Laidlaw [of the *Rosaura*] is a Tower of Strength for which I magnify and praise the Lord daily. The distances are enormous, often 2 days at sea between each island....

> Goodbye <u>Darling</u> Post just off

The above is an extract from a very long descriptive account of the *Rosaura* party's visit to the islands of Tomman, Rennell, Belona and Tulagi, summed up succinctly in Clementine's next cable.

◇ From CSC   [MY *Rosaura*]
[7 March 1935]

LOVE FROM CLEMMIE LOST IN PACIFIC AMONG CORAL REEFS, SAVAGES AND CRIMSON PARROTS. HOW ARE YOU, ALL MY DARLINGS?

On this thrilling voyage to savage peoples and exotic islands, Clementine's constant companion was Terence Philip[1]. Some eight years younger than her, he was suave, good-looking, charming and cultivated. He enjoyed the company of older women, and was much in demand by London hostesses as the perfect (and perpetual) 'spare' man.

Clementine was in her fiftieth year, but she was still slender, graceful and exceptionally beautiful. During the months of this voyage, not surprisingly, she fell romantically in love with him. It was a classic holiday romance – which did not survive (as it was never destined to) – the return to reality.

When, over thirty years later, I was writing her life, she spoke of it to me with detachment, and a touch of amused nostalgia. She acknowledged that Terence Philip had not really been 'in love' with her but, she added, 'he made me like him', and summed it up wryly with a saying which seemed to breathe the Edwardian world of her youth: *C'était une vraie connaissance de ville d'eau*.

After they returned home, Terence Philip came to Chartwell several times, but then his cosmopolitan worldly life claimed him, as her real life – and her only great love, Winston – claimed her.

[1] See p. 367 n. 1.

○ From WSC [typewritten]   Chartwell
8 March 1935

My darling,

CHARTWELL BULLETIN NO. 8

The digger has gone, thank God. We have had a successful week tidying up. The island will look delightful, when all is green again and the lake refills. Next week we shall finish the ha-ha, in a way which I am sure you will like. The orchard is grubbed and only awaits dry weather for the offending roots to be shaken clean and removed. Howes' [the chauffeur's] cottage is approaching completion, and enormously improved inside. . . .

Animal news. The black swan is sitting on six eggs, next to a small duck who is sitting on eleven. The two goats are nibbling industriously. . . .

Randolph's foray at Norwood goes very much as I apprehended. The India Defence League refused to give him any support and only one Conservative member (and he a crack-pot) has appeared on his platform. The place is utterly dead-alive. The papers give very little prominence to the election, and the hope of Randolph, Sarah, Diana, Moppet and Co. seems limited to saving their deposit. To do this he will have to poll at least 4,000 votes. I think they might do this. If so they will probably put the Socialist in. This will of course arouse the wrath of the whole Conservative party, more especially is this so because the Socialist woman candidate is fighting the election on pacifist lines, and the Government tardily, timidly and inadequately have at last woken up to the rapidly increasing German peril. The estimates of the Army, Navy and Air are up by £10 million. The Socialists are moving a vote of censure in the House on Monday and hope to mobilise all the pacifist forces throughout the country against national defence. At such a moment a Socialist victory, however explainable, will be most venomously interpreted on the Continent, and will play its small and temporary part in making things worse.

Diana says that Randolph has been much depressed by the way things have gone and the lack of any of the enthusiasm which sustained him at Wavertree. But that he is working like a black and radiates confidence around him. I have not seen him nor has he communicated with me since he left my table in a rage.

I should have felt very solitary but for the fact that the India Bill and Parliament have taken up so much of my time. . . .

The German situation is increasingly sombre. Owing to the Government having said that their increase of ten million in armaments is due to Germany rearming, Hitler flew into a violent rage and refused to receive Simon[1] who was about to visit him in Berlin. He alleged he had a cold but this was an obvious pretext. This gesture of spurning the British Foreign Secretary from the gates of Berlin is a significant measure of the conviction which Hitler has of the strength of the German Air Force and Army. . . . All the frightened nations are at last beginning to huddle together. We are sending Anthony Eden*[2] to Moscow and I cannot disapprove. The Russians, like the French and ourselves, want to be let alone, and the nations who want to be let alone to live in peace must join together for mutual security. There is safety in numbers. There is only safety in numbers.

If the Great War were resumed – for that is what it would mean, in two or three years' time or even earlier – it will be the end of the world. How I hope and pray we may be spared such senseless horrors. . . .

The cook is going. She sent in her spoon and ladle on her own account. I am very glad. She had the knack to the highest degree of making all food taste the same, and that not particularly good. I subsist on soup which Margaret makes for me secretly in London and is delicious.

I had a lovely letter from Streetie [Margery Street] describing her day with you and how she enjoyed it. . . .

Your ever loving
W

[1] Sir John Simon (see p. 123 n. 2). At this date Foreign Secretary. In the Cabinet reshuffle of 7 June 1935 he became Home Secretary, being replaced at the Foreign Office by Sir Samuel Hoare.
[2] At this date Lord Privy Seal. On 7 June 1935 he was appointed Minister without Portfolio for League of Nations Affairs, and on 23 December that year succeeded Sir Samuel Hoare as the youngest Foreign Secretary since 1791.

O From WSC   Chartwell
9 March 1935

My darling,

This is yr Birthday letter wh I send to wish you many, many, happy returns of April 1. . . . This has been a vy long separation for us; but now that 'your nose is turned homeward', we can look forward to the end of it. . . .

The cat is on my bed and reminds me of her presence by a purr. How I wish you were here too, my darling one. Yr telegram about the crimson Parrots came in yesterday. No doubt you are having a wonderful view of the world: but 'East, west, Home's best'. . . .

Now on yr return journey you will be meeting yr mails, instead of their lagging behind you. You must read the papers thoroughly, as there is so much going on.

Tender love my dearest darling and a thousand kisses from your
ever devoted
loving husband
W
. . .

○ From WSC [typewritten]   Chartwell
10 March 1935

My darling,

CHARTWELL BULLETIN NO. 9

Randolph has been here for the week-end and all is well between us. He evidently feels in a sorry plight, but his firmness of character and courage are proof against many hard blows. . . .

Mary has been roped in to the electioneering and was addressing envelopes with all the rest of our progeny and Moppet last Saturday afternoon. You never saw such a political household. I don't expect any of your dragons fight half as hard. . . .

The pug [Mary's] is getting intolerable. He commits at least three indiscretions a day, and if his actions stain the carpets, his protests when chastised fill the air. . . .

The Norwood election figures [14 March 1935] were as follows: –

Mr Duncan Sandys (Nat. Con)	16,147
Mrs Barbara Gould (Soc)	12,799
Mr Richard Findlay (Ind. Con)	2,698
Majority	3,348

No change.

Randolph's candidate thus forfeited his deposit. I do not think the 2,700 votes was so bad considering that no one gave him the slightest support, and Randolph virtually had to fight alone, carrying everything on his shoulders, . . . This result is of course a setback to him and should teach him prudence, and to work with others without at the same time daunting him. . . .

There are continuous rumours, some of which I believe are true that Ramsay [MacDonald] is going in the near future, and that Baldwin will reconstruct the Government[1]. It is said with some authority that they had hoped to defer this change till after the India Bill is out of the way, and that they would wish to include me in the administration. I am not at all keen on this, and there is a very desperate General Election which lies ahead. One would simply have to take the disgrace of the Government for all the opportunities they have missed.... Ministers are singularly civil, but I really have not excited myself at all upon the possibilities, which obviously are various and numerous....

We have a big meeting at the Albert Hall[2] on Thursday next at which I am the principal speaker. The tickets have gone like hotcakes and I expect we shall pay all the expenses (£4–500) from the sale. I have an Air speech on Tuesday – most important – and the India Bill on Wednesday, so that a heavy week lies ahead....

All the work here is progressing steadily and I hope in another fortnight greatly to reduce the extra labour. If the weather is dry next week I shall returf your orchard instead of resowing....

One of the heifers has committed an indiscretion before she came to us and is about to have a calf. I propose however to treat it as a daughter.

Tender love, my darling one

from

your ever loving

W

[1] Stanley Baldwin succeeded Ramsay MacDonald as Prime Minister on 7 June 1935.
[2] On 21 March 1935, organized by the India Defence League.

○ From CSC   M.Y. Rosaura
18 March 1935   Komodo

My Darling

This morning we arrived here & have reached the climax of our travels.

The Dragon Hunt is on foot – To me it seems unlikely that we capture <u>alive</u> one of these monsters. But long before you get this letter you will have heard. It is most important that the Dragon should be immaculate – If even one scale is knocked off the Zoo will be grieved, as they do not grow new scales.

This morning we landed the huge trap in sections. We then walked single file thro' the breast-high grass for about a mile to the lair of some of these lizards. It is a beautiful spot. Half way up a green velvet hill is a huge upended rock about 40 foot square – At the base are 2 cavernous holes & we could in the dust at the opening distinctly see the track of the monster's tail. So he was at home! We were a party of about 20 including the more efficient members of the crew, 2 most intelligent Dutch Officers whom we lured from their duty off the Island of Flores – Their part is to control the Natives & to act as interpreters – We make a great fuss of them & I think they are enjoying the adventure. We carried with us up the hill a live goat which had been captured earlier in the morning – This poor beast was later slain for bait. I removed myself quickly as I could not bear to see the poor little bleating beast put to death. The trap was erected about 100 yards from the lair. Its floor was covered with fresh grass, the bait was hung at the end, the trap-door fixed to fall with the clash of doom when released by the lizard touching the bait. The whole affair was camouflaged with branches & several young trees which were transplanted. (Luckily the dragons are deaf or they would certainly have heard our efficient preparations!)

A Native was left on watch who is to hare off to the beach as soon as he sees or hears the trap released – He will then blow a note on a horn or rather on an enormous conch shell – The ship's siren will then screech & the whole party however scattered & every native in the island will hear the news....

March 19th

Walter & Vera Broughton started at dawn to explore inland. They did not take me as I am not thought to have enough staying power in the hot sun. The Dutch Officers have gone to recruit Natives etc....

Later. Walter & Vera have returned exhausted from their walk but having seen a Baby Dragon 3 foot long.

. . .

◇ From CSC   M.Y. Rosaura
[22 or 23 March 1935]

TWO DRAGONS CAPTURED. CANNOT UNDERSTAND NORWOOD. IS RANDOLPH LEADER OF NEW PARTY? TENDER LOVE TO ALL.

Clemmie

◇ From WSC   [Chartwell]
24 March 1935

DELIGHTED NEWS. WE WERE GETTING ANXIOUS. BRAVO DRAGONS. NORWOOD NEWS AWAITS YOU BATAVIA. RADIO YOUR PLANS HOMEWARD JOURNEY. TENDER LOVE FROM ALL.

WOW

[continuation of CSC letter started 18 March 1935]

Tuesday March the 26th i.e.: a week later –

This has been an enchanting bewildering & exciting week –

I meant to keep this letter in the form of a diary adding to it day by day, but failed to do it – In this way I could have made you feel the excitement, the suspense, the heat, the repeated disappointments, the fearful smell of the decaying baits – (which of course had always to be approached & watched with the wind blowing towards one). Side by side with all this 'big game' 'Boys' Own Annual' world is the enchantment of this island, which is the most beautiful thing I have ever seen & is perhaps one of the loveliest, wildest, strangest spots in the world. It is deeply indented with bays & lagoons. It has innumerable paradise beaches – some of the finest sand (there is a pink one of powdered coral) some of wild rocks with coral gardens, far lovelier than at Nassau, & accessible – That is if you are not afraid of being absorbed by a giant polyp or tickled by a sea snake 12 foot long – ... The sea is alive with fish – Lively flying ones of different sizes.... In pursuit come gray mullets in shoals & after these again great black fins like sharks – Hovering over all beautiful albatross-looking birds & glorious herons fishing <u>and</u> catching.

The beaches are covered with exquisite shells of all sizes & with great lumps of crimson coral & delicate branches of white tree coral. Beautiful trees like magnolias grow on the beach – At high tide their trunks may be six foot under water – At low tide you sit in their shade among the shells & sand. The island itself is made of rock thickly covered with (what appears to be) green velvet. It is mountainous – Some of the peaks are fantastic in shape & down the gorge are lovely woods, but haunted & impenetrable....

But to leave my enchanted world & to return to the world of sport – Total result of week's hunt: – 5 small dragons – Of these 2 have been liberated – Our allowance was 2 & we have been allowed to keep 3[1] – The longest is about 6 foot & they have not yet developed a very dragon like appearance. This comes with hoary age.... To get a big one I think one would have to live here for a couple of months – On the other hand our photographer Mr Pereira has <u>seen</u> a big dragon 12 foot long & photographed him going off with half a pig in his mouth. He & Vera Broughton have lain in wait for hours in the long grass in the blazing sun near the trap, & near dead exposed & rotting animals to get good pictures –

I spent one hot morning watching & decided upon the other life – But I did see one prehistoric peep of a dragon on a stony beach looking for crabs – I have also found quantities of dragon tracks which I notify to Walter on my return when we meet at meals....

. . .

[1] Komodo dragons. On his return Lord Moyne presented two dragons to the London Zoo. They both lived until 1946; this was considered to be a good survival rate. (Information from London Zoo's archives.)

[continuation of CSC's letter started 18 March 1935]

<u>April the 1ˢᵗ & Pussie's Birthday   Batavia.</u>

My Darling We spent 2 entrancing days at Bali & 2 in the southern part of Java, & here we are at Batavia at 'Journey's End' so far as our joint party is concerned. For the day after tomorrow Walter flies away bearing this letter in his beak. I got your letter at Bali about Norwood. What a great pity – I fear this will take away the glamour of Wavertree, & I'm so grieved my Darling that Randolph should have shewn so little consideration to you who love him so dearly & who have supported & helped him so much. The result which you telegraphed me is a flop. I'm afraid his headstrong foolish action may prejudice your side of the Indian question by alienating people. However it will be only temporary? I'm so glad Epping is all right; tho' it is new for us to have a bitter minority against us there. I'm longing to be back to share all this with you.

Bali is an enchanted island – Lovely temples embedded in green vegetation in every village – Lovely dancers. The inhabitants lead an Elysian life. They work for about 2 hours a day – The rest of the time they play musical instruments, dance, make offerings in the Temples to the gods – attend cock fights & make love! Perfect? isn't it? Southern Java is beautiful but more ordinary & the inhabitants less lighthearted. . . .

This letter is really too long – But it stretches over a fortnight. I will start another when I get the Batavia Mail.

Tender Love
Clemmie

○ From WSC [typewritten]   Chartwell
5 April 1935

CHARTWELL BULLETIN NO. 10
Everything is gradually getting tidied here. . . .

We are a little late with the harrowing, but the field in front of the house has been done twice and manured and rolled. I have bought a tractor which covers the ground four times as fast as the horses, and I hope to get the park done next week. . . .

Mary has developed whooping-cough and barks away with great regularity. She seems quite well otherwise and runs about the garden every day. . . . She will be probably quite well by the time you come back.

I was rather worried about Randolph. He came back from Liverpool after about ten weeks of frantic electioneering and political work, and went to bed with a high temperature, . . . He has now been ill nearly a fortnight[1], with fever practically all the time, eating very little and looking very yellow. But the Doctor says there is no danger and no infection, and Randolph seems in quite good spirits, although depression is one of the symptoms. . . . Poor boy! I go to see him every day, but he has other visitors too. He has obstinately grown a hideous scrubby beard which makes me positively sick to look at. However, he has promised to cut it off when he gets up. . . .

Animals. The black swan should hatch out this week-end. Three of the heifers have calved. . . . I have banished all the dogs from our part of the house. Punch [Mary's pug] is in the nursery. Trouble [Sarah's spaniel] is with Arnold, and Harvey [Randolph's fox-terrier] with Howes. I really think you will have to buy a new strip of carpet outside my landing.

I have had a very hard time with the India Bill. They have taken it four days this week, and they are to be four days next week. . . . We are keeping our end up very well. . . . But they will drive it through like a steam roller and then hope we shall all kiss and make friends. I do not know at all how this will work.

The political sensation of course is the statement by Hitler[2] that his air force is already as strong as ours. This completely stultifies everything that Baldwin has said and incidentally vindicates all the assertions that I have made. I expect in fact he is really much stronger than we are. Certainly they will soon be at least ten times greater than we are so that Baldwin's terms that we should not be less than any other country is going to be falsified. Fancy if our Liberal Government had let the country down in this way before the Great War! I hope to press this matter hard in the next month and a good many of those who have opposed me on India now promise support on this. . . .

I am very tired tonight after this hard week, but have to finish up my articles for the Evening Standard on King George V's reign. Poor Marlborough lingers on the battlefield of Ramillies. I do not think I shall be able to carry him further forward till the month of June when we shall be quit of the India Bill.

My party last week-end was a great success. Venetia [Montagu*], Freda [Dudley Ward] and Diana D.C. [Duff Cooper*] would make anything go, and I hear they all enjoyed themselves very much. Although it was the 31ˢᵗ of March and the weather severe, Venetia and Diana both bathed with me in the pool the temperature of which was nearly 80º. They said they liked it. I have now let it cool off as the weather has turned quite bitter. . . . Venetia as usual cleared everybody out at bezique, but I only lost a tenner.

¹ He was nursed at the Mayfair Hotel.
² Statement made by Hitler during conversations with Sir John Simon and Anthony Eden in Berlin, 24–6 March 1935.

○ From WSC [typewritten]   [Chartwell]
11 April 1935

CHARTWELL BULLETIN NO. 11

Randolph's jaundice has caused a good deal of anxiety, as it did not follow the normal course. . . . This morning his temperature is normal . . . Therefore it looks as if he is getting over whatever it was he had, . . . He will be at least another week in bed. Then I hope to bring him to Chartwell for Easter.

Mary's whooping cough is on the mend. . . . Sarah on the other hand is overdoing it, dancing practically four hours a day as well as going to balls. . . . I have therefore told her that she must not go to a ball on any night when she practises her dancing. She has been very good about it and last night went to bed at 9 o'clock. I expect you will be sorry if she does not go to balls of any kind. However you must deal with this situation when you come back. . . .

My statements about the air last November are being proved true, and Baldwin's contradictions are completely falsified. There is no doubt that the Germans are already substantially superior to us in the air, and that they are manufacturing at such a rate that we cannot catch them up. How discreditable for the Government to have been misled, and to have misled Parliament upon a matter involving the safety of the country.

○ From WSC   Chartwell
13 April [1935]

My darling Clemmie,
    What wonderful letters you write! The Dragon one has just reached me.
Indeed the whole account of yr cruise is thrilling. . . .
    It is splendid to think that when this reaches you on the 20th, you will
be no further off than Suez. Even Colombo seemed near compared to the
recesses of the Pacific. We all long to welcome you back, and the Spring
will dress our valley in its bridal robes.
    You realize no doubt that the Jubilee will absorb yr first week home.
We are of course both bidden to St Paul's, & will I expect have a good
view. There will be other functions: still I hope in the main we can enjoy
Chartwell. . . .
    You will find me waiting for you at Dover pier: & a final mail will reach
you at Marseilles.
    I think a lot about you my darling Pussie 'every little while', and rejoice
that we have lived our lives together; and have still some years of
expectation in this pleasant vale. I have been sometimes a little depressed
about politics and would have liked to be comforted by you. But I feel this
has been a gt experience and adventure to you, & that it has introduced a
new background to yr life, & a larger proportion; & so I have not grudged
you yr long excursion; but now I do want you back.
                    Tender love my own sweet Clemmie from your ever loving
                                                                husband
                                                                    W
                                                                    . . .

○ From WSC [typewritten]   [Chartwell]
13 April 1935

                        CHARTWELL BULLETIN NO. 12
    There is very little to say since the last bulletin. Randolph is decisively
better and only has very slight fever under 99 for a few hours in the
evening each day. . . . He is in great good spirits and is visited by youth
and beauty. He has grown a beard which makes him look to me perfectly
revolting. He declares he looks like Christ. Certainly on the contrary he
looks very like my poor father in the last phase of his illness. . . .
    I have come to a satisfactory arrangement with the London Films and I
think they have behaved very well. In a nutshell, they pay me £2,000 a
year for another year on account of the short films, and £5,000
compensation for the failure of the Jubilee film. . . .
    I completed the Jubilee articles for the Evening Standard and each week
I do an article for the Daily Mail.
    You will be very pleased to see the state of our bills when you come
home, for everything has been paid up every month this year, and there
are only three or four old stagers which exist. . . .
    The brown nanny goat named Sarah died by misadventure. Hill
scattered some nitrate of ammonia on the grass. She ate it and expired.

The white-horned nanny goat named Mary survived, thanks to a timely dose of castor oil. She is expecting a family.

How paltry you must consider these domestic tales of peaceful England compared to your dragons and tuataras. But I think it is very important to have animals, flowers and plants in one's life while it lasts. . . .

All the talk here is about reconstruction as soon as the India Bill is through. Whether that process will lead to my receiving an invitation I cannot tell, and I say most truthfully I do not care. . . .

At sixty I am altering my method of speaking, largely under Randolph's tuition, and now talk to the House of Commons with garrulous unpremeditated flow. They seem delighted. But what a mystery the art of public speaking is! It all consists in my (mature) judgment of selecting three or four absolutely sound arguments and putting these in the most conversational manner possible. There is apparently nothing in the literary effect I have sought for forty years! . . .

On the whole since you have been away the only great thing that has happened has been that Germany is now the greatest armed power in Europe. But I think the allies are all banking up against her and then I hope she will be kept in her place and not attempt to plunge into a terrible contest. Rothermere rings me up every day. His anxiety is pitiful. He thinks the Germans are all powerful and that the French are corrupt and useless, and the English hopeless and doomed. He proposes to meet this situation by grovelling to Germany. 'Dear Germany, do destroy us last!' I endeavour to inculcate a more robust attitude. . . .

More love from
W

P.S. Two black cygnets just arrived.

O From CSC   M.Y. Rosaura
20 April [1935]   Suez

Oh my Darling Winston

The Air Mail is just flitting & I send you this like John the Baptist to prepare the way before me, to tell you I love you & that I long to be folded in your arms.

A week to-day I shall be home. I long to be with you & hear everything you are thinking & doing.

Your loving
Clemmie

Clementine arrived home after her 30,000-mile sea journey on 2 May, just in time for the Silver Jubilee celebrations of King George V and Queen Mary on the 6th.

Of her travel souvenirs the most charming was a Bali dove, a dear little pinky-beige bird with coral beak and feet, who lived in a wicker cage resembling a lobster pot. He survived some two or three years, and when he died

Clementine had him buried under the sundial in the middle of the walled vegetable garden. Round the base are engraved these lines from a poem by W. P. Ker, suggested to Clementine by the traveller and writer Freya Stark:

> HERE LIES THE BALI DOVE
>
> It does not do to wander
> Too far from sober men,
> But there's an island yonder,
> I think of it again.

Chapter XVII

DARKENING HORIZONS

Throughout the later summer months of 1935 the possibility of war loomed. In August Mussolini threatened to invade Abyssinia, and on 24 August the British Government announced that if Italy attacked Abyssinia Britain would stand by its obligations under the Covenant of the League of Nations. On 3 October Italian forces attacked Abyssinia. On 7 October the League voted for economic sanctions[1].

In November there was a General Election (which in the event was to be the last for ten years). Churchill campaigned in support of the Government, while urging the necessity for re-armament. Baldwin's assurance to the voters was, 'I give you my word there will be no great armaments.' The election results on 14 November proved an overwhelming triumph for the Conservatives.[2]

In July Baldwin had asked Churchill to be a member of the Air Defence Research Sub-Committee, a request which he accepted; that appointment, and the acceptance of his help in the election, led Winston to believe that his breach with Baldwin was healed, and he did not conceal his disappointment and frustration when, again, he was excluded from government.

He now planned a long holiday when he could concentrate on *Marlborough*, Volume III, and find sunshine and scenes to paint. Winston and Clementine left England on 10 December for Majorca, via Paris and Barcelona; the Prof (Lindemann*) joined them en route.

While they were travelling the news leaked of the secret and infamous pact made between Sir Samuel Hoare[3] and Pierre Laval[4] whereby large areas of Abyssinia should be ceded to Italy, providing military action ceased. Public opinion, both in France and in Britain, was outraged. Hoare (who had made the agreement without Cabinet approval) resigned, and was succeeded as Foreign Secretary by Anthony Eden*.

Meanwhile the Churchills had returned to Barcelona, from where Clementine set out for home on 19 December. My mother and I spent Christmas at Blenheim, and on 30 December we embarked on our first skiing expedition, to Zürs-am-Arlberg in Austria. Winston spent a not very happy Christmas in Tangier, where there were gathered some friends and acquaintances; but the weather was odious.

---

[1] Italy's allies, Austria, Hungary and Albania, did not participate in sanctions; nor did Germany or the USA, neither of which was a member of the League.
[2] The Conservatives won 432 seats; Labour, 154; Liberals, 21. Randolph, who had contested West Toxteth (a Labour-held Liverpool seat) – this time as the official Conservative candidate – was

defeated. Duncan Sandys, who had married Diana on 16 September, repeated his by-election win at Epping WSC increased his majority.
[3] Sir Samuel Hoare, later Viscount Templewood (1873–1954). Secretary of State for Foreign Affairs (June–December 1935).
[4] Pierre Laval (1883–1945). Entered French Chamber of Deputies as a Socialist, but after the First World War moved towards the right. Prime Minister and Foreign Secretary, 1931–2 and 1935–6. Joined Pétain's Vichy Government in 1940 as Deputy Premier, and became Prime Minister, 1942–4, when he openly collaborated with the Germans. Tried for treason and executed, 1945.

O From WSC   El Minzah Hotel
26 December 1935   Tangier

My darling,

It seems an age since you left a week ago. We have not had a really fine day nor have I opened my paintbox. On the other hand Marlborough progresses: & Oudenarde is nearly finished.

We are just off to Rabat where we sleep en route for Marrakech, 450 miles further South. Ll.G. [Lloyd George*] telephones that the weather was beautiful there, & the hotel good. So off we go in search of the sun. Rothermere & party ... conform to our movements & the potentate makes himself vy agreeable. We play Bezique.

This is only a scribble: for I shall write more at length tonight. Tender love my sweet Clemmie to you & all. . . .

Thine ever loving
W

O From WSC   Hotel Balima
26 December 1935   Rabat

My darling,

I broke off my letter this morning as the cars were waiting. We have had a vy interesting drive through this moist, green, fertile, temperate & sparsely populated land. . . .

I too thought B[aldwin]'s speech most damaging to his position & repute. Eden's* appointment [as Foreign Secretary] does not inspire me with confidence. I expect the greatness of his office will find him out. Austen [Chamberlain] wd have been far better; & I wonder why he was overlooked. Poor man he always plays the game & never wins it!

Duncan [Sandys*] & Diana shd be here on Tuesday & I am bringing them on to Marrakech. Ll.G. says it is delightful. . . .

I have been working vy hard at Marlborough. It interests me, & takes my mind off other things about wh I can't help feeling anxious. I am longing to hear yr news from London & from Blenheim. I felt a little sad & lonely when I realised with a shock that it was Christmas Eve. I suppose you and Maria are now about to set off to Switzerland [Austria]. I do hope you will find it all you hope, & will not be too venturesome on the skis. I am most anxious to hear about Sarah's debut, & how you all got on at Manchester[1]. . . .

The more I think over the European Affair, the more I fear for our future – feebly armed & in the heart of every quarrel! Rothermere is of course horribly gloomy. He showed me a long friendly telegram he had received from Hitler. All vy pretty: but R thinks it is France or even England Hitler will attack – not Russia. R is coming on to Marrakech, & as he gets the papers with uncommon speed we shall be constantly informed. R bet Randolph this morning £500 that he would not be teetotal for the whole of 1936. Randolph took the bet – wh is a blessing. It is a kindly act of R's. He says if Randolph wins 1936 he will bet him £1,000 for 1937. Nothing cd be better for Randolph's purse or his looks.

My darling One I think a lot of you; and wish you were here so that you could pet me – for I do love that. My sweet darling I send you my fondest love and many many kisses from your wandering, sun-seeking, rather disconsolate

W
. . .

Darling pussy I love you so much.
Kiss Maria for me.

. . .

¹ When Sarah finished her training at the De Vos School of Dancing, she secured an audition with the great impresario C. B. Cochran (1872–1951), who took her on as one of his celebrated 'Young Ladies'. The Cochran revue, *Follow the Sun*, opened in Manchester just before Christmas.

O From CSC   Chartwell
29 December 1935

My Darling

I felt so sad for you when I got your telegram saying it was 'pouring' in Tangier. I do hope Marrakech is better.

Since leaving you I have been on the rush. First of all Manchester to see Sarah on the opening night. Then Blenheim, & now Mary & I are starting for our Alpine adventures!

You really would have been proud of Sarah. The dancing performed by the chorus was difficult & intricate & she was certainly in the first flight. She looked graceful & distinguished.

Blenheim was delightful & you were much missed. . . .

Tender Love to you my Darling. How is Vol: III & have you painted some lovely pictures –

Your loving
Clemmie

During the winter of 1935 a family crisis developed which was to overshadow the following year. The male star of *Follow the Sun* was Vic Oliver. Sarah and he had first met when rehearsals started for the show, and they fell in love. Sarah soon announced to her parents that they wished to be married.

Winston and Clementine were strongly opposed to the match: Vic Oliver, born Victor von Samek, of Austrian Jewish extraction, was eighteen years older than Sarah, and was not yet divorced from his Austrian wife.

The next letter must have been written as Clementine (and I) waited to embark at Dover en route for the Alps.

○ From CSC   Dover Harbour
Monday 3.15 p.m. [30 December 1935]

My Darling

I'm writing this in the car while Howes is registering my luggage.

I hated leaving you [in Barcelona]. Please write to Sarah – (but not severely). Remember the effect of the letter you wrote to Randolph 5 years ago. He was very near marrying Miss Halle when I was with him in New York.

But more important than writing is to get from Mr Cochran Mr Vic Oliver's dossier....

Your loving
Clemmie

. . .

○ From WSC [typewritten]   Hotel Mamounia
30 December 1935   Marrakech

My darling Clemmie,

At last the sun! I thought we should never overtake it....

This is a wonderful place, and the hotel one of the best I have ever used. I have an excellent bedroom and bathroom, with a large balcony twelve foot deep, looking out on a truly remarkable panorama over the tops of orange trees and olives, and the houses and ramparts of the native Marrakech, and like a great wall, to the westward [actually eastward] the snowclad range of the Atlas mountains – some of them are nearly fourteen thousand feet high. The light at dawn and sunset upon the snows, even at sixty miles distance, is as good as any snowscape I have ever seen.

Rothermere came on here with his party and we were warmly welcomed by Ll-G, who has been here for three weeks in perfect weather, and proposes to stay till February. Mrs Ll-G and Megan[1] arrive on the 8th. He is busy writing his book and is very splendid and patriarchal. What a fool Baldwin is, with this terrible situation on his hands, not to gather his resources & experience to the public service.

I am painting a picture from the balcony, because although the native city is full of attractive spots, the crowds, the smells and the general discomfort for painting have repelled me.

Diana and Duncan are on their way and I hope they will arrive by Thursday for lunch. After that we shall make some long expeditions....

The French have a large army here of fifty thousand men and the general who commands the division of eleven thousand has been to pay his compliments. I shall get him to arrange for us to go into the districts beyond the Atlas. The French garrison them, and only on certain days of the week do they guarantee the safety of travellers. They have to put out pickets and patrols etc. I think they will take good care of us....

How I wish you were here. The air is cool and fresh for we are fifteen hundred feet high, yet the sun is warm and the light brilliant. It is quite a large city with eight thousand French and one hundred and fifty thousand Moors. It is much the best place I have struck so far. But the whole country is full of interest....

We get excellent French newspapers and so are able to follow the French side of the political drama. There is no doubt we are in it up to our necks. Owing to this vigorous manifestation from the depths of British public opinion [against the Hoare–Laval Pact], the French have come a long way with us against Mussolini, and they will expect a similar service when the far greater peril of Hitler becomes active. We are getting into the most terrible position, involved definitely by honour & by contract in almost any quarrel that can break out in Europe, our defences neglected, our Government less capable a machine for conducting affairs that I have ever seen. The Baldwin–MacDonald regime has hit this country very hard indeed, and may well be the end of its glories. Now the one thing that matters seems to be to try and find seats for those two ragamuffin MacDonalds![2] Luckily I have plenty of things to do to keep me from chewing the cud too much.

✍ New Year's Eve. My beloved I have just heard yr voice on the long distance. It was a vy Miaou Cat & I cd not hear much, but it was sweet to get in touch across all these distances & foreign countries. All my wishes for yr happiness in the coming year.

Rothermere offered me 2 bets. First £2,000 if I went teetotal in 1936. I refused as I think life would not be worth living, but 2,000 free of tax is nearly 3,500 & then the saving of liquor, 500 = 4,000. It was a fine offer. I have however accepted his second bet of £600 not to drink any brandy or undiluted spirits in 1936. So tonight is my last sip of brandy.

It was kind of the old boy to take so much interest in Randolph's health & my own. I think you will be pleased.

My beloved pussy cat, I will write you again vy soon. I have been idle today. No Marl [*Marlborough*], only a little daub & a little bezique. Randolph is of course wanting to fight Malcolm M. [MacDonald]. But I hope he won't be able to – because it would put a spoke in my wheel & do nothing good for him. I do not think he would really when it came to the point.

> Tender love my darling one
> from your ever loving husband
> W

P.S. Many kisses to Maria.
Duncan & Diana arrive tomorrow at Tangier & next day here.

[1] Megan Lloyd George (1902–66), younger daughter of David Lloyd George. Liberal MP for Anglesey, 1929–43 and l945–51. President, Women's Liberal Federation, 1936 and 1945.
[2] Father and son, Ramsay MacDonald (see p. 275 n. 1) and Malcolm MacDonald were both defeated in 1935 Election. Malcolm MacDonald (1901–81) sat for Bassetlaw as Labour MP 1929–31, National Labour MP 1931–5; National Government MP, Ross and Cromarty, 1936–45. Held various government, ministerial and prestigious Commonwealth appointments. WSC made him High Commissioner to Canada in 1941.

Clementine took to the ski slopes in her fifty-first year. For the next three winters she took me either to Austria or to Switzerland in the Christmas holidays; she usually stayed on after I had to return to school.

○ From CSC   Hotel Zürserhof
Tuesday 7 January 1936   Zürs

My darling,

I was so very glad to get your interesting letter (of December 30). Here we are 5,500 feet up above the clouds in the eye of the sun completely enclosed in a little valley. On the steep slopes you can sometimes count over 400 human beings, struggling in the glistening powder-like snow. The ones near the top are the experts; (& there are many grades of them) they look like flies. It takes them 1½ hours to climb up [no ski-lifts then!] & perhaps 12 minutes to swirl down in lovely curves.... Further down are the less good skiers – those who have only been out say 2 years and on the lower slopes are the 'ski babies' among them myself, Maria, Clarissa[1], and since yesterday Venetia [Montagu*], her daughter Judy[2] and another little girl. It is extraordinarily difficult and laborious and it is a mystery to me why it is done at all, but there is a strange fascination about it & tremendous satisfaction at every minute stage of progress....

The idea of joining you in Morocco attracts me very much. For one thing I miss my Pig very much; but I want to stay out here till the 21st and I suppose by then you will be thinking of moving home?...

The political situation at home is depressing, I really would not like you to serve under Baldwin, unless he really gave you a great deal of power and you were able to inspire and vivify the Government. But as you say we are in it up to our necks and that cannot be altered now. All you could do would be to organise our armed forces. The very pussy foots who trust Baldwin are being involved by him (& not by policy but by muddle). Goodbye my darling.

Your loving
Clemmie

[1] Clarissa Churchill, b. 28 June 1920, Jack and Goonie's only daughter. In August 1952 she married, as his second wife, Anthony Eden, later 1st Earl of Avon (see Biographical Notes).
[2] Judy Montagu (1923–72), only child of Edwin and Venetia Montagu. Married, 1962, Milton Gendel; one daughter, Anna, born 1963. Judy and I were much thrown together as children because of our mothers' friendship: we heartily disliked each other till we were about fifteen, when we became devoted friends.

○ From WSC [typewritten]   Hotel Mamounia
8 January 1936   Marrakech

My darling Clemmie,

Of course during last week the excitement here has been about the Ross and Cromarty [Scotland] by-election[1]. The [Conservative] Unionist

Association have unanimously and officially appealed to Randolph to stand against Malcolm MacDonald.... You will see how unfortunate and inconvenient such a fight is to me. 'Churchill v. MacDonald'. If they get in, it would seem very difficult for Baldwin to invite me to take the Admiralty or the co-ordinating [Defence] job, and sit cheek by jowl with these wretched people. I therefore would greatly have preferred Randolph to damp it all down. Instead of this he has had his agent up there feeling around.

Quite apart from this, there is no doubt the thoughts of all Conservatives in the constituency turn naturally to him. It is a great insult to a Scottish constituency to be used as a mere utensil for Baldwin's purposes. Moreover this National Labour business is humbug.... The whole manoeuvre is an abuse of representative government, and I do not at all wonder that the Scottish electors are furious and insulted at being made a dump for these adventurers, whom no English constituency will receive. As I said, I should have been very glad if Randolph had put a stopper on the whole business, so far as he is concerned. But what with the insistent telegrams from the Ross and Cromarty Conservatives, and the press and broadcast references; and with Rothermere, Beaverbrook* and Lloyd George* all goading him on, I really cannot blame him for accepting the official invitation of the local Conservative Association.

Neither do I think the fight hopeless. There will be four candidates. The Simonite Liberals [supported National Government] will fight the Samuelite Liberals [did not support National Government], splitting the Liberal vote at least half and half. A good Socialist candidate will be out to down Malcolm MacDonald at all costs. Randolph who will be the most live, powerful, presentable and also a consistent candidate in the field, might well get the five or six thousand votes which will win the seat. How will Baldwin take it? Will he regard it as a definite declaration of war by me? I have of course expressed no opinion whatever, and Randolph will make it clear he is acting entirely on his own.

Rothermere is sending Oliver Baldwin[2] to write up Randolph, which he is apparently ready to do, and to write down Malcolm, which of course is what all other Socialists revel in. So we shall have Ramsay's son, Baldwin's son and my son – all mauling each other in this remote constituency....

Randolph started last night, and tomorrow will be flying by aeroplane from Casablanca to Barcelona, this being the only means by which he can be in Dingwall [Ross and Cromarty] on Friday. It will be a star contest, and will certainly have the sympathy of Conservatives, and all those who hate 'jobs' and humbug. In addition it will have the Rothermere–Beaverbrook support in a most vigorous manner....

I think the Government greatly weakened by what has occurred over the Hoare–Laval agreement, and Baldwin greatly weakened too. Therefore I expect that either Baldwin will be looking for a chance to clear out, or he will want a strong reconstruction. The Naval Conference[3] is breaking down and Monsell[4] will soon be going. Thus everything comes to a head at once, and Destiny will decide. I thought you would like me to give you my views at length upon this unsought-for event.

This is a wonderful place.... In my opinion it is better than any of the hotels I have stayed in on the Riviera.... The country is wonderful with the fertile red and black soil, gushing streams of water, swarms of picturesque inhabitants, every one of whom is a picture, perfect cloudless days, brilliant sunshine, translucent air.... We are fifteen hundred feet high and the air is crisp, even sharp the moment one is out of the sun. But the sunlight is mellow and warm, and though the days are short, they are brilliant.

Esmond[5] is coming out here, and Rothermere has travelled north like a dutiful father to meet him at Tangier.... He has been good enough to arrange to have all the newspapers brought here each day by air for me and Lloyd George. This is a great convenience for we are only forty-eight hours behind the Times.

I have no plans and propose to stay here till I get bored. I spend the whole day painting and on Marlborough (apart from eating and drinking) but no neat spirits, according to the bet. Randolph is completely teetotal, though it does not seem to make him better tempered.

I have had one letter from you, but I look forward to some full account of your ski-ing, and how Mary is getting on?... Lloyd George is staying here till the end of February. His daily routine is simple. He wakes at five and works on his <u>history</u> (save the mark) till breakfast. He plays golf on a very good course here till lunch. He sleeps from lunch till tea-time. His small wireless gives us what the B.B.C. call the news bulletin, much twaddle, but here and there some facts. He dines early, then bed at 10.15. My roster is a little different, but equally satisfactory....

... The world seems to be divided between the confident nations who behave harshly, and the nations who have lost confidence in themselves and behave fatuously. Mussolini is failing more and more in his Italian campaign. What I told you about the Italians being no good at fighting is being painfully proved. They are throwing away their wealth and their poor wedding rings[6] on an absolutely shameful adventure. How it will end no one can tell. I am very sorry Austen [Chamberlain] was not made Foreign Secretary. I think you will now see what a light-weight Eden* is. The League of Nations Union send me heaps of letters from the constituency clamouring for extreme measures, they having previously disarmed us, so that we are an easy prey!

🐾 It is vy nice having Diana & Duncan here. They are so happy. They say it is a second honeymoon. Anyhow Sunshine, Love, & no expense or household cares ought to be pretty good! The more I see of him, the better I like him. They read political books to each other under the palm trees while I paint. I think you will be surprised to see the pictures I have painted. ... I now have <u>seven</u>....

I am longing to hear yr news....

Tender love my darling pussy cat
Your ever devoted husband
W

P.S. I wonder if the ginger cat misses me!

[1] Occasioned by the resignation of the sitting National Liberal MP. The local Liberal Association (in accordance with the National Government code) had adopted Malcolm MacDonald (see p. 405 n. 2) as their candidate.
[2] Oliver Baldwin (1899–1958), elder son of Stanley Baldwin. Labour MP for Dudley, 1929–31; for Paisley, 1945–7. Succeeded his father as 2nd Earl Baldwin, 1947. Governor of Leeward Islands, 1948–50.
[3] The London Naval Conference, set up in 1930 to limit naval armaments and reduce tension in the Far East, had resumed on 6 January 1936. Japan withdrew on 15 January. The London Naval Treaty, defining categories of ship, permitted tonnages and gun sizes, and requiring advance notification of building programmes, was signed by Britain, the USA and France on 25 March and by the USSR on 1 October 1936.
[4] Viscount Monsell (1881–1969), First Lord of the Admiralty, November 1931–June 1936.
[5] Esmond Harmsworth (1898–1978), son and heir of Lord Rothermere, whom he succeeded as 2nd Viscount, 1940. Chairman of Associated Newspapers Ltd, 1932–71.
[6] On 18 December 1935 Mussolini had appealed to all Italian women to donate their gold wedding rings to help finance the Abyssinian campaign.

O From CSC   Hotel Zürserhof
11 January 1936   Zürs

My Darling

I'm anxiously awaiting news of Randolph & his activities. Yesterday we went on our expedition.... We had a charming guide who carried our food, our coats, 1st aid apparatus, &, poor fellow, in the end almost had to carry me! I gave him a handsome tip which he tried to refuse & said 'it was a pleasure'; which makes me feel he must have rather a dull life – My Darling you would have laughed & also been rather angry if you had seen us clinging like flies on a wall to the sheer slopes! Mary fell down 19 times, we counted, but she said 'only 18½ times'!

To-day I am going in a sleigh as I am really bored with tumbling down!

Tender Love from
Your bruised & struggling but undaunted
Clemmie

O From WSC [typewritten]   Hôtel Transatlantique
15 January 1936   Meknes

My darling Clemmie,

We quitted Marrakech on the 14th with much regret, eighteen days having gone without count of time. Rothermere sent a motor which conveyed us 250 miles northwards to Meknes, where we still are. It is an excellent hotel, and is situated in most beautiful fertile foothills of the Atlas mountains, but does not compare with Marrakech. The weather is definitely colder, the sunlight less mellow and the vegetation Spanish rather than African. There is of course the great native city of Fez which we shall go to see tomorrow or the day after. Rothermere and Esmond [Harmsworth] are here, very friendly to us, and very pessimistic about everything....

You will no doubt have read in the papers all about Randolph. Today he telegraphs that an unimportant Scottish paper alleges I am wholeheartedly supporting his candidature. I am reluctant to disavow him and have let things drift.... I shall not make up my mind upon the matter further until I get home, but I should think that any question of my joining the Government was closed by the hostility which Randolph's campaign must excite. Kismet![1]

At Marrakech Ll.G [Lloyd George*]'s party and ours dined with the Glaoui[2] or Pasha and ate a gargantuan endless Arab feast with our fingers. He is a very able man and keeps a great state in Marrakech. His son, aged 21, lives at Telouet, a hundred miles into the heart of the Atlas mountains. We visited him there by a splendid road with awful precipices on either side, and were entertained in his enormous castle which lies about the level of the snow line in a sombre valley. We were received with a great welcome and had another Arab banquet – I hope my last for a long time.... Ll.G. and I returned the Glaoui's hospitality by giving him a dinner at the hotel which went off very successfully....

I have been idle the last few days as we have been moving so much. Marlborough has advanced but little. I have four articles to do which I must manage somehow on the journey home.

17th January.

...

So here we are on our way in the train approaching Marrakech again amid sunshine once more warm and brilliant....

It is Ll.G's birthday [his seventy-third] and we are all going to dine together to celebrate it....

I am delighted to know that you are enjoying yourself at Zürs. You certainly should do so with such agreeable company. Also to hear you and Mary are progressing in the art of ski-ing. I am afraid I must resign all attempts to emulate you....

... I fear they [the Government] have some grave news about Germany and her aggressive intentions. Certainly our Ambassador at Berlin found a very rough Hitler when he went to talk about an air pact. They are getting stronger every moment. They have chosen to make their Press demonstrate vehemently against the Anglo-French military and naval conversations which were necessary upon the Italian danger.... Rothermere who has long letters and telegrams from Hitler and is in close touch with him, believes that on the 24th or it may be the 21st, Hitler is going to make a most important announcement. This may well be that Germany will violate Articles 46 and 47 of the Treaty and reoccupy the neutral zone [of the Rhineland] with troops and forts. This would immediately raise a very grave European issue, and no one can tell what would come of it. Certainly the League of Nations would be obliged to declare the Germans guilty of 'aggression', and the French would be in a position to demand our specific aid in enforcing sanctions. So the League of Nations Union folk who have done their best to get us disarmed may find themselves confronted by terrible consequences. Baldwin and Ramsay, guilty of neglecting our defences in spite of every warning, may well feel anxious not only for the public but for their own personal skins.

The Naval Conference has of course collapsed. Japan has ruptured it. The good thing is that we and the United States are working hand in glove and will encourage each other to strengthen the navies. Meanwhile Japan is seeking more provinces of China. Already more than half of their whole budget is spent upon armaments. Those figures I quoted about German expenditure on armaments are being admitted in the press to be only too true. One must consider these two predatory military dictatorship nations, Germany and Japan, as working in accord. No wonder the Russian bear is quaking for his skin and seeking protectors among the capitalist powers he deserted in the war, and sought to destroy at the close of it. What – to quote a famous phrase – 'What a fearful concatenation of circumstances.'[3] How melancholy that we have this helpless Baldwin and his valets in absolute possession of all power!...

It is very nice to look forward to another week of sunshine and painting. I expect you will be surprised at my pictures when you see them. They are a cut above anything I have ever done so far. ✍ One more today! I am doing figures so much better than before. Indeed every person here however poor is a picture, & the crowds with their bright varied colours are a pageant.

My darling pussy cat – I must bring you to this place. I am sure we could spend some happy weeks here together in sunshine, when perhaps at home all was gloomy & cold.

I will write again vy soon. Meanwhile give my fondest love to Maria, & tell her how glad I am she is getting on so well in ski-ing.

Your ever devoted & loving husband
W
...

---

[1] Kismet, from Turkish *qismet*, meaning fate, destiny or the fulfilment of destiny.
[2] El Hadji T'hami El Glaoui, paramount Pasha of Marrakech and Hereditary Sultan of the Atlas (d. 1956).
[3] Daniel Webster (1782–1852), American statesman and orator.

On 20 January 1936 King George V died and was succeeded by the Prince of Wales as King Edward VIII. Winston cut short his Moroccan holiday to return home on 23 January. Clementine stayed on in Zürs for several more weeks after I was despatched home to school with her maid.

The Ross and Cromarty by-election was held on 10 February, resulting in a clear win for Malcolm MacDonald (National Labour); Randolph came a poor third after the Labour candidate, and the Liberal candidate lost his deposit[1]. Anti-Churchillians took snide pleasure in the defeat of Randolph and in what they presumed must be the discomfiture of his father.

Altogether, family affairs were somewhat fraught, as shown in Winston's next letter, written from the Chamber of the House of Commons during a debate.

[1] The results were: National Labour (M. MacDonald), 8,949; Labour, 5,967; Conservative (R. Churchill), 2,427; Liberal, 738: a majority of 2,982 for Malcolm MacDonald.

○ From WSC   House of Commons
[Friday] 21 February 1936

My darling,
   The interview took place on Sat[y] at noon. He [Vic Oliver] professed himself quite ready to give the name & address of his mother & sister. His father was a well-known cloth manufacturer at Brünn named Victor Samek. He did not impress me with being a bad man; but common as dirt: An Austrian citizen, a resident in U.S., & here on license & an American passport: twice divorced[1]: 36 so he says. A horrible mouth: a foul Austro-Yankee drawl. I did not offer to shake hands: but put him through a long examination. He described Sarah [who was present] as the 'brainiest & smartest gurl' he had ever met. He said that they would not think of getting married in a hurry, & 'that he would not force his way into my family agst my wishes': but he said they were always seen together at lunch supper etc: evil suggestions might be made, & the best thing was an engagement.
   You may imagine that I confronted him with the hard side of things. I told him that if there was an engagement, it would force me to make an immediate public statement in terms wh wd be painful to them both. I then recapitulated the whole case agst their marriage or engagement. And I said that if they wd not see each other or communicate for one year, & were still in the same mood at the end, I would withdraw my resistance, otherwise I wd do my best to persuade Sarah not to take a fatal step. On this he got up with gt emotion, not without some dignity, & said 'You don't need to do it. I will do it myself'.
   Sarah followed him downstairs & I have not seen her since. But I put Diana on to her & I learn that the idea of an engagement is off: & in my talks to her on the telephone she seems calm & in fairly good spirits. I don't think there is immediate cause to worry.
   I am now going to try to get Sarah out of the revue [*Follow the Sun*], & started on the regular stage. Penelope Ward[2] is working on the Liverpool repertory theatre, & I am finding out more about this from Brendan [Bracken*]. Cochran will I am sure do anything he can to help.
   My darling I am writing this to you while Bob Boothby is speaking just behind me. But I wanted to give you a reasoned account....
   There is no change in the uncertainty about my affairs. Evidently B[aldwin] desires above all things to avoid bringing me in. This I must now recognise. But his own position is much shaken, & the storm clouds gather.
   How are you getting on? I do hope you are happy, healthy & making progress: & that the snow will not melt prematurely.

                              With innumerable kisses & tender love,
                                 Your loving & devoted husband
                                                      W
                                                      ...

[1] Not correct: Vic Oliver was only once married and divorced before he met Sarah.
[2] Penelope Dudley Ward (1914–82), one of the two daughters of William and Freda Dudley Ward (see pp. 227 n. 2; 242 n. 2). Very beautiful and a charmer. A successful actress on stage and screen. Brendan Bracken was a great friend of Freda Dudley Ward and her daughters.

○ From CSC   Sporthotel Lorünser[1]
27 February 1936   Zürs

My Darling, Your letter dated the 21st has only just reached me at Noon – Your account of your interview with Mr Oliver riveted me with renewed horror at the possibility of such a marriage – Sarah must be more than stage struck – In the middle ages it would be thought she was bewitched – My Darling – Here I am doing nothing to avert this disaster; but I feel Sarah will pay more attention to your opinions & to the time & trouble you are taking over her & her affairs. I am like the poor – 'always with her' – I agree with your diagnosis of Mr Oliver – not a bad man, but common as dirt etc. I spent an evening in his company; but before I knew what was impending – So I did not look at him with an all searching eye. But even as a boon companion I was surprised at Sarah's taste. . . .

My Darling – I think Baldwin must be mad not to ask you to help him – Perhaps it is a case of 'Those whom the gods wish to destroy – – – '

As for ski-ing I have come to the conclusion that it is not a pleasure but a vice – I have got it very badly. It is unbelievably difficult & my vanity is nettled that I do not get on faster. The weather is lovely. Glittering sun & heavenly blue skies – Very hot in the middle of the day – Icy at night. But the hotel tho' rather rough & homely is cosy & warm. . . .

Your loving
Clemmie

[1] After my departure CSC had moved into a smaller hotel in the village, to be nearer her friends.

○ From WSC   11, Morpeth Mansions
3 March 1936

My darling,

On Sunday when we went to feed Jupiter [white swan] she would not eat from my hand. On Monday she was dead. She has been on the lake 10 years & was about 3 years old when she came. They only live about 12 years normally. So it was quite natural.

I send you a letter about the Liverpool Repertory Theatre. . . . I told Sarah about it & she said she would vy much like to go as soon as possible after this run of Follow the Sun is over. She has taken quite kindly to the plan. . . . She came down to luncheon on Sunday & seems quite cheerful. I said 'Does what you told me about "no need to worry" still hold good.' She replied 'Oh yes indeed it does'. I hope from her manner that this cloud will presently roll by. Once it has I will say a kind word to the man.

However do not let us count our chickens before we have them all back in the hen coop.

The Defence business is at its height. Baldwin is still undecided[1]. His own choice was Swinton (Cunliffe Lloyd Lister Greame)[2]. But a really ugly snarl from the Commons has I believe scared him from appointing a Peer. On Saturday Bendor [Westminster*] came out of the blue to luncheon at Chartwell, being much worked up on my behalf. He asked Gwynne[3] of the M.P. [*Morning Post*] about it, who said 'there was reason to believe matters wd be settled as he wished'. Now this morning the D.T. [*Daily Telegraph*] comes out as the enclosed, wh is the most positive statement yet & the latest – & from a usually well-informed Government quarter. Anyhow I seem to be still en jeu. I suppose that to-day or tomorrow it must be settled. Betty Cranborne[4] (whom I met at Jack [Churchill*] & Goonie's dining last night) told me that Neville Ch[amberlain][5] said to her last week 'Of course if it is a question of military efficiency, Winston is no doubt the man'. Every other possible alternative is being considered & blown upon. Hoare because of his F.O. [Foreign Office] position & Hoare–Laval pact: Swinton & Hankey[6] & Weir[7] because Peers: Ramsay [MacDonald] because all can see he is a walking ruin: Lord U. ['Useless' (Eustace)] Percy because of himself & his size: Neville because he sees the PM'ship not far off. K[ingsley] Wood[8] because he hopes to be Ch of Exch then, & anyhow does not know a Lieutenant General from a Whitehead torpedo: [Sir Robert] Horne because he will not give up his £25,000 a year directorships – etc. So at the end it may all come back to your poor [sketch of pig].... I do not mean to break my heart whatever happens. Destiny plays her part.

If I get it, I will work faithfully before God & man for <u>Peace</u>, & not allow pride or excitement to sway my spirit.

If I am not wanted, we have many things to make us happy, my darling beloved Clemmie. I will wire if anything 'transpires'.

Your ever loving husband
W

P.S. It wd be the heaviest burden yet. They are <u>terribly</u> behindhand.

[1] The appointment of a Minister for Co-ordination of Defence was mooted in the press and political circles. WSC's name featured prominently as a possible choice. In the event the post was created on 13 March 1936 and Sir Thomas Inskip (see p. 381 n. 3) was appointed.
[2] Sir Philip Cunliffe-Lister, formerly Philip Lloyd Greame, had been created Viscount Swinton on 29 November 1935. See p. 381 n. 7.
[3] H. A. Gwynne, Editor of the *Morning Post*.
[4] Elizabeth (born Cavendish) (1897–1982), wife of Viscount Cranborne (Bobbety), later 5th Marquess of Salisbury (see p. 462 n. 3). Elder daughter of Lord Richard Cavendish, brother of the 9th Duke of Devonshire, and his wife Lady Moyra.
[5] At this date Chancellor of the Exchequer (1931–7).
[6] Sir Maurice Hankey. At this date Secretary to the Cabinet (1919–38). He did not, in fact, become a Baron until February 1939.
[7] William Douglas Weir (1877–1959), cr. Baron, 1918; 1st Viscount Weir, 1938. Shipping contractor and pioneer motor car manufacturer. Adviser, Air Ministry, 1935–9.
[8] Sir Kingsley Wood (1881–1943), Conservative MP 1918–43. Several government offices; at this date Minister of Health (1935–8). Chancellor of the Exchequer in WSC's War Cabinet, from 1940.

Clementine was still away in Zürs when, on 7 March 1936, German troops reoccupied the demilitarized zone of the Rhineland, committing yet another breach of the Treaty of Versailles. The German force had orders to withdraw should any opposition be offered, but Hitler had judged all too well the effect of the spirit of pacifism which infected public opinion in France and Britain weakening their governments' resolve, so nothing – other than protest – was opposed to the aggression.

In early May, Abyssinia was conquered; the Emperor Haile Selassie fled to England, and Mussolini annexed Abyssinia to Italy. In mid-July a revolt broke out in the Spanish army against the left-wing Republican Government; General Franco[1] assumed the leadership of the Nationalists, and a grim civil war ensued in which terrible atrocities were committed on both sides. Britain, France, Germany and Italy were among other European states who signed an agreement of non-interference in Spain. Hitler and Mussolini broke the agreement and supported Franco with massive military aid which would prove decisive in the Nationalist victory in 1939.[2]

On 24 August Winston and Clementine went to stay with Consuelo and Jacques Balsan* at St Georges Motel, near Dreux in Normandy. Winston then went south to stay with Maxine Elliott* at the Château de l'Horizon, and Clementine returned home to Chartwell.

[1] General Francisco Franco (Bahamonde) (1892–1975), Spanish military dictator. One of the leaders of the Nationalist revolt, July 1936; in 1939, having overthrown the Republican regime, he proclaimed himself head of state (Caudillo).
[2] British opinion was divided: neither Conservative nor Labour leaders favoured intervention. About 2,000 British citizens joined the International Brigade and fought for the Republicans.

O From WSC   Château de l'Horizon
5 September 1936

My darling,
    I have been painting all day & every day. I have found a beautiful clear river – the Loup – & a quiet wild spot, & I study the clear water. I have done two variants which I hope you will admire as much as I do![1] Wow! Tomorrow I go to lunch with Muriel [Warde] (who came over here) at Maryland.... After lunch I shall have another go at the little port of St Jean Cap Ferrat – wh you know I have several times attempted.
    The weather has been bright & warm, but tonight there is more wind & also cloud & mist. Loelia [Westminster][2] left yesterday & we have here only Doris [Castlerosse][3], a young French film actress (vy pretty but not vy successful), Lord Queensberry's younger brother (who lost a leg in the war). But many come as usual to bathe & lunch ... (I can't remember them all – or indeed any).... I have just completed the first of my new articles for the News of the W[orld]. I mean to do at least three before I leave. They are vy lucrative. It wd be folly not to work them off in view of many uncertainties.
    I have arranged to go to the [French army] manoeuvres at Aix en Provence on Wed. 9th & 10th. I am to have a formal invitation....
    I am thankful the Spanish Nationalists are making progress. They are the

only ones who have the power of attack. The others can only die sitting. Horrible! But better for the safety of all if the Communists are crushed....

Tender love my sweet Clemmie,
Always your devoted loving husband
Winston
...

[1] One of these is now in the Tate Gallery collection.
[2] Born Loelia Ponsonby, only daughter of 1st Baron Sysonby, she had married the Duke of Westminster, as his third wife, in 1930; they separated in 1935, but were not divorced until 1946.
[3] Born Doris Delavigne, wife of Viscount Castlerosse (later 6th Earl of Kenmare). The marriage was dissolved 1938; she died 1942.

O From CSC   Chartwell
8 September 1936

My Darling Winston

How wise you are to be in the South for here it is autumnal. I have had the furnace let out under the pool as no one bathes, but the filter is kept working so that in the pale fitful sunlight the pool looks like a great aquamarine....

... Wednesday we 'showed the garden' – It was a lovely day – The pool was newly scrubbed & crystal water was pouring in. At first I thought we were to have very few visitors – They came straggling in; but soon they became a steady trickle which continued till at closing time they numbered 526 – £28. 18. 9. for the Hospitals. Half of them visited your Studio – The next day I went over to Woodford & opened a Fête & was made to bowl in a cricket match. I find I can't bowl straight – at least not over arm – it's very annoying. I took over one of Mary's budgerigars[1] in a lovely green cage as a present for Sir James Hawkey's little grand-daughter. That was a great success. When I got home I found Goonie & Clarissa who were followed on Friday by Jack [Churchill*] & Peregrine, so we had a nice cosy family week-end. You were much missed & so was Mary, who is away in Brittany staying with the Grant Forbes[2]. Also there were no dogs as careful Moppet [Whyte*] had before leaving boarded them out at the Vet. William Nicholson* (Cher Maître) also came down so it was very pleasant....

... Sarah has been very sweet & loving, but I fear there is no improvement in that quarter [vis-à-vis Vic Oliver]....

Your loving
Clemmie

I'm lunching at Lympne to-day. Philip [Sassoon*] is sending his aeroplane.

[1] My one and only commercial venture – as proprietress of the 'Happy Zoo' I bred budgerigars and sold them.
[2] James Grant Forbes, an American businessman, and his wife Margaret took Squerryes Court, Westerham, on a long lease in the 1930s. They also had a house, Les Essarts, at St Briac, near Dinard. They had 11 children; I was great friends with my contemporaries among them, and was invited to Brittany several years for glorious seaside visits.

O From WSC   Domecy-sur-Cure
13 September 1936   Yonne

My darling,
   I arrived here this morning. It is 120 kilometres from Dijon by car. We
are in the heart of France: Flandin's[1] home, by the banks of the clear swift-
flowing Cure. We have exhausted the possibilities of conversation on
politics, & I have retired to bed to write to you.
   The eleven days I passed with Maxine [Elliott*] were pleasant – The
weather beautiful, every comfort, & I have painted six beautiful pictures,
besides the three at Dreux. I am sending them home tomorrow or next
day by Mrs P [Violet Pearman, secretary]: but do not unpack them till I
come; for I want to do the honours with them for yr benefit myself. ...
   The manoeuvres were vy interesting. I drove about all day with General
Gamelin[2] the Generalissimo, who was communicative on serious topics.
There was nothing to see, as all the troops were hidden in holes or under
bushes. But to anyone with military knowledge it was most instructive.
The officers of the French army are impressive by their gravity &
competence. One feels the strength of the nation resides in its army.
Tomorrow I go to Paris, dine & sleep at the Embassy & then on Tuesday
go to the fortress line[3]. The military attaché & [Lord] Lloyd are coming with
me. It will be a pilgrimage well worth making. I shall perhaps stay 17th in
Paris, and perhaps make a little 'discours' to the journalists, before
returning.
   Everything gets worse, except that the Nationalists [Franco's army] (as
they insist on being called) are winning. <u>Secret</u>. F[landin] thinks that the
French Communists were paid at the election, not by Russia, but by
<u>Germany</u> – in order to weaken France! Pretty cynical if true. This would
explain why Stalin[4] executed the Bolshevik old guard: i.e. in order to
break the orthodox Communists who were disobeying his orders about
not disturbing France. On this showing it looks as if the Russians are trying
to move to the right – & with sincerity. Of course this is only surmise.
   My darling I got yr letter, & was much pleased by all yr Chartwell news.
I wonder how Diana is getting on. It must be vy near now[5]. ...
[in margin] Indigestion definitely better.
   My darling I hope you got my wire & flowers on September 12. How
time flies! My sweet Clemmie, how much I owe you. With a thousand
kisses, I remain

                                            Your loving devoted husband

                                                                        ...

...

[1] Pierre Etienne Flandin (see p. 381 n. 6). He had ceased to be French Minister for Foreign Affairs
in June 1936.
[2] Gen. Maurice Gustave Gamelin (1872–1958), Chief of Staff of the French Army from 1931;
Inspector-General of the Army and Vice-President of the War Council, 1935–7.
[3] The Maginot Line: an underground fortification system constructed in 1929–38 to protect the
eastern frontier of France against a German thrust, stretching from the Swiss border to the
Luxembourg and Belgian frontiers and into southern France. In 1940 the main German attack
through Belgium outflanked the Line.
[4] Joseph Stalin (1879–1953), Communist leader of the USSR. He eliminated opposition to his
ideology in the 'Great Purge' of 1936.
[5] Diana was expecting her first child. Julian Sandys was born 19 September 1936.

◇ From CSC
[undated pencil note, on plain paper]

I love your beautiful carnations –

Purr ... X X X

While Winston had been on his journeys a drama had erupted at home. On 14 September Sarah left without telling her parents to join Vic Oliver in New York. Naturally this news, communicated by Sarah in a letter to Clementine after her departure, caused her mother the utmost distress, as did the subsequent publicity on both sides of the Atlantic.

During this autumn and winter the saga of King Edward VIII and Mrs Simpson[1] developed: the King's relationship with Wallis Simpson had been known to the higher reaches of the 'establishment', and the world's press had commented upon their affair for many months, but it was not until early December that it was reported in the British newspapers, when a major constitutional crisis developed.

The King turned to Churchill, among others, for advice and support. Winston had known him since his youth and was devoted to him, and he sought by every means to play for time, hoping some solution might be arrived at short of abdication. One idea he canvassed was that of a morganatic marriage[2], but the Cabinet refused to accept this possible solution, nor would it have been acceptable to the Commonwealth.

On this whole issue Clementine profoundly disagreed with Winston – judging the mood and opinion in the country more accurately than he did. She realized that his chivalrous championship of the King's cause was damaging to his own political position, at a time when people were beginning to heed his warnings as to the nation's defences and the dangers presented by the dictators.

[1] Wallis Simpson (born Warfield), later Duchess of Windsor (1896–1986), daughter of Teakle Wallis Warfield of Baltimore. Twice-divorced American socialite. Married Edward, Duke of Windsor (formerly King Edward VIII) in 1937.
[2] By which the King could have married Mrs Simpson, but she would have remained a private citizen, and any children of the marriage would not have been in the line of succession. Morganatic marriage is, however, unknown in England, although practised among Continental royalty, and an Act of Parliament would have been necessary to make this solution to the *impasse* possible.

○ From WSC   Eaton[1]
27 November 1936

My darling,
    We had a jolly day. I shot 112 birds. Indeed a year without Brandy seems to have improved my eye.
    You would not have been particularly amused by the guests, or by the sport....
    Max [Beaverbrook*] rang me up to say he had seen the gent [King Edward VIII], & told him the Cornwall plan[2] was my idea. The gent was

definitely for it. It now turns on what the Cabinet will say. I don't see any other way through.

Good night my darling one. I will telegraph whether I return tomorrow late or Sunday early.

Fondest love,
Your ever loving husband
W

[1] Eaton Hall, the Duke of Westminster's home near Chester.
[2] If the idea of a morganatic marriage had developed, it was suggested that Mrs Simpson should become the Duchess of Cornwall.

Nineteen-thirty-six ended on a muted note for the Churchills: Winston was mortified by the hostility demonstrated in the House when (on 7 December) he had sought to make a plea that no 'irrevocable step' would be taken with regard to the King – he was literally shouted down. Both he and Clementine were deeply affected by the King's abdication on 11 December.

Sarah married Vic Oliver in New York on Christmas Eve.

It was rather a quiet Christmas and New Year at Chartwell; but to our home party were added Diana and Duncan, and their first child, Julian, now three months old.

Chapter XVIII

NONE SO DEAF

Nineteen-thirty-seven opened with Winston staying with Sir Philip Sassoon* at Trent Park, near London, while Clementine was on her way to Zürs.

The first letters of this year are much concerned with the sudden, tragic death of Ralph Wigram[1], aged forty-six, a Counsellor at the Foreign Office. He was one of a small band of servicemen and public servants who, in despair with the Government's policy, and the total inadequacy of the progress being made towards re-armament, supplied (at personal risk to themselves and their careers) details of Government policy, technical details about armaments, etc., enabling Churchill to wage a more effective campaign urging the Government into action and converting public opinion.

[1] Ralph Wigram (1890–1936), Counsellor, Foreign Office, from 1934 and Head of the Central Department. He married (1925) Ava Bodley (1897–1975), daughter of the historian J .E. C. Bodley.

O From WSC
2 January 1937

Trent
New Barnet

My darling,
I fear you had an uncomfortable crossing. Howes said the sea & wind were vy high, the boat small, crowded, French, & that you had no private cabin. I bewailed yr misfortunes, but anyhow they are now over.

I was deeply shocked & grieved to learn from Vansittart[1] by chance on the telephone that poor Ralph Wigram died suddenly on New Year's Eve in his wife's arms. I thought him a grand fellow. A bright steady flame burning in a broken lamp, wh guided us towards safety & honour.

Brendan [Bracken*] & I are going on Monday to the Funeral wh is at Cuckfield near Haywards Heath. Afterwards I shall bring him & Vansittart back to luncheon at Chartwell. I am taking a wreath from us both. Poor little Ava is all adrift now. She cherished him & kept him alive. He was her contact with gt affairs. Now she has only the idiot child.[2] ...

The King's[3] business forms a constant theme. I have worked at Marl. [*Marlborough*] & am also painting a little daub indoors.

420

I hope by now you are safe & teed-up at Zurs –

> With all my fondest love
> Your devoted loving husband
> W
> ...

[1] Sir Robert (later 1st Baron) Vansittart (1881–1957), diplomat. At this date Permanent Under-Secretary of State for Foreign Affairs (1930–8).
[2] Charles Wigram (1929–51), only son of Ralph and Ava Wigram. A Down's syndrome child, he died aged 21.
[3] The former King Edward VIII, now Duke of Windsor.

O From CSC   Flexenhotel
Sunday 3 January [1937]   Zürs am Arlberg

My darling

I arrived yesterday two hours late after a really grim Channel crossing –
I had omitted to reserve a cabin & was fortunate in getting a sofa in the
public women's saloon – People had to lie on the floor & many had to
stand up, so crowded was the boat – But I was <u>not</u> sick ... Mary[1] who had
been with some kind local neighbours at the next village joined me for
luncheon bringing them with her....

... My Darling I do hope you are having a happy visit at Trent. Do not
be sad my Dear One. There is nothing which you have done which in
perspective will not seem generous & courageous – which is indeed the
truth[2] –

Venetia [Montagu*] & her child [Judy] & our niece Clarissa arrive here on
the 7th –

I will write again in a day or two. This is just to bring you my dear Love.

> Your own
> Clemmie

[1] I had gone to Austria ahead of my mother with a party of friends.
[2] This refers to WSC's championship of King Edward VIII (now Duke of Windsor), which had cost
him dear politically, and which his enemies attributed to his hostility to Baldwin. Any understanding of WSC's character refutes this view: he had reacted to the King's dilemma spontaneously,
rallying to his Sovereign – a long-time friend – in his hour of need.

O From CSC   Flexenhotel
Tuesday 5 January 1937   Zürs am Arlberg
4 a.m.

My Darling,

I am horrified & astonished to read in last Saturday's Times an
'appreciation' of your friend Ralph Wigram by Vansittart. Did you know he
was ill? ... I am so very sorry – He was a true friend of yours & in his eye
you could see the spark which showed an inner light was burning –

His poor little wife will be overwhelmed with grief –

In these troubled times one is astonished to be standing up – with head
'bloody but unbowed' –

I wonder if you have seen our Sarah.[1] I'm glad I waited. She is unchanged – as virginal & aloof as ever.

Yesterday at Noon the Sun was dazzling, the sky blue & it was so hot that a cotton shirt with short sleeves & an open neck seemed the only thing to wear on the slopes. . . .

Mary has been promoted & is now more than half way up the Ski school. I am more pedestrian but still creditable.

Your loving,
Clemmie

[1] Sarah and Vic Oliver had left New York for England immediately after their Christmas Eve (1936) wedding. They went down to Chartwell soon after their arrival to see her parents (CSC had delayed her departure for Zürs in order to see them).

O From WSC   Chartwell
7 January 1937

My darling,

Yr second letter arrived this morning. I am so glad you have health, snow & sunshine.

I went to Cuckfield (Sussex) for the funeral of poor Wigram. The widow was ravaged with grief, & it was a harrowing experience. Vansittart & his wife have taken her in for ten days at Denham – a good act. There appears to be no pension or anything for Foreign Office widows: but she says she can manage on her own resources. Her future seems blank & restricted[1]. A sombre world!

After the funeral I brought the Vansittarts & other F.O. people back here to luncheon. Ivor C. [Spencer Churchill][2], Brendan [Bracken*] & P. Maze* came also. The remnants of the influenza-stricken staff rose to the occasion.

Sarah came to luncheon yesterday (Wed) & we had a nice talk. She was vy sweet & loving, & seems to want vy much to keep in touch with us. I told her what we proposed financially. . . . 'Vic' – I suppose we must call him that – is making about £200 a week for 8 or 10 weeks over here. They get special terms at the hotel. But what a life – hand-to-mouth, no home, no baby!

I thought Sarah serious & gentle. Like the ill-starred D of W. [Duke of Windsor] she has done what she liked, & has now to like what she has done. We shall have to take special care & make exceptions for her. She spoke with gt affection of you.

I have been painting indoors a good deal & have been using one end of the drawing room – with a dust sheet. Deakin[3] has been here 4 days & has helped me a lot. He shows more quality & serviceableness than any of the others. . . .

Arnold [farm manager] caught about 15 of the large golden orfes with his landing net when the middle lake was empty. They are wonderful fish – 15 inches long & thick in proportion. I have now 25 in the garden pool. I told them to eat all that they wish. But I expect they will miss their mud & weeds[4].

I go to ... Blenheim for the week end – to paint & look at archives. I shall not go to Italy, & indeed hardly leave this garden till you return. The days pass quickly, for I have so much to do. Marlborough alone is a crusher – then there are always articles to boil the pot!

My darling I do hope you & Mary are going to have good fun. I do feel so happy when I think of you enjoying yourselves. Venetia [Montagu*] shd be with you now. Write me all about it.

Your ever loving husband
W
...

P.S. H.M.G. [His Majesty's Government] are preparing a dossier about the D of W [Duke of Windsor]'s finances, debts & spendings on acct of Cutie [Duchess of Windsor] wh I fear they mean to use to his detriment when the Civil List[5] is considered. 'Odi quem laeseris' (Hate whom you have injured) as the Romans used to say –

W

[1] In 1941 Ava Wigram married Sir John Anderson (see p. 448 n. 7).
[2] Lord Ivor Spencer-Churchill (1898–1956), younger son of 9th Duke of Marlborough.
[3] William ('Bill') Deakin (1913–), research assistant to WSC, 1936–9. Led first British Military Mission to Tito (Yugoslavia), 1943. First Secretary, British Embassy, Belgrade, 1945–6. Director of Researches to WSC, 1946–9. Warden, St Antony's College, Oxford, 1950–68. Author of several books. Married, second, Livia Stela Nasta ('Pussy') of Bucharest, 1943. DSO, 1943. Knighted 1975. Bill and Pussy were great personal friends of WSC/CSC.
[4] These giant goldfish and their descendants hereafter inhabited the pool in the water garden and were a great feature; WSC habitually fed them with live grubs.
[5] The annual provision voted by Parliament for the maintenance of the Monarchy.

O From CSC   Flexenhotel
11 January 1937   Zürs am Arlberg

My Darling

Yesterday we were unblocked[1] & your letter of January the 7th arrived, to my great joy. I am so very glad that Sarah came down to see you & that you had a long talk with her....

Moppet [Whyte*] tells me you are painting a lovely picture of the two little silver sugar urns – (& also of a little gold box?) I am so glad that you went to Blenheim for a visit – Mary [Marlborough] is devoted to you & she & Blandford [Bert] have transformed it into a pleasant home.

My Darling I hope that what with Marlborough weighing you down & the Pot Boilers nagging at you, that you are not worn out – I wish you liked snow – If you saw it glistening under a royal sun & a limpid blue sky I think you might – It is sweet of you to let Mary & me have this holiday. She returns to you next Tuesday & I go on to Davos ...

... There are lots of German tourists here & the feeling is quite friendly to them. They are thought to be having a 'breather' from overstrenuous conditions at home.

Your loving
Clemmie

[1] Zürs had been cut off by heavy snowfalls and avalanches for several days.

◇ From WSC [typewritten]   11 Morpeth Mansions
20 January 1937

Sarah and her husband lunched here yesterday. They are contemplating taking a flat. There is one vacant under Randolph's[1] at about half the rent they are paying in the hotel....

We have not yet given her any present on her wedding and I think if they do decide to have some small fixed abode we might well see them into it....

Yesterday I moved up to the flat to do the fortnightly article. These are getting on quite well.... There must be nearly forty papers publishing it in all the different countries. Some pay only two or three guineas, but they all mount up....

Walter Monckton[2] came to see me today. He is going out to the D of W [Duke of Windsor] on Friday week, and I am to see him again beforehand. He said that the D would very much like me to come out and stay with him, but I said that we would wait and see how the Civil List Pensions went first, and then I would certainly like to go if all was well. But I must not run any risk of compromising on the Civil List Committee.

Herr von Ribbentrop[3] promised the Leeds Chamber of Commerce to dine with them on Monday at their annual dinner, but then he threw them over on account of his preoccupation in Germany. So the Yorkshire Post which is apparently running their affairs made vehement appeals to me to take his place. No one else apparently would serve. (They could not have the German Eagle, so they must have the Blenheim pup. At least that is how I put it to myself!) I therefore consented to meet their wishes. They say it is to be a record attendance.

Parliament has met in a dead-alive condition. I do not feel much desire to take part in their affairs.....

[1] In Westminster Gardens, Marsham Street, London SW1.
[2] Sir Walter (later Viscount) Monckton (1891–1965), barrister. Attorney-General to the Duchy of Cornwall, 1932–47 and 1948–51. Adviser and friend of the Duke of Windsor. Conservative MP, 1951–7; Minister of Labour and National Service, 1951–5; Minister of Defence, 1955–6; Paymaster-General, 1956–7.
[3] Joachim von Ribbentrop (1893–1946), German Nazi politician and diplomat. Hitler's adviser on foreign affairs. Ambassador to Britain, 1936–8. German Foreign Minister, 1938–45. Tried as war criminal at Nuremberg and hanged 1946.

○ From WSC   11 Morpeth Mansions
25 January 1937

My darling,

We have had tremendous rains and the valley is soaking....

Two wild white swans have arrived this morning. Perhaps they will stay on the lake. [in margin ✍: (No.)] A pair of black swans are nesting on the island and have laid a number of eggs. It is very early days for them and I hope they will not get caught by some heavy February frost....

Monckton is coming to lunch on Wednesday. I think there is no doubt that our friend gave Mrs S[impson], now Duchess of Windsor] an enormous sum of money, so that it will be very difficult to have anything in the Civil

List, as this would entail bringing out all the facts and would be most injurious to many interests....

Duncan and Diana and Sarah and her husband all came to lunch on Sunday. Everything has been very quiet there, and I think we have spent very little this month....

I am now on my way to Leeds to make a speech. I do not know how on earth I let myself in for this jaunt. However they say that many more applied to come to see me than for the German Ambassador! Randolph is joining me there. We will sleep at the house of a local worthy.

✍ It went off all right.

◇ From WSC
27 January 1937

WIRE DATE RETURN. AM POSSIBLY GOING ROTHERMERE RIVIERA FOR TEN DAYS PAINTING. MUCH LOVE.

WINSTON

◇ From CSC   St Moritz
28 January 1937

RETURNING ABOUT FEBRUARY FIFTEENTH. IS THAT ALL RIGHT. TENDER LOVE.

CLEMMIE

◇ From WSC

QUITE ALRIGHT. AM MAKING PLANS. PERHAPS BRING YOU BACK MYSELF. ANYHOW MEET PARIS. WRITE ABOUT SNOW EFFECTS FOR PAINTING, ESPECIALLY SUNSHINE. FONDEST LOVE.

W.

○ From CSC   Palace Hotel
Friday 29 January 1937   St Moritz

My Darling –

I was overjoyed when I read your telegram saying that perhaps on your way to [from] the Riviera you might join me here for a few days. Oh please do – I should love it so much & really I believe you would like this place. The air is like champagne & you could sit in the sun & paint without a great coat. You could paint the most fairy-like pale dazzling pictures – The fir trees weighted down with sparkling snow are too beautiful – The snow itself is mauve pink & every shade of warm white – Then you could do a portrait of me like on this postcard – Don't I look big in front of the Alps? I wish I could really master them!...

... The Daily Mail (Continental) says Baldwin has now decided to stay on for another 2 or 3 years! I must say that as the country does not seem to mind the way it is governed by a system of 'trial & error' he might just as well maunder on.

Tender Love my Darling ...

O From WSC
2 February 1937

CHARTWELL BULLETIN

... I think we have had a very cheap month here. The wine has been very strictly controlled and little drunk. We get our fuel in for the central heating in five ton batches at £9.11.0 each.... The last lot lasted three weeks instead of a fortnight, although the weather has been raw and generally damnable. The telephones also show a marked reduction....

The making of the new croquet court[1] is going forward at intervals, but there have been such floods of rain that the men have been much interrupted.

Randolph and I start tomorrow on the 10.25 a.m. aeroplane from Gatwick (weather permitting). It seems to be blowing up for a storm tonight.... I propose to stay with Rothermere till the night of Tuesday 9 or perhaps Wednesday 10, reaching you the next day. You should write to La Dragonnière, Cap Martin. I am much looking forward to painting your lovely coloured snows on which Lavery*, years ago, dilated and enthused me....

Mr Capon [estate agent] ... tells me that there is a lady nibbling around for a house like Chartwell, and even mentioning Chartwell. Capon said he would on no account mention any figure less than £30,000. If I could see £25,000 I should close with it. If we do not get a good price we can quite well carry on for a year or two more. But no good offer should be refused, having regard to the fact that our children are almost all flown, and my life is probably in its closing decade....

I have what seems to be almost absolutely certain information from the most sure sources inside the Cabinet and from B[aldwin]'s intimate entourage that he is resolved to go after the Coronation. He has practically announced it to his colleagues. Neville [Chamberlain] who is already in fact doing the work, will without any doubt or question succeed him. It will be a great relief and simplification of our affairs to have all uncertainty cleared up at that date one way or the other. I really do not care very much which.

Wolmer's[2] dinner was very pleasant and there I met Leathers[3], of whom I have told you, who is the leading man at Cory's and connected with my small Boards. If I am not required for public work he gives me great expectations of important business administrative employment. Then I should be able to do my books more slowly and not have to face the truly stupendous task like Marlborough Vol. IV being finished in 4 or 5 months, simply for current expenses. For 1938–9 we have the History of the English-Speaking Peoples, worth £16,000, but entailing an immense amount of reading and solitary reflection if justice is to be done to so tremendous a topic.

Always yours
W

[1] On the lawn above the Rose Garden. (The present croquet lawn was made after the war, replacing the tennis court.)
[2] Roundell Cecil Palmer, Viscount Wolmer (1887–1971), eldest son of the 2nd Earl of Selborne, whom he succeeded in 1942.
[3] Frederick James Leathers, later Viscount Leathers (1883–1965). Shipowner and director of various steamship companies. Had served at Ministry of Shipping, 1915–18. Member of the Coalition Government as Minister of War Transport, 1941–5.

In the end Winston did not join Clementine at St Moritz. Snow – except as painted from the windows of well-heated rooms – was not really his scene.

The Coronation of King George VI and Queen Elizabeth took place on 12 May 1937. Stanley Baldwin retired on 28 May, and was succeeded as Prime Minister by Neville Chamberlain. In the reconstruction of the Government there was no place for Churchill.

In mid-July Clementine went for about three weeks to a spa at Bad Gastein in Austria.

○ From WSC   The Manor House[1]
25 July 1937   Stoke D'Abernon, Surrey

My darling Clemmie,

I am overwhelmed with work. Three days H of C [House of Commons] last week: the new book in its final birth throes[2]: articles, & always Marlborough: & now ahead on Tuesday next another debate on Inskip's salary[3]. I really don't know how I find all that I need, but the well flows freely: only the time is needed to draw the water from it.

Let this be some apology for my not having written, do not think you have not been always in my thoughts. I do hope the cure is benefiting you....

My darling I send you by this only my fondest love. The sense of gratitude in my heart to you for all you give me is unfailing. God bless you sweet pussie –

Always your ever loving husband
W

. . .

[1] The home of Edgar Vincent, 1st Viscount D'Abernon (1857–1941).
[2] *Great Contemporaries*, which was published in October 1937.
[3] Sir Thomas Inskip (see p. 381 n. 3). Former Attorney-General. At this date Minister for the Co-ordination of Defence (1936–9).

◇ From CSC   Haus Hirt
30 July 1937   Badgastein

My Darling Winston – I was so glad to get your dear letter but saddened by the touching picture of the pig manfully supporting that staggering 10 ton weight on his poor back. I wish you were not so over-worked my Darling. . . .

The proofs of your articles have arrived – Your speeches read splendidly in Hansard.

Venetia [Montagu*] & Juliet [Duff] arrive here in a day or two – I go every day for one very long walk with Doktor Kommer[1] or two shorter ones – The air is lovely – My eyes are giving me trouble; so when I leave here on August the 9th, I shall go to Vienna to see a distinguished oculist, as my London one is really too casual & careless. Otherwise I'm feeling so well I could jump over the Moon; but one likes to see where one is jumping!

Your loving Pussie

. . .

[1] Dr Rudolf Kommer (d. 1943), right-hand man of the Austrian theatre manager and impresario Max Reinhardt. Known to his friends as 'Kaetchen'.

○ From WSC   Chartwell
3 August 1937

My darling One,

   . . .

I was worried by what you said about yr eyes, & if you are near Vienna you shd certainly go & see their best man. If not there are good ones in England. Perhaps it is the waters that have affected you. Anyhow we must clear it up, so that you can jump over the moon with yr eyes open. Darling!

Here all goes peacefully, I am working night & day and the progress on M [*Marlborough*] is enormous – I have done nearly 20,000 words this week alone. Deakin[1] arrives this evening so the pace will not slacken.

Julian [Sandys, nearly one] is vy sweet, but you will have to come back by the 14th if you want to see him. . . .

We need not settle plans for going abroad till you come back.

With fondest love my sweet Clemmie
Always yr loving husband
W

. . .

[1] William Deakin, WSC's principal research assistant (see p. 423 n. 3).

◇ From CSC   London

MANY HAPPY RETURNS MY DARLING ONE AND MAY YOUR STAR RISE

                                                          CLEMMIE

[30 November was Winston's sixty-third birthday.]

◇ From CSC   Hotel Lenzerhorn[1]
27 December 1937   Lenzerheide

My Darling Winston
    Everything is going very well here – Mary is very happy & enjoying the
crisp powder snow, & Duncan [Sandys*] & Diana are having a renewed
honeymoon. They are very sweet together & his devotion to her makes me
like him better – I think when he is in London he is so taken up with his
'Career' & the excitement of Parliament that he has no time to talk to her
or play with her, & she is a lovely fragile little flower which droops when
neglected.
    The Grant Forbes family are here in great force – They are the kind
people who for the last four years have had Mary & Moppet [Whyte*] to
stay with them in the Summer near Dinard. . . .
    On Christmas night we all went to a dance at one of the big hotels & I
provided Champagne for dinner! . . .

                                                          Your loving
                                                          Clemmie

[1] Our third ski-ing holiday: this time my mother took me to Switzerland. WSC spent Christmas
and New Year at Blenheim.

○ From WSC   Chartwell
31 December [1937]

My darling One,
    I am off to Blenheim to-day & so farewell to the Chart for a few weeks.
    I have thought a gt deal about you my darling pussy in the fortnight
since you left. I do hope the New Year will bring you happiness, & that I
may contribute to it. If you do not do too much, the ski-ing ought to give
you health & poise. But I am always anxious about unusual exercise & an
unusual height. So do be moderate at least till you are fit & hardened.
    If when you return you feel you want to take yr voyage to the Bali[1], I
will arrange it for you. But it will be much better if you had a woman
companion. Why not Nellie? I don't like the idea of yr going all alone.
    The Chicago horoscope says I am to 'have a romance' in 1938 or 39! So
don't stay away too long: because my only thought is to have it with you.

All my heart's wishes for a happy New Year. I will ring you up from Randolph's flat on Sunday night before starting [for France].

Tender love my darling
from your loving & devoted husband
W
. . .

[1] CSC had been toying with another exotic journey.

Having stayed for New Year at Blenheim, Winston spent a few days in Paris en route to Maxine Elliott* at the Château de l'Horizon.

O From WSC   British Embassy
3 January 1938   Paris
Secret

My darling Clemmie
    Blum[1] lunched here to-day and we had a long talk, with the Ambassador[2]. Blum began by admitting the bad state of French Aviation & that I had warned him about it 18 months ago. It is difficult to persuade people of facts till too late.
    When Chautemps[3] & Daladier[4] were in London, Neville [Chamberlain, now Prime Minister] told them that we were making 350 machines a month. They were deeply impressed. But now it turns out N.C. was wrongly informed the true figure being only ½! Consequently there is a certain reproaching going on between NC & the Air M. What happened was that poor Neville believed the lie that the Air M. circulated for public purposes & did not know the true figures. This gives you some idea of the looseness w wh we are governed in these vital matters. I had heard all about this from a quarter you can guess Ⓜ [Desmond Morton*][5] so I led the talk into this channel & got full confirmation. It ought to make Neville think. He does not know the truth: & perhaps he does not want to.. ..
    The French were much excited by the rumour I was going to join the Govt. They have been sprouting eulogistic articles – of one of wh I send you a copy.. ..
    My darling how are you going on?. .. I hope you will not run needless risks, or go too far from home. I had a lovely letter from Mary. Do thank her for it & give her many kisses from yr own ever loving husband
W

... Tender love my sweet darling.
P.S. ...
    It would be vy nice if you would write a line to the D of W [Duke of Windsor] and thank him for his Christmas card. You can refer to her as The Duchess thus avoiding the awkward point[6].

More love

[1] Léon Blum (1872–1950), French Socialist politician, and leader of 'Front Populaire', 1936. Prime

Minister, June 1936–June 1937, and again March–April 1938. Interned in Germany in Second World War. Prime Minister, December 1946–January 1947.
[2] Sir Eric Phipps (1875–1945), diplomat. Had been Ambassador Extraordinary and Plenipotentiary to Berlin, 1933–7. Ambassador in Paris, 1937–9.
[3] Camille Chautemps (1885–1963). French Socialist politician. Prime Minister, June 1937–March 1938. Later served briefly in Marshal Pétain's Vichy government, and in 1946 was sentenced for collaboration with the enemy, this sentence being later annulled.
[4] Edouard Daladier (1884–1970), French Minister of War and Defence, 1936–8; Prime Minister, April 1938–March 1940. After the fall of France, interned until 1945.
[5] At this date Head of the Committee of Imperial Defence's Industrial Intelligence Centre (January 1929–September 1939).
[6] i.e. referring to the Duchess of Windsor as 'Her Royal Highness', which by royal decree she was not. Although both WSC and CSC skated round this delicate matter in writing, they both unfailingly bowed/curtsied to the Duchess.

○ From WSC [typewritten]   [Paris]
[3 January 1938]

I add a few notes by way of bulletin.

The New Year party at Blenheim was very agreeable. I did better at Bezique. . . . I came away on the Sunday and dined with Randolph at the flat. We had a regular reunion, Duncan and Diana just arrived from your snows, Vic came up from the flat below . . . Sarah I just missed as she had gone off to Cambridge to rehearse. She is playing the leading part in The Amazing Dr Clitterhouse[1]. She has the 'Star dressing-room'. . . . They all seemed to think that she will be able to make a career [on the straight stage]. . . .

Harraps, the publishers of Marlborough, declare they cannot have a volume of more than 650 pages. I have already got the equivalent of 750 in print or practically finished, so that now I have to cut it down, which is a kind of self-mutilation difficult and painful to do. Still, I think the book will gain by it as it is far too overloaded with extracts, letters, etc. I have been toiling with it the last few days.

You had better write henceforward to Château de l'Horizon, where I shall be till the middle of the month. You must have plenty of snow now and I was very glad to hear from Diana that you are not overdoing it.

More love still
W

[1] Play by Barry Lyndon, 1936.

○ From WSC   Château de l'Horizon
8 January [1938]

My darling Clemmie,
I have been here three days & have not stirred outside the house, except to dine with the Windsors. . . . The first day there was snow at St Tropez! But since then it has been bright & warmer, though now the wind is rising. I have not unpacked my paints yet. The truth is I wanted a rest & also to get rid of my cold. It still hangs about me. But in a day or two I shall poke my nose out of doors in the sunlight. Tomorrow I dine with

Flandin[1] at St Jean Cap-Ferrat. He has lately been diverging somewhat from the policy in Foreign Affairs wh I pursue, & I hope to bring him back to the fold.

To-night the Windsors & Ll.G [Lloyd George*] are coming to dine. The former said they wd like to come, & Maxine [Elliott*] was vy ready to have them. We are a tiny party, but none the worse for that. By special request the monkey has been locked up!...

Mrs P [Violet Pearman, secretary] arrives here tomorrow so I shall feel less helpless than [when] I am alone. The comfort & convenience of this house are perfect. I have that lovely room you had: & have shifted the bed so as to get a side light for writing.... We are only 4 in the house. Maxine's niece Diana & her husband, a Mr Sheean[2]. Last night 14 for dinner, ... I have not been near the Casino. The Paris Embassy was vy pleasant. I like Lady Phipps vy much. She made many inquiries after you, & when you could be persuaded to come.

Last night my darling I rang you up at 7.30. Answer – no cat there. Rang up again at 9 p.m. Answer It was asleep. I am now trying again....

Tender love my darling to you & to Mary. I hope all is going up to yr expectations. Let me know yr movements.

Always yr ever loving & devoted husband
W
...

[1] Pierre Etienne Flandin (see p. 381 n. 6). He had been French Minister for Foreign Affairs, January to June 1936.
[2] Diana Forbes-Robertson, who in 1935 had married the American writer James Vincent Sheean (1899–1975). In his book *Between the Thunder and the Sun* (1943), Vincent Sheean gives interesting accounts of WSC's visits to the Château de l'Horizon.

◇ From CSC   Hotel Lenzerhorn
8 January 1938   Lenzerheide

My Darling
...

Thank-you so much for several delightful letters from you.

I did not know you had had your horoscope taken? Who did it for you? Please on no account have a romance with anyone but 'poor Pussy whose coat is so warm'.... The cold here has been piercing – 27° of frost. But the hotel is cosy & warm. I have hurt a muscle in my shoulder & it is really very painful; so for two days I have left off ski-ing.... I'm afraid it's neuritis. Clarissa [Churchill] has arrived with Priscilla Bibesco[1], Elizabeth's daughter, the image of her & quite as tiresome!

Tender Love
from
Clemmie
...

[1] Daughter of Prince Antoine Bibesco and his wife (born Lady Elizabeth Asquith). See p. 74 n. 2.

○ From WSC [typewritten]   Château de l'Horizon
10 January 1938

My darling Clemmie,
    ...
    The dinner to which the Windsors came was a great success. Ll.G was
the only guest outside the house and Maxine never ceases to declare that
she has not enjoyed any dinner in her own house since the days at
Hartsbourne when she used to entertain the politicians and celebrities. The
Ws are very pathetic, but also very happy. She made an excellent
impression on me, and it looks as if it would be a most happy marriage....
    The dinner with Flandin was very depressing, the food lamentable. But
the account he gave of France was most pessimistic. Making every
allowance for what people feel when they are out of office, and what we
should feel if an extreme Left-Wing Government were ruling the roost in
London, I still came away very seriously concerned about their position,
and consequently our own. It looks as if these French Right-Wing
politicians thought that Germany would become undisputed ruler of
Europe in the near future. All was the fault of the years 1932–35 when
Ramsay [MacDonald], Baldwin and Simon would never make friends with
Germany, nor prevent her rearming. A thousand years hence it will be
incredible to historians that the victorious Allies delivered themselves over
to the vengeance of the foe they had overcome.
    There is much talk about the bad state of the Air Force, upon which a
great deal of information has been sent me through sources of which you
are aware. I do not propose at the present time to say a word upon the
subject. The Ministers are at last realising all these facts which I explained
and predicted in detail two or three years ago....
    I have had to cut nearly 100 pages out of Marlborough which I had in
print, and this has been a very long, tiresome business, like cutting off
your own fingers and toes; but I think the result will be much more
readable. I am longing to get this book finished, but I am still far from
satisfied with it as a whole....
    I shall not stay more than a week at the outside with Daisy [Fellowes],
and unless something very attractive opens up, I shall return home.
Therefore keep me well informed of all your plans....
    ✍ Always my darling your ever loving husband

                                                       W
                                                       ...

P.S.... Love to Mary from whom I have a delightful letter.
The Times today (11th) say the south wind makes avalanches likely.
Do be careful, & don't make long wild expeditions.

○ From WSC [typewritten]   Les Zoraïdes[1]
18 January 1938   Cap Martin

My darling Clemmie,
    I was very glad to hear that you had had a good passage[2], because by
all accounts forty-eight hours before there had been a tempest.

I motored on here yesterday with all my belongings and am very comfortably installed. No one but the family is here....

Everyone here is of course excited about the French Government crisis. I am very glad that the Communists are not to be included in the Government; although with my knowledge of politics and of France, I should not have been alarmed by this, the impression produced in Europe would have been very weakening....

My twelve days with Maxine were most peaceful and agreeable. Although I have spent all my mornings in bed correcting and recasting the proofs, this is not at all fatiguing....

Maxine was genuinely upset at my departure, and made me promise to come back again, and if possible to bring you.... The Windsor–Ll.G. dinner was a great success, and the poor duke gay and charming, although he had to fight for his place in the conversation like other people....

Now the thing to be decided is, whether you will come and join me at Maxine's.... It would be lovely if you would come. There is golf both at Moujins, and the old course, which everybody says is very good.... They say – though I have not seen it – that it is lovely to paint up there. So you could play golf, while I painted.... I have no doubt I could arrange some tennis for you too....

✍ My darling, I am just hoping to talk to you on the telephone, so I will end this with my fondest love. Always your loving husband,

W.

...

[1] Daisy Fellowes' villa.
[2] CSC and Mary had returned home on 16 January.

The plans discussed worked out, and Clementine joined Winston at the Château de l'Horizon for one of her rare visits there: both came home to England early in February.

On 20 February Anthony Eden* resigned from the Government after disagreement with the Prime Minister and other Cabinet colleagues over the Government's approaches to Italy – he wished to see a firmer attitude adopted. Lord Halifax[1] succeeded him as Foreign Secretary.

On 9 March German troops crossed the Austrian border, and on 13 March Hitler entered Vienna. Austria was incorporated into the German Reich – the Anschluss. As Churchill warned, Czechoslovakia would be next on the list.

In early July Clementine went to Cauterets, a watering place near Lourdes, in the French Pyrenees.

[1] Edward Frederick Lindley Wood, 3rd Viscount Halifax (1881–1959). He married, 1909, Lady Dorothy Onslow, daughter of 4th Earl of Onslow. Conservative MP 1910–25; held various government appointments. Viceroy of India, 1926–31. Lord Privy Seal, 1935–7. Lord President of the Council, 1937–8. Foreign Secretary, 1938–40. Ambassador to Washington, 1941–6. Cr. 1st Earl of Halifax, 1944.

○ From WSC [typewritten]   Chartwell
8 July 1938

My darling One,

We have had a strenuous day in the old building. You will not know its interior when you return.... I hope in a few more days to be able to begin installing the tin boxes[1]....

Three reports have come to hand about the swans[2]. One on the way to Sundridge [not far], which we have tried in vain to recapture so far. Another reported in Hampshire and a third on a lake near Dartford. I doubt very much whether we shall be able to get them. It is very tiresome.

The rose-garden is a veritable explosion of colour. I have never seen so many roses in my life. As it has been pouring all day, I have not been out to see your lilies, but I will do so tomorrow....

The cat slept two nights in the work-room under the table on which the dove-cage stood, though without the dove being frightened at all, which is very much to the credit of the cat. It reminds me of Brab's[3] famous saying: 'My Sergeant-Major's wife is sacwed to me.' ...

Arms and the Covenant[4] has not gone as well as we expected. They have sold 4,000, but the price is high, and it is by no means certain that a second edition will be required. The reviews have been very good and I am glad we collected and published the speeches....

I have been here quite alone for the last three days, except that [Desmond] Morton* dined with me last night, and I have no one coming until I go up for the Monday debate. Bernie Baruch came down for lunch before going off by the plane, and I also gave him a dinner in London (5 people). We had a good talk.... The President [Roosevelt*] is breast-high on our side and will do everything in his power to help[5]. Baruch admitted opinion in the States had never yet been so friendly to us. It is a great pity matters cannot be carried further now. Apparently, you always have to have a disaster before anything sensible can be done which would prevent it....

I am dining Monday night with Betty [Cranborne], who has the Edens* [Anthony and Beatrice]. She is full of revolt and, apparently, Lord Salisbury[6] is all for vigorous action. Anthony made a rather truculent speech yesterday, but it is well boycotted by the Tory Press.

I have not yet lost the impression of that lovely play [*Operette*] of Noel Coward's, and I am ashamed to say I have not written him as I meant to do.

✍ My sweet One – It grieves me to hear you are tired & lonely at yr retreat[7]. Now that yr garden is so beautiful & all sorts of things in wh you take an interest are alive & growing, it is vexing that you shd not be here. But I am sure a change wh cuts you out of the household routine and leaves you free to recharge yr batteries is a wise step....

... Last night I opened the Polly's[8] cage to encourage him to sit on my hand. He gave me a frightful peck & got out. It took Edna [a housemaid] (& her young man) an hour to get him back. He is vy naughty. But still a companion.

I keep my weight steady at 5–6 lbs less. But it seems difficult to push it further. I am persevering strictly....

> With my tender love to you my darling Clemmie
> Your ever loving husband
> W

¹ One of the buildings in the garage/stable yard: it was to be used principally to house WSC's ever-growing archives.
² The black Australian swans had gone 'fly-about'.
³ Maj.-Gen. Sir John Brabazon (see p. 74 n. 1, letter of 7 April 1913). WSC's former commanding officer in 1895. Much admired by WSC and the source of many anecdotes. He was unable to pronounce his 'r's.
⁴ *Arms and the Covenant*, published 1938, contains some of WSC's most far-seeing, forceful speeches from 1932.
⁵ Roosevelt had introduced his policy of economic reconstruction (the 'New Deal') in 1933, and in foreign policy was endeavouring to restrain German aggression.
⁶ Her father-in-law, 4th Marquess of Salisbury (1861–1947).
⁷ They must have spoken on the telephone.
⁸ An African Grey parrot of surly disposition: we all bore his scars.

○ From CSC   Gd. Hôtel d'Angleterre
12 July 1938   Cauterets

My Darling
    It was a great joy to get your letter –
    I am longing to see you. The weather is now glorious, brilliant sun with freshness in the air.
    The 'cure' is most thorough & searching & takes 2½ hours in the morning & ¾ of an hour in the afternoon.... I have been here 8 days – the first five days I felt ill & sad, but now the Kat is beginning to perk up....
    I'm sorry Darling you are disappointed at the sale of the Book [*Arms and the Covenant*]. I'm sure it's the price – The sort of people who want to hear that the Government is all wrong are not the rich ones – The Tories don't want to be made to think! It's too painful –
    I hope you have got a lovely grey suit for Versailles etc – I <u>am</u> looking forward to it all ...

> Your loving
> Clemmie

Clementine joined Winston in Paris on 18 July, on the eve of the State Visit to France of King George VI and Queen Elizabeth. Although holding no public position in his own country, and politically in the doldrums, Winston was highly regarded by the French. The Churchills were warmly received by their hosts and preferentially placed at all the functions arranged for the royal visit.

On 3 September the fourth and final volume of Winston Churchill's magisterial life of John, Duke of Marlborough was published.

Chapter XIX

PEACE WITH DISHONOUR

The summer of 1938 had seen continual rising tension between Germany and Czechoslovakia. Churchill kept up his pressure on the Government, and his views reached a wide public through his fortnightly articles in the *Daily Telegraph*, in which he not only dealt with Britain's policy of appeasement, but drew forceful attention to the mounting persecution of the Jews in Germany and in Austria.

In September Hitler demanded the incorporation into the Reich of those parts of Czechoslovakia where the German population predominated. Now it was generally realized in France and Britain that, after their divisions and futility in the face of previous acts of German aggression, a firm stand – however tardy – had to be made.

Chamberlain flew twice to parley with Hitler (15 and 22 September); each time German demands on Czechoslovakia were stiffened, until President Beneš[1] refused to agree, and mobilized the army.

During these days of crisis, there was alarm at the growing threat of war. The Fleet was mobilized; in London trenches were dug in the parks as protection from air raids, and gas masks were distributed.

On 29 September Chamberlain flew to Munich, where he met Hitler, Mussolini and Daladier, the French Prime Minister. The Munich Agreement was concluded, whereby Germany's demands were met, and the interests of Czechoslovakia (which had not been represented at the meetings) were brutally sacrificed. Britain and Germany entered a solemn agreement never to go to war with each other again.

Chamberlain believed he had struck a lasting agreement with Hitler. When he returned to London he was hailed with hysterical relief and gratitude. He said he had brought 'Peace with honour ... peace in our time'. It was neither.

Many people shared in the general sense of relief – but to Winston Churchill and his supporters the Munich Agreement was an act of shame and betrayal. Half the Members of Parliament who spoke in the debate[2] spoke against the Munich Agreement. Duff Cooper*, First Lord of the Admiralty, resigned in protest.

During this fraught summer Clementine received an agreeable invitation: Lord Moyne (Walter Guinness) invited her to go for another voyage in the *Rosaura*. It would be of an entirely different character from the exotic journey in search of dragons in 1934–5. The Government had set up a Royal Commission, of which he was Chairman, to enquire into social conditions in the West Indies. He proposed to take his yacht, accommodating half the

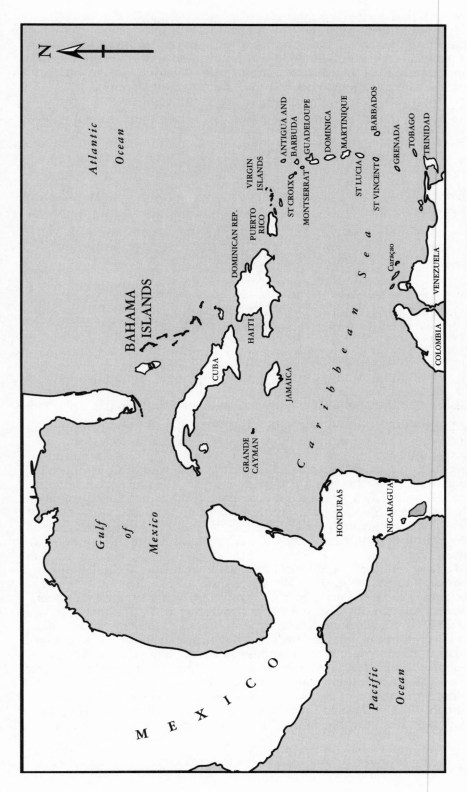

THE WEST INDIES, SHOWING PORTS OF CALL OF MY ROSAURA

members of the Commission in turn, and including one or two private guests.

Clementine had not had a good year health-wise, so this voyage was most opportune; she left England on 25 November 1938 in SS *Carare*, bound for Jamaica, where she joined her host and *Rosaura* on 9 December.

[1] Eduard Beneš (1884–1948). With Thomas Masaryk (1850–1937), builder of new state of Czechoslovakia, created under Treaty of Versailles, and succeeded him as second President, 1935–8. Leader of Czechoslovak government-in-exile from 1939.
[2] 3–5 October 1938.

◇ From CSC   [MY *Rosaura*]
2 December 1938

ALL COUNT OF DAYS AND ANNIVERSARIES LOST IN LONELY VAST ATLANTIC. NO PORT OF CALL TILL JAMAICA, BUT LIKE SIR RICHARD GRENVILLE WE PASSED THE AZORES NEAR FLORES[1]. BELATED BUT LOVING BIRTHDAY HOPES AND WISHES.

                                                 CLEMMIE

[1] From Alfred, Lord Tennyson's The 'Revenge' – a favourite with WSC:
   At Flores in the Azores Sir Richard Grenville lay,
   And a pinnace, like a flutter'd bird, came flying from far away:
   'Spanish ships of war at sea! We have sighted fifty-three!'
and so on ...

◇ From CSC   M.Y. Rosaura
Tuesday 13 December 1938   At sea between Jamaica & Porto Rico

My Darling – On arriving at Kingston last Friday the 9th I spent 3 days with the Governor Sir Arthur Richards[1] & his wife ... motoring with them through the Island on a sort of tour of inspection – The Governor is an agreeable very capable man & is I hear, above the type of Governor to be found in a Colony this size – The island is lovely – mountainous, tropical & wild – politically it seems to be in a very uneasy & disquieting condition – Unfortunately Sir Stafford Cripps[2] has just been there on a visit – He said it was a visit purely for 'pleasure'; but his 'pleasure' was to see privately all the Agitators & ill-wishers, & then to sail away just before the Commission arrived. ...

We have on board Mr Morgan Jones, a very nice little Welsh Labour Member, Professor Engledow, the Agricultural Advisor, Sir Percy Mackinnon, our close neighbour at Chartwell. (He is a Liberal & has been 5 times Chairman of Lloyds – He knew my Father well.) Then there is Doctor Mary Blacklock who is an expert upon Child Welfare & Nutrition. She is very agreeable & gentle with a lovely smile (quite unlike an expert). Mr Lloyd, the Secretary to the Commission is also here – extremely intelligent & well informed – The other half of the Commission are already at Porto Rico where there will be a General Post –

Vera Broughton is of course here, & Walter [Moyne]'s younger son Murtogh – The yacht is full to overflowing – I must tell you (to return to Jamaica) that in a tiny highland village where the Foundation Stone of a

School was being laid the Chairman welcomed me as the wife of the future Prime Minister of England, upon which the whole pitch black Audience burst into 'loud & prolonged cheers' – The Chairman told me that they all know about you & follow your doings in the Jamaican Press – I was thrilled & moved but rather embarrassed, as this rather took off from the Welcome to the New Governor who had never been to the spot before – I am hoping for news....

Your loving
Clemmie

...

¹ Sir Arthur Richards, later Baron Milverton (1885–1978). Capt.-Gen. and Governor-in-Chief of Jamaica, 1938–43. He married (1927) Noelle Brenda Whitehead of Torquay.
² Sir Stafford Cripps (1889–1952), fifth son of 1st Baron Parmoor. Labour politician. Expelled from British Labour Party 1939 for supporting 'Popular Front' against Chamberlain's appeasement policy; sat until 1945 as Independent. Ambassador to Moscow, 1940–2; Minister of Aircraft Production, 1942–5; Chancellor of the Exchequer, 1947–50. Married, 1911, Isobel Swithinbank (later Dame Isobel Cripps).

◇ From CSC   M.Y. Rosaura
Monday 19 December 1938   Tortola British Virgin Islands

My Darling
    Puerto Rico, where we spent 2 days last week has a most lovely approach from the sea as good in its way as Naples – Government House is a great frowning Spanish fortress overlooking the sea; but when you get inside it is gay & smiling with glorious tropical plants growing on its terraces which are I imagine like the hanging gardens of Babylon. A beautiful Evening Party was given there for the Commission & we all had to shake hands with hundreds of guests. There were innumerable buffets with nothing to eat but oceans of iced drinks all of an intoxicating nature, Whisky & Soda, Rum Punch, cocktails etc; so that by midnight [I] was feeling a little dizzy – Then suddenly hot supper appeared – Wherever you were sitting you were handed a plate laden with succulent & varied tit bits a napkin & a fork. Then there was dancing – Exotic Native Music coupled with Mary's favourite tune 'The Lambeth Walk' which had just arrived from London via New York & is all the rage....
    ... [At] Porto Rico one half of the Commission left the yacht ... & we took on board Sir Walter Citrine¹, Dame Rachel Crowdy², Mr Assheton³, a very nice M.P. who I think agrees with your views but is still in thrall to the Tory Whips, & Mr Engledow the Agricultural Expert. We left Porto Rico for St Croix, where we spent two days looking at the sugar plantations etc., & yesterday we spent at St Thomas, a lovely little Island where the Governor of the 3 American Virgin Islands has his house. His name is Cramer – very good-looking, extreme left Wing New Dealer, ...
    He was at Washington when the Commission was nearing the Virgin Islands & Roosevelt* made him fly back to look after us & find out what the Commission was about....

This afternoon we are riding across this small Island which has no cars & no roads.

Tender Love
Clemmie

[1] Sir Walter (later 1st Baron) Citrine (1887–1983). General Secretary, Trades Union Congress, 1926–46; Director, *Daily Herald*, 1929–46. Member of National Coal Board, 1946–7; Chairman of Central Electricity Authority, 1947–57.

[2] Dame Rachel Crowdy (1884–1964), Principal Commandant of VADs, France and Belgium, 1914–19; Chief of Social Questions and Opium Traffic Section, League of Nations, 1919–31; delegate to various international conferences, including International Red Cross Conference, Tokyo, 1934.

[3] Ralph Assheton (1901–84), later 1st Baron Clitheroe KCVO. At this date National Unionist MP for Rushcliffe (Nottinghamshire), 1934–45. Held various government appointments. Financial Secretary to the Treasury, 1943–4. Chairman, Conservative Party Organization, 1944–6.

○ From WSC   Chartwell
19 December [1938]

My Darling,

It seems an age since you left. Yet vy little has happened that matters. I have been toiling double-shifts at the English S.P.s [*History of the English-Speaking Peoples*], & our score tonight is 180,000, or 30,000 above the tally of 1,000 a day from Aug. 1. It is vy laborious: & I resent it, & the pressure.... My life has simply been cottage[1] & book (but sleep too before dinner). I have slept here every night – – & have only been to London for occasional Parl^t Debates –

I send you telegrams frequently: but in yr answers you do not tell me what I want to know – How are you? Are you better & more braced up? How is the voice? Have the rest and repose given you the means of recharging your batteries. That is what I want to know! And even more – Do you love me? I feel so deeply interwoven with you that I follow yr movements in my mind at every hour & in all circumstances. I wonder what you are doing now....

There is a sharp cold spell: the temperature is bloody: Snow covers the scene: the mortar freezes: I envelope myself in sweaters, & thick clothes & gloves: they say it will be worse. A White Christmas! Pray God it be not a Red New Year!

Mary & I go to Blenheim on Saturday (Christmas Eve), & we go to the Circus on Thursday. Then I return here & think to stay till the middle of the month....

I do not think war is imminent for us. Only further humiliations, in wh I rejoice to have no share.

Darling do always cable every two or three days. Otherwise I get depressed – & anxious about you & yr health.

Probably when this reaches you it will be in warm sunshine – How scrumptious!

> My sweet Clemmie,
> Good night & my blessings on you
> Always yr devoted loving husband
> W

...

P.S. Polly is vy cruel to me but the cat is affectionate.

[1] Orchard Cottage, at the bottom of the orchard, which was being built. It was intended to be a possible 'retreat' from the big house in time of crisis.

◇ From CSC   M.Y. Rosaura
21 December 1938

MY DARLING MY THOUGHTS ARE WITH YOU NEARLY ALL THE TIME AND THOUGH BASKING IN
LOVELY SUNSHINE AND BLUE SEAS I MISS YOU AND HOME TERRIBLY.
LOVE.

                                                               CLEMMIE

○ From WSC [typewritten]   Chartwell
29 December 1938

My darling Clemmie

...

I cabled to you about Diana's baby daughter [Edwina]. It came most unexpectedly, was less than eight months old and weighed just over four and a half pounds. She, D, was perfectly well in the afternoon, sitting up and could see me. The baby is tiny but perfect, and by my latest news, thriving.

Duncan [Sandys*] and Randolph are forming a new party to bust up all the old ones. The plan is to have a hundred thousand members, who pay a pound a head a year, but after the first hundred thousand are enlisted they are ready to go on even to a million, or more if necessary. No one may belong who is not doing war preparation work of some kind or who has not fought in the last war. Anyone who disagrees with Randolph or Duncan is to be immediately dismissed, and at any meeting only those are to be allowed to stay who are wholeheartedly in favour of the programme. The programme has not yet been settled. I have promised to accept the Presidency when the first hundred thousand is reached. Meanwhile Mary has joined, and has volunteered for any work.

Otherwise there is no political news worth speaking of.... I am now doing the Wars of the Roses. They are deeply interesting, and have been much too lightly treated by modern opinion. The causes were deep, the arguments equally balanced, and immense efforts were made to avert the disaster which occurred. I have just finished writing about Joan of Arc. I think she is the winner in the whole of French history. The leading women of these days were more remarkable and forceful than the men.

We came back from Blenheim on the Tuesday, not over-staying our welcome. It was very comfortable and pleasant. I won £20 at bezique from Mary [Marlborough] ... Randolph made himself very agreeable all round, and we bestowed and received many gifts.....

All Mary's goats give promise of increase, and February is expected to be the date. We shall have troops of goats browsing on our pastures, ... The parrot is not behaving well, ... He has not bitten me again because I have not given him the chance.... The snow is thawing fast, and we hope soon to see the last of it. I have practically finished the brick-work of the cottage.... Everything else here appears to be quite normal. I continue to lead my routine mechanically, reading the papers and letters, eating, building, correspondence, sleeping, dining and finally dictating until three o'clock in the morning....

✍ My dearest Clemmie, You will be saddened to know that Sidney Peel[1] has died. I do not know the cause. Many are dying now that I knew when we were young. It is quite astonishing to reach the end of life & feel just as you did fifty years before. One must always hope for a sudden end, before faculties decay. But this is a lugubrious ending to my letter. I love to think of you in yr Sunshine. But I hope & pray that some solid gains are being made in yr poise & strength....

Tender love my dearest soul
from your ever devoted husband
W

...

[1] Sir Sidney Peel, 1st Bt (cr. 1936); see p. 5 n. 15. Devotedly in love with CSC from when she was 18 until her marriage; they had been twice secretly engaged.

◇ From CSC
Sunday 1 January 1939

M.Y. Rosaura
Leeward Islands
Antigua – British West Indies

My Darling

We arrived here last Thursday December the 29th –

It is a lovely Island – On the map it looks almost round; but it is really deeply indented with scores of sheltered bays with smooth white sands – At the end of the 18th Century, at 40 separate points, strong Defences were built against the French & you can see the remains of these old forts all round the coast –

There is an historic & romantic old Naval Dockyard set in a beautiful little bay, called English Harbour – Rodney, Hood & Nelson all were here – It is not deep enough for modern ships and the Navy gave it up about 50 years ago – Nelson served here as a young Captain of 25.... To while away the time he married a young Widow who lived in the neighbouring Island of Nevis. He re-visited Antigua in 1805 to re-fit his Ships after chasing Villeneuve across the Atlantic – He then chased him back all the way home & got him at Trafalgar. It is a beautiful but sad and eerie spot with the deserted Dockyard Buildings falling to pieces. The old capstans are there, rotting into the ground & huge iron rings. There is a tiny dock for small ships and great stone pillars which used to support the roof of a gigantic boathouse – all blown away in a Hurricane. I was alone for a while ... and I wondered if I should see the shades of departed heroes & hear the men in the Stores and Workshops[1].

Wednesday January the 4th.
We have now moved to Montserrat a small but lovely & mountainous Island very green & luxuriant. It has been ravaged by 2 hurricanes within four years and an earthquake.

My Darling – Do you know that I am starved for a letter from you. Mary, Horatia [Seymour], Moppet [Whyte*] & Sarah have written but Alas not you, & I am rather miserable. You telegraphed that you had posted a letter by Air Mail leaving Dec: 20th – This should have reached me at Antigua before we left there. And even if I had received it, my Darling, I had left home 4 weeks before – Do you think you could dictate a few words every day to a Secretary & she could send it off twice a week – Never mind about writing yourself – I used to mind about that, but I'm accustomed to typewritten letters now, & would rather have them than nothing. I feel quite quite cut off –

Your loving but sad
Clemmie

Please don't telegraph – I hate telegrams just saying 'all well rainy weather Love Winston'.

[1] In 1954 CSC became President of the successful appeal to restore the Naval Dockyard.

◇ From WSC
4 January 1939 [Chartwell]

YOUR LETTERS DECEMBER 19TH GREATLY ENJOYED BY MARY AND ME. ALL WELL HERE. AM OFF TO MAXINE [ELLIOTT*]'S ON 7TH. CABLE FREQUENTLY. FONDEST LOVE.

WINSTON

◇ From CSC
8 January 1939 M.Y. Rosaura

OVERJOYED AT RECEIVING LETTER. AM BETTER AND HAPPY WHEN I THINK OF YOU. BEWARE CASINO. TENDER LOVE.

CLEMMIE

○ From WSC Château de l'Horizon
8 January 1939

My darling one,
Here I am in radiant sunshine though there is a nip in the air. We crossed – Prof [Lindemann*] & I – in a new Frobisher aeroplane in 1¼

hours, without seeing the sea or the ground – all mist. But they seem to make no difficulty about weather: & landed perfectly.... The journey was vy comfortable & I slept blissfully.

Maxine [Elliott*] was overjoyed to see me.... The Windsors dine tomorrow night. There is much to-do about curtseying to the lady. Feelings run high on the point. But all accounts show them entirely happy and as much in love with each other as ever. I will write you more hereafter.

I propose to stay here for a fortnight and work hard on the book. I have been leading a life of unbroken routine at Chartwell – & have now got in print no less than 221,000 words i.e. 63 days ahead of the vy hard task I prescribed of 1,000 a day from August 1. At this rate I shd cover the whole ground by May, wh wd leave 7 months for polishing. It is a formidable grind; but if accomplished will put things on a vy satisfactory basis.

Mary has been twice out hunting & lives for it. She has been vy sweet and is growing into her beauty. I left all well behind me.... As usual I did not leave Chartwell without a pang. But now that I am here I am sure I shall enjoy it.

Tomorrow the Daily Herald begin distributing the new cheap edition of the World Crisis wh Odham's have printed. It can be sold at 3/9 for each of two volumes – a miracle of mass production. They expect to sell over 150,000! I like to feel that for the first time the working people will hear my side of the tale.

I had a long talk with Anthony [Eden*] before leaving London; he is resolved not to join the Government – & they have so far made him no advances. But there may easily be a big reconstruction after Chamberlain's visit to Rome [11 January], & before the end of the month. I cannot feel that after all I have said, they can be able to swallow me – it wd have to be 'horns & all'. But I can truthfully say I do not mind. It will be much better to await the situation wh will arise after the G[eneral] Election – now probably in October. Meanwhile the book is the thing....

I have received two lovely letters from you & have also been shown those you have written to Maria. You seem to be having a delightful & interesting cruise & seeing all sorts of places off the beaten track. Also the Commission must be an intelligent accompaniment, & I have no doubt you are taking interest in their work. But what you do not say in any of yr letters or telegrams is how you are in yourself. Is the voice better, and are you stronger, & able to get through whole days? Really my pussy cat you have had a vy rough year – toe – throat – tail, and general debility – It is too much. I feel great hopes that the voyage will do you lasting good. But do let me know.

I am deeply grieved that no letters have yet reached you. This is my third, & I am ashamed that I did not begin earlier. I shall now write you every mail.

Good bye my darling Clemmie.

Always your loving & devoted,

W

...

I append some bulletin material wh will supplement my writing.

◇ From WSC [typewritten]   Château de l'Horizon
8 January 1939

[addendum to previous letter]

<u>Secret</u>

Darling Clemmie

I had a full and interesting day in Paris [en route to Riviera]. I had lunch with Reynaud[1] at Versailles where he was recuperating after his exertions and triumphs in French finance. The whole of France is united against Mussolini. Reynaud said that if he touched Djibouti[2] 'France would spring into a fresh and joyous war'. There is an intense desire to take it out of Mussolini for the humiliation inflicted upon them by Hitler [at Munich]. . . .

In the afternoon I had a long talk with the Ambassador [Sir Eric Phipps] and Charles Mendl[3], and then I went to see Blum, who was the most informing of all. They all confirm the fact that the Germans had hardly any soldiers at all on the French frontier during the crisis. And Blum told me, (secret) that he had it from Daladier himself that both Generals Gamelin and Georges[4] were confident that they could have broken through the weak unfinished German line, almost unguarded as it was, by the fifteenth day at the latest, and that if the Czechs could have held out only for that short fortnight, the German armies would have had to come back to face invasion. On the other side there is their great preponderance in the air, and it depends what value you put on that how you judge the matter. I have no doubt that a firm attitude by England and France would have prevented war, and I believe that history will incline to the view that if the worst had come to the worst, we should have been far better off than we may be at some future date.

Blum lives in a flat above which resides Delbos[5], who was brought down en déshabillé to join our talk. Both are very anxious. They fear that Mussolini is determined to have his share of the loot, Hitler having had everything so far and he nothing, and they believe that Hitler is bound to him and will support him. . . . Blum seems to think that these two ruffians will be moving again quite soon. In London there is a good deal of fear that Hitler may turn towards us, and make demands upon us instead of going to the East. . . .

Meanwhile Chamberlain, in endorsing all that Roosevelt*[6] said, has made a great advance to my point of view. Perhaps you will have noticed that he used the very phrase I have been repeating for the last two years, namely 'Freedom and peace', and that he put, as I have always done, 'Freedom' first.

All reports from behind the scenes indicate his great disillusionment with Hitler, and despair about appeasement. Meanwhile, however, the disagreeable muddle in A.R.P. [Air Raid Precautions] continues. The trenches in the parks are full of water. They cannot either fill them in or drain them and make them useful. Indeed, they have had to hire special guardians to keep children from drowning themselves in these muddy troughs. The A.R.P. volunteers are disgruntled and melting away because of the defective organisation. Sir John Anderson[7], although so recently made a minister, is skating at St Moritz, and this is a subject of continued comment in the press. There is a total lack of drive, and Chamberlain does not know a tithe of the neglects for which he is responsible. Indeed, I do not think it would be much fun to go and take these burdens and neglects upon my shoulders, certainly not without powers such as they have not dreamed of according.

Duncan [Sandys*] launched his Party [The Hundred Thousand] with Randolph's assistance, and almost everyone ratted at the last moment, ... Duncan was miserable, and Diana rang me up saying he had lain awake all night. But I told them now that they had taken this plunge, if they could not advance, to mark time, and let it die peacefully, and on no account to make a public retreat; ...

The baby, I hear, continues to thrive. Instead of being four pounds six ounces, which it was when born, it is now four pounds, eleven ounces. It is, therefore, gaining strength more rapidly than the political movement launched at the same time....

Tender love
Darling
Your devoted
W

[1] Paul Reynaud (1878–1966). At this date French Minister of Finance. Prime Minister of France, March–June 1940.

[2] Djibouti, port and capital of French Somaliland (now Afars and Issas), East Africa.

[3] Sir Charles Mendl (1871–1958), Press Attaché, British Embassy, Paris, 1926–40. Married (1) Elsie de Wolfe (d. 1950); (2) Mme Yvonne Reilly (d. 1956).

[4] General Joseph Georges (1875–1951). Had been Chief of Staff to Marshal Pétain, 1925–6; Chef de Cabinet in the Maginot Government, 1929. Created Generalissimo, 1934.

[5] Yvon Delbos (1885–1956), who had been French Minister of Foreign Affairs, June 1936–March 1938.

[6] In a speech to Congress on 4 January 1939 President Roosevelt had called for defence against aggression, while stressing the need for 'methods short of war'.

[7] Sir John Anderson, later 1st Viscount Waverley (1882–1958). At this date Lord Privy Seal with special responsibility for Air Raid Precautions. Home Secretary and Minister of Home Security, 1939–40; Lord President of the Council, 1940–3; Chancellor of the Exchequer, 1943–5. His first wife died 1920; in 1941 he married Ava Wigram, widow of Ralph Wigram.

◇ From WSC [typewritten]   [Château de l'Horizon]
18 January 1939

. . .

It was bright sunshine for two days, but ever since we have had nothing but grey skies and cold winds. This has not, however, worried me because I have stayed in bed every morning and made great progress with the book. We have averaged fifteen hundred words a day, although nominally on holiday. I shall have a lot for you to read when you come home.

The Windsors dine here, and we dine back with them. They have a lovely little place next door to La D[1]. Everything extremely well done and dignified. Red liveries, and the little man himself dressed up to the nines in the Balmoral tartan with dagger and jabot etc. When you think that you could hardly get him to put on a black coat and short tie when he was Prince of Wales, one sees the change in the point of view. I am to dine with him tomorrow night with only Rothermere. No doubt to talk over his plans for returning home. They do not want him to come, but they have no power to stop him.

Just as at Chartwell I divided my days between building and dictating, so now it is between dictating and gambling. I have been playing very long, but not foolishly, and up to date I have a substantial advantage. It amuses me very much to play, so long as it is with their money....

Chamberlain's visit to Rome[2] did no harm. That is the most we can say of it. The question is what are these people going to do now against us. The bomb explosions in London and Manchester[3] are no doubt the Irish trying to get hold of Ulster. How vain it was for Chamberlain to suppose he could make peace by giving everything away! Everything looks as if he and his Government are stiffening up on foreign matters.... It looks almost certain there will be no election before November, which is a great relief, for it would be very awkward at present....

My reports from Chartwell show that the building [Orchard Cottage] is getting on well.... when I get back all will be ready for tiling the roofs, and after that the floors will go down.... It will be a lovely place when it is finished, and I look forward so much to leading you round it when you return....

[1] La Dragonnière, Lord Rothermere's home at Cap Martin.
[2] On 11 January 1939 Neville Chamberlain visited Mussolini, in pursuance of his fervent belief in 'personal contact' and his policy of appeasement; after lengthy conversations no decisions were reached.
[3] Which caused considerable damage and the loss of one life. This marked the start of a campaign by the Irish Republican Army (IRA) to force the British Government to incorporate Northern Ireland into Eire.

◇ From CSC   M.Y. Rosaura
19 January [1939]   Barbados

My Darling

Four days ago I was sitting in the Public Library at Dominica, (this was before getting your last letter) reading up the back copies of the Times, and suddenly there was Sidney Peel looking at me from the middle of the Obituary page – A young photograph, as I used to know him – I closed my eyes; Time stood still, fell away, and I lived again those four years during which I saw him nearly every day – He was good to me and made my difficult rather arid life interesting – But I couldn't care for him & I was not kind or even very grateful – And then my Darling you came, and in that moment I knew the difference –

I am glad you wrote to me about it, because at that moment I longed for you – I wanted to put my arms round you and cry and cry –

We have now reached Barbados, & soon I think I will come home. These islands are beautiful in themselves but have been desecrated & fouled by man.

These green hills covered with tropical bush & trees rise straight out of the sea & fringing the coasts are hideous dilapidated crazy houses, unpainted for years with rusty corrugated iron roofs – Trade stagnating, enough starchy food to keep the population alive but under nourished – Eighty per cent of the population is illegitimate, seventy per cent (in several islands) have syphilis and yaws. The homes of the labourers are small sheds full of holes stuffed with rags or patched with old tin – There is no sanitation of any sort, not even earth latrines; in some places the women have to walk 3 miles to get water – In many places the proportion of doctors to the population is one doctor to 30,000 persons. Labourers' wages are 1/- a day for men & 6d. for women – There is much unemployment & no system of Insurance – And this is a sample of the British Empire upon which the Sun never sets!

I have been reading Prescott's Conquest of Mexico[1] – At the end of his life Cortés[2] was treated with coldness & ingratitude by the Spanish Government. 'He found like Columbus that it was possible to deserve too greatly.' So you see you are in good company. And, Oh Winston, are we drifting into War? without the wit to avoid it or the will to prepare for it – God bless you my Darling –

Your loving
Clemmie

[1] William Hickling Prescott (1796–1859), US historian: *History of the Conquest of Mexico*, 1843.
[2] Hernán Ferdinand Cortés (1485–1547), Spanish *conquistador* who conquered Mexico for Spain.

There is in these last letters from Clementine a recurring note of homesickness: half a world away, under blue skies and amid palm-fringed shores, the dark shadows and anxieties of the scene she had left for a brief space were still constantly present with her. The sordid social conditions in the West Indian islands they visited made a strong and depressing impact. Moreover, among her shipboard companions political tensions lay very near the surface. There was a real 'blow-up' one evening (24 January) in Barbados, touched off by a broadcast from England in which anti-Government opinion was attacked, prompting approval from some of those present, led by Lady Broughton. Clementine felt she could bear it no longer; after explaining herself to her host, she went ashore, and booked herself on a passage on the SS *Cuba* which was due to sail the next day.

Despite the circumstances in which she had left *Rosaura*, her friendship with Walter Moyne would remain unaltered.

◇ From WSC [Chartwell]
30 January 1939

ENCHANTED YOU ARE COMING HOME. FONDEST LOVE FROM ALL.

WINSTON.

At the end of February 1939 the British and French Governments recognized General Franco's Nationalist regime in Spain. The bloody Civil War came to an end on 2 April.

On 15 March German troops crossed the Czechoslovakian border; that night Hitler was in Prague, and the next day the German protectorate of Bohemia and Moravia was announced.

On 7 April Mussolini and his forces invaded and annexed Albania.

There was now a growing body of support for Churchill's views throughout the country. As the summer advanced the demands in the press for his inclusion in the Government grew in volume. Churchill himself took no part in these campaigns, but he kept in close touch with affairs, and corresponded privately with ministers.

This summer Winston spent the greater part of his time at Chartwell, continuing his work on the *History of the English-Speaking Peoples.*

From 14 to 17 August, at the invitation of the French Government, he toured the Maginot Line.

O From WSC   Hôtel Ritz
14 August 1939   Paris

My darling,

This trip promises to be both agreeable & instructive. General Georges, who will command the Army in a war, has put all aside to conduct me. He met the aeroplane & drove me to the restaurant in the Bois where in divine sunshine we lunched; & talked 'shop' for a long time. I am in full accord with the views held here. It is thought that nothing will happen till the snow falls in the Alps, & gives to Mussolini a protection for the winter. This looks like early or mid-September; wh wd still leave Hitler 2 months to deal with Poland, before the mud season in that country. All this is of course speculation, but also reasonable. It seems to fit the German programme, so far as it has been published.

The General is coming here in a few minutes to take me to the Gare de l'Est. We are to travel in a special Michelin train of extreme speed to Strasbourg, dining en route. We are to have 2 vy long days on the line....

I think you had better send any urgent message to me at the Ritz. I will ring up each evening in case. But I do not know exactly where I shall be. We sleep tonight Strasbourg: tomorrow Colmar: & Wednesday Belfort. I shall be back here 3 p.m. on Thursday. I think it is all going to be vy interesting....

Keep all this to yourself.

Always yr ever loving husband
Darling yr devoted
W

...

My mother and I joined my father in Paris at the end of his tour of the Maginot Line (17 August) and we all went to stay with Consuelo and Jacques Balsan* at St Georges Motel. But this most agreeable holiday was short: because of the increasingly grave situation Winston returned to England on 23 August. We followed the next day.

On 24 August the German–Soviet Non-Aggression Pact was announced: Parliament was recalled, and the Fleet ordered to action stations; on 31 August the evacuation of women and children from London was started.

In the early hours of 1 September, German forces invaded Poland. An ultimatum was sent to Germany, to expire at 11 a.m. on 3 September. No answer being received, Britain – followed shortly afterwards by France – declared war on Germany.

That same day Winston Churchill was appointed First Lord of the Admiralty, with a seat in the War Cabinet.

The Board of Admiralty signalled the Fleet: WINSTON IS BACK.

Chapter XX

INTO THE BREACH AGAIN

B y the end of September 1939, the Churchills had moved once more into Admiralty House, Whitehall[1].

The most important family event that autumn was the marriage, on 4 October, of Randolph (now an officer in his father's old regiment, the 4th Hussars) to Pamela Digby, the eldest daughter of Lord and Lady Digby[2].

When war was declared people braced themselves for sudden and terrible events, but the ensuing months saw an uncanny inactivity on land and in the air: this period came to be called the 'twilight war' or the 'phoney war'[3]. The trance-like atmosphere was rudely shattered in early April 1940, when Germany invaded Denmark and occupied the main Norwegian ports. On 14 April British forces were sent to Norway; but the ensuing campaign was a failure, causing unrest and criticism both in and outside Parliament. In a House of Commons debate (7–8 May), Churchill vigorously defended the Government. Forty-one Conservative Members voted against the Government, whose majority slumped from over two hundred to eighty-one.

Chamberlain[4] tried to form a government to include members of the Labour and Liberal parties, but they refused to serve under him. The choice for Prime Minister lay between Lord Halifax and Churchill, the former being preferred by Chamberlain, but he demurred on the grounds of the impossibility in wartime of the Prime Minister being in the House of Lords.

In the early hours of 10 May, Hitler's forces attacked the Netherlands, Belgium and France. That evening King George VI invited Winston Churchill to form a Government. He constructed a National Coalition of the three main political parties.

On 13 May he addressed the House of Commons for the first time as Prime Minister: 'I have nothing to offer but blood, toil, tears and sweat. . . .'

The end of May and early June saw the fall of France and the near-miraculous evacuation of our forces from the beaches of Dunkirk – but with the loss of all their arms and equipment.

In June Churchill flew several times to wherever the crumbling French Government was situated, in strenuous efforts to keep them in the fight. On 22 June Marshal Pétain, who had succeeded Reynaud as Prime Minister, signed an armistice with Germany: Britain was now alone, and facing the threat of invasion.

In these crisis weeks Churchill drove himself – and others – with a flail.

[1] They did not occupy the whole house: the State Rooms were shut up and the two top floors converted to the family's use.

² Pamela Digby (1920–97), daughter of 11th Baron Digby and Pamela ('Pansy') Digby (born Bruce). See also p. 575 n. 2, letter of 16 October 1953.
³ At sea, however, hostilities had begun at once, with the systematic sinking by German submarines and magnetic mines of British merchant shipping. On 14 October the battleship *Royal Oak* was torpedoed and sunk at Scapa Flow. On 13 December, following the fierce battle of the River Plate (Uruguay), the German battleship *Graf Spee* scuttled herself in the mouth of the river.
⁴ Neville Chamberlain (see p. 316 n. 5). He had been Prime Minister since 28 May 1937.

○ From CSC ✉   10 Downing Street
27 June 1940¹

My Darling,
  I hope you will forgive me if I tell you something that I feel you ought to know.
  One of the men in your entourage (a devoted friend) has been to me & told me that there is a danger of your being generally disliked by your colleagues & subordinates because of your rough sarcastic & overbearing manner – It seems your Private Secretaries have agreed to behave like schoolboys & 'take what's coming to them' & then escape out of your presence shrugging their shoulders – Higher up, if an idea is suggested (say at a conference) you are supposed to be so contemptuous that presently no ideas, good or bad, will be forthcoming. I was astonished & upset because in all these years I have been accustomed to all those who have worked with & under you, loving you – I said this & I was told 'No doubt it's the strain' –
  My Darling Winston – I must confess that I have noticed a deterioration in your manner; & you are not so kind as you used to be.
  It is for you to give the Orders & if they are bungled – except for the King the Archbishop of Canterbury & the Speaker you can sack anyone & everyone – Therefore with this terrific power you must combine urbanity, kindness and if possible Olympic calm. You used to quote: – 'On ne règne sur les âmes que par le calme' – I cannot bear that those who serve the Country & yourself should not love you as well as admire and respect you –
  Besides you won't get the best results by irascibility & rudeness. They <u>will</u> breed either dislike or a slave mentality – (Rebellion in War time being out of the question!)

                    Please forgive your loving devoted & watchful
                                                        Clemmie

I wrote this at Chequers² last Sunday, tore it up, but here it is now.

¹ This is the only letter extant between WSC/CSC during 1940.
² Official country residence of British Prime Ministers. See also p. 225 n. 1 (letter of 6 February 1921).

No answer exists to Clementine's letter: perhaps they spoke. But Winston surely took it to heart: for although during the years of his greatest power he could undoubtedly be formidable and unreasonable, many of the people who served him at all levels in those dire years have put on record not only their admiration for him as a chief, but also their love for a warm and endearing human being.

In September 1940 the London Blitz began, and heavy bombing raids would continue nightly until November. In mid-September Winston and Clementine moved out of No. 10 Downing Street[1] into the 'Annexe' flat, specially created out of government offices on the first floor of the building at Storey's Gate, overlooking St James's Park. The whole structure of No. 10 was frail, and the air raid shelter there inadequate in size and safety for the people living and working in the building. The 'Annexe', in a strong, modern stone and concrete building, was further strengthened, and steel shutters positioned over the windows. It was directly over the underground Central War Rooms[2].

On 22 June 1941 Germany invaded Russia, opening up a new vast dimension to the struggle. German armies advanced deep into Russia during July, perpetrating frightful cruelties on the civilian population.

Although Churchill had corresponded for two years with President Roosevelt* (who had been re-elected for a third term the previous November) and they already had a strong link and understanding, both leaders now wished to meet each other face to face.

On 4 August Churchill, accompanied by key colleagues and commanders, left Britain (on the first of his many wartime journeys across the Atlantic) in the battleship HMS *Prince of Wales*, bound for the top secret meeting place, Placentia Bay, off Newfoundland.

---

[1] Into which they had moved in mid-June. Until severe air raid damage was done to No. 10 Winston continued to work in the Cabinet Room and the Private Office. The Churchills continued to use the fortified ground-level sitting room and dining room at No. 10 for luncheons and dinners whenever possible.

[2] The Central War Rooms had been prepared in 1938 in anticipation of massive air attack. Further reinforced, by July 1940 they could accommodate for work and their meetings the War Cabinet and Joint Planning Committee, and included map rooms, cypher offices and switchboard. There were small emergency bedrooms for key personnel. WSC slept there only three times during the war, preferring the Annexe above, with which the War Rooms directly communicated. The Cabinet War Rooms, as they are now known, are open to the public.

A few days before Winston's departure Clementine, who was somewhat anxious about his health, wrote him the following note:

○ From CSC ✉   10 Downing Street
1 August 1941

I feel very strongly that on this all-important journey you should have a

Doctor with you – (The Ship's Doctor – no good – merely like Doctor Jones of the Enchantress) –

Please take Sir Charles Wilson[1] –

. . .

Brendan [Bracken*][2] agrees with me –

[1] On this occasion WSC did not take CSC's advice, but Sir Charles (later 1st Baron Moran; see Biographical Notes) would accompany him on nearly all his subsequent journeyings.
[2] At this date Minister of Information.

With the prospect of Winston being away for about a fortnight, Clementine took the opportunity to have a much-needed rest.

During 1941 her workload greatly increased[1]. Many calls were made on her as wife of the Prime Minister, and there was a steady stream of guests to be entertained, both in London and at Chequers; but she devoted herself to her wartime appointments with great energy and conscientiousness. Now she went for a short rest cure to Champneys, near Tring in Buckinghamshire, a highly regarded health establishment.

Winston's voyage and whereabouts were of course a deadly secret.

[1] From November 1939, Chairman of Fulmer Chase Maternity Home for wives of officers of all three services. From February 1941, President of the Young Women's Christian Association (YWCA) Wartime Fund, to provide welfare for the women's services. In October 1941 she undertook the Chairmanship of the Red Cross Aid to Russia Fund.

From WSC[1]   [HMS *Prince of Wales*
6 August 1941   At sea]

TUDOR NO. 4
... ALL WELL. COMPLETELY IDLE DAY. WE HAVE PICKED UP OUR NEW ESCORT[2] AND ARE NO LONGER LONELY. LOVE. WIRE HOW YOU ARE GETTING ON.

[1] Public Record Office, as yet unlisted.
[2] Owing to heavy seas which slowed down the escorting destroyers, the *Prince of Wales* had forged on ahead: complete radio silence had to be observed until an escorting destroyer joined her from Icelandic waters on 6 August.

From CSC[1]   [Champneys, Tring][2]
7 August 1941

ABBEY NO. 14
I AM GETTING ON WELL. VERY GLAD TO HEAR OFFICIALLY ABOUT RANDOLPH[3]. MY THOUGHTS AND LOVE FOLLOW YOU. CLEMMIE

[1] Public Record Office, as yet unlisted.
[2] The cables and other information from the Private Office reached CSC at Champneys by despatch rider, by whom she also sent back her replies to be radioed to WSC.
[3] Randolph had just been appointed GSO2 (with rank of Major) and put in charge of Army Information in Cairo; he would also be responsible for Press Censorship.

O From CSC [Champneys]
7 August 1941

My Darling
    My thoughts are constantly with you –
    I have just received your message sent by Mr Rowan[1] by dispatch rider –
It said you had spent a day in complete idleness! I can scarcely believe
this; but if it is so I hope you will continue to rest.
    The 'mad-house' is comfortable and well run – I have massage,
osteopathy hot & cold showers etc. etc. – but nothing to eat so far but
tomato juice & pineapple juice – This is the fourth day & I am beginning
to feel rested so that when you come home you should find a completely
renovated (if not rejuvenated) cat. . . .
    Randolph's post as officially described sounds thrilling & terribly
responsible – His duties seem multifarious & will require discrimination,
judgment & tact. But I think Randolph has these qualities – I must write &
congratulate him. . . .
    I do hope my Darling that this momentous journey besides being an
impulse of American resolve will rest & refresh you –
    How I would love to be with you in that beautiful ship – I hope you
often sip the air on the Bridge.

Tender love my Dearest
Clemmie

. . .

[1] Leslie Rowan (1908–72), KCB 1949. Principal Private Secretary to two Prime Ministers: WSC,
1941–5, and Clement Attlee, 1945–7. Subsequently Economic Minister, British Embassy,
Washington, and Second Secretary, HM Treasury, 1951–8. Chairman, Vickers Ltd, 1967–71. A
brilliant and charming man. In 1944 he married a ravishing Wren officer, Judy Love.

O From CSC Champneys
14 August 1941

My Darling –
    This morning early my Wireless told me that at 3 o'clock Mr Attlee[1]
would be making a statement on behalf of the Government & that
simultaneously the same announcement would be given out from the
White House in Washington – Great excitement and anticipation –
    It cannot be a Declaration of War by America? Because the President
cannot do that without Congress?
    I am told that in this Retreat (which I leave this afternoon), the Patients
have been betting whether you have gone to see the President or Stalin! I
will conclude my letter after hearing the broadcast. I go back to Chequers
this afternoon & a dispatch rider is coming there to fetch this letter for the
pouch.
    I am longing to see you my Dear One.
    I pray your journey has been fruitful & that you & the President like
each other.
    This place has done me a great deal of good – I feel rested & refreshed
– 'Wow & Re Wow'. . . .

Last Sunday I inspected a very smart platoon of Home Guard of which the Director of this place is Commanding Officer – They work very hard doing all sorts of exercises creeping about the woods at night & taking the local villages at the point of the bayonet.

3.20. I have just heard your joint declaration[2].

It is grand. God bless you.

Clemmie
. . .

[1] Clement Attlee, later 1st Earl Attlee (1883–1967). Labour MP since 1922 and Leader of the Opposition from 1935. Held various posts in first two Labour Governments. In Coalition Government Lord Privy Seal, 1940–2; Dominions Secretary, 1943–5; Lord President of the Council, 1943–5. Deputy Prime Minister from 1942; Prime Minister, 1945–51. Married, 1927, Violet Millar (d. 1964).

[2] The Atlantic Charter, an eight-point document agreed by WSC and Roosevelt at the Placentia Bay Conference, and later the basis of the United Nations Declaration. It seemed at this time like a blueprint for a better world, and had a stimulating and cheering effect.

On 7 December 1941 the Japanese attacked the US naval base and warships at Pearl Harbor; they also launched attacks on Malaya, the Philippines and Hong Kong. The following day Britain and the United States declared war on Japan. On 10 December Japanese torpedo-carrying aircraft sank the British battleships *Prince of Wales*[1] and *Repulse* off Malaya.

On 11 December Germany and Italy declared war on the United States.

With the entry of the United States into the war, Churchill felt it was imperative for him to see the President again. He and his colleagues left London by train on 12 December to go aboard the battleship HMS *Duke of York* off Gourock, on the Clyde. On arrival in Washington Winston stayed at the White House. In addition to Churchill's talks with Roosevelt* and his close colleagues, the British and American Chiefs of Staff held numerous meetings[2].

[1] In which WSC had travelled to and from the Placentia Bay/Atlantic Charter meeting.

[2] This conference was known as 'Arcadia'.

O From CSC   10 Downing Street
Friday 19 December 1941

My Darling

You have been gone a week & all the news of you is of heavy seas delaying your progress – plans to change into planes at Bermuda, so as to arrive in time, & then those plans cancelled.

I hope you are able to rest in spite of wind & weather and the anxiety in the Far East – How calm we all are – Hong-Kong threatened immediately, Singapore ultimately? perhaps not so ultimately Borneo invaded – Burmah? to say nothing of the blows to America in the Pacific –

Here I am bound to my Russian Fund. We have passed the Million Pound target & that without what will come in from the Flag Days, held not only in London but all over the country. I visited many depôts all over London from dawn till dusk – The people came running everywhere –

They are so good & sweet especially the old & they all asked about you.

Yesterday Mary's leave[1] came to an end; I took her & Judy in your car & deposited them as night was falling at their new camp near Enfield – In the gathering darkness it looked like a German concentration camp. It is a big piece of waste ground surrounded by suburban villas in the distance. – It has a high iron fence all round with barbed wire & locked gates....

... They disappeared in the gloom, & we waited becos' we ... hadn't 'kissed them good-bye' – We waited & waited ... , but Mary had disappeared in search of her barrack Room & I did not see her again as I thought it best not to loiter any more....

Well my beloved Winston – May God keep you and inspire you to make good plans with the President. It's a horrible World at present, Europe over-run by the Nazi hogs, & the Far East by yellow Japanese lice.

I am spending Christmas here at the Annexe & going to Chequers on Saturday the 27th.

Tender Love & thoughts
Clemmie

[1] Mary (19) and her cousin Judy Montagu (18; see p. 406 n. 2) had joined the Auxiliary Territorial Service (ATS) in September 1941 as private soldiers; after technical training they were posted to the same (mixed) anti-aircraft battery at a gun-site near Enfield, on the perimeter of London.

O From WSC [typewritten]   At sea
[undated but clearly 21 December 1941,   but now White House
with addition 24 December]

My darling,

Yesterday, Saturday, finished the longest week I have lived since the war began. We have had almost unceasing gales. For a long time going round the Bloody Foreland in the worst part of the U-boat and Focke Wulf[1] areas we could not make more than six knots unless we threw off our destroyer escort. For 36 hours we were within 5 or 600 miles of Brest, with its bomber squadrons, and it was very fortunate that no Focke Wulf spotted us through the gaps in the clouds. Three days ago we left our destroyers behind as they could not keep up in the rough sea, and in half an hour we hope to meet the American destroyer escort just North of Bermuda. The weather has again turned so rough that we shall no doubt leave them behind too and press on, but even so we now speak of Tuesday afternoon as the likely time for reaching Annapolis[2]. If this is realised, the voyage will have taken ten days, which is a big slice in times like these.

I am very well and have not suffered from seasickness at all, though I took two doses of Mothersill the first day. These ships literally cannot go more than 17 or 18 knots in a really heavy sea. No-one is allowed on deck, and we have two men with broken arms and legs. I have a lovely cabin in the bridge structure as well as my apartments aft. These latter are unusable owing to the noise and vibration. Here it is cool and quiet and daylight. I spend the greater part of the day in bed, getting up for lunch, going to bed immediately afterwards to sleep and then up again for dinner. I manage to get a great deal of sleep and have also done a great deal of work in my waking hours. We have been very well supplied with official telegrams and secret news. We have 27 cypherers on board for this service alone, and all my telegrams from Auchinleck[3] and others are coming through, but of general news one knows but little except what the wireless says, ...

We make a very friendly party at meal times, and everyone is now accustomed to the motion. The great stand-by is the cinema. Every night we have a film. I have seen some very good ones. The one last night, Blood and Sand[4], about bullfighters, is the best we have seen so far. The cinema is a wonderful form of entertainment, and takes the mind away from other things.

About these other things. The worst that has happened is the collapse of the resistance of Hong Kong; although one knew it was a forlorn outpost, we expected that they would hold out on the fortified island for a good many weeks, possibly for several months, but now they seem on the verge of surrender after only a fortnight's struggle[5]. Not very good news has also come in from Malaya. Owing to our loss of command of the sea, the Japanese have an unlimited power of reinforcement, and our people are retreating under orders to defend the Southern tip and the vital Fortress of Singapore. I have given a good many instructions to move men, guns and aircraft in this direction. We must expect to suffer heavily in this war with Japan, and it is no use the critics saying 'Why were we not prepared?' when everything we had was already fully engaged. The entry of the United States into the war is worth all the losses sustained in the East many times over. Still these losses are very painful to endure and will be very hard to repair.

On the other hand there is good news. We made a fine kill of U-boats round Gibraltar, about seven altogether in a week. This is a record. There has never been such a massacre, and it should dunch the spirits of the survivors when they get home to see how many of their companion vessels have been sent to the bottom. But the best of all is Auchinleck's continuous victorious advance. Before the end of the year he will be at Benghazi[6] and well on the road farther West. No doubt there will still be pockets of resistance to mop up, but there is every hope that the whole armed force of the enemy, which amounted to 100,000 Italians and 50,000 Huns, will be dead or captured. That, at any rate, would be a clean job, and gives relief as well as encouragement at an anxious juncture. It is very important for the Americans that we should have proofs that our soldiers can fight a modern war and beat the Germans on even terms, or even at odds, for that is what they have done. This lends weight to our counsels and requests.

I had been hoping till an hour ago to dine with the President tomorrow, Monday, night – and this is not yet impossible – but it is still blowing hard and from my porthole I can see, every minute, tremendous seas pouring over the bows of the ship, while down below can be heard the crash of them striking the sides. We are running obliquely across the waves[7] and sometimes the ship rolls very heavily. However, once you get used to the motion, you don't care a damn.

You can imagine how anxious I am to arrive and put myself in relation to the fuller news and find out what is the American outlook and what they propose to do. Long and not free from risk as the voyage has been, I am glad I did not try to fly, although they make you fine stories of how you can cover the Atlantic in 12 or 14 hours. In the Winter time this is very rare. There are all kinds of difficulties and dangers, and sometimes you are kept waiting 6, 8 or 10 days for favourable weather, so that the tortoise may still beat the hare. Everything is being kept open for the return journey, as I, particularly, do not wish to make up my mind; nor does anyone know how it will be accomplished. As soon as I get established in the White House I will ring you up on the trans-Atlantic cable. I wish particularly to know the length of your stockings, so that I can bring you a few pairs to take the edge off Oliver Lyttleton's coupons[8]....

I have read two books, Brown on Resolution[9] and Forty Centuries Look Down[10]. You would like both of them, particularly the opening part of Brown on Resolution, which is a charming love story most attractively told. The other is a very good account of Napoleon's relations with Josephine, and his excursions of various kinds to and in Egypt. I will bring them both back for you.

I am frightfully fed up with the idea of an extra day being tacked on to all these others, but one has to accept the inevitable. Being in a ship in such weather as this is like being in a prison, with the extra chance of being drowned. Nevertheless, it is perhaps a good thing to stand away from the canvas from time to time and take a full view of the picture....

I hope the [Aid to Russia] Fund is getting on well, and I daresay before I return it will have reached the million mark. I hope you brought off your camouflage trick of publishing the photograph of me buying the badge on your Flag Day on the 17[th][16th][11].

🖎 I have not had a minute since I got here [the White House] to tell you about it. All is vy good indeed; & my plans are all going through. The Americans are magnificent in their breadth of view.

Tender love to you and all – my thoughts will be with you this strange Christmas eve –

Your ever loving husband
W

[1] German fighter aircraft.
[2] State Capital of Maryland, USA, situated on the Severn river, near its mouth on Chesapeake Bay.
[3] Gen. (later Field Marshal) Sir Claude Auchinleck (1884–1981), who in July 1941 had succeeded Gen. Wavell as C.-in-C. Middle East.
[4] *Blood and Sand*, 1941; film based on book of same title by Vicente Blasco Ibanez, directed by Rouben Mamoulian and starring Tyrone Power.
[5] Hong Kong surrendered on 25 December 1941.
[6] Benghazi was reached on 24 December 1941.
[7] A deliberate manoeuvre to minimize detection by U-boats.
[8] Oliver Lyttleton KG, DSO, MC, later 1st Viscount Chandos (1893–1972). President of the Board of Trade, 1940–1. His clothes rationing (coupons) scheme had been introduced on 1 June 1941.
[9] C. S. Forester (1899–1966), *Brown on Resolution*, 1929.
[10] Frederick Britten Austin, *Forty Centuries Look Down*, 1936.
[11] As part of the security surrounding WSC's voyage, a photograph had been taken of him buying a flag from CSC for her Aid to Russia Fund *before* his departure for the USA. The Flag Day was on 16 December, and the photograph duly appeared in the newspapers, showing WSC ostensibly in London on that day.

Winston spent Christmas 1941 at the White House; Clementine was at the Annexe, with Cousin Moppet [Whyte*] for company.

On 26 December Churchill addressed the US Congress for the first time. That night, opening a very stiff window in his bedroom, he felt a pain over his heart and down his arms, and became short of breath. The next morning Sir Charles Wilson [Moran*] diagnosed that he had sustained a mild heart attack, but decided not to tell anyone, not even his patient[1]. It was a cool and correctly judged decision: Sir Charles told Winston that his circulation was 'a bit sluggish' and that he 'must try to ease up a little on his work'. This, of course, was easier said than done.

On 28 December Churchill left Washington by train for Ottawa, where on 30 December he addressed the Canadian Parliament. On New Year's Day 1942 he was back in Washington, and on 5 January he went to Pompano, near Miami in Florida, for a few days' rest; but he worked continuously.

The news from the Far East was grave: on 10 January the Japanese invaded the Dutch East Indies and Burma, pushing down through Malaya.

[1] From Lord Moran's book, *Winston Churchill: The Struggle for Survival*, 1966, pp. 16–17; his diary entry for 27 December 1941. This incident was not known outside a close circle until publication of the book.

O From CSC   10 Downing Street
29 December 1941

My darling Winston

I have been thinking constantly of you & trying to picture & realize the drama in which you are playing the principal – or rather it seems – the only part – I pray that when you leave, that the fervour you have aroused may not die down but will consolidate into practical & far-reaching action.

The news from Malaya is disquieting; & now I see that the Japanese have reached Medan in the north eastern corner of Sumatra just opposite Penang. This is one of the places I visited with Walter [Lord Moyne] on the East Indies cruise....

In the midst of their own preoccupations Malaya 2 days ago cabled me £25,000 for my Russian Fund. I was much moved....

No news of Mary since Christmas Eve when she & Judy blew in for a hot bath & a bite of dinner, & Sarah is completely swallowed up in her W.A.A.F.[1] ...

I hear Anthony Eden*[2] returns to-night – Bobbety[3] lunches with me tomorrow.

Tender love & thoughts my Dear One
Your own Clemmie

[1] This year Sarah and Vic Oliver parted, and he returned to the USA. Sarah joined the Women's Auxiliary Air Force (WAAF) in October as an Aircraft Woman 2nd Class. She trained in photographic interpretation (of aerial photographs) and, commissioned as a Section Officer, was posted to the Photographic Interpretation Unit at Medmenham in Berkshire, where she remained for the rest of the war, engaged in highly skilled and secret work.
[2] Foreign Secretary since December 1935. He had been on mission to Russia.
[3] Robert Gascoyne-Cecil (1893–1972), Viscount Cranborne, later 5th Marquess of Salisbury ('Bobbety'). At this date Secretary of State for Dominion Affairs. His wife was Betty (born Elizabeth Cavendish): see p. 414 n. 4.

○ From CSC   10 Downing Street
6 January 1942

My Darling

Randolph has just walked in looking brown & well & very happy.
Consequently, as I have been talking to him, I have time for only this one
line to bring you my love –

I am happy that you are slipping away to the South for 3 days rest &
sunshine –

I miss you dreadfully – Time seems to stand still.

I am pegging away at my Russian Fund – It now stands at 1¼ Million!

Tender love
Clemmie

Churchill left Washington by air (flying boat) on 14 January for the voyage
home, arriving at Plymouth on the 17th, after a flight of nearly eighteen hours.

On 19 February Government changes were announced: the War Cabinet
was reduced from nine to seven in number. Five of the seven were
unchanged; Clement Attlee became Deputy Prime Minister (a new office).
The principal change was in the appointment of Sir Stafford Cripps to the
War Cabinet, as Lord Privy Seal and Leader of the House of Commons. Lord
Beaverbrook* resigned.[1]

Part of the background to this re-shuffle is revealed in Clementine's next
letter (sent by 'house post'): obviously the matter had been discussed
between herself and Winston, and she had 'blown up'.

[1] Lord Beaverbook had been Minister of Aircraft Production (in the War Cabinet) since August
1940 and had literally worked wonders; but he was a difficult colleague. At the end of June 1941
he had become Minister of Supply and, on 4 February 1942, Minister of War Production. Tension
had arisen between him and Ernest Bevin, Minister of Labour, over the boundaries of their respective powers.

○ From CSC ✉   10 Downing Street
Thursday [probably 12 February 1942]

My Own Darling

I am ashamed that by my violent attitude I should just now have added
to your agonizing anxieties – Please forgive me.

I do beg of you to reflect whether it would not be best to leave Lord
B[eaverbrook*] entirely out of your Reconstruction.

It is true that if you do he may (& will) work against you – at first
covertly & then openly – But is not hostility without, better than intrigue &
treachery & rattledom [sic] within? You would have peace inside your
Government – for a few months at any rate – & you must have that with
what you have to face & do for us all – Now that you have (as I
understand) invited Sir Stafford [Cripps], why not put your money on
him –

The temper & behaviour you describe (in Lord B) is caused I think by the prospect of a new personality equal perhaps in power to him & certainly in intellect.

My Darling – Try ridding yourself of this microbe which some people fear is in your blood – Exorcise this bottle Imp & see if the air is not clearer & purer – You will miss his drive & genius, but in Cripps you may have new accessions of strength. And you don't mind 'that you don't mean the same thing'. You both do in War, & when Peace comes – we can see. But it's a long way off.

Your devoted

Clemmie

In early April Randolph joined a parachute detachment of the Special Air Service (SAS), formed by Major David Stirling[1] with the express object of operating behind the enemy lines in the desert.

[1] Maj. (later Sir) David Stirling (1915–90) DSO, OBE, the eldest of three remarkable brothers. Scots Guards, 1939. Founder, 1941, of the Special Air Service (SAS). Captured and imprisoned in Colditz Castle, 1943–5. Lived Southern Rhodesia, 1945–59. Knighted, 1990.

○ From CSC ✉   10 Downing Street
Saturday 11 April 1942

My Darling

Please don't think I am indifferent because I was silent when you told me of Randolph's cable to Pamela saying he was joining a parachute unit – I'm afraid I agree with Pamela that it's best not to intervene; but I grieve he has done this because I know this will cause you harrowing anxiety, indeed even agony of mind –

I feel this impulse of Randolph's caused by natural disappointment that he has lost his interesting post is sincere but sensational – Surely there is a half-way house between being a Staff Officer and a Parachute Jumper? He could have quietly & sensibly rejoined his Regiment & considering he has a very young wife with a baby[1] to say nothing of a Father who is bearing not only the burden of his own country but for the moment that of an unprepared America, it would in my view have been his dignified & reasonable duty.

I think his action is selfish & unjust to you both, & as regards Pamela one might imagine she had betrayed[2] or left him –

I am really very sorry he has lost his post because his talents & capacities suited him for it; but alas – these were not sufficient to outweigh his indiscretions & the hostilities which he arouses – It's no use offending & antagonising everybody unless you really are indispensable – Even then it's sad to do it –

My Darling – Do you think it would be any use my sending an affectionate cable begging him on your account to re-join his Regiment & give up this scheme in which if he begins one feels he must perhaps persevere – He has already left one Commando [No. 8]; & if he takes up parachuting & then gives it up for perhaps some other Staff job he might be regarded as theatrical & unstable.

He might listen to me, as though he does not care for me, I know he respects me[3].

Your poor loving
Clemmie

---

[1] 'Baby' Winston, born 10 October 1940.
[2] Since the spring of 1941 Pamela had in fact been having an affair with Averell Harriman (see also p. 469 n. 1). At this moment clearly CSC was unaware of this.
[3] Randolph had already joined David Stirling's group. On 27 May, returning from a long-range raid on Benghazi, the truck in which he was travelling overturned. One member of the party was killed and several others, including Randolph, suffered fairly serious injuries. Randolph was several weeks in the military hospital in Cairo, and was then invalided back to England until October 1942.

○ From CSC ✉   10 Downing Street
Saturday 11 April [1942]

Later
Darling –
    Since my long letter, I have had a talk with Pamela on the telephone – I rang her up. She seems so calm & sensible & <u>she</u> feels all is for the best. . . .

Churchill visited President Roosevelt* in Washington between 17 and 27 June 1942. During his visit the devastating and humiliating news was received of the fall of Tobruk, as German forces in Egypt advanced again: by 1 July they were less than 200 miles from Cairo.

In mid-July a record 40,000 tons of Allied shipping were sunk in the Arctic and Atlantic in a single week.

On 2 August Churchill flew to Cairo en route for Moscow.

○ From CSC   10 Downing Street
4 August 1942

My Darling,
    It was both dramatic & mysterious standing in the dark on that aerodrome while your monster bomber throbbing, roaring & flashing blue light taxied away into the blackness – It seemed a long time taking off – Finally we saw its huge dim shape airborne against the row of 'glim' lights which I suppose are there as a guide to planes -- I was assured that these are invisible from the air –

Yesterday the House went into Secret Session for a few minutes while Mr Attlee told the Members of your journey & its two-fold purpose[1]. Colonel [Brigadier] Harvie-Watt[2] tells me that the statement was well received....

... This week-end I go to Dytchley [Ditchley] to stay with the Trees*. I have sent all the servants away for a week's holiday except the tall Housemaid Lena [at Annexe] – She & 'Smoky' [cat] are looking after me....

I think much of you my Darling & pray that you may be able to penetrate & then solve the problem of the Middle East stultification or frustration or what is it?

This first part of your journey is less dramatic & sensational than your visit to the Ogre [Stalin] in his Den; but I should imagine it may be more fruitful in results.

Nancy Astor has made an ungracious & clumsy (I was about to write 'ass of herself' – But I will not compare her to the animal which bore Christ in triumph) speech which has repelled everybody[3] –

All my love & hopes go with this letter
Your
Clemmie
...

[1] To make major changes in the Middle East command, and to fly on to Moscow to inform Stalin that no Second Front (i.e. assault on Europe) could be undertaken in 1942.
[2] Brig. (later Sir) George Harvie-Watt (1903–89), barrister and Conservative MP. Commanded 6th Anti-Aircraft Brigade, 1941. At this date (1941–5) WSC's Parliamentary Private Secretary.
[3] A speech she made at the United Nations Rally in Southport on 1 August, which aroused widespread criticism and resentment largely owing to her statement that the Russians were fighting not for the Allies but for themselves.

O From WSC [typewritten]   British Embassy
9 August 1942   Cairo

My darling One,

I have been so busy at anxious work since I arrived nearly a week ago that I have not found a moment to write.... It was absolutely necessary that I should come here. This splendid army, about double as strong as the enemy, is baffled and bewildered by its defeats. Rommel[1] is living almost entirely on transport, and food and fuel captured from us. He is living from hand to mouth; his army's life hangs on a thread, but meanwhile a kind of apathy and exhaustion of the mind rather than the body has stolen over our troops which only new strong hands, and above all the gleam of victory can dispel. I went to the front on Wednesday; saw the Alamein and Ruweisat positions and was everywhere greeted with rapture by the troops who of course are scattered about an immense area to avoid air attack.

I drove all day with Auchinleck, Ramsden[2], Gott[3] and Coningham[4] (R.A.F.). I had long talks with Tedder[5] and his Admiral, with the Minister of State[6], with Smuts[7] and Brooke[8] continually. We have all been seeing separately the necessary people and collected opinions from all useful quarters. We had no doubt whatever of the changes which I forecast in my

Cabinet telegram. They were necessary to victory and [I] am very glad that except in the matter of calling the Middle East the Near East they have been endorsed by the Cabinet. Smuts was magnificent in counsel. We could work together with the utmost ease. He fortified me where I am inclined to be tender-hearted, namely in using severe measures against people I like. All was then set on Thursday. I had had a long drive alone with Gott, and without making him any offer or suggestion I convinced myself of his high ability, charming simple personality, and that he was in no way tired, as was alleged. One knows at once when one can make friends. Imagine my grief when even while the Cabinet was sitting, I had to telegraph that he had been killed.

He was killed flying in to have a bath and a restful night in Cairo. Although a Corps Commander he just took his place in the ordinary flying-bus, a Bombay.... This seems to me to be very grim, and even sinister considering that I had brought all concerned to realise that he should immediately be given Command of the Eighth Army. [in margin ✍:] You shd write to his wife. I am doing so too.... Here one sees the hand of fate. I had thought that Alexander[9] with his grand capacities for war and Gott with his desert prowess and his hold on the troops would have made an ideal combination. However, the order must ever be 'carry on'. In Montgomery*, who should be here on Tuesday, we have a highly competent daring and energetic soldier, well-acquainted with Desert warfare. If he is disagreeable to those about him he is also disagreeable to the enemy. I am confident that the new arrangement will work well....

Yesterday I spent six hours with the four armoured brigades that are all preparing and are [a] magnificent, well-trained, resolute body of men thirsting for action, but with only a few tanks to train on. I told them (in seven speeches) how the President had given me Shermans [tanks]; how the Navy were bringing them as fast as possible and how in a few weeks they would be the most powerful and best equipped armoured force of its size in the world. At one place they nearly all came from Oldham[10]. They showed the greatest enthusiasm. I intend to see every important unit in this army, both back and front and make them feel the vast consequences which depend upon them and the superb honour which may be theirs. The more I study the situation on the spot the more sure I am that a decisive victory can be won if only the leadership is equal to the opportunity.

Here we live in Capuan luxury. The weather is delightful. My host and hostess [Sir Miles and Lady Lampson][11] are charming; the food pre-war. My rooms are air-cooled. The wonderful air of the desert with its fierce sunshine and cool breeze invigorates me so much that I do not seem to need as much sleep as usual. Of course however, I sleep in instalments which is most refreshing.... I have had all Randolph's friends to lunch with me: David Stirling, who strolled in from behind the German lines, a tall slim dandified figure, recalling 'he was the mildest mannered man that ever scuttled ship or cut a throat'[12]....

... Now Russians have arrived and de Gaulle*, but Smuts I am sorry to say has gone. He has promised to come to England in September to stay at least a month ...

I found Tom Mitford[13] yesterday with the Armoured Brigade and will get him in to dinner when I return from this new adventure.

I start at midnight Monday and have a bath at Teheran, and should reach Moscow (DV) before dark on Tuesday. This is much shorter than I had imagined. I am not looking forward to this part of my mission because I bear so little in my hand, and sympathise so much with those to whom I go.

I informed General Auchinleck by letter yesterday of the decisions taken[14]. He is coming to see me here in a few minutes and I must close this letter without even having had time to read it through.

✍ Both yr darling letters [only one to hand] have arrived. Do send something by every plane that leaves. You may show any parts of this you think suitable to Attlee, Anthony [Eden*] & others in our secrets. But the fewer the better. Tender love my dearest.

This shd reach you in 48 hours. I hope then to be in Moscow.

Always yr ever loving husband
W

. . .

[1] Field Marshal Erwin Rommel (1891–1944), German Commander of North African offensive (nicknamed the 'Desert Fox'); defeated at El Alamein, 1942.
[2] Maj.-Gen. William Ramsden (1888–1969) CBE, DSO, MC. At this date Commander, 30 Corps, Middle East.
[3] Acting Lt-Gen. William Gott (1897–1942) DSO, CB, CBE. King's Royal Rifle Corps.
[4] Air Marshal (later Sir) Arthur Coningham (1895–1948) DSO, DFC, MC. Born Brisbane. Joined Royal Flying Corps, 1916. Second World War, Bomber Command. At this date commanded Desert Air Force, North Africa. Operations Sicily and Italy, 1943. AO C.-in-C., 2nd Tactical Air Force, 1944–5.
[5] Air Vice-Marshal Arthur Tedder, later 1st Baron Tedder (1890–1967), GCB, Commander of RAF Middle East, 1941–3. Later, as Deputy Supreme Commander under General Eisenhower, largely responsible for success of Normandy landings, 1944.
[6] Richard G. Casey, later Baron Casey (1890–1976). Australian diplomat and Liberal politician. At this date Minister of State Resident in the Middle East and member of British War Cabinet, 1942–3.
[7] Jan Christian Smuts (1870–1950) PC, OM, CH, FRS. Commanded Boer Commando Forces in South African War, 1899–1902. Supporter of Allies in both world wars; member of Imperial War Cabinet, 1917–18. Prime Minister of South Africa, 1919–24 and 1939–48. Sat with British War Cabinet, 1943. Honorary Field Marshal, 1941.
[8] Gen. Sir Alan Brooke, later 1st Viscount Alanbrooke (1883–1963) KG, GCB, OM, DSO. Chief of the Imperial General Staff, 1941–6. Chairman, Chiefs of Staff Committee, 1942 onwards. Field Marshal, 1944.
[9] Gen. Sir Harold Alexander, later Earl Alexander of Tunis (1891–1969) KG, GCB, OM, DSO, MC. C.-in-C. Middle East, 1942; Deputy C.-in-C. Allied Forces in North Africa, 1943; C.-in-C. Allied Forces in Italy, 1943–4; Supreme Allied Commander Mediterranean, 1944–5. Field Marshal, 1944. Governor-General of Canada, 1946–52. Minister of Defence, 1952–4.
[10] Oldham, Lancashire. WSC's first constituency, 1900–5.
[11] Sir Miles Lampson, later 1st Baron Killearn (1880–1964), Ambassador Extraordinary and Plenipotentiary to Egypt, and High Commissioner for the Sudan, 1936-46. Married (2), 1934, Jacqueline Castellani.
[12] Quoted from Lord Byron, *Don Juan*, canto III, stanza 41.
[13] Thomas Mitford (1909–45), only son of 2nd Lord Redesdale, CSC's cousin. Brother of the famous Mitford sisters. Killed in action in Burma, 1945.
[14] Among which was the decision to supersede him.

These key changes in the Middle Eastern command made, Churchill set forth on the second stage of his momentous journey. Just after midnight on 10

August he flew from Cairo to Tehran. Accompanying him on this important mission to Moscow was Averell Harriman[1].

While briefly in Tehran Winston, whose alias for this journey was 'Mr Green', sent a telegram to 'Mrs Green'. On 12 August the party flew on to Moscow.

[1] W. Averell Harriman (1891–1986). Son of US multi-millionaire. His public career dated from 1934. Sent by President Roosevelt as his special envoy to monitor Lend-Lease arrangements in Britain and USSR, March 1941. US Ambassador to USSR, October 1943–6. Governor, State of New York, 1955–8. US Ambassador at Large, 1961 and 1965–9. Married (1) 1915, Kitty Lawrence; divorced c. 1929; (2) 1930, Marie Norton Whitney; d. 1970; (3) 1971, Pamela (Churchill), widow of Leland Hayward, whom she had married, 1960 (see p. 575 n. 2, letter of 16 October 1953). Averell Harriman was handsome, urbane and extremely able.

○ From CSC   10 Downing Street
12 August 1942

My Darling
Mrs Green has just received the romantic message saying that you are 'resting in this delightful Persian garden' for a few hours. I am glad you are having a short respite from trouble & anxiety. I am awaiting the announced letter. I hoped it would come in time for me to reply to it – But this note has to go in a few moments so I can wait no longer....

All my thoughts wishes & prayers.

Your loving
Clemmie

...

○ From CSC   10 Downing Street
19 August [1942]

My Darling
I count the days & nights since you flew away in the dark – Eighteen – I pray that all the work you have done will bear fruit. I suppose this will reach you before you wing your way back?

I send you my dear love
Clemmie

Churchill and his colleagues left Moscow on 16 August, flying via Tehran again to Cairo, and finally back to England on 24 August. Of this journey General Douglas MacArthur said: 'A flight of 10,000 miles through hostile and foreign skies may be the duty of young pilots, but for a Statesman burdened with the world's cares it is an act of inspiring gallantry and valour.'[1]

On 23 October 1942 the Eighth Army, commanded by General Montgomery*, attacked at El Alamein, and after twelve days of heavy fighting inflicted a severe defeat on the German and Italian forces under Rommel's command. Thirty thousand prisoners were taken.

Throughout Britain on 15 November the church bells (hitherto only to be rung to warn of invasion) rang out to celebrate the great victory.

[1] Quoted by Martin Gilbert in *Churchill: A Life*, 1991, p. 730. Gen. Douglas MacArthur (1880–1964) was at this date US Supreme Commander, Far East.

Chapter XXI

JOURNEYINGS AND PARLEYINGS

In January 1943 Roosevelt* and Churchill met in Casablanca in Morocco[1]. Churchill left London on 12 January. His code name for this journey was 'Air Commodore Frankland'.

[1] The intention had been for Stalin to complete the 'Big Three', but he could not leave Russia on account of the continued intense fighting outside Stalingrad.

○ From CSC   10 Downing Street
14 January 1943

My Darling
    The 'Annexe' & 'No 10' are dead & empty without you – Smoky [the Annexe cat] wanders about disconsolate – I invite him into my room & he relieves his feelings by clawing my brocade bed-cover & when gently rebuked, biting my toe through it.
    I lunched to-day at 'Bucks' [Club] with Cardie Montagu[1], Crinks[2] & Venetia [Montagu*] – very pleasant.
    Everything is quiet – so far at <u>this</u> end 'the secret' is water-tight. . . .
                                                            Your loving
                                                            Clemmie
                                                                    . . .
I've just come back from having tea with Pamela & Baby Winston [two and a half] – Both looking lovely & blooming.

[1] Lionel Montagu, Edwin Montagu's youngest brother.
[2] Harcourt ('Crinks') Johnstone (1895–1945), Liberal MP; a friend of Venetia Montagu.

○ From WSC [typewritten]   Casablanca
15 January 1943

Darling,
    We arrived here on Wednesday morning after an uneventful journey.
    This, as you know, is a very attractive part of the world. The weather is bright with occasional showers and like a nice day in May for temperature. The hotel is taken over by the American Army, who keep open house

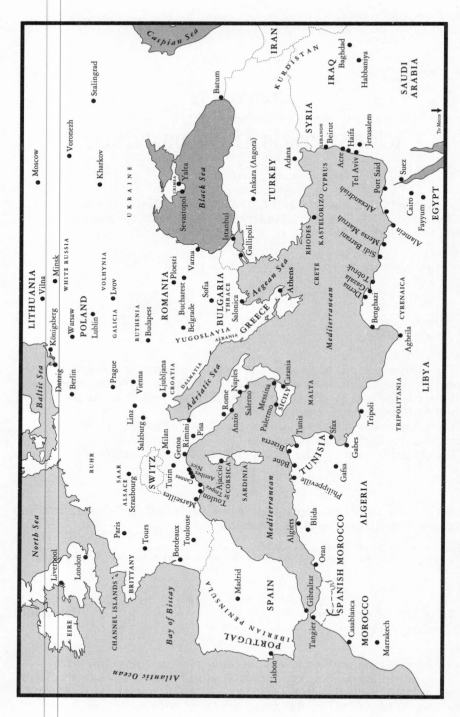

THE WIDE SCENE OF CONFLICT, 1939–1945: EUROPE, NORTH AFRICA, WEST ASIA

there and allow no British to pay for anything. Around the Hotel is a circle of villas. I have a very nice villa, except for getting hot water, but this difficulty has now been overcome.

Don Quixote [Roosevelt*], who arrived yesterday evening, has a magnificent villa which ... is all made on one floor.

The food here is very good, especially on the points where we are weak. There are plenty of eggs and oranges, but of course the milk is not safe so we have to have it out of tins. Most of our stores have been brought from England, but fresh meat and vegetables abound here. The countryside is verdant with lush grass in the meadows and many fine trees, some of which are palms. Around the whole circle of villas is drawn a circle of barbed wire, ceaselessly patrolled by American sentries, and around that again is a circle of anti-aircraft guns.

The two Staffs spent all yesterday collaborating, and ours report to me at intervals how their talks are going. At present they are working on what is called 'off the record', and very rightly approaching the problem in an easy and non-committal fashion on both sides. Meanwhile I am having what has hitherto amounted to a perfect holiday. I am reading that book about England against Napoleon which you said I should like. It is not bad, though its technique consists in reducing great matters to the level of small. I played a good deal of Bezique with Averell [Harriman] who pretended to be entirely ignorant but has inflicted a number of defeats upon me.

Last night I dined with the Don [Roosevelt*] and the Staffs. We were twelve in all. Dickie [Mountbatten][1] was there and Harry Hopkins[2], and the Don's son Elliott. I had a talk with him before dinner, and after dinner around the table we had a regular discussion.... We did not separate till 2 o'clock, though I made several offers to go.

The Don was not at all tired by his journey, which had taken four days. He slept in a different cruiser every night. He is determined to see his troops and has promised me that he will stay for ten days if necessary so that everything can be settled. After all, we have everybody here. We have this tremendous opportunity. If we cannot settle things now how will we ever be able to? ...

I am lunching with the Don, Harry Hopkins and Averell alone. We have touched on several things, plunging right into the matter straight away. I think he was delighted to see me, and I have a very strong sense of the friendship which prevails between us. Sancho P. [Sancho Panza = Harry Hopkins] was looking extraordinarily well, and twice as fit as he was before the combined restoratives of blood transfusions and matrimony were administered to him.

We are completely segregated from the surrounding world. Even the servants are not allowed to go out of the sealed circle, but according to the Don the German radio already has it that I am here with the Staffs, and also alternatively at Marrakech. I expect we shall adjourn thither after a few days. ...

I am waiting for the news of battle from the Eighth Army front. I have every reason to believe they attacked last night. Meanwhile here at a casual glance you would not believe there was such a thing as war, and one might be on the Riviera. However it is wise to let everything develop quietly and without hurry and to allow opposite or divergent points of view [to] melt themselves down. This can only be done by time and patience, but so far it seems a great change to me from my daily grind of papers and decisions. Also, I don't suppose a couple of blank days will do me any harm.

This is a very bad place for careless 'Short-snorters'[3]. There was a regular flourish last night before dinner. The Don produced his, and everyone else was similarly accredited. Luckily I was well prepared.

Forgive these aimless jottings.

Always yr loving
W

[1] Lord Louis Mountbatten, later Admiral of the Fleet Earl Mountbatten of Burma (1900–79). Second son of Prince Louis of Battenberg, who assumed name Mountbatten, 1917. Naval cadet, 1913; midshipman, 1916; commanded HMS *Kelly* 1939. Chief of Combined Ops and Member of British Chief of Staffs Committee, 1942–3; Supreme Allied Commander SE Asia, 1943–6. Cr. 1st Earl Mountbatten, 1947. Viceroy of India, 1947; Governor-General of India, 1947–8. First Sea Lord, 1955–9; Admiral of the Fleet, 1956; Chief of UK Defence Staff, 1959-65. Married, 1922, Edwina Ashley, grand-daughter of Sir Ernest Cassel. Murdered by IRA terrorists in the Irish Republic, August 1979.
[2] Harry L. Hopkins (1890–1946), US social worker and administrator. A close confidant of Roosevelt from New Deal days; he lived in the White House. Following the death of his second wife, Barbara Duncan, in 1937, Eleanor Roosevelt took their six-year-old daughter Diana under her wing. During the Second World War, as Roosevelt's special assistant, he undertook several important missions to UK and the USSR. In July 1942 he married, thirdly, Mrs Louise Macy. A man of enormous charm, he had extremely fragile health.
[3] A light-hearted invention of the Americans. To qualify as a Short-Snorter, the person must have flown the Atlantic, and have had a dollar bill signed by any Short-Snorters present. If one Short-Snorter met another and challenged him to produce his $1 bill, and he couldn't, he had to pay a dollar to each other Short-Snorter present. It shows how at this time it was still relatively uncommon to have made a transatlantic airflight.

[undated, *c*.19–22 January 1943]

FOLLOWING FOR PRIVATE OFFICE FROM MARTIN.[1]

PERSONAL AND PRIVATE. AIR CDE FRANKLAND WISHES YOU TO ENSURE THAT MRS FRANKLAND AND THE SERVANTS GO DOWN TO THE SHELTER IN EVENT OF AIR RAIDS WARNING[2]

[1] John Martin (1904–91), WSC's Principal Private Secretary, 1941–5. Knighted, 1952. Assistant Under-Secretary of State, 1945–56, and Deputy Under-Secretary of State, Colonial Office, 1956–65. British High Commissioner, Malta, 1965–7.
[2] On 18 January 1943 a fresh series of air raids had started on London.

O From WSC [typewritten]   [Casablanca]
24 January 1943

My dearest Darling Clemmie,

After ten days of very hard work for the Staffs, and a good deal for me and the President, we have now covered the whole vast war scene and have reached a complete agreement both between the two countries and between the military and political authorities. This entailed not only the plans but the distribution of material between 5 and 6 different theatres of war all over the world and the timing and the emphasis of all that should be done. [🖉 It is in every respect as I wished & proposed.]

Of course I have seen the President constantly and we have had nearly all our meals together. He came here and dined one night, the special ramps necessary for his movements being rapidly put in beforehand by the American Army Engineers. We had a very agreeable and successful evening, showing him our Map Room[1] which is perfectly fitted and records all the movements, of both ships and troops wherever they may be, from day to day. And then Harry Hopkins produced five negro soldiers who sang most melodiously to us.

Comic relief has been afforded by the attempt to bring de Gaulle* to the altar where Giraud[2] has been waiting impatiently for several days! Giraud made a much better impression on everyone here than was expected. De Gaulle was induced to come here, after much pressure from me, and arrived with his party the day before yesterday. He thinks he is Clemenceau (having dropped Joan of Arc for the time being), and wishes Giraud to be Foch, i.e., dismissible at Prime Minister Clemenceau's pleasure! Many of these Frenchmen hate each other far more than they do the Germans, and all I have met care more for power and place than for the liberation of their country. When a country undergoes so frightful a catastrophe as France, every other evil swarms down upon her like carrion crows.

We have had lovely weather here.... I have taken several walks along the sands and there is a reef with three walls of rocks from which one can watch the splendid breakers rolling in....

Dickie Mountbatten sent for Randolph[3] on his own initiative, having the idea of extending the David Stirling organization into the new Tunisian theatre. I was very glad to see him and have had long talks with him, and also quite a lot of Bezique. He is very well, and the President, who has both his sons[4] here, invited him to come to several of the Conferences on the de Gaulle–Giraud question, where he acquitted himself successfully. [🖉 He wd not discuss his own affairs, but he was delighted with the photographs you sent him.]

I am now about to receive a visit from Generals Giraud and de Gaulle. I fear that all they will be able to establish is a kind of liaison, but perhaps out of that other things may grow. [🖉 (Later: They have been photographed together shaking hands.)]

At noon the President and I are to hold a Press Conference, to which all the journalists in North Africa have been bidden. They are in an exceedingly bad temper [in margin: 🖉 We charmed them all right] and have been doing their best to work up political sensations out of the squalid tangles of French North African politics. After the [Press] Conference the President and I motor together to Marrakech, picknicking on the way. He goes off to-morrow on his five-day journey home by air. I shall probably fly to-morrow night to Cairo, where I am to meet Alexander fresh from his Conferences with Eisenhower[5], and also General 'Jumbo' Wilson[6], who is coming in from Persia. [🖉 It is an easy & simple flight over the Atlas mountains for 37 minutes & thereafter the Desert wh is far preferable to the sea.]

I have arranged that Alexander shall become Deputy Commander-in-Chief to General Eisenhower [for the Tunisian campaign], with the real planning and direction of the main operation. Wilson will succeed him in the Command of the Middle East.

The triumphant arrival of the Eighth Army in Tripoli has made it possible for us to obtain practically all the solutions we wished from our American friends. There is no doubt that these high officers, spending practically twelve hours of the day in each other's company, and speaking the same language, have got to know each other in a way never before achieved between Allies.

I had a sweet letter from Mary. Thank her so much for it.

My indigestion is definitely better, and contrary to everything that was predicted, my house-maid's elbow is going away of its own accord.

Post just going.
Fondest love.
Your loving & devoted husband,
W.
...

[1] WSC had his own Map Room, installed wherever he was living – even when aboard ship. The Map Room had its own permanent staff, headed by Capt. (later Sir) Richard Pim RNVR, and operated round the clock.
[2] General Henri Giraud (1879-1949), gallant and romantic French military figure; captured but escaped in both world wars. In November 1942 a British submarine took him from the Riviera to Gibraltar in time for Operation 'Torch' (Allied invasions North Africa, 8 November 1942). After Admiral Darlan's assassination (December 1942) Eisenhower appointed him local Commander of the Free French forces in Algiers; in 1943 he became Co-President (with de Gaulle) of the National Committee for Liberation and C.-in-C. of the French army, but resigned these appointments some months later following political manoeuvring on the part of de Gaulle.
[3] Randolph, recovered from his injuries (see p. 465 n. 3), had taken part with 1st Army in Operation 'Torch' and was currently in Algiers.
[4] Elliott Roosevelt, army officer, and Franklin Roosevelt, naval officer.
[5] General Dwight D. Eisenhower ('Ike') (1890-1969). Served in US army from 1915. C.-in-C., Allied Forces in North Africa, 1942–4; Supreme Commander Allied Expeditionary Forces in Western Europe, 1944–5; Chief of Staff, US army, 1945–8; Supreme Commander, NATO forces in Europe, 1950–2. 34th President of the USA, 1953–61.
[6] General Sir Henry Maitland ('Jumbo') Wilson, later Field Marshal Baron Wilson (1881–1964), GCB, GBE, DSO. At this date C.-in-C. Persia–Iraq Command; appointed C.-in-C. Middle East, 1943; Supreme Allied Commander Mediterranean, 1944.

From WSC[1]   H.M.S. *Bulolo*
25 January 1943

ADMIRALTY 'STRATAGEM' NO. 238
HUSH – MOST SECRET
WE ARE HERE IN A FAIRYLAND VILLA[2] IN MARRAKECH. WEATHER BRILLIANT. AM GOING TO PAINT A LITTLE THIS AFTERNOON FROM ROOF OF THE SAME VIEW OF THE PINK GATEWAY. MY FRIEND [ROOSEVELT*] HAS GONE. WE MOTORED HERE TOGETHER YESTERDAY 250 KILOMETRES, BEING GUARDED BY SENTRIES ALL THE WAY. THEY ALL ADMIT I HAD NOT OVER-STATED THE BEAUTY OF THIS PLACE. I HOPE TO BE WITH YOU BY WEEK-END.

WINSTON

[1] Public Record Office, Cabinet Papers 120/77.
[2] The 'fairyland villa' was Villa Taylor, residence of the American Vice-Consul. WSC later gave the picture – the only one he painted during the war – to President Roosevelt.

On 30 January Churchill flew from Cairo to meet President Inönü of (neutral) Turkey at Adana. This meeting had the strong support of President Roosevelt*, but Churchill had had to overcome considerable opposition to the plan from his Cabinet colleagues. The object of the meeting was to try to persuade President Inönü to assist the Allies, and to facilitate in particular British bases in Turkey.

From WSC[1]   Cyprus
1 February 1943

FROM AIR COMMODORE FRANKLAND TO MRS FRANKLAND.
WE HAD A GREAT SUCCESS IN TURKEY WHERE WE STAYED IN A COMFORTABLE TRAIN. I MADE FRIENDS WITH THE PRESIDENT WHO IS A VERY CAPABLE AND AGREEABLE MAN. WE FLEW IN THE EVENING TO CYPRUS WHERE WE ARE STAYING WITH THE GOVERNOR. I INSPECT THE FOURTH HUSSARS TOMORROW MORNING AND THEREAFTER TO CAIRO AND SO BY STAGES HOME. RANDOLPH SENDS HIS LOVE AND SO DO I TO ALL. W.S.C.

[1] Public Record Office, Cabinet Papers 120/77.

For the last part of his journey WSC's code name was 'Mr Bullfinch'.

From CSC[1]
[2 February 1943]

TELESCOPE NO. 390
MRS FRANKLAND TO AIR COMMODORE FRANKLAND.
I AM FOLLOWING YOUR MOVEMENTS WITH INTENSE INTEREST. THE CAGE IS SWEPT AND GARNISHED FRESH WATER AND HEMP SEED ARE TEMPTINGLY DISPLAYED, THE DOOR IS OPEN AND IT IS HOPED THAT SOON MR BULLFINCH WILL FLY HOME.

[1] Public Record Office, not yet listed.

From WSC[1]   Mideast [Cairo]
3 February 1943

STRATAGEM NO. 340
KEEP CAGE OPEN FOR SATURDAY OR SUNDAY. MUCH LOVE.

[1] Public Record Office, not yet listed.

From WSC[1]   [Algiers]
5 February 1943

STRATAGEM NO. 357
THE BULLFINCH HOPES TO MAKE A LONG HOP HOME TONIGHT.

[1] Public Record Office, Cabinet Papers 120/77.

○ From CSC   10 Downing Street
Friday Night [5 February 1943]

My Darling
    Welcome Home. The anxiety & tension has been severe.
    What an inspiration was the visit to Turkey – And how glad I am you
did not allow yourself to be deviated from that extra lap of your journey –
    I'm thinking of you flying thro' the tenebrous dark & pray you make a
good land-fall -

                                                        Your loving & expectant
                                                                        Clemmie
                                                                           . . .

Saturday Morning [6 February]. Thank God engine trouble[1] discovered
before you started. I shall come to station to meet you. Please let me get
into train before you come out – I like to kiss my Bull-finch privately &
not be photographed doing it!

[1] The party made a false start on the evening of 5 February: the aircraft developed magneto trouble,
and so an extra night was spent in Algiers. WSC arrived home on 7 February.

After his various testing journeyings in the New Year, Winston became quite
seriously ill with pneumonia; he was nursed at the Annexe, and bulletins
were issued; he recovered well, but the doctors now insisted he should make
his next journey by sea.
    On 4 May 1943 he left London for the Clyde to board the *Queen Mary*[1],
bound for the United States, to visit the President.

[1] The luxury passenger liner RMS *Queen Mary* was used as a troop carrier during the war. WSC
and his colleagues travelled in her several times.

○ From CSC   Dytchley[1]
Sunday 9 May 1943

My Darling
    The news of Tunis & Bizerta[2] broke upon the country at midnight last
Friday. But I was asleep & heard it at seven o'clock on the Wireless
yesterday. It's too thrilling, but no news of any number of prisoners yet. I
suppose they have fled into the peninsula –
    Sarah came to dinner unexpectedly on Friday which was a treat. She

was very silent & mysterious as usual & emitted only a few inarticulate sounds.

I went to a Y.W.C.A. function in Oxford yesterday & came on here for the week-end. The house is mostly shut up but is as pleasant & agreeable as before....

Your loving
Clemmie

[1] The Oxfordshire home of Mr and Mrs Ronald Tree (see Biographical Notes). Modern sources use spelling 'Ditchley'.
[2] On 7 May the 1st US High Command had entered Bizerta, and the 1st British Army had entered Tunis.

From WSC[1]
10 May 1943

PENCIL NO. 31
FROM AIR COMMODORE SPENCER TO MRS SPENCER.[2]
SIX AMERICAN WARSHIPS ARE NOW ESCORTING US AND THREE MORE ARRIVING TOMORROW
MORNING. VOYAGE CONTINUES TO BE MOST PLEASANT. LOVE TO ALL.

[1] Public Record Office, not yet listed.
[2] Code names for this journey.

From CSC[1]   [London]
11 May 1943

ALCOVE NO. 157
FOLLOWING FOR AIR COMMODORE SPENCER FROM MRS SPENCER.
HAVE BEEN THINKING OF YOU SO MUCH AND LOOK FORWARD TO HEARING OF YOUR SAFE ARRIVAL.
WHAT GLORIOUS NEWS FROM NORTH AFRICA.

[1] Public Record Office, not yet listed.

O From CSC   10 Downing Street
13 May [1943]

My darling Winston

How I wish that in this hour of Victory I were with you – So that we could rejoice together & so that I could tell you what I feel about your North African Campaign. You must be deeply moved by these events although you planned them & knew beforehand that they could be achieved –

I'm worried at the importance given by the Press (notably The Times) to the presence of Wavell[1] & his East Indian Naval & Air Colleagues in your Party.

I'm so afraid the Americans will think that a Pacific slant is to be given to the next phase of the War – I have cut out the piece of The Times which disturbs me. <u>Surely</u> the liberation of Europe <u>must</u> come first.

I wonder what impression Wavell has now made upon you. I have never met him but I understand he has a great deal of personal charm. This is pleasant in civilized times but not much use in total War....

16 A.T.S. 'Ack Ack' [Anti-Aircraft] girls were killed in [Great] Yarmouth by hit & run raiders[2]. The hostel where they were congregated was pulverized.

God bless you my Darling.

Mary has gone with her Battery[3] to Bude for a fortnight's firing practice.

Your loving
Clemmie

Have just heard of the terrific raid on Duisburg. Do re-assure me that the European Front will take 1st place all the time.

[1] Gen. Sir Archibald Wavell, later Field Marshal Earl Wavell (1883–1950), PC, GCB, GCSI, GCIE, MC. At this date C.-in-C. India, 1941–3. Previously C.-in-C. Middle East, 1939–41. Later Supreme Commander SW Pacific, 1942. Viceroy and Governor-General of India, 1943–7. Unfortunately he and WSC were never on the same 'wavelength'.
[2] 11 May 1943. In fact 26 ATS were killed in their hostel, and 12 men of various units in the Regimental Headquarters nearby.
[3] In mid-April I had been posted to 481 Heavy (Mixed) Anti Aircraft Battery RA in Hyde Park, London. I was now a subaltern.

13 May 1943 was a day for triumph and congratulation. Churchill, in Washington, received a telegram from General Alexander: SIR, IT IS MY DUTY TO REPORT THAT THE TUNISIAN CAMPAIGN IS OVER. ALL ENEMY RESISTANCE HAS CEASED. WE ARE MASTERS OF THE NORTH AFRICAN SHORES.[1]

On Sunday 16 May victory church bells rang again throughout Britain.[2]

[1] Churchill Papers CHAR 20/111.
[2] They had been rung for the first time on 15 November 1942 in celebration of victory at El Alamein.

O From CSC   10 Downing Street
Saturday 15 May 1943

My Darling

I have just returned from Sarah Churchill's Wedding[1] at St Margaret's Westminster. It was very charming & simple; & little Winston & Mary [Duchess of Marlborough]'s baby son Charles[2] (to whom I am Godmother) wore little white duck sailor suits & walked together up the aisle. During the service Winston decided it was a bore standing; so he lugged a hassock out of a pew into the aisle & sat on it –

The reception was in a lovely house in Belgrave Square belonging to that rather wormish but harmless Mr Chips Channon[3] – Jack [Churchill*] was a tower of strength & acted as Usher & general factotum.

Your telegram to the bride arrived at Downing Street ... so we had it telephoned to the Bride at the Party & it gave great satisfaction.

Talking of telegrams – that was a splendid one the King sent you. I am so glad about it. I do wish you were here my Darling so that we could jump for joy at this great & glorious Victory. And Alexander's telegram has just come out in the evening papers. . . .

I rather think Randolph is trying for a 'rapprochement' with Pamela[4]. He sent little Winston an 'airgraph' letter & said at the end 'take care of your Mother' – How I wish that could happen. Perhaps it will.

Tender Love my own Darling Winston
Clemmie

[1] Lady Sarah Spencer-Churchill (1921–), eldest daughter of the 10th Duke of Marlborough, married Lt Edwin Russell of the US Naval Reserve; divorced 1966.
[2] Born 1940.
[3] Henry ('Chips') Channon (1897–1958), Conservative MP. Parliamentary Private Secretary to Under-Secretary of State for Foreign Affairs, 1938–41. Knighted 1957. His diaries were published posthumously: *The Diaries of Sir Henry Channon*, ed. Robert Rhodes James, 1967.
[4] Randolph and Pamela's marriage had soon run into difficulties, largely on account of his debts and drinking, and Randolph's discovery of Pamela's affair with Averell Harriman.

○ From CSC   Chartwell
20 May 1943

My Darling

Your address to Congress[1] was grand & a masterpiece of 'walking delicately' –

It warmed me to hear your voice so strong, resonant & resolute.

Yesterday I went with the Attlees to St. Paul's to give thanks for Tunisia – The Service was short & restrained & the Cathedral was cold as Charity, but when we emerged into brilliant sunlight & clanging bells & whirling pigeons & sweet clapping city stenographers who, sensing a ceremony, had stayed on after their work, one's blood began to flow & one's pulses to beat in time with great events.

Diana had her baby[2] in one swift hour. Doctor & Nurse only just in time. She looks lovely & well but such a crashing labour is a bit of a shock & she must be well nursed. She & Duncan are over the moon with joy. I have just now come to the cottage for a week to enjoy the heavenly spring weather – Chartwell has on her bridal dress – She is a lovely untidy bride – 'A sweet disorder in the dress kindles in clothes a wantonness'[3].

We have had four sleepless nights caused by nuisance raids – Alerts at Midnight, 2 & 4, with the Parks' guns & Prof [Lindemann*]'s rockets barking & shattering[4].

Last night down here 2 big bombs, I don't know where, shook the little cottage – They say it is the Army down the valley who shew lights & attract them – Here, guns not crashing but muttering in the distance, but a constant drone of 1 enemy plane at a time <u>seemingly</u> circling round & round!

Tender Love Darling
from
Clemmie

. . .

[1] WSC addressed the US Congress, for the second time, on 19 May.

[2] Celia Sandys, born 18 May. Her third and last child.
[3] Robert Herrick (1591–1674), 'Delight in Disorder'.
[4] Nearly all the bigger London parks had anti-aircraft batteries and also rocket batteries in them.

From WSC[1]   Washington
23 May 1943

PENCIL NO. 212
AIR COMMODORE SPENCER TO MRS SPENCER. PRIVATE AND PERSONAL.
    YOUR LOVELY LETTERS ARRIVE EVERY DAY BUT I HAVE BEEN TOO HARD PRESSED TO WRITE. I
HAVE BEEN STAYING AT THE EMBASSY FOR A FEW DAYS TO SEE A LARGE NUMBER OF PEOPLE,
BRITISH AND AMERICAN, WHO ARE IMPORTANT. I GO BACK TO SLEEP AT THE WHITE HOUSE
TONIGHT IN ORDER TO SETTLE OUR BUSINESS, WHICH HAS GONE WELL, FINALLY WITH OUR
FRIEND.
    YOU MUST BE HAVING A LIVELY TIME AND SO MUST MARY.
    FONDEST LOVE TO ALL.

[1] Public Record Office, not yet listed.

O From WSC [typewritten]   In the Airplane
28 May 1943   Gibraltar[1]

My darling Clemmie,
    You really have been splendid in writing to me. Hardly a day has
passed that I have not had a letter to give me so much pleasure and
delight. I, on the other hand, have been most remiss but I really have been
hunted altogether beyond the ordinary. Not only have I had all the big
business about which I came, but I naturally took advantage of all the time
the President could give me, which was a very great deal, and in addition I
undertook to see a large number of people, both British and Americans.
For this purpose I went to the Embassy for the week-end and did not
accompany the President to his SHANGRI-LA in the forests of the Blue
Ridge[2].
    I took an immense amount of trouble with the Speech and did not think
much of it till it was delivered, but it certainly had a most electrifying
effect. . . . They never had had anything like the kind of accounts I give to
Parliament, and were delighted to be so considered on this occasion.
    At the Embassy one afternoon about 40 Senators and Members of both
parties came, including some of the leading Isolationists. Nothing could
exceed their cordiality, which was evidently entirely sincere.
    In my long talks with the President I naturally discussed American
politics. Although after 12 arduous years he would gladly be quit of it, it
would be painful to leave with the war unfinished and break the theme of
his action. To me this would be a disaster of the first magnitude. There is
no-one to replace him, and all my hopes for the Anglo-American future
would be withered for the lifetime of the present generation – probably for
the present century. On the other hand, the Constitution says there must

be an election, and even now when it is twenty months away [November 1944] all thoughts are turned to the question of who is to hold the power. We should certainly not allow such a state of affairs in our country, but a written Constitution makes slaves of its subjects and is in this case totally unfitted to the waging of war.

Harry Hopkins and his wife[3] were most agreeable and friendly, and evidently in the highest favour. Mrs Roosevelt* however was away practically all the time, and I think she was offended at the President not telling her until a few hours before I arrived of what was pouring down on her. He does not tell her the secrets because she is always making speeches and writing articles and he is afraid she might forget what was secret and what was not. No-one could have been more friendly than she was during the two or three nights she turned up.

They all made great complaint I had not brought you with me, and made me promise that next time you must surely come.

It was very hot in Washington and if I had not had a specially-cooled room I should have been very uncomfortable....

My friendship with the President was vastly stimulated. We could not have been on easier terms. There is no doubt that the speech I made showing the success which has attended our joint efforts, and his part in it, strengthened his position, and I hope he will take my advice and make some statements of this kind himself from time to time. There are many other things he could do which would be highly beneficial, but I was very careful not to presume outside my proper sphere.

I got the President to let General Marshall[4] come with me in order that the work I am now about to do at Algiers should run evenly, and that there should be no suggestion I had exerted a one-sided influence. I think very highly of Marshall. He wrote a paper the day before yesterday in the airplane on general strategy. It was one of the most masterly I have seen, and with which I am in the fullest accord. There is no doubt he has a massive brain and a very high and honourable character.

Much depends on the talks which are now about to open, and which will implement in the tactical sphere the decisions of strategy and policy which we reached with so much general agreement.

We had an absolutely perfect journey in two hops of 7 & 17 hours respectively, and reached this wonderful place [Gibraltar] yesterday at 5 p.m. We were a few minutes too late to go on to Algiers before dusk but the General (Mason MacFarlane)[5] made us very comfortable and fired off all his cannons at an anti-aircraft practice, which was most impressive.

I am now off to visit the Rock and the batteries, and finish up at my new airplane[6] which is waiting, having acquitted itself very well on the outward journey. We hope to reach Algiers in a flight of about 2½ hours.

I was delighted to hear of Diana's good news and that all is well there.

I am afraid you have been having disturbed nights lately. But the enemy's spite is only equalled by his feebleness, while we are hitting him really massive and frightful blows....

I was enchanted by The King's letter and thought it charming of him. I must try to make my exceedingly complicated and highly sensitive hen lay a few more eggs[7].

They are all pressing me now to go, so I must close,

✍ with many kisses & tender love
your ever loving husband
W

P.S. I am bringing you home various desirable objects including 2 dresses & Bernie B[aruch] has added some other things –

[1] After his talks with the President, WSC decided to go to North Africa to discuss Italian invasion priorities with Gen. Eisenhower (see p. 476 n. 5). He flew to Algiers via Newfoundland and Gibraltar.
[2] Blue Ridge, in Maryland, later known as Camp David.
[3] Harry Hopkins (see p. 474 n. 2, letter of 15 January 1943).
[4] Gen. George Marshall (1880–1959), US general and diplomat. Chief of Staff of United States Army, 1939–45; Secretary of State, 1947–9; Secretary of Defense, 1950–1. His proposed European Recovery Program, 1947, became known as the Marshall Plan. Awarded Nobel Peace Prize, 1953.
[5] Lt-Gen. (later Sir) Mason MacFarlane (1889–1953) KCB, DSO, MC. Governor and C.-in-C., Gibraltar, 1942–4.
[6] A Lancaster bomber converted for WSC's use and called 'The York'.
[7] WSC was referring to the ULTRA (top secret) source of information deriving from the decryption of information from the ENIGMA machine cypher, the secret of which was brought to Britain on the outbreak of war by Polish cryptographers. It was operated largely by signals operators, university mathematicians and cryptographers at Bletchley Park in Buckinghamshire. WSC afterwards called them 'my geese that laid the golden eggs but never cackled'.

○ From WSC [typewritten]   Algiers
29 May 1943

My darling One,

We flew on here yesterday, under strong escort, from Gibraltar in my new York, which is certainly marvellously comfortable and efficient. A serious oversight is that the Frigidaire only works when the plane is flying. Consequently, if you stop anywhere for a night all the food goes bad. This problem is being dealt with.

Here I am in Admiral Cunningham's[1] delightful villa on the hills above Algiers harbour. The flowers and flowering trees are splendid. The sun is bright and warm, though not fierce, and a delicious cool breeze springs up from the sea. The harbour yesterday was full of ships taking 10,000 German prisoners to England or America (I do not know or care much which!).

De Gaulle* is to arrive to-morrow and everyone here is expecting that he will do his utmost to make a row and assert his personal ambition. He will run up against a pretty tough combination if he does not play straight. General Georges[2] is here. I encouraged him to escape from France and we brought him by secret means to Algiers ten days ago. It gave me great pleasure to meet him and Giraud at luncheon to-day and in their company I recaptured some of my vanished illusions about France and her Army.

Randolph was summoned to meet me at the airport and dined with all the Generals and potentates last night. I never saw him looking so fit and well. His complexion is perfect being bronzed and burnt by the sun. He has also lost a lot of weight and looks the picture of health. It will be a pleasure to me to have him with me for a few days.

I cannot sufficiently praise the charm of this scene and climate and I think I may fairly claim a few days' repose here during which I shall not waste my time, ...

Always yr ever loving husband

W

[1] Admiral Andrew Cunningham, later Admiral of the Fleet 1st Viscount Cunningham of Hyndhope (1883–1963), KT, GCB, OM, DSO. Naval C.-in-C. Expeditionary Force, North Africa, 1942. Appointed C.-in-C. Mediterranean, 1943. First Sea Lord and Chief of Naval Staff, 1943–6.
[2] See p. 448 n. 4. An admired military pre-war contact and friend.

August 10–24 saw the meeting of President Roosevelt*, Churchill and Mackenzie King (Prime Minister of Canada) at the First Quebec Conference ('Quadrant'). Clementine and I (as ADC) accompanied Winston.

The first meeting of the Big Three (Roosevelt*, Churchill and Stalin) was planned for November in Tehran[1]. But the President and Churchill decided they must meet before this. Churchill left England on 11 November for his rendezvous with Roosevelt.

[1] Capital of Persia (Iran), which had been officially neutral until signature of Tripartite Treaty of Alliance (Persia, UK, USSR), 29 January 1942.

From WSC[1]
21 November 1943

FROZEN NO. 57
COLONEL WARDEN TO MRS WARDEN.[2]

HAVE HAD FOR FIVE DAYS BAD COLD ON CHEST NOW DEFINITELY MASTERED. THIS AND BAD WEATHER DECIDED ME TO GO ON IN SHIP AND AM JUST REACHING ALEXANDRIA AFTER SAFE VOYAGE. WE HAVE BEEN HANDED ON FROM POINT TO POINT BY AIR COVER AND SEAPOWER WITHOUT ANY MOLESTATION. AM STILL GRIEVING OVER LEROS[3] ETC. IT IS TERRIBLE FIGHTING WITH BOTH HANDS TIED BEHIND ONE'S BACK.

HAD GREAT WELCOME FROM WORKMEN IN MALTA DOCKYARD.

LOVE FROM SARAH AND ME. RANDOLPH WITH HIS REGIMENT.

[1] Public Record Office, not yet listed.
[2] Code names for the journey.
[3] In the wake of the Allied invasion of the Italian mainland (3 September) and the surrender and signing of an armistice with Italy (8 September), a number of Italian-held islands in the Dodecanese were occupied by British forces. The Germans counter-attacked, and Leros was re-captured after a gallant fight on 17 November: 5,000 British soldiers were taken prisoner.

From WSC[1]
23 November 1943

FROZEN 99
COLONEL WARDEN TO MRS WARDEN.
. . . SARAH HAS BEEN WRITING FULLY. MY COLD IS GONE AND COUGH IS BETTER. WEATHER HERE IS DELIGHTFUL. HAVE JUST TAKEN ADMIRAL Q [ROOSEVELT] TO SEE SPHINX.
FONDEST LOVE. W.

[1] Public Record Office, not yet listed.

O From CSC   10 Downing Street
23 November 1943

My Darling,
    I'm afraid that so far your journey has not been pleasant or refreshing – Your cold must have made you miserable & uncomfortable & then I know Leros must cause you deep unhappiness – But never forget that when History looks back your vision & your piercing energy coupled with your patience & magnanimity will all be part of your greatness. So don't allow yourself to be made angry – I often think of your saying, that the only worse thing than Allies is not having Allies![1] . . .
    I went the other day to call upon poor widowed Madame Sikorska[2]. She is an agreeable, & must have been, a beautiful woman – She shewed me a photograph of her daughter aged 26 who was killed in the same crash.
    Max [Beaverbrook*][3] was most amusing about the Cabinet in your absence – it seems that Archie [Sinclair][4] is quite out of hand, & 'Prof' [Lindemann*][5] has suddenly become verbose too! So that the Meetings go on for ever.
    To-day Mr Morrison[6] is going to tell the House about the Mosleys[7]. I hope it goes all right.
    Anthony [Eden*][8] brings you this letter with my dear love. I'm more lonely this time than ever before, because I have tasted of the excitement & interest of travel in War Time in your company[9].

                                                        Your devoted
                                                        Clemmie
                                                            . . .

[1] WSC had had a severe disagreement with Gen. Eisenhower over the support required for British forces to occupy and hold the Dodecanese islands. The President was invoked, and WSC's demands were not agreed.
[2] Wife of Gen. Wladyslaw Sikorski (1881–1943), Polish soldier and statesman. C.-in-C. Free Polish Forces and premier of Polish government-in-exile in London from 1940 until his death in an air crash taking off from Gibraltar, 4 July 1943.
[3] Since 24 September 1943 Lord Privy Seal (in War Cabinet).
[4] See p. 88 n. 3. Since 11 May 1940 Secretary of State for Air (not in War Cabinet).
[5] Now 1st Baron Cherwell. Since 30 December 1942 Paymaster-General (not in War Cabinet).
[6] Herbert Morrison, later Baron Morrison of Lambeth (1888–1965). Labour MP since 1923. At this date Home Secretary (1940–5). Later Leader of the House of Commons and Lord President of the Council, 1945–51; Foreign Secretary, March–October 1951.
[7] Sir Oswald Mosley (see p. 254 n. 1), Leader of the British Union of Fascists, and his wife Diana (born Mitford, CSC's cousin) had been detained in 1940 under Regulation 18B and were in

Holloway Prison. On 20 November 1943 they were released and transferred to house arrest on grounds of his ill-health.
[8] Foreign Secretary since 22 December 1940 (in War Cabinet).
[9] CSC had accompanied WSC when he went to Canada and the USA for 1st Quebec Conference (10–24 August 1943).

O From WSC [typewritten]   Casey Villa[1]
26 November 1943   Cairo

My darling,

Sarah[2] assures me that she has kept you up to date with her accounts of our journey. We came through the whole way safely and uneventfully on the RENOWN[3], but many guardian angels were employed on the sea and in the air to ward off evil. I have completely recovered from my cold. It has left behind a nasty cough which occurs in the morning when I awake but does not bother me during the daytime.

We have now been five days here and so far have only really tackled the Chinese end of the business[4]. However, a good deal has gone on behind the scenes in the sense of bringing the British and Americans nearer together on the great and grim issues with which we are confronted. Tomorrow at first screech of cock we start for CAIRO THREE [Tehran] and we shall stay there I hope three or four nights. U.J. [Uncle Jo – Stalin] meets us on the evening of the 28th. It has not been possible to come to grips with our main problems without knowing what are his views and wishes.

Nothing could exceed the amicable relations between me and Admiral Q [Roosevelt*], and indeed throughout all our large parties of British and Americans. Thus differences of outlook may be reconciled by agreements which also spell action....

I got on excellently with Madame Chiang Kai Shek[5] and I withdraw all unfavourable remarks which I may have made about her. She has brought me from China a long scroll, which is a picture by a fine artist of the Ming dynasty.... I send you a copy of a letter which I have just sent her by Sarah, who will deliver the goods. The cat[6] is a very nice one, bigger than my little one, but with a somewhat less quizzical expression on its face....

I am burning to take part in the debate on 18B[7], and if I were at home now I would blow the whole blasted thing out of existence. So long as Morrison presents the case as exceptional treatment for Mosley naturally he is on difficult ground and people can cry 'Favour'! He really would lose very little to sweep the whole thing away, which he could do by the overwhelming arguments I have mentioned to him in the various telegrams which you will have seen by now.

Let me know how public opinion is going on different things. Of course I know it is said in London that I was frustrated in my conduct of the war in the Mediterranean during the last two months. It is not for me to challenge this. I cannot pretend to have an adequate defence of what actually occurred. I have been fighting with my hands tied behind my back, but now I hope to get better arrangements and procure the necessary decisions for future blows on a good scale....

I have not yet succeeded in gripping affairs as I hope and mean to out here, but I have a feeling things will go the way I want. Tomorrow we start so very early that I am now going to sleep for an hour before dining with the Embassy in Cairo.

✍Tender love my darling Clemmie. How I wish you were out here w me to see the variegated show.

Your ever loving
W
...

¹ The residence of Richard G. Casey, Minister of State Resident in the Middle East (see p. 468 n. 6).
² Sarah had been given leave from her WAAF unit to accompany her father as his ADC; this was her first wartime journey with him.
³ WSC and party had travelled a roundabout route via Gibraltar, Algiers and Alexandria.
⁴ Generalissimo Chiang Kai-shek (1887–1975), Chinese Nationalist general and statesman, at this date President of China, was in Cairo to confer with WSC and Roosevelt.
⁵ Madame Chiang Kai-shek, born Mayling Soong (1897), wife of the Generalissimo, whom she married 1927. Youngest daughter of the Chinese merchant and Methodist missionary Charles Jones Soong, she was American-educated and a forceful personality.
⁶ The 'cat', I surmise, was a superior copy of the well-known Egyptian feline.
⁷ WSC had a deep loathing for this regulation, justified only on grounds of national security in 1940, under which persons could be detained without charge or trial.

O From CSC   10 Downing Street
Friday 26 November 1943

My Darling
Yesterday Mr Morrison lunched with me. He seemed battered by what he is going thro' in the Mosley affair. I felt very sorry for him as I think he is shewing political courage of quite a high order. The manifestations¹ have been surprising & various. The crowds at various points in London quite large but good-tempered; I ran into hundreds streaking² thro' Parliament Square – good looking girls & middle-aged men rather like a foot-ball crowd –

I comforted poor Morrison as well as I could – he has to go thro' quite a lot yet before he emerges. He enjoyed my little luncheon party ...

I have also been seeing Mr Bevin³ who seemed a bit in a temper with Herbert Morrison.... Mary's Battery is more than decimated by influenza & she has had to convert a barrack room into a Hospital for 20 girls with high temperatures....

Tender love from
Clemmie

Smuts visited her Battery last week & was charming to the ranks.

¹ Following the Home Secretary's announcement on 18 November that the Mosleys were to be released, on the grounds of his ill-health, and placed under house arrest, 20,000 factory workers had handed in a petition to No. 10 Downing Street and had stood in Whitehall in protest. On 23 November, while Mr Morrison was defending his action in the House of Commons, hundreds of demonstrators had gathered outside the House, their representatives lobbying MPs against the decision. A mass protest meeting held in Trafalgar Square on 28 November demanded that Mosley be returned to gaol.

[2] The word 'streaking' did not have the same connotation then as now!
[3] Ernest Bevin (1881–1951), Labour politician, creator and General Secretary of the Transport and General Workers' Union, 1921–40. Minister of Labour and National Service and member of War Cabinet, 1940–5; initiated the 'Bevin boys' (those chosen by ballot to work in coal mines as war service); Secretary of State for Foreign Affairs, 1945–51.

From WSC [typed copy][1]   Tehran
28 November 1943

FROZEN NO. 508.
  COLONEL WARDEN TO MRS WARDEN
  PERSONAL AND MOST SECRET.
  ARRIVED SAFELY OVER MOUNTAINS AT CAIRO 3 [TEHRAN]. MELLOW SUNSHINE IN THE GARDEN.
CONTACTS ALL MOST FRIENDLY. BY AN UNFORTUNATE COINCIDENCE MY VOICE HAS LEFT ME
THROUGH A DAMN COLD ON THIS SOMEWHAT UNUSUAL OCCASION. ADMIRAL Q. [ROOSEVELT*] HAS
BEEN PREVAILED UPON TO COME INTO OUR JOINT ANGLO-RUSSIAN ENCLAVE WHICH IS STRONGLY
GUARDED AGAINST GERMAN ENTERPRISE. HOPE TO ENTERTAIN ALL COLLEAGUES NOVEMBER 30TH.
LOVE.

                                                                        W.

[1] Original in Public Record Office, Cabinet Papers 120/120.

O From CSC   [London]
[29 November 1943]

FOR COLONEL WARDEN FROM MRS WARDEN
AM DISTRESSED ABOUT YOUR VOICE. I HOPE THE SUNSHINE WILL REVIVE IT. PLEASE SALUTE
ADMIRAL Q FROM ME. ALL MY LOVE AND THOUGHTS UPON THIS MOST MEMORABLE OF BIRTHDAYS[1].
CLEMMIE.

[1] WSC celebrated his 69th birthday on 30 November at a dinner party at the British Legation in Tehran, attended by both President Roosevelt and Marshal Stalin and their top colleagues. Sarah and Randolph were also present.

From WSC[1]   [Tehran]
29 November 1943

FROZEN NO. 515
  COLONEL WARDEN TO MRS WARDEN.
  VOICE RETURNED. ATMOSPHERE MOST CORDIAL BUT TRIANGULAR PROBLEMS DIFFICULT. BOTH
POTENTATES ARE COMING TO MY BIRTHDAY DINNER ALSO CAPTAIN WARDEN [RANDOLPH] AND
SECTION OFFICER OLIVER [SARAH]. LOVE.

[1] Public Record Office, Cabinet Papers 120/120.

From WSC[1]   [Tehran]
30 November 1943

FROZEN NO. 530
    COLONEL WARDEN TO MRS WARDEN.
    DELIGHTED TO RECEIVE TWO MORE OF YOUR LETTERS. WE STAY HERE TILL THE 2ND. THE
ATMOSPHERE AT MEAL TIMES IS GENIAL BUT THE TRIANGULAR CONFERENCES ARE GRIM AND
BAFFLING.

[1] Public Record Office, Cabinet Papers 120/120.

From WSC[1]   [Tehran]
1 December 1943

FROZEN NO. 544
    COLONEL WARDEN TO MRS WARDEN.
    LOVED YOUR TELEGRAMS AND LETTERS.
    AM JUST GOING DOWN TO RECORD [SIC] DINNER. EVERYONE MOST KIND. WE ARE ALL
STAYING ON TILL 3RD. THINGS HAVE TAKEN A VERY GOOD TURN. TENDER LOVE TO YOU ALL.

[1] Public Record Office, Cabinet Papers 120/120.

O From CSC   10 Downing Street
2 December 1943

My Darling
    I'm overjoyed to get your message that 'things have taken a very good
turn'. Allelluia! Allelluia! ...
    I'm just going to turn on the 7 o'clock morning radio when I expect to
hear 'the news' released – – – I've just heard the announcement of the
Conference held 'Somewhere in North Africa'. It's described as purely
Chinese & ends by saying that you & the President & the Generalissimo
[Chiang Kai-shek] have left for unknown destinations – What a relief! (I
mean that the 1st part is released to the hungry public.)
    Colonel Harvie-Watt[1] came in yesterday evening to describe the Mosley
Debate[2]. He seemed most satisfied – Another relief.
    General Smuts was really delightful at luncheon yesterday. Bobbety[3] &
Betty [Cranborne] came, & Sir Stafford & Lady Cripps. . . .
    The Field Marshal [Smuts] brings you this letter – Sarah has written me
the most delightful & colourful accounts of your doings & hers. . . .
                              Your loving but 'black out & winter wearied'
                                                             Pussy
                                                               . . .

[1] See p. 466 n. 2. At this date WSC's Parliamentary Private Secretary.
[2] 1 December 1943. The Amendment to the Address was beaten by 327 to 62.
[3] Viscount Cranborne (see p. 462 n. 3). At this date Secretary of State for Dominion Affairs.

Winston had not been well during these latest travels, which had already covered three weeks and three changes of place, climate and lodging. The strain and frustration (two's company, three's none) of the Tehran Big Three Conference in particular had added enormously to the burdens he was carrying.

Back in Cairo from Tehran, it was quite clear to his entourage that, as well as suffering from 'gyppy tummy', Winston was utterly exhausted; nevertheless he could not be deflected from his fixed intention to visit the battle-front in Italy before flying home. Clementine hoped he would have a few days' rest.

From WSC[1]   [Cairo]
8 December 1943

FROZEN NO. 426
COLONEL WARDEN TO MRS WARDEN.
  AM MUCH BETTER. PROPOSE LEAVING HERE FRIDAY NIGHT AND STAYING FOUR OR FIVE DAYS WITH EISENHOWER IN TUNIS AND ALEXANDER IN ITALY. I HAVE TO REMODEL ALL THE MEDITERRANEAN COMMANDS. THEN A DAY AT ALGIERS WITH THE FROGS AND SO HOME BY SEA UNLESS WEATHER IS VERY TEMPTING. ANTHONY [EDEN*] STARTS TONIGHT AND WILL BE AVAILABLE FOR THE DEBATE IN PARLIAMENT. TELL WHAT SHOULD BE TOLD TO DEPUTY P.M. AND OTHERS. THANK MARY FOR HER LETTER.

[1] Public Record Office, not yet listed.

From CSC[1]   [London]
10 December 1943

GRAND NO. 550.
  DO NOT HURRY HOME BUT HAVE A GOOD REST AFTER ALL THE EXCITEMENT, BURDENS AND EFFORT. THEN WE WILL HAVE A COSY FAMILY PARTY AT CHEQUERS [FOR CHRISTMAS]. ALL MY LOVE.

                                                   CLEMMIE

[1] Public Record Office, Cabinet Papers 120/126.

Churchill and his colleagues flew from Cairo to Tunis on 11 December, intending to spend one night with General Eisenhower[1] on their way to Italy. On arrival at the 'White House'[2] Winston felt so weary and ill that he went straight to bed. The following day Lord Moran* telegraphed for a pathologist[3], a consultant[4] and two nurses to come from Cairo.

[1] See p. 476 n. 5. At this date C.-in-C. Allied Forces in North Africa.
[2] Eisenhower's villa on the coast, near the ruins of ancient Carthage.
[3] Col. R. J. V. Pulvertaft.
[4] Brig. D. E. Bedford. Serving in the Middle East, but Consultant for Heart Diseases at the Middlesex Hospital, London.

From WSC[1]   [Carthage]
12 December 1943

FROZEN NO. 463
  COLONEL WARDEN TO MRS WARDEN.
  I AM LAID UP HERE AT CARTHAGE WITH TEMPERATURE OF 101 AND RATHER VIOLENT
NEURALGIC SORE THROAT, DUE, I THINK, TO A DRAUGHT IN THE AIRPLANE. I SHALL
THEREFORE STAY IN BED AND RECOVER FOR TWO OR THREE DAYS. ALEX[2] HAS FLOWN OVER AND WE
HAVE ALL THE AUTHORITIES HERE. I FEEL QUITE WELL IN SPITE OF MY AILMENT. THIS VILLA
IS RIGHT OUT ON A PROMONTORY WITH THE SEA ALL ROUND AND THE WEATHER IS SUNSHINY AND
BRACING. I AM SURE I HAD BETTER TRY TO GET WELL HERE RATHER THAN HURRY HOME....
  HOPE TO BE BACK BY CHRISTMAS.
  LOVE.

                                                                            W.

[1] Public Record Office, Cabinet Papers 120/120.
[2] General Alexander (see p. 468 n. 9). At this time C.-in-C. Allied Forces in Italy.

From CSC[1]   [London]
15 December 1943

GRAND NO. 599
  FROM MRS WARDEN TO COLONEL WARDEN.
  DARLING, I WISH I WERE WITH YOU. I KNOW YOU WILL LIE LOW AND DO EVERYTHING LORD
MORAN* SAYS.... ALL MY LOVE.

                                                                        CLEMMIE

[1] Public Record Office, Cabinet Papers 120/126.

From WSC[1]   [Carthage]
15 December 1943

FROZEN NO. 486
  COLONEL WARDEN TO MRS WARDEN.
  THERE SEEMS TO BE NO DOUBT I HAVE GOT ANOTHER TOUCH OF PNEUMONIA BUT I AM BEING
WELL LOOKED AFTER AND HAVE FAITH IN MY M. AND B. [2]
  LOVE FROM ALL.

                                                                            W.

[1] Public Record Office, Cabinet Papers 120/120.
[2] M&B stood for May & Baker, the pharmaceutical company: WSC called it 'Moran and Bedford'.
This relatively new sulphonamide drug was the first effective treatment for pneumonia.

Winston was now very ill.

  Sarah was watching her father sleep: 'Once he opened his eyes, and must
have caught my troubled look before I had time to mask it. He looked at me

without speaking for a moment; then said: "Don't worry, it doesn't matter if I die now, the plans of victory have been laid, and it is only a matter of time", and fell into a deep sleep once more.'[1]

[1] Sarah Churchill, *A Thread in the Tapestry*, 1967, p. 69.

15 December 1943   [Carthage]

FROZEN NO. 494.[1]
[MESSAGE TO NO. 10 PRIVATE OFFICE FROM JOHN MARTIN:]
COLONEL WARDEN HAS DICTATED THE FOLLOWING MESSAGE FOR MRS WARDEN. I SHOULD HOWEVER WARN YOU THAT LORD MORAN DOES NOT AGREE WITH THE FIRST SENTENCE. I THOUGHT IT BETTER NOT TO TROUBLE PATIENT WITH ARGUMENT ON POINT.
[MESSAGE TO MRS WARDEN BEGINS:]
THE BLOOD TESTS THIS MORNING WERE CONSIDERED SATISFACTORY AS INDICATING HEALTHY BUT NOT SERIOUS REACTION. TEMPERATURE BETWEEN 101 AND 102. DOCTOR BEDFORD A HIGH LONDON CONSULTANT ON CIRCULATION AND CHEST IS ARRIVING THIS AFTERNOON, HAVING BEEN SUMMONED BY MORAN TWO DAYS AGO. WE CERTAINLY ARE NOT SHORT OF ANY OF THE TALENTS. SARAH IS READING PRIDE AND PREJUDICE TO ME. RANDOLPH HAS RETURNED, WHICH IS VERY NICE.
2. IN CASE I GO TO CONVALESCE AT MARRAKECH IT MIGHT BE WORTH WHILE TO SEND OUT A MODEST PACKAGE OF PAINTING MATERIALS. THE CHER MAÎTRE [SIR WILLIAM NICHOLSON*] WOULD ADVISE YOU ON WHAT WAS NECESSARY. THE DAYS ARE LONG AND WEARY.

[1] Public Record Office, Cabinet Papers 120/120.

On 16 December Clement Attlee, Deputy Prime Minister, made an announcement of Churchill's illness in the House of Commons; and the first bulletin was issued.

There was a flurry of cables.

From CSC[1]   [London]
16 December 1943

GRAND NO. 691
MRS WARDEN TO COLONEL WARDEN.
I AM SO GRIEVED THAT YOU ARE WEARY AND UNCOMFORTABLE AND ANXIOUSLY AWAIT FURTHER NEWS.... I AM UNHAPPY ABOUT THE NEW DEVELOPMENT BUT COMFORTED YOU ARE IN GOOD HANDS. I KNOW YOU WILL TAKE EVERY CARE OF YOURSELF.
I HAD ALREADY ARRANGED FOR PAINTING MATERIALS TO GO OUT FOR YOU TO USE DURING YOUR CONVALESCENCE, AND THEY WOULD HAVE LEFT LAST NIGHT BUT FOR THE WEATHER. I HOPE THEY WILL GET OFF TONIGHT WITH ADDITIONS BY THE CHER MAÎTRE.
ALL MY LOVE.

                                                            CLEMMIE

[1] Public Record Office, Cabinet Papers 120/127.

From WSC[1]   [Carthage]
16 December 1943

FROZEN NO. 700
FROM COLONEL WARDEN TO MRS WARDEN.
  ALTHOUGH YESTERDAY WE HAD A NEW COMPLICATION IN SOME HEART FLUTTERINGS, I AM ABLE
TO SAY TODAY THAT THERE IS A QUITE DEFINITE IMPROVEMENT AT ALL POINTS AND BY ALL
TESTS. MY OWN FEELING IS THAT I AM AT THE TOP OF THE HILL....
  WHEN I GET OVER THIS IMMEDIATE TROUBLE I PLAN TO GO TO MARRAKECH FOR CHRISTMAS,
WHERE THERE IS A BEAUTIFUL VILLA AVAILABLE AND WHERE THE WEATHER IS PREDICTED TO BE
CLEAR, WARM AND BRIGHT. IF YOU COULD COME IT WOULD BE LOVELY....
  SARAH IS DOING AWFULLY WELL WITH PRIDE AND PREJUDICE. LET ME KNOW HOW YOU FEEL
ABOUT COMING OUT.
  MUCH LOVE. W.

[1] Public Record Office, not yet listed.

16 December 1943[1]   [Carthage]

  FOR MRS WARDEN [FROM RANDOLPH AND SARAH]
  PAPA HAD EXCELLENT NIGHT AND HIS CONDITION IS MUCH IMPROVED.... WHY DON'T YOU
JOIN HIM AT MARRAKECH WHEN HE IS WELL ENOUGH TO GO THERE. HE HAS TALKED OF IT
SEVERAL TIMES.
  WE ARE GLUED TO PRIDE AND PREJUDICE. HE SAYS YOU ARE SO LIKE ELIZABETH.
  ALL OUR LOVE TO YOU AND THE FAMILY.

[1] Public Record Office, Cabinet Papers 120/120.

16 December 1943[1]   [London]

GRAND NO. 627
  MRS WARDEN TO MRS OLIVER [SARAH].
  THANK YOU BOTH FOR YOUR TELEGRAM.
  I AM FLYING TO YOU TONIGHT IN LIBERATOR A L 514 WITH MISS HAMBLIN* AND JOCK
COLVILLE*[2]. CODE WORD FOR DEPARTURE WILL BE PIP WHICH WILL BE TELEGRAPHED AS SOON AS
WE ARE SAFELY OFF.... I AM TELLING YOU THIS SO THAT YOU ARE WARNED IN ADVANCE, BUT
ON NO ACCOUNT TELL YOUR FATHER BEFORE I ARRIVE AS DETAILS OF JOURNEY MAY CAUSE HIM
ANXIETY....
  LOVE TO ALL.

                                                                          CLEMMIE

[1] Public Record Office, Cabinet Papers 120/127.
[2] WSC's Private Secretary from May 1940. Jock had returned to WSC's Private Office from the RAF
(he later rejoined his squadron in time for the D-Day operations).

Clementine and her party left that night from Lyneham in Wiltshire, wearing
padded flying suits, in an unheated Liberator, in swirling fog – and, flying

via Gibraltar, landed at Tunis the following day. They arrived at the 'White House' to find Winston distinctly improved.

17 December 1943[1]   [Carthage]

```
FROZEN NO. 712
  PRIVATE OFFICE FROM MARTIN.
  THE FOLLOWING FOR SUBALTERN MARY CHURCHILL.
  YOUR MOTHER IS HERE. ALL IS JOYFUL. NO NEED TO WORRY.
  TENDER LOVE, PAPA.
  ALSO FOR MRS DUNCAN SANDYS SAME MESSAGE.
```

[1] Public Record Office, Premier Papers 4/74/3.

Official bulletins were issued regularly. By 23 December Winston was on the mend, but his condition had caused deep concern, and he was still far from well, though eager to leave for Marrakech for his convalescence.

○ From CSC ✉   [White House, Carthage]
Christmas Eve 1943

My Darling One
    May I plead with you to make the 27th our first flying day? – Not on the grounds of your health for I believe that is being well taken care of, but on the grounds of kindness of heart....
    ... Christmas means so much to the great mass of humanity, & those who are not fortunate in being together like ourselves value their little celebrations with their comrades, while they think of their wives & children at home.

                                                                      Clemmie

Winston heeded his wife's pleading. Christmas luncheon was the first meal he took outside his room. He was attired in his splendid quilted dressing-gown decorated with blue and gold dragons. Five Commanders-in-Chief and their staffs were guests of the Churchills, plus his own entourage.
    On Boxing Day Randolph returned to Cairo, and on 27 December Winston, Clementine and their party flew to Marrakech. Here the ever-generous and hospitable Americans had placed at their disposal Villa Taylor, the residence of the US Vice-Consul, which Winston and President Roosevelt had visited after the Casablanca Conference.
    On 28 December the following statement was issued from No. 10 Downing Street: 'The Prime Minister continues to make very satisfactory progress. It is not expected that any further bulletin will be issued. '
    Now thanked we all our God.

Chapter XXII

TIDE OF VICTORY

W inston stayed in Marrakech recuperating for nearly the whole of January 1944, increasingly taking up his workload, and keeping in touch with commanders and other colleagues who visited him in relays. He and Clementine returned home on 18 January.

During the spring to summer months the final preparations for Operation 'Overlord' (the Allied cross-Channel invasion of Europe) dominated the thoughts of all the commanders and planners, and a sense of mounting urgency prevailed.

The original date for D-Day – 5 June – had to be postponed for twenty-four hours owing to weather conditions; this added to the anxiety and tension.

On 4 June the Allies entered Rome.

O From CSC ✉¹   10 Downing Street
Monday Morning [5 June 1944]

My Darling
I feel so much for you at this agonising moment – so full of suspense, which prevents me from rejoicing over Rome! I look forward to seeing you at dinner –
Write a nice letter to the poor King!²

Tender Love from
Clemmie
. . .
Just off to her Hospital

. . .

¹ CSC had had to leave London early to attend a committee meeting of the Fulmer Chase Maternity Home, for which she had worked since 1939.
² There had been a tussle of wills between WSC, his top colleagues and, ultimately, the King over WSC's desire to witness the D-Day landings at close hand on D+1. Opposition to this scheme was understandably strong, but the King settled it all by pointing out that as head of the three fighting services he himself had prior and absolute claim to be present. In the event WSC went to France on 12 June, visiting Gen. Montgomery at his caravan headquarters in the field.

That evening Winston and Clementine dined alone together. After dinner he went to his Map Room where, just before going to bed, she joined him. He said to her: 'Do you realise that by the time you wake up in the morning twenty thousand men may have been killed?'[1]

[1] Incident recounted in Gerald Pawle, *The War and Colonel Warden*, 1963, p. 302. Mercifully, the casualties on D-Day were not as horrific as had been feared: about 4,300 British and Canadian, and 6,000 American. (*The Oxford Companion to the Second World War*, 1995).

○ From CSC   Chequers
[undated, probably 16 or 17 June 1944]

Mary rang up – They have had alerts all day & 2 hours ago the Battery fired. They could not see the P.A.C.[1] – It was a non visual target. They were watched by a large crowd which had assembled [in Hyde Park] to watch an American Base-Ball Match.
. . .

[1] On the night of 12–13 June the Germans had launched the first wave of their 'secret weapon' – a pilotless aircraft (PAC) with a high-explosive warhead. Officially known as 'V-1', these horrible machines were instantly dubbed 'Doodlebugs' by their intended victims.

On 10 August 1944 Churchill (pseudonym 'Colonel Kent' this time) flew from London to Italy to confer with the commanders on the spot. On the way he looked in on Duff and Diana Cooper*[1] in Algiers. Staying with them was Randolph, who was convalescing from injuries incurred when the aircraft in which he was travelling from Bari to Yugoslavia on 16 July crashed in flames on landing near the village of Topusko: he was one of nine survivors out of nineteen[2].

With him Winston had a letter for Randolph from his mother about family matters, which he did not deliver.

[1] Duff Cooper was from 1942 British Minister in Algiers.
[2] On 20 January 1944 Randolph had parachuted into Yugoslavia with Brigadier Fitzroy Maclean to the headquarters of the partisan leader Marshal Tito. In early July Maclean had appointed Randolph Head of the British Military Mission to Croatia. He was on his way there to take up his post when his aircraft crashed.

Brig. Fitzroy Maclean, later Sir Fitzroy Maclean of Dunconnel, 1st Bt (1911–96), KT, CBE. Diplomat, traveller, author and soldier. At British Embassy, Moscow, 1937-8; wrote *Eastern Approaches*, 1949. Conservative MP, 1941–74. WSC's personal envoy to Tito and his Yugoslav partisans, 1943–5. Parliamentary Under-Secretary and Financial Secretary, War Office, 1954–70. Married, 1946, Veronica Fraser, second daughter of 16th Baron Lovat and widow of Lt Alan Phipps, RN. He and his wife became great personal friends of WSC/CSC.

○ From WSC   In the Air over Algeria
[12 August 1944]

My darling One,
    I did not have the heart to deliver yr letter to R when I saw him. It was only for about an hour or so. No reference was made by either of us to

family matters. He is a lonely figure by no means recovered so far as walking is concerned. Our talk was about politics, French & English, about wh there was plenty of friendly badinage & argument. I am sure he wd have been profoundly upset & all his pent up feelings wd have found a vent on me. Please forgive me for not doing as you wished. Where words are useless Silence is best. However if you wish to send the letter I will forward it to him from Italy.

So far we have had a lovely passage. The weather is hot & the thinnest & fewest clothes are necessary.

We shd arrive in about 4 hours at Naples.

> Tender love my darling Clemmie.
> Your ever loving husband,
> Winston

. . .

From WSC[1]   [Naples]
13 August 1944

CHAIN NO. 22
FOLLOWING FROM COLONEL KENT TO MRS KENT.
AM STILL IN NAPLES DISCUSSING THINGS WITH TITO[2] AND THE BAN[3]. WE HAVE A VERY COMFORTABLE VILLA, THE WEATHER IS HOT. I BATHED YESTERDAY AT ISCHIA AND WE ARE OFF THIS MORNING TO BATHE AND LUNCH AT CAPRI. WE RETURN AT TEATIME TO TITO. I MOVE NORTHWARDS TOMORROW. ALL WELL. HOPE YOU ARE NOT GETTING MUCH BOMBARDMENT. . . . TENDER LOVE.

[1] Public Record Office, not yet listed.
[2] Marshal Tito (Josip Broz) (1892-1980), Yugoslav Communist leader. Became prominent during Second World War as partisan leader against the Nazis. Established provisional government, 1943, and Federal Republic, 1945. Yugoslavia's first Communist Prime Minister, 1945; and, from 1953, President.
[3] Ban of Croatia. Dr Ivan Subasic, a former Governor of Croatia, who had emerged as Prime Minister of a new Royal Yugoslav Government formed to try to come to terms with Tito's (Communist) partisan regime.

O From CSC   10 Downing Street
15 August 1944

My darling Winston

I quite understand that you did not feel you could give Randolph my letter, & I am glad you did not as there might have been a fresh scene.

But now he has not heard from me at all & it looks as if I were sulking – I agree that 'where words are useless, silence is best'. But I hoped that my few very mild & moderate words might turn out not to be quite useless. You see, one shrinks from <u>saying</u> anything to Randolph because one wishes to avoid a scene. Consequently he is not acquainted with one's point of view – For instance I am sure he will be surprised to learn that we minded the Baby being taken away from Chequers. I do think he ought to know this. Because then there is just the chance that he may be a little more considerate in future[1].

Will you not read my letter to him again? & then decide yourself whether to send it or not –

If I have to see Randolph again I should feel less embarrassed if he had read my letter than if he thought I had never even troubled to put down my thoughts on paper –

Your loving
Clemmie

[1] Randolph and Pamela's marriage was by now in ruins, a cause of concern and distress to WSC and CSC. Evidently arrangements for 'Baby' Winston (nearly four) had gone awry; it would seem that Randolph (who had been recently in England) had intervened, causing mortification and upset to his parents. However, 'Baby' Winston would return to Chequers with his nanny by the end of August.

○ From CSC   10 Downing Street
16 August 1944

My darling Winston

You will see from this enclosed letter how delighted little Winston is with the clock-work train. On Friday I am going from Chequers to see him, lunch with the Melchetts[1] & play with the train. I shall also see Pamela who will be out of quarantine[2]. . . .

I was distressed to see from some minutes, shewn me by John Martin, that General de Gaulle had taken advantage of your courtesy & behaved with his usual calculated rudeness[3] – Please do not allow this to wound you. I love to feel you are basking in delicious & I hope not too ardent sunshine.

Mr Winant[4] spent a night at Chequers last week-end, & last night Edwina [Mountbatten][5], Mr Butters [an official] & I escorted Mr Morgenthau[6] round some of the Shelters & First Aid Posts. He is a funny vague old thing & it is difficult to imagine him managing a whelk stall – but perhaps the Treasury is easier with no competition! He broadcast to America last night & told them about flying bombs & all our arrangements to combat them & to alleviate suffering.

Tender Love
from
Clemmie

[1] At Colworth House, Bedfordshire, home of Henry Mond, 2nd Baron Melchett (1898–1949), Deputy Chairman, Imperial Chemical Industries, 1940–7, and his wife Gwen (born Wilson, of Johannesburg, South Africa). Friends of WSC/CSC; she was also a great friend of RSC.
[2] Pamela had contracted scarlet fever while at Colworth.
[3] WSC had invited de Gaulle to come and see him: the General refused to do so.
[4] John G. Winant (1889–1947) ('Gil'), US Ambassador at London since April 1941 (to 1946). Had become a great friend of the family.
[5] See p. 256 n. 2. Now Superintendent-in-Chief, Red Cross and St John Ambulance Brigade.
[6] Henry M. Morgenthau Jr (1891–1967), US Treasury Secretary and originator of controversial 'Morgenthau Plan' for pastoralization of post-war Germany.

O From WSC [typewritten]   Italy [Naples]
17 August 1944

<u>PERSONAL</u>

My darling,
    We have had a busy but delightful time since we arrived here. A very
comfortable guest-house, formerly the villa of a wealthy Fascist, now in a
concentration camp, was got ready for us. I have here been able to see or
entertain all the principal officers of the Army, also Kathleen Harriman[1]
and Dorothy Macmillan[2]. The few days we spent in Naples were relieved
by a lovely expedition to the Island of Ischia on the first day, and the
second to Capri. I thought the Blue Grotto wonderful. We have had
altogether four bathes which have done me all the good in the world. I
feel greatly refreshed and am much less tired than when I left England.
    On the 14th I flew with two of my party to Ajaccio. (Do you remember
when we went to see Napoleon's house there in 1910?). General Wilson
and Admiral John Cunningham[3] had to stay in the Headquarters' ship in
order to be able to go to any place if things went wrong, but I went out in
a destroyer, ... The journey takes five hours, and a little after one o'clock
we found ourselves in an immense concourse of ships all sprawled along
20 miles of coast with poor San Tropez in the centre.
    It had been expected that the bombardment would continue all day[4],
but the air and the ships had practically silenced the enemy guns by 8
o'clock. This rendered the proceedings rather dull. We traversed the whole
front and saw the panorama of the beautiful shores with smoke rising from
many fires started by the shelling and artificial smoke being loosed by the
landing troops and the landing craft drawn up upon the shore. But we saw
it all from a long way off. If I had known beforehand what the conditions
would be I would have requested a picket-boat from the RAMILLIES, when
I could have gone with perfect safety very much nearer to the actual
beaches.
    I got frightfully sunburnt, but on the way back I read that novel Berlin
Hotel[5] which I thought absolutely thrilling – one of the best I have read 'in
years'. We got back to the Headquarters' ship at Ajaccio at about 10, and
then heard that all the landings except one had been successful. The three
American Divisions were safely ashore without any serious losses. The
beaches are now free from fire and further disembarkation of vehicles and
cannon, etc., is proceeding smoothly. The whole thing had run like a
piece of clock-work. Everybody arrived punctually at exactly the right
place. I telegraphed to the President [Roosevelt*] congratulating him on
this success.
    If you reflect upon what I have said at different times on strategic
questions you will see that Eisenhower's operations have been a diversion
for this landing instead of the other way round as the American Chiefs of
Staff imagined. Several German Divisions have gone to the North, but
there are still heavy forces in front of the Army. I think it probable that
Eisenhower will take Paris before General Patch takes Marseilles[6]. If I had
had my way the armies now cast on shore 400 miles from Paris would
have come in at St Nazaire in about a week and greatly widened the front

of our advance with corresponding security against German movement east of Paris. This will all become blatantly apparent to the instructed. One of my reasons for making public my visit was to associate myself with this well-conducted but irrelevant and unrelated operation.

I told the Private Office to show you the insolent letter de Gaulle sent in reply to my civil gesture by proposing a meeting, which I did in response to the enthusiastic thanks which Massigli sent me on my last speech in the House. Naturally at times like this I do not let them influence my political judgment but I feel that de Gaullist France will be a France more hostile to England than any since Fashoda[7].

After returning from Ajaccio we spent another night here in Naples seeing people and dealing with correspondence. You will have read about the interviews with Tito. I think the old Ban and he got on almost too well together. It may well be a case of Tito first, the Ban second and the King[8] nowhere. However, the great thing is to unite all forces against the Germans. Unhappily Tito is now using the bulk of the ammunition we give him to fight the Serbs. However the meetings did a lot of good and made Tito, I think, more desirous of respecting our wishes.

We have now started off by motor to the battlefield of Cassino[9], where we will meet Alexander and Wilson who have come there and will give us lunch. I fly then with Alexander to his Headquarters near Siena, where he has put a house at my disposal. I purpose to stay there till the 21st when I fly to Rome to see Papandreou[10] from Greece, the Pope [Pius XII], Bonomi[11], Badoglio[12] and perhaps the ancient Orlando.

What tremendous events are taking place in France! The Eike–Monty operations appear to be the greatest battle of the war and may result in the destruction of the German power in France. Such a victory will have effects in many directions, one of which undoubtedly will be more mutual respect between the Russians and the Anglo-American democracies.

I hope to return home by the 27th. There will then only be a week before we sail on the QUEEN MARY for OCTAGON[13], formerly called QUADRANT. I hope you and Sarah are going to come as she has never seen that part of the world, and I know Mary would not leave her battery whilst it is in action. This visit of mine to the President is the most necessary one that I have ever made since the very beginning as it is there that various differences that exist between the Staffs, and also between me and the American Chiefs of Staff, must be brought to a decision. We have three armies in the field. The first is fighting under American Command in France, the second under General Alexander is relegated to a secondary and frustrated situation by the United States' insistence on this landing on the Riviera. The third on the Burmese frontier is fighting in the most unhealthy country in the world under the worst possible conditions to guard the American air line over the Himalayas into their very over-rated China. Thus two-thirds of our forces are being mis-employed for American convenience, and the other third is under American Command. The casualties in Burma amounted in the first six months of this year to 288,000 sick and 40,000 killed and wounded. These are delicate and serious matters to be handled between friends in careful and patient personal discussion. I have no doubt we shall reach a good conclusion, but you will see that life is not very easy. None of this should deter you from coming to the Citadel [in Quebec]. Indeed, I think your presence and that of Sarah would be a help as well as a pleasure.

✍ (Later)

We have now reached Siena & are vy comfortable – Alex is gay & charming in spite of the vexation of watching his splendid Army pulled to pieces by American strategy.

I hope to remedy this. With tender love

Your ever loving husband

W

...

¹ Kathleen Harriman, Averell Harriman's daughter.
² Lady Dorothy Macmillan (1900–66), born Lady Dorothy Cavendish, daughter of 9th Duke of Devonshire. Married, 1920, Harold Macmillan, at this date Minister Resident at Allied Headquarters, North-West Africa.
³ Admiral Sir John Cunningham (1885–1962). C.-in-C. Mediterranean and Allied Naval Commander Mediterranean, 1943–6. First Sea Lord and Chief of Naval Staff, 1946–8. GCB, 1946; Admiral of the Fleet, 1948.
⁴ Operation 'Anvil': Allied landings in South of France on 15 August. Following 'Overlord' serious differences had arisen between the British and US planners and Chiefs of Staff on strategy in the Mediterranean. The British saw 'Anvil' as a distraction from Gen. Alexander's advances in Italy. The President and the US Chiefs of Staffs' view prevailed: this was a low moment in Anglo-American wartime relations.
⁵ Vicki Baum, *Hotel Berlin*, 1944.
⁶ Marseilles was liberated by French troops on 23 August. On 25 August French troops entered Paris (French Resistance forces in the city had risen in revolt on the 23rd).
⁷ A reference to the Fashoda Incident of 18 September 1898, in the Egyptian Sudan, one of a series of territorial disputes in Africa between Great Britain and France.
⁸ King Peter of Yugoslavia (1923–70). Came to Britain after German invasion of Yugoslavia and headed royal government-in-exile. He was deeply opposed to Marshal Tito's Communist partisans.
⁹ Monte Cassino, town and monastery in central Italy, a key point in the German winter defensive line blocking the Allied advance to Rome, and the scene of four months' bitter fighting; taken by the Allies on 18 May 1944.
¹⁰ Georgios Papandreou (1888–1968), veteran Greek Liberal politician, staunch anti-Communist, headed Greek government-in-exile from 1942. Prime Minister briefly on his return, 1944, and again 1963 and 1964–5; arrested following military coup, 1967.
¹¹ Ivanoe Bonomi (1873–1951), anti-Fascist Italian politician who, as Chairman of Rome Committee of National Liberation, on the liberation of Rome in June 1944 forced the removal of King Victor Emmanuel and his Prime Minister, Badoglio (see n. 12). Prime Minister of Italy, 1944–5; elected President of the Italian Senate, 1949.
¹² Marshal Pietro Badoglio (1871–1956), Italian army officer, appointed Chief of the Supreme General Staff, June 1940; resigned after fiasco of Italy's invasion of Greece, December 1940. Became Prime Minister following arrest of Mussolini, July 1943; forced out of office by Committee of National Liberation, June 1944.
¹³ 'Octagon', the second Quebec Conference, September 1944. 'Quadrant' was the first Quebec Conference, August 1943.

○ From WSC [typewritten]   Italy
18 August 1944

My darling Clemmie,

Alexander met us yesterday near Cassino and took us round the various points from which the battlefield could be studied, explaining as he went along. I was deeply impressed by the savage mountain obstacles of which one cannot get any idea except on the spot. Knowing the campaign as I do I could recognize many of the key features. Afterwards General Wilson arrived by air from Corsica, and we had a picnic and a pow-wow under a canopy in a lovely olive-grove overlooking these plains and valleys which, although much greener, singularly resemble the North West Frontier.

We then came on by air to the Headquarters near Siena....

Alex lives in his caravan as do most of our principal Generals in this war. He came to dine with me last night and I am going to dine with him to-night.

I am just off to see a bit of the line near Florence where fighting is still going on[1]. A thunderstorm and heavy rain is now on and I do not know how it will affect our plans. (Later: It has spoiled them.)

You should ask the Private Office to let you see the various telegrams now passing about the Russian refusal either to help or allow the Americans to help the struggling people of Warsaw[2], who will be massacred and liquidated very quickly if nothing can be done. These messages speak for themselves. If there is a massacre in Warsaw the whole world will criticize the Soviets, and will do so with more freedom if the battle in France proves, as I hope, to be a far larger and more intense military event than anything which Russia has produced. I am most painfully affected by this Polish incident.

I have decided to send your letter on to Randolph. I hope to see him in Rome during the few days I am there.

With all my love,
Your ever loving
W

[1] Florence was taken by Gen. Alexander's forces on 19 August 1944.
[2] WSC is referring to the Warsaw uprising, which had begun on 1 August 1944 and was to last 63 days; it was an attempt to seize control of the city before it could be occupied by the advancing Soviet army. The British Government sent air-drops of ammunition and supplies, and WSC appealed to Stalin to help the resurgent Poles – an appeal which was met with chill indifference. The Soviets having refused to allow the Allies to airlift supplies from Soviet bases, the Polish patriotic forces were forced to surrender on 2 October. Tens of thousands of Poles were killed during the fighting; the Germans then systematically deported the rest of Warsaw's population and destroyed the city itself. The Soviet army subsequently occupied the whole of Poland.

From WSC[1]
18 August 1944

CHAIN NO. 119
COLONEL KENT TO MRS KENT.
  PERSONAL AND PRIVATE. BOTH YOUR LETTERS AND ENCLOSURES RECEIVED. I AGREE WITH YOUR REASONS FOR SENDING YOUR LETTER [TO RANDOLPH] FORWARD, AND HAVE DONE SO. I HAVE SENT YOU TWO LONG LETTERS TODAY.

[1] Public Record Office, not yet listed.

From WSC[1]   [Italy]
28 August 1944

CHAIN 245
  FOLLOWING FROM COLONEL KENT TO MRS KENT. PERSONAL AND PRIVATE.
  AM JUST STARTING AND HOPE TO BE AT THE ANNEX EARLY 29TH. MY DELAY WAS CAUSED BY MY
WAITING TO SEE THE OPENING OF THE BATTLE ON ADRIATIC SIDE OF ITALY WHICH WITH
ALEXANDER'S GUIDANCE I DID TO MY ENTIRE SATISFACTION. [2]
  LONGING TO SEE YOU.

[1] Public Record Office, not yet listed.
[2] On 26 August Gen. Alexander began a new offensive; WSC was with him and spent a day after
his own heart – close to action.

Winston arrived back in England from Italy on 29 August in the grip of a
suddenly developed high fever: a small patch on his lung was diagnosed.
He was nursed at the Annexe, and no bulletins were issued: only a close
circle of people knew he was ill. He was better in a few days.

On 5 September, a barely recovered Winston, accompanied by Clementine
and, of course, Lord Moran*, left London with his colleagues to go on board
the *Queen Mary* at Greenock, outward bound for Halifax and the Second
Quebec Conference ('Octagon').

After listening to ship's radio early in the morning of 7 September,
Clementine sent this note to WSC's cabin.

○ From CSC ⊠   [aboard *Queen Mary*]
7 September 1944

Darling – How are you this morning?

What a rousing news Bulletin this morning! Calais, Boulogne, Dunkirk,
Le Havre more & more closely invested – 19,000 Prisoners to the poor unnoticed British! Is the Moselle the frontier between France & Germany?
because if so we are in the Reich[1].

Then side by side with the announcement about the Home Guard[2], the
Americans (with an eye I suppose to the [Presidential] Election) announce
demobilisation! Wurrup & Alleluia!

                                                                    . . .

[1] In fact the German frontier was crossed by the Americans at Trier on 11 September.
[2] On 5 September the War Office had announced that although the Home Guard were still necessary, plans had been prepared for standing them down when appropriate.

The 'Octagon' party arrived back in England on 26 September. Eleven days
later Churchill was off on his travels again: he felt the necessity of talking
to Stalin on several pressing matters. Late on the night of 7 October,

accompanied by Anthony Eden* (Foreign Secretary), he flew off from Northolt, headed for Moscow.

Winston's next letter must have been written just after taking off at Northolt in the dark early hours of 8 October. He had evidently had a 'rufflement' with Clementine.

○ From WSC   [In the air]
[8] October [1944] 1.30 a.m.

My darling One,

I have been fretting over our interchange at luncheon yesterday.

I am sure that no one thought of it as more than my making my own position clear, and that it all passed in the ripple of a most successful party.

Anyhow forgive me for anything that seemed disrespectful to you, & let yr morning thoughts dwell kindly on

yr penitent
apologetic
& ever loving
W

. . .

From WSC[1]   [Moscow]
11 October 1944

HEARTY NO. 36
    FOLLOWING FOR MRS KENT FROM COLONEL KENT.
    GENERAL ATMOSPHERE HERE IS MOST FRIENDLY BUT THERE ARE MANY VEXATIOUS POINTS TO SETTLE.... I AM VERY WELL AND WEATHER TODAY IS BRILLIANT. LOVE TO ALL.

[1] Public Record Office, Premier Papers 4/76/1.

○ From WSC [copy][1]
13 October 1944

HEARTY NO. 62
    FOLLOWING FROM COLONEL KENT FOR MRS KENT.
    EVERYTHING IS GOING WELL HERE AND THERE IS GREAT CORDIALITY. LIFE IS HOWEVER THE SAME, AND I DID NOT GET TO BED TILL 4 A.M. THIS MORNING. I HAVE A HOUSE IN MOSCOW AS WELL AS IN THE COUNTRY, BOTH SPLENDIDLY SERVED. I AM JUST OFF TO THE COUNTRY HOUSE, 45 MINUTES AWAY, AS WE ARE GOING TO HAVE A QUIET NIGHT TO-NIGHT. LOVE TO ALL.

[1] Original in Public Record Office, Premier Papers 4/76/1.

○ From WSC   Moscow
13 October 1944

Beloved,

Here I am at the Country House with Averell[1] (whom I have just
defeated in 4 games, 2 Rubis) [Bezique] & Kathleen [his daughter], who is
writing a series of missives. This is just a line to tell you how I love you &
how sorry I am you are not here. I told Kathleen to tell you all the nice
things she has heard about you. I do hope that you are happy w yr & my
Maria[2]. Give her my dearest love. It is wonderful to get the London papers
the same day at about 6 pm. But the couriers also bring heavy bags & in
between meals of 12 or 14 courses & conferences of various kinds I am
hard at it. I am vy well except for a little Indy [indigestion].

The affairs go well. We have settled a lot of things about the Balkans[3] &
prevented hosts of squabbles that were maturing. The two sets of Poles[4]
have arrived & are being kept for the night in two separate cages.
Tomorrow we see them in succession. It is their best chance for a
settlement. We shall try our utmost. I have had vy nice talks with the Old
Bear [Stalin]. I like him the more I see him. Now they respect us here & I
am sure they wish to work w us – I have to keep the President in constant
touch & this is the delicate side.

Darling you can write anything but war secrets & it reaches me in a few
hours. So do send me a letter from yr dear hand.

Your ever loving husband,
W
. . .

Love special to Mary, Sarah & the Sandies [Diana and her family].

[1] Averell Harriman (see p. 469 n. 1). US Ambassador at Moscow, 1943–6.
[2] While WSC was in Russia I had a week's leave and was able to keep my mother company.
[3] Stalin and Churchill agreed a rough and ready division of proportional interests and spheres of
action in the Balkans: Romania, 90% Russian; Greece, 90% British; Yugoslavia and Hungary, 50%
Russian, 50% British; Bulgaria 75% Russian.
[4] In July 1944 Stalin had established a Polish Committee for National Liberation at Lublin, in eastern
Poland. On 31 December 1944 the Lublin Committee became the Provisional Government of the
Polish Republic: it was distinct from and hostile to the Polish government-in-exile, long-estab-
lished in London.

○ From CSC   10 Downing Street
Sunday 15 October 1944

My Darling

I've just been listening to the early 'Radio' news & there was a vivid
description of your visit to the Moscow Opera House in company with 'the
old Bear' – I wish I could have witnessed this hard-won recognition of
your untiring & persistent work –

All three Kittens, Sarah, Diana & Mary, send their tender & devoted love.
Riga & Athens[1] are ripe plums fallen; How I wish we could wrench

Rotterdam & Cologne – I pray we are not condemned to a winter of trench warfare among the waterways & mud of the Low Countries.

Tender love. I hope to see you soon[2].

Clemmie

. . .

[1] The Russians had entered Riga (capital of Latvia) on 13 October, and on the same date British troops entered Athens.
[2] WSC arrived back from Moscow on 22 October 1944.

The next letter and group of telegrams are concerned with the serious situation in Greece, and particularly in Athens.

The Greek guerrilla forces (largely controlled by the Greek Communist Party) had played a major part in the struggle against the German occupying forces; but as these withdrew, the Communists (EAM and ELAS)[1] prepared to seize control, and prevent the return of King George II of Greece and the Greek government-in-exile headed by the Liberal Georgios Papandreou: this intention Churchill was determined to foil. To this end, a British force had been despatched to Greece in October 1944 to secure the authority of an all-party provisional government under Papandreou which would organize democratic elections.

In the first week of December violent fighting broke out in the streets of Athens between Communists and pro-Monarchist groups. The commanding officer of the British force was General Scobie[2], whose orders were to clear the streets and to restore order and the authority of the provisional government: reinforcements were sent with all haste from Italy.

[1] The most formidable political (EAM) and guerrilla (ELAS) combination of Communist Greek resistance.
[2] Lt-Gen. (later Sir) Ronald Scobie (1893–1969) KBE, MC. GOC Greece, 1944–6.

○ From CSC ✉   10 Downing Street
4 December 1944

My darling Winston

Please do not – before ascertaining full facts repeat to anyone you meet to-day what you said to me this morning, i.e. that the Communists in Athens had shewn their usual cowardice in putting the women & children in front to be shot at – Because altho' Communists are dangerous, indeed perhaps sinister people, they seem in this War, on the Continent, to have shewn personal courage –

I write this only because I may not see you till tomorrow & I am anxious (perhaps over-anxious).

Your loving & devoted
Clemmie

'Tout savoir, c'est tout comprendre, tout comprendre, c'est tout pardonner.'[1]

[1] From Mme de Staël, *Corinne*, 1807, Bk XVIII, ch. 5.

British intervention in Athens provoked criticism in the British press and in Parliament, and widespread hostile comment in the American press[1]. In a debate in the House of Commons on 8 December, Churchill vigorously defended the Government's policy and actions, and demanded a vote of confidence (which was carried by 279 to 30 votes).

The gravity of the Greek political and military situation was such that by the third week in December Churchill decided he must intervene on the spot himself; therefore, taking Anthony Eden* with him, he flew to Athens on the night of Christmas Eve.

My father's dramatic departure from Chequers, where a family party was assembling for Christmas, caused great disappointment to us all. My mother – so stoical, and so used to stern priorities – was deeply upset, and wept.

Churchill and his colleagues flew[2] via Naples and landed at Athens airport. There to meet him were General Alexander, Rex Leeper[3], General Scobie and Harold Macmillan[4]. During their visit Churchill and his immediate party lived aboard HMS *Ajax* in Phaleron Bay.

[1] In accordance with the 'deal' made at the Moscow talks (see p. 506 n. 3), the Russians meticulously refrained from active or political involvement with the Greek Communists.
[2] In the American C54 Skymaster, newly converted for his use – a great improvement on the York.
[3] Reginald ('Rex') Leeper (1888–1968), diplomat. At this date British Ambassador at Athens (1943–6). Married, 1916, Margaret Dundas. Knighted, 1945.
[4] Harold Macmillan, later 1st Earl of Stockton (1894–1986). Conservative MP from 1924; Prime Minister, 1957–63. At this date Minister Resident at Allied HQ, N.W. Africa, 1942–5. Married, 1920, Lady Dorothy Cavendish (see p. 502 n. 2).

From WSC[1]   [Pomigliano, near Naples]
25 December 1944

MASON NO. 2
  FOLLOWING FOR MRS KENT FROM COLONEL KENT.
  LOVE AND MANY THOUGHTS FOR YOU ALL AT LUNCHEON TODAY. I AM SORRY INDEED NOT TO
SEE THE TREE. VERY GOOD PASSAGE SO FAR AND WE CAN GO THE WHOLE WAY IN THE BIG
PLANE.

[1] Public Record Office, Cabinet Papers 120/169.

O From WSC [copy][1]   [Athens]
26–7 December 1944

MASON NO. 8
TOP SECRET – HUSH
FOLLOWING FOR MRS KENT FROM COLONEL KENT
[PART 1]
WE HAVE HAD FRUITFUL DAY AND SO FAR THERE IS NO NEED GIVE UP HOPE OF SOME IMPORTANT
RESULTS. HMS AJAX IS VERY COMFORTABLE AND ONE CAN GET A VIEW OF THE FIGHTING IN
NORTH PIRAEUS AT QUITE SHORT RANGE. WE HAVE HAD TO MOVE A MILE FARTHER AWAY AS WE
WERE GETTING TOO MANY OF THEIR TRENCH MORTAR BOMBS IN OUR NEIGHBOURHOOD. I WENT
INTO THE EMBASSY UP THAT LONG ROAD FROM PIRAEUS TO ATHENS IN AN ARMOURED CAR WITH

STRONG ESCORT AND I ADDRESSED ALL THE PLUCKY WOMEN ON EMBASSY STAFF WHO HAVE BEEN
IN CONTINUED DANGER AND DISCOMFORT FOR SO MANY WEEKS BUT ARE IN GAYEST OF MOODS.
MRS LEEPER IS AN INSPIRATION TO THEM.
[PART 2]
YOU WILL HAVE READ ABOUT THE PLOT TO BLOW UP HQ IN HOTEL GRANDE BRETAGNE. DO NOT
THINK IT WAS FOR MY BENEFIT. STILL, A TON OF DYNAMITE WAS PUT IN SEWERS BY
EXTREMELY SKILLED HAND AND WITH GERMAN MECHANISM, BETWEEN THE TIME MY ARRIVAL WAS
KNOWN AND DAYLIGHT. I HAVE MADE FRIENDS WITH ARCHBISHOP[2] AND THINK IT HAS BEEN VERY
CLEVER TO WORK HIM IN AS WE HAVE DONE, LEAVING THE CONSTITUTIONAL QUESTIONS FOR
FURTHER TREATMENT LATER.
[PART 3]
CONFERENCE AT GREEK FOREIGN OFFICE WAS INTENSELY DRAMATIC. ALL THESE HAGGARD GREEK
FACES ROUND THE TABLE AND ARCHBISHOP WITH ENORMOUS HAT MAKING HIM I SHOULD THINK 7
FEET HIGH, WHOM WE GOT TO PRESIDE. THE AMERICAN RUSSIAN AND FRENCH AMBASSADORS WERE
ALL VERY GLAD TO BE INVITED. YOU WILL HEAR SPEECHES ON RADIO NO DOUBT, OR SEE THEM
PRINTED IN WEDNESDAY'S PAPERS. ELAS[3] ARRIVED LATE, 3 IN ALL. THEY CERTAINLY LOOK A
MUCH BETTER LOT THAN THE LUBLIN ILLEGITIMATES[4]. THANKS WERE PROPOSED WITH MANY
COMPLIMENTS TO US FOR COMING BY THE GREEK GOVT, AND SUPPORTED BY ELAS
REPRESENTATIVES, WHO ADDED REFERENCE TO GREAT BRITAIN 'OUR GREAT ALLY' – ALL THIS
WITH GUNS FIRING AT EACH OTHER NOT SO FAR AWAY.
[PART 4]
AFTER SOME CONSIDERATION I SHOOK ELAS DELEGATES' HAND[S] AND IT WAS CLEAR FROM
THEIR RESPONSE THAT THEY WERE GRATIFIED. THEY ARE THE VERY TOP ONES. WE HAVE NOW
LEFT THEM TOGETHER AS IT WAS A GREEK SHOW. IT MAY BREAK UP AT ANY MOMENT. WE SHALL
WAIT FOR A DAY OR TWO IF NECESSARY TO SEE. AT LEAST WE HAVE DONE OUR BEST. YOU CAN
SEND LETTER BY MOSQUITO [RAF] BAG ALMOST EVERY DAY. I DO HOPE THE CHRISTMAS TREE
WAS A SUCCESS. FONDEST LOVE TO YOU AND ALL. PLEASE SHOW ANY PARTS OF THIS TELEGRAM
WHICH ARE RELEVANT TO INTIMATE COLLEAGUES.

[1] Original in Public Record Office, Cabinet Papers 120/169.
[2] Archbishop Damaskinos (George Papandreou) (1891–1949), whom WSC asked to preside over
the conference. A popular neutral figure. Regent of Greece, 31 December 1944–28 September
1946, pending plebiscite and return of King George II.
[3] The guerrilla wing of EAM (see p. 507 n. 1, commentary).
[4] See p. 506 n. 4.

From WSC[1]   [Athens]
28 December 1944 4.50 a.m.

TOP SECRET – HUSH
MASON NO. 23. PERSONAL.
   COLONEL KENT TO MRS KENT.
   ... YOU SHOULD ASK THE PRIVATE OFFICE TO SHOW YOU THE LENGTHY ACCOUNTS WHICH WE
HAVE SENT HOME. TODAY WEDNESDAY HAS BEEN AN EXCITING AND NOT ALTOGETHER FRUITLESS
DAY. THE HATREDS BETWEEN THESE GREEKS ARE TERRIBLE. WHEN ONE SIDE HAVE ALL THE
WEAPONS WHICH WE GAVE THEM TO FIGHT THE GERMANS WITH AND THE OTHER, THO' MANY TIMES
AS NUMEROUS, HAVE NONE, IT IS EVIDENT THAT A FRIGHTFUL MASSACRE WOULD TAKE PLACE IF
WE WITHDREW. ...

[1] Public Record Office, Premier Papers 3/208.

O From CSC [copy][1]   London
28 December 1944

LABEL NO. 30
PERSONAL AND PRIVATE
MRS KENT FOR COLONEL KENT.
I HAVE BEEN MOVED AND THRILLED TO READ OF ALL THAT HAS HAPPENED WHILE YOU WERE IN
ATHENS. I AM SO GRATEFUL THAT YOU ARE WELL AND LONG FOR YOUR RETURN. ALL MY LOVE,
                                                                        CLEMMIE.

[1] Original in Public Record Office, Premier Papers 3/208.

From WSC[1]   [Athens]
29 December 1944 1.15 a.m.

MASON NO. 28
  FOLLOWING FOR MRS KENT FROM COLONEL KENT.
  DELIGHTED TO RECEIVE YOUR MESSAGES. I WAS FEELING LONELY. HOPE TO BE WITH YOU AT
DINNER TOMORROW. [AND HE WAS ...] TENDER LOVE.

[1] Public Record Office, Cabinet Papers 120/169.

In the New Year of 1945, with the German armies being compressed from
both west and east within their own frontiers, it was clear that the end of the
conflict was near, and Churchill pressed urgently for a meeting with Stalin
and Roosevelt* in order to grapple with the issues which would arise in the
wake of victory.
    Marshal Stalin's doctors forbade him to leave the Soviet Union, and so it
was that the ailing President Roosevelt and the septuagenarian Churchill (the
oldest of the trio), journeyed to the chosen rendezvous at Yalta, in the
Crimea[1].
    Travelling again as 'Colonel Kent', Churchill set out in Skymaster on 29
January; Sarah accompanied him as ADC. During the night Winston sprang
a high temperature: instead, therefore, of leaving Skymaster when it landed
at 4.30 a.m. (30 January) at Malta, he stayed on the aircraft until later in the
morning when he felt better, and transferred to the cruiser HMS *Orion*.
    'Mrs Kent' was kept in touch by telegram.

[1] A resort on the Black Sea which, in conversation with Sarah, WSC was to dub 'The Riviera of
Hades'. From Martin Gilbert, *Churchill: A Life*, 1991, p. 819.

O From CSC   10 Downing Street
Tuesday 30 January 1944[45]

My Darling,
    I was much relieved to get the signal that you had reached Malta safely,
flying with a blizzard on your tail – But we didn't get the news till 9.30

though you arrived at 4.30 – a seven hours' flight! What a marvellous difference being able to fly across France instead of round Spain & Portugal & Gibraltar.

I'm pursuing my enquiries about the <u>delectable</u> little London house[1].... There is one drawback you must consider – All the neighbouring houses are damaged & will need repair – What about the noise of hammering?

I hope you will rest well these two spare days so as to be fresh for the ordeals of the Conference. Make Sarah take care of herself – She looked so pale & worn last night. Seven inches of snow fell last night but it's much less cold – The radio announced this morning that coal distribution by Army lorries begins to-day! It didn't mention who thought of this[2].

Your loving
Clemmie

[1] Just before leaving for Yalta (27 January) CSC had taken WSC to view a house in Kensington – No. 28 Hyde Park Gate, SW7 – to which he took a great fancy. CSC had done some discreet house-hunting during the winter, as she did not want the end of the war to find them without a London base.
[2] During January there was an acute coal shortage. CSC's suggestion to WSC that the Army should be used to transport coal had evidently been conveyed to the right quarters.

From WSC[1]   [Malta]
1 February 1945

JASON 32
  FOLLOWING FOR MRS KENT FROM COLONEL KENT.
  QUITE WELL AGAIN BUT SPEND MOST TIME IN BED IN ORION COMFORTABLE CABIN. MISS YOU
VERY MUCH. THE WORLD IS IN A FRIGHTFUL STATE. WE SEEM TO HAVE CHOSEN THE MOST
UNSUITABLE PLACE FOR MEETING. 16 AMERICAN COLONELS ARE TO BE QUARTERED IN ONE ROOM.
HOWEVER PERHAPS IMPROVEMENTS MAY BE MADE AT LAST MINUTE.

[1] Public Record Office, not yet listed.

O From WSC [typewritten]   H.M.S. ORION [Malta]
1 February 1945

My darling Clemmie,
1. I was so glad to get your letter and one from Diana which arrived yesterday morning. Sarah tells me she has written to you both yesterday and today so that you should know our news, which is scanty. I had a serious alarm coming over lest I was going to have another attack, for my temperature went to 102½ in the night. But it all passed off agreeably the next day and now I am in my usual health.... It would indeed have looked silly to have come all this way and put everyone to so much trouble and then be unable to do my share of the work which awaits us.
2. Yesterday I had General Marshall to luncheon alone and had a long and very pleasant talk with him touching on important things. Today Admiral King[1] was my companion. But of course I have not so many points of business to discuss with him as with his military confrère. Both

are in great form and all the conversations at the Conferences have been most friendly and agreeable.

3. Last night I dined with the Governor [of Malta] at a large dinner party at which Stettinius[2], Averell [Harriman] and Anthony [Eden*] were also guests. Harry [Hopkins] has arrived and tonight he, Stettinius, Anthony and Cadogan[3] are coming to dine with me.

4. I have very comfortable quarters here, Orion, and have spent most of the time in bed. . . . The Captain asked me to have a photograph taken with the entire crew who were massed behind me streaming right up over the turrets to the upper works and the mast. . . . Harry Hopkins' boy[4] turned up and was here taking photographs. He joined in with the other cameramen. I lingered on the deck as the Malta sunshine was very pleasant, and the shattered buildings which encompass us at every side, for we are in one of the creeks, showed their fine warm yellow-ochre shapes.

5. I have nearly finished the book by Beverley Nichols[5], . . . called Verdict on India. I think you would do well to read it. It is written with some distinction and a great deal of thought. It certainly shows the Hindu in his true character and the sorry plight to which we have reduced ourselves by losing confidence in our mission. Reading about India has depressed me for I see such ugly storms looming up there which, even in my short flight, may overtake us. I have had for some time a feeling of despair about the British connection with India, and still more about what will happen if it is suddenly broken. Meanwhile we are holding on to this vast Empire, from which we get nothing, amid the increasing criticism and abuse of the world, and our own people, and increasing hatred of the Indian population, who receive constant and deadly propaganda to which we can make no reply. However out of my shadows has come a renewed resolve to go fighting on as long as possible and to make sure the Flag is not let down while I am at the wheel. I agree with the book and also with its conclusion – Pakistan[6].

6. I was astonished to see the language which the Socialist Chairman of Committees, Major Milner [Deputy Speaker], allowed to be used about Anthony [Eden*] and me in our absence by the little band of insulters who have been so forward about Greece. Every day come the proofs of how right we were, and I see in today's Times, which reached me several hours ago, that they have learned something from facts. It may be that we shall hearken to the wishes of His Beatitude[7] and look in at Athens for a few hours on our homeward journey. The bitter misunderstandings which have arisen in the United States, and in degenerate circles at home, are only a foretaste of the furies which will be loosed about every stage of the peace settlement. I am sure in Greece I found one of the best opportunities for wise action that this war has tossed to me from its dark waves.

7. I am free to confess to you that my heart is saddened by the tales of the masses of German women and children flying along the roads everywhere in 40-mile long columns to the West before the advancing Armies. I am clearly convinced that they deserve it; but that does not remove it from one's gaze. The misery of the whole world appals me and I

fear increasingly that new struggles may arise out of those we are successfully ending.

8. All the news from MAGNETO (our destination [Yalta]) continues to prove that the Big Three in their first and most important action have managed to pick out the very worst place in the whole world for their Meeting. Sixteen American <u>Colonels</u> sleeping in one room gives an idea of the accommodation which the very high-grade rank and file of our expedition must expect. I am proposing that we go forward with the smallest number and deposit the great bulk of our joint forces in the ships we have at Sevastopol. Among these is the liner FRANCONIA, which has been to some extent staffed from the Queen Mary and is I am sure equipped with every comfort. It <u>only</u> takes three and a half hours from where we shall be to reach her along a very bad road....

9. Randolph, who was coming to Bari [from Yugoslavia] in any case to have his teeth attended to, will very likely look in here tomorrow[8]. The President arrives at the first light of dawn and I shall go to see him as soon as he desires it. We do not reach our destination till after dark on the 3rd. They say an immense amount of work is being done on the roads and that it is quite practicable to cross the mountains[9]. The weather here is a vast improvement on anything at home although there are often clouds. Keep your eye on the coal shortage as long as it lasts, and keep prodding at them to give the necessary military lorries etc. I shall hope to write again tomorrow.

> ✍ Tender Love my darling
> I miss you much
> I am lonely amid this throng
> Your ever loving husband
> **W**

[1] Fleet Admiral Ernest King (1878–1956), C.-in-C. US Fleet and Chief of Naval Operations, 1942–5. He believed the war could be won by the US navy in the Pacific if it were given greater resources.
[2] Edward R. Stettinius, Jr (1900–49). At this time US Secretary of State (1944–5).
[3] Sir Alexander Cadogan (1884–1968) OM. At this date Permanent Under-Secretary of State for Foreign Affairs (1938–46).
[4] Robert Hopkins, aged 22, elder son of Harry Hopkins.
[5] Beverley Nichols (1898–1983), *Verdict on India*, 1944.
[6] The State of Pakistan – Muslim – which came into being on India's independence, 1947.
[7] Archbishop Damaskinos (see p. 509 n. 2), now Regent of Greece.
[8] Randolph arrived on 2 February and saw WSC, but did not go on to Yalta.
[9] Between Sevastopol and Yalta, more than six hours' drive.

From WSC[1]   [Malta]
2 February 1945

JASON NO. 63
FOLLOWING FOR MRS KENT FROM COLONEL KENT.
MY FRIEND HAS ARRIVED IN BEST OF HEALTH AND SPIRITS[2]. EVERYTHING GOING VERY WELL. LOVELY WARM SUNSHINE. WE ARE ON THE WING AT DAWN.

[1] Public Record Office, Premier Papers 4/78/1.
[2] WSC was the only person who thought so. Numerous accounts exist of how shocked people

who saw the President were at the change in him since the Second Quebec Conference and Washington (September–October 1944). WSC had modified his view by the end of the Conference.

○ From CSC   10 Downing Street
2 February [1945]

My darling Winston

I have been spared the agonising anxiety of your journey with the high temperature and the violent change from chill to heat in the plane. I pray there may be no recurrence, but I fear the six hour drive will be a severe ordeal even, if when you arrive there is warmth, quiet & comfort, I'm afraid your staff will be a long way off – I hope that neither Miss Layton[1] nor Miss Sturdee[2] will have to share rooms with 16 American Colonels!...

Here is a note on the coal situation – It seems to be well in hand....

I'm afraid your conversations may be difficult. I think of you continually my Darling & often look at the Bull-dog[3] – I thought he winked yesterday.

Your loving
Clemmie

...

A lovely letter from Sarah.

3 Rockets[4] in one morning on Chingford [WSC's constituency], but hardly any casualties.

[1] Elizabeth Layton, one of WSC's personal secretaries from May 1941 to 1945, when she went to South Africa to marry Frans Nel, whom she had met in London after his release from prisoner-of-war camp. She wrote an excellent book about her time with WSC, *Mr Churchill's Secretary*, published in 1958.
[2] Nina ('Jo') Sturdee, Private Secretary to WSC from 1942 to 1953. MBE, 1953. Married, 1962, 6th Earl of Onslow (d. 1971).
[3] During the war the French artist Camille Bombois (1883–1970) gave CSC a strikingly powerful painting of a bulldog with a patch over one eye and a most intent look, as a token of the artist's admiration and tacit support for WSC. It hung in WSC's study at Chartwell for many years after the war. CSC sold it at Christie's in 1977.
[4] The first V-2 rockets had fallen in the London area on 8 September 1944. Developed by the Germans in parallel with the V-1, the V-2's trajectory was pre-set, and fuel cut off when the missile had reached the requisite speed to reach the target; its velocity was such that no anticipatory defensive action was possible.

○ From CSC   Chartwell
3 February 1945

My darling Winston

It's marvellous getting your letter the day after you've written. I am so very thankful that you are well again, & now I'm feverishly awaiting the news of your arrival at Magneto [Yalta]. My heart sank when I heard of the crash of one of your Conference planes[1]. I feel very sad about it. I'm told that Mr Loxley's young wife had (the day before the grim news) given birth to a still-born child – So she has not even her baby to comfort her. And Anthony [Eden*]'s charming doctor – you remember that very tall man – & many others of his entourage[2]. Thank God Miss Sturdee was not on the plane; she might well have been.

I send you a letter from Mary – Sarah has written me two enchanting & entrancing letters which rival any letters as light literature of a very high level –

Tender Love & grapple close to the President. . . .

Your Clemmie

. . .

[1] On 2 February one of the planes flying out with participants to the conference crashed off the island of Lampedusa, with 7 survivors out of 20.
[2] Peter Loxley was a young Foreign Office official. The victims included also Anthony Eden's doctor and one of his detectives.

From WSC[1]   [Yalta]
4 February 1945 12.30 p.m.

JASON NO. 109
FOLLOWING PERSONAL AND PRIVATE FROM COLONEL KENT FOR MRS KENT.
ARRIVED SAFELY [3 FEBRUARY] AFTER GOOD JOURNEY AND LONG DRIVE. BRIGHT SUNSHINE AND NO SNOW. U.J. ['UNCLE JO' = STALIN] IS COMING TO SEE ME AT 3 O'CLOCK. ALL WELL. SARAH SENDS HER LOVE.

[1] Public Record Office, Premier Papers 4/78/1.

From WSC[1]   ARGONAUT[2]
6 February 1945

JASON NO. 151
FOLLOWING FOR MRS KENT FROM COLONEL KENT.
WEATHER IS QUITE GOOD HERE AND YESTERDAY WAS BRIGHT. LONG AND MUCH HEAVY BUSINESS. PROBABLY FIVE OR SIX DAYS MORE.
MUCH LOVE FROM BOTH TO ALL.

[1] Public Record Office, not yet listed.
[2] Code name for the Yalta Conference.

O From WSC [copy][1]   [Yalta]
12 February 1945

JASON NO. 376
FOLLOWING PERSONAL AND PRIVATE FOR MRS KENT FROM COLONEL KENT.
I HOPE YOU WILL LIKE COMMUNIQUE PUBLISHED TOMORROW MORNING. WE HAVE COVERED A GREAT AMOUNT OF GROUND AND I AM VERY PLEASED WITH THE DECISIONS WE HAVE GAINED. STAYED LAST NIGHT AND STAYING TONIGHT ON FRANCONIA[2] IN GREAT COMFORT AT SEVASTOPOL. VISITING BALACLAVA[3] THIS AFTERNOON. FLYING ATHENS TOMORROW FOR A NIGHT THENCE 14TH ALEXANDRIA FOR FINAL TALKS WITH PRESIDENT. THEREAFTER NEAR PYRAMIDS SEEING HAILE SELASSIE[4] AND IBN SAUD[5] ETC.

HOPE TO START HOME 17TH OR 18TH. ALL WELL. LOOKING FORWARD MUCH TO SEEING YOU AT CHEQUERS WEEKEND.

ALL LOVE.

[1] Original in Public Record Office, Premier Papers 4/78/1.
[2] The liner *Franconia*, berthed at Sevastopol, was used as headquarters and base for many of the conference staff; see WSC's letter of 1 February 1945.
[3] Where WSC visited the battlefield. The Battle of Balaclava, famous for the Charge of the Light Brigade, was fought on 25 October 1854, during the Crimean War against the Russians.
[4] Haile Selassie (Prince Ras Tafari) (1892–1975), Emperor of Ethiopia, 1930–74.
[5] Ibn Saud (Abdul Aziz) (1880–1953), King of Saudi Arabia from 1932.

O From CSC   10 Downing Street
12 February 1945

My Darling
    . . .
    John Peck[1] has just brought in the terrific announcement[2] which is to be released to-night at 9.30 on the Radio. It's really grand –
    I long to see you my Darling – Sarah has been writing such lovely, long letters[3].
    Yesterday Peter Portal[4] & his charming wife Joan lunched with me. He was in great spirits – She has just returned from a visit to France where she stayed with Peter's opposite number General Vallin & his wife – She moved during a week among French service families & was shocked by the want & cold on every side among their civilian relations –
    People here are getting upset at the conditions in France. Quite apart from the humanitarian aspect don't you think it's dangerous to have the whole Nation cold, hungry & unemployed. Do you think you could influence General Marshall or the President to release enough lorries to distribute the food & coal already in France – I know the War must come first, but if presently you have to use troops to guard lines of communication & to put down riots it will be as broad as it's long – Both 'Houses' are working up steam & the Press is writing some moderate & some exaggerated articles. At least I hope they are exaggerated. I notice in the Statement to be released to-night there is a paragraph promising help – But it ought to come swiftly. There is, it seems, a great deterioration since November the 11th [1944] when we saw Paris exalted – That was three months ago –
    . . . with my love,

                                                                              Clemmie
                                                                                  . . .

[1] John Howard Peck (1913–95), longest-serving Assistant Private Secretary to WSC, from Dunkirk 1940 to Potsdam 1945. Knighted, 1971. British Ambassador at Dublin, 1970–3.
[2] The official communiqué on the outcome of the Yalta Conference encompassed the post-war division of Germany; the defining of the Polish frontier; and the setting up of the inaugural Conference of the United Nations in San Francisco (25 April–26 June 1945).
[3] Extracts from Sarah's brilliantly descriptive letters to her mother about this journey, as about others she made with her father, are to be found in her autobiography, *Keep on Dancing*, 1981.
[4] Sir Charles ('Peter') Portal, later Marshal of the Royal Air Force 1st Viscount Portal of Hungerford (1893–1971) KG, GCB, OM, DSO, MC. Chief of the Air Staff, 1940–5. Married, 1919, Joan Welby. He and his wife became great friends of the Churchill family.

O From CSC   10 Downing Street
13 February 1945

My darling Winston

I'm filled with happiness gratitude & pride – What a wonderful result
equal to a major military Victory or a whole victorious campaign – And I
am convinced brought about by you –

I know you will be grieved that Fircroft, my Convalescent Home,
belonging to my Maternity Hospital[1] has been savaged by a V2 rocket
which fell 100 yards away. Thank God not a soul killed or injured, but the
poor young Mamas & their little babies homeless – for the moment. It
happened last Sunday morning at 5 o'clock. Joan Portal [also on the
Committee] & I rushed down at once & made the best arrangements we
could. The repair service is wonderful – There were 20 workmen mending
the roof taking out smashed doors & window frames when we arrived –
The rain was pouring in – ceilings down & cracked.

Strangely enough the same night a rocket burst in the air half a mile
from Chartwell & metal rained down from the skies – Harris[2] & Moppet
[Whyte*] picked up masses of sharp aluminium fragments all over the
garden, tennis court & garage yard.

The poor cows had their feet cut! but soon recovered.

Courier going – All my Love to you & my beloved Sarah

Clemmie

[1] Fulmer Chase Maternity Home for wives of officers of all three services, of whose House
Committee CSC had been Chairman since 1939.
[2] New head gardener at Chartwell in succession to Albert Hill, who had died of leukaemia in June
1944, aged 49, after 18 years' service with the Churchills.

After the Yalta Conference ended on the morning of 11 February, Winston
and Sarah drove back along the six-hour road to Sevastopol, and went aboard
Franconia. Here they rested for two days.

On 14 February, en route for Alexandria, the party flew to Athens, to call
upon Archbishop Damaskinos (now Regent of Greece). Here Randolph
joined his father again.

Seven weeks previously Churchill had been conveyed in an armoured
vehicle through a city rent by civil war; now he drove with the Regent in an
open car, with people rushing to greet their unannounced but instantly
recognized visitor. Harold Macmillan[1] estimated there were about 40,000
people in Constitution Square. Churchill made the cheering multitude an
emotional, impromptu speech.

That night the Acropolis was floodlit in his honour, for the first time since
the German occupation.

The following day Churchill and his party flew to Alexandria, where he,
Randolph and Sarah in small launches sped out to sea to go aboard USS
Quincy, where they lunched with President Roosevelt*. Churchill wrote later
of their leave-taking: 'The President seemed placid and frail. I felt that he had

a slender contact with life. I was not to see him again. We bade affectionate farewells.'[2]

Churchill flew to Cairo, where he remained for three days.

[1] See p. 508 n. 4. From his *War Diaries*, 1984 (14 February 1945).
[2] Notes dictated by WSC, Churchill Papers, CHUR 4/363. President Roosevelt died suddenly at Warm Springs, Georgia, on 12 April 1945.

From WSC[1]   [Cairo]
16 February 1945

JASON NO. 558
  FOLLOWING FOR MRS KENT FROM COLONEL KENT.
  ATHENS WAS A MOST MARVELLOUS EXPERIENCE. I HAVE NEVER SEEN ANYTHING LIKE THE SIZE
OF THE CROWD OR SO MUCH ENTHUSIASM. AM NOW NEAR THE PYRAMIDS RECEIVING POTENTATES.
  PLANNING REACHING YOU SUNDAY AFTERNOON WEATHER PERMITTING....
  MUCH LOVE FROM ALL.

[1] Public Record Office, Premier Papers 4/78/1.

From WSC[1]   [Cairo]
17 February 1945

JASON NO. 577
  FOLLOWING FOR MRS KENT FROM COLONEL KENT.
  WEATHER CONDITIONS IN ENGLAND MAKE IT DESIRABLE TO PUT OFF RETURNING AT ANY RATE
FOR ONE DAY, BUT POSSIBLY TWO. MOST INTERESTING INTERVIEWS WITH ONE EMPEROR[2], TWO
KINGS[3] AND ONE PRESIDENT[4].
  LOVE TO ALL.

[1] Public Record Office, Premier Papers 4/78/1.
[2] Emperor Haile Selassie of Ethiopia (see p. 516 n. 4).
[3] King Ibn Saud of Saudi Arabia (see p. 516 n. 5) and King Farouk I (1920–65), King of Egypt, 1937–52, when forced to abdicate.
[4] Shukri al-Kuwatli (1891–1967), President of Syria, July 1943–March 1949 and from 1955 until union with Egypt, 1958–61.

Churchill and his party set out for home in Skymaster in the small hours of 19 February; because of thick fog they were diverted to Lyneham in Wiltshire. From there Winston drove for three hours to Reading, where he awaited Clementine in the Manager's office of the Station Hotel. My mother wrote to me on 21 February that there she found him ensconced 'imbibing whisky and soda. He is marvellously well – much, much better than when he went off for this most trying and difficult of Conferences'[1].

Chapter XXIII

WORLDS APART

In April 1945 Clementine, at the invitation of the Soviet Government and the Soviet Red Cross, went on a five-week goodwill tour to Russia on behalf of her Red Cross Aid to Russia Fund[1]. Accompanying her were Mabel Johnson[2] and her own secretary, Grace Hamblin*.

On 27 March Winston went to Northolt to see Clementine and her party fly off in Skymaster to Cairo, on the first leg of their journey to Moscow.

[1] By May 1945 the fund had reached £7 million and was still growing.
[2] Secretary to the Red Cross Aid to Russia Committee; a close colleague who became a great friend of CSC.

○ From CSC   Minister Resident in the Middle East
28 March 1945   Cairo

My Darling

Ned & Joan Grigg[1] are kindness itself – Ned saw Lord Wavell[2] on his way thro'; & says he does not mean to make trouble but has a scheme for bringing Congress into the War against Japan – He has no use for Gandhi[3]....

We are off to-night –

Your devoted
Clemmie

[1] Sir Edward Grigg (see p. 117 n. 1), at this time Minister Resident in the Middle East, 1944–5.
[2] Field Marshal Sir Archibald Wavell (see p. 480 n. 1, letter of 13 May 1943), who was in Cairo on his way back to India, where he was Viceroy and Governor-General, 1943–7.
[3] Mohandas Karamchand (Mahatma) Gandhi (1869–1948), leader of Indian National Congress. Organized hunger strikes and civil disobedience campaign against British rule in India; several times arrested and imprisoned. Assassinated by Hindu fanatic, January 1948.

○ From CSC   Office of the Minister Resident (M.E.)
Good Friday, 30 March 1945   Cairo

My Darling,

Last night when we were having dinner & were all set for our flight an adverse weather report came in & it was postponed for 24 hours, which is a little trying.

The kindness & warmth of Joan & Ned Grigg makes staying here a restful pleasure – All the same I have done a good deal! I have visited the principal Y.W.C.A. in the town; ... to-day [Isabel Catto][1] is taking me to Tel-El-Kebir to see 3 of her Clubs & Hostels....

I loved your speech about Ll.G. [Lloyd George*][2]. It recalled forgotten blessings which he showered upon the meek & lowly.

Your loving
Clemmy

... I also visited the big Military Hospital. Poor men, some had not seen home or chick or wife for 3½ long years. But they smiled –

[1] Isabel Catto (1912–97), daughter of 1st Baron Catto. At this date in charge of YWCA establishments in and around Cairo; President, World YWCA, 1955–63. Became a great friend of CSC.
[2] Earl Lloyd George had died on 26 March 1945, aged 82. On 28 March WSC made a moving tribute to him in the House of Commons.

Clementine celebrated her sixtieth birthday in Cairo. Before she left home Winston had given her the most beautiful diamond-encrusted heart-shaped brooch.

○ From CSC   Minister Resident in the Middle East
Easter Sunday 1 April [1945]   Cairo

My Darling Winston

Your lovely Birthday telegram was handed to me in Church this morning by Lord Killearn [British Ambassador] – I was so pleased. I <u>think</u> we <u>may</u> get off to-night. There has been a 'Hanseen' [*khamsin*], which is a great wind which blows the sand right up in the air sometimes to 6,000 feet so that it's like a gritty fog & of course one can't fly....

I have taken a great liking for both Ned & Joan Grigg – It seems to me they are an excellent counterpart to our somewhat lush Ambassador!...

... There's a plane just starting for home, so no more except all my love to you & Sarah – I do rejoice in her freedom[1].

Your loving & devoted
Clemmie

...

[1] Sarah had been granted a decree nisi from Vic Oliver on 28 March 1945.

Since the Yalta Conference the threat of Soviet domination in Eastern Europe was becoming a stark reality. Relations between Britain and the Soviet Union had become so tense over the Polish question[1] that Winston had had very real qualms about the wisdom of letting Clementine go to Russia. However, her visit afforded a welcome opportunity for smiles, not scowls.

To greet her on arrival were Mr and Mrs Maisky[2], our Ambassador Sir Archibald Clark Kerr[3], and Averell Harriman, the United States Ambassador.

[1] On 27 March 14 Polish leaders representing all the non-Communist parties were arrested, having been taken under promise of safe guard to a Soviet army establishment near Warsaw; later they would be taken to Moscow as prisoners and, in mid-June 1945, put on trial.
[2] Ivan Mikhailovich Maisky (1884–1975), the former Soviet Ambassador to London, 1932–43, and his wife Agnes (who was an English woman, Ivy Low). CSC had had many contacts with Madame Maisky concerning her Aid to Russia Fund. 'Agnes' could be quite brusque – graciousness was not part of her make-up – but CSC used to give as good as she got, and they became friends.
[3] Sir Archibald Clark Kerr, later 1st Baron Inverchapel (1882–1951). Ambassador to the USSR, 1942–6.

O From WSC   [Foreign Office]
2 April 1945

LOVELY ACCOUNTS OF YOUR SPEECH AND RECEPTION RECEIVED HERE. AT THE MOMENT YOU ARE THE ONE BRIGHT SPOT IN ANGLO-RUSSIAN RELATIONS. FONDEST LOVE. I AM FORWARDING YOU A LETTER FROM MARY.

O From WSC   [Foreign Office]
4 April 1945

DELIGHTED TO RECEIVE YOUR TWO LETTERS FROM CAIRO AND ALL REPORTS OF YOUR RECEPTION. PLEASE TELEGRAPH DAILY. I AM ASKING AMBASSADOR TO KEEP ME INFORMED OF YOUR MOSCOW CONTACTS. HAVE BEEN EXTREMELY HARD-PRESSED WITH VARIOUS SITUATIONS AND HAVE HAD NO CHANCE TO WRITE BUT WILL TELEGRAPH YOU AGAIN TOMORROW. I AM SURE YOU WILL UNDERSTAND THAT AS THESE TELEGRAMS ARE ALL CODED AND DECODED I DO NOT LENGTHEN THEM BY EXPRESSIONS I PUT IN LETTERS.   W.

O From CSC   Moscow
5 April 1945

VISIT PROGRESSING FAVOURABLY AND MOST ENJOYABLE. TUESDAY, I WAS RECEIVED MOST AMIABLY BY MR MOLOTOV[1] IN THE KREMLIN. HE REFERRED TO PRESENT DIFFICULTIES BUT SAID THEY WOULD PASS AND ANGLO-SOVIET FRIENDSHIP REMAIN. WENT TO THE OPERA. YESTERDAY, WEDNESDAY, VISITED FACTORY AND ATTENDED LOVELY BANQUET GIVEN IN MY HONOUR BY MR AND MADAME MOLOTOV. IT WAS THRILLING. ARCHIE [CLARK KERR] MOST COSY AND HELPFUL AND GENERAL CATROUX[2] CAME TO TEA YESTERDAY. TENDER LOVE, CLEMMIE.

[1] Vyacheslav Mikhailovich Molotov (V. M. Skriabin) (1890–1986), Soviet Communist statesman. Chairman of Council of People's Commissars (Prime Minister), 1930–41; Foreign Minister, 1939–49 and 1953–6.
[2] Gen. Georges Catroux (1879–1969), distinguished French soldier and diplomat. At this date French Ambassador to USSR, 1945–8.

○ From WSC   London
6 April 1945

YOURS OF APRIL 5:
AM RELIEVED EVERYTHING IS GOING WELL WITH YOU. AMBASSADOR WILL SHOW YOU
TELEGRAMS. PLEASE ALWAYS SPEAK OF MY EARNEST DESIRE FOR CONTINUING FRIENDSHIP OF
BRITISH AND RUSSIAN PEOPLES AND OF MY RESOLVE TO WORK FOR IT PERSEVERINGLY. YOUR
DELIGHTFUL LETTER OF MARCH 30 HAS ARRIVED ... ALL MY LOVE.

                                                             W.S.C.

○ From WSC [typewritten]   10 Downing Street
6 April 1945

My darling Clemmie,
    Since you were swirled away into the night, I have had the most
exacting time. What with looking after Bernie Baruch and all the
Dominion Premiers, as well as overwhelming toil, I have not found a
minute to write. It is now Friday, and I have just finished my sleep and am
going down to Chequers, where Smuts is spending the week-end with
me. . . . I arranged for Sarah to attend on me for week-ends on duty while
you are away, to help with our various official guests.
    On Tuesday last Smuts dined with me alone at the Annexe. On
Wednesday I gave a dinner at No. 10 to a lot of finance people, including
the Chancellor of the Exchequer[1], the Governor of the Bank [of England][2],
Lord Keynes[3], Max [Beaverbrook*] and Brendan [Bracken*], to hear Baruch
talk, which he does to great purpose, ... A great deal of this 'pep' talk was
agreed with by my friends above-mentioned. But I keep on asking myself
all sorts of awkward questions. How are we to balance our Budget? How
are we to place our exports where they are wanted; and how are we to
make up across the exchange for all our losses of foreign investments; and
how are we to buy the balance of our food, etc? ...
    The President [Roosevelt*] sent me several messages by Baruch, and
now that Harry [Hopkins] is ill and Byrnes[4] has resigned, my poor friend is
very much alone and, according to all accounts I receive, is bereft of much
of his vigour. Many of the telegrams I get from him are clearly the
work of others around him. However yesterday he came through with a
telegram, which perhaps Archie [Clark Kerr] has shown you, as I told him
to do, which certainly ends up with a flash of his old fire, and is about the
hottest thing I have seen so far in diplomatic intercourse. I have told
Archie to keep you well informed, but this will have to cease when you go
away from Moscow. You will not have a cypher, and much of this stuff is
dynamite. The same is true of letters. I do not feel able to write freely
because I do not know how letters will be forwarded from Moscow. My
telegrams also will be sent en clair from the Embassy. Well you know how
great our difficulties are about Poland, Rumania, and this other row about
alleged negotiations. I intend still to persevere, but it is very difficult.
    What puzzles me is the inconsistency. There is no doubt that your visit
is giving sincere pleasure. Gusev[5] called at the Foreign Office yesterday, as
Anthony [Eden*] thought, to begin a long attack, but instead he spent a

long time in conveying a message from his Government in praise of you and your work, and asking whether they might offer you the Order of the Red Banner of Labour, which was of course approved....

I have also had a wrangle between our Staffs and the Americans, in which I participated with telegrams to the President, about a change of plan Eisenhower introduced on the Western Front, ... The only times I ever quarrel with the Americans are when they fail to give us a fair share of opportunity to win glory. Undoubtedly I feel much pain when I see our armies so much smaller than theirs. It has always been my wish to keep equal, but how can you do that against so mighty a nation and a population nearly three times your own? ...

I hope that Montgomery's* advance will drain the Boche out of Holland, and that we shall soon begin to throw in food. At any rate for a whole week there have been no bombs or bangs[6]. I have moved the Cabinets back to No. 10[7], and have also had one or two meals there. I am giving orders for the rehabilitation of that dwelling, otherwise we shall not be able to use it this year....

One big goldfish was retrieved from the bottom of the pool at Chartwell. All the rest have been stolen, or else eaten by an otter. I have put Scotland Yard on the work of finding the thief. I fear we shall never see our poor fish any more, ...

The greater part of my Government have departed; or are about to depart to various countries on one excuse or another.... I am myself in the best of health, but I have not found a minute to spare for the two or three interesting books I have at my bed-side. Indeed I am far behind this weekend in the ordinary Boxes.

I have had also to deal with [Conservative] Party matters. We have upwards of 540 candidates already chosen, and it is quite possible that the Election will take place at the end of June or July. Everyone is resigning himself to this unpleasant fact.

Last night I gave a dinner ... of thirty-five people in the big dining room of No. 10 to the Dominions representatives, War Cabinet, Chiefs of Staff and others. There was the greatest good temper.... There is no doubt that Victory is an intoxicating draught. All these men from all over the Empire arrive with eyes glowing with admiration, and have nothing but praise for our conduct during these terrible years. The sense that the end may be near in Europe entrances all minds, and will give us, I trust, the impetus to overcome the many labours and uncertainties that lie ahead....

Next Wednesday The King comes, and this will I expect be the last of the dinners of our war-time Cabinet[8], famous I think I may call it. The Wednesday following Mary Marlborough is to give me a dinner at Buck's Club, where gaiety will be the order of the night.

I fear this is a most aimless account of my doings. Like the entry in Mark Twain's diary: 'Got up, washed, went to bed.' Looking back on the days, they seem little more than that.

Then look at the questions looming ahead and the number of decisions which I shall have to take personally in the formation of a new Government[9], with all the personal pangs and pinches entailed. However so far everyone seems quite ready to be told where they get off or get in....

I am sending out a call for M.P.s and candidates to come home from all fronts unless actually engaged in fighting. . . .

— — —

Monday morning.
April 9.

During the weekend I have had much good news about you from Moscow, and Clark Kerr telegraphs that your visit there did the utmost good at a most difficult time. . . . I do hope you will be sensible and not overdo it. Insist upon days of leisure. They will understand. Otherwise you may be killed with kindness. The Soviet Press make a great fuss of your visit. . . .

I think there is very little doubt that the Government will break up shortly[10]. Bevin has made a very hostile speech (answered today by Brendan [Bracken*]), and it is clear he will not work with us. Generally the Party men are anxious to get at each other, and matters have gone so far that life inside the Cabinet will not be agreeable and might easily become inefficient. The prodigious advances we have made in Germany may easily bring matters to a close. I expect the General Election about the middle of June, with the announcement of a dissolution in May. . . .

✍My darling one I think always of you & am so proud of you. Yr personality reaches the gt masses & touches their hearts. With all my love constant kisses

I remain ever yr devoted husband
W

. . .

[1] Sir John Anderson (see p. 448 n. 7). Chancellor of the Exchequer, 1943–5.
[2] Thomas Catto, 1st Baron Catto (1879–1959). Governor of Bank of England, 1944–9.
[3] John Maynard Keynes, 1st Baron Keynes (1883–1946), distinguished economist. Leader of British delegation at Bretton Woods conference, which set up International Monetary Fund.
[4] James Francis Byrnes (1879–1972), US Secretary of State, 1945–7.
[5] Fedor Tarasovich Gusev (1905–87), who had succeeded Maisky as Soviet Ambassador to London, September 1943.
[6] The last (1,050th) V-2 rocket hit England on 27 March 1945, when its launching base was destroyed by Allied bombing attack.
[7] The Cabinets had been held in the underground Cabinet War Rooms while there was a risk of air raids. See p. 455 n. 2.
[8] During 1944–5 the King dined with WSC and Cabinet colleagues in the downstairs fortified dining room at No. 10 on six occasions: these are recorded on a plaque in the room.
[9] It was planned that with victory in Europe a new 'Caretaker' Government would be formed by WSC, as leader of the majority Conservative Party, to hold the fort pending a General Election.
[10] WSC had hoped that political unity could be maintained until all our enemies had been defeated; but he now accepted that the wartime Coalition Government would break up once victory in Europe (now rapidly approaching) was achieved.

In the week Clementine was in Moscow before starting on her tour she fulfilled a packed programme of engagements, the highlight of which was her meeting with Marshal Stalin. She brought him as a present from Winston a gold fountain pen: 'My husband wishes me to express the hope that you will write him many friendly messages with it.' My mother told me he accepted the gift smilingly, but said: 'I only write with a pencil . . .'[1]

On the night of 8 April Clementine and her companions boarded the special train provided for them by the Soviet Government, to set out on their nearly month-long journey.

[1] From Clementine Churchill, *My Visit to Russia*, a booklet published by Hutchinson in 1945 and sold in aid of 'Mrs Churchill's Aid to Russia Fund'.

○ From CSC   Leningrad
[9 or 10 April 1945]

THINK LENINGRAD IS THE MOST BEAUTIFUL CITY I HAVE EVER SEEN. WE ARE INSTALLED IN A LOVELY VILLA IN THE SUBURBS AND ARE ABOUT TO START OUR TOUR. I MISS MY QUIET EVENINGS WITH YOU. PLEASE PASS ON ALL TELEGRAMS TO MARY BY POST AND TELL HER SHE IS CONSTANTLY IN MY THOUGHTS. ALL MY LOVE.

CLEMMIE

○ From CSC   Leningrad
[11 April 1945]

YESTERDAY WE VISITED A SCIENTIFIC INSTITUTE DEVOTED TO THE HEALTH OF CHILDREN. TO IT IS ATTACHED A HOSPITAL WHERE WE SAW MANY CHILDREN STILL BEING NURSED BACK TO HEALTH FROM THE EFFECTS OF PROLONGED STARVATION DURING THE BLOCKADE OF LENINGRAD[1]. . . . THE NEVA STILL HAS A THIN COATING OF ICE BUT THE WEATHER IS LOVELY. . . . THE MAYOR VISITED US AND DRANK YOUR HEALTH. HE AFTERWARDS TOOK US TO THE BALLET. . . . HAVE THE ROCKETS CEASED? LOVE.

CLEMENTINE

[1] From 8 September 1941 to 27 January 1944.

○ From WSC   [Foreign Office]
13 April 1945

I AM VERY GLAD YOUR VISIT TO LENINGRAD WAS SO PLEASANT AND INTERESTING. MARY'S M.B.E. IS GAZETTED. YOU SAW PERHAPS THAT POOR TOM MITFORD[1] DIED OF WOUNDS, AND BASIL DUFFERIN[2] WAS KILLED. HERE EVERYTHING IS QUIET EXCEPT POLITICS. LOVE. I HAVE JUST HEARD THE GRIEVOUS NEWS OF PRESIDENT ROOSEVELT'S DEATH[3].

[1] Thomas Mitford (see p. 468 n. 13), only son of 2nd Baron Redesdale, died in Burma.
[2] Basil Hamilton-Temple-Blackwood, 4th Marquess of Dufferin and Ava (1909–45).
[3] WSC received the news of the President's death at midnight on 12 April.

Passing briefly through Moscow on the afternoon of 13 April, on their way to Stalingrad, Clementine learned the news of President Roosevelt's* death; she went to the British Embassy and had a short telephone conversation with Winston before resuming her journey.

○ From WSC   London
14 April 1945

... YOU HAVE NOT YET SENT ME THE ACCOUNT OF YOUR TALK WITH STALIN. MANY
CONGRATULATIONS ON YOUR DECORATIONS[1]. AT THE LAST MOMENT I DECIDED NOT TO FLY TO
ROOSEVELT'S* FUNERAL ON ACCOUNT OF MUCH THAT WAS GOING ON HERE. ANTHONY [EDEN*] HAS
GONE INSTEAD. I HAVE HAD A VERY NICE TELEGRAM FROM PRESIDENT TRUMAN[2] OPENING OUR
RELATIONS ON THE BEST CONDITIONS. W.S.C.

[1] CSC was awarded the Order of the Red Banner of Labour, and Miss Johnson the Medal of Labour.
[2] Harry S. Truman (1884–1972), 33rd President of the United States, 1945–52. Democrat. US Senator
(Missouri), 1934; Vice-President, 1944; became President on Roosevelt's death, April 1945, and
was re-elected for second term, November 1948.

○ From CSC   Kislovodsk
[17 April 1945, 13.50 hours]

MR PIGALEV THE CHAIRMAN OF THE COUNCIL OF STALINGRAD SENDS YOU HIS GREETINGS AND
HIS EARNEST HOPES OF FRIENDSHIP BETWEEN OUR TWO COUNTRIES.... THE NORMAL POPULATION
OF STALINGRAD IS HALF MILLION AND THERE ARE STILL THREE HUNDRED THOUSAND PEOPLE
LIVING HERE. TWO GREAT FACTORIES HAVE BEEN REBUILT AND ARE MAKING STEEL AND
TRACTORS AND EMPLOYING ABOUT THIRTY THOUSAND PEOPLE. THEY HAVE REBUILT A FEW
SCHOOLS WHICH HAVE TO WORK IN TWO SHIFTS. HOSPITAL ACCOMMODATION IS EXTREMELY
LIMITED BUT THEY ARE REBUILDING THEM AS QUICKLY AS POSSIBLE. WE SAW A WOODEN
PREFABRICATED VILLAGE BEING RUN UP WHICH WILL HOUSE TWENTY THOUSAND PEOPLE. THEY
ARE REBUILDING THEIR CITY WITH THE SAME SPIRIT OF DETERMINATION WITH WHICH THEY
FOUGHT THE GERMANS[1].... ALL MY LOVE.

                                                              CLEMMIE

[1] The battle of Stalingrad lasted from 13 September 1942 to 2 February 1943.

○ From CSC   Kislovodsk
[17 April 1945, 20.08 hours]

WE HAVE ARRIVED IN THE CAUCASUS AND ARE STAYING IN A LOVELY SPA IN A HIGH VALLEY
BETWEEN TWO RANGES OF MOUNTAINS.... THE GERMANS WERE HERE FIVE MONTHS DURING
WHICH TIME THEY PUT TO DEATH MANY LEADING DOCTORS AND SCIENTISTS. WAS TOLD THAT
SOME OF THE XRAY UNITS PROVIDED BY MY FUND HAD BEEN TAKEN AWAY BY THE GERMANS.
THESE I SHALL OF COURSE REPLACE AND SHALL TRY TO PROVIDE FOR SOME OF THEIR OTHER
NEEDS.... LOVE.

                                                              CLEMMIE

○ From CSC   Kislovodsk
[18 April 1945]

LAST NIGHT WE ATTENDED THE LOCAL THEATRE WHERE THERE WAS A SPRIGHTLY AND AMUSING
COMEDY..... THE AUDIENCE WERE RAPTUROUS IN THEIR WELCOME AND THREW BUNCHES OF

VIOLETS FROM THE GALLERY. THIS MORNING WE SPENT VISITING SANATORIUMS FULL OF
SEVERELY WOUNDED RED ARMY SOLDIERS. THE WHOLE TOWN TURNS OUT TO GREET US EVERY TIME
WE GO OUT AND I AM CONTINUALLY AMAZED AND MOVED BY SO MUCH ENTHUSIASM.... I WANT
YOU TO KNOW THAT THIS TREMENDOUSLY WARM FEELING SEEMS UNIVERSAL.... LOVE.

Clemmie

○ From WSC   London
19 April 1945

   SARAH AND I ATTENDED THE SERVICE AT ST PAUL'S FOR ROOSEVELT*, WHICH WAS VERY
IMPRESSIVE. THE WEATHER HERE IS BRIGHT AND DELIGHTFUL. EVERYONE IS AS MUCH
ASTONISHED BY IT AS BY THE RAPIDITY WITH WHICH GERMANY HAS BEEN OVERRUN. MY WORK
HAS BEEN VERY HEAVY, BUT THE HOUSE OF COMMONS IS VERY KIND TO ME.... I SEND YOU
BEST LOVE FROM ALL.

○ From WSC   [Foreign Office]
20 April 1945

   DELIGHTED TO GET YOUR TELEGRAM FROM KISLOVODSK AND TO LEARN OF ALL THE KINDNESS
WHICH HAS BEEN SHOWN YOU BY THE RUSSIAN PEOPLE. IN THIS FRIENDSHIP OF OUR TWO
PEOPLES THE GREATEST HOPE FOR THE WORLD RESIDES. HERE WE ARE ALL SHOCKED BY THE
MOST HORRIBLE REVELATIONS OF GERMAN CRUELTY IN THE CONCENTRATION CAMPS. GENERAL
EISENHOWER HAS INVITED ME TO SEND PARLIAMENTARY DELEGATION. I ACCEPTED AT ONCE AND
IT WILL START TOMORROW. THEY WILL GO TO THE SPOT AND SEE THE HORRORS FOR THEMSELVES
– A GRUESOME DUTY.... NELLIE IS IN DEEP ANXIETY ABOUT GILES[1] WHO HAS BEEN MOVED
AGAIN WITH THE OTHERS TO SOME SECRET PLACE. MUCH LOVE FROM ALL OF US.

[1] Giles Romilly (1916–67), Nellie Romilly's elder son. As *Daily Express* correspondent was captured
by Germans at Narvik and interned, April 1939. On discovering his identity the Germans isolated
him. In 1941, following an escape attempt, he was transferred to Colditz Castle, where he remained
until April 1945.

○ From CSC   Rostov-on-Don
[20 or 21 April 1945]

YESTERDAY WE VISITED ESSENTUKI AND PYATIGORSK, TWO MORE HEALTH RESORTS. THE WHOLE
OF THE CAUCASUS IS FILLED WITH HOSPITALS AND SANATORIUMS TO NURSE THE WOUNDED OF
THE RED ARMY BACK TO HEALTH.... THE GERMANS DESTROYED VERY FEW BUILDINGS BUT IN
PYATIGORSK THEY SHOT FIVE THOUSAND CIVILIANS INCLUDING A HUNDRED DOCTORS AND
SCIENTISTS AND MANY WOMEN AND CHILDREN AND ALSO BURNED A VALUABLE REFERENCE LIBRARY
OF ONE HUNDRED AND FIFTY THOUSAND BOOKS. HERE AGAIN THE POPULATION TURNED OUT IN
GREAT NUMBERS.... EVENTS SEEM TO BE MOVING TO A CLIMAX IN THE WEST BUT WE GET NO
DETAILED NEWS. LOVE.

CLEMMIE

○ From WSC   Foreign Office
21 April 1945

HAVE JUST SPENT DAY IN BRISTOL GIVING DEGREES[1] TO BEVIN AND A. V. ALEXANDER[2].
TERRIFIC CROWD AND JOYOUS RECEPTION. I ALSO WAS MADE A FREEMAN OF THE CITY. MANY
ENQUIRIES WERE MADE ABOUT YOUR TOUR. THE GERMAN WAR IS MOVING VERY QUICKLY BUT IT IS
FOR THE COMMANDERS IN THE FIELD TO LET US KNOW WHEN THEY CONSIDER THE EFFECTIVE
RESISTING POWER OF THE ENEMY IS BROKEN AND WHEN THE PERIOD OF MOPPING-UP WAR CRIMINALS
HAS BEGUN.... WE DO NOT WANT TO HAVE PREMATURE REJOICINGS AND WE MUST ALWAYS REMEMBER
THE STRUGGLE WITH JAPAN THAT LIES AHEAD. INTENSE HORROR HAS BEEN CAUSED BY THE
REVELATIONS OF GERMAN BRUTALITIES IN THE CONCENTRATION CAMPS. THEY DID NOT HAVE TIME
TO COVER UP THEIR TRACES. DELIGHTED TO HEAR OF THE CONTINUED SUCCESS OF YOUR TOUR.
MACHINE [SKYMASTER] WILL BE READY FOR YOU FROM 1ST MAY ONWARDS. LOVE. WINSTON.

[1] WSC had been Chancellor of Bristol University since 1929.
[2] Albert Victor Alexander, later 1st Earl Alexander of Hillsborough (1885–1965), Labour MP, soldier
and Baptist lay preacher. First Lord of the Admiralty, 1929–31, 1940–5 and 1945–6; Minister of
Defence, 1947–50; Leader of Labour Peers, House of Lords, from 1955.

○ From CSC   Rostov-on-Don
[21 April 1945]

YESTERDAY WE ALL TOOK A DAY'S REST STOP AT PYATIGORSK.... WE HAVE NOW ARRIVED IN
ROSTOV ... WHICH ALAS HAS BEEN GRIEVOUSLY WRECKED BY THE GERMANS. EVERY BRIDGE OVER
THE DON HAS BEEN DESTROYED AND WE CROSS ON A TEMPORARY ONE. THE PRINCIPAL OBJECT OF
OUR VISIT HERE IS TO SEE THE TWO HOSPITALS WHICH ARE BEING EQUIPPED BY MY FUND....
LOVE.

                                                             CLEMMIE

○ From WSC   Chequers
23 April 1945

JACK [CHURCHILL*], WHO WENT TO WEYMOUTH WITH PEREGRINE [HIS YOUNGER SON], HAD A
HEART ATTACK IN THE YACHT CLUB YESTERDAY. HE IS BETTER NOW AND HORDER[1] WHO HAS
VISITED HIM HAS ARRANGED TO BRING HIM TO LONDON IN AN AMBULANCE TOMORROW.... HIS
CONDITION IS DANGEROUS BUT THERE IS DEFINITE HOPE OF STABILISATION....
2. NELLY CAME TO ME IN DEEP ANXIETY ABOUT GILES WHO, WITH LORD LASCELLES[2], AND
OTHER PROMINENTI[3] WERE REMOVED FROM THE PRISONER OF WAR CAMP IN GERMANY A FEW HOURS
BEFORE THE LIBERATING AMERICANS ARRIVED AND CARRIED TO AN UNKNOWN DESTINATION, NO
DOUBT AS HOSTAGES. THERE IS NOTHING TO BE DONE AS IT WOULD ADD TO THEIR DANGER IF
WE SHOW THAT WE MINDED.
3. SARAH WAS WITH ME AT BRISTOL ... AND IS NOW HERE AT CHEQUERS WHERE WE HAVE
CAMROSE[4] AND WINANT[5].... ANTHONY [EDEN*] WIRES FROM WASHINGTON THAT AVERELL
[HARRIMAN] WAS LOUD IN PRAISE OF YOUR ACHIEVEMENTS IN MOSCOW AND SAID THAT YOU HAD
MADE A VALIANT AND TACTFUL CONTRIBUTION TO WORLD RELATIONS. THE BRILLIANT WEATHER
HERE CONTINUES. LOVE,

                                                             WINSTON

[1] Thomas Jeeves Horder, 1st Baron Horder (1871–1955), distinguished physician.
[2] Viscount Lascelles (1923–), son of 6th Earl of Harewood and HRH Princess Mary, the Princess

Royal; King George VI's nephew. Served during Second World War in Grenadier Guards, wounded and taken prisoner. Succeeded his father as 7th Earl, 1947.
[3] Persons related to important public figures who had been secluded in Colditz as being of possible 'hostage' value.
[4] William Berry, 1st Viscount Camrose (1879–1954), Chairman and Editor-in-Chief of *Daily Telegraph* and various newspapers and journals. A close colleague, friend and supporter of WSC.
[5] Gil Winant, US Ambassador (see p. 499 n. 4).

○ From CSC   Sevastopol
[23 April 1945]

WE HAVE [LEFT] ROSTOV AND ARE NOW ON OUR WAY TO THE CRIMEA. YESTERDAY WAS MOST INTERESTING. WE VISITED THE SECOND HOSPITAL AND HELD A CONFERENCE WITH THE MEDICAL AND HEALTH AUTHORITIES AND SETTLED A GREAT DEAL OF BUSINESS.... WE WERE MOBBED BY FRIENDLY CROWDS. EVERYWHERE WE SEE SMILING FACES.... LOVE. CLEMMIE.

○ From CSC   Simferopol
[28 April 1945]

I HAVE JUST HEARD THE GLORIOUS NEWS OF THE MEETING OF THE RED ARMY WITH THE ALLIES[1] AND BY YOUR STATEMENT ON THE WIRELESS IT SEEMS THE END IS NEAR. I LONG TO BE WITH YOU DURING THESE TREMENDOUS DAYS AND I THINK OF YOU CONSTANTLY. ALL MY LOVE.
                                                                        CLEMMIE

[1] At Torgau on the Elbe, 26 April 1945.

○ From WSC   London
2 May 1945

1. DELIGHTED WITH ALL YOUR TELEGRAMS. SKYMASTER STARTS FOR YOU TONIGHT WITH MANY PAPERS AND MESSAGES.... STAY TILL 10TH IN MOSCOW IF YOU WISH BUT AFTER THAT I AM VERY GLAD YOU WILL COME STRAIGHT HOME.... SEVERAL CRISES ARE COMING TO A HEAD AND AS YOU SEE BOTH OUR GREAT ENEMIES ARE DEAD[1]. MY WORK HAS BEEN EXTREMELY HEAVY AS I AM LOOKING AFTER THE COMMONS AND THE FOREIGN OFFICE[2] AS WELL AS THE ORDINARY DAILY ROUND. MY HOURS ARE SHOCKING BUT I AM VERY WELL. YOU DO NOT SEEM TO HAVE RECEIVE[D] MY TELEGRAM ABOUT JACK [CHURCHILL*]'S HEART ATTACK WHICH HAS CAUSED ME MUCH ANXIETY. HE IS MAKING PROGRESS.... I SEE HIM NEARLY EVERY DAY.
2. THE AMBASSADOR WILL SHOW YOU MY TELEGRAMS WITH STALIN. OUR PERSONAL RELATIONS ARE VERY GOOD AT PRESENT BUT THERE ARE MANY DIFFICULTIES AS YOU WILL SEE. YOU SHOULD EXPRESS TO STALIN PERSONALLY MY CORDIAL FEELINGS AND MY RESOLVE AND CONFIDENCE THAT A COMPLETE UNDERSTANDING BETWEEN THE ENGLISH-SPEAKING WORLD AND RUSSIA WILL BE ACHIEVED AND MAINTAINED FOR MANY YEARS, AS THIS IS THE ONLY HOPE OF THE WORLD. TENDER LOVE.
                                                                        WINSTON

[1] Mussolini had been executed by partisans on 28 April; Hitler shot himself in the bunker of the Chancellery in Berlin on 30 April.
[2] The Foreign Secretary, Anthony Eden, was in San Francisco for the inaugural conference of the United Nations.

○ From CSC   Odessa
[2 May 1945]

WE ARE IN ODESSA AND HAD INTENDED STAYING HERE TWO DAYS, BUT IN ORDER TO SEE MORE
OF OUR PRISONERS OF WAR WE ARE STAYING ON TILL TONIGHT WHEN WE LEAVE FOR MOSCOW ...
THIS IS A LOVELY CITY BUT EVERYWHERE WE SEE THE SAME PAINFUL DESTRUCTION.... WE
HAVE JUST HEARD THAT HITLER IS DEAD.... ALL MY LOVE. CLEMMIE.

○ From WSC   Foreign Office
3 May 1945

GILES [ROMILLY] IS FREE AND SAFE, ALSO JOHNNY DODGE[1] HAS ACTUALLY ARRIVED. [FIELD
MARSHAL] ALEXANDER'S VICTORY RESULTED IN A MILLION GERMANS BEING TAKEN PRISONERS.

[1] Stepson of WSC's cousin, Lionel Guest, son of 1st Baron Wimborne.

○ From WSC   [Foreign Office]
5 May 1945

I HEAR YOU ARE TO ARRIVE AT MOSCOW ON THE 5TH.... THE AMBASSADOR HAS MY AUTHORITY
TO SHOW YOU THE TELEGRAMS ABOUT THE POSITION. YOU SEEM TO HAVE HAD A TRIUMPHANT
TOUR AND I ONLY WISH MATTERS COULD BE SETTLED BETWEEN YOU AND THE RUSSIAN COMMON
PEOPLE. HOWEVER THERE ARE MANY OTHER ASPECTS OF THIS PROBLEM THAN THOSE YOU HAVE
SEEN ON THE SPOT....
2. JACK [CHURCHILL*] IS VERY ILL AND THE NEXT FEW DAYS ARE CRITICAL AND POSSIBLY
DECISIVE.
3. IT IS ASTONISHING ONE IS NOT IN A MORE BUOYANT FRAME OF MIND IN PUBLIC MATTERS.
DURING THE LAST THREE DAYS WE HAVE HEARD OF THE DEATH OF MUSSOLINI AND HITLER;
ALEXANDER HAS TAKEN A MILLION PRISONERS OF WAR; MONTGOMERY* TOOK 500,000 ADDITIONAL
YESTERDAY AND FAR MORE THAN A MILLION TO-DAY; ALL NORTH-WEST GERMANY, HOLLAND AND
DENMARK ARE TO BE SURRENDERED EARLY TOMORROW MORNING WITH ALL TROOPS AND SHIPS,
ETC; THE NEXT DAY NORWAY, AND THE U-BOATS WILL, I BELIEVE, GIVE IN; AND WE ARE ALL
OCCUPIED HERE WITH PREPARATIONS FOR VICTORY-EUROPE DAY. MEANWHILE I NEED SCARCELY
TELL YOU THAT BENEATH THESE TRIUMPHS LIE POISONOUS POLITICS AND DEADY INTERNATIONAL
RIVALRIES. THEREFORE I SHOULD COME HOME AFTER RENDERING THE FULLEST COMPLIMENTS TO
YOUR HOSPITABLE HOSTS. DO NOT DELAY BEYOND THE 7TH OR 8TH EXCEPT FOR WEATHER. ON NO
ACCOUNT LEAVE IN BAD WEATHER....

○ From CSC   Moscow
5 May 1945

HAVE JUST RETURNED TO MOSCOW AND SEEN ALL YOUR TELEGRAMS NONE OF WHICH COULD BE
FORWARDED, SO THAT IT IS ONLY TODAY I KNOW OF JACK'S SERIOUS ILLNESS WHICH GRIEVES
ME VERY MUCH. I AM FULL OF JOY AT THE OVERWHELMING VICTORIES OF ALEXANDER AND
MONTGOMERY. I LONG TO BE WITH YOU, BUT WE HAVE SOME NECESSARY ENGAGEMENTS TO FULFIL
AND SOME LOOSE ENDS TO TIDY UP AFTER WHICH I SHALL JOYFULLY FLY HOME.... IN THE

MIDST OF ALL THIS MILITARY GLORY I KNOW THAT YOU ARE HAVING HARASSING AND SOMETIMES
SAD EXPERIENCES. I WILL TELEGRAPH YOU DAY BY DAY.

On 7 May Clementine and Mabel Johnson received their decorations at the
hand of Mr Shvernik, First Vice-Chairman of the Supreme Soviet of the USSR.

It was anguishing for Clementine to be separated from Winston in these
hours of glory. In Britain, 8 May was celebrated as Victory in Europe (VE)
Day.

○ From CSC   Moscow
8 May 1945

ALL MY THOUGHTS ARE WITH YOU ON THIS SUPREME DAY MY DARLING. IT COULD NOT HAVE
HAPPENED WITHOUT YOU. ALL MY LOVE. CLEMMIE.

On 8 May, at the Embassy in Moscow, Mr Frank Roberts[1] (the Ambassador
being absent) quickly organized a religious service. At luncheon the other
guests were Madame Catroux, the wife of the French Ambassador, and
Monsieur and Madame Herriot:[2] he had just been liberated by Russian troops
from prison in Germany.

[1] Later Sir Frank Roberts (1907–98), GCMG, GCVO. British Minister in Moscow, 1945–7. Deputy
Under-Secretary of State for Foreign Affairs, 1951–4; Ambassador to Yugoslavia, 1954–7, to the
USSR, 1960–2, to Federal Republic of Germany, 1963–8. Wrote *Dealing with Dictators*, 1991.
[2] Edouard Herriot, former Prime Minister of France (see p. 289 n. 2, letter of 10 January 1925).
Openly opposed to the Vichy regime of Pétain, he had remained in France after the capitulation
to help with the Resistance, but was put under house arrest and later deported to Germany. Freed
by Russian troops, April 1945.

○ From CSC   Moscow
8 May 1945

MY DARLING. HERE IN THE BRITISH EMBASSY WE HAVE ALL BEEN LISTENING TO YOUR SOLEMN
WORDS. GOD BLESS YOU. M. HERRIOT IS HERE AND SENDS YOU HIS DEVOTED GREETINGS.
ALLELUIA. ALL MY LOVE. CLEMMIE.

On the evening of 9 May – Victory Day in Russia – Clementine broadcast on
Moscow Radio.

On 11 May she and her companions bade farewell to their hosts, and flew
away in Skymaster for England. Sarah and I went to meet her (I had been
whisked back home from Germany to be with my father on VE+1); Winston,
too, was at Northolt to welcome her home (just in time – Skymaster had to
do one or two delaying circuits before landing!).

Chapter XXIV

BLESSING IN DISGUISE

The Coalition Government resigned on 23 May 1945, and Churchill became Prime Minister again of a (Conservative) Caretaker Government until the results of the impending General Election could be known.

Polling Day was on 5 July, after which a gap of nearly three weeks ensued to allow the gathering in from all over the world of 3 million servicemen's and servicewomen's votes.

During this pause Winston and Clementine, plus myself, went for a short holiday in France. Winston then flew to Potsdam for the Big Three Conference (17 July–2 August).

From WSC[1]   [Potsdam]
15 July 1945

TARGET NO. 25
ARRIVED AFTER BUMPY JOURNEY TO FIND DELICIOUS SUMMER WEATHER, HOTTER THAN HENDAYE.
I HAVE A BEAUTIFUL HOUSE OVERLOOKING A LARGE LAKE AND SURROUNDED ON EVERY SIDE BY
FORESTS. ALTHOUGH WE ARE NO GREAT DISTANCE FROM BERLIN THERE IS NO TRACE OF
DEVASTATION....

                                                    FONDEST LOVE. W.

[1] Public Record Office, Cabinet Papers 120/193.

From WSC[1]   [Potsdam]
18 July 1945

THE FIRST TWO DAYS OF INTENSE HEAT HAVE BEEN FOLLOWED BY GREY SKIES AND A DROP OF
15 DEGREES.
EVERYTHING HAS OPENED WELL SO FAR BUT OF COURSE WE HAVE NOT REACHED ANY OF THE
SERIOUS ISSUES. WE ARE BESIEGED IN OUR IMPENETRABLE COMPOUND BY A HOST OF REPORTERS
WHO ARE FURIOUS AT NOT BEING ABLE TO OVERRUN US. IT IS IMPOSSIBLE TO CONDUCT GRAVE
AFFAIRS EXCEPT IN SILENCE AND SECRECY.
    ... MARY[2] IS A GREAT HELP TO ME. TENDER LOVE. W.

[1] Public Record Office, Cabinet Papers 120/193.
[2] I was acting as his ADC.

He flew home in time to receive the Election results on 26 July. By midday it was clear that it was to be a landslide victory for the Labour Party[1]. At 7 p.m. Churchill went to Buckingham Palace and tendered his resignation to the King. At 7.30 p.m. the King invited Clement Attlee to form a Government.

After the Election the Churchills moved out of No. 10 and the Annexe with all due speed. Chartwell was uninhabitable, and the purchase of 28 Hyde Park Gate not yet completed: Diana and Duncan (Sandys*) lent them their flat in Westminster Gardens.

Meanwhile kind and thoughtful 'Alex'[2] offered them a villa on the shores of Lake Como. Clementine would not leave her task of struggling back into Chartwell, so Sarah went with her father; the party[3] flew out to Italy, in Alex's Dakota, on 2 September.

[1] Final results were: Labour, 393 seats; Conservatives, 213; Liberals, 12. Labour majority, 146. The family candidates – Randolph at Preston, and Duncan Sandys at Streatham – were both defeated. WSC himself had a 17,000 majority at Woodford (Epping re-named) over his one opponent, an Independent: the main political parties had not run candidates against him.
[2] Field Marshal Alexander since 1944 and now Supreme Allied Commander, Mediterranean. (See p. 468 n. 9.)
[3] With them were Lord Moran; WSC's secretary, Elizabeth Layton; Sawyers, his valet; and two detectives.

O From WSC [typewritten]   Lake Como
3 September 1945

My darling Clemmie,
   This is really one of the most pleasant and delectable places I have ever struck. It is a small palace almost entirely constructed of marble inside. It abuts on the lake, with bathing steps reached by a lift. It is of course completely modernized, and must have been finished just before the War, by one of Mussolini's rich commerçants who has fled, ... Every conceivable arrangement has been made for our pleasure and convenience. Sarah and I have magnificent rooms covering a whole floor, with large marble baths and floods of hot and cold water.
   ... Yesterday we motored over the mountains to Lake Lugano, where I found quite a good subject for a picture. I made a good beginning and hope to go back there tomorrow, missing one day. I have spotted another place for this afternoon. These lakeshore subjects run a great risk of degenerating into 'chocolate box', even if successfully executed.
   ✍I have been thinking a lot about you. I do hope you will not let the work of moving into these 2 houses wear you down. Please take plenty of rest.

With fondest love,
Your devoted husband
W

. . .

☐ From CSC   [67 Westminster Gardens
4 September 1945   Marsham Street, London SW1]

My darling Winston,
    On Saturday the day you flew away, I went to Woodford to open a
Vegetable Show held by the local Allotment Holders – It was a gray
uncertain afternoon & I thought of you and Sarah in the windy, rainy,
misty skies – Driving along the road [to the constituency] so familiar for
more than twenty years, I thought how the War had changed it – Many of
the humble but neat little homes were shattered, all were battered &
squalid – In every space, where before had been busy shops & houses,
huge menacing Venereal Disease posters were erected – After passing half
a dozen of these – suddenly I saw a new design – the picture of an insect
(upside down so that you could see his mandibles & count his crawling
feet) magnified to 12 feet and across it written 'Beware the Common Bed
Bug!'
– – –
    Mary's Birthday is on Saturday the 15th – I enclose her address[1]. ...
    My love to Sarah – I do hope her nettle-rash has not only subsided, but
has really vanished so that she can enjoy everything – And I do hope your
painting is fun & does not give you indigestion[2] – I expect you are bathing
too?
    When you see Alex pray give him my respects & admiration –
                                                             Your loving
                                                             Clemmie

[1] Since June, 481 Battery had removed from outside Antwerp to a disused airfield at Wenzendorf,
about 50 miles from Hamburg. Our role was now receiving vehicles of all kinds from military
units no longer requiring them. We were under canvas again.
[2] From too much sitting at an easel. WSC suffered frequently from indigestion.

○ From WSC [typewritten]   Lake Como
5 September 1945

My darling,
    We have had three lovely sunshine days, and I have two large canvases
under way, one of a scene on the Lake of Lugano and the other here at
Como. ...
    Alex arrives tomorrow, and I am looking forward very much to seeing
him. I cannot say too much for the care and authority which he has
bestowed on making my visit pleasant. For instance, I am guarded by the
4th Hussars. 24 men and two officers[1] travelled 400 miles (I blush to say)
from Austria to be my personal protectors here, ...
    ... The men are all picked men, but were very keen to come and are
particularly smart and intelligent. My aide-de-camp Major Ogier – he is
only 24 – is most attentive and tireless in planning painting and bathing
expeditions with picnic lunches. Last night General Heydeman, who
commands the 2nd Military District, came and dined. This house is
nominally his Headquarters, though he has never used it and keeps it for
the Field Marshal. ...

An air of complete tranquillity and good humour pervades these beautiful lakes and valleys, which are unravaged by war. There is not a sign to be seen in the countryside, the dwellings or the demeanour or appearance of the inhabitants which would suggest that any violent events have been happening in the world. I am, of course, immediately recognized, even by a small party of young girls right out in the mountains, and everywhere am clapped and cheered, pressed with demands for autographs and so on. The feeling of the population towards the British Army seems very good, and I understand everything works most smoothly. Of course, however, the Italians are very good at making themselves agreeable. They are a handsome race in these mountains, with a great many fair-haired people, both men and women. The children are well-nourished, and nobody seems to have suffered in any way. The Partisans are frequently to be seen in their half-uniform carrying their weapons. I am told that in this part of the country they were very strong and ardent, and that there were hardly any Germans, so that they were also successful. The people have the air of having won the war (if there was a war), and make the V-sign to me with gusto. All they want is a large influx of tourists to make their happiness and prosperity complete. Meanwhile the place of these is supplied by large British, American, New Zealand and South African leave resorts established in all the hotels for officers and men. On the road near this house is painted a large sign 'American Bar – English spoken'.

It has done me no end of good to come out here and resume my painting. I am much better in myself, and am not worried about anything. We have had no newspapers since I left England, and I no longer feel any keen desire to turn their pages. This is the first time for very many years that I have been completely out of the world. The Japanese War being finished[2] and complete peace and victory achieved, I feel a great sense of relief which grows steadily, others having to face the hideous problems of the aftermath. On their shoulders and consciences weighs the responsibility for what is happening in Germany and Central Europe. It may all indeed be 'a blessing in disguise'[3]. . . .

I long to hear from you how you are progressing on your two fronts, and whether Whitbread[4] is continuing to give you satisfaction, and when the German prisoners are going to come[5]. . . . How are the Beaverbrook chickens[6]? Have they laid any eggs yet? . . . I fear you must be very near the end of the lemon-scented magnolias.

The sun is beginning to gleam fitfully through the clouds, so perhaps we are going to have a painting afternoon.

✍Darling a tiresome thing has happened to me. When I was vy young I ruptured myself & had to wear a truss. I left it off before I went to Harrow & have managed 60 years of rough & tumble. Now however in the last 10 days it has come back. There is no pain, but I have had to be fitted w a truss wh I shall have to wear when not in bed for the rest of my life[7] – Charles [Moran*] got a military surgeon from Rome who flew & has been w us for the last 3 days.

I do hope you are having a good rest & not taking things too seriously. I have still had no letters or papers & have not the slightest idea what is going on –

Always yr loving husband
W
...
Sarah is a joy to <u>all</u>

[1] Maj. John Ogier and Lt (later Capt.) A. D. D. ('Tim') Rogers. Tim became a great friend, and later used to stay with us.
[2] Japan surrendered on 14 August 1945.
[3] These were my mother's somewhat bleak words of comfort to my father with regard to the election result: at the time he had riposted, 'It certainly seems very well disguised!'
[4] Henry Whitbread, who worked for WSC at Chartwell for 18 years, before and after the war, as a general outdoors help; he was one of those who taught him bricklaying. An ex-company sergeant major, and an outspoken socialist, he was much liked and depended upon by WSC.
[5] As in the First World War, many German prisoners worked on farms until their repatriation.
[6] Max Beaverbrook had given WSC/CSC some pullets and a cock to assist Chartwell housekeeping.
[7] In fact WSC was successfully operated on for hernia in June 1947.

☐ From CSC   67 Westminster Gardens
6 September [1945]

My darling Winston & Sarah

No letters yet from either of you, & I expect mine take as long to reach you –

But I am kept informed by the Press that you have painted 2 pictures from the shore of the Lake near your 'three storied villa' & that you sometimes go out in a motor boat & that you drive about in a yellow car, & that your privacy is being respected, & that there are guards round the villa, & that you have had secret meetings with Italian royalists, & that there is no truth in these rumours, & that you sometimes sit on a terrace & talk to your 'Physician Lord Moran' & to your 'daughter Sarah'!

The workmen have begun mending the roof etc of the new house [28 Hyde Park Gate], & the Press (Evening Standard) forced their way in & photographed the rooms & threatened to reveal what you had paid for it[1] [in margin: I can't think how they found out]; but I telephoned & asked them not to publish anything & they desisted –

People seem disappointed but resigned over the slow demobilisation....

Your loving
Clemmie

[1] There was a limit to what could be spent on house repairs.

○ From WSC [typewritten]   Lake Como
8 September 1945

My dearest One,

Alex and his aide-de-camp ... have left us after staying two nights. I hope Alex will come back again next weekend. He certainly enjoyed himself painting, and produced a very good picture considering it is the first time that he has handled a brush for six years. I have now four pictures, three of them large, in an advanced state, and I honestly think they are better than any I have painted so far. I gave Alex your message and he was very pleased.

The painting has been a great pleasure to me, and I have really forgotten all my vexations. It is a wonderful cure, because you really cannot think of anything else. This is Saturday, and it is a week since we started. We have had newspapers up till Wednesday. I have skimmed through them, and it certainly seems we are going to have a pretty hard time. I cannot feel the Government are doing enough about demobilization, still less about getting our trade on the move again. I do not know how we are ever to pay our debts, and it is even difficult to see how we shall pay our way. Even if we were all united in a Coalition, gathering all the strength of the nation, our task might well be beyond our powers. However, all this seems already quite remote from me on this lovely lake, where nearly all the days are full of sunshine and the weather bright and cool.

Much better than the newspapers was your letter, with its amusing but rather macabre account of the journey to Woodford. I am longing to hear how our affairs are progressing. I do hope you are not overtaxing yourself with all the business that there is to do. We shall certainly not forget about Mary's birthday; . . .

Considering how pleasant and delightful the days have been, I cannot say they have passed quickly. It seems quite a long time since I arrived, although every day has been full of interest and occupation. I have converted my enormous bathroom into a studio with makeshift easels, and there all this morning Alex and I tried to put the finishing touches on our pictures of yesterday. . . .

He begged me to stay on here as long as I like, but . . . I expect in another ten or eleven days I shall be very keen to get home again. Sarah has been a great joy, and gets on with everybody. She and I both drive the speed-boats. They are a wonderful way of getting about this lake, and far safer than the awful winding roads around which the Italians career with motorcars and lorries at all sorts of speeds and angles.

Charles [Moran*] plays golf most days. There is a very pretty links here, and he has fierce contests with himself or against Bogey. His devoted care of me is deeply touching. . . .

✍My darling I think a gt deal of you, & last night when I was driving the speed-boat back there came into my mind your singing to me 'In the gloaming' years ago. What a sweet song & tune, & how beautifully you sang it in all its pathos. My heart thrilled w love to feel you near me in thought. I feel so tenderly towards you my darling, & the more pleasant & agreeable the scenes & days, the more I wish you were here to share them & give me a kiss.

You see I have nearly forgotten how to write with a pen. Isn't awful my scribbles?

Miss Layton has heard from her 'boy friend' in S. Africa that she is to go out there ... immediately if possible to marry him. So she is vy happy....

Always yr loving husband

W

...

☐ From CSC   67 Westminster Gardens
11 September 1945

My Darling

I'm so distressed about the truss – I hope it is comfortable & does not worry you. Did you strain yourself or stretch unduly – And will you now be able to do your exercises which are so potent a preventative of indigestion? Please take great care of yourself –

I have big news. Mary is home from Germany for good & has applied for a posting in London or near-by....

I'm so happy to see from your letter that you are enjoying the beauty of the Lakes & the comforts & elegance of the Villa – I have had a most amusing letter from Sarah describing her apricot coloured & mirrored bathroom –

Work is progressing rather slowly but I hope surely on the Chartwell & London fronts – Whitbread is industrious & thorough & smiling – Max [Beaverbrook*]'s hens are beautiful & have laid a few (a very few) eggs, of exquisite flavour but of diminutive size – about the size of a pigeon's egg.... But Moppet [Whyte*] says they will get bigger & more numerous presently –

No German prisoners yet till after the Harvest. It will be lovely when the lake Camouflage is gone & also the barbed wire....

I must hurry because your mail is just off. I'm sending 2 bottles of brandy as requested. I hope they are the right sort?...

Your loving
Clemmie

...

○ From WSC [typewritten]   Lake Como
18 September 1945

My darling One,

I hope you will not mind my change of plans. The weather has been so good and the prospects seem so favourable that the opportunity of having another four or five days in the sunshine was too tempting to miss. Alexander was delighted that his plane should carry Moran* and Sarah home and return for me....

I really have enjoyed these 18 days enormously. I have been completely absorbed by the painting, and have thrown myself into it till I was quite tired. I have therefore not had time to fret or worry, and it has been good to view things from a distance. I think you will be pleased with the series of pictures, eight in all, [🖉above line:] (now nine!) which I have painted. I am sending them home by Sarah, who will give you all our news. I hope you will be able to keep them in their packet till I come, for I am so much looking forward to showing them to you and Mary one by one myself. If of course you cannot bear it, I shall forgive you. I am sure you will consider they are a great advance, particularly the later ones. I am confident that with a few more months of regular practice, I shall be able to paint far better than I have ever painted before....

Montag[1] has just left, having been with us four days. He was most helpful in his comments. I do not entirely agree with his style, and when he paints himself it is disappointing, but he has a vast knowledge and one cannot paint in his presence without learning....

I have made great friends with these two young officers of the 4th Hussars. The Lieutenant, Tim [Rogers], is a great character, a Southern Irishman and devoted to horses.[2] He will scout on ahead of us on each stage of our journey and find a sleeping-place.[3] We shall come along behind, and stop off at any scene that catches my fancy. My party is now very small. I only have Sawyers[4] and Sergeant Davies [detective]. We are all men, so it will not be difficult for us to fend for ourselves along the route. We have every facility in the way of cars....

🖉Sarah has been a joy. She is so thoughtful, tactful, amusing & gay. The stay here wd have been wrecked without her.

Ever yr loving husband,
W

...

[1] Charles Montag (1880–1956). Swiss-born painter and art connoisseur who lived mostly in Paris, arranging exhibitions of French art and advising individual collectors. WSC met him in 1915, and over the years Montag often accompanied WSC on painting holidays and advised him in letters. Their friendship lasted until his death in 1956.
[2] His father and he, in succession, owned the famous Airlie Stud near Dublin. When WSC took up racing Tim was of great assistance.
[3] WSC planned to drive with a now much reduced party along the Riviera from Genoa to Cannes, painting en route, before returning home.
[4] Frank Sawyers, WSC's butler/valet, 1939–46. He went everywhere with WSC during the war, and despite a somewhat timid appearance was very stalwart under all the untoward circumstances in which he found himself. He looked after WSC with nanny-like care and devotion, and was awarded the Defence Medal in WSC's Resignation Honours List, August 1945.

□ From CSC   67 Westminster Gardens
Friday 21 September 1945

My darling Winston
    It was lovely seeing Sarah looking so brown & well; but I am glad you prolonged your holiday & are driving slowly along that coast you love so well – I'm pining to see the pictures but am resisting the temptation of peeping before you arrive....

Mary has ... got a job in London demobilising A.T.S. She went to it two days ago but can visit us in the evenings....

Your loving
Clemmie

O From WSC [typewritten]   Villa Sous le Vent
24 September 1945   Antibes[1]

My darling,

Here is some account of my doings.

We motored [from Como] in four hours to Genoa through lovely country with a particularly striking view of Pavia over the Ticino River and arrived after dark to find the local British colonel in charge of the district installed in the marble palace which belonged to Pirelli[2].... There it stands on a rocky bluff overlooking the sea and the bathing place where I got a beautiful clear water of the palest green to try to paint. I worked hard for two days at the illusion of transparency and you shall judge when you see the result how far I have succeeded.

The weather was delightful and it seemed to me very foolish to go home on the 24th. We, therefore, sent Tim Rogers (Lt.) and Major John Ogier on ahead to reconnoitre the neutral State of Monaco. Their report was highly pleasing and the manager of the hotel which is only half full was delighted to receive us on reasonable terms.... Every important bridge over the valleys leading down to the sea has been smashed to pieces by bombing or naval artillery and all kinds of deviations had to be made. Nevertheless in five hours we came through and arrived in the lap of luxury at Monte Carlo. The square in front of the hotel and the Casino is very empty and dead looking but the Monégasques gathered in crowds and welcomed me on every occasion with the greatest fervour. We had our meals on the veranda facing the Casino but I did not transgress the 80 paces which separated me from that unsinkable institution....

General Eisenhower sent his aide-de-camp to see me on arrival, asking me to come on to his villa at Antibes which was vacant and fully staffed. I therefore moved in here after two days at Monte Carlo. My two young officers and I are now in this beautiful place surrounded by every comfort and assistance. In four or five days I propose to return to Monte Carlo and to stay there until the 5th or 6th of October when I shall be back to have a few shadow Cabinet meetings[3] and settle the policy of the opposition before Parliament meets....

When Alex returns home at the end of this month he and Margaret should be invited to lunch with us in the new house. After lunch we will show him the Como pictures together with the new series now developing on the Riviera. He is most anxious to see them. I had his own picture varnished and framed and sent to GHQ. It is quite good and he thoroughly enjoyed the hours spent upon it.

I have all this batch of newspapers now up to the 21st and am wading through them.... I was sure there would be a complete deadlock at the Foreign Ministers' conference[4], but I hardly expected the Russians to come out so boldly with a demand for one or more of the African colonies of the Italians in the Mediterranean for a naval and air base.... I do not myself see any serious objections to their having these places if they will be reasonable in other directions.... However, I have no doubt that these demands will cause a great stir. The Bolshevization of the Balkans proceeds apace and all the cabinets of Central, Eastern and Southern Europe are in Soviet control, excepting only Athens. This brand I snatched from the burning on Christmas day [1944]. The failure of the conference will, of course, have bad results. The Russians have no need of agreement & time is on their side because they simply consolidate themselves in all these countries they now have in their grasp. I regard the future as full of darkness and menace. Horrible things must be happening to millions of Germans hunted out of Poland and Czecho-Slovakia into the British and American occupied zones. Very little is known as to what is happening behind the Russian iron curtain, but evidently the Poles and Czecho-Slovakians are being as badly treated as one could have expected....

There will be no lack of topics to discuss when we [his party colleagues] all come together again. Meanwhile, this rest and change of interest is doing me no end of good and I never sleep now in the middle of the day. Even when the nights are no longer than 5, 6 or 7 hours, I do not seem to require it. This shows more than anything else what a load has been lifted off my shoulders....

With tender love
Your devoted
W

...

[1] General Eisenhower's villa.
[2] Giovanni Pirelli (1848–1932) or one of his two sons; he was founder of the Italian tyre manufacturing firm.
[3] WSC was now Leader of the Opposition.
[4] The Allied Powers Council of Foreign Ministers (UK, USA, USSR, France and China), meeting in London, 11 September–2 October 1945.

On Winston's return to England in the first week of October, 28 Hyde Park Gate was ready to receive him: it was to be their London home for the rest of his life. They moved back into Chartwell (suitably re-arranged to meet lean post-wartime conditions) during the late autumn.

In December Sarah was demobilized from the WAAF; she and Vic Oliver had been divorced the previous March, and she now resumed her acting career. Randolph and Pamela were divorced in December 1945.

Nineteen-forty-six was apparently a letterless year, the Churchills travelling and holidaying together.

In November 1946 Chartwell was bought by a group of anonymous donors[1] and presented to the National Trust, with the proviso that Winston and Clementine could remain there for their lifetimes.

In 1946–7 Winston acquired Chartwell Farm (in the valley) and Parkside Farm, both marching with Chartwell; he also purchased Bardogs Farm at Toys

Hill, and a market garden at French Street, in the near neighbourhood: he now farmed about 500 acres in all.

Mary was demobilized in April 1946, and on 11 February 1947 married Christopher Soames*.

On 23 February, Jack Churchill*, Winston's beloved only brother, died aged sixty-seven. (His wife Goonie had died in 1941.)

[1] It was Lord Camrose (see p. 529 n. 4), so long a friend and counsellor, who, horrified to learn that WSC was contemplating selling Chartwell because of the expense of running it, assembled a group of friends and admirers who made this munificent and imaginative project possible. Much later the names of these benefactors became known, and are recorded on a plaque at Chartwell.

☐ From CSC   Hôtel du Pavillon[1]
11 August [1947]   Auray [near Morbihan, Brittany]

My darling Winston

This brings you all my love – I see from the French newspapers that you have been attacking the Government –

The weather is perfect, the beds comfortable, the food delicious the sanitary arrangements deplorable! & no hot water except a trickle at 7 in the morning. The country wild & beautiful – The hotels (few & far between) packed 3 or 4 in a room....

... Yesterday we went to Lorient & in the distance saw the German submarine pens, 15 of them visible from where we stood on a bridge –

[Le] Havre has been knocked end-ways, & on our road to Rennes we saw Lisieux, Falaise & numerous villages much destroyed....

Your loving
Clemmie

I wish I were feeling stronger as I should then enjoy this 10 times more.

[1] CSC was on a motoring holiday in France with Sylvia Henley (see Biographical Notes) and some of her family.

○ From WSC   Chartwell
11 August 1947

My darling One,

...

When I got back from the House on Friday I found a field being cut, & so joined Christopher [Soames*][1] with my gun. In one minute I shot 1 rabbit with one shot – the first I have fired for nine years! I am off now to supervise the tidying up of Bardogs. Never did so small a farm harbour such masses of manure. The weather is lovely & I hate to be drawn to town....

Mr Graebner[2] & Mrs Longwell of Life & Times [Time-Life] were here for lunch yesterday (Sunday). They brought as goodwill offerings Cigars, Brandy, a Meisner ham & lot of chocolate for you. We did a great deal of business. I work all day & night at the book with Bill D.[3] and it is bounding ahead. I must get the decks cleared for the coming [parliamentary] battle.

My darling I do hope you are enjoying yrself in sunshine & are bathing & basking. 'Cast care aside'[4]. What we may have to face cannot be worse than all we have crashed through together. I send you my fondest love. You are ever in my thoughts.

Yr devoted loving
W.
. . .

[1] My husband, having been invalided out of the Army, took on the management of WSC's farms. We lived in the charming farmhouse by the farmyard for the first ten years of our married life.
[2] Walter Graebner, London representative of *Time-Life*. Henry Luce, the owner of *Life*, had bought the serial rights for WSC's war memoirs in the United States; serialization began in April 1948. Author of *My Dear Mister Churchill*, 1965.
[3] Bill Deakin (see p. 423 n. 3) had returned, a seasoned warrior after his life with Tito and the Partisans, to resume helping WSC – now as head of the team assisting with his war memoirs.
[4] From one of his favourite hymns, 'Fight the good fight'.

☐ From CSC   [Auray]
12 August 1947

My darling Winston
    The weather is lovely here & my travelling companions are very agreeable – Sylvia Henley* you know, tho' not so well as Venetia [Montagu*] – Her daughter Rosalind[1] is now a charming woman of 40.... The party is completed by her son Anthony, a nice boy of 15 for whose birthday I have given My Early Life which you inscribed for him before I left –
    Rosalind is a Doctor of Science & is with a team of other learned birds (mostly male) employed by the Privy Council on Research Work –
    They are now trying to find the cure for 'the Common Cold' so far without result – She works in a big Laboratory at Hampstead & lives next door to it. She knows a good deal about Doctor Nunn May[2], the Communist who is serving ten years for giving 'Atom' secrets to the Russians – She says he never should have been employed by the Government as he made no secret of his views that all scientific secrets should be shared – even in war time! – by all mankind –
    We are now off to Quiberon Bay. I feel stronger. A month of this would set me up for the rest of my life.

Tender Love
from your poor old
Clemmie

[1] Dr Rosalind Pitt-Rivers (1907–90); FRS, 1954.
[2] Dr Alan Nunn May (1912–), nuclear physicist and spy, convicted in Montreal, 1946, of passing atomic secrets and material to the Russians in 1943, and jailed for ten years.

☐ From WSC [typewritten]   Chartwell
13 August 1947

My darling One,
    We had a flare-up about the Government's demanding a blank

cheque.... I propose to broadcast Saturday night, in a tone of which you will, I think, approve.

It is delicious here. I have just been bathing with Mary and Christopher [Soames*] and Julian [Sandys, aged eleven]. Six new cows have arrived which Christopher bought. They look very fine....

Bennie [Westminster*] and his new wife[1] came down here yesterday and spent the whole afternoon going round the farm. She is charming and he as sunlit as ever. They were very disappointed you were not here....

Everything here is pretty grim and poor little Attlee is hard-pressed. I have no feelings of unfriendliness towards him. Aneurin Bevan[2] is making the running to gain power by extreme left-wing politics. If this proves true, we must certainly expect a political crisis, in addition to the economic collapse, which is worse than ever, and for which the Government have no plan....

The harvest is proceeding with tremendous vigour and in perfect weather. Most of the fields are already cut and stooked and some have been put up on tripods. Christopher is very good and at it all day long. The lettuces in the walled garden were sold for £200, though they cost only £50 to grow. Thus it may be that the garden will pay its expenses and even be a contributor to the farm.... The hot-houses are dripping with long cucumbers. The grapes are turning black and a continuous stream of peaches and nectarines go to London. I have one a day myself – 'le droit du seigneur'....

The Mule [Sarah] has promised to come and stay with me for a day or two. I expect her Hollywood plans will have come to an end through the Government tax on American films. It seems to have been done in the worst possible way – so as to cause the utmost irritation in America and procure a minimum dollar relief for the British nation. They really are awful fools....

Darling I have <u>just</u> heard (Aug 13) that you are returning 17th instead of 25th. How lovely!... You will find everything bright & happy here.

Always yr devoted
W
...

[1] The Duke of Westminster ('Bendor') had recently married his fourth wife, Anne Sullivan, who gave him great happiness until his death in 1953.
[2] Aneurin ('Nye') Bevan (1897–1960), son of a Welsh miner. Labour MP from 1929. As Minister of Health 1945–51, inaugurated the National Health Service. Later chief Labour spokesman on foreign affairs and deputy leader of Labour Party.

In mid-December 1947 Winston went to Marrakech[1] for a month to combine concentrated book work with painting; he took Sarah with him. Clementine stayed at home and spent Christmas with Christopher and me at the farm.

[1] Draconian currency regulations were in force, and WSC and his party, on this and other book-writing occasions, were the guests of his publishers, Time-Life International, and the *New York Times*: thus no breach of British currency regulations was involved.

○ From WSC [typewritten]   Hôtel de la Mamounia
12 December 1947   Marrakech

My darling One,
Sarah will have told you of our festivities in Paris[1]. There is genuine
sorrow at Duff [Cooper*]'s departure and certainly there will be a sense of
inadequacy in his successor....
The flight was perfect in every way and we have been welcomed here
in a suitable fashion by the French authorities. The weather is cold out of
the sun, but the sunlight is brilliant and warm. I shall have to take much
care about not catching cold....
I painted this afternoon for a couple of hours from the roof of the hotel
where there are two or three lovely views and I do not expect to move
beyond the precincts for several days. Sarah and Bill [Deakin] have made
excursions in the town and in the Arab quarters.... Judging from the first
start I have made to-day, I think I am going to paint better than I have
done before. The days are very short however, for the effect does not
come on till 2.30 and it is dusk and chilly at 5.... The Atlas are
magnificent and as glorious as ever in the evening light.
The Moroccans are enjoying the experience of voting for the first time,
but it is clearly understood that the military government is supreme.
England and politics seem very distant here. I continue to be depressed
about the future. I really do not see how our poor island is going to earn
its living when there are so many difficulties around us and so much ill-
will and division at home. However I hope to blot this all out of my mind
for a few weeks....
✍Tender love my dearest Clemmie. I do hope you will be peaceful &
happy, and will often think of yr ever loving

W
...

[1] They travelled to Marrakech via Paris, where they attended Duff and Diana Cooper's farewell
party: he had been Ambassador at Paris since 1944. He was succeeded by Sir Oliver Harvey, a
career diplomat (p. 563 n. 1).

□ From CSC   28 Hyde Park Gate
16 December 1947

My darling Winston
I am happy that the Sun is shining with you – Here we are muffled in
drizzle & mist, <u>but</u> it is quite warm & muggy. Whereas I am nervous about
the sharp cold which comes from the Atlas – I remember the delicious air
(like champagne) & I feel it will do you good <u>if only</u> you don't catch cold.
Please take great pains not to. The only part of your time table which
matters is the time you come in – Ought not that to be about four
o'clock?...
I dined with the young Birkenheads[1] to meet Mr Marshall[2]. It was a
really delightful party. I sat between 'General' Marshall & Lord Camrose, &

the others were Lady Camrose, Oliver Stanley[3], Bob Laycock[4] & his lovely 'Angie', and Patricia Sherwood, another daughter of Lord & Lady Camrose.

The Conference[5] had ended in dismal failure half-an-hour before but Mr Marshall did not refer to it once. He talked much about you & President Roosevelt* with whom it seems he often disagreed & whom he sometimes did not consult – He said that he – the President – would direct his mind like a shaft of light over one section of the whole subject to be considered, leaving everything else in outer darkness – He did not like his attention being called to aspects which he had not mastered or which from lack of time or indolence or disinclination he had disregarded – Mind you he did not actually use these words, but the gist & I thought much more were implied.

The House of Commons was thoughtful, sad and respectful about Mr Baldwin[6] – Gallacher[7] shewed real feeling. It would seem that even Communists have bowels of compassion. . . .

Yesterday I went to have tea with little Winston [now seven] – He is charming with his Mama, & I spent a happy hour in Pamela's flat. . . . In the New Year I am taking Winston to see Treasure Island. . . .

Mary & Christopher [Soames*] have invited me to stay with them for Christmas, and on the Saturday we are inviting all the children on the Chartwell Estate (there are 23 children) and their mothers to tea & a conjuror – I fear you will not be able to toil through this long letter in my not always clear handwriting, but let Sarah read it aloud to you.

Your loving Clemmie

. . .

[1] Frederick Winston Smith, 2nd Earl of Birkenhead (1907–75) and his wife Sheila (born Berry, daughter of 1st Viscount Camrose).
[2] General George Marshall, initiator of the Marshall Plan, 1947 (see p. 484 n. 4).
[3] Oliver Stanley (1890–1950). Conservative MP, 1924–45. Held various government appointments before and during Second World War.
[4] Maj.-Gen. (later Sir) Robert Laycock (1907–68), KCMG, CB, DSO. A brilliant and attractive soldier. Chief of Combined Operations, 1943–7; Col. Commandant, Special Air Service, from 1960; Governor and C.-in-C. Malta, 1954–9. Married, 1935, Angela Dudley Ward, daughter of Freda Dudley Ward (see p. 227 n. 2).
[5] The London Conference of Powers on Germany, which had opened on 25 November, broke down on 16 December due to the USSR's demands for reparations.
[6] Earl Baldwin of Bewdley (see p. 263 n. 2) died on 14 December 1947.
[7] William Gallacher, who had opposed WSC at Dundee in 1922 (see p. 265 n. 3).

O From WSC [typewritten]
18 December 1947

Hôtel de la Mamounia
Marrakech

My darling Clemmie,

We have been here a week today. The weather is lovely and increasingly warm. . . . At 10 o'clock in the morning it is possible to lie in bed, as I am doing now, with the French windows wide open on to the balcony. I have been working very hard, rather too hard, in fact. My routine is: Wake about 8 a.m., work at Book till 12.30, lunch at one, paint from 2.30 till 5, when it is cold and dusk, sleep from 6 p.m. till 7.30, dine at 8, Oklahoma[1] with the Mule – who was given a credit of £28 and has been completely stripped (I have given her another credit, but she says she will not accept it). At 10 or 11 p.m. again work on Book. Here I have been rather naughty; the hours of going to bed have been one o'clock, two, three, three, three, two, but an immense amount has been done and Book II is practically finished. I am not going to sit up so late in the future.

The painting has not gone badly but I only have these two and a half short hours of good light. Three daubs are on the way.

We have followed exactly the same routine each day, but I think we shall go for a picnic on Saturday. Yesterday the Comte d'Hauteville and his wife (he is the Colonel commanding the whole of this district with both military and civil powers) came to luncheon with us. They are persons of quality.... We are going to lunch with them on Sunday. Tonight we dine with the Glaoui[2]. He is the same age as me. He has sent large crates of grapefruit, oranges, and mandarins, and enormous jars of butter, jam, and honey, and a basket of dates.... I have invited Mrs Deakin[3] to come on here for Christmas as this will enable me to keep Bill till at least the New Year....

They are very attentive in the Hotel; the only fault has been the bathwater not being hot, but this is being attended to. The food and wine are beyond criticism. Generally I am much settled down and very glad to be here, and to feel that I have a good long spell ahead of me, away from the distractions of British politics, and the sense of gathering gloom in our affairs which oppresses me.

... ✍Do tell me about Chartwell. Dictate me a Chartwell Bulletin, with a supplement by Christopher [Soames*]. I hope you are getting all you want done (Have mercy!), ...

Tender love my dearest Clemmie & every wish that my heart can signal for yr health, peace & happiness.

Always yr devoted husband

W

...

[1] An American card game (akin to gin rummy) much enjoyed at this time by the Churchill family and guests.
[2] El Hadji T'hami El Glaoui, paramount Pasha of Marrakech (see p. 411 n. 2).
[3] 'Pussy' Deakin, wife of Bill Deakin, WSC's chief research assistant.

O From WSC [typewritten]   Hôtel de la Mamounia
24 December 1947   Marrakech

My darling Clemmie,
    The weather continues to be cloudless and lovely. The air is cold, and in the shade or when the sun goes down it is biting. I am very careful to wrap up warmly and never paint after 5 o'clock. I have five [✍above line: six now] pictures on the stocks. They are really much better, easier, looser, and more accomplished than those I painted twelve years ago[1] (which I also have with me). I think you will be interested in them....

    ... The progress I have made [war memoirs] is immense. Book I is practically finished and so is Book II [of Volume I]. I believe they will cease to be burdens on me except for minor corrections by the end of the year. It would have been quite impossible for me to do this work if I had not buried myself here, where every prospect pleases, and only the twenty-four hours are too short. As I have often told you, I do not need rest, but change is a great refreshment.

I am so glad you had such an interesting dinner to meet General Marshall. I think we have made good friends with him. I have long had a great respect for his really outstanding qualities, if not as a strategist, as an organiser of armies, a statesman, and above all a man. Cripps[2] seems to me to be taking a far more responsible view of his duties than his predecessor, the dirty Doctor[3], did, and his speech about the Royal Grants[4] was courageous and dignified. I do not think the Debate has done any harm. All will be forgotten, and they will get their £5,000 a year extra....

With fondest love, my sweet & darling Clemmie
Your ever devoted husband
W
...

[1] On his first visit to Marrakech in 1935–6.
[2] Sir Stafford Cripps (see p. 441 n. 2), had succeeded Dr Hugh Dalton as Chancellor of the Exchequer on 13 November 1947.
[3] Dr Hugh Dalton, later Baron Dalton (1887–1962). Chancellor of the Exchequer, 1945–7. Resigned following a pre-Budget disclosure to a lobby correspondent.
[4] The Civil List. Following the marriage of Princess Elizabeth to Lt Philip Mountbatten RN, Duke of Edinburgh, in November, Sir Stafford Cripps had on 17 December proposed in the House of Commons that £25,000 be added to the Civil List. An amendment to reduce this by £5,000 was defeated.

☐ From CSC   Chartwell Farm
Boxing Day 26 December [1947]

My Darling

Here I am most hospitably entertained by Mary & Christopher [Soames*] in their comfortable & pleasant farm house.

We spent a happy & peaceful Christmas Day & we drank your health & Sarah's before we fell to on the fat turkey....

... Last Tuesday I took Edwina & Julian [Sandys] to the Big Circus at Olympia & they loved it. It was Edwina's 9th birthday. She is a very pretty little girl & may be a 'Beauty' one day I think. Diana came too & we really had a delightful afternoon.

Your second letter came two days ago; & it makes me happy to feel that your paws are buttered – Everybody here is sneezing & coughing & I am indeed glad you are having these few weeks' respite from the English Winter....

Your loving
Clemmie
...

Despite Winston's protestations that he was wrapping up warmly and never painting after 5 o'clock (rather too late – the icy cold from the Atlas mountains bites like a wolf), he did catch cold, and developed bronchitis in the New Year. Lord Moran* flew out, as did Clementine on 3 January. Happily, however, Winston soon recovered.

○ From WSC   [Chartwell]
15 June 1948

Darling
    You did promise Sept 12 1908 'To Love, Honour, & <u>Obey</u>.'
    NOW herewith are <u>Orders</u>
    5.15   You come up here to <u>rest</u>. E.Y.H. [car registration letters] will
            bring you & is waiting
    7.30   Dinner
    8.30   Journey to 28 [Hyde Park Gate]
    9.40   Bed & a <u>read</u>.
                                                    Given at Chartwell G.H.Q.
The Tyrant

○ From WSC ✉   La Cröe[1]
12 September 1948   Cap d'Antibes

My Beloved,
    I send this token, but how little can it express my gratitude to you for making my life & any work I have done possible, and for giving me so much happiness in a world of accident & storm.
                                                    Your ever loving and devoted
                                                                            husband
                                                                                W
                                                                               . . .

[1] On their 40th wedding anniversary WSC and CSC were staying with the Duke and Duchess of Windsor.

This next memorandum was written by Clementine in her capacity as Chairman of the Chartwell Literary Trust[1].

[1] The Chartwell Literary Trust was set up by WSC to benefit his children and grandchildren from the proceeds of his war memoirs. CSC was Chairman, with the 'Prof' (now Lord Cherwell) and Brendan Bracken as co-trustees.

□ From CSC [typewritten]
5 October 1948

W.S.C. from C.S.C.

I would like to discuss with you the plan for the Chartwell Literary Trust to buy Randolph a house.

Randolph and I have seen four houses. The first was extremely suitable and slipped through our fingers because we made too low an offer. . . .

Of the three remaining houses only one is good value and therefore a suitable investment for the Trust. At first I thought it too big for Randolph until he explained to me that he intends to marry again, and also that he would like to have room to put up little Winston. If we take Randolph's possible remarriage into consideration we must also suppose that there might be a baby. . . . May I tell the Prof [Lindemann*, now Lord Cherwell] and Brendan [Bracken*] that you approve of my negotiating for this house?[1]

---

[1] 12 Catherine Place, Westminster, London SW1, where June and Randolph lived for some time.

On 2 November, Randolph married a most beautiful girl, June Osborne[1]. At the end of October 1949 their only child, Arabella, was born.

Just before the New Year of 1949 Winston and Clementine and Sarah went to the Hôtel de Paris in Monte Carlo for about a fortnight. Sarah at this time was deeply in love with Antony Beauchamp[2], who was invited to join the party. Neither of her parents 'took' to Antony, although Clementine then – and later – tried to come to like him; but from the first Winston was resolutely hostile. Clementine's rather bleak note reflects the strain and embarrassment of the visit.

---

[2] June Osborne (1922–80), daughter of Col. Rex Osborne, DSO, MC, of Malmesbury, Wiltshire. Randolph and June were divorced in 1961. On 17 June 1980 June took her own life: she had inoperable and terminal cancer.

[2] Antony Beauchamp (1918–57), son of Florence Entwistle, the photographer 'Vivienne'; changed his name on embarking on his own career as a society photographer. In Second World War was a war artist/photographer and was with the 14th Army in Burma. He and Sarah married in October 1949. Their marriage soon ran into difficulty.

□ From CSC ✉   Hôtel de Paris
[undated, early January 1949]   Monte Carlo

Winston

Our party does not seem to be going very well & I wonder if there is any way of resolving the situation –

Antony Beauchamp arrived last Sunday [2 January] and Sarah would feel embarrassed to ask him to leave us until he has been here a week.

I myself am finding the atmosphere of Monte Carlo sad and depressing & would like to go home, leaving say Sunday – or Saturday [9 or 8 January].

Sarah would be glad & willing to bear you company until you travel home next Wednesday [12 January][1] –

Clemmie

[1] In fact they all seem to have travelled home together.

The next two letters are classic examples of how Clementine, when she wanted to make a special point with Winston, often committed her arguments to paper even if they might be under the same roof.

There was restiveness in Conservative Party circles at this time on various matters, including suspicion concerning Churchill's frequent consultation with Lord Beaverbrook* on political policy. Winston and Clementine planned a visit in the spring of 1949 to the United States, where he had important speaking engagements. Max Beaverbrook had invited us all to fly on to Jamaica to stay with him at his house near Montego Bay.

☐ From CSC ⊠   28 Hyde Park Gate
5 March 1949
My Darling
   I am so unhappy over Jamaica & I must seem to you, and I fear to Mary & Christopher, as a spoil-sport. But as I said to you in my letter yesterday (which I tore up perhaps before you had time to assimilate it) I feel that for you, at this moment of doubt and discouragement among your followers, to stay with Max [Beaverbrook*] will increase that doubt & discouragement. It would seem cynical and an insult to the Party –
   You often tease me and call me 'pink' but believe me I feel it very much. I do not mind if you resign the Leadership when things are good, but I can't bear you to be accepted murmuringly and uneasily – In my humble way I have tried to help – the political luncheons here, visits to Woodford, attending to your Constituency correspondence – But now & then I have felt chilled & discouraged by the creeping knowledge that you do only just as much as will keep you in Power. But that much is not enough in these hard anxious times –
   My Darling – Please take Mary with you to America – It would give her such joy and I think it's most important for her & Christopher to be together & to share every possible experience while they are young and passionate –
   I still hope that you may decide against Jamaica, but I cannot venture to persuade you. I only know, that feeling as I do, it would be wrong for me to go.

Your loving
Clemmie

Winston heeded Clementine's views, and excused himself on the grounds that he really could not absent himself so long from the home scene.

We all travelled out on the *Queen Elizabeth* on 18 March. Winston made a speech in New York and, going on to Washington, saw President Truman.

Churchill was to address the Massachusetts Institute of Technology (MIT) in Boston on 1 April, where the President had intended to be present; however, because of unforeseen circumstances he was prevented from attending. Winston therefore decided to return to New York immediately after his speech instead of staying on for a second day, as he had been invited (and had accepted) to do. Clementine and Randolph, who were with him, sent him this joint memorandum: again, Winston heeded advice, and carried out the programme that had been arranged.

□ From CSC/RSC ⊠   [Boston, Mass.]
[undated, before 1 April 1949][1]

We hope you do not mind us making the following point. When President Truman ran out of coming here you could perfectly well have decided not to remain for the second day. Very handsomely, however, you said you would go through with the original plan, so as to help to make it a success, and incidentally to show that your own plans were in no way dependent on President Truman.

Having decided to stay, surely you must go through with the programme as planned, even though it is very tiresome? Enormous pains have been taken about the banquet to-morrow night, and it seems that the early hour was inevitable. The country has been combed for the finest food and wines, and we are both sure that it will not be as bad when it happens as it seems in advance.

If you were not to go it would spoil the whole show....

[1] Original letter unseen by Editor. Quoted from Martin Gilbert, *Winston S. Churchill*, vol. VIII, *Never Despair*, 1988, p. 465.

A General Election was due at some time in 1950, but the Churchills' winter holiday in Madeira was abruptly curtailed by the announcement on 11 January of the Dissolution of Parliament prior to the Election, which would take place on 23 February. As Leader of the Opposition, Churchill returned at once to England, by flying-boat. Clementine, however, stayed on for a short while, arriving home by sea on 20 January.

○ From WSC [typewritten] ⊠   Chartwell
19 January 1950

My Darling,

Welcome home! And what a pack of toil and trouble awaits you! I have not thought of anything in the week since I returned except politics, particularly the Tory Manifesto on which we have had prolonged discussions. One day we were nine hours in the dining room of No. 28.

The Socialists are forcing the Election on to the most materialist lines. All bold treatment of topics in the public interest is very dangerous. The Liberals are running over four hundred candidates, of which at the outside seven will be elected, apart from the sixty others who are working with us.

The Gallup Polls I showed you on the diagram have taken a big dip. Instead of being nine points ahead we are only three. This I think is due to Christmas and the fact that none of the evils of Devaluation[1] have really manifested themselves yet and are only on the way. How many seats the Liberal 'splits' will cause us cannot be measured. All is in the unknown. However there would be no fun in life if we knew the end at the beginning....

I have an immense programme but not more than I can carry....

You will like to see Randolph's admirable opening speech[2]. They now say that Foot[3] is going to bolt to a safer seat. [He didn't.] Randolph is coming for the weekend. June is staying in the constituency to electioneer with Arabella [aged eighteen months].

I was grieved to learn this morning from Christopher [Soames*] that he has a duodenal ulcer[4].... The doctor hopes he will be able to fight. If not, Mary will have to fill the gap.

I am so glad your voyage home was comfortable, but it would have been disastrous if I had not been on the spot here during this difficult week when so many grave decisions had to be taken, not of what to <u>do</u> – that would be easy – but of what to <u>say</u> to our poor and puzzled people. I am much depressed about the country because for whoever wins there will be nothing but bitterness and strife, like men fighting savagely on a small raft which is breaking up. 'May God save you all' is my prayer[5].

Come home & kiss me
Your ever loving
W

. . .

[1] The Labour Government had devalued the pound on 18 September 1949.
[2] Randolph had been adopted as Conservative and Liberal-National candidate for the Labour-held Plymouth (Devonport) constituency.
[3] Michael Foot (1913–), journalist and politician. Labour MP Plymouth (Devonport), 1945–55; Ebbw Vale, 1960–83. Various ministerial appointments; Leader of Opposition, 1980–3. A mercurial left-winger; he and Randolph had worked together on the *Evening Standard* and were on good (if combative) terms, and were to remain friends always.
[4] Christopher had been adopted as Conservative candidate for Bedford constituency, where the Labour member had a small majority. He recovered enough to be able to fight and win the seat back for the Conservatives with a majority of 2,000. He held the seat until 1966.
[5] The 1950 General Election results were: Labour, 315; Conservatives, 298; Liberals, 9; others, 3: an effective Labour majority of 5 (discounting the Speaker).

Clementine, with her secretary Penelope Hampden-Wall[1] as a companion, went for a springtime tour in Italy.

[1] Penelope Hampden-Wall was CSC's secretary from 1948 to January 1951.

○ From WSC   28 Hyde Park Gate
18 April 1950

My darling One,

Randolph, June & little W came for the night. All passed off well, but
there is evident tension. She never looked prettier, but is on the verge of
tears: R I thought seemed 'masterful'. However I think they mean to have
another try.

I am so sorry that you have had disappointing weather. I do hope you
have enjoyed the change of scene & the relief of household cares, & that
you will come back refreshed. I have passed a peaceful ten days at the
Chart, & plunged deeply into my task of finishing Vol. IV.... I never had a
chance to squeeze a tube to any purpose. Mary & Christopher [Soames*]
were a blessing and often came to meals. The days flashed away, & now
here I am back in 28 [Hyde Park Gate] w the Budget opening upon us,
and crisis prowling round the corner, and the Primrose League[1] & [Royal]
Academy Dinner hanging like vultures overhead.

I have thought much about you my sweet darling and it will be a joy to
have you back. Your flowers are growing beautifully on the Chartwell
balcony [terrace] & here the cherry tree is a mass of blossom. All yr
arrangements have worked perfectly in yr absence and no one cd have
been more comfortable than yr P. [Pig or Pug].

With tender love
Your ever loving husband
W

P.S. The Chartwell Bulletin is att[d] & will give you more news. I hope to see
you before the week is out. X X X

[1] Primrose League, founded by Lord Randolph Churchill in 1883 as a fund-raising and supportive
organization for the Conservative Party in memory of Benjamin Disraeli, whose favourite flower
was the primrose.

A new and important feature in Winston's life appears in this Chartwell
Bulletin – horse racing.

Fired by Christopher's love of horses and the turf, Winston himself had
entered the racing scene: registering in 1949 in his own name Lord Randolph
Churchill's colours[1], he acquired a grey French colt, Colonist II, which won
thirteen races and large sums in prize money for his delighted owner before
being sold to stud in 1951. Largely organized by Christopher, Winston soon
had other horses in training.[2] Presently he acquired a small stud farm at
Newchapel Green, Lingfield, Surrey (not far from Chartwell), where he bred
racehorses, and was remarkably successful[3]. In 1950 he was greatly gratified
to be made a member of the Jockey Club.

[1] Pink, chocolate sleeves and cap. Lord Randolph had been a keen racing man and owned the
filly L'Abbesse de Jouarre (cheerfully known as 'Abscess on the Jaw' by the punters and book-
makers), which won the Oaks in 1889.
[2] WSC's trainer was Walter Nightingall, whose stables were at Epsom.
[3] Maj. A. E. Carey-Foster, a brilliant vet, managed the Newchapel Stud (bought in 1955) and was
largely responsible, with Christopher, for finding and breeding WSC's horses. Among the celebrated horses bred here were High Hat and Vienna.

○ From WSC [typewritten]
April 1950

CHARTWELL BULLETIN

. . .

The waterfalls and filters are all running in good order. As coke is off the ration it would be possible to heat the swimming pool this year, but this would mean erecting the chimney again, or at least half of it – eight feet. . . . Moreover I myself cannot bathe, so I have not done anything about it. . . .

All the fish, big and small, and the ten black swans are well and send their compliments. The father swan has fallen in love with one of his daughters, and I think they mean to make a nest on the island. . . .

On Saturday week I went round the farms with Christopher. I was very much impressed by the improvements made and the tidiness. . . .

Even greater improvement is taking place in the quality of the two milking herds. At Bardogs there are forty-five calves from a month to eighteen months old. All are pedigree and will be worth far more than their predecessors. There are twelve jerseys in milk, looking very well and pretty. . . . The shorthorn herd [at Chartwell Farm] is also steadily improving, and practically all the rubbish [inferior stock] has been got rid of. . . .

April 29 will be a big day for us. Colonist II runs in the 'Winston Churchill' Stakes at Hurst Park, and the same day Cyberine, his sister, runs for the first time there too. I hope you will come with me to see these two horses running. So far all this shows a quite substantial profit, and the whole outfit could be sold for two or three times or more what we gave for it. In addition there are twelve hundred pounds of winnings with Weatherby's. Of course I do not expect Colonist II to win the 'Winston Churchill' Stakes. He will meet the best horses in the world there[1].

Sir Gerald Kelly[2] and the R.A. Committee picked out of the seven sent to them to choose from[3], the following four which you may remember: your Carezza sketch (No. 1); the snow scene out of the studio window; a very old one of the Calanque at Cassis; and, to my surprise, Mont Ste. Victoire, which was one of our Christmas cards. I think it was better to send in four and not six. . . .

I have completely turned off politics these last ten days in a struggle to deliver Volume IV in good condition on May 1. . . . If there is no General Election till October I shall hope to have Volume V far enough advanced to earn the fifth instalment. But no one can tell what will happen. Cripps [Chancellor of the Exchequer] opens his Budget tomorrow and we may get some indication from it about Government tactics.

Various visitors came to lunch or dinner: Lord Woolton[4], with whom I had a very good talk; Camrose, . . . and Randolph, June and little Winston stayed the night. Pamela L[ytton] came for the weekend which was very agreeable and peaceful. Mary did the honours. . . .

I am now on my way to the Duchess of Kent's[5] luncheon and am going up to London thereafter as it is only forty minutes. . . .

I send you a cutting from the MANCHESTER GUARDIAN which I thought very interesting about Germany. It is incredible what follies Bevin[6] has committed. No one but he could have managed to quarrel at the same time with Germans <u>and</u> French, with Russians <u>and</u> Americans, with Arabs <u>and</u> Jews. I do not think the poor old creature can last long in office, whatever happens.

... On the whole I think the foreign situation is darkening somewhat, and it is thought that this year will see Soviet intensification at least of the 'cold war'. There is nothing we can do about it.

✍With all my love,
W

P.S. The Duchess of Kent's luncheon went off all right..... . Our hostess was looking beautiful, she paints and gets fun out of it. Otherwise it looks like life in dignified twilight. There were lots of children.

[1] Colonist did win this race! – and 12 others for WSC. CSC was never enthusiastic over his racing life, but it gave him enormous pleasure and interest. By the time of his death he had had 70 winners.
[2] Sir Gerald Kelly (1879–1972), President of the Royal Academy, 1949–54.
[3] In 1947 WSC had submitted under the pseudonym 'David Winter' two pictures to the Royal Academy Selection Commitee, the true identity of the artist being revealed only after the pictures had been accepted. In 1948 he was elected Honorary Academician Extraordinary. WSC regularly thereafter exhibited in the Summer Exhibition.
[4] Viscount (later 1st Earl of) Woolton (1883–1964), at this date Chairman of the Conservative Party (1946–55). Had been wartime Minister of Food, 1940–3.
[5] HRH The Duchess of Kent, born Princess Marina of Greece (1906–68), widow of HRH The Duke of Kent, killed in RAF aircraft crash, 1942. She lived in Iver, Buckinghamshire.
[6] Ernest Bevin (see p. 489 n. 3), now Foreign Secretary, until March 1951. He died a month later.

☐ From CSC ✉   28 Hyde Park Gate
Wednesday Morning 22 November 1950

My Darling,

I am sad that Queen Juliana[1] should have felt hurt in her personal feelings & offended in her National Pride by your absence at Dover – (The Lord Warden of the Cinque Ports[2] is the first person to greet a foreign Sovereign visiting these shores).

I must also take some blame for having too easily agreed (or was it even perhaps my suggestion?) that we should not go to the Guildhall to-day & join in the City welcome. I fear that this smaller defection will be noticed now.

It will grieve me if we should lose the affection of Queen Juliana & particularly of her Mother[3] who flew here specially to honour you & to give you the precious casket of Marlborough letters[4] – And you are the God Father of the little half-blind daughter[5] whom they cherish most of all.

Do you think Darling you would wait upon the Queen or if that is impossible write to her in your own 'paw' & say you are sorry.

Don't say you are too old! becos' you are as young as a gamecock, & the whole World knows about the flight from Copenhagen to London & on to Newmarket & Blackpool[6].

It was just a slip, because you <u>are</u> Monarchist No 1 & value tradition form & Ceremony –

Your
Clemmie . . .

[1] Queen Juliana (1909–), Queen of the Netherlands from 1948 to 1980, when she abdicated in favour of her daughter Beatrix (b. 1939). She paid a State Visit to Britain, 21–4 November 1950.
[2] WSC had been appointed Lord Warden of the Cinque Ports by King George VI in 1941.
[3] Queen Wilhelmina (1880–1962), Queen of the Netherlands from 1890 to 1948, when she abdicated in favour of her daughter Juliana (see note 1 above). Took refuge in Britain after the German occupation of Holland, 1940.
[4] A priceless collection of letters between John Churchill, 1st Duke of Marlborough, and the Grand Pensionary Antonie Heinsius of Holland during the War of the Spanish Succession, 1702–14.
[5] Princess Christina, b. 1947. In 1975 she married Jorge Guillermo of New York.
[6] WSC and CSC visited Denmark, as guests of the King and Queen, 9–12 October 1950. On arrival back at Northolt, WSC immediately boarded another aircraft and flew to Newmarket to watch Colonist II win the Lowther Stakes. Later that same day he flew to Blackpool, where the Conservative Party Conference was taking place. All these movements figured largely in the press.

Winston once again went to Marrakech for Christmas and the New Year, working and painting. Clementine spent Christmas in London – but was not solitary or dull. In the first week of January 1951 she flew out to join him.

☐ From CSC   28 Hyde Park Gate
Tuesday 19 December 1950

My Darling,
    I am sitting in the Studio of Number 27[1] helping to trim the 14 foot Christmas Tree – It is going to look lovely. Penelope [her secretary] & Bullock [chauffeur][2] are doing most of the work, balanced on a ladder –
    On Christmas Day we shall be sitting down 20 to luncheon & we shall be thinking of you & drinking your health. The guests are Duncan [Sandys*] & Diana & their 3 children, Duncan's Mother & Step Father Mildred & Freddie Lister; Randolph & June, Nellie, Giles & Mary Romilly, Peregrine [her nephew], our neighbour & tenant Mollie Long, Sylvia Henley* & her two daughters & son-in-law. The Tree will be lit & presents distributed in the afternoon after the King's Broadcast.
    Little Winston has arrived & tomorrow Pamela brings him to tea with me & then we are all going to see 'The Crazy Gang' – Rufus [the poodle] is well & happy but misses you. . . .

Your loving
Clemmie

. . .

[1] No. 27 Hyde Park Gate had been bought by the Churchills soon after the war; the dividing wall was pierced through, and it was used for offices and studio storage. The top two floors were made into a maisonette which was rented out.
[2] Joe Bullock, part-time chauffeur, 1946–65. Made available 'on demand' to WSC with a Humber saloon by Sir William Rootes, later 1st Baron Rootes (1894–1964), Chairman of Rootes Motors Ltd.

○ From CSC   28 Hyde Park Gate
23 December 1950

My Darling
I hope this letter will reach you Christmas morning – It brings you my
love and Christmas Thoughts.
I love to think of you basking in the <u>morning</u> and <u>mid-day</u> Sun, not I
hope the <u>afternoon</u> Sun, which I dread for you because it sinks so
quickly –
The lumbago is slowly yielding to treatment & I hope when I see you I
shall be an active leaping Cat & not a crippled Cat.

Miaow
All my Love
Clemmie

○ From WSC [typewritten]   Hôtel de la Mamounia
25 December 1950   Marrakech

My darling Clemmie,
      . . .
We had a great dinner with the Glaoui. The D'Hautevilles[1] came and
both Miss Sturdee [secretary] and Miss Gemmell[2] [secretary]. Everybody
liked shoving their paws into the dish and remembered with pleasure that
fingers were made before forks. The Glaoui is as old as I am but quite
lively. He pretends to know neither French nor English, but I believe he
understands everything that is said, at least in French. After dinner there
were dances – three troupes of five each with tomtoms, . . . I never saw
dancing, music, or the human form presented in such unattractive guise –
the women with sullen expressions on their faces, stamping their feet
on the floor, the men in the same vogue but more repellent. All were
dressed up in quilts and blankets – they looked like bundles of cotton
waste. . . . The music brays and squawks and tomtoms, and the singing,
which was maintained throughout, was a masterly compendium of
discords. . . .
I have been painting for a few hours every day. We went to Ourika
where the river comes out of the mountains, and the pebbles – you
know. . . . Meanwhile I have advanced the picture by working from
photographs in the studio. I have one other picture on the stocks. . . .
Everybody enjoyed themselves very much last night at the Christmas
celebrations. I turned up at the hour appointed – a quarter to 12 – and
was introduced to the company, who loudly applauded, to the strains of
Lilli Marlene. (I am terrified of this getting into my mind again. I have
several antidotes ready.) . . .
My day is most tranquil and I do absolutely nothing that I do not want
to. The food is the best you can get. I have discovered Marennes oysters –
excellent. I get at least eight or nine hours sleep. The weather is sharply
cool and there are too many clouds. However I hope for a sunshine spell
not only in the garden, but in the foothills of the Atlas. . . .

The one thing that has gone best of all is the one thing that is most needful – namely the book. I have been here tonight eight days, and eight chapters of Volume VI, Book 12, have been sent to the Printer....

... I earnestly hope that all is well at Chartwell. The little fish, the Black Mollies[3], the golden orfes in the pools (but they do not eat now), the black swans (I hope the lakes are unfrozen and they can go back to their various domains). All these I think of, and then there is the sulky, ill-mannered cat, and poor dear Rufus. I hope he had a good howl but I expect he is reconciled by now to my absence.

Much depends for us all upon the impending battle in Korea[4]. I hope they have made a proper defensive line across the peninsula, with minefields and barbed wire and machine guns, well posted with a good artillery organized in the rear....

✍I hope this tale will please you. I came here to Play, but so far it has only been <u>Work</u> under physically agreeable conditions.

You have my fondest love, I do pray that all is well with all of you: I am looking forward to come [coming] home again. But here I have no distractions & can make astounding progress with my mainstay,

Give my love to all

> & believe in your devoted & ever loving
> husband
> W

P.S. My eyes are closing – Good night.

[1] See WSC's letter of 18 December 1947. D'Hauteville was the French officer commanding the district (military and civil).
[2] Cecily Gemmell ('Chips') was WSC's Private Secretary, 1947–52.
[3] After the war WSC became entranced by tropical fish, and he eventually had a considerable number of tanks for them in his Chartwell Study. While he was Prime Minister, 1951–5, the whole 'aquarium' was moved to Chequers. (At Chartwell now there is a 'token' tank of tropical fish in the study, to mark this interest.)
[4] The Korean War, 1950–3. An escalation of the Cold War, when in June 1950 North Korean troops crossed into South Korea at the 38th Parallel (an artificial frontier created in 1945 for purely military reasons, by the USA and USSR, who had withdrawn their troops in 1949).

In mid-May 1951 Clementine had a major gynaecological repair operation: all went well, but a long period of convalescence was required, which she began at Chartwell, and continued in France, at Hendaye, a seaside resort near Biarritz: I went with her.

☐ From WSC [typewritten]   [Chartwell]
3 August 1951

My Darling,

We had a rotten day at Goodwood. Nightingall [his trainer] should not have proposed running COLONIST only ten days after his effort in the Festival Stakes. He was undoubtedly an overworked horse. Also he lost a shoe early in the race and hurt himself, though not seriously.... WHY

TELL, who was only being trained to the racecourse, ... when the gate went up, the poor lamb turned the other way and started fifty lengths behind everybody. ...

The Session has ended, thank God, but no one knows what is going to happen next. The uncertainty is a bore, as one cannot make clear-cut plans about the farm, etc.

I am plunged in Volume V, which I am trying to deliver in time for the Book-of-the-Month Club in America, which sells 350,000, to take it for November. ... The British edition of Volume IV comes out to-day, or rather tomorrow, August 4, and is reviewed in all the papers to-day. ... I am sending a hundred copies of the book to our friends. I am virtually re-writing the early chapters of Volume V as I deal with them. They take four or five hours apiece, and there are twenty in each book. You may imagine I have little time for my other cares – the fish, indoors and out-of-doors, the farm, the robin (who has absconded[1]). Still, I am sleeping a great deal, averaging about nine hours in the twenty-four. ...

I am dead set on taking the Freedoms of Deal and of Dover in the morning and afternoon of August 15, leaving with Christopher [Soames*] by the ferry after midnight, and expecting to meet you and Maria at the Lotti Hotel in Paris ... on the 16th. Then the night train to Annecy. ...

I send you the Hansard of the Debate on Persia, in which I spoke, with this letter ... by Randolph, who goes forth tomorrow. His visit passed off all right, and I think Winston [aged eleven] ... enjoyed going to the races and spotted a winner which no one else had thought of. The reason was because it belonged to the Aga Khan, whose sons were with him in the school at Switzerland. This is as good a reason as any other.

Give my best love to Maria, and please don't get drowned by the billows of the Bay of Biscay.

The Birleys[2] are arriving at 5 o'clock, and I shall have to sit up in a chair for two hours a day.

[1] There was for several months in the Water Garden a resident robin, who regularly took food from WSC's hand, which greatly delighted him. A short documentary film was made of this touching relationship.
[2] Sir Oswald Birley (1880–1952). Celebrated portrait painter, and a most charming man. He and his beautiful, entrancing wife Rhoda (died 1981), who also painted, became great friends of WSC and CSC. Birley painted WSC in all four times, the first being in 1946.

☐ From CSC   Hôtel Eskualduna
Sunday 5 August 1951   Hendaye

My darling Winston,
How proud and happy you must be of the warm and glowing reception of The H of F. [*Hinge of Fate*, vol. IV of his war memoirs]. The Continental Daily Mail was the first I read, followed by the Times proper and its Literary Supplement. And I have the Book with me to read, as a Book, & not in fragments.

Mary & I are happy here; & we are at this instant basking in the Sun – (not a very hot Sun, but Oh! so welcome after six days of lowering clouds ...).

Randolph is at Biarritz & is coming over presently to lunch with us at a 'Bistro' we have found in the town –

There the food is <u>delicious</u> which cannot be said of the food at our hotel – But the bedrooms are spacious & there is nothing between my bed and America except the Atlantic Ocean which sometimes lulls one to sleep & sometimes thunders & roars like great guns –

Randolph sent your letter last night; & I am sad about your racing disappointment – Miaow....

Tender Love from
Clem ...

We all met in Paris at the Lotti, as planned, and travelled on by train to Annecy, where the weather was so appalling that after a week we decamped *en masse* to Venice, where we had a memorably happy holiday.

Chapter XXV

NO. 10 AGAIN

The Labour Government having struggled with a majority of only six since February 1950, the Prime Minister, Clement Attlee, called for another General Election, which took place on 25 October 1951: it resulted in a majority of seventeen for the Conservatives[1].

Winston Churchill became Prime Minister once more on the evening of 26 October. While he was forming his Government, Clementine sent him this note.

[1] The election results were: Conservatives, 321; Labour, 295; Liberals, 6; Irish Nationalist, 2; Irish Labour, 1. On the family front, Christopher Soames at Bedford and Duncan Sandys at Streatham were both re-elected. Randolph, fighting Michael Foot for the second time at Plymouth (Devonport), was again defeated.

☐ From CSC ✉   Chartwell
Monday Evening [29 October 1951]

My Darling –

Do not be angry with me – But first – do you not think it would be wiser to give Duncan [Sandys*] a smaller post – Se^try of State for War is so very prominent – then do you think it wise to have him working immediately under your orders as Minister of Defence[1]. If anything were to go wrong it would be delicate & tricky – first of all having to defend your son-in-law, & later if by chance he made a mistake having to dismiss him[2] –

Forgive me I think only of your welfare, happiness and dignity

                                                                              . . .

[1] Until March 1952 WSC combined the office of Prime Minister with that of Minister of Defence (as in the war).
[2] Duncan Sandys became Minister of Supply on 31 October 1951, a junior post to that of Secretary of State for War.

At Christmas there was a big family party at Chequers, and on 31 December Winston, with a large entourage, departed for the United States and Canada, on board the *Queen Mary*.

☐ From CSC   10 Downing Street
8 January 1952

My darling Winston,
    It is now ten days since I said Good bye to you at Waterloo Station. It makes me very happy to feel how well things are going and shaping –
    I will tell you how I have been occupied –
    I returned to Chequers on the Sunday morning after you left & continued to entertain the remainder of our Christmas Party – On the 2nd I returned to 'No 10' – since when I have had pleasant contacts with Randolph.... And yesterday I returned from spending a delightful weekend with Mary & Christopher [Soames*] at the Farm. I inspected Page [farm bailiff]'s cottage which has been beautifully renovated for the new bailiff's wife. I also visited your tropical fish who are well & full of colour. To-day I'm giving a luncheon party....
    I'm looking forward to staying with the Harveys[1] in Paris – I go by the Ferry on Sunday night the 13th returning the following Wednesday night –
    This is rather a dry catalogue like the page of an engagement book torn out!
    But I send you my dear Love and thoughts
                                                            Your devoted
                                                            Clemmie

[1] Sir Oliver Harvey, later 1st Baron Harvey of Tasburgh (1893–1968). British Ambassador to France, 1948–54. He married, 1920, Maud Williams-Wynn.

☐ From CSC   London
18 June 1952

MARY AND I LISTENED TOGETHER TO YOUR SPEECH[1] WITH EMOTION. WE BOTH SEND OUR LOVE.
CLEMMIE.

[1] WSC addressed the US Congress on 17 January 1952.

○ From WSC   4 East 66th Street[1]
20 January 1952   [New York]

My Darling
    Sir Roger Makins[2] is flying home today & I send this line w him to tell you how much you have been in my thoughts & how much I love you.
    I have just finished what seems to be the most strenuous fortnight I can remember; & I am staying quiet here for 48 hours to recover. I never had such a whirl of people & problems, and the two speeches[3] were vy hard & exacting ordeals. Now I sail for home going on board Q.M. [*Queen Mary*] midnight 22.
    Beatrice Eden[4] came to dinner last night. She seems as young and attractive as she was when I saw her last abt 10 years ago. She cd give no intelligible explanations of her mental attitude though she tried vy hard to

do so. She says Anthony has no heart – She does not seem to have much herself. She is coming over to England in March. She is a real puzzle....

The Presidential Election [November 1952] is now going to amuse the Americans for the next nine anxious months. They in their turn will have the dose we have swallowed in the last 2 years. But I suppose the Russians have their troubles too. I hope so anyway.

I look forward so much to seeing you next Monday week. Let us dine alone at No. 10. Tender love my darling Clemmie,

Your ever loving husband
W

...

[1] Apartment of Bernard Baruch (see p. 328 n. 1).
[2] Sir Roger Makins, later 1st Baron Sherfield (1904–96). Entered Foreign Office, 1928. At this date Deputy Under-Secretary of State, 1948–52. British Ambassador to the United States, 1953–6.
[3] On 14 January, in Ottawa, WSC spoke at a banquet in his honour given by the Government of Canada.
[4] Beatrice and Anthony Eden (see Biographical Notes) had been divorced in 1950, after which she lived in the USA. She died in 1957.

O From WSC   4 East 66th Street
21 January 1952   [New York]

Darling,

It is splendid (as I cabled) that you will meet me at Southampton.... I have only one piece of urgent business wh I may have to settle before starting either by train or car. This may settle itself beforehand. The enclosed telegram to Tommy Lascelles will explain the possible urgency[1]....

Sarah[2] was really vy good yesterday – the opening, ... She does 4 a month – one of wh is all her own acting. The fee is $2,000 each time!... She seems vy happy & is looking beautiful.

I shall indeed be delighted to get home. I never remember 3 weeks taking so long to live; although it has been all kindness & compliments.

With fondest love
Your loving husband
W

...

[1] The telegram sent to Sir Alan Lascelles, Private Secretary to King George VI, on 20 January would have been concerned with the King's deteriorating health. The King had lung cancer (although this was not publicly known), and his left lung had been removed in September 1951. Combined with the threat of thrombosis, which had been hanging over him since 1948, the months since his operation were deeply anxious ones for those 'in the know'.
[2] Sarah and Antony Beauchamp were now working in the USA. She was just starting a TV series of dramatic programmes for the Hallmark Company (creators and distributors of greetings cards).

Winston and his party arrived back on 29 January at Southampton, where Clementine and I were on the quayside to welcome him.

On 6 February King George VI died in his sleep at Sandringham.

During this summer Clementine was not well and had to cancel all her engagements for nearly three months. On 7 July she flew to Rome with Mary Duchess of Marlborough en route for Monte Catini, near Florence, to do a cure at the health spa there.

☐ From CSC
7 July 1952

[B.O.A.C. airletter]
In flight

My Darling

We reach Rome in half an hour. A marvellous flight at over 17000 feet – Lovely miraculous skies, horrid Alpine peaks, delicious food – I love you.

We flew over poor little Dieppe, the Arc de Triomphe, Dijon, the Lake of Geneva, Turin, & are now fast approaching Rome –

Tender Love
from
Clem Pussie Bird

. . .

○ From WSC [typewritten]
July 1952

10 Downing Street

Max [Beaverbrook*] dined with me at No. 10 the other night. We were alone and I had a very agreeable talk. He is very anxious to order the lift[1] to be got ready to put in, so that whenever it is convenient we can have the carpentering done. . . .

They showed me the plans, which you discussed with the Ministry of Works, for reviving the State Rooms and dining room at No. 10[2]. . . . There are a few minor improvements the Ministry of Works suggest. I think it is a brilliant conception and should be done in the public interest, as it is a great pity these rooms are not available for use. We really ought to have them for the Coronation year. Look at all the distinguished people I have had to entertain in our poor little attic. I am sure they are surprised at the difference between the accommodation and the menu.

The only time the changes can be made is during the ten weeks' holiday. Once finished, this would not commit you to using them until you felt inclined. There would be no need for more servants, except perhaps one in the kitchen, as the State Rooms would continue to be cleaned as at present. However I think the structural changes should be made in the Recess and we could stay where we are [i.e. in the upstairs flat] until you felt able to move down[3].

[1] The lift at Chartwell was a present from Max Beaverbrook. It was installed by the Drawing Room entrance (ground floor, i.e. Front Hall level) and ascended to the Bedroom and WSC's Study level (first floor).
[2] During the Attlees' occupancy of No. 10 a self-contained flat had been created on the second floor; the State Rooms on the first floor were used only for parties, when all the staffing and catering were done by government hospitality.
[3] When the Churchills returned to No. 10 in 1951, CSC was most reluctant to change the 'Attlee' arrangement. But the flat was quite inadequate, except for really small numbers, and with the Coronation in the offing she agreed for plans to be made with the Ministry of Works for the house to be lived in as previously.

☐ From CSC   Grand Hôtel & La Pace
9 July 1952   Montecatini Terme

My darling Winston,
    Yesterday's Times has just reached us announcing Eisenhower's initial
success at Chicago[1]. I hope it is an augury.
    Mary & I have started our 'cures' – They begin at 7.30 in the morning at
a palatial establishment surrounded by a lovely garden. . . .
    It's very very hot but we are bearing up. . . .
    The flowers are lovely & strangely enough it's not at all burnt up. There
are crickets & frogs who keep up a constant chorus –
    The food is delicious but great moderation is enjoined. . . .
                                                            Your loving
                                                            Clemmie
                                                                . . .

[1] Gen. Eisenhower (see p. 476 n. 5) had just scored a victory in a procedural dispute over contested
candidates at the Republican Convention in Chicago; on 11 July he would win the Party's nomination for President.

○ From WSC   10 Downing Street
11 July 1952

My darling Clemmie,
    Yr '17,000' feet letter was vy welcome and I look forward to an account
of how you are & what it is all like. . . . Are you playing Okla[homa] w
Mary? I do hope the weather is not too hot. Here it is cooler & cloudy.
    Another week of toil is over & I am off to Chartwell in an hour. How I
wish I were going to find you there! I feel a sense of loneliness and miss
you often, and wd like to feel you near. I love you vy much my dear
sweet Clemmie. But I am sure you needed the 'Off Duty' break to recover
buoyancy & resilience. I am most anxious to get yr report. . . .
    It is a vy bleak outlook – with all our might, majesty, dominion & power
imperilled by having to pay the crashing Bill each week. I have never seen
things so tangled & tiresome. But we must persevere.
    I am relieved at Ike's progress over Taft[1]. Once the American election is
over we may be able to make real headway. Either Ike or the Democrat[2]
wd be all right. A Taft–MacArthur[3] combine wd be vy bad. . . .
    . . . Give my love to Mary Marl[borough] and believe me always
                                                Yr devoted loving husband
                                                            W
                                                        X X X X
                                                            . . .

[1] Senator Robert Taft (1889–1953), US right-wing Republican senator (Ohio) from 1939, was a
candidate for the presidential nomination (as he had been in 1944 and 1948). An isolationist, he
had expressed the view during the war that he would rather see a German victory than American
involvement. He failed to obtain the nomination.
[2] Adlai Stevenson (1900–65). Governor of Illinois, 1949–53. Twice defeated by Eisenhower
(Republican) as Democratic candidate for the Presidency, 1952 and 1956.
[3] General of the Army Douglas MacArthur (1880–1964). Commander of US forces in Far East, from
1941; C.-in-C. Allied forces, S.W. Pacific Area, from April 1942; Supreme Commander, Allied

Powers in Japan, and C.-in-C., UN forces in Korea, until 1951, when President Truman relieved him of his commands. He failed to secure the Republican nomination for the Presidency in 1952.

☐ From CSC   Grand Hôtel & La Pace
Saturday 12 July 1952   Montecatini Terme

My Darling, last night I heard Sarah's voice from Rome[1] – She is forwarding your letter, which has not yet arrived – I follow your public doings from the Continental Daily Mail & The Times.... The excitement over the Convention is now over, but has been bewildering & contradictory – I can see that the few Americans here would just as soon have had Taft, but now it's <u>over</u> they have switched! If they had been in Chicago they might have switched <u>before</u> the end – Even Mary M[arlborough] was all over the place & kept saying what a fine man Taft is & what a bad speaker is Eisenhower.

Well Well – ! I said a prayer before and a thanks to God after –

Your loving
Clemmie
. . .

It's 100° again to-day but I'm getting used to the extreme heat & quite like it –

[1] Sarah and Antony were going to Capri, where CSC was to join them as their guest.

☐ From CSC   Grand Hôtel & La Pace
17 July 1952   Montecatini Terme

My Darling, Yesterday I was in Florence; so I went to 'l'Ombrellino' Alice Keppel's villa, which now belongs to her daughter Violet Trefusis – It was shut up, but I went & sat on the Terrace (with those graceful gray statues) which seems to float above the city – It was rather sad & nostalgic – I remember 8 or 10 guests always in the house, & gay luncheon parties of 20 or even more – Now I think only a small wing is open....

Tender Love my Darling from your
Pussy

. . .

○ From WSC   Chartwell
21 July 1952

My darling One,

The end of the Session is approaching and will give relief to a vy harsh & worrying strain. Inside our circle we toil continuously at plans to pay our way. The problems are baffling & bewildering because of their number & relationship. What to cut, & all the hideous consequences of the choice. Food, Arms, Housing? or all three? Indeed we were left a dismal inheritance! Beneath all the party malice there is a realization of the facts. But the nation is divided into 2 party-machines grinding away at one another with tireless vigour.

Anthony [Eden*]'s absence adds to my burdens. He has had a sharp dose of jaundice & has lost a stone & a half. His doctor wants him to rest for another week & I am pressing him to do so. Salisbury[1] has been vy tiresome – frail health, private business, and combined with these a defeatist frame of mind. However I hope to bring things to a satisfactory close.

It will be a welcome change to have a lull – busy tho' that must be.

Bernie [Baruch] comes here next Friday for a long week end, when I have an important speech to prepare & much to settle: but Mary & Christopher [Soames*] will help & I expect all will pass off well.

The sun is shining & the weather bright & cool. The gardens are lovely. (They are to be opened on the 23rd as you know.) The fish are doing well. (seven baby black Mollies) I have managed to get a good long week-end (Thursday night till Monday afternoon).

X   X   X

I am afraid the gt heat of Italy may have been a burden to you my darling. I do hope that when you join with Sarah & Antony you will not do too much & that cooler breezes will blow.... I miss you vy much & am often lonely & depressed. Your sweet letter wh reached me yesterday was a joy. I have been wondering how to draw a Clem Pussy Bird ever since. I enclose a daring attempt.

Tender love my dearest
from your devoted husband
W

[1] 5th Marquess of Salisbury ('Bobbety'); see p. 462 n. 3.

□ From CSC   British Embassy
25 July 1952   Rome

My Darling,

Mary M[arlborough] will bring you this letter and all my love –

I leave this afternoon for Naples where Sarah & Antony are meeting me –...

I have not yet heard if Mr Stevenson has been nominated by the Democrats as their Champion – He seems, to the outsider, much their best man –

Yesterday evening I walked for a little on the Appian Way – But it is spoilt; the old stone road with the ruts made by the Roman Chariot wheels is asphalted, & overhead instead of larks are a forest of telegraph wires.

Your loving
Clemmie

...

O From WSC   Chartwell
4 August 1952

My darling One,

With intense relief I have got back here with 10 weeks before Parl meets again. The last month has been vy trying. But now we have a chance to swing the scenes and to try to make better plans. We have saved about £125ᵐ from the torturing exchange and have taken another step to solvency. It seems hard indeed that we shd get no credit for saving the country from Bankruptcy. And even that will require prolonged vigilance. Anthony Eden* is back[1] & I have felt his absence vy much. He looks thin & is I fear frail. Still we shall have a holiday – or at least a change.

Rain has come & the arid fields are freshened. Yr croquet lawn[2] is the greenest spot for miles. The L.S. [lemon scented] magnolia is just beginning its beautiful crop. I see a wealth of buds & several are trying to climb in to my window. Yr garden is looking lovely & so is yr terrace. I think you will be pleased with all you see....

The row between Attlee & Bevan is flaring up vy nicely & it is a pleasure to see the newspapers full of Socialist splits instead of only our shortcomings....

Duncan [Sandys*, Minister of Supply] has done vy well & is recognised by all to have won his position as a leading figure on our side.

It is too hard for my horses to be galloped, but we hope to have some races in Septʳ & Octʳ. The fish (indoors and out) are well & pretty. I feed them all myself. The labour is not unwelcome, after too much politics....

Forgive these disjointed scribblings, wh I send by the bag to meet you in Rome on Tuesday.

I love you so much & miss you & long for yr return – We will just do nothing but sit & purr.

Your ever loving & devoted
husband
W
...

Give much love to Sarah.

[1] A few days after this letter Anthony Eden and Clarissa Churchill (Jack's only daughter, aged 32) came to Chartwell to tell WSC of their engagement. As soon as CSC arrived home from Italy she set about organizing their wedding reception, which would be held at No. 10 on 14 August.
[2] In 1951 the tennis court had been turned into a croquet lawn.

The Coronation of Queen Elizabeth II took place on 2 June 1953. But from the beginning of the year there had been much additional entertaining and important events involving Winston and Clementine; and from the end of April a double burden of work and responsibility descended on Winston because Anthony Eden* had become seriously ill.

The strain took its toll. On 23 June, towards the end of a dinner at No. 10 given in honour of Signor de Gasperi, the Italian Prime Minister, Winston had just made a short but brilliant off-the-cuff speech, and the company was moving to the Drawing Rooms, when he suffered a stroke: at this point the symptoms were not clear, and Christopher (Soames*) helped him to a chair. De Gasperi, on being told that the Prime Minister was greatly fatigued, was most understanding and left quite soon, followed by the other guests. My father's speech was slurred and he was unsteady on his feet, but we managed to get him upstairs to his bedroom, where he seemed to be considerably recovered.

Lord Moran* came in the next morning early, and diagnosed a stroke; but Winston seemed better and, amazingly, presided at a Cabinet meeting, where none of his colleagues thought anything was amiss[1]. The next day (Thursday 25 June) the effects of the stroke were more marked, and it was thought advisable that he should go to Chartwell, where greater privacy could be assured.

Churchill had been due to leave on 30 June for Bermuda, where a meeting (publicly announced) between President Eisenhower and the French and British Prime Ministers was to take place: a decision had therefore to be made. On Saturday 27 June a communiqué was issued to the effect that Churchill was 'in need of a complete rest, and that he must abandon his journey to Bermuda, and lighten his burdens for at least a month'[2]. No medical reasons were given.

Meanwhile Winston's condition deteriorated: Lord Moran thought he might well not live through the weekend. However, in a day or two he was visibly better, and his recovery proceeded (although somewhat spasmodically), to the relief and amazement of the close circle who knew the truth.

Of course this illness raised the whole question of his retirement. Winston set himself a target – the Conservative Party Conference at Margate in October, at which, as Leader of the Party, he must make a major speech: that would be the test.

On 24 July he was well enough to be driven the three-hour journey to Chequers; and he started attending to political and literary work. Eight weeks after his stroke Churchill presided at a Cabinet meeting in London on 18 August; but his progress was uneven, and he suffered fatigue and bouts of depression.

Clementine bore the brunt of all this, and her anxiety concerning his political intentions was great. She also had the misfortune at this time to fall and crack some ribs – not serious, but very painful.

The Queen had invited Winston and Clementine to be her guests at Doncaster Races for the St Leger, and then to travel on up with her and Prince Philip on the Royal Train to Balmoral. His doctors and Clementine thought this expedition would be too tiring – and indeed might jeopardize his recovery. Winston (at Chequers) and Clementine (at No. 10) had 'words' on the subject: Winston telephoned her later the same evening to apologize. The next day she wrote to him.

---

[1] Harold Macmillan noted in his diary on 2 July: 'I certainly noticed nothing beyond the fact that he was very white. He spoke little, but quite distinctly...': *Tides of Fortune*, 1969, p. 516.
[2] Signed by Lord Moran and Sir Russell Brain, the distinguished neurologist.

☐ From CSC   10 Downing Street
3 September 1953

My darling Winston,
    It was sweet of you to ring me up last night & to say loving & forgiving words to me –
    I would like to persuade you to give up Doncaster & Balmoral.
    First Doncaster. You will be watched by loving but anxious & curious crowds – It would be rather an effort to keep up steady walking – It may be a longish way to the Paddock & there will be much standing about. Altho' you sit in the Queen's Presence in intimate Court Circles – If you sat in public when she was standing it would be noticed.
    Then Balmoral –
    You are improving steadily though slowly; but I fear you are not up to a night in the train and so on yet. And you don't want to have a set back before the Margate Speech; but rather you must husband your strength for that important event, & for Parliament. . . .
    I will be with you this afternoon –

                                                    Your devoted
                                                    Clemmie

    For the record: Winston and Clementine both went to the races! It was 12 September – their forty-fifth wedding anniversary. It was a happy day, and they enjoyed their visit to Balmoral afterwards, and he – although tired – was buoyed up by the excursion.
    On 17 September Winston went for two weeks to La Capponcina at Cap d'Ail (Lord Beaverbrook's* villa). Clementine stayed at home nursing her cracked ribs. Christopher and I went with my father for company.

O From WSC   Cap d'Ail
18 September [1953]

Darling,
    All is beautiful & sunlit here. There is a sense of peace & quiet. Nothing but yr presence is lacking. The children swim, & I have plunged in[to] Coningsby[1]. I am going to have a smack at a canvas this afternoon. There is no scarcity of official papers. . . .
    Fondest love Darling Do not worry about anything for a space but think again about coming here when the children leave. . . .

                                                    With all my love
                                                    Your loving husband
                                                    W

                                                        . . .

[1] Benjamin Disraeli, *Coningsby*, 1844.

☐ From CSC   Chequers
20 September 1953

My darling Winston,
    I was much pleased to get your letter so soon after your arrival – I hope
you are happy painting & sitting in the Sun, & that Mary & Christopher are
having lovely bathing. . . .
    Nellie [Romilly] is here & we are playing croquet – Tomorrow we go to
Stratford-upon-Avon to see Richard III & The Taming of the Shrew – Grim
bloody tragedy, followed by a knock-a-bout turn.

                                                                                    Your loving
                                                                                    Clemmie
We have just lunched with Randolph – very pleasant.

O From WSC   Cap d'Ail
21 September [1953]

My darling one,
    The days pass quickly & quietly. I have hardly been outside the garden,
& so far have not had the energy to paint in the sunlight hours. . . . I do not
think I have made much progress, tho' as usual I eat, drink & sleep well.
I think a great deal about you & feel how much I love you. The kittens
[Mary and Christopher Soames*] are vy kind to me, but evidently they do
not think much of my prospects. I have done the daily work and kept
check of the gloomy tangle of the world, and I have dictated about 2,000
words of a possible speech for Margate in order to try & see how I can let
it off when it is finished to a select audience. I still ponder on the future
and don't want to decide unless I am convinced.
    Today I went into Monte Carlo and bought a grisly book by the author
of All Quiet on the Western Front[1]. It is all about concentration camps, but
in good readable print, wh matters to me. It is like taking refuge from
melancholy in horror. It provides a background. I have read almost ¾ of
Coningsby, but the print was faint and small. I am glad I did not have to
live in that artificial society of dukes & would-be duchesses with their
Tadpoles & Tapers. . . .
    Esmond[2] came to luncheon yesterday and was vy friendly & not a bit
vexed about poor Randolph's performance[3] – published verbatim as you
have no doubt seen in the Bevanite rag [Tribune]. . . . O'Brien[4] the TUC
President has been here today. He is a sensible man and I gave him a
good dose of Tory Democracy – quite as good a brand as your Liberalism.
    Forgive this scrawl in bed with a tiny Biro. I can do better, but I so
rarely write with my own paw. Please continue to love me or I shall be vy
unhappy. I suppose you and Nellion will now be off to Stratford. . . . Write

me about it all. I long to hear from you. Burn this scribble. It is worse than I really am.

Ever your loving & as yet unconquered
W

P.S. Once more all my love & with a better pen – like the one you gave UJ [Uncle Joe – Stalin] & he told [you] he always wrote in pencil....

[1] Erich Maria Remarque. The book WSC was reading was *Spark of Life*, 1952.
[2] Esmond Harmsworth, who had succeeded his father as 2nd Viscount Rothermere in 1940. See p. 409 n. 5.
[3] At a Foyle's Literary Luncheon Randolph had made a violent attack on press proprietors (particularly naming Lord Rothermere, owner of the *Daily Mail*) and various editors for peddling pornography. His speech was published in *Tribune*, 18 September 1953.
[4] Tom O'Brien (1900–70). General Secretary, National Association of Theatrical and Kine Employees, from 1932. President, TUC, 1952–3. Knighted 1956.

☐ From WSC Cap d'Ail
23 September 1953

HAVE AT LAST PLUNGED INTO A DAUB. HOPE YOU HAVE GOT MY LETTER. MUCH LOVE. W

☐ From CSC Chequers
24 September 1953

My darling Winston,

By the time you get this letter Christopher & Mary will have left you, & Jock & Meg [Colville*] will have arrived to keep you company –

Your letter reached me only this morning; as of course when you are not here there are no cars going & coming – I wish my dearest that you did not feel so sad and melancholy – I feel at our age it takes a little time to become acclimatized to the soft relaxing air of the Riviera – It would probably be good if you could be there a month – But that's not possible –

It will be lovely to welcome you back & I am making all arrangements for us to spend the week-end ... at Chartwell; as I know that is what you would like....

Randolph lunched here & is with me now. I don't think he has any idea of what we all think of his ill-natured blunder – He is such good company when in a good mood, & we have played highly competitive croquet both yesterday & to-day which we both enjoyed. I'm sending you a letter from him....

All my Love Darling –
Your devoted
Clemmie
...

O From WSC   Cap d'Ail
25 September 1953

My darling,
Mary & Christopher leave now & will carry this to you. I shall follow on
the 30th. It was very nice talking on the telephone to you tho' I found it so
difficult to hear.... I have taken the plunge in painting and certainly feel
the necessary vigour & strength to be as bad as I used to be. This is a
relief because it is a gt distraction and a little perch for a tired bird....
    Nothing cd be more comfortable than this villa [La Capponcina], and all
arrangements are perfect. I have only left the garden twice, and the days
pass vy quickly. I continue to reorder my path. As usual there seems to be
something to be said on both sides. It is rather like a Home Secretary
pondering about his own reprieve.
    I am so glad you are going down to Chartwell tonight. Do write me the
local news about it all – including the little yellow cat[1], with whom I
thought I was making progress thanks to matutinal grouse[2].
    I do hope my darling you have found the interlude restful and pleasant.
I must admit I have had a good many brown hours. However the moment
of action will soon come now.
    I wish you were here for I can't help feeling lonely.
                                                        Your ever loving husband
                                                                        W
                                                                        . . .

P.S. I have begun Père Goriot[3] in French.

[1] One of the successors to the beloved 'Mr Kat'. WSC always had 'marmalades' at Chartwell, and
the National Trust now ensures that there is always a resident 'yellow' cat.
[2] In season, WSC often had cold grouse for breakfast – which he shared.
[3] Honoré de Balzac, *Le Père Goriot*, 1834.

Winston returned from France on 30 September, and concentrated on the all-
important speech. On 10 October he delivered a fifty-minute address to the
Conservatives assembled at Margate and under the eyes of the world media
(for rumours about his health had been rife). The speech and its delivery
were a brilliant success: 'retirement' talk faded away.

O From WSC   10 Downing Street
13 October 1953

My darling,
    I do hope you are enjoying yourself[1]. The French are not pleased with
me; nor indeed did I expect them to be[2]. But I don't think they will
revenge themselves on you. The Pug [Lord Ismay][3] will certainly approve.
Duffie [Duff Cooper*, former British Ambassador to France] will be
adverse.
    The Kitten is behaving admirably & with its customary punctilio! Rufus is

becoming gradually reconciled. Generally the domestic situation is tranquil....

I was lonely last night but Pitblado[4] dined. I am reading The Dynasts[5] & getting into it.

A long good Cabinet this morning – It is curious how much less formidable things look round the Cabinet table, than they do in the newspapers.

With all my love my beloved Clemmie from

Your devoted husband
W

...

[1] CSC was staying in Paris with the Ismays, who had become close friends.
[2] In his Margate speech WSC had welcomed Germany 'back among the great powers of the world'.
[3] Gen. Hastings ('Pug') Ismay (1887–1965), cr. 1st Baron Ismay of Wormington, 1947. Chief of Staff to Minister of Defence (WSC), 1940–5. He married, 1921, Laura ('Darry') Clegg. At this date the Ismays were living in Paris, where he was Secretary-General of the North Atlantic Treaty Organization (NATO), 1952–7.
[4] David Pitblado (1912–97), Principal Private Secretary to the Prime Minister (Attlee and Eden), 1951–6; Joint Principal Private Secretary (with John Colville) to WSC, 1951–5. Knighted 1967.
[5] Thomas Hardy, *The Dynasts*, epic poem in three parts, 1903, 1906, 1908.

O From WSC   10 Downing Street
16 October 1953

My darling One,

I am just off to Chartwell, but come back Sunday to give the Foreign Ministers[1] a final luncheon. Their talks seem to be going allright, but there are a lot of tiresome things happening, & next Tuesday the Parl[t] meets again to help us.

It is all settled about the Nobel Prize [for Literature]. £12,100 free of tax. Not so bad!

I think we shall have to go to Stockholm for a couple of days in December & stay with the King & Queen there.

I am writing in the Cabinet room & the little cat is holding the notepaper down for me. I miss you vy much. One night I had dinner in bed as I did not want anyone but you for company. I do hope you are enjoying yrself and finding the days interesting.

I am dining with Mary [at Chartwell Farm] tonight & tomorrow, and she lunches with me on a chicken pie on Saturday. Pamela C[hurchill][2] lunched w me yesterday. How agreeable she is! I had not seen her for years. She told me she had seen you at dinner at the Pug's [Ismay's].

Tender Love my darling
from yr devoted husband
W

...

[1] The Foreign Ministers of Britain, the USA and France met in London, 16–18 October 1953.
[2] Pamela and Randolph had divorced in 1945, and at this period she was living in Paris. In 1960 she married Leland Hayward, American film agent and producer; he died in 1971, and that same year she married Averell Harriman (see p. 469 n. 1); he died, 1986. Pamela Harriman was US Ambassador to France from 1994 until her sudden death in 1997.

○ From WSC ⊠   10 Downing Street
20 October 1953

My darling – Welcome Home! I am resting in bed, before my H of C
reappearance[1] & many questions. I am following the Margate plan
including a Moran*[2] wh he advised.
    I do hope you have got the better of yr cold: If I am asleep when you
arrive, it wd be good of you to leave me till 2.30 when I dress for the
House at 3. Questions 3.15. But probably I shall be awake longing to see
you. Tender love

                                                                    W
                                                                   ...

[1] On 20 October WSC went to the House of Commons for the first time since his stroke, to answer
Prime Minister's Questions.
[2] A 'Moran' was the name given by WSC to a special stimulant pill prescribed by Lord Moran for
him to take before a major speech.

The Bermuda Conference (cancelled because of Churchill's stroke) was
rearranged to take place in the first week of December. On 30 November
Winston celebrated his seventy-ninth birthday: the next day he left London
for Bermuda – a flight of seventeen hours. Christopher (Soames*) accompanied him as his Parliamentary Private Secretary[1].
    Unfortunately the new Conference dates collided with the annual presen-
tation in Stockholm of the Nobel Prizes by the King of Sweden, but there
could be no question as to which event should take priority. The Swedes
were most understanding, and a special invitation was sent to Clementine
asking her to receive the Prize for Literature on her husband's behalf. I was
invited to accompany her.

[1] Christopher in fact fulfilled this role with WSC from 1950, when he was elected to Parliament;
he was officially appointed, 1952–5.

□ From WSC   [Bermuda]
[2 or 3 December 1953]

EXCELLENT JOURNEY. ALL WELL. GOAT[1] SPLENDID. LOVE. W.

[1] Guard of Honour on WSC's arrival was found by Royal Welch Fusiliers, whose mascot is a white
goat.

□ From CSC   10 Downing Street
5 December 1953

My darling Winston,
    Although this is my first letter, I have been thinking of you constantly
since you flew away at Mid-night on December the 1st – A telegram has
just come from you saying that the work is 'heavy'. I do pray that it will

also be fruitful. The newspapers have very good photographs of you (looking well & jaunty) greeting Monsieur Laniel[1] & later General Eisenhower....

This afternoon I went to see Sydney Butler[2] at the Westminster Hospital – There is no facial disfigurement & it seems that in the terrible circumstances everything has gone as well as possible – But it will be a long time till she is well –

I have had several letters from guests saying how much they enjoyed your Birthday Party –

I hope you are being good and attending to & following Charles [Moran*]'s advice.

Tender Love my Darling from
Clemmie

. . .

[1] Joseph Laniel (1889–1975), Prime Minister of France, June 1953–June 1954.
[2] Sydney Butler, wife of R. A. Butler, whom she married in 1926; the only child of Samuel Courtauld. She died of cancer in 1954.

☐ From CSC   10 Downing Street
8 December 1953 2 p.m.

My Darling,

Mary & I are leaving for Stockholm in ten minutes & I have just time to send a line for 'the bag' which leaves this afternoon.

I hope that now the heavy work of the Conference is over you will have a little sunshine & rest before flying home. It's very hard to judge by the newspapers what has been achieved – The general impression is that the French have been as tiresome obstructive & odious as usual – I'm sure you were right to insist on this meeting.

I long to see you Saturday.

Your loving
Clemmie

. . .

After this most testing and dramatic year, we all assembled thankfully again at Chequers for a glowing Christmas.

Chapter XXVI

TIME TO GO

C lementine had borne up valiantly under the pressures of 1953 – the Coronation celebrations, and then the weeks of agonizing anxiety following Winston's stroke; however, towards the end of the year she started having trouble in her right arm and shoulder, eventually diagnosed as neuritis. In the spring of 1954 her condition became acutely painful, and towards the end of May she went to Aix-les-Bains to do a three-week cure; with her, as fellow-patient, went her secretary Grace Hamblin*, who had been having rheumatic problems.

☐ From CSC   Hôtel des Iles Britanniques
22 May 1954   Aix-les-Bains

My darling Winston
   We have been here exactly 48 hours; but it feels much much longer. In a day or two we shall have got bedded down to the routine & then time will fly.
   ... I have (yesterday & to-day) read the Figaro & the Monde – I see things are not going at all well, & that you were obliged to make a statement in the House about France not having informed us about their separate contact with Washington – I hope you have not minded the sour remarks in the Admiralty's Official History[1] – I suppose the Admirals enjoyed making their protest; but one certainly does not feel (nor does Le Monde) that they would have done better without you! You must be an eagle & 'suffer little birds to sing' ...
   ... It is bitterly cold; worse than England; but just now I saw a fitful gleam of pale sun-shine.
   The treatment is most exhausting; but I'm told that in a week we shall be used to it – The Thermal Establishment is crowded, (even at this unfashionable time of year) with pitifully crippled & ill people; so that one is ashamed of one's own little aches & pains....
   Please Darling circulate this letter to Mary & Diana & Sarah etc.
                                                        Your very loving
                                                            Clemmie

I am treated with great respect & politeness, but it is clear that High & Low are deeply upset with England, & indeed with everything!...

¹ Stephen Roskill, *War at Sea*, 2 vols, 1954, 1957.

O From WSC [typewritten]   10 Downing Street
25 May 1954

Darling
    The weekend at Chequers was a great success. Diana [Sandys]¹ admirable. Jock [Colville*] in particular was enormously impressed with his long talk with her.... Anthony [Eden*] and Clarissa enjoyed themselves, but poor Clarissa is, as you probably know, too ill to go back to Geneva². The Doctors have diagnosed duodenal trouble. I had very good talks with Anthony and we are in pretty close agreement on the Geneva issues, though of course I want to be very careful not to have a break with the Americans. They are the only people who can defend the free world even though they bring in Dulles³ to do it....
    ... Monday was Payment of Members⁴ in the House. It all worked out as I wished and had planned. The Tory Party are said to be very angry, but they seem quite friendly in the Smoking Room and considering they were free to do whatever they liked and get paid a monkey [£500] for it, I think they will get over any moral sulkiness. I am trying to have the debate on Friday about the Quebec Agreement⁵ (about which there was that row in the House) withdrawn, as Attlee made a special and public appeal to me in the House to do so.... Today after all the excitement of Payment of Members, in which I avoided speaking, I have had Billy Graham⁶ for half-an-hour, to see me. He made a very good impression and his latest triumph has been to convert the Archbishop of Canterbury.... I think he finds anti-Communism a pretty good ally to salvation in the United States. After this quite agreeable meeting I had the Duke of Windsor to luncheon, who looked very well and made himself most agreeable. The American historians are bringing out some beastly documents ... , but they will do no harm, and I expect it is only put in to add some sensationalism to what would otherwise be a boring book. Talking of War historians, I have an overwhelming case against the Admiralty historian⁷. He belongs to the type of retired Naval Officers who think that politicians should only be in the Admiralty in time of War to take the blame for naval failures, and provide the Naval Officers with rewards in cases of their successes, if any.
    Thursday, alas, I have to address the Women at the Albert Hall....
    This is a toil which lies ahead of me, and I do not conceal from you that original composition is a greater burden than it used to be, while I dislike having my speeches made for me by others as much as I ever did ...
    Alas, I have had two bits of bad luck. The black swans have hatched out and there is only one alive and swimming about with its parents.... The fox was certainly not guilty. However even one is very attractive riding on its Mama's back. The other piece of bad luck is more serious; RED WINTER, the Irish horse in whom I have a half share has a chill and is

probably unfit to run in the £6,000 race which was one of our principal fixtures next Thursday. . . .

I have had Miss Portal[8] to put this down for me as I could not possibly have written it with my own hand during these exceptionally busy days.

[1] In 1953 Diana had suffered a severe nervous breakdown.
[2] The Edens were spending most of their time now in Geneva, where the Conference on Indo-China and Korea was taking place.
[3] John Foster Dulles (1888–1959), US Secretary of State since 1953.
[4] In a free vote on 24 May a resolution to raise MPs' salaries from £1,000 to £1,500 was carried by 280 votes to 166. WSC incurred the wrath of the Opposition by rejecting it on 24 June, but on 8 July a compromise was reached whereby Members were to receive £2 for every day Parliament was sitting, even if not present (£288 extra per year).
[5] The Quebec Agreement of 1944, whereby Britain and the USA pledged never to use the atomic bomb against each other and that neither would use it against a third party without the other's consent.
[6] William Franklin (Billy) Graham (1918–), the American evangelist who held huge rallies world-wide to which many thousands of people flocked.
[7] Captain Stephen Roskill (1903–82), naval historian and later Fellow of Churchill College, Cambridge.
[8] Jane Portal, one of WSC's secretaries from 1949 to 1955. A niece of both R. A. Butler and Lord Portal of Hungerford. In 1975 she married Lord Williams of Elvel.

O From WSC [typewritten]   10 Downing Street
28 May 1954

My Darling
    Your second letter arrived yesterday morning. I was deeply interested in the account you give of your treatment. It seems very severe. . . . I hope and pray you are making progress. How is the Hambling [Grace Hamblin*] getting on? Is she having a stronger or a weaker dose than you?
    . . . There is a real row in the Tory Party about the payment of Members, and there is no doubt it is very unpopular. . . . At the Women's Conference on Wednesday, there was an outburst, and the one poor lady (an M.P.'s wife) who pleaded the case for the increase was not only interrupted but booed, a procedure unusual at women's meetings. When I went to the Albert Hall the next day (yesterday) I tackled the question and was received with the utmost goodwill and respect, though they did not like it. I took an awful lot of trouble making up my speech, and it certainly went over most successfully. I spoke for 42 minutes, and was not at all tired (through taking one of Charles' tablets[1]). . . .
    I began dictating this going down to Kempton where PRINCE ARTHUR was running, & finished it coming back. He was said to have a very good chance, . . . but the mass overtook him and he came in only fourth. . . . Randolph and June also came and I think enjoyed themselves. . . .
    The police have now made a report on the death or disappearance of the cygnets. They say the criminals were carrion crows. . . . The big red fish in the garden pool are threatening to spawn, and I have got the Zoo expert coming over tomorrow to advise how best we ought to handle this very difficult problem. . . .
    I have only given one luncheon party, of eight. It was in honour of Odette[2], whom Randolph located. He and June came, and so did Christopher [Soames*] and Mary, . . .

✍Otherwise I have dined & lunched with Christopher & Jock [Colville*] for company and played a good deal of Bezique. Christopher had a lesson this morning & I shall soon see if he is a good pupil. I am writing in my bed at Chartwell, after having a little sleep. I will write to you again Sunday & in the meanwhile send you all my fondest love.

Your ever loving husband –
W

15 stone exactly on yr machine
but rather battered & vy sore eyes

[1] Called by WSC a 'Moran'. See p. 576 n. 2.
[2] Mme Jacques Pol Roger, widow of the head of the famous Pol Roger champagne business. A most enchanting, attractive person. WSC met her in 1947 at the British Embassy, Paris, and she became a devoted friend of WSC and CSC – and is to this day much beloved also by all the family in different generations.

O From WSC [typewritten]   Downing Street
31 May 1954

My darling,

We had a jolly weekend. Mrs Landemare[1] distinguished herself as usual. Violet [Asquith*/Bonham Carter] made herself most agreeable, and Mary made everything go well. Sarah came down for luncheon and dinner yesterday and Antony [Beauchamp, her husband] for dinner. We had three films, ...

Things are not going too well at your place, (G[eneva]), though there is still a hope of producing something. The Frogs are getting all they can for nothing, and we are getting nothing for all we can. I think my aeroplane journey [to USA] may be very necessary. Meanwhile at home the M.P.s' salaries or expenses, because the choice is still open, causes much concern, ...

I think we have made the best possible arrangements for the spawning. The Zoo man fully approved. Vincent[2] has planted a lot of little flowering water weeds in the shingle amongst the stepping stones in the shallow part, offering the big fish attractive glades for their approaching honeymoon....

I am longing to get your next letter, and hope you will have some encouraging results to report....

✍All my love my dearest One. I think of you often amid the daily cares.

Your ever loving husband
W
...

[1] Mrs Georgina Landemare, the Churchills' cook. In the 1930s she came for special weekends to Chartwell, but from the outbreak of the war she became full-time. She retired officially in 1953, but still came on occasions to help out during 1954.
[2] Victor Vincent, head gardener at Chartwell from 1948 to 1979.

O From WSC [typewritten]   10 Downing Street
5 June 1954

My darling One,
    I was delighted to get your telegram saying that you are coming home on the 12th. I trust it means that everything has gone as well as you expected. I hope to meet you at the Airport and drive you to Chequers....
    Wednesday (2nd) was an active day. Cabinet till 12.30 p.m. Six or eight Ministers wanted to go to the Derby, and I said they were 'under starter's orders'. I went, and lunched with the Derbys[1]. It is wonderful how she has got over her terrible wounds. I could see no trace whatever on her neck of the bullet which so nearly severed her jugular vein. I saw Sydney [Butler], who is very gay and valiant. Rab [Butler*] confided to me that he had bad news. I do not write it. In the evening we had a further two hours Cabinet about the M.P.s' Pay, about which there is a tremendous – petty row in the Tory Party....
    After that I presided as Colonel at the Fourth Hussars Balaclava centenary dinner. They were all very devoted. Ogier and Tim Rogers[2] were both there.
    Today also has been lively. Anthony [Eden*] returned and gave us a full account of the gloomy and confusing prospects at Geneva, where the French are paralysed and the Americans very difficult. The Communists are playing their winning hand with civility.... We had a two hours' Cabinet on this sombre situation before going on to the more squalid but not less bewildering trouble of M.P.s' Pay. Anthony lunched with me afterwards and we have a very perfect understanding, I think, about everything.
    I then rushed off to Hurst Park where we had decided at the last moment to run PRINCE ARTHUR in the 'Winston Churchill' Stakes.... For one thrilling second a hundred yards from home he took the first place; he was third, but even that paid his expenses for a good many months, (£144.5.0.) It was very exciting and I was very glad to have gone....
    I am now on my way back to Chartwell.... The children at Frinton [on-Sea] have enjoyed themselves enormously, and Maria consented to let Christopher [Soames*] come back and look after me.... I stay at Chartwell till Tuesday when I come again to Hurst Park to see PIGEON VOLE run in a smallish race; he has a good chance of winning. Thereafter an Audience [with the Queen] and then an English-Speaking Union Dinner with a nine minutes' broadcast. I have to come up again for the Trooping of the Colour on the 10th....
    I have got a new weighing-machine. It stands next to yours in my bathroom. It says I am 14 stone and a half compared to the previous version of 15 stone on your machine and 15 stone & a ½ on the broken-down one at Chartwell. The two in London are to be tested on Tuesday next and if your machine is proved to be wrong you will have to review your conclusions, and I hope abandon your régime. I have no grievance against a tomato, but I think one should eat other things as well.

✍6th June Sunday,
Darling, I rejoice you are coming home on Saturday for a Chequers week end. . . .

Always your ever loving husband
Winston

. . .

[1] Edward John Stanley, 18th Earl of Derby (1918–94) and his wife Isabel. The Countess had been shot by a footman, who had also shot and killed the butler and under-butler: he was found guilty but insane.
[2] John Ogier and Tim Rogers, the 4th Hussars officers seconded to look after WSC when he was holidaying in Italy in September 1945. See p. 536 n. 1, letter of 5 September 1945.

☐ From CSC   Hôtel des Iles Britanniques
8 June 1954   Aix-les-Bains

My Darling,
The Monde is exercised about your relations with the Tory Party – It recounts in detail the pros & cons of the increased payment of Members of Parliament – And it feels that you are above all these petty considerations & are meditating on the great problems which affect humanity as a whole. It concludes the article by saying that in one week you have had the bad luck to lose Sir John Mellor[1] and a black swan; & that you are much affected by the loss of the young bird[2] – (I thought this would make you laugh.)
Cure over to-day, Hooray! Must now recover from Cure which has been quite something! Longing to see you Saturday.

Tender Love
Clemmie

[1] Sir John Mellor, 2nd Bt (1893–1986), Conservative MP for Sutton Coldfield, Warwickshire, had renounced the Government Whip on 2 June in protest against proposed increase in MPs' salaries.
[2] One of the black swans had flown off; it was eventually located in Holland.

In August 1954 Clementine went to the Riviera with Rhoda Birley; Sir Oswald had died in 1952, and Rhoda remained a delightful friend and companion.

☐ From CSC   Ste Maxime-sur-Mer
3 August 1954   Beauvallon

JUST ARRIVED. LOVELY SPOT. DELICIOUS WEATHER. LOVE FROM RHODA AND CLEMMIE.

☐ From WSC   [Chartwell]
3 August 1954

DELIGHTED ALL WELL AND ATTRACTIVE. WEATHER WARM HERE. MY COLD BETTER. BEST LOVE FROM WINSTON AND CHARTWELL GARRISON.

☐ From CSC   Ste Maxime-sur-Mer
4 August 1954   Beauvallon

HOW IS THE COLD DARLING? DON'T LOOK AT NEW MOON THROUGH GLASS. LOVE. CLEMMIE

☐ From WSC   [Chartwell]
5 August 1954

COLD BETTER. NO MOON VISIBLE. HOPE ALL WELL. LOVE. WINSTON.

☐ From WSC   [Chartwell]
8 August 1954

NO NEWS. WEATHER BAD. COLD LINGERS. CYPRUS SILLY. ALL WELL. WE DO HOPE YOU ARE
HAVING SUN SHINE. FONDEST LOVE.

                                                                        W.

○ From CSC   Golf Hôtel
9 August 1954   Beauvallon s/Mer

My darling Winston,
    Your sad telegram has just come – I wish we could give you some of
our sunshine; though to say the truth this is not super-abundant....
    Rhoda & I are hunting (in our rattle-trap little car) for a villa for you next
year!...
    Please kiss Mary for me & Charlotte Clementine[1]. I enclose a recipe for
Christopher.
    Rhoda is a friend of Captain Cousteau[2] the famous under-sea explorer –
His H.Q. are at Toulon & we are going in a day or two to visit him & his
famous ship the Calypso from which he conducts his experiments. His
wife goes down with him & I can see Rhoda means to dive too. I don't
think I shall – You wear a lung on your back & can go down 300 feet
without a line & stay 2 hours – Ask Miss Gilliatt[3] [secretary] to telephone
quickly for his book, The Silent World by Captain Cousteau.
    This letter is for the whole 'Chartwell Garrison' & brings my dearest
Love –

                                                                  Clemmie
                                                                      ...

[1] Charlotte Clementine Soames (our fourth child) had been born at Chartwell Farm on 18 July
1954.
[2] Jacques Cousteau (1910–97), French naval officer and underwater explorer; inventor of aqualung
diving apparatus and technique of underwater television. Founder of the French Navy Undersea
Research Group and commander of the oceanographic research vessel *Calypso* since 1950.
[3] Elizabeth Gilliatt, Private Secretary to WSC 1946–55.

○ From WSC [Chartwell]
10 August 1954

My Darling,

. . .

Here I stay in bed most of the time and only go out to feed the fish. Gabriel [CSC's Siamese cat] gets on vy well with everyone except his yellow rival. He is vy friendly to me & Rufus and most attractive. My cold has now gone down onto my chest & turned into a cough, and Charles [Moran*] (who comes nearly every day) watches it vigilantly. . . .

The Hamblin [Grace Hamblin*] has just given me the latest reports about poor Nellion[1]. The hospital say they are satisfied w her progress under the rays. She can go out in the afternoons & Tribe [chauffeur] is at her disposal. It is thought better that she sleep at the hospital. . . . I have sent her my love & flowers.

I do nothing, and enjoy it. It is nice having no plans except what one makes from day to day & better still hour to hour. . . .

One gets no consolation at this moment from the animal world. All the Chartwell rabbits are dead[2] & now the poor foxes have nothing to eat, so they attack the little pigs and of course have eaten the few pheasants. It is said they will perish & migrate & that then there will be no one to cope with the beetles and rats. Christopher [Soames*] paints a gloomy picture.

On the other side the Swans are well, & the Zoo came down yesterday to clip their wings so that they cannot fly away if they dislike what is going on around them. Christopher and I have jointly invested nearly £1,000 in <u>8</u> Swedish 'Land race' pigs: out of wh he expects to make a fortune. They live at Bardogs and have remarkable figures . . .

Their hams are much admired and there are only about 1,200 of them in our Pig population of 5 millions. The Boar is said to be worth 5 or 6 Hundred £s, and in two years we hope to make a fortune. . . .

My darling one I brood much about things, and all my moods are not equally gay. But it does cheer my heart to think of you in the sunlight and I <u>pray</u> that Peace & Happiness may rule yr soul. My beloved darling come back soon refreshed & revived, & if possible bring the Sun with you as well as your lovely smile.

W

P.S. I do not sign myself by my usual portrait, as I am not anxious to compete w the Landrace type.

[1] Nellie Romilly, CSC's sister. She had cancer and died on 1 February 1955.
[2] Myxomatosis, the disease fatal to rabbits, was raging in southern England.

□ From WSC [Chartwell]
11 August 1954

YOUR LETTER OF 9TH ARRIVED. PLEASE NO DIVING. LOVE. W.

☐ From CSC   Golf Hôtel
Friday 13 August 1954   Beauvallon s/Mer

My darling Winston,
   It was a joy to receive your letter. I had been feeling rather starved. . . .
   Tomorrow we go to Marseilles to dive with Captain Cousteau; but we
shall not go deeper than 10 meters, as it is very difficult to swim down
deep without being weighted – (I hope you are reading his book?) One
wears a foam rubber suit to keep out the cold. We shall see octopuses; but
I shall not encourage any familiarity. . . .
   . . . Rhoda sends her love

                                                          Your Clemmie
                                                               . . .

○ From WSC ✉   10 Downing Street
19 August 1954

Welcome Home, My Darling
   I do hope you have got real good as well as pleasure out of yr trip. We
await you tonight with eagerness. All is well here except the weather.
   I lunched yesterday with Mary & the children. They are a wonderful
brood. Jeremy [born 1952] is a portent. I have not seen his like before. It is
a lovely home circle and has lighted my evening years. . . .
   We bought another Landrace pig for £300 on Tuesday at a sale where
many of them were sold for £700 or more. A litter fetches £2,000.
Christopher [Soames*] is much excited about it all and may well be on a
good thing. . . .
   Osbert Peake[1] came to dine & sleep last night and Christopher and I had
4 hours' vy informative talk w him about OAP [Old Age Pensions], which
is the dominant feature of next year's Cons[ervative] Programme. . . .
   Peake hates old people (as such) living too long and cast a critical eye
on me. . . . I felt vy guilty. But in rejoinder I took him in to my study and
showed him the 4 packets of proofs of the History of the E.S. Peoples wh
bring 50,000 dollars a year into the island on my account alone. 'You don't
keep me. I keep you'. He was rather taken aback. . . .

                                      Longing to see you my Beloved
                                              Your devoted husband
                                                          Winston

---

[1] Osbert Peake, later 1st Viscount Ingleby (1897–1966). At this date Minister of Pensions and
National Insurance, 1953–5.

From the moment Churchill became Prime Minister again in 1951 there was
a question mark as to how long he would remain in office. After his serious
stroke in 1953 he made an astonishing recovery, and at his best he was still

pre-eminent. Nevertheless he was not the man he was, and there were strong feelings within the Government, including among Cabinet colleagues, that he should fix a date for his retirement, which would allow his 'heir apparent', Anthony Eden*, time to play himself, and a new team, in before the General Election (due before the end of 1955).

Winston himself was undecided: he felt deeply that he had unfinished business in the sphere of world politics which only he could conduct, and throughout 1954 he continued to procrastinate as to when he would retire. In June he told Eden he would hand over in the autumn, but in July (despite being aware that some of his closest colleagues thought he should go) he changed his mind, and on 24 August wrote to Eden telling him that he intended to remain as Prime Minister until the General Election in November 1955. Winston knew that Clementine would deeply deplore this further putting off of the moment of his departure; she had long wanted him to retire, and she herself was wearied out and far from well. He sent her a copy of his letter to Eden with the note that follows.

□ From WSC ✉   10 Downing Street
25 August 1954

My darling One,
    I did not worry you with the enclosed yesterday. Harold [Macmillan; Foreign Secretary] thought I ought to send it. It has gone. The responsibility is mine. But I hope you will give me your love.

Your ever loving
W

It was Clementine's custom when at Chequers to 'look in' on Winston, who habitually worked in bed in the mornings, on her way downstairs. This note to her indicates how strung-up – and perhaps over-touchy – she was in these difficult days.

○ From WSC ✉   Chequers
25 August 1954

My darling beloved Clemmie,
    Do forgive me for my lapse this morning. I was preoccupied with dictating a message to Ike. I only wanted the Portal [Jane] not to go back to the Office but wait in the next room while we had a talk. I was enraptured by yr lovely smile of greeting, & longing to kiss you. All this I spoiled by my clumsiness & gaucherie. I cherish your morning comings & I beseech you to be noble & generous as you always are to your thoroughly penitent & much ashamed, but loving & hopeful

W

P.S. You have been so bright & splendid here and I have thanked God to see you much stronger. I will try to do better.

This missive shows Clementine in indulgent mood.

○ From CSC ⊠   Chequers
[September 1954]

A Petition . . .
   The 'White parlour' is the ladies' Bower & the <u>private</u> sitting room of the
Wife of the Prime Minister.
   Would it be possible for the Prime Minister when he confabulates with
men, to use: –
   1) 'the Prime Minister's Study' (opposite dining-room)
   or
   2) the long Gallery upstairs – ?

                                                                      . . .

[WSC has written on this note:]
   I was only trying to catch a fat mouse for the Cat, . . .
   I will not trespass again.

                                                                      W.

In his address to the Conservative Party Conference on 9 October, Churchill
had given no hint as to his retirement plans. On 18 October he re-shuffled
his Government.
   Clementine's heart had never been in Winston's last lap as Prime Minister;
although she showed a brave face in public, behind the scenes her morale
was often desperately low (exacerbated by neuritis, which had increasingly
afflicted her from the end of 1953); and she was immensely touchy and difficult. Winston himself could be maddening, and on occasions behaved like
a spoilt child; but now there were times when Clementine harried him too
much, and could be unreasonable and unkind. Although there were some
explosive scenes, Winston on the whole showed unusual forbearance, recog-
nizing that he had imposed this extra mileage on her. Both were always eager
to repair rifts.
   Here is an 'olive twig' from Winston – very probably slipped under her
door.

○ From WSC ⊠   10 Downing Street
[undated, probably 1954]

Darling –
   Fondest love.
   I am so sorry I was awkward at dinner.
   My heart was full of nothing but love but my thoughts were wayward.
                                                        Your ever devoted
                                                                      W

November 30 was Winston's eightieth birthday, and it was veritably a national – as well as our family's – day for celebration.

The family gathered at Chequers for Christmas – our last one there.

○ From WSC ⊠   Chequers
25 December 1954

My Beloved Darling,
    Buy yourself something you like out of this [a fat cheque], and keep the rest for a Christmas without a

All my love
Winston

On 8 March 1955 Churchill confirmed to Eden* that he would resign on 5 April. On 11 March a telegram from Sir Roger Makins (British Ambassador at Washington) reported that President Eisenhower suggested that he, Chancellor Adenauer[1] and Churchill might meet in Paris in early May, and following on this the President mooted that plans might be envisaged for a meeting with the top Russians. This apparently changed situation led Churchill to tell Eden (on 13 March) that the April date fixed between them must now be regarded as in abeyance.

[1] Konrad Adenauer (1876–1967), Chancellor of the Federal Republic of Germany, 1949–63.

○ From WSC [typewritten]   10 Downing Street
15 March 1955

Most Secret
Burn or Lock up

My Darling Clemmie,
    The Cabinet [on 14 March] met for the purpose of approving the answer to be sent to the long Makins telegram I showed you. However, Anthony [Eden*] had been unable to compose a draft, and we had a wandering talk over the whole field, at the end of which he asked whether this made any difference in the planned dates on which we had agreed. I pointed out that it was unprecedented to discuss such matters at Cabinet, and most of the Ministers seemed very embarrassed. I made it clear that I should be guided by what I believed was my duty and nothing else, and that any Minister who disagreed could always send in his resignation. The poor Cabinet, most of whom knew nothing about the inner story[1], seemed

puzzled and worried. Of course, as you know, only one thing has influenced me, and that is the possibility of arranging with Ike [Eisenhower] for a top level meeting in the near future with the Soviets. Otherwise I am very ready to hand over responsibility. I thought this Makins message offered a new chance, and that is why I am testing it. Thus the Cabinet ended, and I had to concentrate on my speech. Later in the day Winthrop Aldrich[2] brought a message to the Foreign Office from Washington to the effect that Ike was not willing himself to participate in a meeting with Russia. Whether this referred to a top level meeting at a later date or not is still uncertain. It may only apply to the immediate meeting of the Four Powers referred to in the Makins note, but this I understand is to be, like all the other failures, upon the Foreign Office level. We are now going to meet again today to settle the answer to America. Of course, if it is clear that Ike will not in any circumstances take part in the near future in a top level meeting, that relieves me of my duty to continue, and enables me to feed the hungry[3]. This will soon settle itself....

I do hope the rest is doing you good[4], and will keep you informed.

All my love
Your ever-loving husband
W

[1] i.e. that a date, 5 April, had been agreed between WSC and Eden.
[2] Winthrop Aldrich (1885–1974), US Ambassador to Britain, 1953–7.
[3] Presumably Anthony Eden – hungering for office.
[4] CSC was at Chequers, trying to throw off a flare-up of her neuritis.

Once it was clear that President Eisenhower would not involve himself in a meeting with the Russians, there remained no reason for Winston to change the originally agreed date for his resignation.

All of us who were close to him understood so well that he should be low and sad as the day drew near. Although my mother was intensely relieved that the decision had been finally taken, she knew what this moment must mean for Winston. In my diary on 19 March I recorded her comment to me: 'It's the first death – and for him, a death in life.'

There were many mechanical arrangements to set in place ...

☐ From CSC [typewritten] ✉   Chequers
25 March 1955 [Friday]

<u>PRIME MINISTER from C.S.C.</u>

This week-end will be the last that we shall spend and sleep at Chequers. We shall want to say Goodbye to everybody here and I am sure you will like to say something to them.

Next week-end we had planned to spend in London because of the Birthday party you are giving for me on Friday April the 1st, and because the Queen is coming to dinner on the Monday, and of course I should want to be all that day in London trying to make the arrangements as perfect as possible. I wonder if you would like to come down to Chequers to lunch on Sunday the 3rd, after which we could make our farewells, and then go back to Downing Street? If you liked we could ask a few people to dinner there on Saturday the 2nd and again on Sunday the 3rd.

I am sending you this minute so that you have time to consider it before we meet here tomorrow evening.

Clemmie

O From WSC [typewritten & annotated
      in his own hand] ⊠   [10 Downing Street]

31 March 1955
APRIL.
<u>Sunday 3rd</u> . . . . Chequers for Luncheon.
                    [Monday 4th][1]
<u>Tuesday 5</u> . . . . 6.30 Audience.
                                         <u>Announcement of my</u>
                                              <u>resignation on radio that</u>
                                              <u>night.</u>
<u>Wednesday 6th</u> . . . . Luncheon at No. 10.
                                              Mrs Pamela Churchill to
                                              luncheon.
                 4 p.m.   Staff cocktails
                5.0–6.0p.m.   Sir Winston leaves for
                                                Chartwell

While the above is going on the name of the successor is announced, probably afternoon of Wed. 6. The letter to Mr John Harvey[2] which may have been sent some hours earlier will be opened by him, and made public by me to the newspapers (if any)[3] & radio on Thursday morning. Is it possible for me to give Christopher [Soames*] and Mary dinner at Chartwell on Wednesday night? Film?

I do not want to be in London on Thursday or Friday, nor to leave for London Airport[4] via Downing Street, I shall be much pestered by people wishing to say goodbye, and I shall be asked to go to the House of Commons to see the 1922 Committee, etc. [in margin ✍: I might even be made to come to <u>H of C</u>] Whereas I simply propose to disappear and remain in strict privacy at Chartwell till I board the airplane for Sicily. Whatever you like can be fitted in with this. There is not the slightest reason why you should not remain here [No. 10] until Saturday morning. However it would be lovely if you would come to Chartwell as soon as you can Thursday or Friday, and if we could go to the Airport from there – . . .

I must have at least two days at Chartwell as I have all the business affairs and farm affairs to settle . . . : [in margin ✍: Also I want to be out of London.]

Arrangements for transferring no. 10.

Much may be labelled before Saturday the 9th but nothing should be moved. I do not wish to be present in the house as my Successor may wish to hold a Cabinet. I propose to inform him that the Cabinet Room will be at his disposal on __Thursday__, if that will be convenient. As Mr Pitblado [Private Secretary] is staying he will be at the Successor's disposal. . . . I propose to suggest to my successor that we should be completely clear of the house by Friday the 15th, the Cabinet Room & office being at his disposal meanwhile.

W.

[1] WSC made no reference in this relentless dictated countdown to the splendid dinner and reception he and Clementine would give on the evening of Monday 4 April for the Queen and Prince Philip. (No deeper meaning need be attached to this omission – his mind was concentrated on the seemly sequence of smaller and mainly domestic matters.)
[2] John Harvey (1920–), WSC's Constituency Chairman, 1954–6.
[3] There was a major strike in the newspaper industry from 25 March, lasting for nearly a month. Only the *Manchester Guardian* continued to appear.
[4] WSC and CSC planned to take a holiday in Sicily immediately after his resignation.

These arrangements – and one senses how much it cost Winston to chart out so trenchantly the last steps of these final days – were fulfilled with punctilio and grace.

And after the party for his personal staff at No. 10, Winston drove away down to Chartwell.

To a young reporter waiting there he said:

'It's always nice to come home.'

Chapter XXVII

SEEKING SUNSHINE

The holiday in Sicily was not a success, despite the agreeable company of the Prof (Lindemann*, now Lord Cherwell) and Jock Colville*: it poured with rain most of the time, and Clementine's neuritis gave her no respite. They had intended to stay three weeks, but came home after a fortnight.

In their absence the date of the General Election was announced for 26 May[1].

During this summer Clementine was in a thoroughly exhausted and depressed state. To the strain of the last lap of Winston's Prime Ministership was added the continuing pain of neuritis in her right arm and shoulder, now made worse by pain from her left wrist, which she had fractured in a fall in June. In August she went to St Moritz in Switzerland to undertake a recommended cure. Her secretary Heather Wood[2] accompanied her. Later I went out to keep her company.

[1] In the Election the Conservatives were returned with an increased majority: Conservatives, 345; Labour, 277; Liberals, 6; Sinn Fein, 2. Conservative majority, 60.
[2] CSC's secretary from June 1953 to March 1956.

☐ From CSC   Suvretta House
5 August 1955   St Moritz

My Darling, It was very sweet of you to come with me to the Airport. It sent me off happy in my laborious effort to regain my health. . . .

I tucked up comfortably in the station hotel [at Zürich] for 2 hours & then began the rather tedious 5-hour journey (with a change) to St Moritz – Dinner in the train was delicious & we were made most welcome in this very comfortable hotel –

The pain is considerable but supportable; I have given myself one injection[1], but hope soon to do without – Tomorrow I'm seeing the Spa Doctor to see if he can soothe the neuritis away with some magic peat or pine baths –

All my love Darling
Your devoted
Clemmie.

I'm spending to-day in my room so as to get used to the altitude –

[1] CSC's doctor had prescribed pethidine injections which she gave herself to alleviate pain.

○ From WSC   Chartwell
5 August [1955]

Darling,
    Monty [Montgomery*] came to lunch today. He was vy amusing & made most thorough inquiries about you. I told him all there was to tell. We all went down to the Pool with Jeremy[1] who was a gt success.
    I am eagerly awaiting news of you & hope to receive some on Monday. It may well be that you will have a set back for a few days and that then the attacks of pain will lessen.... Anyhow do not Despair. I beg you not to do that. I am <u>sure</u> you will find a remedy. I know it may be hard, but you have valiant blood.
    This is the third letter I have tried to write to you and always failed. I love you so much and am determined to persevere.
    It will be easier when I have one of your own dear letters to begin on.
                                        Always your loving husband
                                                          W

[1] Our second son Jeremy Soames (now three and a half) was one of Monty's godsons.

□ From CSC   Suvretta House
8 August 1955   St Moritz

My Darling,
    Thank-you for several telegrams; & soon I am hoping for a letter –
    I'm beginning to feel better for which I thank God....
    ... The scenery round here is magnificent but a little drastic for my taste; chains of lakes overhung by frowning mountains the tops generally wreathed in clouds, but sometimes rearing themselves against an intense blue sky. <u>When</u> the sun shines it is really delicious, very hot, the air like champagne –
    I hope Darling you are happy
                                        Your loving & devoted
                                                     Clemmie
This afternoon Mr Einstein[1] is taking me to explore the Bernina Pass....

[1] Lewis Einstein, a courtly old American widower. He lived in Paris, but came regularly to St Moritz, and he and CSC made friends.

○ From WSC   Chartwell
8 August [1955]

My darling, I was so glad to get your letter.... Now it has come I take up my pen to answer, aided by Toby[1] who is sitting on the sheet of notepaper insisting on lapping the ink from my pen in order to send you a personal message.... He is a wonderful little bird. He pecked and scribbled with his beak and what I have written so far is as much his work as mine. He has gone back to his cage now (by my bedside) so perhaps I may write better. (I have also had my pen refilled.)

Monty evidently enjoyed himself and has given me a letter to send you. He has asked to come on Sunday 11th September. You may well be here & high time too.... (Toby is back again on my hand). This is really a joint message so I made him sign it.

I have had Hodge[2] down for a couple of days & in a quarter of an hour expect Bill Deakin.... I am diluting him with Nemon[3] who comes at about 4....

My dearest One, you have all my love. Do write to me & don't give up hope.

Your ever devoted husband
W

[1] A blue budgerigar, given to WSC by Dido Cairns, Christopher's sister, for Christmas 1954. He was a great character, and a feature of WSC's life.
[2] Alan Hodge (1915–79), joint editor of monthly magazine, *History Today*. He led team of young historians who assisted WSC with the revision and production of *A History of the English-Speaking Peoples*.
[3] Oscar Nemon (1906–85), brilliant sculptor. Commissioned by the Queen to create a bust of WSC for Windsor Castle in 1952. Subsequent statues/busts by him are in the Guildhall (1955) and in the Members' Lobby of the House of Commons (1969). Several foreign countries have WSC statues by him. Nemon became a friend of the family.

○ From WSC   Chartwell
10 August [1955]

Darling,

Your letter of the 8th has reached me this morning. I am enchanted that you feel better. This is really good news after only three days. Let me know what the local doctor says after his blood tests, and also what he prescribes....

I have been working at my book[1], & Christopher [Soames*] and Mary have made all sorts of plans to fill in the 11 days (wh begin tomorrow) which I am bound to say seem attractive. Violet [Asquith*/Bonham Carter] is coming here for Saturday, today we have the Ismays....

Anthony & Cleopatra [the Edens*] have chosen the 10th September for their visit .... They only stay one day. I do hope you will be back flourishing. Monty lunches on the 11th September & I am trying to persuade them not to go till after lunch.

Tender love my dearest Clemmie.
Your devoted husband,
W.

Toby has signed

[1] *A History of the English-Speaking Peoples*, 4 vols, 1956–8. Started in the mid-1930s in succession to *Marlborough,* and virtually completed at the outbreak of war. It was put aside until after the completion of WSC's war memoirs. Interrupted again by his prime ministership in 1951; he started revising chapters while convalescing from his stroke in 1953, and within 48 hours of his resignation in 1955 he resumed work on its final stages.

□ From CSC   Suvretta House
Saturday 13 August 1955   St Moritz

My Darlings (The plural includes Toby!)

I came away with the first <u>8</u> Chapters of your Book [*A History of the English-Speaking Peoples*]. I began reading it the day before yesterday & have nearly finished it. I am thrilled – I think ordinary people will love it & they will now 'take to' History as they did to painting[1]. Please send me out a further instalment by Mary – I must keep up with it....

I am so thankful, and excited because this is the first morning practically free from pain – I think the peat packs must now be working in a <u>benevolent</u> way – The first two treatments produced swelling & pain....

Darling I hope you are well – I feel you are happy surrounded and cherished by so many who love you....

Your devoted
Clemmie

[1] CSC is referring to *Painting as a Pastime*, published in 1948. A number of people were encouraged to paint for themselves after reading this charming small book.

□ From CSC   Suvretta House
16 August 1955   St Moritz

My Darling,

. . .

My acquaintance Mr Einstein who takes Heather Wood & me for drives has become argumentative over Cyprus[1] – He says we have behaved badly to the Greeks over it years ago in our efforts to please the Turks – He implemented his remarks with numerous dates & incidents – I felt rather cross as I felt I couldn't say the only thing I could think of, i.e. 'Of course Americans always want us to give everything away' –

Instead I remarked (I hope) with dignity, 'If you will put your thesis shortly in writing I will provide you with the answer!' He was also controversial about the Dardanelles & about Singapore! So I have decided he is hostile & I am chucking my next engagement with him! But you might send me a concise justification of our possession of Cyprus.

Enraged Clem Bird

[1] Cyprus (population 80% Greek Orthodox Christian, 20% Turkish Muslim) had been since 1954 in a state of unrest, Greek Cypriots desiring union with Greece (*enosis*), which was strongly opposed by the Turkish minority. To safeguard British Middle East interests the Eden Government decided Cyprus must remain British. Following terrorist activities and general unrest, a state of emergency was declared (1955) and a strong force of British troops sent to keep order.

○ From WSC   Chartwell
20 August 1955

My darling,

Mary comes home to-day & stays with me[1]. She leaves on Monday & will bring you all the news....

Your letter dated 18 has just reached me. It tells me what I wanted. There has been a definite improvement during the fortnight. This is anyhow to the good, and I feel you are right to postpone yr return. . . .

I shd be a bit stiff with Einstein. We <u>saved</u> Greece from being inside the Iron Curtain by our personal exertions. Cyprus has never had any pledges from us that she shd be handed over to the Greeks, who have never had her. Although I do not say that this is a decisive argument, we have embarked upon a clearance plan [of troops] fm Egypt which is based upon our base in Cyprus, & we are not likely to choose this moment (above all others) to compromise it. The Greek revilings leave me quite cold – or indeed hot me up. I will see if I can put something more down for Mary to bring.

Tender love my dearest one. I am struggling along with my book – most bucked up by yr approval –

All my love & many kisses
Your devoted & loving husband
W

. . .

P. S. I go out harvesting every day in the new Land Rover

[1] I had been staying in the North with Christopher, our children were at the seaside, and the Farm House shut up.

☐ From CSC   Suvretta House
24 August 1955   St Moritz

My Darling, It is a great joy having Mary with me.

Yesterday we went for a drive with Mr Einstein – We both set upon him about Cyprus (with the help of your letter), after which he became quite amenable.

– – – I have just been speaking to you on the telephone. . . .

I'm getting on with the cure & feel stronger, but can't walk more than ½ a mile which is mortifying –

I'm just going to start out on the new chapters you have sent me – I love your book –

Darling Winston take care of yourself –

Your loving & devoted
Clemmie

. . .

the 25th
Mary has just been having a lawn-tennis lesson from a very good professional. . . .

God bless you my Darling, and us both –
Clemmie

○ From WSC [typewritten]   Chartwell
28 August 1955

My darling,

    I am so glad that my letter was of some use in dealing with Mr Einstein. He is not the great Einstein, who died earlier in the year. This I should have known.

    Christopher [Soames*] leaves this afternoon. His visit has been very pleasant. We went to Windsor races yesterday, and won a good victory [with Pinnacle]....

    I sent you two more chapters yesterday. I am so glad you like the book. I am much encouraged by it. You now have the whole of Book II, ending with 'The Black Death', which reduced the population of the world by at least a third at a time when it was certainly not over-crowded. Let me know how you get on, ...

    Let me repeat yr ending. God bless you my darling, and us both.

                                               Winston

□ From CSC   St Moritz
[27 August 1955]

HURRAH FOR PINNACLE. LOVING THOUGHTS TO YOU BOTH.

                                       CLEMMIE AND MARY

In mid-September Winston and Clementine went to La Capponcina at Cap d'Ail, lent to them by Max Beaverbrook*. Clementine stayed until mid-October, before returning home: the neuritis still lingered.

○ From WSC [typewritten]   La Capponcina
26 October 1955   Cap d'Ail

My darling,

    The weather is very pleasant – bright and calm. The only change is that it has become a little cooler. I am very glad that Sarah is coming out again on Friday....

    I am bidden tomorrow to lunch with [Emery] Reves* and Madame R. at the St Pol [de Vence] Restaurant, which I believe is where you went the other day, and I will look at the Matisse Chapel after lunch.

    ✍Darling, your Doctor's account is very vague. Perhaps Sarah will bring me details. I send this letter by Hodge[1] & Kelly[2] who are returning home today, so it shd reach you tonight & is quicker than a telegram. I am certainly better & am sure I shall be able to do the speeches all right – within the limits[3]....

... The time passes fairly quickly here. I have been every night to the Casino! & not a word in the Press, & am still playing on my winnings. When they stop I shall stop too.

Darling one, I think of you so much & of how we are to lead a happy life. I was quite content with Nov. 15 as my date for going home. It will be interesting to get in touch with political affairs again....

Sarah will bring me news of Diana[4]. I have none now. She is vy dear to me.

I am afraid this is a vy discursive letter, but I know you will receive it with kindness & I hope pleasure.

Always my tender love my dear one & many many kisses.

Your devoted husband
W
...

[1] Alan Hodge, literary assistant (see p. 595 n. 2).
[2] Denis Kelly, young barrister who came during 1946 to help WSC with his war memoirs, continuing as his assistant for *A History of the English-Speaking Peoples*.
[3] WSC had suffered a 'spasm of the artery' on 2 June 1955 at Chartwell. For several days he suffered the effects in minor inconveniences; but he was well enough to go to London on 8 June to take his seat in the new Parliament: speeches, however, were an anxiety – and several loomed.
[4] This summer had seen a recurrence of Diana's mental and nervous illness.

□ From CSC   28 Hyde Park Gate
27 October 1955

My Darling

I am so much pleased to get your lovely long letter; and Sarah will bring you this one. She will have a pleasant journey with Bill Deakin [principal research assistant] & have fun with you and him –

I feel your long stay in the benign climate of the South of France has done you good –

Christopher is thrilled, because Anthony E[den*, Prime Minister] accosted him in the Members' Lobby & let him understand (though not in so many words) that the future was rosy – He (Anthony) explained elaborately why the Ministerial re-construction was delayed[1]....

The neuritis is much better, but I have got a very bad cold; so I am staying in my lovely bed-sitting room well wrapped up –

Your loving
Clemmie
...

[1] Christopher Soames was appointed Under-Secretary of State for Air on 20 December 1955.

O From WSC [typewritten]   La Capponcina
9 November 1955

My Darling,

I am looking forward to returning on Monday and seeing you all again. I think you will find me better, and I have no doubt about getting through all right on Friday at Hawkey Hall [in his constituency]....

We have engaged ourselves in reconnoitring houses[1], but without any result. Do not be alarmed therefore by anything you read in the Nice-Matin.

Will you give us dinner on Monday night. It would be nice to ask Anthony M.B. [Montague Browne*] and his wife, and of course I should like to see Randolph and June, and Mary and Christopher if they are free.

I am leaving my speech till I return. The Government seem to be getting through their Parliamentary difficulties all right, but it is difficult to judge from out here.

✍Darling One, I think so much of you & hope & trust you are making progress. I love you vy much my dearest Clemmie & feel sure you reciprocate these sentiments wh spring from my heart.

Your devoted husband
W

. . .

[1] WSC nursed a plan to acquire a villa on the Riviera, where he now desired to spend more and more of his time. CSC viewed this prospect with dismay: two houses in England seemed more than enough to her. Of course whenever WSC sallied forth to look at a prospective house it was always picked up by the local press.

☐ From CSC ✉   28 Hyde Park Gate
14 November 1955

My Darling,

I would have liked to be at the Airport to greet you; but I want to be fresh for to-night & so I will await you here.

The time has been long without you and I long to be with you again.

Your loving
Clemmie

. . .

In early January 1956 Clementine's health was so poor that she entered University College Hospital for a complete check-up; her stay there was expected to last a few days, but she caught a streptococcal infection, and was in hospital for nearly three weeks.

Meanwhile Winston (as had been planned before Clementine became so ill) paid the first of many visits to Emery and Wendy Reves* at La Pausa, their beautiful house at Roquebrune[1].

In mid-February Clementine and Sylvia Henley*, who had also been ill, went for a convalescent sea voyage to Ceylon.

Winston hoped so much to lure Clementine to La Pausa to recuperate, but she preferred to make her own plans.

¹ Originally built by the Duke of Westminster ('Bendor') for Coco Chanel.

○ From WSC   La Pausa
17 January 1956

My darling,

I have had so much pleasure & relief at hearing good news of you. Things sound so bad and to be at a distance is vy trying – But this morning when I was awakened at half past nine to hear from Doctor Rosenheim that your temperature was normal I was filled with joy.

I have passed the time since I arrived three-quarters in bed & come down to meals. Reves* & Wendy are most obliging. They ask the guests I like and none I don't. A few people have written, & so we had last night Daisy Fellowes & her young man Hamish Edgar. Daisy was vy sprightly.... She is wonderfully well maintained & kept us all agog. Her young man is coming to play bezique with me this afternoon at 4....

... On Wednesday we all go to lunch or dinner with R.A.B. [Butler*] if the weather (which is unbroken clouds) permits. Thursday we are going to paint still-life or garden according as the sun shines.

My darling one, I send you all my love....

With all my heart,
Your loving husband
W

(own paw)

○ From WSC   [La Pausa]
17 January 1956

My Darling,

All the children go home today by one route or another. Arabella¹ & Celia² were both vy sweet to me. Diana will give you accounts. She seems vy well & mistress of herself. Randolph brought Onassis³ (the one with the big yacht) to dinner last night. He made a good impression upon me. He is a vy able and masterful man & told us a bit about Whales. He kissed my hand!

I have passed another morning in bed at the Book. I had a peep outside yesterday, but today the sun has definitely begun to shine & I shall take a walk in the garden after luncheon....

I am so grieved & worried by the news that your throat has not cleared up entirely and that you had a temperature....

My dear One I would so much like to kiss you now. I send you my love

by this. You see I have written it by my own paw & no one has seen it.
The children will take it home.

All my love
Your devoted
W

[1] Arabella Churchill (1949–), Randolph and June's only child.
[2] Celia Sandys, Diana and Duncan's younger daughter (see p. 482 n. 2).
[3] Aristotle ('Ari') Onassis (1906–75), Turkish-born Greek shipowner. Built up the world's largest independent shipping line, and in the 1950s pioneered the construction of supertankers. His first marriage (1946) to Athina Livanos (1929–74; see p. 628 n. 3) ended in divorce, 1960. After a long relationship with the opera singer Maria Callas, in 1968 Onassis married Jacqueline Kennedy, widow of US President John Kennedy.

□ From CSC   London
17 January 1956

THANK YOU DARLING FOR YOUR TWO LOVING LETTERS. AM JUST COMING ROUND THE BEND AND
HOPE TO WIN THE RACE. PLEASE SEND ME FOR PROFESSOR ROSENHEIM ONE HUNDRED OF YOUR
BEST REPEAT BEST CIGARS. LOVE. CLEMMIE.

□ From WSC
17 January 1956

I REJOICE YOU ARE BETTER. HAVE SENT CIGARS. LOVE. WINSTON.

○ From CSC   28 Hyde Park Gate
29 January 1956

My darling, I am ashamed that this is my first letter to you. But I have been
so sick & weary that I have not been able to hold a pen or read a book.
But now I am really better. It is just 6 days since I left that unspeakably
dreary hospital –

Your Pamela [Lytton[1]] has just been to luncheon with me, looking
exquisite & pretty in spite of her intense pain – We exchanged the names
of our drugs & I have put her on to demanding pethidine from her doctor
– I, for my part, am going to explore one of her pain killers.

When I know more about Ceylon I will tell you.

Your loving devoted
Clemmie Cat
. . .

P.S. I am shocked at the idea that the Government mean (perhaps) to 'jam'
Athens Radio[2]. I can't imagine anything more ineffective – And all the time
we have been scolding Russia for 'jamming' us – It's lucky the Government
have got a long term before them or I think Gaitskell[3] would get them out.
I don't think Sir John Harding[4] is equal to that brilliant scoundrel
Makarios[5].

[1] Wife of 2nd Earl of Lytton (see p. 5 n. 17).

[2] Although at the time the Government neither confirmed nor denied reports of the jamming of Anglophobic Greek broadcasts to Cyprus, it was admitted later (28 March) in the House of Commons that this had taken place and that it had been 'effective'.

[3] Hugh Gaitskell (1906–63), Leader of the Labour Party since December 1955. Former Chancellor of the Exchequer, 1950–1.

[4] Field Marshal Sir John Harding, later 1st Baron Harding of Petherton (1896–1989), Governor and C.-in-C. Cyprus, 1955–7.

[5] Makarios III (Mikhail Christodoulou Mouskos) (1913–77), Cypriot politician and Greek Orthodox archbishop since 1950. Suspected of collaboration with the Greek Cypriot resistance organization EOKA, he was exiled to the Seychelles by the British, 1956–7. Later President of the Republic of Cyprus, 1960–77.

○ From WSC   La Pausa
30 January 1956

My Darling,

Assuming you have made up your mind to start with Sylvia [Henley*] on the 17th [February], I shall come home on the 10th to see you off...

I had hoped to persuade you to come out and convalesce out here & that you wd meet Wendy who is a vy charming person. But I feel that with Sylvia & the Ceylon sun your plan is a good one, and the weather here in February is vy half & half (today & yesterday unfit for human consumption) and once you have got through the Bay of Biscay you will have a good convalescent cruise. Be vy careful about Ceylon & do not treat it like England.

Give me warning of any change because my plans depend on yours, my dearest One. I spend the days mostly in bed, & get up for lunch and dinner. I am being taken through a course of Manet, Monet, Cézanne & Co by my hosts who are both versed in modern painting, and practise in the studio.... Also they have a wonderful form of gramophone wh plays continuously Mozart and other composers of merit, and anything else you like on 10-fold discs. I am in fact having an artistic education with vy agreeable tutors.

Darling, unless I hear to the contrary we meet on the 10th at 28 [Hyde Park Gate].

All my love
Your devoted husband,
W

...

□ From CSC   P & O Himalaya
Sunday 19 February 1956

My Darling

Tomorrow we shall be at Gibraltar. We passed the Bay of Biscay with scarcely a ripple –

But Sylvia & I have not left our cabins – Sylvia because she is exhausted by the masses of penicillin.... I have stayed below to keep her company.

We are both very happy in each other's company, but we are longing to reach the warm weather –

I think of you much my Darling and admire your dignity in political matters & your philosophy –

Will you please consider & weigh the following proposition – That I should go straight home reaching Tilbury on April the 11th & that the same day or a day or two later you should join me at Chartwell.

By that time you will have had another month in the South of France, & England is lovely in April – 'Oh to be in England now that April's here', wrote Rupert Brooke [actually Robert Browning!]. If Mr Onassis invited you & a party, you could have a little Easter Cruise with Mr Reves* and Wendy & Mary & Christopher [Soames*] etc. But somehow I don't want to be beholden to this rich powerful man, & for the news to be blazoned. Similarly, tho' to a lesser degree, I don't want to stay at 'La Pausa', though one day I would like to meet 'Wendy'. – Also I want this journey to last as long as possible, & to get off at Marseilles & rattle along either by train or car to Monte Carlo, then stay with that unconventional[1] & uneasy ménage does not allure me – Please forgive me; but you can't teach an old dog new tricks – But I am happy that you should be there in the sunshine which surely must come.

Darling I love you very much....

Sylvia is deep in your book & is enthralled.

Your loving and devoted
Clemmie

. . .

[1] Emery Reves and Wendy Russell were married in 1964; but were generally referred to by the Churchill family and their staff and *milieu* as Mr and Mrs Reves.

○ From WSC   28 Hyde Park Gate
27 February 1956

My darling One,

It is hard to catch you with a letter at your different ports of call, so I have telegraphed. I do hope you are both feeling better and that the Indian Ocean has been warm. As you voyage southwards you carry my thoughts with you....

I spent the long weekend at Chartwell mostly alone. It was not fit for more than one peep out. I walked however round the ponds – 3 inches of ice – and down to the Farm ... & they all [Soameses and house guests] came to dine & see the film on Saturday. It was a vy good one, The Four Feathers, with lots of good pictures of the battle of Omdurman. These stirred my memory, though accuracy was not achieved.

I had made all arrangements for going back to Roquebrune on Monday, March 5, ... I thirst for warmth, and Chartwell even with Mary & Christopher & Dido[1] does not make up for the snowy landscape my window reveals. The thaw however seems to have begun here too & will I trust continue.

I came back this morning to attack the Debate on Foreign Affairs which are in a fog. Tomorrow & Wednesday Defence is the subject. I shall vote with the Government. . . .

I will write about your landing at Marseilles [on return voyage] & bringing Sylvia [Henley*] with you to stay for a few days at La Pausa. I do hope she liked Vol I. She is, I am sure, a good judge.

Tender love my darling Clemmie from yr old & battered [pig]

Your devoted husband
W

---

[1] Dido Cairns (1918–97), Christopher's elder sister, who married Major Hugh Cairns MC in 1939 (he died 1996). She and Christopher were devoted to each other, and WSC and CSC liked her very much. (See also p. 595 n. 1, letter of 8 August 1955.)

○ From WSC   La Pausa
3 [March] 1956

My darling,

Here I am, with Diana [Sandys] & Anthony [Montague Browne*], in gt comfort but nursing a sore throat with the aid of Dr Roberts[1], who is I think a good man. (I had him last time, you will remember.) Meanwhile you shd have reached Colombo & I hope are already safely ensconced. I await a letter. . . .

I had an interesting time in London, & saw a lot of Christopher & Maria & also of the P.M. [Anthony Eden*]. He is having a hard time & the horizon is dark whichever way one looks. The Defence debate was an awful flop. . . . ; the condition of the air force; the state of the navy; all very disturbing. W.M. [Walter Monckton][2] was not good at this difficult task – to which he is completely new; and Nigel Birch[3] was deservedly shouted down.

Christopher [now Under-Secretary of State for Air] goes into action next Monday & will I trust establish himself. He has a gt chance.

I give you my impressions gained in my corner seat[4], which is most respectfully kept open for me by Hinchinbroke[5], and wh I fill at the critical moment.

I have brought Toby [his budgerigar] out here! He can go home whenever I choose. There is no restraint in England now – so I took him along. He is a bit subdued, but I think it is only the change of scene. . . .

I must close this letter now my dearest Clemmie.

Your ever loving husband,
W

. . .

---

[1] Dr John Roberts, ex-RAF, who had an English practice in Monte Carlo, and who always looked after WSC when he was on the Riviera. Both WSC and CSC liked him very much; Lord Moran was contemptuous of him – and, I suspect, jealous.
[2] See p. 424 n. 2. At this date Minister of Defence (December 1955 to October 1956).
[3] Nigel Birch, later Baron Rhyl (1906–81). At this date Secretary of State for Air (December 1955–January 1957).
[4] WSC's time-honoured seat in the 1930s: the corner seat below the gangway.
[5] Victor Montagu, Viscount Hinchinbroke (1906–95). Sat in the House as Conservative MP 1941–62, under his courtesy title. A friend of Diana's, he came quite often to Chartwell in the early 1930s. Succeeded his father as 10th Earl of Sandwich, 1962, but renounced the peerage for life two years later.

☐ From CSC   The Temple Trees
Monday 5 March 1956   Colombo

My Darling, We arrived here Saturday & are staying with Sir John
Kotelawala[1] in his guest house in his garden – We have not seen him yet
because he is away electioneering; but an amiable & capable Secretary
looks after us – Tomorrow we are to be received by the Governor General
– In the afternoon we leave for Kandy – – –
   Later. We have just been to the Zoo which is said to be the most
beautiful in the world – The animals are glossy & well kept & it is a bower
of flowers – The Elephants are of all sizes down to babies 30 inches high
which are fed on a bottle.
   Goodbye my Darling. I will write again soon –

                                                                   Your loving
                                                                      Clemmie
                                                                         . . .

There is a bad drought, and it's very hot.

[1] Col. Sir John Kotelawala (1897–1980), Prime Minister and Minister of External Affairs, Ceylon,
1953–6.

☐ From CSC   King's Pavilion
10 March 1956 7 p.m.   Kandy

My Darling –
   Here we are half way between Polonnaruwa & Colombo. To-night we
are the guests of the Governor General, Sir Oliver Goonetilleke[1] (he is not
here) – He received us in audience at Queen's House Colombo the day
after our arrival – He is an agreeable man & I should think a wise one. He
gave me a special message for you to convey to Anthony Eden*. He thinks
it disastrous that although we have a Naval Commander-in-Chief at
Trincomalee (which has one of the largest natural harbours in the world),
we have no ships there at all, so he says! It's very close to India, & Nehru[2]
is watching the situation with an acquisitive eye. Do find out about this.

                                                                   Your loving
                                                                      Clemmie
                                                                         . . .

[1] Sir Oliver Goonetilleke (1892–1978), Governor-General of Ceylon, 1954–62.
[2] Jawaharlal Nehru (1889–1964). Educated at Harrow and Trinity College, Cambridge. Imprisoned
for dissidence for 18 years between 1921 and 1946. President at various times of Indian National
Congress. First Prime Minister and Minister of External Affairs of India after Independence from
1947.

○ From WSC   La Pausa
11 March 1956

My Darling,
I was so glad to get yr letter of the 5ᵗʰ & to realize that we are only 5 or 6 days apart. . . .
Now the weather has clouded over again here & I have hardly been out of doors since I arrived. Perhaps it is saving up for yr landing on April 5 at Marseilles. The Reves* will be delighted to put you & Sylvia [Henley*] up. . . . It is vy comfortable here & Wendy makes herself most agreeable. I work in bed at the book every morning. . . . This is the way to get the job finished, I am sure. . . .
. . . Diana is staying now till the 13ᵗʰ and Christopher [Soames*] & Mary are planning to come out on the 27ᵗʰ. And we can make arrangements all to go home together after the Easter Recess. However if this does not attract you I shall have done my best.
I am glad that the 'Zoo' is so attractive, but I think it wd be better not, repeat Not, to bring more than three 30 inch elephants to Chartwell! . . .

                                          Best & Fondest Love
                                          Your devoted husband
                                                    W

. . . I have had a cough & sore throat but am recovered thanks to Dr Roberts & penicillin.

□ From CSC   The Mount Lavinia Hotel
16 March 1956   Ceylon

My Darling, Your letter has come, suggesting that Sylvia & I should get off at Marseilles & join you & Mr Reves* & Wendy at La Pausa.
Fundamentally I'm better; . . . But I do feel I need an uninterrupted voyage home. . . . So I shall await you with much longing either at Hyde Park Gate or Chartwell. I shall have much to tell you about this island – The rich are now being heavily taxed, but the condition of the poor peasant is pitiable –
The Election is being conducted with barefaced self-interest. . . .
We are being treated with the most lavish hospitality by the Prime Minister Sir John Kotelawala – We have a young Civil Servant attached to us, who is our 'Shadow' –
The crows here & everywhere are quite menacing. They almost hop on to your breakfast tray & dispute with you your slice of pineapple.

                                                    Your loving
                                                    Clemmie
                                                       . . .

☐ From WSC   La Pausa
31 March 1956

MANY HAPPY RETURNS OF THE DAY.[1] DO THINK OVER WHETHER YOU WILL NOT COME ON HERE FROM MARSEILLES. WE CAN GO HOME TOGETHER BY AIR ON 10TH OR 11TH. LOVE.

                                                   W

[1] 1 April was CSC's seventy-first birthday.

☐ From CSC   [SS] Stratheden
3 April 1956

SO SORRY DARLING BUT CANNOT SORT AND REPACK CRUMPLED AND INADEQUATE CLOTHES, SO AM MAKING STRAIGHT FOR HOME. ALL MY LOVE.

                                             CLEMMIE

☐ From CSC   At sea
Easter Sunday [1 April] 1956   S.S. Stratheden
                                                    Suez

My Darling,
    Your letter reached me at Aden – I was so glad to get it....
    I have had a quiet pleasant birthday with a lovely telegram from Randolph, June & Arabella –
    The ship's wireless news tells me that you are now Mayor of Roquebrune[1] – I wonder if you went to the Town Hall or if the Municipality came to the Villa as at the Capponcina [when he was made Mayor of Cap d'Ail]....

                                          Tender love
                                            Clemmie

[1] WSC was received by the *Municipalité* of Roquebrune at a charming sunlit ceremony. His hosts and Christopher and myself, who were staying at La Pausa, accompanied him.

○ From WSC ✉   28 Hyde Park Gate
12 April 1956

My Darling,
    'Welcome Home.' I long to see you & kiss you.
    You will find me putting the finishing touches on my speech[1]....
                                 Your ever loving husband
                                           W

[1] At a meeting of the Primrose League at the Albert Hall on 13 April, over which he presided.

For the greater part of August, Clementine went again to St Moritz, where she had found great benefit previously.

The Suez crisis was brewing up.

○ From WSC [typewritten]   28 Hyde Park Gate
30 July 1956

My darling One,

Christopher [Soames*] was quite right in his judgment about flying. He rang up the proper authorities and was told that the clouds, which were 6,000 feet in England, were 3,000 feet in the neighbourhood of Düsseldorf. We started amid gusts, which the plane encountered with a few bumps, and reached our destination in one hour and fifty minutes....

We were received with the utmost courtesy in Düsseldorf, and were all invited to luncheon with the Stewards at the hotel.... The French horses were quite good. The paddock was invaded by the mob, who pressed around our horse, causing him to stream with sweat long before he even got to the course. We had a ten minutes hail and rain storm before the race, which made the ground even more boggy than it was after the heavy rain. As you know, Le Pretendant's form largely depends on hard ground, but here he was slipping all over the place. The Irish horse ridden by Lester Piggott was just behind us at the tail.

It all passed off very pleasantly, however. The Germans paid the expenses, and the Ambassador met us and accompanied us all the time....

I am on my way to the Royal luncheon, and afterwards am going to the House [of Commons]. Eden* says he wants to see me, as he has much to tell. Personally, I think that France and England ought to act together with vigour, and if necessary with arms, while America watches Russia vigilantly[1]. I do not think the Russians have any intention of being involved in a major war. We could secure our rights in the Arab world, and France has every reason to resent Nasser's attitude and action in regard to Algeria.

I do hope you will take a good rest and acquire height usage, and will recover from the bumpy journey and the long and very tiring motor drive.

With all my love
Your ever devoted husband
W

[1] Forces of the newly elected President Nasser of Egypt had seized the Suez Canal on 26 July 1956.

□ From CSC   Palace Hotel
1 August 1956   St Moritz

My Darling,

Your letter has just come full of interesting information....

Your flight to Düsseldorf was a gallant adventure, & I grieve that you were not rewarded by good fortune....

I fear that A.E. [Anthony Eden*] will wait for America, who for the 3rd time will arrive on the scene very late.

I hope you may be able to influence him.

The weather here is lovely though crisp, & I wish you were here to enjoy it – The sun is hot & high between 9 and 3 – After that chill descends on this high World –

I am still very tired, but I'm sure in a few days I shall recover –

Yesterday I went for a short drive with my old crony, Mr Einstein, but we were both of us too exhausted to enjoy it! ...

With my dear Love
Clemmie

...

○ From WSC [typewritten]   Chartwell
3 August 1956

My darling One,

Your letter of the 1st arrived the morning of the 3rd, which is pretty good. Tomorrow is the 4th of August[1], a date which used to be very memorable in our minds....

Give my regards to Mr Einstein. I am very glad he has turned up to give you company....

I am pleased with the policy being pursued about Suez. We are going to do our utmost. Anthony [Eden*] told me everything, and I even contemplated making a speech, but all went so well in the Thursday debate that this would have been an unnecessary hazard. As I am well informed, I cannot in an unprotected letter tell any secrets, but I feel you may rest assured that there will be no ground of complaints on what we try to do. The French are very sporting, and it is nice to feel they are working with us, and that we and the Americans are both agreed. We have taken a line which will put the canal effectively on its international basis, and will also make it secure until long after 1968. Anthony has told my Anthony [Montague Browne*] to keep himself fully informed from Downing Street, and I am actually reading large bundles of telegrams from day to day.

Violet [Asquith*/Bonham Carter] is coming to spend the night of Bank Holiday with me, and thereafter I have Juliet[2] on Friday the 11th. I propose to ask Pamela [Lytton] for the following week.... Randolph has gone off to America after giving me a dreadful beating up about supporting such a Government as this. I took the brunt of it off myself by a film, and he was himself astonished the next morning (Wednesday) when he saw the newspapers, which I could not reveal to him until they were published. There is only one opinion in the House of Commons, and this fully covers the use of force as and when it may be necessary.

⚓My dearest Clemmie, do persevere in getting back yr strength & we can make some plans together. With all my love,

Your devoted husband
W
...

¹ Date of declaration of war, 1914.
² Lady Juliet Duff (see p. 327 n. 1).

□ From CSC   Palace Hotel
9 August 1956   St Moritz

My Darling, I have been reassuring & comforting myself by reading again your letter of August the 3rd – Because to me, the Suez situation seems perplexing and deteriorating. . . .

Do explain to me why Israel has not been bidden to the Conference¹. I listened to Anthony [Eden*] last night – It was hard to hear but I'm afraid I was disappointed by what I <u>did</u> hear – There was no inspiration. . . .

The leg & foot are static but any day now I hope for improvement. I have a balcony to my bedroom which is pleasant.

Your devoted & loving
Clemmie
...

¹ 1st London Conference on Suez, which opened on 16 August 1956.

○ From WSC [typewritten]   Chartwell
11 August 1956

My darling One,

The weather is awful. We had one lovely day, not a cloud from dawn to dusk, . . .

Like you, I am anxious about the situation in the Middle East. I suppose the reason why they did not bring Israel in [to the London Conference] was that they were afraid she would become uncontrollable. But she is there in the background, and I have no doubt that if it comes to war she will join in. One can never be quite sure whether a number of 'volunteers' will not be mixed up with the Egyptians, who manage the Russian aeroplanes and tanks. There is no doubt that this would involve hard fighting, but I think we will have enough troops on the move. Naturally I am worried about this pow-wow, which was to have finished by the end of August at the latest. I do not see myself how it is to be closured and wound up, and I am not sure that Selwyn Lloyd¹ is the man. However, there is nothing for it but to go on with the programme. The President [Eisenhower] is quite right in saying that if he stays out America will balance Russia. The unity of Islam is remarkable. There is no doubt that Libya, to whom we have paid £5,000,000 a year, like Jordania, to whom we paid £10,000,000 or more, are whole-heartedly manifesting hostility. You will be home before anything serious happens....

I am so glad you are having sunshine. It is indeed dreary gazing out through rain-spotted windows on the grey mists that wrap the weald of Kent. I have been reading a lot about Disraeli, because I must have a chapter on Disraeli and Gladstone to come after the American Civil War book....

✍4 p. m.

Juliet [Duff] is here, & she has brought her own book with her, & sends you lots of love. We are sitting in yr rose garden which is really <u>hot</u>.

All my love
Yr devoted husband
W

. . .

[1] John Selwyn Lloyd, later Baron Selwyn-Lloyd (1904–78). At this date Foreign Secretary, 1955–60.

O From WSC ✉   28 Hyde Park Gate
12 September 1956

My darling One,
    Some Flowers to salute our 48th anniversary!

All my love
W

O From WSC [typewritten]   La Pausa
24 September 1956

My dearest,

. . .

Here all is peaceful and I am glad to say that the whole book team is hard at work....

I am wearing Bernie [Baruch]'s hearing-aid every day when in company and I find it a great relief. It is complete and in perfect order and I think I shall get used to the habit of using it. I quite agree that it is a necessity.

I have not tried any painting yet, although there has been plenty of sunlight. The Prefect and his wife are coming to dine on Thursday next. So far we have had no strangers as company.

I had a letter from Anthony [Eden*] thanking me for the cigars, and incidentally showing a robust spirit. I am so glad they are going to the Security Council immediately.... I must say I am very glad the burden does not rest on me.

I stay in bed all the morning, and am very pleased with the way the book [*A History of the English-Speaking Peoples*] is getting on, and I think you will be both pleased and surprised at the way the work is going.

✍My darling One, It is such a pleasure to receive your letters – The handwriting is so strong and you can dash them off with a vigour wh shows that your troubles and their consequences are now steadfastly relegated to the background. . . .

My tender love
Your devoted husband
W

. . .

Toby [budgerigar] sends his salutations wh I enclose. . . .

☐ From CSC   28 Hyde Park Gate
9 October 1956

My Darling – 'Prof' [Lindemann*/Lord Cherwell] rang me up to say how much he had enjoyed visiting you & that during his five days at La Pausa the weather had been lovely. I am so very glad –
    I feel ashamed & mortified by Randolph's libel action[1] – I fear he will lose, which will be expensive; if he wins, I expect the damages will be one ¼d –
    'Prof' said, however, that you were not using your hearing aid. Oh – I do hope you will.
    Mary & I are going to Kempton Park with Christopher [Soames*] to see your Horse run.

Tender Love my Darling from
Your Clemmie

. . .

[1] Randolph had brought a libel action against *The People* for having described him in an article (printed during the May 1955 General Election) as a 'paid hack'. In the witness box he made mincemeat of the defence counsel. The jury awarded Randolph £5,000 (£65,000 in 1990s terms) and his legal costs.

○ From WSC [typewritten]   La Pausa
12 October 1956

My dearest One,
    I am so glad you and Mary are going to see the horse run on Saturday. I hope it will not rain and that Le Pretendant will fulfil our hopes[1]. You might tell Christopher to send me a telegram, or better still ring me on the telephone, whatever happens.
    The weather is very good. Yesterday was one of the finest days I have seen out here. I invited hosts and guests to lunch with me at the Vistaero [Restaurant], which is really a most beautiful villa perched on a peak from which you can look down a thousand feet or more. We came home and I went for my usual daily walk in the garden. . . .
    I admit I was astonished that Randolph won his action, and at the damages. It is quite true that he is not a 'paid hack', but I did not think that a jury would draw so firmly the very refined distinction between his vocabulary and the People's. He seems to have acquitted himself well in the box. I have written him a letter of congratulation.

I was so glad to hear from your own lips that you have made a recovery from the many evils which haunted you. I do hope it will last.

With my fondest love
I remain
Your devoted husband
W

(more like a mouse than a pig)

[1] Le Pretendant won, beating the Queen's horse High Veldt by half a length in the Cumberland Lodge Stakes at Kempton Park, on 13 October 1956.

On 20 October 1956, while at La Pausa, Winston suffered a black-out, and was unconscious for twenty minutes; he had sustained a stroke – a cerebral spasm. No bulletins were issued, though there were rumours that he was not well: it was given out that he was suffering from a chill. Clementine went out to France to be with him. However, he was recovered enough to fly home on 28 October. Although this incident had no long-lasting visible effects, nonetheless it marked a decline in Winston's health and spirits.

Chapter XXVIII

'KEEP RIGHT ON TO THE END OF THE ROAD'

Winston stayed much of January, February and March 1957 with Emery and Wendy Reves* at La Pausa. During this time Clementine made one of her rare visits there.

○ From WSC   La Pausa
24 January 1957

My darling,
   I send you herewith the notification from Lloyd's that they have bought me £29,900 odd of shares immune from duty at my death. I hereby give it to you as I promised & hope you will long live to enjoy it....
   I am vy glad to be able through my own exertions to be able to testify in this way my love & gratitude to you.

Your ever-devoted husband,
Winston S. Churchill

□ From CSC   28 Hyde Park Gate
26 January 1957

My Darling –
   How can I thank you for your thoughtful & loving care for me –
   Mr Moir [lawyer] came to see me this morning & I entrusted him with the papers.
   You may be sure that I shall not fritter away this generous endowment.
   Tomorrow, Sunday, I am going to Chartwell Farm to visit Mary, the Chimp [Christopher Soames*] & the children – Jeremy fell off a chair 3 days ago & fractured his collar bone. He is all right, but it's a worse break than was thought before the X Ray was developed....

Your very loving & devoted
Clemmie
. . .

○ From WSC   La Pausa
[17 March 1957]

Darling – Here is a damnable thing – The House I wrote to you about was offered by the agents at <u>thirty</u> million francs; but now that my name is mentioned to the owner – a swindling Italian prince, he has put it up to <u>forty-seven</u> million. Of course I will not touch it on those terms. So we are all at sea again.

Anthony [Montague Browne*] is off today to look at 2 Houses at Cannes. There is one at 25 millions and one all on one floor. But I do not like the idea of Cannes vy much.

It is vy nice to think I shall be home again in 60 hours. Darling one, I look forward to dining with you so much.

                                                    Tender love from
                                                           Winston
                                                             . . .

Winston returned home in time to celebrate Clementine's seventy-second birthday on 1 April.

In May he made a speech to the Primrose League at the Albert Hall and attended the Royal Academy Banquet. On 19 May he flew back to Roquebrune: Clementine preferred to stay at home, where she had agreeable plans of her own.

○ From WSC   La Pausa
21 May 1957

Darling –

We are arrived and all is well. To-day the skies are without a cloud & the temperature is warm. . . . I am going to get up and paint in half an hour. . . . Sarah and A.M.B. [Anthony Montague Browne*] are very happy & will write you for themselves. . . .

Wendy was obviously disappointed to learn that you wd not come, but would see you at Capponcina[1] in September. I was exhausted yesterday and slumbered well.

Your visit to me the night before I left was vy precious. Do not let the idea that I am 'mean' to you tease your mind[2]. As a matter of fact I take every lawful opportunity of passing money to you in a way which will avoid the 67% toll wh the State will almost certainly take at my death, & will continue to do so as long as I am able. Your life of devotion & kindness to me has made my own one both happy and successful. . . . I am weary of a task wh is done & I hope I shall not shrink when the aftermath ends.

My only wish is to live peacefully out the remaining years if years they are. But you, dearest one, have the sunlight of a glorious spell before you in all probability. So be happy & do not let misconceptions of me darken & distort your mind.

> With all my love and many kisses X X X
> I remain
> Your loving husband
> W

[1] La Capponcina, Lord Beaverbrook's villa at Cap d'Ail.
[2] Perhaps CSC had been 'at him' about money for current bills. As we have seen, WSC was certainly not 'mean' in the long-term arrangements he made for her. Among other provisions, he left her all his post-July 1945 papers (the Churchill Papers), which she in turn bequeathed to Churchill College, Cambridge. He also left her the copyright in his pictures.

□ From CSC   28 Hyde Park Gate
Tuesday 28 May 1957

My Darling,

. . .

I had a most agreeable visit at Hatfield[1], and Betty [Salisbury] sent you a great deal of love – It was thrilling to meet Adlai Stevenson after all that one had heard.... I sat next to him & had a most interesting conversation. The men remained in the dining-room an hour after the women had withdrawn; . . .

Mr Stevenson was cautious in his approach to Anglo-American relations, but I sensed that he thought we & the French had gone down in the World – I should think he holds much the same views as Violet Bonham Carter [Asquith*] on Suez (and Cyprus), but he is not emphatic & voluble. He asked me if I knew your views – I said you thought things had been badly bungled – He then referred to the coolness he felt here in England towards America – So I was able to say that you felt warm towards his country & that we should not be parted by Russian intrigues intended to make us fall out....

It has been bitterly cold here; but now the cruel wind is abating – I hope with you the sun shines –

> Your very loving
> Clemmie

. . .

[1] Hatfield House, Herts, ancestral home of the Marquess of Salisbury.

○ From WSC   La Pausa
1 June 1957

My darling

I am vy glad to hear about yr visit to Hatfield & the conversation with Adlai [Stevenson]. His succession to Ike [Eisenhower] wd no doubt be popular in England. But it is the Americans who have to choose!

Now I write to you on another glorious 1st of June[1]. The weather is a little better – I painted for 2½ hours yesterday. Today I gave a luncheon to the company.... Wendy seemed unhappy at our going to the Capponcina in Sept, but cheered up when I said it was only for a month & I wd come back afterwards.

You will have gone to Ireland[2] before I write again in all probability. I hope you will enjoy yr stay there. Let me know about the Irish people. I am worried about them. They come to England in large numbers instead of building up their own country....

What fun it was winning two races in one day! Quite an event for a beginner. Christopher is vy clever about horses & the stud[3] has become numerous & valuable: & pays for itself so far.

Always your loving husband
W

. . .

[1] Anniversary of the British naval victory over the French, in the Channel, 1 June 1794.
[2] To stay with Sir Alfred and Lady Beit at Russborough, Co. Wicklow. Clementine Beit was CSC's cousin, the daughter of Lady Helen (Ogilvy) Mitford; see also pp. 56 n. 2, undated letter; 122 n. 2.
[3] At Newchapel Green, Lingfield, Surrey. See p. 554 n. 4.

☐ From CSC   Stour[1]
The Glorious First of June – 1957   East Bergholt, Suffolk

My Darling,

I came here yesterday afternoon with Sylvia [Henley*] –

Randolph has made such improvements here – You must come & see it again.

It's a really hot day – delicious – So I know fine weather has at last reached you.

Randolph is just going to take me to do a little local sight-seeing. I go back to Hyde P. Gate this afternoon & the house here then fills up for the week-end....

Your loving
Clemmie

. . .

[1] In 1955 Randolph had bought a lovely house – Stour, at East Bergholt, in Suffolk. To everybody's surprise he took enthusiastically to country life, particularly gardening. He was to live at Stour until his death there in 1968.

☐ From CSC   28 Hyde Park Gate
4 June 1957

My Darling,

For a birthday present from us both I sent Randolph a pair of garden chairs to put on the terrace in front of his house, which overlooks that peaceful view of Dedham Church, so often painted by Constable – He is delighted with them.

This morning I was rung up by Clarissa from their tiny cottage where she and Anthony [Eden*] have at last fetched up after so many trials and tribulations[1] – I think their courage and dignity in adversity are making a deep impression –

We have had a glorious heat wave – but Alas – it lasted but 3 days – or was it 4 days? And now it is cold & bleak again – I want so much to see you my Darling – your new bath is being put in to-day. I hope you will be able to roll about in it comfortably!

Your loving
Clemmie

. . .

[1] On 9 January 1957 Anthony Eden had resigned because of ill-health, and was succeeded by Harold Macmillan. The Edens had no home, apart from this small cottage, Rose Bower, in Broad Chalke, Wiltshire, belonging to Clarissa.

○ From WSC   La Pausa
5 June 1957
Derby Day

Darling

. . .

I am absorbed in Wuthering Heights.[1] There is no doubt it deserves its fame. One can see it is a good book. I am ¾ the way through.

Here we have mainly clouds & I spend my mornings in bed. But in the occasional gleams I have painted 2 landscapes which are worth bringing home to show you.

Christopher [Soames*] comes the day after tomorrow (Friday) & I am looking forward to seeing him and hearing his news....

I read what you say about Clarissa & Anthony [Eden*] and agree with it. They bear their lot with courage....

The French are dawdling & dithering over their new government & their large deficit. Algeria is in a shocking situation.... The politicians must be enjoying their 'Crisis'. I hope they will pull through & beat the Algerian terrorists.

I envy you your heatwave. The world has become as muddled as its people about the weather, and it is a relief to find the shelter of Victorian literature, when the alternative wd be to stare out at really bloody prospects from the windows....

My dearest one, I love you from a gloomy background I fear. The only thing that cheers me this morning is the new bath of wh you write. I shall look forward to wallowing in it.

Tender love my darling. Your devoted husband
W

. . .

XXXXXXXXXXX for you.

[1] *Wuthering Heights* by Emily Brontë, 1847.

Winston returned home in the second week of June, and spent the rest of the summer in England. He had a full programme: the Garter Service at Windsor; an expedition to the races; he spoke in his constituency; addressed a large audience at a United Europe meeting at the Albert Hall, and the American Bar Association at the Guildhall.

On 3 July the 'Prof' (Lindemann*/Lord Cherwell) died in his sleep. Winston and Clementine were deeply sad; they had been friends for over thirty years. Both he and Clementine went to his funeral at Christ Church, Oxford.

Winston and Clementine spent September at La Capponcina; on 1 October Winston moved to La Pausa, and Clementine returned home.

○ From WSC   [La Pausa]
7 October [1957]

My darling,

    . . .
    Yesterday (Sunday) we went over to Mortola[1], . . . The owners were most agreeable. The poor lady was charming – crippled though she be. . . . I felt vy sorry for her. She was absolutely charmed to see me. I clambered up to the square terrace, & we all sat and talked. She had sent her conveyances. It was Queen Victoria's special Chair, in which I was wheeled about from the top to the bottom (the sea) & the bottom to the top, & saw everything, accompanied by the whole family – husband, son, his wife and my own party. (The Reves* had to go back from [to] the house because Wendy had terribly high heels. But they enjoyed themselves vy much with all they saw.) It is indeed a wonderful spot. . . .

                                                                    With tender love
                                                                     my dearest one
                                                          Your ever loving husband
                                                                                W

                                                                                . . .

[1] La Mortola, house and garden at Ventimiglia, Italy, not far from the French–Italian border, built and created by Sir Thomas Hanbury from 1867. Under his son, Sir Cecil Hanbury, the gardens thrived, and the collection, reaching some 6,300 specimens, became world-famous. Sir Cecil died in 1937; on her death in 1972 his widow, Mrs Dorothy Hanbury-Forbes, bequeathed the house and gardens to the state. Now known as the Giardino Botanico Hanbury (Hanbury Botanical Gardens), Mortola Inferiore.

□ From CSC   28 Hyde Park Gate
8 October 1957

My Darling,
    I'm thrilled and delighted that you visited La Mortola – I wish I had been with you & seen you in Queen Victoria's chair – How was it propelled? A pony? 2 gardeners? Electricity? I'm so glad you enjoyed it. I believe that in the 'Good old days' 20 gardeners were employed – Now there are but 3. . . .

What do you think of the Earth Satellite?[1] I heard it on the Wireless – It sounded ominous – How right 'Prof' was about the technical superiority of the Russians. I read that the socket of the Satellite has become disconnected, but that they are both whizzing round together, & that the socket is losing speed gradually – I think it is most uncomfortable & alarming!

On Thursday I go to Birmingham, to lay the foundation stone of a new Y.W.C.A. Building – I am being entertained at luncheon by the Lord Mayor before the Ceremony....

Three of our grandchildren have Asian (or Asiatic) flu: Edwina, Celia and Winston.

> Your loving
> Clemmie
>
> . . .

[1] The Soviet Union had launched the first earth satellite – the 'Sputnik' – on 4 October 1957.

O From WSC [La Pausa]
[undated, probably 11 October 1957]

Darling,

Your letter has just arrived. I send the answer back by Anthony [Montague Browne*]. It shd reach you to-day. Queen V's chair was pushed by the entire Mortola family & the 3 gardeners.

The Satellite itself etc does not distress me. The disconcerting thing is the proof of the forwardness of Soviet Science, compared to the American. The Prof [Lindemann*, Lord Cherwell] was as usual vigilant and active. Plenty of warnings were given but we have fallen hopelessly behind in technical education[1], & the tiny bit we have tends to disperse & scatter about America & the Dominions. This is the mechanized age, & where are we? Quality – of the Front rank indeed we still possess. But numbers are lacking. The necessary breeding ground has failed. We must struggle on; & looking to the Union with America....

I have painted two (2) pictures, one is rather good.

> Tender love & many kisses X X
> from your devoted husband
> W
>
> . . .

[1] It was WSC's great anxiety about the backwardness of British science and technology in comparison with Russia which had caused him, encouraged and helped by the Prof and Jock Colville, to be the Founder of Churchill College, Cambridge, in 1958 – a scientific, technological and engineering foundation. He contributed £25,000 from his Eightieth Birthday Presentation Fund.

From the mid-1950s Sarah had started having a drink problem, which however did not surface in public until now. In August 1957 Antony Beauchamp had committed suicide, and although they had been separated for nearly two years, Sarah was deeply affected by his death. Returning to

Hollywood, where she had television film contracts, she lived alone for much of that winter, in a seaside cabin house at Malibu, within easy reach of the studios in Los Angeles. On 14 January 1958 the British press reported that Sarah had been arrested and charged with being drunk; there were unpleasant photographs and accounts of the incident. In the subsequent court case a few days later, she pleaded guilty and was given a $50 fine. Winston was at La Pausa: he minded very much – but my mother was shattered.

○ From WSC [typewritten]   La Pausa
18 January 1958

My darling,
    The muff[1] is a great success here. I use it at all meals, and on the whole it achieves its purpose. It is vy cold.
    ... I have spent the greater part of my days in bed, but sit for a couple of hours in the sunshine from 2.30 till 4.30. It is very pleasant & bright.
    I agree with you that Sarah got out of it as well as she could.... I will keep you informed of any correspondence with her. Personally I hope she will find it possible to come here as soon as she has finished her local [US] engagements....
    We had another lovely day today – the third running, and for the moment the prospects are good. I hope you will find it possible to come, if only for a few days....
    I have been reading a Russian novel[2], which has made a great impression in America as it is critical of the Russian world and yet the author has apparently been permitted by the Russian government to publish it and print an edition of thirty thousand copies for Russian use. This is a step in the right direction, and we should watch it with attention....
    ✍ ... [Sarah] has arranged to come in the first week of February.
                                        With all my love my dearest darling,
                                                    Yours devotedly
                                                          W

[1] CSC had given WSC a beautiful fur muff, as he suffered so much from cold hands.
[2] Boris Pasternak, *Doctor Zhivago*, 1957 (English translation, 1958).

□ From CSC   28 Hyde Park Gate
19 January 1958

My Darling, You have been gone 5 days; but it seems much longer –
    To distract my heart and mind from grief (there is no news of Sarah), I have been cultivating the younger generation. Celia (Sandys) came to luncheon with me bringing with her two school friends of the same age (14). I took them all to a play, which we all enjoyed, & then they came back here to tea –

Yesterday I repeated this with Mary Romilly[1] and her two children –
They are Nellie's grandchildren – We went to a pantomime & they enjoyed
it very much. . . .

Sylvia [Henley*] has been spending to-day (Sunday) with me, which is
very pleasant. I hope your fine weather has lasted. It's very cold here &
the forecast is that this will last for several days.

I've just been seeing & hearing Rab Butler*[2] on Television – <u>Not</u> good.
He was being questioned by an impertinent young man & I found the
performance undignified & shy-making –

Your loving
Clemmie

[1] Wife of Giles Romilly (see p. 527 n. 1), from whom he was separated.
[2] At this time Home Secretary.

☐ From CSC   28 Hyde Park Gate
25 January 1958

My Darling,
    I have just telegraphed to Wendy to ask if I may come & stay at La
Pausa on February the 18th for a week.

I have seen in the Daily Mail that 1,221 persons visited your Exhibition
in one day at Kansas City[1], & that this is a record. I am so happy about
this. . . .

I lunched with Pamela Churchill the other day to say Goodbye to young
Winston [nearly eighteen] before he went back to Eton. He is now
beginning to grow, & he has a man's voice, low & rather attractive –

I took Edwina [Sandys, now just nineteen] & a party of her friends to the
theatre another night & we all came back to dinner here – It was great fun
& we all enjoyed it. She knows some very agreeable & intelligent young
men –

To-night I'm taking Diana out to a play.

I so much want to see you Darling –

Your loving
Clemmie

. . .

[1] A travelling exhibition of WSC's paintings had opened in Kansas City on 21 January 1958; it
would then go to the Metropolitan Museum, New York, and other important American cities,
before travelling to Australia and New Zealand.

☐ From WSC [typewritten]   [La Pausa]
31 January 1958

I send you the letters I have exchanged with the President[1] of which I
talked to you on the telephone. I did not see what else I could do. It will
be a very short visit to America, only a week, of which three and a half
days will be spent at the White House and the rest with Bernie [Baruch],

either in New York or at his country place. I do hope you will be able to come with me, but I shall quite understand if you feel that a double flight across the Atlantic is more than the experience will be worth. I hope and trust, however, that you will come.

I am sitting here in the garden under the balcony. We have only had one cloudy day, and all the rest have been lovely and sunny and really not cold. I expect March will be very warm out here, and I am keeping it un-planned.

[1] President Eisenhower had invited WSC to visit him at the White House, Washington.

□ From CSC   28 Hyde Park Gate
12 February 1958

My Darling,
    I'm afraid Brendan [Bracken*][1] is very ill –
    Mr Moir [lawyer] told me that he had been to see him at Westminster Hospital – I wrote to Brendan to cheer him up & to say I hoped he would soon be well. . . . You will want to write to him, but do not alarm him about his condition – Perhaps not say I told you? . . .
    Poor Sarah – The more one quarrels with the Press, the more they tease one. Actually I don't think the American breed are much worse than ours –
    My Darling, I've got a bad sore throat & am going to consult old Doctor Barnett [her GP] – I don't want to arrive next Tuesday under the weather –
                                                                    Your loving
                                                                    Clemmie
                                                                        . . .
I've had a nice little letter from Sarah[2], but only about shampooing her hair & your picture of oranges & lemons which I much want to see.

[1] He was indeed, with cancer.
[2] Who was staying at La Pausa.

On 18 February 1958 Winston developed a chest cold which rapidly became pneumonia. By fortunate coincidence Clementine arrived at La Pausa for her planned visit (due to last a week, it prolonged itself into a month). Lord Moran* flew out, and bulletins were issued. Winston responded well to treat-ment, but suffered a relapse in March, and was not well enough to return home until 3 April. He now accepted, to his great disappointment, that he must postpone his projected visit to the United States to see President Eisenhower.

Although Winston made a good recovery, this illness took its toll of his strength, and from now on he had a full-time male nurse[1].

[1] Roy Howells, a charming and gentle person who remained with WSC until his death in January 1965. His recollections, *Simply Churchill*, were published in 1965.

☐ From CSC   28 Hyde Park Gate
2 July 1958

My Darling,

I like to think of you having a happy peaceful time at Blenheim, varied with fierce exciting Battles at Bézique –

Last night I rang up the Westminster Hospital and spoke to Brendan [Bracken*]'s Nurse.

Since you saw him he has been worse (with nausea & other miseries), but yesterday was a better day – I sent him (through the Nurse) affectionate messages from you and me.

Perhaps on Thursday, after lunching with Violet Bonham Carter [Asquith*] and before receiving the Israeli Ambassador at 5.30, you might pay him another little visit?[1] I told the Nurse we would telephone on Thursday.

Your loving & devoted
Clemmie

. . .

[1] WSC visited Brendan twice more before he returned to the South of France on 1 August to stay with Max Beaverbrook at La Capponcina. The news of Brendan's death, on 8 August 1958, greatly saddened WSC: they had been friends for 40 years.

○ From WSC   La Capponcina
8 August 1958

Darling,

The days pass monotonously but pleasantly & quickly. More than a week has gone since I arrived. I have done nothing but play bezique with Anthony [Montague Browne*] – several games a day! – and have won thirty shillings. . . .

It is vy hot & beautiful, & time passes swiftly. I long to have you here – I am sure you would find it agreeable. 'Toby' [his budgerigar] is on my bed at the moment & I have had a large cage constructed which serves as an exercise ground for him.

We have been deeply moved by Brendan's death – but I am sure it was best for him. His will about no memorials[1] for him made us [WSC and Max Beaverbrook*] resist a return journey tomorrow wh we had contemplated.

Darling one I am eagerly looking forward to seeing you. I rejoice that the doctors give a good report, & that progress continues steady to the eye[2].

This is an awful scrawl, but I write in bed & have almost lost the art of legibility.

Always your loving & devoted husband
W

[1] Brendan Bracken left instructions in his will that there should be no memorial to him, and that all his papers should be destroyed.
[2] CSC had been free from the wearing neuritis for about a year, but in the summer of 1958 she was beset by shingles, which affected her face, eyelid and eye. This painful complaint was to afflict her spasmodically for some time.

☐ From CSC   Chartwell
9 August 1958

My Darling – You are much in my thoughts –
    You will miss Brendan [Bracken*] so much and so will Max
[Beaverbrook*] – Please give him a message of sympathy.
    I am sorry there is to be no Memorial Service for him – So many would
have liked by their presence to pay a tribute of affection and respect.
    I'm packing up & leaving Chartwell, & till I leave Tuesday (at cock-
crow!) I shall be at Hyde Park Gate. Diana is coming up from the Isle of
Wight to spend Monday with me – It's very sweet of her.
    ... I will write to you from Tangier[1] – Meanwhile I am your poor
devoted

                                                                            Clemmie

[1] CSC was headed for a visit to Bryce and Margaret Nairn. Bryce Nairn CBE (1903–78) had been
British Consul in Marrakech in 1944 when the Churchills were staying there, and they all made
great friends; Margaret Nairn was a gifted painter. They met again after the General Election in
July 1945, when WSC and CSC holidayed near Hendaye and Bryce Nairn was then British Consul
at Bordeaux; now he was Consul-General at Tangier (1957–63).

☐ From CSC   In the Air between Madrid & Gibraltar
12 August 1958   [en route for Tangier]

My Darling, I'm in the middle of a wonderful flight & am expecting to
touch down at Gibraltar in about 20 minutes –
    I follow your social engagements & your 'toilettes' in the Daily Press –
Luncheon & cards & Greta Garbo on the Onassis yacht dressed in pure
white!
    Sarah returned at 3 hours' notice from Zürich[1] last evening – She dined
with Diana & me & then went on to her little house[2] – She reappeared at
7.30 this morning & both daughters came & saw me off –
    We are just landing –

                                                                            Au Revoir
                                                                            Clemmie
                                                                               ...

[1] This year Sarah spent several months at the Bircher-Benner Clinic in Zürich, grappling with her
general health.
[2] In the summer of 1958 the Chartwell Trust (set up by WSC for the benefit of his children and
grandchildren) had bought a small house for Sarah in Randolph Mews, London W9.

☐ From CSC   British Consulate General
18 August 1958   Tangier

My darling Winston,
    This little letter will reach you only a day or two before me[1]. This is a
most interesting place & I love being with the Nairns, who are most kind
& interesting....
    I have just heard from Brendan's Executors that in his Will he has left

me his set of military China Horses[2] – I am touched that he wished me to have a token of his friendship –

Your loving & devoted
Clemmie

. . .

[1] On 23 August CSC flew from Tangier to join WSC at La Capponcina.
[2] A collection of porcelain equestrian figures made at the Potschappel factory near Dresden in 1875. One is of Napoleon, and the others members of the French Imperial Army. They are at Chartwell in CSC's bedroom.

After celebrating their Golden Wedding on 12 September at La Capponcina, Winston and Clementine went for the first of many cruises they would enjoy on board Ari Onassis's fabulous yacht, *Christina*.

In mid-October Winston was again at La Pausa.

○ From WSC   [La Pausa]
14 October 1958

My darling one,
    . . . All is peace & quiet here. It is six months – so they calculate – since I was last here. They all send appropriate messages. I am passing the morning in bed – reading a book about ancient Greece wh is rather good. Tomorrow I shall try to paint, and Murray[1] is getting the outfit ready. But I am doubtful, inert & lazy.
    I wonder what you will be doing & when you will set off for Chartwell. Would you give some food to the fish? They are vy appreciative. And the black swans. I never visited them this time. It was too wet for the car [to go across the fields], & I do not care about walking – much.
    You have all my fondest love my dearest. The closing days or years of life are grey and dull, but I am lucky to have you at my side. I send you my best love & many kisses.

Always your devoted
W

. . .

[1] Detective-Sergeant Edmund Murray (1917–96), WSC's detective from 1950 to 1965. A colourful personality. He had served in the French Foreign Legion. Himself an amateur painter, he helped WSC with all his painter's paraphernalia.

☐ From CSC   28 Hyde Park Gate
16 October 1958

My Darling,
    I was so very glad to get your letter, although you seemed a little sad. Do not be sad, my Dear One. I hope your sunshine will return. Here it is fine though of course not so warm as with you. . . .

Next Saturday I am going to Hamsell Manor[1], to stay with Mary & Christopher [Soames*] – Monday I shall stay at Chartwell ... I will certainly feed your fish & the black swans.

I have been invited to Paris to witness the great Honour which is being shewn to you[2] – And we will return together.

I had a charming picture (from a newspaper) of you & Tina[3] reproduced & I am sending it to you framed in silver to give Tina – I know she will love it. ...

The days are flying & soon I hope to see you safe & sound.

Your loving
Clemmie
. . .

[1] In 1957 Christopher and I and our four children had moved from Chartwell Farm (which we had outgrown) to Hamsell Manor, at Eridge Green, near Tunbridge Wells; it was about 40 minutes' drive from Chartwell. In October WSC wound down his farming activities, selling both Chartwell Farm and Bardogs.
[2] On 6 November 1958 Gen. de Gaulle would invest WSC with the Croix de la Libération. Founded by de Gaulle, it was the highest award made only to those who had served with the Free French or with the Resistance. Only two Britons were appointed: King George VI and WSC.
[3] Athina Onassis ('Tina') (1929–74), daughter of Greek shipowner Stavros Livanos. First wife of Ari Onassis, whom she married, 1946; divorced, 1960. In 1961 she married (as his second wife) the Marquess of Blandford ('Sunny'), later 11th Duke of Marlborough; divorced, 1971. She married, third, 1971, Stavros Niarchos; he had previously been married to her sister Eugenie (died 1970). Tina died from a drug overdose in 1974, aged 45. She was beautiful, lively, kind and charming, and both WSC and CSC were very fond of her.

On 6 March 1959 Winston flew to Nice to stay with Emery and Wendy Reves* at La Pausa for a month.

During this time a 'One Man Show' (a signal honour accorded by the Royal Academy to their Honorary Academician Extraordinary) opened in March in the Diploma Gallery.

O From WSC [typewritten]   La Pausa
8 March 1959

Clemmie, Beloved One,

I arrived in due course and was met by the Préfet and Emery Reves*. I found Nice and Roquebrune and all between wrapped in fog and shrouded impenetrably by clouds. ...

Wendy, who came to meet me, was delighted to get your letter, and she will no doubt answer it herself. ...

✍My darling, I think a great deal about you & our troubles. I hope for a letter soon to tell me about Sarah[1]. I think they treated her vy roughly at Liverpool & roused her fiery spirit. I hope she will convince you that her affliction is a part of the periodic difficulties which are common to women at the change of life, & above all that she will persevere at her profession.

I am so sorry for the burden this casts on you, & hope that staying with Mary & Christopher will relieve your troubles. Dearest my thoughts are with you. It all falls on you: 'Poor Lamb!' With all my love I remain a wreck (but with its flag still flying) & send you my best love and many kisses. I await your letter.

I found Toby safely here & he just got on my elbow to remind me that I must mention him in writing to you, or he wd be offended.

Your loving husband
Winston
X X X X X X X X

---

[1] On 6 March 1959 Sarah was fined £2 in Liverpool for being drunk and disorderly. She was playing the lead role in *Peter Pan*, which had opened in London before Christmas and was now on tour. Needless to say, the publicity was mortifying.

☐ From CSC   28 Hyde Park Gate
10 March 1959

My Darling,

I have just returned from the Private View of your pictures – The two rooms were crowded, & everyone seemed delighted – I am so glad – I think the Exhibition will provide entertainment for many in these bleak Spring days....

Sarah came to dinner Sunday night, as also did Diana – Sarah was quiet, dignified & quite sober. Not a word was said about the events at Liverpool.

I pray she will be able to complete her present engagement (another 3 weeks). Her doctor, whom I spoke to on the telephone, fears she is in a bad way – He thinks she can hold out for about 10 days, but fears another 'incident' before the end of the tour. He begged her when her present contract ends to do a serious cure. She replied she would 'rather die' than do so. He pointed out that she might not get any more theatrical or film offers, & she then said she would retire into 'private life' & paint & write –

Anthony [Montague Browne*] saw her off at the station for her present lap (Wolverhampton) – He gave her luncheon before at a quiet restaurant. He is a good friend.

Your devoted
Clemmie

☐ From CSC   28 Hyde Park Gate
11 March 1959

My Darling,

I have been reading your letter [of 8 March] a second time –

Neither Sarah's solicitor, Mr Hardcastle (whom I sent up post haste to help her), nor her theatrical manager, Mr Patrick Desmond, think she was roughly treated at Liverpool. Both these men are devoted to her & her interests, & they told me that the Police at Liverpool had done everything they could to conceal Sarah's identity & to get her to plead 'Guilty'; in which case she would have been allowed to slip away after paying the minimum fine....

Perhaps you were thinking back to the Hollywood incident 2 years ago when she was so vilely ill-treated by the American police....

Mary & Christopher have been invited to 'dine & sleep'[1] at Windsor. It will be just before her baby arrives – I hope she is not 'brought to bed' at Windsor –

Your devoted
Clemmie

[1] A ministerial visit; at this date Christopher was Secretary of State for War (since January 1958). We stayed at Windsor Castle, 21–22 April. Rupert Christopher Soames, our fifth and last child, was born at Hamsell Manor on 18 May.

○ From WSC [typewritten]   La Pausa
13 March 1959

My darling,
I have been thinking about the Sarah incident and I have come to the conclusion that it went off as well as it could be expected. I am very glad that Sarah is to do another three weeks in the provinces, and I hope she will realise how much it means to her if she can clear her reputation by good behaviour in the future....

We have been invited to go to the Palace[1] for luncheon on Monday and all three have accepted. Tomorrow, Saturday, we lunch with the Préfet. The day after we shall go on board the yacht [*Christina*], and on Friday we lunch with Daisy Fellowes.

✍It is fine today though windy. I have spent long hours in bed. Toby has just bitten off this flick of blue [a feather] which he sends you with his love,

And mine dearest
Your loving husband
Winston

[1] As guests of Prince Rainier of Monaco and Princess Grace.

□ From CSC   28 Hyde Park Gate
13 March 1959

My Darling,
Long before you get this letter you will have heard that yesterday, Thursday, when your pictures were shewn to the General Public 3,210 people visited the Exhibition – The crush was so great that last night a third room was allocated & the pictures were all re-hung. The Academy officials are wildly excited & say this is a record for a 'One Man' Show. Last year there was an Exhibition of drawings by Leonardo da Vinci and 1,172 came on the opening day. Poor Leonardo! I will keep you posted if these large numbers keep up –

Your loving
Clemmie

Everyone I meet is shocked at Ike's statement about using the hydrogen bomb on Russia & dispensing with ground forces[1]. I think we shall soon miss Dulles[2]!

[1] President Eisenhower, speaking in Washington, 11 March 1959, against Congress moves to restore cuts in the armed forces, stated that a 'ground war' in Europe could not be won and that the USA would therefore need to resort to 'other means'; he recognized, however, that nuclear warfare would be self-defeating.
[2] John Foster Dulles (see p. 580 n. 3). He was about to retire as Secretary of State (April 1959).

□ From CSC   28 Hyde Park Gate
14 March 1959

My Darling, I see (to my great relief) in to-day's Times that at last it is sunny in the South of France & that the temperature is 65° – So I like to think of you basking in the sun.

Presiding over your pictures at the Royal Academy is a very good bust of you in bronze by David McFall[1], the sculptor who did your statue for Woodford so badly at first, & deplorable photographs of which were published in all the newspapers – But now he has re-modelled the head of the statue & it is good – Monty [Montgomery*] is unveiling it on October the 3rd –

Tender Love Darling
from your devoted
Clemmie

[1] David McFall (1919–88). Exhibitor at Royal Academy from 1943. The statue is a standing figure.

O From WSC [typewritten]   La Pausa
16 March 1959

Dearest Clemmie,

Your two letters of the 13th and 14th have both arrived, and I am delighted by their contents. . . .

Wendy has started a new cure for my habit of dropping food upon my coat front. She presented me with a gold snap locket which fastens securely the table napkin upon my coat front. This has only to be placed in position on my coat for all danger to be averted. She gave it to me on my arrival, and I am using it regularly with good results. . . .

We have had two days of brilliant weather, and I walked each day in the garden. Yesterday Paul Maze* and his wife came to lunch. He talked a good deal about painting, and will come and paint with me. . . .

I think it will be best to put the celebration of your Birthday off until Sunday, April 12, at Chartwell. I choose Sunday because then Sarah will be able to come. Also it will give me more time to make the necessary arrangements after I return on Monday the 6th. Let me know if this will be convenient.

Tender Love my darling
Your affectionate loving
W

O From CSC   28 Hyde Park Gate
16 March 1959

My Darling,
    Sarah dined with me yesterday, Sunday night. We were alone – She was
affectionate and pleasant, but I thought she looked ill. Last week the play
was at Wolverhampton, this week it is Birmingham – After that Nottingham
& then Bristol. That I think is the end. I pray she may hold out – At Bristol
all the students of the University of which you are Chancellor will be
going to see Peter Pan. I hope she gives a good performance....
    Your pictures are attracting record crowds. In 4 days, i.e. Thursday,
Friday, Saturday & Sunday (a half day) 12,283 people visited the
Exhibition. They stayed an average of 50 minutes.
    On Sunday afternoon the queue stretched right along Piccadilly – There
was a procession coming along of Anti-Hydrogen bomb demonstrators
going to a Meeting – They got mixed up with the queue going to see your
pictures – This amused the Academy officials a good deal!...
    My eye has been giving me a good deal of trouble; so on Wednesday
I'm going to see a new oculist, Mr Rycroft[1]. I do hope he can help me.
                                                        Love from
                                                        Your devoted
                                                        Clemmie

[1] Benjamin Rycroft (1902–67), eminent opthalmic surgeon. Knighted 1960.

Back in London, Winston suffered another spasm (slight stroke) on 13 April.
His doctors advised strongly against any speaking engagements, but he was
determined to address a meeting already arranged in Woodford for 20 April
– which he duly did. He spoke for twenty-two minutes to a crowded meeting
of his constituents, announcing at the end of his speech[1] that he was ready
once again to offer himself as their candidate in the forthcoming General
Election; this was received with tumultous cheers.
    Then in early May he carried out his postponed journey to the United States
to see President Eisenhower. He travelled with Anthony Montague Browne*
and his valet-nurse; he specifically did not wish Lord Moran* to accompany
him, as he strongly resisted the idea of appearing as an invalid.
    In Washington he stayed for three days at the White House, where the
President received him with care and kindness. During his stay he made a
short speech or two. People were impressed by his resilience and good form.
    After Washington, Churchill visited Bernie Baruch in New York, flying
home on 11 May. We, at home, were of course on tenterhooks throughout
this expedition.

[1] For some little time now WSC's speeches had been largely written for him by Anthony Montague
Browne; but the thinking behind them was essentially his, and he always carefully perused and
corrected the drafts, often supplying inimitable Winstonian touches.

○ From WSC   The White House
5 May [1959]   Washington

My dearest Clemmie,
    Here I am. All goes well & the President is a real friend. We had a most
pleasant dinner last night, & I caught up my arrears of sleep in <u>eleven</u> (11)
hours. I am invited to stay in bed all the morning & am going to see Mr
Dulles[1] after luncheon. Anthony [Montague Browne*] will send you more
news. I send my fondest love darling.

                                           Your loving husband
                                                        W

[1] John Foster Dulles, recently retired as US Secretary of State, who was seriously ill with cancer
and died on 24 May 1959.

□ From CSC   28 Hyde Park Gate
5 May 1959

My Darling,
    This morning at seven o'clock, I heard your voice, strong, clear &
resonant – You were greeting the President and the U.S.A.
    I hope this visit will be a great pleasure to you & that you will feel
well –
    I thought you looked well when I said Good-bye to you on board that
sensational plane[1] – I watched the 'take off'. It shot straight into the sky at
45° & I was told that before it got to the end of the landing strip you were
1,500 feet up –
    I enclose the latest figures for your Exhibition. Before you return they
<u>should</u> be over 100,000 –
    Toby is pattering all over this letter. He says if you don't come back
soon, he will like me best. Beautiful but unfaithful bird!

                                              Your loving
                                                Clemmie

                                                    . . .

[1] This was WSC's first flight in a jet aircraft, the De Havilland Comet.

□ From CSC   28 Hyde Park Gate
7 May 1959

My Darling,
    Not one word from you & Anthony after the short message announcing
your safe arrival –
    However I follow your doings in the Press –
    I am so very glad you went to see Mr Dulles & General Marshall[1], &
what fun the helicopter must have been! There's a charming photograph of
you being driven by the President in an electric golf car round the grounds
of his Farm.

This morning I went to see my oculist – He reports slow & steady progress & hopes to be able (when all trace of the shingles have gone) to operate on the drooping lid about the middle of July[2].

I send you a great deal of affection.

I love to think you are having a happy interlude.

Your devoted
Clemmie

. . .

[1] Gen. George Marshall (see p. 484 n. 4), who was very ill from a stroke, and unable to speak; he died on 16 October 1959.

[2] At the end of August CSC underwent a successful operation to remedy the drooping eyelid.

The General Election took place on 8 October 1959. The Conservatives were returned for a third term with an increased majority of 100, winning 365 seats; Labour won 258, the Liberals 6, and there was a single Independent member. Harold Macmillan remained as Prime Minister. Churchill's result at Woodford – a majority of 14,797 – showed a reduction of just over 1,000 on 1955; this probably reflected a degree of discontent among his own supporters who felt his retirement was overdue.

Aged eighty-four and seventy-four respectively, Winston and Clementine fought their fifteenth election campaign together: it was to be the last.

Chapter XXIX

LENGTHENING SHADOWS

I know of no letters between my parents in 1960 – they were together nearly all this year. They both went on *Christina* cruises with Ari Onassis in the New Year, and then later in the summer.

In the middle of November 1960, shortly before his eighty-sixth birthday, Winston had a fall at home in London, banging his head and back, and breaking a vertebra at the top of his spine; he did not go to hospital, but was not well enough to attend his eldest granddaughter's – Edwina Sandys' – wedding to Piers Dixon[1] just before Christmas. However, he reappeared in the House of Commons at the end of January 1961.

In February Winston went to the Hôtel de Paris in Monte Carlo, as was now his wont: a visit which was marred by the escape through an open window of Toby, his cherished budgerigar.

[1] Piers Dixon (1928–), son of Sir Pierson Dixon, diplomat. British Ambassador to France, 1960–4. He and Edwina were divorced in 1973. They had two sons.

☐ From CSC   28 Hyde Park Gate
15 February 1961

My Darling –
    I do grieve for you over Toby – I keep hoping against hope that I shall hear he has been recovered safe and well – [Alas, he never was.]
    It was sweet of you to write to me in your own 'paw' –
    Here I am struggling to get well – Injections, Heat Ray treatment for the refractory ear etc. We shall win through in the end –
    Yesterday was like Midsummer – I think of you constantly
                                                    Your loving and devoted
                                                                Clemmie

Clementine's health was pretty ragged now: minor clinical complaints combined with general nervous fatigue, anxiety and depression made it necessary for her to go into the Lindo Wing, St Mary's Hospital, Paddington, for nearly all March. Winston came back from his sunshine in Monte Carlo to see her shortly before he embarked at Gibraltar in *Christina* for a cruise

– this time to the Canaries and the West Indies, ending up in New York. Clementine was content for him to go, knowing he would be happy in the company of friends[1], and well cared for.

[1] The other guests were Anthony and Nonie Montague Browne and their nearly eight-year-old daughter Jane, and Lord and Lady Moran. WSC was accompanied also by two nurses.

O From WSC   S.Y. Christina
20 March [1961]

My darling Clemmie,
    Here is a line to keep us posted in my own handwriting – all done myself! And to tell you how much I love you: We have travelled ceaselessly over endless seas – quite smoothly for weeks on end.... This is the moment for me to show you that I still possess the gift of writing & continue to use it. But I will not press it too far.

                                                              Ever your devoted
                                                                             W

O From WSC   S.Y. Christina
31 March 1961

HAVE HAD AGREEABLE VOYAGE IN GRENADINES AND ANTHONY AND CLARISSA [EDEN*][1] LUNCHED ON BOARD. WE ARE NOW BOUND FOR JAMAICA AND HAITI. IF CONVENIENT FOR YOU I PROPOSE TO FLY HOME ON APRIL 13. WE WILL TRAVEL VIA NEW YORK[2] WHICH IS SHORTEST AIR ROUTE. LOVE. WINSTON

[1] The Edens now lived most of the time on the small island of Becquia in the Grenadines. Anthony Eden would be created Earl of Avon in July this year.
[2] This would be WSC's last visit to the USA. Christina was two days in New York's Hudson River; WSC stayed on board. Bernard Baruch, now 90, came to visit him.

O From WSC   S.Y. Christina
3 April 1961

NORMAN BROOK[1] DINED WITH US YESTERDAY AT KINGSTON. WE ARE NOW AT MONTEGO BAY. SO MUCH LOOKING FORWARD TO SEEING YOU AND MUCH HOPE FOR NEWS. TENDER LOVE. WINSTON

[1] Sir Norman Brook, PC, GCB, later 1st Baron Normanbrook (1902–67). At this date Secretary of the Cabinet, 1947–62; Joint Secretary of the Treasury and Head of the Home Civil Service, 1956–62.

Clementine had been a worse correspondent than Winston during this time apart; but her four-week spell in hospital, and then one or two pleasant convalescing visits to family and friends, had achieved an improvement in her general health, and when Winston reached home on 14 April (having flown from New York) he found her much better, and with her 'batteries recharged'.
    Winston now would make frequent, usually short, visits to the Riviera,

staying in a beautiful penthouse suite in the Hôtel de Paris, put at his disposal by Ari Onassis. During his June 1961 visit, there is only one (welcome home) note from Clementine: either she really did not write, or the letters have been lost.

○ From WSC
[undated, *c.*6 June 1961]

[Hôtel de Paris]
Monte Carlo

My darling One,
  I write, as I promised, to salute you with love and kisses. You will recognise the handwriting, for it is my own. It is a feat.
  We got here all right, and I am sitting up in bed looking at the view which you know so well. The sun is shining brightly and perhaps it will continue to shine. I hope so.
  I am going out for a drive this afternoon in the mountains and look forward to it.
  I send you this letter with all my love and hope you will like to get it.

All my kisses
Yours ever
W

○ From WSC
[undated, June 1961]

[Hôtel de Paris]
Monte Carlo

My darling, I am writing you a letter with my own paw, from lovely sunshine. We are all going to bask in it from the balcony. I hasten to send you this assurance of my devotion – How I wish you were here.

Tender love,
W

Winston's relish for life was not extinguished: in June he returned home from Monte Carlo for four days to see one of his horses run at Ascot.

□ From CSC ✉
13 June 1961

28 Hyde Park Gate

Welcome Home my Darling –
You will find me waiting for you here.

Clemmie

○ From WSC   Hôtel de Paris
25 June 1961   Monte Carlo

My darling Clemmie,

I am looking forward a great deal to coming home [26 June]. We have had wonderful weather here, but you seem to have had a fine show too. There is nothing like England when it chooses to be good. I am most eager to get back & to sit in the sunlight.

Here we have had a jolly time. Every day we have ranged the country & climbed some new fortress. There is no lack of them, & the French are proud of their defences in this much fought over land.

I have <u>not, so far</u>, visited the Casino. But I think I will go before I go.

Tender love my darling. I am longing to kiss you.

You are a sweet duck.

                                            Winston

○ From WSC   Hôtel de Paris
[undated, August 1961]   Monte Carlo

My dearest Clemmie,

Here is a letter in my own paw. All is vy pleasant and the days slip by. We are steadily wiping off old friendship's debts with lunches & dinners. I find it vy hard to write a good letter – and wonder at the rate with which my friends accomplish their daily tasks. It is amazing they can succeed so well.

But now here I have written what is at least the expression of my love, Darling. When I was young I wrote fairly well, but now at last I am played out.

You have my fondest love

                                    Your devoted
                                            Winston

P.S. I am daily astonished by the development I see in my namesake[1]. He is a wonderful boy. I am so glad I have got to know him.

[1] Winston, Randolph's son, now nearly 21 and an undergraduate at Christ Church, Oxford.

○ From WSC   [Monte Carlo][1]
[undated, ?December 1961]

My darling,

Here I am with a pen in my hand & a full sheet of paper before me. I believe I could write a whole letter jobbed in a strong hand together without difficulty; and I think I will take this business up again.

We are now half way through our journey [visit] & are already counting the days when the red bricks of Chartwell will shine before us. I am a shocking scribbler & the more I try to write a letter the worse it looks. I love you vy much indeed my darling Clemmie, but I think I have lost the art of writing, & when the page is finished I am quite ashamed of all my remaining efficiency as an author, but I am sure you will like to receive this. Many kisses X X X X

Winston

[1] WSC was in Monte Carlo, 1–13 December 1961. Anthony Montague Browne and Diana Sandys were his companions.

Winston and Clementine spent Christmas 1961 at Chartwell with a family party: it was to be the last Chartwell Christmas.

New Year 1962 saw a 'house post' greeting.

☐ From CSC ✉   Chartwell
[1 January 1962]

A Happy New Year Darling Winston and all my Love

Clemmie

Towards the end of June 1962, Winston went to the Hôtel de Paris in Monte Carlo for an expected stay of several weeks; two days after his arrival there he fell in his bedroom and broke his hip. He was operated on and put in plaster the same day at the Monaco hospital; he said to Anthony Montague Browne*, 'Remember, I want to die in England. Promise me that you will see to it.'[1] Anthony rang No. 10, and the Prime Minister (Harold Macmillan) sent an RAF Comet air ambulance, and, despite the French doctors' dismay, Winston flew home on 29 June, the day after the accident. Clementine, who had been kept closely in touch, although aware of the inherent risks in moving him so soon, wanted Winston home – and thoroughly supported his decision.

On his return, Winston was taken straight from the airport to the Middlesex Hospital, where he would be for nearly two months.

[1] Anthony Montague Browne, *Long Sunset*, 1995, p. 312.

☐ From CSC   London
28 June 1962

DARLING I AM SO GRIEVED, BUT MUCH RELIEVED YOU ARE FLYING BACK HOME TOMORROW. FOND AND TENDER LOVE. CLEMMIE

☐ From CSC   28 Hyde Park Gate
24 July 1962

My Darling,
    I have just returned from the Garden Party [at Buckingham Palace].

The Queen was solicitous about you & sent you a special message.
I saw Anthony & Clarissa [Eden*], who are looking forward to seeing you tomorrow.

Your loving
Clemmie

. . .

By the time Winston returned home to No. 28 Hyde Park Gate, Clementine had organized major changes to accommodate his greatly diminished mobility. From now on his bedroom was on the ground floor, and a lift was installed so that he could descend to the garden-level dining room; on fine days he loved to sit out in the garden.

Although he made a remarkable recovery from this accident – attending an Other Club dinner on 1 November – yet it marked a definite further stage in his slow decline. A sad remaining witness to this are his letters: from 1961 his handwriting at times is noticeably less confident – and there are fewer, and shorter letters – but after breaking his hip Winston's handwriting became very wandery. The short notes are full of affection and concern, if occasionally somewhat muddled – but the message shines through. Clementine herself, although her handwriting is still fluent and bold, latterly had become a meagre letter-writer: her long wearying battle with neuritis and later health troubles contributed to this.

○ From WSC   [Hyde Park Gate]
3 October [1962]

Darling

Please let me know how you are. I do hope you are getting on & will soon be thriving again.

Yours ever
Pig

○ From WSC   [Hyde Park Gate]
[October 1962]

Darling,

I hope you are going on well & that we may come together again tomorrow. I have found it quite lonely & will rejoice to see us joined together in gaiety and love. Dearest one I place myself at your disposal & intend to take a walk in the park hand in hand.

With many kisses
Ever loving
W

○ From WSC   [Hyde Park Gate]
[undated, but dated by CSC
8 April 1963]

My darling One,
    This is only to give you my fondest love and kisses <u>a hundred times</u>
<u>repeated</u>. I am a pretty dull & paltry scribbler, but my stick as I write
carries my heart along with it.

Yours ever & always,
W

While my father was in Monte Carlo, my mother spent Easter 1963 with us
at Hamsell Manor. During her stay she discussed with Christopher a matter
which for some time now had caused her acute concern – namely, my father's
retirement from the House of Commons. It was out of the question that he
could fight another election campaign, but with a General Election on the
horizon (in 1964) his Woodford constituency officers, although loyal to him,
felt increasingly the need to appoint a successor. Winston, however, largely
avoided discussion of this matter, which was extremely distasteful to him. As
a result of Clementine's talk with him, Christopher wrote his father-in-law a
reasoned letter.

○ From CSC   28 Hyde Park Gate
19 April 1963

My Darling Winston,
    Thank-you so much for your loving letter.
    I am so glad you are having a pleasant interlude; but I look forward
much to your return on the 25th – I hope Darling you are thinking carefully
about the letter Christopher wrote to you – He read it to me before he
despatched it & I agree with all he says.
    I don't see how you can stand next year without campaigning & fighting
for your seat – And it would be kind to let your Executive Council know
now, before they become too restive –

All my Love Darling
Clemmie

Winston returned from France on 25 April, and Clementine met him at the
airport. The next day, however, she was in the grip of an infection and was
unable to be present when Mr and Mrs Moss (the latter now Winston's
Constituency Chairman) came to luncheon. Anthony Montague Browne* was
also there.

☐ From CSC ⊠   28 Hyde Park Gate
Friday 26 April [1963]

My Darling,
    I have a bad sore throat – & am infectious & so shall not come down
[stairs] to-day.
    You know your Chairman, Mrs Moss, is coming to luncheon to-day
hoping for a decision –
    Don't forget that you promised your Executive that you would at the
next General Election make way for a younger man –
    I am so sorry to be indisposed just when you return. It made me so
happy to see you yesterday my Darling.

                                                        Your loving
                                                        Clemmie
                                                            . . .

Although Mrs Doris Moss (whom both Winston and Clementine very much
liked) had fairly recently talked to Winston about his retirement, yet now
again, she left without his having given her a positive response. But the arguments had not been unavailing, and Winston – however reluctantly – bowed
before them. A few days later, on 1 May, he wrote to Mrs Moss telling her
he would not stand for Woodford at the next Election. For him it was a bitter
decision.

○ From WSC   Chartwell
[June 1963]

My Darling,
    There is no doubt that [what] the favourite would be of Lady Dunn[1]. She
would like above all wedding presents one of my own pictures & you
have 500 under your hand and choice.

                                                        Ever your loving one
                                                        W

[1] On 7 June Max Beaverbrook married Lady Dunn (Christofor), the widow of Sir James Dunn.
Winston guessed at once what would be the best present for her.

In the middle of June Winston returned to Monte Carlo, and on 21 June he
embarked in *Christina* for a cruise round the Greek islands: it was his eighth
voyage with Ari Onassis in that fabulous boat, and it would be his last.

☐ From CSC   Chartwell
15 June 1963

My Darling Winston,
   The day after you left Summer departed & it was really bitterly cold –
Now a little sunshine has returned; but not enough.
   I hope you are well and happy –
   Soon after you receive this letter you will be embarking on that glorious
boat the Christina with pleasant company.
   Sylvia Henley* is here with me keeping me company over the week-
end. To-day we went over to Hamsell to lunch with Christopher and Mary.
                                                         Tender Love
                                                              from
                                                           Clemmie

O From WSC [typewritten]   Hôtel de Paris
18 June 1963   Monte Carlo

Darling Clemmie
   Thank you so much for your letter, which I received today. I do hope
you are having a good rest and that the weather is better.
   Here we have had on the whole sunny days, and I go for a daily drive
with Anthony [Montague Browne*]. We also sat in Max [Beaverbrook*]'s
garden [at La Capponcina] one afternoon, and the white cat sat with us.
   Jock and Meg [Colville*] and Nonie [Montague Browne] join us
tomorrow, and I think we sail on Thursday night or Friday.
   It has certainly been very pleasant and amusing using these very
comfortable and princely rooms. I do wish that you had been filling the
odd room.... ✍ I do hope you will come in the long run – I shall
persevere.
                              With all my love & many kisses X X X X X
                                                         Your devoted
                                                              W

There was a note to greet Winston on arrival at the airport on his return.

☐ From CSC   Chartwell
4 July 1963

My Darling,
   The Time has seemed long without you –
   I shall be on the door-step to welcome you Home.

                                                         Your devoted
                                                           Clemmie

○ From CSC ✉
12 September 1963

> My darling Winston
> To-day we have
> been married 55 years
> September the 12ᵗʰ 1908
> September the 12ᵗʰ 1963

> Your loving
> Clemmie

Although the constituency situation had been resolved, the strain and worry of it had taken its toll, and as this summer progressed Clementine became seriously unwell. She worried also about Winston, who was increasingly frail and who, on 12 August, suffered a slight stroke (a clot). He had recovered quite well, but each such episode left its mark on his vitality and strength.

During September Clementine became more and more depressed, exhausted and agitated: it was decided she must have a complete break from Chartwell.

☐ From CSC [typewritten] ✉
17 September 1963

Winston.
Now that I have been indisposed for such a long time, and have been really ill for a month, the doctors want me to go away for a change. So on Friday I am going to stay with Mary at Hamsell for a fortnight.

> Your loving
> Clemmie

○ From WSC [typewritten]
[22 September 1963]

My dear Clemmie,
Thank you so much for your telegram. I only send you a line to break my silence, and to hope you are getting well in the care of the Family, and send you my fondest love.

> Yours ever,
> W

○ From WSC [typewritten]   [Chartwell]
27 September 1963

My darling
We rejoice at the better shining weather today, and I look forward to quite a number of friends who are coming on other days who also

promise to give me pleasure. I hope indeed you will be well and cheerful soon, and I look forward greatly to our meeting.

Yours ever,
W

☐ From CSC   Hamsell Manor
28 September 1963

My Darling,
Thank-you for your dear letter which arrived by Express. I am so glad you are having pleasant visitors –
I look forward to seeing you my Dear One next week.

Clemmie

○ From WSC [typewritten]   [Chartwell]
30 September 1963

My darling,
I am glad you are about to come here and very pleased that you will select Friday as the day. I shall be delighted to see you again, and hope that it will mark a sign of a truly bright time and give me a few days which, like others in their turn, will be sweet and happy.

With all love
Your devoted
W

Nineteen-sixty-three was marked by tragedy in our family. In July, Sarah's husband, Henry Audley[1], to whom she had been married for little more than a year, died suddenly in Granada, Spain.

On the night of 19–20 October, Diana died in London from an overdose of sleeping pills[2]. When this tragic event took place Clementine was in the Westminster Hospital under treatment for her nervous condition, which had worsened at the end of the summer. Neither she nor Winston could go to Diana's funeral; but both went to her crowded memorial service at St Stephen's, Walbrook, on 31 October.

The next notes must have been written some time now.

[1] Henry Touchet Tuchet-Jesson, 23rd Baron Audley (1918–63), whom Sarah had married, as his second wife, in 1962. It was her third marriage. They seemed so happy together.
[2] Duncan Sandys and Diana had been divorced, after nearly 25 years of marriage, in 1960. Duncan had married Marie Claire, Viscountess Hudson, in 1962.

○ From WSC   Chartwell
[undated, *c.* late October 1963]

My darling,
    To acknowledge your lovely letter [not to hand] and to send back my
grief at yours. Clemmie, you must expect it at these sad times. I am sure
you are having worse. Here is my best of love, & a struggle to gain it.
                                                          Yours always
                                                                W

□ From CSC ⊠   28 Hyde Park Gate
Tuesday [22 or 29 October 1963]

My darling Winston
    Thank-you for your sweet note –
    The Doctor has been & I am to stay 2 or 3 days in bed –
    Sylvia [Henley*] is coming to luncheon with you tomorrow & would love
to play bézique.
                                                            Fond Love
                                                             Clemmie

□ From CSC ⊠   Chartwell
[undated]

A little love message from Clemmie
    I am so sorry that I am laid up & so cannot see you

The last letter we have in the long dialogue is from Clementine in the spring
of 1964: she had largely recovered her health, and was again able to cope
with life.
    The suggestions reported in her memorandum to Winston were realized.

□ From CSC [typewritten] ⊠
18 April 1964

Winston
    The Government and the Members of the Opposition have been
thinking what would be the best way of marking the end of your time in

Parliament. They propose that you should be given a Vote of Thanks. This would be passed unanimously by the House, and then a special Committee consisting of the Prime Minister, the Leader of the Opposition and the Leader of the Liberal Party would wait upon you here at Hyde Park Gate to hand you a copy of the Resolution.

Would you be agreeable to this?

Clemmie

Winston Churchill was present in the House of Commons for the last time on 27 July 1964; he had been a Member of Parliament almost continuously for over half a century.

On 28 July a deputation headed by the Prime Minister, Sir Alec Douglas-Home, and among whom were the Leader of the Opposition, Harold Wilson, and the Leader of the Liberal Party, Jo Grimond, called upon Sir Winston Churchill and presented him with the Resolution which, earlier that day, had been carried by the House of Commons *nemine contradicente*:

That this House desires to take this opportunity of marking the forthcoming retirement of the right honourable Gentleman the Member for Woodford by putting on record its unbounded admiration and gratitude for his services to Parliament, to the nation and to the world; remembers, above all, his inspiration of the British people when they stood alone, and his leadership until victory was won; and offers its grateful thanks to the right honourable Gentleman for these outstanding services to this House and to the nation.

This small but historic ceremony took place in the dining room at 28 Hyde Park Gate, witnessed by Clementine and some of their children and grand-children. It was a muted, yet fit, ending to a long, long day.

Winston Churchill died on 24 January 1965, in his ninety-first year. He was accorded a State Funeral in St Paul's Cathedral by the Queen. He lies in Bladon churchyard just outside the park walls of Blenheim Palace, where he had been born.

Clementine died on 12 December 1977, in her ninety-third year. Her ashes were laid in Winston's grave.

Bladon churchyard is now a place of pilgrimage.

> Sleep after toil, port after stormy seas,
> Ease after war, death after life does greatly please.[1]

---

[4] Edmund Spenser, *The Faerie Queene*, Bk I, c. IX, xl.

Biographical Notes

These notes have been compiled and written largely by the Editor. They are haphazard in choice inasmuch as they reflect the importance of the individuals concerned to the lives of Winston and Clementine Churchill; but some relevant personages do not appear here, if their role emerges clearly in the letters. The Notes do not aim to be comprehensive, and the judgements expressed are essentially subjective.

M.S.

AIRLIE, Countess of (1830–1921): Henrietta Blanche Stanley, daughter of Edward John, 2nd Baron Stanley of Alderley, and Henrietta Maria, daughter of 13th Viscount Dillon. CSC's grandmother. Married David Graham Ogilvy, 10th Earl of Airlie (1826–81) in 1851. A cultivated woman of strong character and quasi-Liberal views whose company was enjoyed by politicians, writers and philosophers of the day. Of her six children, the following appear in these letters: Lady Blanche Ogilvy, who married Henry Hozier* and was the mother of CSC; Lady Clementine Ogilvy, who married Bertram Mitford, 1st Baron Redesdale; David, later 11th Earl of Airlie; Lady Maude Ogilvy, who married Theodore Whyte, and whose younger daughter was Maryott ('Mop', 'Moppet' or 'Nana') Whyte*. During the forty years of her widowhood, Blanche Airlie was the ruling force in her family.

AITKEN, Max *see* BEAVERBROOK, Max

ASQUITH, Herbert Henry (1852–1928). Liberal statesman. Classics First Class, QC. Elected to Parliament in 1886, he was appointed Home Secretary in Gladstone's Government, 1892–5. Served as Chancellor of the Exchequer, 1905–8. Succeeded Sir Henry Campbell-Bannerman as Prime Minister in April 1908. During his eight-year premiership were carried through the great Liberal constitutional and social reforms such as the People's Budget of 1910; the Parliament Act of 1911; and the Irish Home Rule Bill of 1912. Asquith headed the Coalition Government formed in May 1915, but was displaced by Lloyd George* in December 1916. Created 1st Earl of Oxford and Asquith, 1925. Resigned the Liberal leadership in 1926. His first wife, Helen Melland, by whom he had five children, among them Violet (Asquith*, later Bonham Carter) and Raymond (killed 1916), died in 1891. In 1894 he married Margaret (Margot) Tennant, youngest daughter of Sir Charles Tennant, 1st Baronet. They had two children. Asquith was a master of parliamentary debate; brilliant, urbane and pleasure-loving, he was also morally and physically courageous (violent assaults on numerous occasions by suffragettes left him unmoved). Variously nicknamed 'The Block', 'Squiffy', 'The Sage'.

ASQUITH, Violet (1887–1969), daughter of H. H. Asquith* by his first marriage; she was deeply devoted to her father and passionately loyal to him. In 1915 she married Maurice (later Sir Maurice) Bonham Carter (her father's Private Secretary), a scientist and civil servant, who died in 1960. Violet Bonham Carter was a fervent Liberal protagonist, and a brilliant orator; but she subordinated her political opportunities to her family life. In the Thirties she campaigned on behalf of the persecuted Jews in Germany and the countries overrun by the Reich. She was energetic in her support of WSC in demanding rearmament and a firm stance in the face of the dictators. Lady Violet was President of the Liberal Party Organization, 1944–5, and a Governor of the BBC, 1941–6; she was created Baroness Asquith of Yarnbury in 1964. Her book *Winston Churchill as I Knew Him*, a brilliantly perceptive study, was published in 1965. As a young minister in H. H. Asquith's government (1908–15) WSC saw a great deal of Violet Asquith and they formed a friendship which, despite one or two political stand-offs, lasted throughout their lifetimes.

AVON, 1st Earl of *see* EDEN, Anthony

BALSAN, Consuelo (1877–1964), daughter of William K. Vanderbilt of New York. In 1895, when she was eighteen, she was coerced by her mother into a loveless marriage with the 9th Duke of Marlborough*. She bore him two sons. In 1906 she left him, and, establishing herself in Sunderland House, Curzon Street, London, immersed herself in serious social work. In 1920 Consuelo divorced the Duke, and in 1921 married Jacques Balsan (1874–1956), a lieutenant-colonel in the French air force, with whom she was truly happy. The Balsans lived in France (at Lou Sueil, at Eze on the Riviera, and at St Georges Motel, near Dreux in Normandy) until forced to leave in 1940 by the arrival of the Germans; they went to the United States, where they lived thereafter in Florida and Long Island. Jacques Balsan died in 1956. Consuelo's autobiography, *The Glitter and the Gold*, was published in 1953. She is buried at Bladon, close to Blenheim Palace.

BEAVERBROOK, 'Max' (1879–1964): **William Maxwell Aitken.** Born in Canada, the son of a Presbyterian minister, he made a fortune out of cement mills. Entered British politics, becoming Unionist MP for Ashton-under-Lyme, 1910–16. Private Secretary to Bonar Law. Knighted 1911; created 1st Baronet, 1916, and 1st Baron Beaverbrook, 1917. First met WSC while Canadian Government Representative at the Front in 1916. Member of British War Cabinets of both Lloyd George and Churchill: Chancellor of Duchy of Lancaster and Minister of Information, 1918; in the Second World War he was Minister of Aircraft Production, 1940–1; Minister of State, 1941; Minister of Supply, 1941–2; and Lord Privy Seal, 1943–5. Beaverbrook entered the world of journalism in 1919, buying a majority interest in the *Daily Express*, and developed it into the most widely read daily newspaper in the world. In 1921 he founded the *Sunday Express*, and in 1929 bought the *Evening Standard*. He married first, in 1906, Gladys Drury of Halifax, Nova Scotia, who died in 1927; secondly, in 1963, Marcia Anastasia Christoforides (always called Christofor), widow of Sir James Dunn QC, who survived him.

Max Beaverbrook was an extraordinary personality, arousing extremes of reaction in people. He had a gnomic appearance, and an impish streak in his character. His friendship with WSC survived periods when they were hardly on speaking terms, usually due to politics: the Beaverbrook press supported appeasement. However, in the end they were always reconciled. Their friendship was much disapproved of by 'top Tories': in the 1945 election the tone of the Beaverbrook papers led to the quip that Max 'wanted the jockey to win but not the horse'!

CSC from the first had a keen distrust of Max, although she once said of him that he was a 'good foul-weather friend'. She frequently warned WSC of the harm Max could do him. After the Second World War Max was most generous and hospitable, and often had WSC/CSC to stay – or lent them his beautiful house, La Capponcina, at Cap d'Ail. In later years CSC sheathed her sword, succumbing gracefully to Max's perennial charm and blandishments.

BIRKENHEAD, 1st Earl of *see* SMITH, Frederick Edwin

BONHAM CARTER, Violet *see* ASQUITH, Violet

BRACKEN, Brendan (1901–58). Born in Ireland (Templemore, Tipperary), son of a builder and stonemason. Journalist; Unionist/Conservative MP, 1921–51. Parliamentary Private Secretary to Prime Minister (WSC), 1940–1; Minister of Information, 1941–5; First Lord of the Admiralty, 1945. Chairman of *Financial News*; Managing Director of *Economist*. Created 1st Viscount Bracken in 1952. He never married.

Met WSC in 1923 and increasingly became his political confidant, champion and crony. For many years CSC distrusted Brendan; she thought him an adventurer, and disliked his brash charm; nor did she appreciate as droll the rumour (easily disprovable) which circulated that Bracken was WSC's illegitimate son. However, she gradually came to appreciate his loyalty as a friend. After the war particularly, she relied on his sage counsel on many family matters, but she was always mistrustful of his political advice.

BUTLER, Richard Austen (1902–82), eminent statesman. KG, CH, PC. Always known as 'Rab'. Conservative MP for Saffron Walden, 1929–65. Created Baron Butler of Saffron Walden (life peer) 1965. A staunch supporter of Neville Chamberlain and his appeasement policy, he was aghast at WSC's succession as Prime Minister; but he came to admire him, and they worked well together. As Chairman of the Conservative Party Research Department and the Party's Advisory Committee on Policy, 1945–64, and Chairman of the Party, 1959–61, Butler played a major role in the renaissance of Conservatism after the defeat of 1945. He held all the senior ministerial posts, including the Exchequer, Foreign Office and Home Office; as Minister of Education in 1944 he fathered the Education Act which bears his name. Twice, in 1957 and in 1963, Butler was within a hair's breadth of being chosen as Prime Minister. But his tenure as Master of Trinity College, Cambridge, from 1965 to 1978 made a happy and dignified coda to his brilliant career. 'Rab' was twice married: first, in 1926, to Sydney Courtauld, only child of Samuel Courtauld (died 1947), who died 1954; secondly, in 1959, to Mollie, widow of Augustine Courtauld (died 1959), who survives him. 'Rab' was a talented amateur painter.

CHERWELL, 1st Viscount *see* LINDEMANN, Frederick Alexander

CHURCHILL, John Strange Spencer (1880–1947): 'Jack', second son of Lord and Lady Randolph Churchill**. Married in 1908 Lady Gwendeline Bertie ('Goonie'), fourth daughter of 7th Earl of Abingdon; they had two sons and one daughter. Served in Light African Horse during the Boer War, and was wounded; mentioned in dispatches, and awarded Queen's Medal with five clasps. Oxfordshire Yeomanry, 1905–21. In the First World War served on Western Front and went to Gallipoli with General Sir Ian Hamilton; later joined Field Marshal Lord Birdwood's staff, returning with him to France in 1916. Mentioned in dispatches; DSO, 1918. After the war he became a stockbroker. Although six years Winston's junior, the two brothers from their schoolroom days throughout their lives were mutually devoted, and their wives, Clementine and Goonie, became close confidantes. In the First World War the two families shared Jack and Goonie's house in Kensington. Jack and Goonie ('the Jagoons') and their children came often to Chartwell. During the Second World War Goonie, suffering from cancer, went to live in the country, where she died in 1941; their London house having been rendered uninhabitable by bombing, Jack (who continued to work in the City) lodged in any nook or cranny available in the Downing Street/Annexe complex. His devotion and loyalty to his elder brother was equalled only by his self-effacing discretion. Winston was deeply saddened by his death in February 1947.

CHURCHILL, Lady Randolph (1854–1921): Jeanette ('Jennie') Jerome, WSC's mother. A renowned beauty, second daughter of Leonard and Clara Jerome of New York. She and her sisters Clara (later Frewen) and Leonie (later Leslie) were brought up largely in Paris, where Mrs Jerome chiefly resided. In April 1874 Jennie married Lord Randolph Churchill*. She bore her husband two sons: Winston (WSC), born prematurely on 30 November 1874, and John* ('Jack'), born in 1880. Lord Randolph died in 1895. In 1900 Lady Randolph married fashionable George Cornwallis-West, a man twenty years younger than herself; she divorced him in 1913. In 1918 she married Montagu Porch, a member of the Nigerian Civil Service – again a man half her own age. Worldly and extravagant, Jennie's beauty, vitality and charm made her a star in the firmament of Edwardian society. Winston loved her devotedly and uncritically. Clementine from early days cast a cool look at her mother-in-law, and particularly deplored her extravagance which weighed heavily on her sons. But in later years she was won over by Jennie's buoyancy and courage in the face of the troubles which beset her. Throughout this book she is referred to as either 'Jennie' or 'Lady Randolph'.

CHURCHILL, Lord Randolph Henry Spencer (1849–1895), third son of the 7th Duke of Marlborough. WSC's father. Conservative politician and brilliant orator. He entered Parliament in 1874 as MP for Woodstock. In April the same year he married 'Jennie' Jerome of New York (Lady Randolph Churchill*); their first son, Winston (WSC), was born prematurely on 30 November, and a second son, John* ('Jack') in 1880. From 1876 to 1880 Lord Randolph acted as unofficial Private Secretary to his father, then Lord Lieutenant of Ireland. In 1880, together with three other Conservatives, he formed a group known as the 'Fourth Party' advocating 'Tory democracy', a policy at first opposed by older members of the party, such as Lord Salisbury, but which later became widely accepted. His brilliance and meteoric career won him a large popular following in the country. Appointed Secretary of State for India in Lord Salisbury's Government of 1885–6, in July 1886 he became Chancellor of the Exchequer and Leader of the House of Commons, but resigned impetuously six months later following a struggle with the War Office over his Budget reducing the service estimates; he never held office again, although he remained in the House of Commons until his death. Lord Randolph's chief interest in the last years of his life was racing. He died in January 1895 after a long and distressing illness then diagnosed as general paralysis of the insane (a derivative of syphilis). Recent medical research indicates that he may have suffered from a cerebral tumour. Winston admired and revered his father and longed to have a closer relationship with him. He wrote a much-praised life of his father: *Lord Randolph Churchill* (2 vols), first published in 1906.

COLVILLE, John Rupert, 'Jock' (1915–87). Jock Colville was in the Prime Minister's Private Office in 1940 when Winston Churchill succeeded Neville Chamberlain. Starting from a standpoint of dislike, mistrust and political hostility, Jock became over a period of time (well recorded in his diaries) a devoted admirer and close friend to both WSC and CSC and their family. Coming from the same social world, WSC found Jock instantly congenial, but also came to rely on his brilliance and professionalism. He greatly admired Jock's determination to join the RAF, despite his poor eyesight, but deplored his departure from the Private Office, to which however Jock returned after participating in the invasion of Europe air combats of 1944. In 1948 Jock married Lady Margaret ('Meg') Egerton, and she too became a much-loved friend of the Churchills. WSC summoned Jock Colville back to be joint head of his Private Office, 1951–5. Throughout the remaining years of WSC and CSC's lives Jock and Meg's friendship was a joy to them. Jock was the principal motivator of the idea of Churchill College, Cambridge, founded by WSC in 1958. His publications include: contribution to *Action This Day – Working with Churchill*, 1968; *Man of Valour*, 1972; *Footprints* *in Time*, 1976; *The New Elizabethans*, 1977; *The Churchillians*, 1981; *The Fringes of Power: Downing Street Diaries 1939–55*, 1985.

COOPER, Lady Diana (1892–1986): Diana Manners, third daughter of the 8th Duke of Rutland. She was the outstanding beauty of her day, and a fascinatingly unorthodox character. In the First World War she nursed at Guy's Hospital. In 1919 she married Alfred Duff Cooper*, they between them having worn down her parents' opposition. In order to make money to fulfil Duff's ambition of leaving the Foreign Office and entering politics, Diana first played in films, but from 1923 she took the lead role of the Madonna in Max Reinhardt's production of *The Miracle* (a mimed play set to music by Engelbert Humperdinck). The play toured in the United States, Britain and the Continent on and off for twelve years.

Diana was a prolific letter-writer: to Duff when apart (*A Durable Fire*, their letters to each other edited by their grand-daughter Artemis Cooper, 1983); and to such friends as Conrad Russell and Evelyn Waugh (*Mr Wu and Mrs Stitch*, also edited by Artemis Cooper, 1991). Mrs Algernon Stitch in Waugh's novels was modelled on Diana Cooper. Diana herself wrote deliciously and idiosyncratically, and published three volumes of her memoirs: *The Rainbow Comes and Goes*, 1958; *The Light of Common Day*, 1959; and *Trumpets from the Steep*, 1960.

COOPER, (Alfred) Duff (1890–1954), politician, diplomat, *homme de lettres*. PC, GCMG, DSO. Son of Sir Alfred Cooper FRCS and Lady Agnes Duff, a daughter of the 5th Earl of Fife. Educated at Eton and Oxford; entered the Foreign Office in 1913: reserved occupation, only released for military service in 1918, when as a lieutenant in the Grenadier Guards he won the DSO. Created 1st Viscount Norwich, 1952. In June 1919 he married Lady Diana Manners (Cooper*), a daughter of the 8th Duke of Rutland; their marriage of thirty-three years lasted till Duff's death in 1954, and was characterized by their unvarying love and devotion for each other, though not by unvarying fidelity.

Duff Cooper entered Parliament in 1924; he held various government appointments including Secretary of State for War, 1935–7, and First Lord of the Admiralty from 1938 until he resigned in protest after the Munich Agreement. In WSC's wartime government, he was Minister of Information, 1940–1. In 1942–4 he was British Minister in Algiers and from 1943 the Government's Representative with the French Committee of Liberation, and was Ambassador to France, 1944–7; in these two last appointments he succeeded in restoring and maintaining Anglo-French relations to a remarkable degree. He was a man of erudition and charm. Among his works of literature and history were: *Talleyrand*, 1932; *David*, 1943; *Operation Heartbreak*, 1950; and his autobiography, *Old Men Forget*, 1953. He also wrote some beautiful poetry. Duff and Diana had one child, John Julius, born 1929, who succeeded his father as 2nd Viscount Norwich.

DE GAULLE, Charles (1890–1970), French general, leader of Free France. Served as infantry officer in the First World War; wounded three times and taken prisoner, 1916. In the inter-war years his military career was notable for his books on strategy and military theory which were regarded as controversial. Brigadier-General, 1 June 1940; on 6 June appointed Under-Secretary for National Defence. It was at this time that de Gaulle first met WSC, upon whom he made a strong impression. When Reynaud resigned as Prime Minister (16 June) and his successor Marshal Pétain asked the Germans for an armistice, de Gaulle left France in an RAF aircraft and came to London, from where he broadcast his famous *Appel du 18 juin*, calling on his compatriots to continue the struggle and to join the Free French Forces under his leadership. WSC backed de Gaulle from the first (the entire Free French movement was funded by the British Government). However, during the course of the war Churchill and de Gaulle were often at loggerheads, when the Frenchman's arrogant and intransigent demeanour only served to increase the difficulties between them. WSC too became exasperated and was unreasonable: their relationship was several times near breaking-point. But WSC never ceased to regard de Gaulle as the saviour of France, while the General recognized in him the valiant leader of freedom, and never forgot his crucial support for himself and the Free French in 1940; and later, when de Gaulle met with lack of approval and support from President Roosevelt and the American hierarchy, he appreciated Churchill's firm backing. In 1958 he invested WSC with the Croix de la Libération (the highest order of the French Resistance).

CSC and the General had a high regard for each other. She once berated him roundly at a luncheon for expressing views ill-becoming an ally and a guest in this country: the following day he sent her a vast flower arrangement.

On returning to France on 14 June 1944, de Gaulle rapidly established his leadership and the authority of the French Committee for National Liberation (CFLN), set up in Algiers in 1943, and was himself rapturously received by the populace on 26 August. The CFLN, which had soon been accepted by the Allies as the *de facto* government of France, was formally recognized by the United Kingdom and United States in October 1944.

Elections in October 1945 for a Constituent Assembly marked the end of the Third Republic. In 1946 de Gaulle resigned. Called back to office when civil war threatened in Algeria; May 1958, Prime Minister; President Fifth Republic, 1958–69, when he retired. Died November 1970.

EDEN, Anthony (1897–1977), KG, PC, MC. Eton and Christ Church, Oxford (First Class Honours, Oriental Studies). Served First World War, 1915–19 (MC, 1916). Conservative MP for Warwick and Leamington, 1923–57. Parliamentary Private Secretary to Sir Austen Chamberlain when Foreign Secretary, 1926–9. Baldwin favoured him, and he rose rapidly in the 1930s through the posts of Lord Privy Seal and Minister without Portfolio for the League of Nations to Secretary of State for Foreign Affairs, 1935–8, when he resigned over differences with the Prime Minister, Neville Chamberlain, chiefly in regard to Fascist Italy. He was Secretary of State for Dominion Affairs, 1939–40, and in Churchill's wartime Government was Secretary of State for War, 1940, for Foreign Affairs, 1940–5, and also Leader of the House of Commons, 1942–5. On Churchill's return to power in 1951 Eden was once again Foreign Secretary, Deputy Prime Minister and acknowledged 'heir apparent', 1951–5. He succeeded Churchill as Prime Minister in April 1955, but resigned in January 1957 through ill-health, which had latterly beset him. He was created 1st Earl of Avon, 1961. He married first, in 1923, Beatrice Beckett; they were divorced in 1950 (she died in 1957). They had two sons: Simon, the elder, an RAF Pilot Officer, was killed in Burma, 1945; Nicholas succeeded his father in 1977 as 2nd Earl; he died 1985, when the title became extinct. Eden married, secondly, in 1952, Clarissa Churchill, WSC's niece, who survives him.

Anthony Eden was a man of great good looks and debonair mien, highly cultivated and of winning charm. He and WSC were friends and good colleagues in the war (apart from a few skirmishes), but during WSC's last tenure of office, 1951–5, when increasingly the question of his final retirement was in many people's minds, the relationship between him and Eden became tense at times, and in the last year before he resigned WSC had strong feelings of resentment at what he conceived to be Eden's over-eager anticipation of succeeding him; it was an unhappy time. But their friendship was restored, and nothing was more genuine than WSC's and CSC's concern for both Anthony and Clarissa in the aftermath of the Suez crisis, and the illness which forced Anthony's sudden resignation in January 1957.

ELLIOTT, Maxine (1868–1940). American actress and renowned English society hostess. Born Jessie Dermot, daughter of an immigrant Irish sea captain, she went on the stage after a first failed marriage, changing her name to Maxine Elliott, and became very successful in her genre (popular musical plays). In 1896 she married

Nat Goodwin, the celebrated comedian and actor–manager. They came often to London, where her theatrical and social success was dazzling; she was befriended by Mrs George Keppel and introduced into the highest social circles. In 1905, following her divorce, Maxine Elliott bought Hartsbourne Manor. During the First World War she did valuable relief work for refugees. After the war she returned to the American stage, but retired soon afterwards, selling Hartsbourne and moving to Paris. In the 1930s she created Le Château de l'Horizon at Golfe Juan, near Cannes, where she lived and entertained lavishly; she died there in 1940.

GUEST, Frederick Edward, 'Freddie' (1875–1937), third son of 1st Baron Wimborne (Ivor Bertie Guest*). PC, CBE, DSO. Served on the White Nile and in South Africa, 1900–1. Entered Parliament in 1910 as a Liberal, and joined the Conservative Party in 1931. ADC to Sir John French, 1914–16, he became Secretary of State for Air, 1921–2, and did much to promote aviation in the United Kingdom. He married Amy Phipps of Pittsburgh in 1905. Cousin of WSC: they often played polo together, and CSC used to stay with the Guests in Leicestershire for hunting before the First World War. The Churchills shared the Guests' house, Templeton, Roehampton, for some months during the winter of 1919–20.

GUEST, Sir Ivor Bertie, 2nd Baronet (1835–1914), created 1st Baron Wimborne in 1880. Married Lady Cornelia Spencer-Churchill (1847–1927), eldest daughter of the 7th Duke of Marlborough and WSC's aunt. They had five sons and two daughters. Two of their sons, Ivor (later 2nd Baron Wimborne)* and Freddie Guest*, were great friends of WSC. They had houses at 22 Arlington Street, London, and Canford Manor, Wimborne, Dorset. CSC felt a general antipathy towards the 'Guest tribe', but she was very fond of Aunt Cornelia.

GUEST, Ivor Churchill (1873–1939), eldest son of Ivor Bertie Guest*. Served in the South African War and entered Parliament in 1900, first as a Liberal MP and later as a Conservative. He was Paymaster-General, 1910–12; Lord Lieutenant of Ireland, 1915–18. Married the Hon. Alice Grosvenor, daughter of 2nd Baron Ebury, in 1902. Raised to the peerage as Baron Ashby St Ledger in 1910, he succeeded his father as 2nd Baron Wimborne in 1914, and was created 1st Viscount Wimborne in 1918. Cousin of WSC. Renowned as a 'pouncer'.

HALLE (pronounced 'Halley'), **Katharine** (1904–97) of Cleveland, Ohio. Always known as 'Kay'. Devoted friend of Randolph for nearly forty years. Kay was much liked by WSC and CSC and always welcomed at Chartwell or in London. Her warmth and kindness extended to all Randolph's family in several generations, to whom she was immensely hospitable in Washington, DC, where she lived in Georgetown.

Kay Halle was a keen Democrat and supporter of President Roosevelt*, and was for many years a prominent Washington political hostess. An ardent admirer of Winston Churchill, it was she who initiated, campaigned for and assisted on its way through Congress the Act conferring on him honorary American citizenship, bestowed on 9 April 1963 by President Kennedy.

After Randolph's death in June 1968 Kay Halle collected and published a book of tributes to him by many of his varied friends entitled *Randolph S. Churchill: The Young Unpretender*, 1971. She also published *Irrepressible Churchill: A Treasury of Winston Churchill's Wit*, Cleveland, 1966; London, 1985.

In 1967 Kay Halle was invested with the Honorary OBE.

HAMBLIN, Grace (1908–). The daughter of the head gardener of a neighbouring property, she was educated at Crockham Hill Church of England School and later at a secretarial training college. Grace Hamblin came to the Churchills as a holiday 'help-out' in the Chartwell office in 1932, and remained in their employment until 1966. She worked at Chartwell until 1939, when she went to London, and was CSC's personal private secretary throughout the war. Grace accompanied CSC to the first

Quebec Conference (1943) and on her journey to Russia (March–May 1945). She was awarded the OBE in 1945. After the war Grace was again based at Chartwell, and managed the domestic and estate life there until WSC's death in 1965. In 1966, when the National Trust took over Chartwell, she became the first Administrator, until her retirement in 1973. A woman of loyalty, charm, discernment and discretion, WSC and CSC were equally devoted to her, as are all our family. She lives on the Green in Westerham.

HENLEY, Sylvia (1882–1980) OBE, a daughter of the 4th Baron Stanley* of Alderley, later 4th Baron Sheffield of Roscommon. In 1906 she married Colonel Anthony Henley; he died in 1925. She was CSC's cousin and lifelong friend; WSC was also devoted to her. Sylvia Henley gave years of dedicated service in the field of hospital administration, and was connected with King's College Hospital, London, for over twenty years; a ward there is named after her. She was a gifted needlewoman. She had an incisive mind and a forthright manner.

HOZIER, Colonel Sir Henry Montague (1838–1907), third son of James C. Hozier of Newlands and Mauldslie Castle, Lanarkshire. Educated at Rugby and Edinburgh Academy, he showed early distinction as a soldier, passing first in and first out of Staff College; he served in China and Abyssinia, was attached to the Germany army during the Austro-Prussian war of 1866 and as Assistant Military Attaché to the Prussian forces in the Franco-Prussian War, 1870–1, being decorated with the Iron Cross by the Emperor Wilhelm I. He subsequently wrote two books, *Seven Weeks' War* and *History of the British Expedition to Abyssinia*. He left the Army in 1874 and became Secretary to the Corporation of Lloyd's of London, an office which he held for thirty-two years with outstanding distinction. A first marriage had ended in divorce, and in 1878 he married Lady Blanche Ogilvy, eldest daughter of the 10th Earl of Airlie. He was knighted in 1903. Although they were never divorced, Henry and Blanche Hozier were separated from 1891. The four children, Kitty (born 1883), Clementine (born 1885) and the twins, Bill and Nellie (born 1888), are now held not to be the issue of Henry Hozier (see Introduction, p. 3.)

JEROME, Jennie *see* CHURCHILL, Lady Randolph

LAVERY, Sir John (1856–1941), painter. Knighted, 1918; RA, 1921. Married first, in 1890, Kathleen McDermott (died 1891), with whom he had one daughter; secondly, in 1910, Hazel Trudeau (born Martyn), an American. She had one daughter, Alice, by her first marriage. Hazel Lavery was a gifted artist in her own right; a strikingly beautiful woman, she was the model for many of her husband's paintings, and it was her head which was reproduced on the first Irish Free State banknotes. Lavery's pictures are in many public galleries in Europe and America. In 1932 he became President of the Royal Society of Portrait Painters. In 1915 when WSC became enthralled by painting, John and Hazel Lavery, friends and close neighbours of the Churchills in London, were his first mentors. In the early Twenties the Laverys were deeply involved in Irish Nationalist politics: he was a Belfast-born Roman Catholic, and she had Irish blood in her veins; both ardently wished to see a peaceful and constitutional solution to the Anglo-Irish problem, and they used their connections in Ireland (both north and south) and England to try to achieve better understanding, by bringing members of the British Government and establishment into touch with the Irish Nationalist leaders at social occasions in their house. They were in close touch with WSC (in 1921 and 1922 Minister for the Colonies) and fostered the vitally important relationship between him and Michael Collins (of the Irish Republican Army and later a minister in the Sinn Fein government). John and Hazel Lavery remained close friends always with WSC and CSC.

LINDEMANN, Frederick Alexander (1886–1957), 'The Prof'. Physicist. PC, CH, FRS. Son of an Alsatian father and an American mother; his father had emigrated to Britain in the 1870s, and he was educated in England and then in Germany. During 1915–18 he worked in the Physical Laboratory of the RAF. Having learned to fly in 1916, he personally investigated the causes of aircraft spin – then a major cause of fatal accidents. Professor of Experimental Philosophy (Physics), Oxford, 1919–56, presiding over the Clarendon Laboratory, which under his aegis became a foremost research centre. He and WSC first met in 1921, and quickly forged a friendship. 'The Prof' had the capacity of explaining the most rarefied scientific problems with clarity and of making them comprehensible to the layman. Before, during and after the war he would advise and instruct WSC in technical, scientific and economic matters. Personal Assistant to the Prime Minister, 1940–5; Paymaster-General, 1942–5 and 1951–3. Created 1st Baron Cherwell, 1941; 1st Viscount Cherwell, 1956. His close access to WSC when Prime Minister however aroused jealousies, and 'The Prof' himself waged fierce vendettas against those (mainly in the scientific field) who displeased him; he also had his built-in prejudices about race and colour.

He was a welcome and frequent guest of WSC and CSC and their family at Chartwell. (CSC particularly enjoyed his company, as he was a first-class tennis player.) 'The Prof' was a vegetarian, a teetotaller and a bachelor. But despite a conventionally forbidding exterior and reserved manner, he could exude warmth, and his benevolence and hospitality at Oxford to undergraduates in his orbit was celebrated.

LLOYD GEORGE, David (1863–1945). Welsh Liberal statesman, pioneer of social reform. Together with WSC, responsible for (*inter alia*) the introduction in Britain of old age pensions and unemployment insurance. Entered Parliament in 1890. Supported the Boer cause in the South African War. President of the Board of Trade, 1905–8; Chancellor of the Exchequer, 1908–15. The rejection by the House of Lords of his 'People's Budget' of 1909 triggered a constitutional crisis and the Parliament Act, 1911. Minister of Munitions, 1915–16, he succeeded Kitchener as Secretary of State for War in July 1916, and in December the same year engineered Asquith's resignation, becoming Prime Minister of the Coalition Government. He reconstituted the War Council and created a unified military command, and prosecuted the war with energy. Lloyd George subsequently played a major role in the Versailles peace treaty negotiations. The 'khaki election' in December 1918 saw a fatal split in the Liberal Party (from which it never recovered) between the Asquithian and Lloyd George Liberals; the latter carried the day, and Lloyd George became Prime Minister again of a Coalition Government. But his later policies, particularly his support for an Irish Free State, and his pro-Greek stance in the Turkish crisis of 1922, led to distrust within his own party. He resigned in 1922 and never held political office again; but he sat in the House of Commons until his elevation to the peerage as 1st Earl Lloyd George of Dwyfor in 1945 – the year he died. He and WSC were friends and colleagues; but CSC, although admiring him politically, mistrusted him, as clearly emerges from her letters.

MARLBOROUGH, Duchess of *see* BALSAN, Consuelo

MARLBOROUGH, 9th Duke of (1871–1934): Charles Richard John Spencer-Churchill, always known as 'Sunny'. A cousin and close friend of WSC, he succeeded to the title in 1892. Paymaster-General of the Forces, 1899-1902, he served in the South African War as ADC to General Sir Ian Hamilton, and subsequently held the appointments of Under-Secretary of State for the Colonies, 1903–5, and Parliamentary Secretary, Board of Agriculture, 1917–18. In 1895 he married the beautiful Consuelo Vanderbilt (later Balsan*) of New York. She bore him two sons, the 10th Duke of Marlborough and Lord Ivor Spencer-Churchill; and her money assured the programme of beautification and restoration of Blenheim Palace and its gardens. In 1906 Consuelo left her husband, divorcing him in 1920. In 1921 Marlborough married Gladys Marie Deacon (1881–1977) of Boston, Massachusetts; she was a Roman Catholic, and in 1926 the Duke was received into the Roman Catholic Church, after which his first marriage was annulled. By 1931 their marriage was in ruins, and in 1933 Gladys left Blenheim for ever. From 1938 to 1962 she lived the life of an eccentric recluse at Chacombe in Banbury, Oxfordshire, calling herself 'Mrs Spencer'. She died in 1977 in St Andrew's Hospital, Northampton, aged ninety-six. The Duke died of cancer in 1934, aged sixty-three.

MARSH, Sir Edward Howard, 'Eddie' (1872–1953). KCVO. Son of Professor Howard Marsh, Master of Downing College, Cambridge. A Classical scholar and civil servant, he entered the Colonial Office in 1896. He served as Private Secretary to WSC, 1905–15, 1917–22 and 1924–9; also as Private Secretary to H. H. Asquith*; to J. H. Thomas; and to Malcolm MacDonald. Trustee of the Tate Gallery (to which he bequeathed his collection of pictures), 1937–44. He was a patron of the arts and literature; among his elegant works are translations of *Fables de La Fontaine*, 1931, and the *Odes* of Horace, 1941. He was a close friend and literary mentor of WSC, and CSC was devoted to him; Eddie and 'The Prof' (Lindemann*) signed the Chartwell visitors' book over a longer period and more often than any other persons. Eddie died unmarried.

MAZE, Paul (1887–1979). Painter. Born in Le Havre and educated both in France and England, he was completely bilingual. A French conscript soldier in the First World War, he acted as an unofficial liaison officer for the Royal Scots Greys. Although only a *sous-officier* (sergeant), he gained the confidence of senior commanders. Maze had the unusual distinction of being awarded military decorations by both the French and the British. He married twice: first, in 1921, Margaret Nelson, the widow of a friend killed in action, from whom he was divorced in 1949; second, in 1950, Jessie Lawrie. Maze lived mostly in England, where his painting came to be much admired. He and WSC had met in 1916, at the front, but their real friendship began when Maze asked WSC to write a preface to his war memoirs, *A Frenchman in Khaki*, in 1934. WSC greatly liked Paul Maze's ebullient personality, and valued his advice on painting. For a time in the 1930s Paul Maze came a good deal to Chartwell, but CSC did not share her husband's liking for him, and after a while the visits ceased. WSC and Maze kept in touch, however, and the latter greatly supported WSC's anti-appeasement policy and his pro-French stance.

MONTAGU, Venetia (1887–1948), a daughter of the 4th Baron Stanley* of Alderley, later 4th Baron Sheffield of Roscommon. In 1915 she married Edwin Montagu (died 1924); they had one daughter, Judith Venetia, later Mrs Milton Gendel (1923–72). Venetia, in her mid-twenties, was from 1910 a close friend of H. H. Asquith*, who was almost twice her age; from 1912 they corresponded often, and from 1914 until her marriage he wrote to her almost daily, often about secret Cabinet matters and about his colleagues. Like her sister, Sylvia Henley*, Venetia was a cousin and lifelong friend of CSC, and much liked by WSC. She had a more worldly disposition than her sister, and had a great gift for companionship. She entertained a clever, amusing circle of friends at her beautiful house, Breccles, in Norfolk.

MONTAGUE BROWNE, Anthony ('AMB') (1923–). CBE, OBE, DFC. Educated at Stowe and Magdalen College, Oxford. Pilot, RAF, 1941–5. Entered Foreign Service, 1946. Married, first, in 1950, Noel (Nonie) Arnold-Wallinger; one daughter; divorced, 1970; second, in 1970, Sheila Macklin (born Milligan). Private Secretary to WSC as Prime Minister, 1952–5. Seconded as Private Secretary to WSC, 1955–65. After retiring from official public life in 1955, WSC remained a world figure, and it was essential that his affairs, public and private, should be handled by someone of standing, trained in the ways of public service: AMB fulfilled this role to perfection; he was also a charming companion and won the affection, trust and gratitude of our whole family. After WSC's death AMB went into the City and business. By special arrangement he had retained his status in the Foreign Office; nevertheless his long and devoted service to my father was to the detriment of his career. AMB was one of the founding Trustees and Council Members of the Winston Churchill Memorial Trust in 1966, and from 1980 to 1997, Chairman of its Council; he is still a Trustee. His book, *Long Sunset*, was published in 1995.

MONTGOMERY, Bernard, 'Monty' (1887–1976). KG, DSO (1914). Son of a bishop, Rt Revd H. H. Montgomery, KCMG. Entered army in 1908. Severely wounded, 1914. Between the wars he served in India, Egypt and Palestine, and his ability was recognized, although his curt and abrasive manner made him enemies and detractors. In 1927 he married an army widow, Elizabeth Carver; they had one child, David (born 1928, now 2nd Viscount Montgomery). She died tragically from an insect bite in 1937. In France in 1940, Montgomery's conduct and ability in the crisis were observed by his then corps commander, Lieutenant-General Brooke (later Sir Alan Brooke, CIGS): promotion and high commands followed. From December 1941 Montgomery commanded South Eastern Command, from where he was summoned to Egypt in August 1942 to take command of the Eighth Army. Montgomery galvanized a dispirited army, and October 1942 saw the brilliant victory of the Battle of El Alamein. Thereafter 'Monty's' star shone brightly – and in his capacity to rally and inspire his soldiers, he was second to none. But he always aroused antagonism from those he disdained or swept aside, and he quarrelled almost incessantly with the American commanders during the invasion and liberation of Europe. He was promoted Field Marshal in 1944 and created 1st Viscount Montgomery of Alamein in 1946.

Monty's personal relations with WSC were essentially good, and after the war and WSC's fall from power he established himself as a loyal personal and family friend. CSC liked him very much, but never hesitated to rebuke him when he made some typically intolerable remark; which he always took very well – he liked and admired her. He was benevolence itself to myself and my family. One sensed he was a lonely man, and he valued the warm affection of a family group.

MORAN, Charles (1882–1977): Charles Wilson, MC. Consulting Physician and Dean of Medical School, St Mary's Hospital, Paddington, and President of the Royal College of Physicians, 1941–50. WSC's doctor from 1940, he accompanied WSC on nearly all his travels from 1941 and looked after him until his death. Created 1st Baron Moran, 1943. Wrote a brilliant book about fear called *The Anatomy of Courage*, 1945. But he was much criticized by many, both in and out of the medical profession, for publishing *Winston Churchill: The Struggle for Survival*, 1966, based on his diaries and recollections of his association with WSC, and commenting on and quoting many of the personages he met during these years. Moran also described WSC's medical condition and illnesses in detail: CSC had specifically asked him not to publish these recollections, and was greatly upset when the book appeared, as were all our family.

MORTON, Major Sir Desmond (1891–1971), MC, KCB. Shot through the heart (where the bullet lodged) in the 1914–18 war, his survival was something of a continuing miracle. ADC to Field Marshal Sir Douglas Haig, 1917–18; he and WSC met at this time and became friends. Director of Industrial Intelligence Centre, 1930–9. Personal Assistant to Prime Minister, 1940–6. Delegate to Inter-Allied Reparations Agency, 1946; and other appointments. He was a devout Roman Catholic and a confirmed bachelor. During the 1930s he supplied WSC with much valuable information concerning Germany's economic situation and undercover rearmament. He was a close neighbour of the Churchills at Edenbridge, and frequent unremarked visits were easy. He was also warmly welcomed at Chartwell by CSC, as he was a first-rate tennis player. With the coming of the Second World War and Churchill's Prime Ministership, Morton's close personal association with him gradually diminished, although he acted as a liaison between WSC and the Free French and de Gaulle, and was WSC's contact with the Allied governments in exile; he was also a link between WSC and certain branches of the Secret Service. Morton, however, became increasingly embittered by what he saw as WSC's neglect, and in *Churchill and Morton* by R. W. Thompson, published in 1976 (after Morton's death), in the exchange of letters between Morton and Thompson this bitterness had full rein.

NICHOLSON, William (1872–1949). Painter. Knighted, 1936; refused election to the Royal Academy. By the time he came into the Churchills' life, he was an established and celebrated portrait-painter; and, as a landscape and still-life artist, known for the refinement of his subdued tones and pale clear colourings. Some friends of WSC and CSC in 1933 commissioned Nicholson to paint a conversation piece to mark their Silver Wedding, and thereafter he became a favourite friend of the whole family and a frequent visitor to Chartwell up to the outbreak of the war. He was a man of immense charm and originality: we dubbed him the *Cher Maître*; CSC particularly welcomed his influence on WSC's painting style and technique in softening his palette. WSC himself said that William Nicholson was 'the person who taught me most about painting'.

REVES, Emery (1904–81). Born a Hungarian Jew, Imre Revesz. Founded an agency for the press syndication of political articles, at first in Berlin; forced to leave Germany in 1933, he opened a new office in Paris. Reves first met WSC in 1937, from which time he was instrumental in the publishing of articles by him in many European countries. Reves became a British subject in 1940, and once again escaped the Germans and fled from Paris to London in June of that year. Most of his close relations were murdered in German-occupied Yugoslavia. Reves spent most of the war in the United States, where he published *The Anatomy of Peace*, declaring his belief in the abandonment of nation states in favour of a system of world government, which ideal he pursued for the rest of his life. After the war, Reves handled the American rights in WSC's war memoirs, and himself bought the world rights in these, and also in *A History of the English-Speaking Peoples*.

From 1949 Reves's companion was Wendy Russell, a beautiful and vivacious American model, whom he married in 1964. Between 1956 and 1959 WSC stayed often, and for weeks at a time, with Emery and Wendy in their beautiful house, La Pausa, at Roquebrune, near Monte Carlo. CSC stayed there on relatively few occasions: she did not like the Reves's *ménage*, and had an antipathy to the Riviera. Emery and Wendy were most welcoming to any members of the family, and Wendy and Sarah, in particular, became great friends.

Winston Churchill and Emery Reves: Correspondence 1937–64, edited with an introduction and notes by Martin Gilbert, was published in 1997.

ROOSEVELT, (Anna) Eleanor (1884–1962), born Hall, niece of Theodore Roosevelt (26th President of the USA, 1901–9). In 1905 she married Franklin Delano Roosevelt*, a distant cousin. A strong Democrat, she was deeply involved in social reforms. Following her husband's crippling attack of polio (1921), Eleanor Roosevelt expanded her political role throughout his governorship of New York State and his election as President (1933). She pursued her own line, which even in wartime was strongly slanted to social problems; the President called her his 'eyes and ears'. Her newspaper column, 'My Day', was widely syndicated. After her husband's death in 1945, she became US Representative to the United Nations General Assembly, 1946–52, and chairman of the United Nations Human Rights Commission, 1947–51. Her several books included an autobiography, published in 1962.

ROOSEVELT, Franklin Delano, 'FDR' (1884–1945), 32nd President of the United States, and the only one to be elected for a third term (in 1940) and a fourth (in 1944). A distant cousin of President Theodore Roosevelt (1858-1919). He married Anna Eleanor Hall (Eleanor Roosevelt*), the latter's niece, in 1905.

WSC and FDR had met briefly towards the end of the First World War when the latter was US Secretary of the Navy and WSC Minister of Munitions. They had virtually no contact in the ensuing years, until in 1939 the President initiated what would come to be one of the most famous exchanges of letters in world history, when he wrote to Churchill on 11 September: WSC leapt at the opportunity for private communication, which was to continue until the President's death in April 1945, in letters, transatlantic telephonings, cables and some dozen personal meetings.

There has been much discussion as to how 'real' was the extent of the two men's much publicized friendship. It is idle to ask whether, had they met in 'normal' times, they would have been 'friends'. Their relationship was forged in the crucible of war: it was – at the very least – a highly successful 'friendship *de convenance*'. But mutual admiration and – above all – mutual identity of purpose, welded together two very different styles and personalities. My father truly loved and esteemed Franklin Roosevelt, and was deeply sorrowful when he died.

SANDYS, Duncan Edwin (1908–87). Entered Diplomatic Service, 1930. Conservative MP, 1930–45 and 1950–74: PC, 1944; created 1st Baron Duncan-Sandys (life peer), 1974. Married, first, in 1935, Diana Bailey (born Churchill); they were divorced, 1960 (she died 1963); one son, two daughters; secondly, 1962, Marie-Claire, Viscountess Hudson (born Schmitt, of Paris); one daughter. WSC esteemed and liked him, and after Duncan was disabled from military service in a motor accident in 1941 gave him several government appointments: most importantly Chairman of War Cabinet Committee for defence against flying bombs and rockets; Minister of Works, 1944–5. Minister of Supply, 1951–4; Minister of Housing and Local Government, 1954–7; Minister of Defence, 1957–9; Minister of Aviation, 1959–60; Secretary of State for Commonwealth Relations, 1960–4 (and Colonies, 1962–4). Founded the European Movement, 1947. Founder and President of Civic Trust, 1956. After the war WSC and Duncan collaborated closely on the European Movement and the Strasbourg Assembly. With the break-up of Duncan and Diana's marriage the relationship between WSC and Duncan inevitably became less close, but was always cordial.

SASSOON, Sir Philip (1888–1939). Son of 2nd Baronet and Aline, daughter of Baron Gustave de Rothschild; succeeded father as 3rd Baronet, 1912. Unionist MP from 1912. Private Secretary to Field Marshal Sir Douglas Haig, December 1915–18. Under-Secretary of State for Air, November 1924–9 and 1931–7. First Commissioner of Works from 1937. Millionaire, aesthete, politician. An 'air' enthusiast, he owned his own plane, and encouraged research and development in aircraft design. Sassoon owned a priceless art collection, and was a patron of the American painter John Singer Sargent (1856–1925). WSC and CSC often stayed with him either at Port Lympne, on the Kent coast, or at Trent Park, New Barnet, near London. Sassoon greatly helped and encouraged WSC in the early years of his painting by his own knowledge and taste; he used to lend WSC pictures from his collection to study and copy. Sassoon's sister Sybil was married to the 5th Marquess of Cholmondeley; they were both also great friends of the Churchills.

SHEFFIELD OF ROSCOMMON, 4th Baron *see* STANLEY OF ALDERLEY, (Edward) Lyulph

SMITH, Frederick Edwin, 'F.E.' (1872–1930). Brilliant advocate and orator. Conservative (U) MP for Walton (Liverpool), 1906–19; Solicitor-General, 1915; Attorney-General, 1915–19; Lord Chancellor, 1919–22; Secretary of State for India, 1924–8. PC, 1911; knighted, 1915; created 1st Baron Birkenhead, 1919; 1st Viscount Birkenhead, 1921; 1st Earl of Birkenhead, 1922. Married Margaret Furneaux, 1901; she died, 1968. His close friendship with WSC over many years was never affected by their political differences. They were joint founders, in 1911 of the Other Club, of which Rule 12 reads: 'Nothing in the Rules or intercourse of the Club shall interfere with the rancour or asperity of party politics.' CSC never liked 'F.E.' (although she was very fond of his wife Margaret); she thought he was coarse, and disapproved of his heavy drinking and gambling, particularly fearing his influence upon Randolph, to whom he was godfather.

SOAMES, Christopher (1920–87). PC, GCMG, GCVO, CH, CBE; Croix de guerre avec palme; Grand officier de la Légion d'Honneur. Educated Eton; emerging from Royal Military College, Sandhurst (Coldstream Guards), in 1939, he served in Middle East, Italy and France until 1945. Assistant Military Attaché in Paris, 1945–6. Conservative MP for Bedford, 1950–66. Parliamentary Private Secretary to the Prime Minister (WSC), 1952–5. Junior ministerial posts at Air Ministry and Admiralty, 1955–8. Secretary of State for War, 1958–60. In 1960 entered Cabinet as Minister of Agriculture, until 1964. Ambassador to France, 1968–72; a Vice-President of the European Commission (Brussels), 1973–7. Created 1st Baron Soames (life peer), 1978. Lord President of the Council and Leader of House of Lords, 1979–81. Last Governor of Southern Rhodesia in period leading up to independence of Zimbabwe, 1979–80. At odds with the Prime Minister (Mrs Thatcher), he resigned from the Government, at her request, in July 1981. In the intervals of his political career Soames pursued business interests as a Director of Decca Ltd, and of N. M. Rothschild & Sons Ltd. He was Chairman of ICL (UK), 1984–7.

In 1947 Christopher Soames married Mary Churchill; they had three sons and two daughters. He quickly formed a warm relationship with his father-in-law. CSC was at first wary of him, but became truly fond of him, and in later years relied upon his help and advice. Christopher's closeness to WSC fuelled his already awakened interest in politics, and was a priceless education, and the springboard from which he launched out into his own political career. From the first, Europe and Britain's accession to the European Community would be central to his theme. Christopher's great capacity to enjoy life made him a splendid friend and companion: he loved hunting, riding and racing, he was a brilliant shot, and a fine fisherman. He played bridge very well, he was a great gourmet – and himself an excellent and instinctive cook.

STANLEY OF ALDERLEY, (Edward) Lyulph (1839–1925), son of 2nd Baron Stanley of Alderley. Succeeded his brother Henry in 1903 as 4th Baron. In 1909, on the death of a kinsman, he became 4th Baron Sheffield of Roscommon, by which title he was thereafter known. Married, 1873, Mary Bell CBE, CSC's 'Great Aunt Maisie'; she died 1929. Four daughters appear in these letters: Margaret Stanley (Goodenough); Sylvia Stanley (Henley*); Venetia Stanley (Montagu*); Blanche Stanley (Serocold). CSC often stayed, both as a child and as an adult, with these Stanley relations, to whom she was devoted.

TREE, Ronald, 'Ronnie' (1897–1976). American by birth, he was born and lived the greater part of his life in England, and was a British subject. His mother was a Marshall Field (she married secondly, in 1901, the 1st Earl Beatty). He married, first, Nancy Field (born Perkins), a niece of Nancy, Viscountess Astor; they had two sons. Nancy Tree was clever, charming and a brilliant decorator and gardener; she died in 1994, aged ninety-seven. Nancy and Ronnie divorced soon after the Second World War; he married, secondly, in 1947, Marietta Fitzgerald (1917–91), a widow, the daughter of Bishop Malcolm Peabody. A civil rights campaigner, she was a chief aide to Adlai Stevenson in his presidential campaigns of 1952 and 1956. Ronald Tree was Conservative MP for the Harborough constituency of Leicestershire, 1933–45; he supported Churchill's policy of anti-appeasement. He held a number of parliamentary private secretaryships. In 1940–2 WSC and CSC, their family and entourage were guests of the Trees at Ditchley in Oxfordshire at times of full moon, as a security measure, Chequers being deemed too visible from the air. Tree wrote a book, *When the Moon was High*, 1975, describing these occasions. In 1949 he sold Ditchley and lived thereafter in the United States. After the war CSC kept in touch with Ronnie, to whom she was devoted.

VANDERBILT, Consuelo, later Duchess of Marlborough *see* BALSAN, Consuelo

WESTMINSTER, 2nd Duke of (1879–1953): Hugh Richard Arthur Grosvenor GCVO, DSO. Always known as 'Bendor' (correctly spelt 'Bend'Or') – the name of one of his grandfather's most successful racehorses; he bore the nickname from infancy. He succeeded his grandfather, the 1st Duke of Westminster, in 1899. He and WSC became lifelong friends while serving in the Boer War. In the First World War the Duke formed (and paid for from his own resources) his own squadron of armoured cars. He was awarded the DSO after a raid in the North African desert. He married four times. He had one son (died as a child) and two daughters by his first marriage. In 1947 he married as his fourth wife Anne Sullivan, who survives him. He had various homes: Grosvenor House and Bourdon House, London; Eaton Hall, Chester; Lochmore, Sutherland; Mimizan, Les Landes, France; and a beautiful yacht, *Cutty Sark*. A great character and personality, and a superb host, he has been described as 'the last *grand seigneur*'.

WHYTE, Maryott Honoria (1895–1973), younger daughter of Theodore and Lady Maude Whyte (see under Countess of Airlie*). CSC's first cousin. The Whytes were badly off, and their two daughters had to earn their living. Their brother, Mark, was killed in action in 1918. Maryott trained as a children's nurse at the famous Norland Institute in London. Soon after Marigold's death in the summer of 1921, Maryott (variously to be called 'Mop', 'Moppet' or 'Nana') came to take charge of the Churchills' nursery; the elder children needed supervision. But an imperative need for Nana's care arose when WSC and CSC's last child, Mary, was born in September 1922: the 'Benjamin' of the family, I was soon Nana's sole charge. From 1929 I was entirely Chartwell-based, attending local day schools. Since my parents were often away, Nana provided continuity and organized my daily life; she was the greatest influence in my early years. She always played a considerable role in Chartwell life, and in the immediate post-war period she cooked for my parents at weekends. In 1952 she finally retired, after thirty years, and lived in a house in Westerham, given her by my parents.

WILSON, Charles *see* MORAN, Charles

WIMBORNE, 1st Baron *see* GUEST, Sir Ivor Bertie

WIMBORNE, 2nd Baron, later 1st Viscount *see* GUEST, Ivor Churchill

Nicknames and Aliases

Admiral Q	President F. D. Roosevelt*
Alderney bull	4th Baron Stanley* of Alderley, later 4th Baron Sheffield
Alderney cows	The female Stanleys of Alderley
Alex	Field Marshal Sir Harold Alexander, later 1st Earl Alexander of Tunis
All-Highest, The	George Curzon, later 1st Marquess Curzon of Kedleston
AMB	Anthony Montague Browne*
Amber Dog/Pug	WSC
Bendor/Bend'Or/Bennie/Benny	Hugh Grosvenor, 2nd Duke of Westminster*
Block, The/Old Block	H. H. Asquith*, later 1st Earl of Oxford and Asquith
Blue Tooth/Bluey	Rt Hon. Harold Baker
Bobbety	Viscount Cranborne, later 5th Marquess of Salisbury
Bongey/Bongie	Sir Maurice Bonham Carter
Brab	Major-General Sir John Brabazon
Bullfinch, Mr	WSC code name on homeward journey from Casablanca Conference and Turkey, February 1943
Bumble Bee	Sarah Churchill
Canary, The	Major Cyril Patteson
Chimp, The	Christopher Soames, later Baron Soames
Chumbolly/Chumboly/C.B.	Randolph Churchill
Clem-Pussy-Bird	Clementine Churchill
Crankie	Lieutenant-Colonel Sir Eric Crankshaw
Cutie	Wallis Simpson, Duchess of Windsor
Dan Leno	The Churchills' cook (1909)
Don Quixote/the Don	President F. D. Roosevelt*
Duckadilly, The	Marigold Churchill
Eagle, The	One of the children's nurses (1909)
Fairy Queen, Faery Queen	Grace Curzon (Lord Curzon's second wife)
F.E.	F. E. Smith*, later 1st Earl of Birkenhead
Fiend, The	Admiral of the Fleet Sir John Fisher, later 1st Baron Fisher
Frankland, Air Commodore and Mrs	WSC/CSC code names, Casablanca Conference and his visit to Turkey, January–February 1943

gent, the	HRH The Duke of Windsor
Goonie	Lady Gwendeline Churchill
Green, Mr and Mrs	WSC/CSC code names during his visit to Cairo and Moscow, August 1942; and Tehran Conference, November–December 1943
Grimalkin, Mrs	CSC (Shakespeare's she-cat, *Macbeth*)
Hambling, The	Grace Hamblin*
Ho	Hoe Farm, near Godalming
Hodgy Podgy	Nurse Hodgson
Ike	General, later President, Dwight D. Eisenhower
Imbroglio, The	Daisy Fellowes (Mrs Reginald Fellowes)
Jagoons	Jack and Goonie Churchill* and family
K	1st Earl Kitchener of Khartoum
Kat/Cat	CSC
Kent, Colonel and Mrs	WSC/CSC code names on his visits to Italy, August 1944; Moscow, October 1944; Athens, December 1944; and Yalta Conference and Malta, January–February 1945
Linky	Lord Hugh Cecil
Lulu/Loulou	Lewis Harcourt, later 1st Viscount Harcourt
Ma Jeffreys	Lieutenant-Colonel George D. Jeffreys
Maria	Mary Churchill
Meat	Major-General Sir H. C. Lowther
Moggs/Moggie	Viscountess Gage (born Imogen Grenfell), wife of 6th Viscount Gage
Monty	General Bernard Montgomery*, later 1st Viscount Montgomery of Alamein
Moppet/Mop	Maryott Whyte*
Mule, The	Sarah Churchill
Nana	Maryott Whyte*
Nellinita, The/Nellion	Nellie Hozier, later Romilly
'Oc'	Arthur Asquith
Ogre, The	Marshal Joseph Stalin
Old Bear, The	Marshal Joseph Stalin
Old Malay, The	Admiral of the Fleet Sir John Fisher, later 1st Baron Fisher
Old Snowie	Gardener at Chartwell
Old Tabby	A. J. Balfour
Pawser	CSC
Pebbin	Peregrine Churchill
Pig/Pug	WSC
Prime, The	H. H. Asquith*, later 1st Earl of Oxford and Asquith
Prof, The	F. A. Lindemann*, later 1st Viscount Cherwell
Pug	General Hastings Ismay, later 1st Baron Ismay
Puppy Kitten/P.K.	The Churchills' nickname for some of their unborn or infant offspring
Rabbit, The	Randolph Churchill

R.L./Revered Leader	David Lloyd George*, later 1st Earl Lloyd George of Dwyfor
Rock	Earl of Rocksavage, later 5th Marquess of Cholmondeley
Rosy/Rosie	Rear-Admiral Rosslyn Wemyss
Sage, The	H. H. Asquith*, later 1st Earl of Oxford and Asquith
Sancho P.	Harry Hopkins
Seals, The	The Sea Lords
Spencer, Air Commodore and Mrs	WSC/CSC code names on his visit to Washington, May 1943
Streetie	Margery Street
U. J. (Uncle Jo)	Marshal Joseph Stalin
Warden, Colonel and Mrs	WSC/CSC code names, 1st Quebec Conference, August 1943; visit to North Africa and Tehran Conference, November 1943
Wuthering Heights	Charles Emmett

Bibliography

AIRLIE, Mabell, Countess of, *Thatched with Gold: The Memoirs of Mabell, Countess of Airlie*, ed. Jennifer Ellis, London, Hutchinson, 1962

BALSAN, Consuelo Vanderbilt, *The Glitter and the Gold*, London, Heinemann, 1953

BLUNT, Wilfrid Scawen, *My Diaries*, 2 vols, London, Martin Secker, 1919, 1920

—— 'Secret Memoirs', W. S. Blunt Papers, Fitzwilliam Museum, Cambridge

BONHAM CARTER, Violet, *Winston Churchill As I Knew Him*, London, Eyre & Spottiswoode, 1965

—— *The Letters and Diaries of Violet Bonham Carter*, vol. I: *Lantern Slides, 1904–14*, ed. Mark Bonham Carter and Mark Pottle; vol. II: *Champion Redoubtable 1914–45*, ed. Mark Pottle, London, Weidenfeld & Nicolson, 1996, 1998

BROCK, Michael and Eleanor, eds, *H. H. Asquith: Letters to Venetia Stanley*, Oxford, Oxford University Press, 1982

BUTLER, David and FREEMAN, Jennie, *British Political Facts 1900–1960*, London, Macmillan, 1964

CHURCHILL, Clementine, *My Visit to Russia*, London, Hutchinson, 1945

CHURCHILL, Randolph S., *Winston S. Churchill*, vols I–II, 1966, 1967; also *Companion Volumes I, II*, 1967, 1969; London, Heinemann

CHURCHILL, Sarah, *Keep on Dancing*, London, Weidenfeld & Nicolson, 1981

—— *A Thread in the Tapestry*, London, André Deutsch, 1967

CHURCHILL, Winston S., *The Chartwell Bulletins January–June 1935*, ed. Martin Gilbert, The International Churchill Society, Hopkinton, New Hampshire, 1989

—— *Painting as a Pastime*, London, Odhams/Ernest Benn, 1948

—— *The Second World War*, 6 vols, London, Cassell, 1948–54

—— *Thoughts and Adventures*, London, Butterworth, 1932

CHURCHILL, Winston S. (b.1940), *His Father's Son: The Life of Randolph S. Churchill*, London, Weidenfeld & Nicolson, 1996

COLVILLE, John, *Fringes of Power: Downing Street Diaries 1939–1955*, London, Hodder & Stoughton, 1985

The Companion to British History, ed. Charles Arnold-Baker, Tunbridge Wells, Longcross, 1996

COOPER, Artemis, *A Durable Fire: Letters of Duff and Diana Cooper, 1913–1950*, London, Collins, 1983

—— *Mr Wu and Mrs Stitch: The Letters of Evelyn Waugh and Diana Cooper*, London, Hodder & Stoughton, 1991

FIELD, Leslie, *Bendor: The Golden Duke of Westminster*, London, Weidenfeld & Nicolson, 1983

FORBES-ROBERTSON, Diana, *Maxine*, London, Hamish Hamilton, 1964

GILBERT, Martin, *Churchill: A Life*, London, Heinemann, 1991

—— *Winston S. Churchill*, vols III–VIII, 1971–88; also *Companion Volumes III–V*, 1972–82; London, Heinemann

—— *The Churchill War Papers*, vol. I: *At the Admiralty, 1939–40*; vol. II, *Never Surrender, 1940*, London, Heinemann, 1993, 1994

—— *Winston Churchill and Emery Reves: Correspondence 1937–1964*, Austin, Texas, University of Texas Press, 1997

GOODWIN, Doris Kearns, *No Ordinary Time*, New York, Simon & Schuster, 1994

INGRAM, Kevin, *Rebel: The Short Life of Esmond Romilly*, London, Weidenfeld & Nicolson, 1985

KIMBALL, Warren, *Forged in War*, London, HarperCollins, 1997

LEVINE, Naomi B., *Politics, Religion and Love*, New York and London, New York University Press, 1991

LONGFORD, Elizabeth, *A Pilgrimage of Passion*, London, Weidenfeld & Nicolson, 1979

LOWE, Norman, *Mastering Modern British History*, London, Macmillan, 1984

MACMILLAN, Harold, *Tides of Fortune* (*Memoirs*, vol. III), London, Macmillan, 1969

—— *War Diaries*, London, Macmillan, 1984

MAJOR, Norma, *Chequers: The Prime Minister's Country House and its History*, London, HarperCollins, 1996

MARTIN, John, *Downing Street: The War Years*, London, Bloomsbury, 1991

MONTAGUE BROWNE, Anthony, *Long Sunset*, London, Cassell, 1995

MORAN, Lord, *Winston Churchill: The Struggle for Survival*, London, Constable, 1966

NEL, Elizabeth, *Mr Churchill's Secretary*, London, Hodder & Stoughton, 1958

The Oxford Companion to the Second World War, ed. I. C. B. Dear and M. R. D. Foot, Oxford, Oxford University Press, 1995

PAWLE, Gerald, *The War and Colonel Warden*, London, Harrap, 1963

PEARSON, John, *Citadel of the Heart*, London, Macmillan, 1991

PILPEL, Robert, *Churchill in America 1895–1961: An Affectionate Portrait*, London, New English Library, 1977

REID, Percy G., *Townsman of Westerham*, Folkestone, Regency International Publications, 1969

RIDLEY, George, *Bend'Or Duke of Westminster*, London, Robin Clark, 1985

ROBERTS, Brian, *Randolph: A Study of Churchill's Son*, London, Hamish Hamilton, 1984

ROSE, Kenneth, *The Later Cecils*, London, Weidenfeld & Nicolson, 1975

SHEEAN, James Vincent, *Between the Thunder and the Sun*, London, Macmillan, 1943

SOAMES, Mary, *Clementine Churchill by Her Daughter Mary Soames*, London, Cassell, 1979

—— *Winston Churchill, His Life as a Painter*, London, Collins, 1990

STAFFORD, David, *Churchill and Secret Service*, London, John Murray, 1997

THOMPSON, R. W., *Churchill and Morton*, London, Hodder & Stoughton, 1976

TREE, Ronald, *When the Moon Was High*, London, Macmillan, 1975

VICKERS, Hugo, *Gladys, Duchess of Marlborough*, New York, Holt, Rinehart & Winston, 1980

Index

In this index individuals are entered under the name most commonly used in the text and in their Biographical Notes (indicated by a *). There are two exceptions where entries are split: Edward, Prince of Wales/Edward VIII/Duke of Windsor and Mary Churchill/Mary Soames. Knighthoods and service ranks acquired later than the last mention or subsequent to the period covered by the book are included in the main entry in brackets. Maiden names, where relevant, are also in brackets. As in the text, the courtesy titles 'Rt Hon' and 'Hon' have been omitted. The following abbreviations have been used: CSC (Clementine Churchill); DC (Diana Churchill); MC (Mary Churchill); RSC (Randolph Churchill); SC (Sarah Churchill); MS (Mary Soames); WSC (Winston Churchill); WWI and WWII (First and Second World Wars).

To avoid overloading an already long index with trivial mentions, principally those of close members of the family, who in some chapters figure on almost every page, major and most relevant references only have been included.

The works of Winston Churchill will be found in their alphabetical sequence; also the titles of books, plays and films commented on in the letters, with their authors in brackets (where known).

In the entries for Winston and Clementine Churchill, and their close family, personal references are grouped under headings, in logical or chronological order. Otherwise sub-headings are entered in the order in which they appear in the text rather than alphabetically.

Abbey Division (Westminster) by-election (1924) 278, 279, 280
Abdication crisis 418–19
Abercorn, James Hamilton, 3rd Duke of 324, 325n
Abercorn, Rosalind (Bingham) Duchess of 324, 325n
Abingdon, Montagu Bertie, 7th Earl of 11n, 101
Abyssinia (now Ethiopia) 401, 415
Acton, Arthur Mario 316, 317n
Acton, Harold (Sir) 317n
Acton, Hortense 317n
Aden 366
Adenauer, Konrad 589
Admirable Crichton, The (Barrie) 25
Admiralty, the: WSC as First Lord of (1911–15) xvi, 57–110 *passim*; (1939) 452, 453; official history 578, 579n
Admiralty House 58: WSC/CSC move into (1913) 69, 70, 72, 73, 86n; they leave (1915) 110; move into again (1939) 453
Agadir Incident 51, 52, 53

Aid to Russia Fund *see* Red Cross Aid to Russia Fund
Air Defence Research Sub-Committee 401
Air Estimates (1921) 230
Air Force, bad state of (1938) 433
Air Raid Precautions (ARP) (WWII) 447
air raids 474, 480, 481; *see also* Blitz
Airlie, Bridget (Coke), Countess of (wife of 12th Earl) 299, 300n
Airlie, David Ogilvy, 12th Earl of 299, 300n
Airlie*, Henrietta Blanche (Stanley), Dowager Countess of (wife of 10th Earl; CSC's grandmother) 4, 6, 10n, 56, 648; critical of CSC's handwriting 57
Airlie, Mabell (Gore), Countess of (wife of 11th Earl) 57
Airlie Castle 4; CSC at 56–7
Aitken, Max *see* Beaverbrook*, 1st Baron
Aix-en-Provence: French army manoeuvres at (1936) 415, 417
Aix-les-Bains: CSC at 578, 583
Ajaccio (Corsica) 500